PSYCHOLOGY
AND YOU

Third Edition

PSYCHOLOGY
AND YOU

Third Edition

Judith W. McMahon

**Webster University
St. Louis, Missouri**

Tony Romano

**William Fremd High School
Palatine, Illinois**

National Textbook Company
a division of NTC/CONTEMPORARY PUBLISHING GROUP
NTC Lincolnwood, Illinois USA

Cover Photo   Diana Ong/SuperStock

Published by National Textbook Company, a division of NTC/Contemporary Publishing Group, Inc.,
4255 West Touhy Avenue, Lincolnwood (Chicago), Illinois 60712-1975 U.S.A.

Manufactured in the United States of America

10 58/55 06 05

Student Edition: ISBN 0-314-14090-5

Contents in Brief

Contents

Chapter 2 Methods of Psychology 26

Chapter Features
. . . .

Chapter Features

· ·

Chapter 6 Consciousness

Chapter Features
....

In Focus
**Natural Cycles
and Entrainment** 162

In Focus
**Comparing REM to NREM
Periods of Sleep** 167

In Focus
**Three Major Theories
about Why
We Dream** 168

In Their Own Words
Sigmund Freud 170

In Focus
**Comparing Nightmares
to Night Terrors** 172

Case Study
Losing Sleep 174

Thinking Critically
about Psychology
**Can We Relive
Childhood?** 178

Applying Psychology
to Life
**The World of
Consciousness** 182

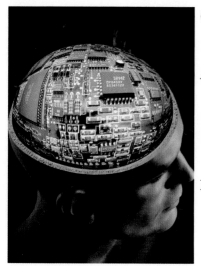

Chapter 8 Information Processing and Memory

Chapter Features

Chapter 9 Intelligence and Creativity 254

Chapter Features

Chapter Features
....

Chapter 12   Adulthood and Aging   348

Chapter Features

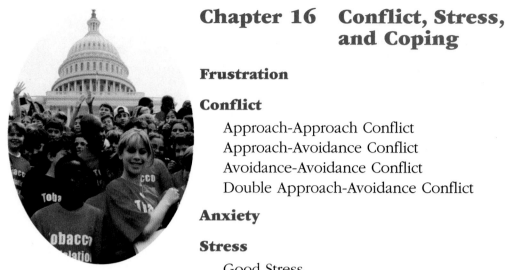

Chapter 16   Conflict, Stress, and Coping

Chapter Features

Chapter 18   Treatment and Therapy   538

Chapter Features

Preface

Psychology encompasses broad areas of research about human behavior, information that should be available to all high school students who want to understand themselves and their world better. The goal of this text is to create active intellectual and emotional involvement by the student, not only in learning about psychology, but in life as well. The authorship of this text holds to a philosophy and approach that seeks always to keep the students' welfare and understanding in mind. This edition retains all of the original elements designed to stimulate students' interest and enhance their knowledge of the field. We believe that you will find it highly informational, up-to-date, and "user-friendly."

We are very excited about the new features we have added to this revision, features that we think will be especially appealing to high school students. Each chapter now contains a substantial direct quotation from an important expert in a particular field covered in that chapter. These quotes, titled "In Their Own Words," were carefully selected to illustrate a major point or theory found in the text material. Each chapter also contains a case study, a discussion of particular instances, people, or events that expands on or gives additional details about a topic covered in that chapter. Another feature was added to each chapter in response to the continuing and growing interest in critical thinking. This feature, called "Thinking Critically about Psychology," offers the student a point-by-point explanation of what critical thinking is and how it might be applied to a specific issue.

Learning abstractions and learning practicality do not have to be separate things. Almost every page of this book ties in scientific issues with corresponding applications to daily life. The special feature—one for each chapter—called "Applying Psychology to Life" applies some of the principles found in the chapter to everyday issues and concerns. Additional devices designed to keep interest high and improve retention are the inclusion of anecdotes, historical facts, unusual events, and humor, plus a writing style that talks to the students, taking them step by step through the subject matter.

With input from teachers who used previous editions of *Psychology and You,* each chapter was gone over carefully and updated and tightened or expanded or reworked in many places. For example, the chapter on conflict and stress and the chapter on the healthy personality were collapsed into one chapter for this edition. There is expanded coverage of the nervous systems, brain scans, the limbic system, and the prefrontal area of the brain. We also added material on emotional intelligence, multiple intelligences, and the issue of repressed memories of abuse. The chapter on abnormal psychology has been enlarged to include discussions of the childhood disorders ADHD and autism. A new section on the insanity defense has been added, and the section on substance abuse now includes nicotine plus the other substances previously covered. For the chapter on personality we added a discussion of trait theorists and one on the use of personality tests in hiring. Other topics that have either been expanded or added for this revision include resisting peer pressure, the effects of yo-yo dieting, savant syndrome, and current perspectives on gender roles. The overall content also complies with the American Psychological Association's guidelines for high school psychology texts.

This edition is extremely current. There are nearly 300 new references, including articles from 1999 journals. New references can be found in every chapter and they cover all major areas in the field. For example, the section on psychotherapy discusses the most recent findings on effectiveness, of both treatment approaches and types of professionals. We also added a section on courtship signals, which is a highly visible area of recent research. Our coverage of multicultural concerns has been expanded to include new discussions of cultural attitudes toward aging, cultural emphases on competition and aggression, and the role of stereotypes in cross-cultural understanding. As was true for the second edition, multicultural issues also appear in various other places throughout the text.

Each chapter contains learning devices and exercises designed to enhance the students' understanding and retention of material. In creating these, Tony Romano, a high school teacher with a master's degree in psychology, has done his usual outstanding job. Especially noteworthy are his In Focus features, which condense and bring together subject matter that might be confusing or especially difficult. Mr. Romano has long been involved in setting up psychology science fairs for the counties in which he teaches, and his knowledge and skills are evident in the work he has done here.

Tony Romano also developed the wraparound teacher's edition and the teacher resource material.

Every effort has been made to be sure that you are getting the best possible psychology text for high school students. Several professors, clinical psychologists and experienced high school teachers from across the country reviewed this edition and made many excellent suggestions for changes. Their help and encouragement are warmly appreciated and gratefully acknowledged.

REVIEWERS

Tracy S. Bennet, Ph.D.
Licensed Clinical
    Psychologist
Simi Valley, CA

David Boersma
Evergreen Park
    Community
    High School
Evergreen Park, IL

Rhonda Coleman,
    M.Ed.
Reading Specialist
Los Angeles, CA

Dr. Dennis Coon,
Santa Barbara City
    College
Santa Barbara, CA

Dr. D.A. Gershaw
Arizona Western
    College
Yuma, AZ

Sondra Gray
Chesapeake Senior
    High School
Pasadena, MD

Neil Lloyd
Carl Schurz High
    School
Chicago. IL

Ruth Martin
Memorial High School
Madison, WI

Jim Matiya
Carl Sandburg High
    School
Palos Park, IL

David Mejia
West High School
Denver, CO

Iris Roberts
Jefferson City High
    School
Jefferson City, MO

James Rostello
Olathe North High
    School,
Olathe, KS

Charles Schallhorn
Ball State University
Muncie, IN

Dickee Six
Bath High School
Bath, MI

Marie T. Smith
Thomas S. Wootton
    High School
Rockville, MD

Barbara G. Wiggins
Robert E. Lee
    High School
Montgomery, AL

Swazette D. Young
Bowie High School
Bowie, MD

Without the patience, cooperation, and support of the Department of Behavioral and Social Sciences at Webster University, this project could never have been completed. The help and good advice of Professor William Huddleston Berry, department chair, proved especially invaluable.

The National Textbook Company has been very enthusiastic about the text and provided an enormous amount of assistance. Clyde Perlee and Carole Grumney were instrumental in development of the first two editions of this text and I will always be grateful for their advice and support. For this edition I would like to thank Lynn Bruton and Lynda Kessler for editorial guidance. I want to thank Mario M. Rodriguez, Lee Anne Dollison, and Bette Darwin for their design and production work, and Jan Seidel for the many hours spent in photo research.

Finally, to those of you who have used the book before, we hope that this revision pleases you. To first-time adopters, welcome. We are about to embark on an exciting educational journey, and we are delighted to have you all along.

Unit 1

In this Unit...

xxx

Approaches to Psychology

CHAPTER 1

The Field of Psychology

Because of scientific progress in the 1800s, humans began to be viewed as creatures who could be studied and understood. Since then, the human body and mind have been explored in detail. In this chapter, we cover some of these explorations, trying to describe human nature as it was seen by scientists in the past and as it is understood now.

The World of the Psychologist

The field of psychology is quite popular these days. The number of college students majoring in psychology increased dramatically from the mid-1980s to the mid-1990s (McDonald, 1997). Over the last 25 years or so, the number of psychologists in the work force has more than tripled (Pion et al., 1996). It seems that there are more psychologists around than ever before. But what exactly do all these psychologists do?

For most people, a psychologist is someone who sits across from you, listens to your problems, and tries to help. There are about 100,000 psychologists in the United States, and roughly 45 percent do in fact deal with personal problems. But that leaves more than half of the group doing something else (Pion et al., 1996). What are the rest of them doing? Well, some try to understand what the world is like for children or adolescents or older people—that is, what are their worries, hopes, needs, and so forth. Some help design spacecraft cabins so dials and switches are in the right place and so the captain in an emergency won't hit the "up" button instead of the "down" button. Still others study the effects of various drugs, while some counsel alcoholics or drug abusers. Another group works with delinquents, while others try to figure out what causes delinquency in the first place. Psychologists work in educational systems. They try to understand exactly what we measure with an IQ test (since we're still not completely sure); they try to keep the good students moving forward and help struggling ones get themselves together; they try to improve both teaching and learning. Some psychologists handle rape and suicide crises, while others try to figure out why such things happen and how best to prevent them.

As you may have guessed by now, this list could go on and on. Figure 1.1 (on the next page) shows the major areas of psychology. And at the end of the chapter, you'll find a fairly detailed outline of the tasks involved in some of the major fields of psychology.

Defining Psychology

At first, when we look at all the things that psychologists do, it doesn't seem possible to come up with a single definition for what psychology is. But there actually is one that fits them all: **Psychology** is the scientific study of mental processes and behavior. The term *behavior* is not used here in its simple, everyday sense. It refers to almost *any* activity. Thus, the blink of an eye is behavior, and so is sweating. Mental processes are everything that the mind is capable of doing. They include such things as thinking, learning, remembering, believing, forming attitudes, wishing, imagining, and so on. For example, when we observe that someone avoids stepping on cracks in the sidewalk (behavior) because the person thinks that stepping on one will cause something terrible to happen (mental process), we are in the world of psychology. Thus, studying behavior and mental processes usually means trying to figure out why they occur.

The meaningful study of any subject requires some kind of structure. In science, theory provides that structure. A **theory** is a general frame-

▲ *Some psychologists study the workplace environment or consumer behavior. Others help people with their problems by leading group therapy sessions.*

psychology the scientific study of mental processes and behavior

theory a general framework for scientific study; smaller aspects can be tested

▶ **Figure 1.1** *Where Psychologists Work*

Where Psychologists Work

- University, college, school, and other educational settings — 32%
- Business, industry, and self-employed settings — 42%
- Nonprofit organizations — 16%
- Government — 10%

Some Specialized Fields in Psychology

Educational	Teaching
Media	Experimental
Adulthood and aging	Psychological testing
Engineering	Physiological
Rehabilitation	Developmental (children)
Community	Personality and social
Psychology and the law	behavior
Psychopharmacology	Clinical (abnormal)
Mental retardation	Industrial and
Consumer behavior	organizational
Psychology of women	Exercise and sport
Psychology of men	Environmental

work or idea about the nature of something. Because it covers so much, a theory is usually too complicated to be directly tested or researched. However, smaller aspects of it can be. When enough of these smaller parts prove true, the theory itself is supported. A theory, then, is something like a tree, and its branches and leaves are testable ideas or assumptions.

In sciences such as chemistry and physics, theories are fairly straightforward. In psychology, though, things can get pretty confusing. After all, there may be many causes for a particular behavior. For example, people can be violent if they come from a family in which they have learned to deal with arguments by beating each other up. But there are also cases in which a person suddenly goes into a rage for no apparent reason. This might be a physical problem. As we will discuss in Chapter 3, there is a part of the brain that, when stimulated, causes a person to become extremely violent. In 1966, a man with a brain growth on this area climbed atop a tower at the University of Texas carrying rifles and ammunition and picked people off one by one. By the time the police got him, he had shot 44 people, killing 14 of them. So psychologists study the physical as well as the psychological aspects of behavior (Valenstein, 1973).

Focus

Four "Cool" Questions

Critical thinking means carefully examining and evaluating ideas or claims in order to reach sound conclusions. All sciences demand critical thinking, and psychology is no exception. Thinking critically also means being objective and not letting the emotions or ideas you have already formed decide the case (Romain, 1997; Wade & Tavris, 1993). Listed below are four questions that we believe will help you think critically about psychological research and theory.

1. **What specifically is being claimed or stated?** This question requires you to carefully define and summarize the position being taken. Don't oversimplify or overstate the case.

2. **What is the objective evidence for and against this claim?** When evaluating evidence, you cannot let your emotions interfere. You may think or hope that the evidence supports a particular viewpoint, for instance. However, if the evidence is not there, or if it is very weak, you must take that into account.

3. **What other interpretations might be made instead?** Here, your job is to consider other perspectives, other ways of looking at the evidence.

4. **What are the most logical conclusions to draw?** In answering this question, you will probably have to put up with some uncertainty. In psychology, we often cannot draw absolute conclusions. Instead of thinking in black-and-white terms, we prefer various shades of gray.

If we focus on a key word in each question we get a list that looks like this:

- Claim?
- Objective evidence?
- Other interpretations?
- Logical conclusions?

The first letter of each of these key words put into a word spells out "COOL." This is a "cool" way to remember these steps when we want to analyze an issue. As you read the chapters in this text, you will be given specific opportunities to practice critical thinking skills. These "COOL" questions will guide you through the process.

According to the dictionary, what are two meanings for the term *criticism?* Which meaning underlies the term *critical thinking?*

Research Versus Applied Psychology

Depending on how much attention you were paying to the very beginning of this chapter, you may or may not have noticed that there are two basic types of psychologists. One group studies the origins, causes, or results of certain behaviors. Another group uses such information to deal with people and solve problems directly. Psychologists in the first group are called **research psychologists.** Since psychologists in the second group make direct use of (or "apply") psychological studies, they are called **applied psychologists.** As we will discuss in Chapter 6, airlines have discovered a rather serious problem: pilots are falling asleep in the cockpit as you ride along at 30,000 feet. Research psychologists who study sleep patterns and basic body rhythms have determined why this happens. Applied psychologists consult with airlines and suggest ways to fix the pilots' schedules in order to avoid the problem.

research psychologists psychologists who study the origin, cause, or results of certain behaviors

applied psychologists psychologists who make direct use of the findings of research psychologists; they deal directly with clients

5

Focus Questions

• Who pioneered the science of psychology?

• How did psychologists of the past explain human behavior?

History of Psychology

For our purposes, psychology has the goal of understanding the human being, how and why we operate the way we do. To understand what psychology is today and how it got there, you need a brief history.

At the beginning of the 1800s, science as a whole was in its infancy. Psychology had not really begun to be a science in the formal sense. But in the 1800s, **Charles Darwin** went on a five-year sea journey around the world. He had two feet of walking space in his cabin and was seasick the whole time. When he was on land, though, he noted that animals he knew well at home in England had developed differently in other places due to climate or food sources. Eventually, he suggested that animals, including humans, had evolved and changed. His theory has been causing argument since 1859 when it was first published. He was so worried about the effect his book might have on religion that he hid his manuscript from his wife for 14 years for fear that it would upset her (Stone, 1980; Adams, 1969). The importance of Darwin's theory for our purposes lies in the fact that it inspired scientists to study animals in an attempt to understand humans better, something psychologists still do all the time. Indeed, there are certain similarities between humans and animals. Although the individual units in the brain differ in size and location, the overall structure of the human brain is quite similar to that of the chimpanzee, for instance. Since other animals are less complex than human beings, scientists of Darwin's era assumed that if we understood how they worked, we could apply this information to ourselves.

By the mid-1800s, it looked as if science was going to be able to understand almost everything—including the human being. Our species was going to be examined and understood in detail. At least that was the goal, but as you know, people are more than a little difficult to pin down.

▲ *Charles Darwin: " I love fools' experiments. I am always making them." (1887).*

Wilhelm Wundt

Wilhelm Wundt (pronounced VOONT) (1832–1920) is called the "father of psychology" because in 1879, he started the first laboratory for studying humans. Like many famous people, he got off to a rocky start. Darwin's father, for example, had called his son a bum and had told him he was too lazy and stupid to ever amount to anything. Albert Einstein, one of the world's greatest mathematicians, kept failing high school math as well as college entrance exams. When he finally got through school, he claimed it had injured his mind. So, too, with Wundt; he spent most of his time in class daydreaming and failing, for which his teachers kept slapping him in the face (literally). Fortunately, a few teachers saw the promise of greater things in him and helped him to pull himself together. He eventually wrote so many books and articles that if you read 50 pages a day, it would take you three years to get through them all. Several well-known early American psychologists studied under Wundt or were strongly influenced by him (Benjamin, Durkin, Link, Vestal, & Acord, 1992; Fancher, 1979).

In Wundt's time, sciences like chemistry were having success in breaking things down into parts. Wundt thought he might be able to break down the human mind in the same way. In other words, since chemists had found that water can be broken down into two parts hydrogen and

▲ *Wilhelm Wundt: "The work which I here present to the public is an attempt to mark out a new domain of science" (1873).*

one part oxygen, maybe the same type of thing could be done with the human mind. If that was possible, psychologists would understand the basics that go into making up our feelings and thoughts.

Wundt's idea was to train people to be very accurate in describing the sensations they got from objects they touched. For instance, if you pick up something like a shoe, what sensations (sights, smells) does it cause? What images or memories? What emotions (love, hate, distaste, and so on) does it bring out? If you pick up a cat, what kinds of responses does that bring? Wundt hoped that, with responses to enough different objects, he would find certain things in common. These would be the basic elements that humans use to build the thoughts they have.

There is no question that Wundt had an excellent idea here. Unfortunately, it didn't work. The number of descriptions he and his assistant got kept getting larger and larger. At one point, people had described 44,000 different sensations, with only a small number in common.

What went wrong? Actually, nothing. Wundt was learning that the human is so complex that mechanical measurement alone won't work. The only way anyone can deal with things like emotions and sensations is to ask people what they feel. This process is called **introspection,** which means "looking into" yourself and telling what is there (Bringmann & Tweney, 1980). Once you do that, though, rigid science becomes less rigid. Even today we have to rely on introspection when trying to get information about complex feelings.

introspection the process of looking into yourself and describing what is there

But Wundt's work was not all a waste of time. He and his followers showed that some things about the human can be measured in a scientific fashion and that if you are clever enough, you can get information in an objective fashion that is fairly reliable (Mueller, 1979).

Psychologists today will always try to be as objective as possible, even when they have to rely on introspection. But sometimes relying on introspection is not necessary. For instance, in Chapter 2, we will show you how an experiment is done. The issue we will deal with is an interesting one: Are males *really* better at playing video games than females? The results might surprise you, but we don't want to give them away here. In any case, such a study does not require introspection even though, as you will discover, it deals with very complex social and personal issues.

Sigmund Freud

In the late 1800s and early 1900s, **Sigmund Freud** (FROID) (1856–1939), an Austrian physician, developed one of the first comprehensive theories of personality. His special areas of interest were how personality develops, what can go wrong, and how to fix it. His theory is based on the effects of unconscious conflicts within the individual. In other words, we are influenced by things we are not aware of. We are also influenced by our experiences in early childhood. In Freud's view, problems that appear in adolescence or adulthood can be traced to things that happened in the first five or six years of life.

Freud's theory had a huge impact on psychology through the 1950s. Its popularity then declined from the 1960s through the 1980s. Recently, though, psychology has renewed its interest in unconscious processes (Greenwald, 1992; Kihlstrom, Barnhardt, & Tataryn, 1992). The current emphasis is somewhat different from Freud's. However, his work as a pioneer of this subject definitely set the stage.

▲ *Sigmund Freud: "A man like me cannot live . . . without a dominating passion. . . . It is psychology" (1895). Here Freud is seen with Anna, who continued her father's work in psychoanalysis.*

William James: "Psychology is the science of mental life" (1890).

John B. Watson: "No one today knows enough to raise a child" (1928).

William James

William James (1842–1910), a philosopher and Harvard professor, was one of the founders of American psychology. In 1890, he published a very important and widely used textbook on psychology. It took him 12 years to write, was 1,400 pages long, and filled two volumes. James himself apologized for the book's length. In fact, he even suggested parts the reader might skip to keep from getting bored (James, 1890).

James was interested in how humans function and adapt to their environment. Rather than breaking consciousness down into its elements, he preferred to look at human experiences as complete wholes. For example, he tried to understand thinking as a "stream" of ideas, not a series of separate thoughts. As far as James was concerned, each person perceives and reacts to the world slightly differently. While basic rules of behavior may apply in general, psychology must never lose sight of the individual (Leary, 1992).

John B. Watson

Working mostly in the 1920s, **John B. Watson** (1878–1958) was one of the first American psychologists to study the impact of learning on human emotion. Because of his emphasis on learning, he is associated with behaviorism, an approach covered in more detail shortly. Watson believed that what we feel and do depends on connections and associations we have made. For instance, we are afraid of something because we have associated bad or unpleasant experiences with it. Most people would agree that learning plays a major role in our lives. According to Watson, though, nearly everything we are is caused by learning. Put another way, we are what we learn to be.

Watson believed that careful, structured parenting could prevent most psychological problems from ever happening. Frustrated by the haphazard methods most parents used, he wrote a book on child rearing. The goal of his book was to teach parents how to apply scientific learning principles in bringing up their children (Watson, 1928).

Learning theory was a major early force in psychology. It has been greatly expanded since Watson's time, and its popularity continues to this day. Several useful treatment approaches in mental health come from this school of thought.

 ## Pause for Thought

1. How does this text define *psychology*?
2. Why were Darwin's discoveries important to psychology?
3. What important theory did Sigmund Freud propose?
4. What special approach to psychology is associated with John Watson?

Critical Thinking

5. Why might people think that introspection is unscientific?

Present-Day Psychology

Focus Question

- What approaches do today's psychologists use to describe human nature?

Since the early years, psychology has expanded dramatically. Many theories about what humans are and how we develop have arisen. Some have dropped by the wayside, but a number of approaches are still important today. We have chosen six of these important approaches to cover here and again in more detail later in the book. The first thing you will notice is that these theories to some extent contradict one another. The fact that they do not agree is all right, however, since we don't have anything close to the final answers about human nature. Thus, each of them is a good guess with some support—but not the last word. Also, sometimes one theory fits a particular situation where another might not. So while most psychologists tend to lean toward one approach, they often borrow here and there from other theories, developing their own combination. This process is called **eclecticism** (ek-LEC-tuh-cism).

eclecticism the process of making your own system by borrowing from two or more other systems

In Focus

Eclecticism

The eclectic is like a child in a candy store who knows that getting only one kind of candy will not be quite satisfying enough.

Which jar would best explain your behavior during class?

The Biopsychological Approach

Why do people behave as they do? Although many view behavior in strictly psychological terms, other psychologists view behavior as **biopsychological** (*bio*—physical, including nerve cells, chemicals, muscular responses, and so on + *psychological*). Suppose you are on a camping trip and decide to find a secluded place under a tree just to enjoy nature. You sit down, leaning back against the tree. You are watching something to your left that has captured your attention. But then you hear a muffled noise and feel something on your right leg. You look down and, to your horror, see that a snake is using your leg as a pathway on its travels. You instinctively jump up, shaking your leg and gasping.

Biopsychologists examine behavior like this in terms of the physical changes that take place. When you see a snake or other scary creature, your heart starts beating rapidly, your muscles tense, your breathing becomes shallow, and you start to perspire. In this case, your body undergoes a full emergency reaction. Eventually, you calm down, and your body goes back to normal. Biopsychologists study the physical processes that take place when you panic *and* when you relax.

Another example of the biopsychological approach can be seen in research on depression. We know that significant losses and stress are often involved. Biopsychologists, however, emphasize other factors. Their focus is on changes in the brain's chemistry that occur in depression. Understanding this aspect of depression has led to important and useful methods of treatment.

The Behavioral Approach

The **behavioral approach** states that we are the products of learning and associations. We are the end result of all the different events we have been exposed to throughout life, the types of responses we have

biopsychological approach an approach that views behavior as strongly influenced by physiological functions

▲ *For most people, this is a sight guaranteed to start a chain of physical reactions.*

behavioral approach an approach that views behavior as the product of learning and associations

▲ *Behaviorist B. F. Skinner studied pigeons in his research on learning.*

made to them, and the consequences of making those responses. Whether or not you get involved in delinquent behavior, for instance, depends on the types of punishments or rewards that have been part of your life up to the time you make the decision. If the praise and rewards for *not* doing forbidden things have been great enough, this will successfully counteract the desire to do something forbidden, such as vandalizing someone's property. But if you have gotten attention over the years mostly for doing things that are not allowed, then the rewards for doing them can be greater than the rewards for not doing them.

John B. Watson was an early behaviorist, but one of the most famous recent behaviorists is **B. F. Skinner** (1904–1990). Skinner disliked philosophy and focused only on what could be seen. He believed we are controlled by the environment in the sense that we become whatever the environment forces us to be—good or bad (Skinner, 1967). Shortly before his death, Skinner wrote a paper about his concerns over the direction psychology was taking. Psychology, in his view, was moving away from the study of observable behavior. He felt that the emphasis on things we cannot see or study directly, such as cognition and unconscious processes, threatens to make psychology less scientific (Skinner, 1990).

In Their Own Words . . .

B. F. Skinner's *focus was on discovering the laws of behavior and applying them. In his own words:*

Science is more than the mere description of events as they occur. It is an attempt to discover order, to show that certain events stand in lawful relations to other events. . . . But order is not only a possible end product; it is a working assumption which must be adopted at the very start. We cannot apply the methods of science to a subject matter which is assumed to move about capriciously. Science not only describes, it predicts. It deals not only with the past but with the future. Nor is prediction the last word: to the extent that relevant conditions can be altered, or otherwise controlled, the future can be controlled. If we are to use the methods of science in the field of human affairs, we must assume that behavior is lawful and determined. We must expect to discover that what a man does is the result of specifiable conditions and that once these conditions have been discovered, we can anticipate and to some extent determine his actions. (Skinner, 1953, p. 6)

Interpreting Primary Sources

Skinner refers to "lawful relations" and "lawful behavior." What do you think the word *lawful* means in this case: (a) moral, (b) legal, or (c) predictable? Give reasons for your answer.

The Psychoanalytic Approach

Perhaps the best known of all theories, that of Sigmund Freud, considers our inner selves to be cesspools of forbidden desires. Freud developed a theory that centered around sexual and aggressive impulses that are hidden in our unconscious from early childhood. These impulses live below the surface of consciousness and from there control our everyday behavior in ways we are not aware of. For example, if you were very angry at your mother but knew better than to say anything, you might, when you call out to get her attention, say, "Oh, Bother!" The unconscious has replaced the "M" with a "B," showing your real feelings. Since these impulses are hidden, in order to understand them and have more choice about them, we have to *analyze* them with the help of a therapist. Thus, this approach to our behavior is called **psychoanalysis.**

Currently, psychology's interest in unconscious processes does not focus on sex and aggression, as Freud did. Instead, psychologists try to understand what kinds of perception, thinking, and memory go on below our level of awareness and without our conscious control (Greenwald, 1992). Nevertheless, many of Freud's ideas are still around. His influence can still be felt today.

psychoanalysis a system that views the individual as the product of unconscious forces

▲ *Believe it or not, having fun is part of actualizing your potential.*

The Humanistic Approach

The **humanistic approach** to human behavior arose largely in reaction to problems some psychologists had with both psychoanalysis and behaviorism. The term *humanistic* comes from *humane*. So, this group of psychologists believes that people are basically good and that our very nature is such that we could reach perfection—if all went right.

To the humanists, each of us is like the perfect seed. If we get the right amount of water, nutrients, and sunlight from the environment, we will become a perfect flower. Personal growth is internal and very individual. We are in control of our destinies, and all of us can make our lives worthwhile. Unlike the behaviorists, the humanists believe that the environment does not *force* us to become anything; instead, it acts as a background for our internal growth. How we handle the death of a loved one, for instance, is an individual thing in which we call on our own internal resources to make the best of it.

The most famous humanist is **Carl Rogers** (1902–1987). He studied for the ministry before switching to psychology. Possibly this influenced his beliefs, because he saw people as worthwhile creatures with free will and choice (Rogers, 1986, 1961). To him, every human has the potential to become great in his or her own (however small) way, something he called our *actualizing,* or directional, tendency.

The Cognitive Approach

The fifth approach is one of the most popular in psychology today. It is called the **cognitive approach.** The word *cognition* refers to thinking or using mental processes. Once you understand that, the cognitive approach will be clear. For cognitive psychology, the most important human ability is that we can take information from the environment, analyze it, and come up with a solution to almost any problem. So, we are first and foremost thinking creatures able to compare the past with the present and make judgments. We humans are special because we can change our thought patterns after looking at different problems and deciding on the best approach.

To the cognitivist, our personalities are, to some extent, made up of the different kinds of sentences (thoughts) we have inside our heads. If you pay close attention, you will notice that there are many times during the day when you are carrying on a conversation with yourself inside your head. In fact, you are, in a sense, sitting there listening while this goes on, even though it's coming from you. These sentences can sometimes get us in trouble, as when we keep saying, "This math is completely impossible to understand." The cognitivists believe that if we replace such internal sentences with more useful ones like, "Joe Smaltz is not that smart and *he* can do math, so I can, too," it will have an impact on how well we do (Hilgard, 1980; Haugeland, 1978).

humanistic approach an approach that views people as basically good and capable of helping themselves

cognitive approach an approach that emphasizes how humans use mental processes to handle problems or develop certain personality characteristics

The Sociocultural Approach

In recent years, psychology has begun to look more closely at how much we are influenced by our culture. Thus, the **sociocultural approach** studies the impact of specific social, ethnic, racial, and religious groups on behavior. For example, it's clear that a suburban white girl and a Native American boy on a tribal reservation live in very different worlds. They probably have different experiences and opportunities, activities and values, dreams and goals. They also follow different rules and have different expectations. Each child's culture influences how she or he spends time and plans for the future, what is learned, and so on. However, they are both affected by the overall American culture as well.

Which cultural and social differences are the most important? What areas of life do these differences affect? How can we measure these effects? Do we need special ways of dealing with certain problems? These are some of the questions a person taking a sociocultural view of behavior might ask.

For a time, this approach looked mostly at such issues as racial prejudice and the fairness of IQ testing for different groups. Now, however, it has spread to nearly every area of psychology. One major concern is how to counsel people from cultures different from our own. Another has to do with education. Still others include such things as motivation and emotion, crime and criminal justice, family systems, and smaller social groups and their impact (Pedersen, 1991).

In Their Own Words . . .

To **Carl Rogers**, all humans have an innate tendency to fulfill their potential. He called this the actualizing, or directional, tendency.

The actualizing tendency can, of course, be thwarted or warped, but it cannot be destroyed without destroying the organism. I remember that in my boyhood, the bin in which we stored our winter's supply of potatoes was in the basement, several feet below a small window. The conditions were unfavorable, but the potatoes would begin to sprout—pale white sprouts, so unlike the healthy green shoots they sent up when planted in the soil in the spring. But these sad, spindly sprouts would grow 2 or 3 feet in length as they reached toward the distant light of the window. The sprouts were, in their bizarre, futile growth, a sort of desperate expression of the directional tendency I have been describing. They would never become plants, never mature, never fulfill their real potential. But under the most adverse circumstances, they were striving to become. . . . In dealing with clients whose lives have been terribly warped . . . I often think of those potato sprouts. So unfavorable have been the conditions in which these people have developed that their lives often seem abnormal, twisted, scarcely human. Yet, the directional tendency in them can be trusted. (Rogers, 1980, pp. 118–119)

Interpreting Primary Sources

Rogers used the example of how most plants will turn toward light to explain how he believes people try to fulfill their potential. What does this excerpt tell you about Carl Rogers's values?

Pause for Thought

1. Which psychological approach states that we are the product of learning and associations?
2. What are the basic beliefs of the humanistic approach to psychology?
3. Which psychological approach is the newest?

Critical Thinking
....
4. Which psychological approach do you believe is the most scientific, and why?

sociocultural approach an approach that views behavior as strongly influenced by the rules and expectations of specific social groups or cultures

Thinking Critically about Psychology

A Critical Look at Child Abuse

Let's try an example of thinking critically about a psychological issue so you can see how this process might work. Here is a statement many of us have heard before: "Most people who were physically abused in childhood abuse their own children later on. In fact, this is the major cause of child abuse."

1. **What specifically is being claimed?** First of all, this statement refers to "most people." That does not mean all such people, so a single exception would not make the statement false. It does say "most," though, so unless it holds true for a majority of cases, the claim is not valid or accurate. Second, the statement says that parents' having been abused as children is the most important reason that child abuse occurs. If other factors are equally important causes of child abuse, then the claim is not accurate. So, we have two issues to examine. The first is whether most people who were abused as children abuse their own children. The second is whether this situation is the most important cause of child abuse.

2. **What is the evidence for and against this claim?** There is no way you could know the answer at this point, so let us supply it for you—very, very briefly. To begin with, we know that abusive parents more often have a history of having been abused as children than nonabusive parents (Trickett & Susman, 1988). We also know, however, that at least two-thirds of those people who were abused in childhood nevertheless are good parents themselves. This is even more likely to be the case if, as children, they had an adult in their lives that they could trust and count on (Papalia & Olds, 1995; Egeland & Sroufe, 1981).

As for whether an abusive history is the most important cause of child abuse, we know that a number of other factors are also related. For instance, marital problems, extreme poverty, and substance abuse all contribute to this tragic situation. Ignorance about how to parent and about what children are able to do and understand at different ages also plays a role.

◀ *Conflict exists in every family. Fortunately, however, abuse does not.*

3. **What other interpretations might be made?** At least one other interpretation can be made at this point. A chaotic family life filled with conflict and problems can increase the likelihood that child abuse will occur. On the other hand, having the ability and opportunity to develop a stable family life and learn new parenting skills reduces the risk that parents will abuse their children (Peterson & Brown, 1994).

4. **What are the most logical conclusions to draw?** Conclusions that seem reasonable to us are the following ones. The original statement is not completely accurate or valid. It is true that people who were physically abused in childhood are at higher risk for being physically abusive to their own children. However, most of them are able to overcome their histories and become good parents. This is especially so if they do not have serious ongoing problems in their adult lives. While a history of abuse is a

▲ *Family counseling can improve parenting skills and reduce the risk of child abuse.*

contributing factor, it is only one such factor and others may be equally important. It may take a little practice to get used to thinking this way. Once you get the hang of it, though, it can become almost second nature. Then you will have a skill that you can use not only in your schoolwork, but in other areas of your life as well.

Applying Critical Thinking Skills

You can conclude from this feature that child abuse is less likely to occur when parents have good parenting skills. What parenting skills or knowledge do you think could be taught in school?

See if *COOL* works for you....

Claim?

Objective evidence for and against claim?

Other interpretations?

Logical conclusions?

Case Study

Before Psychology

For a few thousand years, knowledge about human behavior came from arguing and discussing rather than from scientific evidence. The Greek philosopher Aristotle taught that the highest form of reasoning and thinking took place in the heart. This early claim is echoed today when a lover says, "My heart yearns for you." While the Greeks knew we had a brain, they thought of it as a big gland that was placed near the nose to help cool down the forces of life that descended from heaven and entered the body (Bergland, 1985).

The Greeks also noticed that if you take blood from a vein and let it sit in a glass, the blood separates into a blackish clot at the bottom, then a layer of yellow fluid, and finally a thin layer of white on top. This fact was the basis of the early belief that personality comes from what you have in your blood. If you have too much of the black material ("black bile") flowing through you, it makes you depressed and sad. The Greeks called this *melancholy,* a term we still use today. Too much yellow material, and you are bitter, angry, and hot tempered. Too much white material, and you become dull and sluggish. (There is some truth to this last claim: the white part comes from cells that increase when you have an infection, which *can* make you feel dazed.)

The Greeks thought personality could be changed by "bloodletting," using leeches or a knife to pierce the skin in order to allow evil spirits to escape. This could work—but not for the reason they thought. If you take enough blood out, a person weakens, and his or her personality seems to change for a while until he or she begins to recover. Then it's back to the same old self. This removal of blood as a "treatment" was popular for many years. In fact, George Washington in the late 1700s suffered from bouts of melancholy or depression unless he stayed active, so he often had blood removed, and he claimed that it made him feel better (Flexner, 1974).

You can't fault the Greeks because there were no scientific procedures developed to study behavior. No one knew how to begin. Meteorites and stars sailing through the skies were thought to be battles going on between the gods. Beliefs in such powers led to astrology, the prediction of behavior by observing the position of planets and stars. Each day was controlled by one of seven different planets, in order, one after the other. This is where our seven-day week comes from. The sun is Sunday, the moon is Monday, and so on.

▲ *Aristotle taught his students that reasoning and thinking took place in the heart.*

Why do so many people continue to believe in astrology, even though there's not a shred of scientific evidence to support it? Human behavior is so complex that it's easier to create simple theories that sound good, even if they remain unproven. One goal of psychology is to counter that urge to jump to easy conclusions, and to provide *scientific* answers to the questions humans have been asking for centuries.

Review the Case Study

What are some "simple" theories people still believe today?

In Focus

Six Important Theories in Psychology

Theory	Description	Approach to Studying Alcohol Abuse
Biopsychology	Behavior viewed in terms of biological responses	Is alcoholism a disease? What role does heredity play? How does alcohol affect the brain?
Behaviorism	Behavior viewed as a product of learned responses	Is alcoholism learned? Can it be unlearned? Can new habits replace drinking habits?
Psychoanalysis	Behavior viewed as a reflection of unconscious aggressive and sexual impulses	Is heavy drinking an indication of some conflict raging in the unconscious? Does drinking release inhibitions, allowing unconscious desires to surface?
Humanism	Behavior viewed as a reflection of internal growth	Do people drink because they don't feel a sense of worth? Does alcohol provide false esteem?
Cognitive Psychology	Behavior viewed as a product of various internal sentences, or thoughts	What thoughts lead up to episodes of heavy drinking? If analyzed, can drinking patterns be changed?
Sociocultural Psychology	Behavior viewed as strongly influenced by the expectations of social groups or cultures	How does alcoholism differ among cultures? What societal pressures might cause alcohol abuse?

Suppose a millionaire wanted to fund research to find answers to these questions. To which psychologists should the millionaire give money?

Analyzing Your Neighbor

Strange things always go on next door or down the block. And everyone knows about them. So now, we will look at the problem that John, who lives down the block, has, and we'll examine it using each of the six approaches discussed. In this way, you'll get a better understanding of how each approach views the person.

John is 40 years old and lives still with his mother. He has never been married but has a good job as an engineer. His life seemed to be going well—until one day a month ago his boss chewed him out for not doing something right. During the last month, John has been worried and depressed because he has started to forget things. He told his mother, who told Ethel who lives next door, and now everybody knows. Here are examples of what has been happening to him: He was supposed to turn in plans for a new project but forgot they were due. He had always

Focus Question

• What kinds of questions do psychologists ask?

Psychologists would make different recommendations to help John with his problems, depending on their approach.

remembered his mother's birthday, but this time he completely forgot about it, hurting her feelings, even though she pretended not to be upset. A month ago, a few days after the incident on the job, he met a woman he really liked and set up a date with her for later in the week. But he had forgotten that he was going to be out of town then, so he had to cancel the date.

Biopsychological Analysis

Psychologists know that memory is stored better if the learner is excited at the time of the event. Chemicals that aid in storage are much higher with excitement, anger, fear, or hope. But John's condition is such that just the opposite is going on; he is depressed. Depression lowers the level of brain chemicals that aid in memory. Therefore, John's memory problem is seen by biopsychologists as the result of a physical malfunction resulting from the trouble at work and other chaos in his life.

Behavioral Analysis

The behaviorists see the problem differently. When John was in grade school, he was comforted and hugged by his mother, not scolded, when he did things like forgetting to bring a book home to study for a test the next day. Not only that, but she let him stay home the next day because he "didn't feel well." So, over time, John has learned very bad habits. Something in John's present life is worrying him, just as an exam the next day used to do. Now he is doing the same thing that worked well in the past; he is not forgetting textbooks, but he is forgetting other things to try to get love and attention from his mother.

Psychoanalytic Analysis

The psychoanalysts focus on desires and needs such as sex and aggression. John is suffering from a conflict. He wants to stay with his mother but knows that if he has a close relationship with the other woman, which he also wants, he will someday have to leave home. Since the two desires cannot live side by side, he is getting more frustrated and aggressive toward others. This is shown by his forgetting his mother's birthday. But the more the conflict goes on, the more guilty he gets, so he tries to forget this "bad" side of himself. He forgets many things in his effort to hide from the ongoing basic conflict raging in his unconscious.

Humanistic Analysis

For the humanists, John will soon continue with his fine work as an engineer. But his inner world has suffered a number of setbacks. It was going so well, but now he is more and more distracted. Exactly what is it that is causing John so much worry? His individual self has been injured. His personal growth has been slowed because he made mistakes and got upset about them and because he is starting to bring another woman into his personal life, which requires major adjustments. These distractions are causing the forgetting. But he still has the same basic internal strength and purpose. He will soon recover and get back on course if given patient understanding and a chance to regain his footing.

Cognitive Analysis

Cognitive psychologists focus on thinking skills rather than on previous learning or unconscious impulses. For them, John will have to sit down and take out a piece of paper and analyze (a cognitive process) exactly what his life is like. He has to focus on the kinds of things he is saying to himself that are causing him so much trouble. For example, he is convincing himself he is forgetful. He is talking himself into hopelessness because he made a mistake at work. He is telling himself he can never do anything right. If, however, he makes a formal, logical plan of action and decides what he is going to do about this "other woman" in his life, then his memory will improve all by itself.

Sociocultural Analysis

Sociocultural psychologists focus on cultural influences on our behavior. They would want to know what special social pressures exist in this man's particular world.

In John's subculture, being publicly chewed out is a serious disgrace and a threat to one's self-image. Also, when a father dies, his son, married or single, is expected to live with and care for his mother. So John's depression makes sense after he has suffered public humiliation. His boss needs to know the importance of what happened so that John can get back some of his self-esteem. John's forgetting his mother's birthday and having to cancel his date were caused by social conflict. The overall American culture is pressuring him to marry and set up his own family. His own culture is pressuring him to stay with his mother and take care of her, as a dutiful son is supposed to do. Part of the answer lies in everyone's having a better understanding of the special conflicts John faces. Another part of the answer lies in John's making some decisions about which social demands are the most important to him.

In Their Own Words . . .

It may seem that figuring out what is in someone's unconscious mind would be nearly impossible. **Sigmund Freud** *didn't think so.*

When I set myself the task of bringing to light what human beings keep hidden within them . . . by observing what they say and what they show, I thought the task was a harder one than it really is. He that has eyes to see and ears to hear may convince himself that no mortal can keep a secret. If the lips are silent, he chatters with his finger tips; betrayal oozes out of him at every pore. And thus the task of making conscious the most hidden recesses of the mind is one which it is quite possible to accomplish. (Freud, 1953, pp. 77–78)

Interpreting Primary Sources

According to Freud, how are hidden conflicts expressed, or "made conscious"?

Pause for Thought

1. A psychologist who assumed that medicine taken by a patient had affected the patient's behavior would be following which approach?
2. How might a behaviorist explain why some people pretend to be ill to get sympathy?

Critical Thinking
. . . .
3. Which approach do you think assumes that the individual has the most control over his or her behavior?

APPLYING
Psychology to Life

Careers in Psychology

I n case you become interested in psychology as an occupation (which we hope will happen), here is a review of some major areas in the field. Most of these occupations will require an advanced degree, meaning a master's degree (two to three years beyond the regular four years of college) or a doctorate (four to five years beyond).

Clinical/Counseling Psychologists

Clinical or counseling psychologists work with people who have marital, personal, or mental problems, using specialized techniques to increase their clients' self-confidence and to reduce behaviors that are causing them trouble. These psychologists give psychological tests and help people to understand themselves and others better. They may work in private practice, in a mental hospital or clinic, in industry, or in a school system.

School/Educational Psychologists

Some educational psychologists work in the school setting. The tasks are varied. Some help design and improve the learning

▲ *Psychological testing is often done by clinical psychologists.*

systems and curricula involved in education. Some work directly with the students, helping them with personal or learning problems or with the choice of a career. Others try to improve the quality of the school system as a whole and act as educational advisers to the administration.

Environmental Psychologists

Environmental psychologists work in industry or for the gov-

ernment. Their task is to study the effects of the environment on people. They look at the effects of disasters, overcrowding, and toxic materials on the health and welfare of the population as a whole or on individual families. They also study such things as how best to design an environment (such as a factory) in order to keep those working there reasonably comfortable.

Developmental/Child Psychologists

As you will find when you read the chapter on child psychology, children live in a world all their own and have sets of rules often beyond adult comprehension. Psychologists in this area study child development, but they also often work in clinics or private practice to help disturbed children or to help parents who are trying to understand the problems they face in living with and rearing these "foreigners."

Industrial Psychologists

Psychologists in this area "take sides," so to speak. They work with management to try to improve working conditions, to obtain greater efficiency from the work force, to increase sales, and to keep the company's image positive with the public. They also work with employees on any issues they might have, from difficult work conditions to problems at home.

Engineering Psychologists

Psychologists in this area work to design systems that help people become more efficient. These psychologists do everything from studying how to design the instruments on a machine or an automobile for greatest efficiency to figuring out the best physical design for a shopping mall so that people are able to get in and out efficiently and pleasantly.

Experimental Psychologists

These psychologists work in industry or universities. They perform research to understand better how the human operates physically or psychologically. This work may include the study of drugs, of physical reactions, and of the effect of certain laboratory events on human beings or animals. The goal of all of these studies is to add to the literature—that is, the books and articles that are studied by other psychologists as well as made available to the public. For example, an experimental psychologist might try to answer the question, "What leads to a heart attack?"

Teaching

Teaching psychology can involve any of these fields. That is what the authors of this book do. It's the most exciting field in the world. We hope some of you will try it someday. The rewards of communicating with others and helping them to understand are truly remarkable.

▲ One theme park sponsored a stress management program for "coaster-phobics"—people who are afraid of roller coasters. The program, led by a Harvard-trained psychologist, included tension-relieving exercises.

Summary

1. Psychologists work in just about every setting you can imagine. About 45 percent help people with personal problems.

2. Psychology is the scientific study of mental processes and behavior. Psychologists use theories (general ideas) as a framework for research. There are two basic types of psychologists—those who do research and those who apply the research.

3. Charles Darwin's theory, published in the mid-1800s, suggested that animal studies might help us understand humans.

4. . Wilhelm Wundt started the first human psychology laboratory in 1879. He tried to break the human mind down into basic parts, but both the mind's complexity and the need for introspection kept him from reaching his goal.

5. William James wrote an important early psychology textbook. He tried to understand how we humans function and adapt to our environment.

6. Sigmund Freud developed a comprehensive theory of personality. His emphasis was on unconscious conflicts in early childhood.

7. John B. Watson studied the effect of learning on emotions. He wrote a book on child rearing based on his ideas.

8. Eclecticism is the process of developing one's own system by borrowing from two or more other systems.

9. At least six important approaches guide our understanding of human behavior today:

    a. The biopsychologists see behavior as mostly influenced by bodily and chemical processes.

    b. The behaviorists, such as B. F. Skinner, see us as creatures who are formed and controlled by what we learn and the associations we make.

    c. The psychoanalysts find us controlled by unconscious impulses, especially sex and aggression.

    d. The humanists, such as Carl Rogers, see people as basically good and able to achieve almost anything. For them, each of us is special and in control of his or her destiny.

    e. The cognitivists focus most on the thinking brain, which can talk itself into (and out of) almost any belief or behavior.

    f. Sociocultural psychologists emphasize the influence of specific cultures on attitudes and behavior.

10. Psychologists use critical thinking skills to evaluate theories and research. This means carefully and objectively weighing evidence to arrive at sound conclusions.

Vocabulary

psychology
theory
research psychologists
applied psychologists

introspection
eclecticism
biopsychological approach
behavioral approach

psychoanalysis
humanistic approach
cognitive approach
sociocultural approach

Review Questions

Fill in the Blank

On a sheet of paper write the word or words that best complete each statement.

1. A general framework for doing more specific research is called a ▓▓▓▓.
2. Psychologists who use research to solve practical problems are called ▓▓▓▓.
3. Psychologists who study the causes of behavior are called ▓▓▓▓.
4. ▓▓▓▓ is considered the father of psychology.
5. A famous psychologist who studied how people function and adapt to their enviroment was ▓▓▓▓.

True/False

On a sheet of paper, answer each statement true *or* false. *If false rewrite to make it true.*

6. B. F. Skinner was an early behaviorist who wrote a book on child rearing.
7. Psychology is no longer interested in the study of unconscious processes.
8. The overall structure of the human brain is remarkably similar to the structure of a chimpanzee's brain.
9. The process of introspection helped Wilhelm Wundt categorize sensations into five main areas.

Matching

On a sheet of paper, match terms in right column with definitions in the left column. Answers may be used more than once.

10. Rewards and punishments control behavior.
11. Physical changes are emphasized.
12. Humans are basically good.
13. The unconscious plays a great role in behavior.
14. The enviroment is all-important.
15. Ethnic and religious backgrounds influence behavior.
16. Humans control their own destinies.
17. A person's thoughts are emphasized.
18. Chemical changes in the brain influence behavior.
19. Sexual and aggressive impulses control behavior.
20. "Self"-talk directly influences personality.

a. behavioral approach
b. psychoanalytic approach
c. cognitive approach
d. biopsychological approach
e. humanistic approach
f. sociocultural approach

Discussion Questions

1. How could both a research psychologist and an applied psychologist be involved in studying stress? Explain. Offer examples of what each type of psychologist might do.

2. Each of us constructs "theories" about behavior based not on research but on our own experiences. Describe one of your "theories," and discuss what parts of the theory you might like to test if you were a psychologist. Sample: "When it begins to drizzle, male drivers tend to turn on their windshield wipers, turn them off, and turn them on again as needed. Females, on the other hand, turn the wipers on and leave them on." This is a silly theory, of course, but you could test its numerous assumptions: Are females more safety conscious than males? Are females lazier? Are males more fidgety? And so on.

3. John is afraid to fly in airplanes. Explain John's fear from the point of view of the behavioral approach and the cognitive approach.

4. Of the six approaches to studying and understanding behavior discussed in this chapter (biopsychological, behavioral, and so on), with which do you tend to agree the most, and why? With which do you agree the least? Explain.

5. Maria wants to ask for a raise but becomes uncontrollably anxious every time she even gets near her boss. Using the six approaches discussed in this chapter, briefly describe how each might explain this simple behavior.

6. Someone studies your palms and claims she can read your future. She sees deep lines intersecting and informs you that your ambitions run deep and that you will be wealthy by the time you are 30 years old. Analyze the person's claims using the four steps outlined in the In Focus feature and modeled in the Thinking Critically about Psychology feature.

Activities and Projects

1. For this first activity, we want you simply to write down 40 questions that you want answered by this text or course. The questions can range from simple to complex, from general to personal. Some examples: Why are my parents becoming grouchy lately—is it a midlife crisis? Why am I hungrier in the winter? Does hypnosis really work? Forty questions may seem like a lot at first; but you'll be surprised at how quickly you complete this activity, since psychology deals with so many interesting issues. Feel free to skim through the text for ideas. If your list of questions seems to end at about 25, leave it, and come back to it in a day or two until you *can* complete it. It might be interesting to save this list or post it in the classroom and, at the end of the year, check how many of the questions were answered.

2. Write a dialogue between two psychologists who disagree on the nature of humans. One psychologist could be a proponent of the cognitive approach, for example. The other might believe more in the behaviorist approach. Try to make the dialogue as realistic as possible. The two could argue, let's say, about why gambling seems to be on the rise or why students drop out of school.

3. Often, the information that an applied psychologist borrows or uses from a research psychologist may seem practical at first but then may not turn out that way. For example, Watson wrote a book to teach parents how to apply scientific learning principles in raising their children, but it is difficult to determine how successful this was.

These kinds of parenting books are still being written today. Your task is to find out how effective they seem to be by interviewing two or three parents with preschool children. Of course, you will need to find parents who consult these books from time to time and who might have an opinion on the topic. A good area to focus on might be discipline.

An alternative to interviewing could be to read various sections from a parenting book or two and write a report on *your* reactions.

4. In the next chapter, you will learn how psychologists gather information about behavior and the environment through scientific experimentation. For now, we want you to gather information about the environment through informal observations. Visit two of the following sites (or choose your own sites): grocery store, train station, fast-food restaurant, factory, doctor's office, office building. Take notes on as many of the following categories as possible: (a) colors used, (b) music played, (c) arrangements of products, (d) arrangement of furniture, (e) other details you may notice.

Next, analyze your observations. *Why* does a store have red walls and low lighting? How will this influence your behavior? Does it make you want to hang around or leave quickly? Does it keep you awake or put you to sleep? Don't worry too much about the "correctness" of your analysis. The purpose of this activity is not to search for "right" answers but merely to make you more aware of how psychology is all around you.

These are the kinds of observations you might note if visiting a grocery store: (1) Milk, located at the back of the store, is a popular item. As you walk through the entire store to get to it, you might buy other items. (2) Children's cereals are stacked on the bottom shelf so children, at their eye level, can point out the boxes to their parents. (3) Snack items located at the checkout counter encourage impulse buying while you wait.

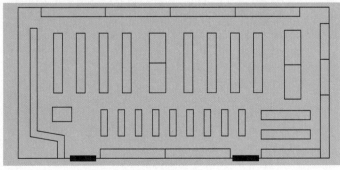

Typical Grocery Store Layout

Divide your report into two parts. Part One should be an *analysis* of your sites, as described in the previous paragraphs. Part Two should be a *critique* of your sites. For example, do you agree that slow music should be played at a particular site? Why or why not? In your critique, be sure to include suggestions on how to improve the design of the site. If you visited a family restaurant, you might suggest that it supply crayons and paper for kids to keep them busy (and, yes, quiet).

5. The Applying Psychology to Life feature at the end of the chapter lists several types of psychologists. Contact a psychologist who fits into one of the categories listed and interview this person. Have a list of questions prepared beforehand. Possible questions: (1) What kind of education is necessary for your particular job? (2) Would you recommend one kind of graduate school over another? (3) Are there many jobs available today in your type of work? (4) What would a typical day at work be like for you—or is there no such thing as "typical"? (5) What motivated you to enter this line of work? Write a report of your interview.

6. Select an issue in psychology that might be controversial. Examples include whether ESP exists, whether people can really have multiple personalities (called dissociative identity disorder), whether the mind can repress and later recall some tragic incident, and so on. Find two or three articles on your topic, and write a four-paragraph report using the "COOL" critical thinking skills introduced in this chapter. Paragraph 1: What is being claimed? (There may be many claims, some opposing each other. Just pick one.) Paragraph 2: What objective evidence is presented for and against this claim? Paragraph 3: Are there any other possible interpretations of this evidence? Paragraph 4: What is the most logical conclusion?

Try to find just a few articles that seem to represent both sides of the issue. Your "logical" conclusions then will be based on limited evidence, and acknowledging this may affect your reasoning. One last option: you might want to interview someone who *has* read dozens of articles, and then count this as one of your sources.

CHAPTER 2

To avoid bias and false conclusions, psychology, as a science, tries to be as objective and factual as possible in its studies. This chapter covers some of the research methods that are used to gain information about people and animals. These methods are designed to prevent the personal bias of the researcher from distorting the conclusions reached.

Methods of Psychology

Scientific Methods

In a year, Americans consume roughly one *billion* dollars' worth of pain relievers, such as aspirin. Pain relievers come in many forms: They may be tablets, capsules, or crystals that dissolve in water. They may be coated, buffered, or built up with other "added ingredients." It is a huge business and advertisers fight vigorously for every cent they can wrench from us. Their techniques often involve TV commercials using questionable "studies" and distorted charts, diagrams, and claims. How well do these products really work? The only way to find out is to perform an actual, unbiased study of a product.

Psychologists do these kinds of studies because the question immediately arises, "How much, if any, pill-taking brings about a cure based on the power of suggestion?" The goal of the researchers is to be completely objective. For instance, you would have to be careful about the age and sex of the subjects studied. Their overall health would have to be explored. If a handful of people in the group you were studying happened to have a major illness or a disease that caused pain, the pain reliever would probably affect them differently than it would a person who was in good health but had a headache. And you would have to determine whether it was actually the pain remedy that was responsible for the cure.

If we take an average of the studies in this area of pain relief, it turns out that roughly 50 percent of pain is "cured" by the power of suggestion (Frank, 1974). This is discovered when the experimenter uses one group that is given the real medicine and a similar group that is given a "medicine" with nothing in it that could cause a change. This second "fake medicine" is called a **placebo** (pla-SEE-boh). By comparing the cure rate between the two groups, we discover that 50 percent are getting better just because they get a pill they *believe* will bring relief.

The patients' expectations obviously play a major role here. Often, researchers' expectations have an impact as well. For instance, knowing that one group is only getting a placebo might change the experimenter's attitude. Then the patients' responses might be interpreted differently. Such a situation might well affect the accuracy of the results. It's better, then, if neither the patients nor their examiners know which group is which. When this is the case, the study is called a **double-blind study.** This means that neither the participants nor the researchers know which group anyone belongs to until the study is finished.

Psychological studies provide broad scientific information about what we do, why we do it, and what changes go on during the process. Studies do not attempt to establish what is "right" or "wrong" as much as to provide accurate information. For example, some people might decide that since 50 percent of the people get better without a painkiller, this group should not take pills for a headache. That, however, would be a highly questionable judgment, because other studies show that when people take a pill they *believe* will help them, their body chemistry actually changes to provide pain relief—even for those taking pills that contain no pain reliever. Thus, fake pills can be necessary for triggering the body's own internal pain relievers.

One of our major goals in the first part of this chapter is to acquaint you with some of the terminology used in experimentation. This is best done by discussing a few different studies.

• How do psychologists use the scientific method to study behavior?

▲ *The power of suggestion affects cure rates.*

placebo a "medicine" that has no active ingredients and works by the power of suggestion

double-blind study a study during which neither participants nor researchers know to which group any subject belongs

Basic Procedures: A Study of the Effects of the Moon

An area of interest that has been around since ancient times involves the belief that the moon influences our behavior. In fact, the word *lunacy* (insanity) comes from the word *lunar,* which means "of the moon."

One study compared mental hospital admissions with the phases of the moon to see if there might be some relationship between a full moon and abnormal behavior. Researchers compared mental hospital admission rates for the days during the full moon phase with the rates for ten days before and ten days after the full moon (Blackman & Catalina, 1973). They did find what seemed to be a relationship between the full moon and "lunatic" behavior. (See Thinking Critically about Psychology on page 30.)

Hypothesis

hypothesis a statement of the results that the experimenter expects

We will use this study to help you become familiar with the terminology used in experimentation. The researchers started with a **hypothesis** (hy-POTH-ah-sis), which is a statement of the results they expected to get. In this case, the hypothesis was that there would be a relationship between the occurrence of the full moon and an increase in mental hospital admissions.

Choosing Subjects

subjects people or animals on whom a study is conducted.

Subjects are people (or animals) on whom research is conducted. In this study, the subjects were people being admitted to a mental hospital.

Variables

variables factors that change in an experiment

Every study has **variables.** The term *variable* refers to things that can change (vary). In the present research, the variables were the phases of the moon and the rate of mental hospital admissions. Researchers want to examine how one variable changes, as the other changes. So, in this study, they asked, "During different moon phases, does the admission rate vary?"

Sometimes there are hidden or unexpected variables to guard against. There was one in the moon study that was not discovered until after the study was over, and it invalidated the results. The time period after the full moon happened to include a weekend. Hospital admissions drop over weekends. As a result, there was a sudden drop in admissions that was not connected with what was being studied—the moon's phases. Hence, we cannot conclude based on this study that the moon has an effect on people's mental health. When the experiment was run again, eliminating a weekend, the moon's phases no longer showed up as having any relationship to admission rates. Researchers always have to watch out for this kind of problem (Campbell & Beets, 1980).

The finding of the second study is disappointing because most of us like to believe in the exotic. To date, studies of many kinds have found that no clear connection exists between the moon and mental problems or criminal behavior, except in horror movies (Rotton & Kelly, 1985).

A Study of Stereotypes

Focus Questions
....

- What is a stereotype?
- What are independent and dependent variables?

To acquaint you with some more terms, we will examine an issue that relates to how we perceive other people. A stereotype is a set of fixed, generalized beliefs we hold about a given group. These beliefs are often inaccurate. Nevertheless, we tend to assume that everyone from that group shares the same characteristics. For instance, if you believe that elderly people are crabby, you will probably expect that behavior from a friend's grandmother when you meet her for the first time. We will study stereotypes in more detail in Chapter 20.

Research: Men, Women, and Management

It has been shown repeatedly that stereotypes are strongest when people have little or no other information about a particular member of a group. For example, women traditionally have been perceived as unsuited for jobs in management. Imagine that you don't know anything about two people except that one of them is the president of a large company. Now imagine that one of these people is a man and the other a woman. Wouldn't you be likely to decide that the company president is the man rather than the woman? Most of us would be. One of the troubles with stereotypes is that they frequently result in discrimination. People may be treated unfairly simply because they belong to some group or other. In business, then, an individual woman may be denied the opportunity to prove herself because of a stereotype about women in general (Heilman, 1984; Martinko & Gardner, 1983).

▲ *Stereotyped roles for men and women are fast disappearing. Today, females may work in construction or play football, and many nurses are male.*

29

Thinking Critically about Psychology

Effects of Moon Phases

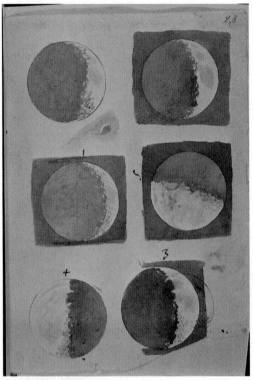

▲ *Galileo prepared these drawings of the phases of the moon for one of his books.*

For most people, learning to use the critical thinking process effectively takes time and practice. If any skill is to be developed, it must be used regularly and with the intent of improving it. This is true for critical thinking just as it is for sports, music, or keyboarding. In Chapter 1, you learned four "cool" questions to use for examining claims: (1) What specifically is being claimed or stated? (2) What is the objective evidence for and against the claim? (3) What other interpretations might be made instead? and (4) What are the most logical conclusions to draw?

To help you develop your critical thinking skills, apply the four critical thinking questions to the following statement. *"Phases of the moon affect human behavior in such a way that mental hospital admissions, emergency room visits, and illegal acts increase during the appearance of a full moon."* Use the information in this text, independent research, and your own careful logic to complete this activity.

To further help you get started, we will briefly summarize some information for you to examine. We have already discussed in the chapter a study of phases of the moon and admission rates to mental hospitals on page 28. We should also note that emergency room personnel and police officers sometimes claim that during a full moon the pace of their jobs becomes much more frantic. They state that they see more cases and stranger cases than is true at other times. Again, there is no scientific evidence to support this idea.

After you have completed your own critical thinking exercise, you may read the example provided on the next page.

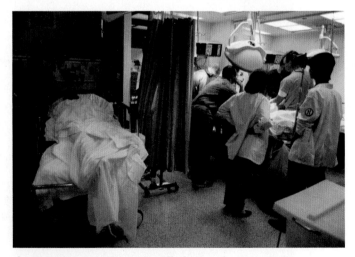

▲ *Are emergency rooms really busier during a full moon?*

Section 1B

Psychology

What specifically is being claimed or stated?

Phases of the moon affect human behavior in such a way that mental hospital admissions, emergency room visits, and illegal acts increase during the appearance of a full moon.

What is the objective evidence for and against the claim?

Legend and folk wisdom tell us that some people act strangely or differently when under the influence of the full moon. This is reflected in myths about witches and werewolves. No scientific proof of these stories exists, however. Also, as stated in the text, hospital personnel and law enforcement officials claim that reports of injury and crime increase during periods of a full moon. (This evidence is anecdotal, meaning that these are merely stories from individuals. Anecdotal evidence can be interesting, but it is not scientific. It does not prove anything.)

The text cites research that found "no clear connection between the moon and mental problems or criminal behavior" (Rotton & Kelley, 1985). In addition, a recent survey of studies on this topic found only two that offered any support at all for the claim. And follow-up studies failed to duplicate these earlier findings (Holmes, 1997).

What other interpretations might be made instead?

Why do people continue to believe the moon affects behavior? It can be difficult to dispute an idea that has been woven into culture and mythology. People want to believe in the exotic and the strange. So they may more readily accept some statements that lack scientific proof. In addition, we often see what we want to see, rather than what is really there. Police officers, emergency room staff, and others may take more notice when something unusual happens during a full moon than at some other time. They also may ignore all those full moons when nothing much occurred. Consequently, it seems to them that this relationship exists, but it actually does not.

What is the most logical conclusion to draw?

No relationship has been scientifically shown to exist between the phases of the moon and human behavior.

See if COOL works for you....

Claim?

Objective evidence for and against claim?

Other interpretations?

Logical conclusions?

Applying Critical Thinking Skills

In what ways was your analysis of the effects of the moon similar to the example provided above? In what ways did it differ? Did you reach the same logical conclusion?

▲ *As more women assume management roles, stereotypes should begin to break down.*

independent variable the factor that the experimenter manipulates or changes in a study

dependent variable the factor in a study that changes or varies as a result of changes in the independent variable

One study of this issue had an equal number of men and women evaluate candidates for promotion to a managerial job. The subjects were given the job description and fictional summaries of several applicants' past professional experience. Half of the applicants were male, half female. The subjects were then asked to rank the applicants in order. All of the candidates had good work histories and were described as successful in their previous jobs. The only difference, then, was gender, which the subjects could figure out by the applicants' names. We still aren't ready for the results, though. There is another twist to this story. The subjects differed from each other in one important way. Some of them had personal experience working under a female manager; the rest did not.

So, what were the results of this study? What questions would we like to have answered? Well, the first one might have to do with whether male or female candidates were ranked higher. Since stereotypes are strongest when there is little information about a person, and since in this study the subjects were given a lot of information about each candidate, it might not surprise you to learn that there was no evidence of a bias against the women applicants. (In fact, the women got slightly better ratings than the men did!) The more intriguing question to us, though, and the one we want to focus on, is whether having worked for a woman in the past made a difference. It did, and in a somewhat unexpected way. The subjects who had never worked for a woman before ranked the men and women equally. The subjects who had personal work experience with female managers ranked the women applicants significantly higher than they ranked the men. In other words, these people were more *in favor of* women as managers, something you might not expect to happen (Pazy, 1992).

It's always risky to draw broad conclusions from a single experiment. However, this study is backed up by many others that have made the same observation—namely, the more personal experience we have with members of a group, the less likely we are to apply stereotypes to them.

Variables: Independent and Dependent

This study shows the importance of two special kinds of variables that are part and parcel of scientific experiments. The first is called the **independent variable,** meaning that the researcher changes or varies this factor in a study. In the experiment just described, the independent variable is a subject's experience working for female managers. The experimenters varied this by dividing the subjects into those with such experience and those without it and then looked at the responses of these two groups. The other special kind of variable is called the **dependent variable,** meaning that it will change as a result of what the other factor does. You might think of it as being dependent on the independent variable. Put another way, the results you get depend on what else has happened. In this study, the ranking of men and women changed as a result of the experience of the people doing the ranking. Thus, the dependent variable is the ranking of male and female candidates for promotion.

Focus

Independent Versus Dependent Variables

How can you tell which is the independent variable and which is the dependent variable? Most hypotheses include the words *IF* and *THEN*. Here's a sample:

IF a request is made by a person in a uniform,
THEN more people will agree to this request than to a request made by someone without a uniform.

IF refers to the independent variable (what is controlled).
THEN refers to the dependent variable (what is measured).

Even when the words IF and THEN are not actually used, they are implied. For example, consider the hypothesis "People are more likely to obey instructions from someone who is near them than from someone who is far away." The IF part, the independent variable, is nearness. The THEN part, the dependent variable, is obedience. The hypothesis could be rewritten this way: "**IF** someone is nearby rather than far away, **THEN** that person is more likely to be obeyed."

Try to identify the independent and dependent variables in the following example: "People tend to jog faster than usual when others are around to watch."

Field Studies

Not all research is carried out in a laboratory. A study that is done away from the laboratory is called a **field study,** because it happens away from the laboratory or "in the field."

Studying Jet Lag

As we will discuss in Chapter 6, a current and serious problem is the effect of rapid transportation on pilots and passengers. The disturbances created are called "jet lag" because the rhythm of the body lags behind (or runs ahead of) the time of day at the destination. In other words, a person's internal time clock is still set on the time at home while the person is engaging in activities on a different schedule at a different place (eating lunch at 4 P.M., for example). Our bodies are very sensitive to any kind of shift in the time of day when we eat, sleep, or work. The result of major shifts in time are fatigue, stomach distress, dizziness, and mental confusion.

For example, jet air travel causes a disruption in the normal cycle of behavior when we fly across the ocean. Flights across the ocean are usually made at night. The airlines claim that the passenger will arrive at his or her destination "ready for a day's work." That's not really true. Here's what actually happens. If you leave from New York and are flying east, you will cross

Focus Question

• How do psychologists apply the scientific method when studying behavior in the field?

field study research that takes place outside the laboratory

five time zones and arrive in Europe five hours out of synchronization with your own body's time clock. Thus, if you arrive at 9 A.M. London time, it actually is 4 A.M. at home. Your body is operating on home time. And 4 A.M. is the low point in the day for almost everyone; it is the time when your body is least able to cope with any kind of stress. It will take you at least several days to get into synchronization with London time, yet you are expected to operate at full efficiency right away when you are weakest and least able to do so (Moore-Ede et al., 1982). So this shift in light and darkness, and the changes in habits that it causes, will create all the symptoms associated with jet lag. These effects have been demonstrated over and over and are the subject of considerable concern, even when they involve shorter time zone changes such as those that result from crossing the United States. But perhaps some people are still skeptical of these claims. How do we set up an experiment that will clearly show that the problem comes from rhythmic changes rather than just from the fatigue of flying itself?

▲ *The man in the top photo avoided the pitfalls of jet lag by never getting off the ground. The* Concorde, *however, can cross several time zones in a relatively brief trip.*

experimental group the group on which the critical part of the experiment is performed

control group the group that does not participate in the critical part of the experiment

To examine whether the effects arise from the disruption of body rhythms, the scientist uses the same experimental procedures that are followed inside the laboratory. To illustrate that the effects are not from fatigue, the experimenters can look at the different reactions of two groups of subjects. The first group will fly to Europe, crossing the time zones. This group is called the **experimental group,** since the critical part of the experiment is being performed on them. A second group is needed, however—one that does *not* cross time zones. In this way, we can note how the effects of the trip differ for the two groups. So, we have to *control* the critical part of the investigation, the flying across time zones. "Control," then, refers to removing, for one group, the factor being studied. (Note that this was done in the study on pain relievers. One group was given a "medicine" that did not contain any medically active ingredients so that it could be compared with the group that received the real painkilling medications.) Thus, we form what is called a **control group.** Our control group will fly an equal time and distance but to South America. The shift in light and darkness and the alteration of sleep and eating times *do not* occur for this group because there is no time change.

What we discover is that the control group does not suffer the physical effects of jet lag, which show up dramatically in the experimental group. Hence, we have demonstrated that the problems come from time changes, not the length of the flight itself.

To go over it once more: The independent variable is the alteration of the usual light-dark cycle by using a time-changing flight path, and the dependent variable is the result of the alteration: fatigue, poor decision making, and disturbances of the body's rhythmic cycles. The control group, which does not undergo the specific factor we are studying, is then contrasted with the experimental group—which *does* undergo the critical variable.

Fighting Insomnia

So many technical terms can be difficult to grasp at first, so we will review them with an additional experiment. In this one, we want to determine if people who have trouble sleeping (insomnia) can be helped by taking a "sleeping pill" before going to bed.

The experimenter assembles two groups of insomniac subjects and administers sleeping pills to one group and placebos to the other group. Here are the experimental setup and the results:

Hypothesis. *X* amount of sleeping pills helps the otherwise healthy person with insomnia to sleep better.

Subjects. The subjects of the experiment are two groups of people in similar physical health, within the same age range, and with similar sleep problems.

Independent Variable. (This is the variable that the experimenter changes.) The experimenter regulates the "medicine," with one group receiving genuine sleeping pills while the other receives a placebo.

Dependent Variable. (This is what results from the experimenter's varying or changing the independent variable.) The results can *vary* among better sleep, worse sleep, and about the same amount of sleep.

Control. (This is the removal of factors other than the independent variable that might cause the results.) The experimenter will not use people who are sick, people with severe allergies, or people who are very old. Any one of these factors could alter the real effects of the medicine in the average person with insomnia.

Control Group. (This group consists of subjects who are like those in the experimental group except that they do not participate in the crucial part of the study.) The control group in this study consists of those subjects who receive a placebo, thinking it is a sleeping pill.

Experimental Group. (These are the people who participate in the crucial part of the study.) The experimental group consists of those subjects who get *X* amount of sleeping pills.

Results. The hypothesis turns out to be incorrect in a real-life study. Thus, we reject the hypothesis that those who receive the sleeping pill will sleep better. What is found is that subjects taking the sleeping pill over a period of days will still have insomnia, only worse. And the sleep they do get is less restful than the sleep the control group gets.

These results occur because most tranquilizers and sleeping pills interfere with dreams. They cause the person to feel worse because without dreams, sleep loses much of its "curative effect" (Hartmann, 1984). This subject is discussed in more detail in Chapter 6.

▲ *Insomnia can be a real nightmare. Does counting sheep really work?*

Experimental Procedure

Hypothesis
IF "A" (the independent variable) is present or changed,
THEN "B" (the dependent variable) will occur or change.

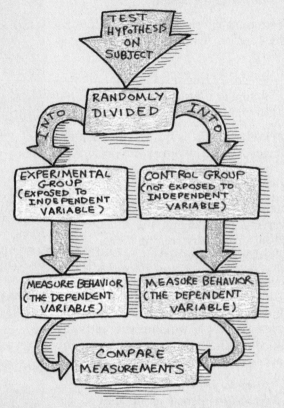

The diagram shows one control group. Is it possible to include more than one control group in an experiment?

 Pause for Thought

1. Why is it important to use placebos and a double-blind approach in some studies?
2. Assume that researchers find that people's memories are sharpest right after they've eaten lunch. What hidden variables may have affected these results?

Critical Thinking

3. How might you use the scientific method to study factors that affect obedience? Devise a simple study, and identify the following: hypothesis, subjects, independent variable, dependent variable, experimental group, and control group.

Other Methods for Studying Behavior

In this section, we want to acquaint you with other methods that psychologists use to study behavior.

Survey Method

A **survey** involves asking questions of a carefully selected group of people. This allows you to gather information on feelings, opinions, or behavior patterns. Surveys can be done by mail (using questionnaires), in person, over the phone, or via television using a responding device set up in the home. Which method is used is not as important as the kind of people chosen to participate in the research. Suppose we wanted to find out if people think that there is too much crime and that the prison sentences given to criminals are too light. If, say, 30 percent of our sample is made up of ex-convicts, we will get a distorted view of the general population's opinion on this subject—to say the least.

Since we can't interview everyone, a **sample,** or small group, must be chosen that represents the general population. The sample should be composed of a correct proportion of people from various races, sexes, social classes, and age groups. When this small group truly reflects the characteristics of the larger population, it is called a **representative sample.** Such a representative sample can produce results that are amazingly accurate. The Gallup Poll, for instance, is careful to include people from all the various groups in the U.S. population. As a result, the poll is an excellent predictor of the actual presidential election results.

The way a question is phrased can also be of major importance. Advertisers are infamous for phrasing questions in such a way that they get results favorable to their points of view. For instance, an advertiser might

- What is the survey method?
- How do psychologists use observation, case study, and testing to study behavior?
- What is the difference between longitudinal and cross-sectional studies?

survey a method of research that involves asking subjects questions about their feelings, opinions, or behavior patterns

sample a group that represents a larger group

representative sample a group that truly reflects a selected characteristic of a larger population

▲ *Opinion polls are a type of survey. How the samples are selected is critical to the accuracy of the results.*

ask, "Which aspects of car X [the advertiser's car] do you like better than car Y?" This question forces a biased answer. After the survey, the advertiser places ads that ignore the original question and how it was phrased and, instead, say something like, "Ninety percent of people surveyed said they preferred car X over car Y!" Such advertisers would be afraid to ask the more meaningful question, "Do you prefer car X or car Y?"

Using a questionnaire sent through the mail can pose a big problem that may distort the results—namely, filling out the questionnaire takes time and trouble. Hence, many people will not bother to fill it out and mail it back. Usually, only those with an ax to grind or a special devotion to the issue will go to the trouble of responding. In some surveys, as few as 20 to 30 percent of the questionnaires are returned. It is hard to put much faith in such a low response rate. Too many opinions are missing.

naturalistic observation a research method that involves studying subjects without their being aware that they're being watched

Naturalistic Observation

In **naturalistic observation,** researchers secretly observe the subjects of the study—animal or human—in daily activity, carefully recording their behavior. The advantage to this method is that the creatures will behave as they normally do, since they don't know anyone is watching them. Both people and animals behave differently in the presence of an outsider. Thus, it is possible to get more realistic information on behavior through naturalistic observation. For example, observing male and female monkeys interacting with one another and as a "family" shows that males do a great deal more pushing and shoving of one another than do females, a situation similar to that found among humans. If the monkeys are in the laboratory or are aware of your presence, they do not act out their full repertoire of behavior. For humans, as we will discuss in Chapter 20, laboratory studies on the effects of violent TV programs strongly suggest that such TV shows cause violent behavior to increase. But naturalistic observation of people viewing violence yields results that don't always match the laboratory results; in some cases, people become less violent after a violent program. Thus, a whole different perspective is provided by this method.

▲ *Although the researcher can see these children, the children cannot see her. From inside the classroom, the window looks like a mirror. In this way, naturalistic observations of the children can be made.*

One of the flaws of naturalistic methods is that the observer is not able to talk with or interact with the human subject. In some cases, the observer may be making an incorrect interpretation of exactly what is going on, since the subject is never asked.

Interviews

interview a research method that involves studying people face to face and asking questions

A common method for studying people and how they feel about things in the present is to **interview** them. Quite a bit of personal, detailed information can be obtained with this technique. The biggest problem here is trying to sort out fiction from fact, since the interviewee is going to be on his or her best behavior and will try to present information in the most favorable light. More often than not, for example, when people are asked what kind of television they watch, they will claim they are glued to the set viewing educational material on public TV rather than a soap opera or a block-buster film filled with murder, mayhem, and mischief. If what they told us were true, the public television channel would be the one most watched, which it never is, and the commercial networks would be broke, which they are not. Even so, a fair amount of reasonably accurate personal data can be gained through the interview.

Another problem is that the interviewer always has to be on guard against his or her own biases in a face-to-face situation. All of us carry around subtle and not-so-subtle prejudices against certain types of people, certain age groups, certain modes of dress, and so forth. There is no doubt that these factors have an influence not only on the types of questions we ask but also, and more important, on the interpretation we give to an answer. An answer that seems clever or original from interviewee A might be interpreted as flippant or rude coming from interviewee B.

▲ *Interviews can be done in a variety of settings, including a bench in a park.*

Case Study Method

The **case study method** involves developing information about a person's long-term background, often for purposes of psychological treatment. The goal is to find out as much as possible about how the individual's personality has evolved from the early years in order to shed light on what might be the origin of present-day problems. This method is subject to the same distortion as the interview, but it is still a useful way to get a rough idea of how a person views the world. People who are very pessimistic might not know they are giving away the fact that they see most things so bleakly; but if you talk to them for even a short period of time, you get clues that suggest the presence of this attitude. If you are lucky, you will also get some background information that suggests how they became such black-cloud creatures.

In real life, the psychological interview or case study method is most often used to get an overall sense of how a person approaches problems and what his or her general feelings are. The psychologist generally doesn't rely too much on the specific content of what a person claims is the truth.

One word of warning about case studies—you cannot generalize from their findings. You *can* get a fair amount of detailed information about a particular person or situation, and that is the advantage of case studies. However, what is true for one case may or may not be true for others.

Psychological Tests

One way to overcome bias in an interview is to use objective **psychological tests.** An example is the IQ test. All of us have experienced the phenomenon of being mistaken about the intelligence of people we meet for the first time. They seemed to be very dull (or bright), but later we discover that we have misjudged them just because they looked

case study method research that collects lengthy, detailed information about a person's background, usually for psychological treatment

psychological tests objective methods for observation and measurement of subjects in various areas, such as intelligence

the way they did or dressed in a certain fashion. Problems of this kind can be avoided by using the IQ test, since it has a fixed set of questions *and* answers for scoring. It leaves no room for personal bias to enter into the interpretation of the results. The test takers either answered the questions correctly or they didn't. In a way, then, the psychological test is a kind of fixed, rigid interview with minimal opportunity for personal distortion. As we will discuss in Chapter 9, the test is a much better method than the interview for finding out a person's intellectual potential.

Tests of personality or job aptitude are, again, more objective than interviews, but when we move into these rather vague areas, the tests are often not as useful as observation of a person on the job or in interaction with others. Too often, people exaggerate the amount of information these tests provide. Such tests cannot predict behavior in the complex human with a high degree of accuracy, even though they can uncover important information that might be missed in an interview. The best of all worlds, then, is to combine and compare the results of the interview and the psychological test.

Longitudinal and Cross-Sectional Studies

In addition to the fact that there are all these different methods for investigating behavior, you should be aware that there can also be different goals behind such investigations. For example, in some cases, researchers want to know how large groups feel about a problem that is current today but are not concerned with how the opinions developed or changed over time. In other cases, researchers want to examine a pattern over time in groups in order to observe any changes that might occur. For example, you may have heard that intelligence notably declines with age. This seemed to be true from early studies examining the issue. How were these studies done? Since the goal was to compare intelligence levels for people of different ages throughout the life span, the experimenters took subjects from different age groups, running from late childhood through old age, administered IQ tests to each age group, and then looked at how the results changed from one age group to another. This technique is called the **cross-sectional method** because a cross section (or representative sample) was taken from each major age group.

These findings on intelligence, however, turned out to be incorrect. There was a major flaw in the way the study was designed that no one saw at first. Using the cross-sectional method required that the researchers use different people to represent different age groups. Therein lay the problem. The older people in the sample were from a generation that did not know as much as the generation following it. It seems that your generation will know more than we do, that we know more than our parents did, that our parents knew more than their parents, and so forth. (As long as we have to face up to this, we take some consolation in the fact that *your* children will know more than you do.) As a result, the cross-sectional method was measuring and comparing the older people, who had less knowledge to begin with, with younger people, who had more information. Thus, it *appeared* that as a person got older, intelligence declined.

How was the error discovered? To understand, you need to know that there is another system of conducting studies, called the **longitudinal** (lon-juh-TUE-di-nal) **method.** In the longitudinal method, the researchers

▲ *These similarly aged people are taking part in a cross-sectional study.*

cross-sectional method a method of research that looks at different age groups at the same time in order to understand changes that occur during the life span

longitudinal method a method of research that studies the same group of people over an extended period of time

Methods of Research

	Advantages	Disadvantages
Laboratory Study	Researcher can be completely objective. Method usually provides accurate information.	Setting is somewhat artificial, may not reflect the "real world."
Field Study	Setting is more realistic than in a laboratory.	It is often difficult to control all variables.
Survey Method	Researcher can gather information on feelings, opinions, and behavior patterns. Results can be amazingly accurate.	Survey's sample may not be representative of population as a whole. Questions used may not be phrased objectively. Interpretation of results may be distorted.
Naturalistic Observation	Behavior studied is completely natural.	Researcher cannot interact with subjects and may interpret subjects' responses incorrectly.
Interview	Researcher can obtain personal, detailed information.	Subjects' responses may not be completely honest. Researcher's biases can influence behavior.
Case Study Method	Method provides background information that may shed light on present behavior.	Subjects' responses may not be completely honest. Researcher's biases can influence behavior.
Psychological Test	Tests provide accurate, objective information—there is little chance of distorting results.	Tests are limited in the amount of information they can obtain.
Longitudinal Method	Method provides information needed for certain kinds of research, such as studies on development.	Method is expensive and time consuming.
Cross-Sectional Method	Samples used are usually representative of population as a whole. Method is less expensive and less time consuming than longitudinal method.	Method is not appropriate for some types of research, such as studies on developmental changes over time.

If you were a psychologist and you wanted to study whether reading to children would affect their reading ability once they entered school, which of these methods would be most useful and which would be least useful? Answer this question by ranking the methods from 1 (most useful) to 9 (least useful).

follow the *same* group of people through the years, measuring them again from time to time. You can immediately see why this method is not used very often, given the length of time and the expense involved. But sometimes it is necessary, as in this example about intelligence or in child development research.

When the longitudinal studies were applied to the *same* group of people over the decades, researchers discovered that the cross-sectional studies were wrong. They found that in general, people maintain approximately the same level of intelligence as they age. Of course, there is a slowing of reaction time and a moderate amount of memory loss when a person is quite old, but overall there is little decline in a person's mental abilities over his or her life span. Similar studies show that old people who are cranky, selfish, forgetful, and rigid in old age were that way when they were 30 and often when they were 15 years old.

Most psychological studies are cross sectional. But every now and then, longitudinal research still appears today.

Ethics of Experimentation

Throughout this book, you will read about studies that have required deceiving subjects or deliberately creating frustration and anxiety in people to see how they react in certain situations. These studies have been justified on the grounds that the researchers were seeking more information about the human being. The more knowledge we have of ourselves, the better off we will probably be, and the more likely it is that we can be helped or that we'll understand problems that arise.

But serious issues come up with this kind of research. How far can and should an experimenter go in trying to find answers? For example, in Chapter 20, we will discuss an experiment designed to determine the causes of deplorable conditions in prisons. The experiment in question was performed with college students. For a time, it *literally* turned the college-student "guards" into vicious people and the college-student "prisoners" into helpless, miserable creatures. After the experiment, there was greater understanding of what causes today's prison conditions, but some of the subjects were psychologically scarred from finding out that they could act the way they did. Was it ethical and worth it? We don't know; the matter is still being argued back and forth.

Ethical Principles

The American Psychological Association has established ethical guidelines for experimenters (see Figure 2.1). We want to cover the main points here to help you make your own decisions about what is ethical (American Psychological Association, 1992).

1. *Subjects must always have the right to decline participation in an experiment or withdraw their participation at any time.* This ethical principle is rarely violated. No one should ever be forced to take part in an experiment. Still, there can be hidden pressure: "If I don't participate, what will the teacher think of me? Will my grade be affected?" In cases where participation in research is a course

Focus Question

• What guidelines do psychologists need to follow when they conduct experiments?

Basic Ethical Guidelines for Psychological Researchers

- Do no harm.
- Ensure that participation is voluntary.
- Remove any misconceptions caused by deception (debrief).
- Provide results and interpretations to participants.
- Maintain confidentiality.
- Accurately describe risks to potential subjects.

▲ *Figure 2.1* *Basic Ethical Guidelines for Psychological Researchers*

42

requirement, some other fair option must be made available to the students.

2. *Openness and honesty are essential to experimentation.* Here is a typical problem in this area: Studies have been designed to examine under what circumstances a subject will cheat. The subjects are observed—unknown to them—in situations where cheating is possible. If the experimenter is honest with them, they will know they are being observed and will not cheat. How do we conduct this kind of study and still remain ethical? The general rule is that if researchers cannot disclose everything at the beginning of the study, they must do so as soon as possible afterward—a procedure known as debriefing. They are obligated to clear up any misconceptions their subjects may have.

3. *Information obtained about a subject during the course of a study must remain confidential.* The major exception to this rule applies when an agreement to the contrary has been made beforehand. When it is likely that other people will have access to the information, the experimenter must inform the subject of this possibility. Sometimes, though, the experimenter can't foretell with certainty just who will have such access. How far should confidentiality procedures be taken, and with what kinds of information?

4. *The experimenter has the duty to assess carefully the possibility of any potential risks, physical or mental, to participants; inform them of existing risks; and correct or remove any undesirable consequences of participation.* This rule covers both immediate and long-term effects. If an experimenter does a study in which subjects are made to feel inferior (as would be the case with a deliberately difficult test), then the subjects must be told the true nature of the test at the end of the study. Sometimes, however, as in the prisoner-guard experiment, the degree of potential risk is almost impossible to anticipate. Even though that experiment was terminated early, the damage had already been done. In cases like this, there doesn't seem to be any way to help participants completely forget how they behaved during the experiment itself.

In Their Own Words . . .

Psychologist **Martin Seligman** *conducted experiments with dogs while studying learned helplessness, the learned inability to overcome obstacles or avoid punishments. Applying electric shock to the animals was part of the procedure. Here is how Seligman described his attitude toward animal experimentation.*

Because our society's attitudes toward animal experimentation have changed since the 1960s, as have my own, I want to say a few words here about the ethics of such work. My views differ from those of many of my fellow scientists. Because producing animal suffering is wrong, it can be justified only if the experiments promise to help alleviate much more suffering in humans (or animals), and only if there is no other feasible method. My belief three decades ago was that research into learned helplessness showed such promise, and I turned out to be right. New therapies and new ways of preventing depression were developed as a result of this work. . . . But I also maintained that as soon as we had documented the basic facts in dogs and had found out how to cure and prevent helplessness, we should stop our experiments on dogs. This we did in the late 1960s, as we began to apply our findings to help human beings. (Seligman, 1995, p. 3)

Interpreting Primary Sources

Do you agree with Seligman's justification of animal experimentation in his work?

Experimentation with Animals

People all over the country are expressing concern about experimentation with animals. Since animals have many things in common with humans, researchers frequently study them in order to find out more about

Case Study

Experimenter Effect

What is the sum of 4 times 6 minus 5? How about 9 plus 21 divided by 2? What are the chances that a horse could correctly solve both these problems? In the case of Clever Hans the wonder horse, the chances were very high!

His owner, Mr. von Osten, a German math teacher, would present these kinds of math problems to the horse, and Hans would respond by tapping his foot the correct number of times (Rosenthal, 1965). Psychologists, of course, became interested in studying Hans and immediately introduced a few controls. As you might expect, they wondered if Hans's owner was intentionally or accidentally sending signals to his horse, so they asked him to leave the room while they ran their tests. Even with his owner absent, however, Hans didn't miss a beat. He seemed to be counting and calculating.

Could the experimenters themselves be sending subtle signals to Hans? Further testing revealed just that. As it turns out, if Hans could not see the questioner, or if the questioner did not know the answer, Hans was less than amazing. Psychologists eventually discovered why. Each time the questioner presented a problem, he would look down at Hans's foot. Apparently, this was the horse's cue to begin tapping. When Hans reached the right answer, the questioner would always look up amazed, and Hans would immediately stop counting. Hans was so sensitive to the lowering and raising of the head that he would tap faster when the questioner leaned his whole body forward and stopped when the questioner simply raised an eyebrow (Rosenthal, 1969).

Psychologist Robert Rosenthal has written about Hans and has also conducted numerous studies to show how an experimenter can sub-

▲ *Clever Hans (from the Archives of American Psychology, University of Akron).*

tly affect the results of an experiment, a phenomenon known as *experimenter effect,* or *experimenter bias.* Rosenthal (1966) hired several lab assistants and instructed them to observe and time rats as they ran through a maze. The rats were randomly chosen and equal in their ability to run mazes, but Rosenthal identified some of his rats as bright and others as dull. After several sessions, records showed that the bright rats were learning the maze significantly faster than the dull rats. Since the rats were not actually bright or dull, the lab assistants must have *created* the results they expected. They may have handled the rats differently or adjusted their training rituals in small ways, and the rats reacted accordingly.

Dozens of studies have shown that experimenter bias can affect humans too. When experimenters believe that some student subjects are high in intelligence while others are low in intelligence, the students who are treated as bright will actually score higher on intelligence tests (Rosenthal, 1969). The experimenters unintentionally communicate their beliefs to the students, and the students respond to these expectations.

Maybe some practical lessons can be gained from these studies. If a teacher's expectations can influence learning, this occurs only after students' own expectations are changed. This complicated process creates what is known as a self-fulfilling prophecy. If we label ourselves as good readers, for example, we'll start to act that way and we will eventually *become* better readers. Maybe we can all become more "clever" if we just start believing it!

Review the Case Study

What are some steps that experimenters can take to avoid bias while conducting research?

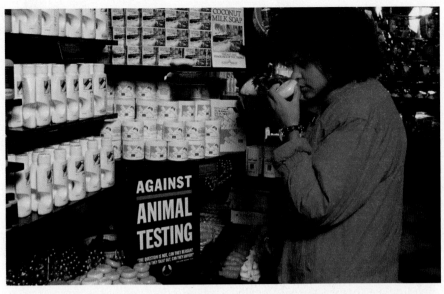

◀ *Ethical questions about using animals in experiments are a concern in psychology as well as in many other fields.*

ourselves. At the same time, they are not merely objects or abstract creatures with no feelings. Some people believe that any physical or psychological suffering caused an animal must be aimed at removing a problem in the human that is equal to or greater than the suffering caused the animal (Fox, 1983).

Some have pointed out that as the brighter creatures, humans have a moral obligation to protect animals rather than use them. Many people feel that since animals are part of the ecology of the planet, scientific researchers must show basic respect for them. Otherwise, scientists will not be taken seriously as individuals trying to foster the greater good of the world (Fox, 1980b).

According to a national survey of psychologists, most support the use of animals in research. They do not, however, support or approve of animal studies that cause pain or result in the death of their subjects (Plous, 1996). Fortunately, the bulk of evidence obtained about the majority of experiments in psychology suggests that animal treatment is humane, but humans must always be on guard against abusing their power over helpless creatures.

Pause for Thought

1. When using surveys, why do researchers use a sample of the population? What are two potential problems with surveys?
2. What is naturalistic observation? Identify one advantage and one disadvantage of using this method.
3. What are two potential problems with both interviews and the case study method?
4. What is the purpose of debriefing after an experiment?

Critical Thinking
. . . .
5. You are awarded several thousand dollars to study intelligence. How might you use both psychological tests and longitudinal studies?

APPLYING
Psychology to Life

Socialized Sex Differences?

There is no hotter topic among the general population as well as in the scientific world than that of differences between the sexes. (We will discuss this topic in some detail in Chapter 13.) Overall, we find that there are far more similarities between the sexes than differences. One area of difference does stand out, however, and this

is called *spatial ability*. Spatial ability is the ability to imagine how things look in space and to manipulate these objects mentally or physically. Thus, playing video games is a good measure of this characteristic. By and large, males take delight in the fact that females, as a group, don't compare well with males on this task.

While we can't disagree with this fact, it clearly requires a more detailed examination. One of the major criticisms of the suggestion that innate differences are involved is the possibility that females either aren't interested in tasks involving spatial skills or, more likely, that society puts pressure on them to stay away from such activities.

Can Females Improve Skills with Practice?

We are going to describe a real experiment on video games and male-female skills. The goal is to try to help you think through the basic problem and some of the issues that come up along the way in such a study. Then we'll give you the results of the study (Gagnon, 1986).

Fifty-eight students at Harvard University participated in the study, 34 males and 24 females. The purpose of the exploration was to determine if practice made any difference in video-game skills. If females don't play the games very often, could this be a factor in their relatively poor performance? In the study, one of the tasks to be per-

▲ *Are females really inferior at playing video games?*

formed was to play a video game called "Targ," which involves moving a spaceship through a maze while fighting off enemy ships.

An Experiment to Test for Improved Skills

As we proceed, touching on several questions about the study, try to answer each question for yourself before reading on.

What is the first step in the experiment?

First, a hypothesis is formed and subjects are selected. In this case, subjects were categorized as "expert" or "novice" on video-game playing to form a background for analyzing their results later on.

Do you need a control group?

Yes. A control group was used and was given no time to practice after a pretest of their skills on the machine. Using a control group reduces the possibility that any other factors will influence the results. The control group, then, took the pretest on the machine to establish a starting point, did nothing for a week, and then took a posttest on the machine. The experimental group took the pretest, got two-and-a-half hours of practice on the machine over the period of a week, and then took the posttest on the machine to detect any changes that might have occurred.

Here is what the experiment looked like in diagram form:

Experimental group:
Pretest → 2 ½ hours of playing → Posttest

Control group:
Pretest → Wait during week → Posttest

Before starting, the experimenter had to perform another task to do the job properly: she had to obtain as much information on the subjects' school histories as possible.

What might she need to know, given that society might be influencing the results? That is, what school courses does society consider "masculine" that might be related to these skills?

The experimenter obtained from the subjects information regarding the math, science, and "engineering-type" courses they had taken, since these courses could be related to spatial skills.

What Were the Results of the Study?

With practice, the improvement rate for females was such that there was no significant difference in learning between males and females. In other words, females clearly can learn such skills rapidly. The second finding suggested that spatial skills are something that

improve with practice and that cumulatively get better over time. Third finding: the number of math and science courses taken is related to improvement in video-game skills. Fourth: the control group did not improve in their skills (which was to be expected but was a necessary part of the experiment).

This study has clear social significance. It strongly implies that we are dealing with a socially induced difference in spatial skills between males and females rather than with some kind of innate difference. In and of itself, the study is not conclusive, but it adds a bit of information to the broad study of male and female differences. It also helps call into question the assumption that females are less capable of dealing with so-called masculine pursuits of this type.

▲ *Do males take more science and math classes than females because they play more video games?*

Summary

1. In the scientific method of psychological research, first the hypothesis is formed and the subjects are chosen; then the subjects are divided up into an experimental group and a control group.

2. A variable is any factor in an experiment that changes. The variable that is regulated by the experimenter is the independent variable. The second variable is the dependent variable, which is the change that occurs as a result of what the experimenter does with the independent variable.

3. Field studies are conducted away from the laboratory, but they still adhere as much as possible to the rigid rules of experimentation.

4. A survey is used to ask questions of carefully selected people in order to understand opinions and feelings. The questionnaire is one such method.

5. Naturalistic observation avoids interfering with the subject's behavior and focuses on hidden observation in order to record how the subject behaves when not aware that it is being watched.

6. The interview involves the face-to-face collection of people's ideas, actions, background, or behavior. The case study is somewhat similar in that it collects specific background information covering a greater period of years in order to help develop a picture of the person, usually to aid in psychological treatment.

7. Psychological tests are objective methods of gathering information about people. The questions are determined beforehand, and the range of answers is restricted.

8. The longitudinal method of research requires considerable time and expense. The same group of people is examined over and over during a lengthy period of time, often many decades. The cross-sectional method also studies the effects of time, but it uses people from different age groups and tests them all at the same time in order to provide the desired information.

9. Psychological research must conform to the ethical guidelines of the American Psychological Association. Subjects may decline or withdraw their participation. Researchers must be honest, maintain confidentiality, assess risks, and correct any undesirable effects on their subjects.

Vocabulary

placebo	dependent variable	naturalistic observation
double-blind study	field study	interview
hypothesis	experimental group	case study method
subjects	control group	psychological tests
variables	survey	cross-sectional method
stereotype	sample	longitudinal method
independent variable	representative sample	

Review Questions

Fill in the Blank

Read the following sample study and fill in the blanks. Answer on a sheet of paper.

Psychologists wanted to find out if people are less likely to help in an emergency if there is a full moon. An "emergency" situation (a flat tire) was staged for 20 males and 20 females, all in cars. One-half of the subjects (group A) were tested when there was a full moon. The other half (group B) were tested when the moon was not full. Helping was defined as "seeing the flat tire, stopping, and getting out of the car to assist in any way."

1. Hypothesis = ▓▓▓▓
2. Subjects = ▓▓▓▓
3. Dependent variable = ▓▓▓▓
4. Independent variable = ▓▓▓▓
5. Control group = ▓▓▓▓
6. Experimental group = ▓▓▓▓

True/False

On a sheet of paper, answer each statement true or false. If false, rewrite to make it true.

7. Placebos have some medicinal ingredients but not enough for the brain to detect.

8. The experimental group is exposed to the independent variable.

9. The control group is exposed to the dependent variable.

10. In a double-blind study, the experimenter does not know which subjects are in the control group and which are in the experimental groups.

Matching

On a sheet of paper, match the answer from the second column that best fits the description in the first column. Answers may be used more than once.

11. Results can be distorted to mislead others.

12. Chance of personal bias distorting results is minimized.

13. Researcher has to be careful about own biases.

14. A representative sample from each age group is taken.

15. Subjects can act "normally."

16. Subject's past is studied in order to help with present problems.

17. This is not very useful for studies on long-term development.

18. Only a sample of the population can be studied.

19. This can be expensive.

20. As this is a face-to-face situation, subject may put up a false front.

21. A great deal of information about a subject's background is gathered.

22. Subjects are studied for a long period of time.

23. Researcher does *not* interact with subjects.

24. An intelligence test is one example of this.

a. psychological test
b. interview
c. longitudinal method
d. survey method
e. naturalistic observation
f. cross-sectional method
g. case study method

Discussion Questions

1. In your own words, explain the conclusions of the "men, women, and management" study. Make a list of other factors that might influence the results. Explain how these factors could make a difference. Decide how you might be able to control them.

2. Let's say that you started off conducting an experiment on why people do not help in emergencies. Immediately after the experiment is completed, you decide to interview those people who did not help. What potential problems might you have with these interviews? Explain.

3. The chapter describes several methods that psychologists use in their research. If you wanted to study the effects of alcoholism on the family, which of the methods described would you use, and why? Briefly describe how you might conduct this research. Why would you probably *not* conduct your research in the laboratory?

4. Which method of research would you probably use to study the effects of mild stress on job performance? Explain. Briefly describe how you might conduct this research.

5. Leo is an animal rights activist. He believes we should stop *all* experimentation on animals and find alternative means. He argues that if animals somehow could choose, they certainly would not choose to be part of the experiments. They suffer; they are part of the ecology; they should be given more extensive rights. Sam, on the other hand, believes we should experiment on animals as much as we like. He argues that only with this attitude will we ever develop vaccines and cures that will improve the quality of life. He admits that animals will obviously not experience this quality of life at first; but in the long run, even they will benefit. Both of these views are extreme, but with which do you tend to agree, and why?

6. Skim through this text and find a description of some experiment. Briefly summarize the experiment, and then identify the following: hypothesis, subjects, independent variable, dependent variable, experimental group, and control group. Then answer this question: Does the experiment seem to meet the ethical guidelines established by the American Psychological Association? Explain.

Activities and Projects

1. This chapter describes one study that examines stereotypes in the workplace. (See "Research: Men, Women, and Management.") You're going to find out if some of the principles in that study apply to you and your classmates. First, make a list of stereotypes about high school students. Include as many characteristics as you can think of. Make three copies of your list and pass these out to three different people. Tell each person to check the items that apply to most teens. Ask a classmate to complete one copy, an adult who doesn't work with teens to complete another, and an adult who does work with teens to complete the final copy. Then compare all your results. What conclusions can you draw? Finally, compare your conclusions with the conclusions from the stereotype study described in the chapter.

2. Reread "Research: Men, Women, and Management." You're going to conduct a similar study, but you'll tailor it for a high school setting. The procedure is fairly simple. Create a ballot for class president with two fictitious names on it, one male and one female. Make lists of qualifications for both candidates that are very similar in quality, then ask subjects to vote for one candidate at the bottom of the sheet. Half of your ballots should have the male candidate on the left; the remaining ballots should have the male on the right. But don't switch the qualifications—only the names! If you have unconsciously listed better qualifications on one side, this switch should control for that. (When you switch the names, though, don't forget to change any *he*

and *she* pronouns in the lists!) Finally, write out brief, word-for-word instructions for your subjects so that *you* don't subtly influence your results. After the voting is completed, compare your vote totals to see if any sort of sex bias has occurred. You'll need to pass out ballots to quite a few subjects to get any meaningful results. To help you analyze your results, you may want to ask your subjects why they decided on one candidate over the other. They may give you an idea or two about other directions that future research could take—or they may help you revise your ballots.

3. Conduct a simple experiment to test the following hypothesis: Older people have slower reaction times than younger people. Maybe this seems obvious, but common sense is often wrong.

   For the purposes of this experiment, *younger* will refer to high school students, while *older* will refer to 30-year-olds. Procedure: Ask 10 *younger* subjects and 10 *older* subjects to play a simple video game that measures reaction time. Compare results, and write a report. Before conducting the experiment, show your plans to your instructor to iron out any problems.

   Try to avoid miscellaneous variables that might affect your results. (A) Pick subjects randomly. In other words, don't pick friends that you know are good at video games. You probably want to ask your subjects if they've had any experience with the video game you decide to use. If they are familiar with the game, you should probably disqualify them as subjects. (B) Run a few practice trials before you collect data to find out if there are any flaws in your procedure. You might find that younger people are better at the video game *controls* you give them because they've had more experience with those. So you may even want to switch how you measure reaction time. Maybe just use a stopwatch and ask each subject to complete some hands-on task. (C) Treat all subjects in an identical manner. Write out and read directions to each subject to maintain consistency.

4. Interview one or both of your parents or other caregivers regarding some of the child-rearing methods they used in raising you. You might ask them how they tried to motivate you to do chores, how they tried to stop you when you misbehaved, and which techniques worked and didn't work. Ask them how their methods changed as you grew older. Finally, ask them about their reasoning behind each method: *Why* did they send you to your room? *Why* did they offer a prize after you performed a series of chores? *Why* did they treat you and your sister differently? Write a two-part report of your interview. *Part A:* Summarize the content of the interview. Include your reactions and a few quotes. *Part B:* Analyze the interview process. Did any of the strengths and weaknesses of interviews discussed in the chapter come into play? Be specific.

5. As noted in this chapter, surveys gather information on feelings, opinions, or behavior patterns. Write your own 10-item survey to find out the feelings and opinions of at least 30 freshmen and 30 seniors at your school. The survey should deal with a single subject of your choice. For example, it might be interesting to find out how freshmen view dating and to contrast that with how seniors view it. Other possible subjects: parents, clothes, friendship, work, studying. Once you decide on a subject, write 10 objective questions. Do *not* include open-ended questions that allow participants to fill in the blanks. You might get 100 different answers in these blanks, and responses would then become difficult to analyze. Your objective questions may have multiple-choice answers. Or you may use a scale similar to this one:

   If you use the scale, you will write 10 statements below the scale and have participants place a corresponding number next to each statement. Sample statements: "The male should initiate and pay for the first date." "A movie theater is a good place to go for a first date."

   Draw a simple chart summarizing all your responses, and then analyze your results. Compare and contrast the freshmen responses with the senior responses. Any surprises? Were there any questions that could have been phrased more carefully? Explain.

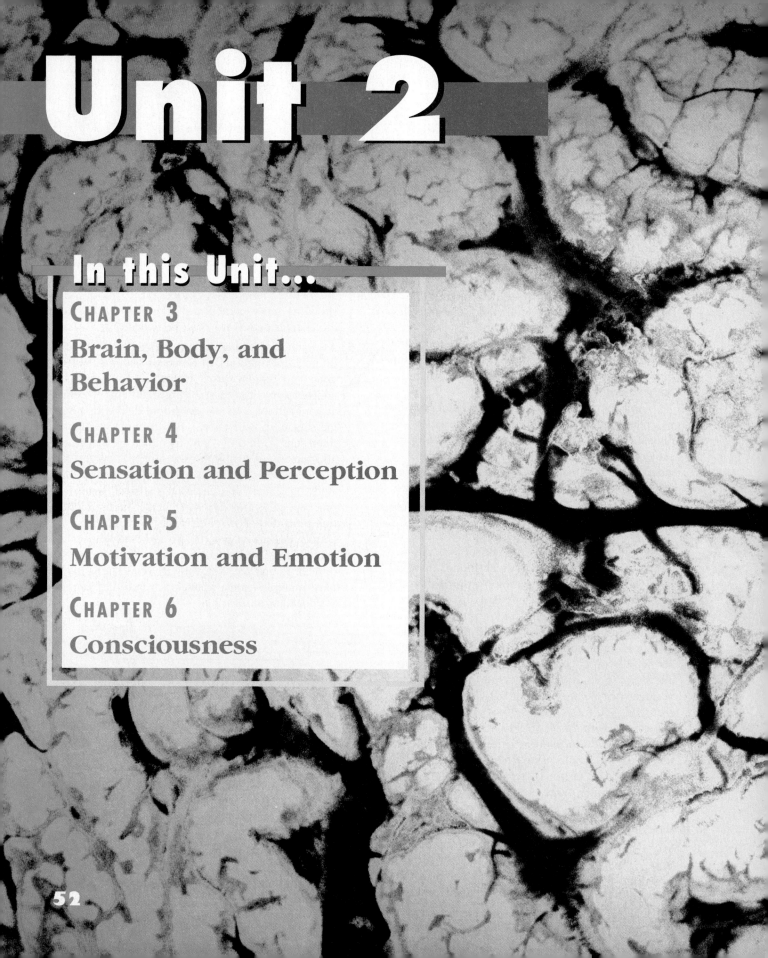

Unit 2

In this Unit...

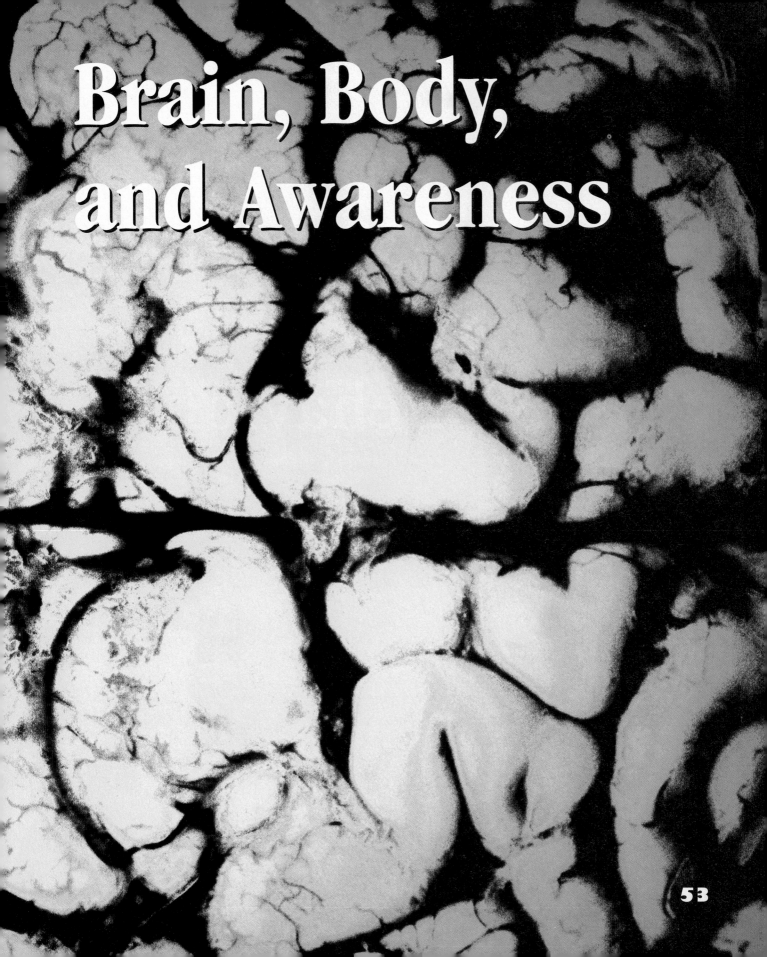

Brain, Body, and Awareness

CHAPTER 3

Brain, Body, and Behavior

Many behaviors that seem "psychological" are in fact the result of some activity of the brain or endocrine system. The human brain is remarkable in what it can do. It allows a combination of animal-like behaviors to come from the "lower" brain and very elaborate thought processes to come from the higher brain. This chapter will show that the brain plays an important part in everything we do.

Observing the Brain in Action

Let's start with an experiment. Put your right arm straight out, palm downward. Next, bring your hand in toward your head and put your finger gently into your right ear, saying, "I stretch my hand forth; I bring my hand back." Finally, take your finger out.

You have just done something that is almost beyond belief, it is so remarkable. Here is what happened: Your brain analyzed the instructions. Next it sent a message to your arm. Then it called on the area that controls hand movements and put your finger into your ear. It didn't miss the ear and make you wind up with a finger in your eye or nose. While that was going on, the brain searched through the memory banks for the words you needed, put them together, and then used the speech areas of the brain to make those words.

The experiment is not over, though. Probably if you sense you were tricked into doing something weird, you now feel stupid, or irritated, or puzzled. These are emotions coming from yet another part of the brain. The brain decides whether you were treated fairly and triggers an emotional response that will vary, depending on how you interpreted the experiment.

There were a couple of reasons for our "experiment." First, in daily life, we all too often take for granted the wondrous thing that we are. In truth, it is worth considering how amazing it is that you are able to do what you just did. Second, as we move through the chapter, we wanted to be able to use a concrete example of something you have done, rather than talk in general terms about the workings of the brain.

Examining the Brain

Psychologists study the brain in detail because it is the part of us that controls every thought, action, and feeling. The brain, which looks something like tightly compressed macaroni, is the most demanding organ of the body. If you spend a long time studying, it takes more energy and causes more aches and pains than jogging. The brain uses 20 percent of all our oxygen, eats up most of the sugar we take in, and operates on 20 watts of electrical power. The brain is made up of about 100 billion nerve cells. Even though very elaborate, its basic workings are not hard to understand if you follow the description in this chapter step by step.

The Cerebral Cortex

The **cerebral cortex** is the outermost layer of the brain. This unit controls very high level thought (*cerebral* means "relating to thought or intelligence"). If the cortex were untwisted and spread out, it would be about the size of a large bath towel. We know of nothing in the universe that can equal its processing abilities. The nerve cells in the brain can connect with one another in so many ways that if you emptied dump trucks full of computers night and day until you'd filled up a football stadium, the pile would not even come close to equaling our brain power.

▲ *Michelle Kwan, world champion ice skater, demonstrates some amazing interactions between the brain and the body.*

Focus Questions
....

- What is the cerebral cortex and what does it do?

- What are the four main lobes of the cerebral cortex?

- What happens if you sever the connection between the hemispheres of the brain?

cerebral cortex the outermost layer of the brain; controls high-level mental processes such as thought

fissure a depression marking off an area of the cerebral cortex

hemisphere one half of the cerebral cortex; each half controls the opposite side of the body

corpus callosum a large bundle of nerve fibers that transfer information from one half of the cerebral cortex to the other

▲ *Many parts of the brain are involved in a complicated chess strategy.*

lobes major divisions of the cerebral cortex

frontal lobe division of the cerebral cortex that contains the motor strip, prefrontal area, and frontal association area

parietal lobe division of the cerebral cortex that contains the sensory strip

motor strip band running down the side of the frontal lobe that controls all bodily movements (called motor functions)

sensory strip band running down the side of the parietal lobe that registers and provides all sensation

The Hemispheres

Imagine that a friend of yours is sitting in a chair, and you are standing behind him or her. Looking down at the top of the head, *if* you could see through hair, skin, and bone, you would notice an interesting characteristic of the brain. It is divided into halves. In the middle, from front to back, is a depression, called a **fissure.** This fissure marks the division of one half of the brain from the other. Each half is called a **hemisphere.** *Hemi* means half, so we have two halves of a sphere. These are referred to as the right and left hemispheres. Each one controls the opposite side of the body—that is, the left hemisphere controls movements and sensations on the right side of the body, and the right half controls the left side.

If you were to pull these two halves apart, about midway down, you would see a bundle of fibers called the **corpus callosum** (KORE-pus kah-LO-sum). This unit contains several million nerve fibers that help each half of the brain communicate with the other, transmitting all kinds of information (Myers, 1984). We'll get back to this structure and talk more about the hemispheres shortly. First, however, it's important to understand the functions of different areas of the brain.

The Lobes

The cerebral cortex is divided into four major sections, called **lobes.** To show you where they are, we need to look at the brain from the side. Figure 3.1 shows a side view of the left hemisphere, but the right hemisphere would show basically the same structure. If you think of this side view as resembling a boxing glove, you won't get confused about where the front and back parts are. (It even has a thumb!) About midway from the front to the back is another depression, or fissure. It marks off the boundary between two lobes of the cortex. The frontmost area is conveniently called the **frontal lobe.** The area behind it is the **parietal** (pah-RYE-eh-tul) **lobe.** Notice in Figure 3.1 that there is a colored section on either side of the fissure. The section that is located in the frontal lobe is called the **motor strip.** Every part of the body that is capable of moving is represented on this strip. That is why it is called "motor"; the word *motor* means "relating to movement." During surgery, if the brain is exposed, the surgeon can stimulate different parts of this motor strip with an electrically active wire. Depending on the area touched, the arm, the leg, or the finger will move, the nose will twitch, and so forth.

The colored section located in the parietal lobe is called the **sensory strip.** If this is stimulated in an exposed brain, the person feels a sensation in some area—the leg, ear, mouth, and so forth—depending on the specific area that the electricity hits. So, for the experiment you did at the beginning of this chapter, you used the sensory strip to tell you when your finger actually hit your ear. The motor strip controlled the movement of your arm and finger.

The very back of the brain is devoted to making sense out of what we see. This area is called the **occipital** (ox-SIP-ih-tul) **lobe.** When you were reading the first part of this chapter, images of the words you saw went through the lenses of the eyes and landed on the backs of the eyeballs. What was received was coded and then sent through nerves to the occipital lobe.

◀ *Figure 3.1*   *The Cerebral Cortex*

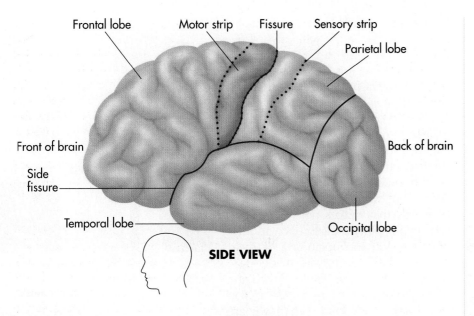

SIDE VIEW

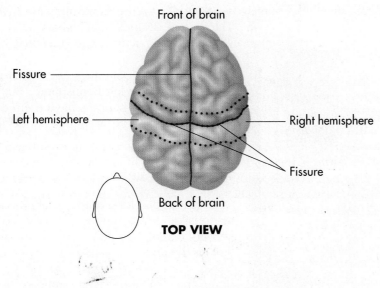

TOP VIEW

occipital lobe division of the cerebral cortex that interprets visual information

    The brain sits in a fluid that acts like a shock absorber, giving it some room to move back and forth and sideways. Sometimes that isn't enough, however. If you've ever been hit really hard in the front part of your head, you saw all kinds of images in front of you for a second (seeing "stars"). This is because the blow sent the brain sloshing backward, crashing the occipital lobe into the skull. The collision stirred up the electrical system of this visual area and created these strange images. If you've never been hit, you can still see this area in operation. Lie on your bed in a dark room for about 10 minutes. Then open your eyes and *VERY GENTLY*(!) touch the edges of your eyeballs. This will send electrical impulses to the occipital lobe that will create odd images "right before your very eyes."

    The part of the cerebral cortex in Figure 3.1 that looks like the thumb of a boxing glove is the **temporal** (TEM-pore-ul) **lobe.** The temporal lobe contains the major centers for hearing. Some of the centers related to speech are also located here, although there is overlap with other lobes to handle all the different aspects of language. If you are actually speaking,

temporal lobe division of the cerebral cortex responsible for hearing and some speech functions

for instance, a place in the frontal lobe's motor strip will also be involved. If you are reading a speech, the occipital or visual area will be activated. There is a circular spot whose sole job is to create sentences. It organizes words in the proper sequence so the meaning can be understood. If someone is unlucky enough to damage this area of the brain, he or she can still speak, but what is said is a jumble of words that makes no sense. So, when you spoke the sentence about your hand at the beginning of the chapter, the speech was made up by this unit. It was spoken with the help of the motor strip, even if you didn't say it out loud. When we are "talking" silently to ourselves, as we all do, the same units are involved. The actual sounds that others hear come when you also activate the voice box in your throat.

▲ *The speech areas of the brain are in action during a debate.*

For most people, these speech areas are only found in the left hemisphere. But about 25 percent of left-handers have them only in the right hemisphere. We'll talk about "lefties" shortly.

The Frontal Lobe

The frontal lobe of the cerebral cortex is responsible for a number of very complex and fascinating functions. One of these functions is the ability to "see" or be aware of ourselves when we remember things we have done. Just behind your forehead lies the **prefrontal area** of the frontal lobe (shown in Figure 3.2). This part of the brain enables us to re-experience past events in our personal lives. Whenever you "mentally travel in time," you are using the prefrontal area of your brain (Wheeler, Stuss, & Tulving, 1997).

Coming up with strategies or plans of action is another function of the frontal lobe. Once the words you received while reading the first part of this chapter were processed by the visual area, this information was sent all the way straight ahead to an area of the frontal lobe called the **frontal association area,** which is also shown in Figure 3.2. The frontal association area is very heavily packed with nerve cells because its task is very complex: to

prefrontal area part of the frontal lobe that enables us to re-experience personal past events

frontal association area part of the frontal lobe that engages in elaborate associations or mental connections; it plays an important part in integrating personality and in forming complex thoughts

In Their Own Words . . .

Richard Restak *is an expert on the diagnosis and treatment of diseases of the nervous system. In his book* Brainscapes, *Restak describes major advances in knowledge of the brain. In one passage, he notes that "the Cray 2 computer [a very large and powerful computer] has the processing power of only a small rodent." He describes the connecting capacity of the nerve cells of the brain in this way:*

Counting these connections [within the cerebral cortex] at the rate of one connection per second would take 32 million years to complete. Even a section of the brain no bigger than a match head contains about a billion connections. Combining these into all of their various connections results in the number ten followed by millions of zeros. And to put that number into perspective, the number of positively charged particles in the whole known universe is only ten followed by eighty zeros. (Restak, 1995, p. 41)

Interpreting Primary Sources

Why do you think Restak included so much detail about all the possible connections in the brain? Do you think he accomplished his goal?

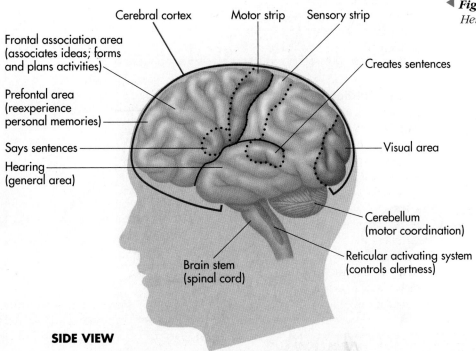

◀ **Figure 3.2**   *View of Left Hemisphere*

Frontal association area (associates ideas; forms and plans activities)

Cerebral cortex

Motor strip

Sensory strip

Creates sentences

Prefontal area (reexperience personal memories)

Says sentences

Hearing (general area)

Visual area

Brain stem (spinal cord)

Cerebellum (motor coordination)

Reticular activating system (controls alertness)

SIDE VIEW

interpret what is going on and tell us what to do and what to feel. It decided how you reacted to our "experiment," for example. In many ways, the frontal association area seems to form the core of the personality, since so many decisions are made there.

In the 1840s, a railroad worker with the unlikely name of Phineas P. Gage was injured in a freakish accident, which gave us clues into the nature of the frontal association area. He was pushing some dynamite into a hole with a four-foot-long iron bar in the shape of a toothpick, about an inch in diameter. The dynamite went off, firing the bar upward through his jaw, through the frontal association area, and on out. Remarkably, he survived, because none of the vital parts that control breathing, movement, or physical control had been damaged. Still, the injury to his frontal association area resulted in some *major* changes. While he had been friendly and normal, suddenly he became someone who swore all the time, undressed wherever he felt like it, urinated in public, and had temper tantrums. Thus, this complex area of the brain must play a large part in what we call social control as well as in our basic personalities.

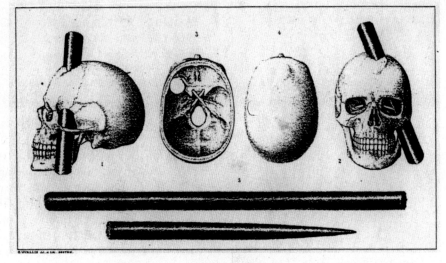

▲ *The damage to Phineas Gage's brain was substantial, as was the size of the iron bar that caused it.*

Tasks of the Two Hemispheres

Typical Right-Hemisphere Task

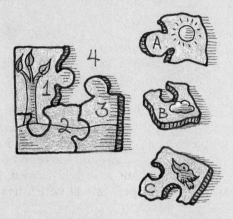

Which of the pieces comes closest to fitting into space 4 on the left?

Typical Left-Hemisphere Task

Which of the following is correct?
a. The outlaw was hung on Boot Hill.
b. The outlaw was hanged on Boot Hill.

The right hemisphere specializes in spatial functions such as piecing together a jigsaw puzzle. The left hemisphere specializes in the verbal skills needed to answer a "language" question.

What will the left hemisphere contribute as you solve the puzzle problem above? What will the right hemisphere contribute in the language problem?

The frontal association area also tries to make sense of the environment. Someone who has major damage in this part of the brain may know what is happening but may not be able to bring together all the aspects of the situation. For example, a man with damage here can watch someone: (1) take a bullet, (2) put it in a gun, (3) cock the gun, and (4) aim the gun at him. He will not show any concern. He understands each act by itself but is not able to put them all together (Jouandet & Gazzaniga, 1979).

The size of the frontal lobe likely reflects intelligence level from one species to another. Since we can't "talk to the animals," we will probably never know for sure, but it is interesting that the amount of the brain devoted to the frontal area depends on how advanced the animal is. Thus, it is 7 percent in the dog, 15 percent in the chimpanzee, and one third in the human (Wheeler, Stuss, & Tulving, 1997).

If you want, you can actually see the frontal lobe in operation. Try this experiment, but pick a reasonably pleasant person to try it on. While the subject is standing in a line, go up and bump him or her from behind. Wait five seconds after the person turns around before you apologize. Note that the person will spend this time (a *long* time for the brain) looking at you, going back and forth mentally, while the frontal association area decides if what you did was on purpose and whether he or she should get mad.

Hemispheres and Handedness

Ten percent of the population is left-handed. Because they are different from others statistically, people wonder how they "got that way." Earlier, we mentioned that the left hemisphere controls the right side of the body and vice versa. That *is* true, but we were referring only to major body movements. When dealing with small, fine movements, such as writing or putting your finger in your ear, one hemisphere has **dominance.** In other words, one hemisphere is always the preferred one to use. Most people are left-hemisphere dominant and right-handed. But if the right hemisphere is dominant, then the person will be left-handed for all fine movements.

Left-handedness does not seem to be inherited—at least not in the same sense as something like eye color, which follows a clear family pattern. Sometimes in identical twins, who have exactly the same heredity, there will be one left-handed twin and one right-handed twin (Corballis & Morgan, 1978).

The genetic instructions that make the brain must be complex beyond imagination. We suspect that for some reason, accidental or otherwise, the part of the "program" that develops the brain gets slightly different signals for the left-hander and shifts the dominance to the right hemisphere. If the shift isn't complete, a very few become what is called "ambidextrous" (left- and right-handed). For these people, the instructions get "stuck" in the middle of the two hemispheres, so to speak.

The intelligence of right- versus left-handed people is about the same; that is, there seems to be about the same percentage of bright, average, and dull people in both groups. But statistically, the left-hander will probably do better in art, music, and mathematics. And the odds increase that the speech areas will be in the right rather than the left hemisphere. Left-handers also tend to be better actors: Try keeping track for a while of the number of leading men and women in movies and TV who are left-handed. We will explain why this is so in a few paragraphs.

Before going on, though, we should mention the myth that if a left-hander is forced to use the right hand in childhood, this may cause insanity. That's not true. But what a nuisance it can be, and so uncomfortable. People used to think that something was wrong with left-handers (there isn't anything wrong, any more than with right-handers), so parents sometimes tried to change their left-handed children. It's hard enough to grow up as it is without adding the burden of making children uncomfortable trying to do things in an "unnatural" way (Geschwind, 1983).

dominance control; either the right or left hemisphere of the cerebral cortex is dominant in each individual; hence, one of them is preferred and controls the majority of actions performed

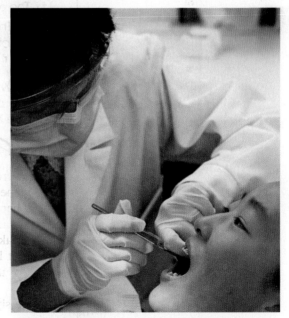

▲ *At times, both hands are required to do the task properly.*

Thinking Critically about Psychology

Creativity and the Cerebral Hemispheres

▲ *Even though these boys are playing right-handedly, their right hemispheres are very much involved in making music.*

Students often come into a psychology class with a number of wrong ideas, believing certain false statements because "everyone knows" they are true. You will find, though, that many things that "everyone knows" are not actual facts. We may have heard these things from other people or read them in newspapers or magazines, but that does not mean they are valid. One example of this is the often-heard statement that *creativity is located in the right hemisphere of the brain*.

For this critical thinking exercise, we want you to examine that statement carefully. Use the information contained in this chapter, independent research, and your own good reasoning to apply the four "COOL" questions to this statement. After you have completed this exercise, read the example provided on the next page.

Section 1B

Psychology

What specifically is being claimed?

Creativity is a function solely of the right hemisphere of the brain.

What is the objective evidence for and against this claim?

According to the text, left-handed people are statistically more likely to do better in art, music and mathematics. This supports the belief that creativity is right-hemisphere centered. The text also notes, however, that there are more right-handed musicians and artists than left-handed. This obviously results from the fact that about 90% of the population is right-handed. Clearly, many right-handed people are highly creative in these fields.

There are many kinds of creativity to consider. For example, what about writing poetry or novels? These are creative acts, yet language functions are located in the left half of the brain. In addition, analytic problem solving can be creative as well. This function is also located in the left hemisphere.

What other interpretations might be made instead?

We know that creative functions are found in both halves of the brain. Also, it is probably not helpful to think of these functions being completely isolated in their own separate hemisphere. We know that the two halves of the brain can easily and quickly communicate with each other. Research has shown that the two hemispheres work together in almost everything we do (Hoptman & Davidson, 1994; Hellige, 1990). Why should creative acts be any different from other complex activities we engage in?

What are the most logical conclusions to draw?

Creativity takes many forms, some of which are primarily the function of the right hemisphere. But other forms of creativity are primarily left-hemispheric functions. So the original claim is not supported. Given the brain's complexity and the rapid communication between hemispheres, it seems likely that both halves of the brain are involved in most creative activities.

Applying Critical Thinking Skills

In what ways was your analysis of right-brained creativity similar to the one above? In what ways did it differ? Did you reach the same logical conclusion?

See if **COOL** works for you....

Claim?

Objective evidence for and against claim?

Other interpretations?

Logical conclusions?

▲ *Can you identify these famous lefties?*

Tasks of the Cerebral Hemispheres

Scientists have wondered for hundreds of years about why the brain has two halves. There must be some reason. Only recently have we begun to understand what this reason might be.

We have already mentioned that nerve fibers in a unit called the corpus callosum hold the two hemispheres together. Patients have sometimes had to have the corpus callosum cut surgically to stop electrical disturbances in the brain. Differences between the functions of the cerebral hemispheres have been noted in these patients. Experiments were set up in which information was fed through a part of the eyes that led to only one hemisphere or the other. This was possible because with a severed corpus callosum, most communication between the two halves is cut off. Hence, only one-half of the brain would get the message.

One experiment involved a woman with a split brain. Her right hemisphere was shown a photo of a nude woman, while the left hemisphere "saw" nothing. The woman blushed and laughed nervously. When asked why she was blushing, she said she didn't know! In a second experiment, a picture of a spoon was shown to a man's left hemisphere. He was asked what he had seen and correctly said "spoon." Next, the picture of a spoon was shown to his *right* hemisphere. He was asked what he saw. He couldn't *say* what it was. But with his left hand he could pick out a spoon from objects on the table to indicate what he saw (Gazzaniga, 1970). What do these findings mean?

It seems that the left hemisphere (for right-handers and most left-handers) handles verbal or speech material (see Figure 3.3). So, when the man saw the spoon only with the right hemisphere, he couldn't *say* what it was (left hemisphere). The right hemisphere deals with objects in space, art, music, and some mathematical reasoning, as well as emotional material. Hence, the woman had an emotional reaction because of what she saw in the right hemisphere but couldn't say what it was (left hemisphere). For those who are left-handed, since the right hemisphere will dominate, the odds increase that they will be better at and deal more with their right hemispheres. This, in turn, increases the chances that they will do well in art, music, architecture, or the physical and emotional art of acting—all *non*verbal activities (Springer & Deutsch, 1985).

Before leaving this topic, we want to make a final comment. A lot has been written in the popular press about right-brain versus left-brain thinking and learning. Many people assume that the differences between the hemispheres are great and that each operates in a very specialized way. That is not quite true. The hemispheric functions we have discussed

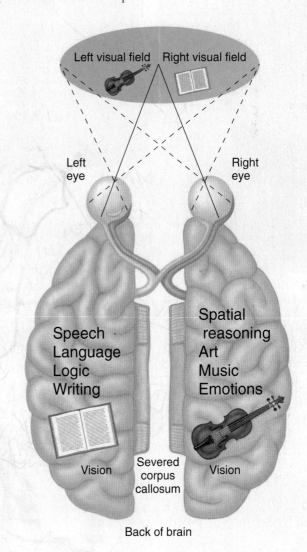

▲ *Figure 3.3* *Assumed Areas of "Specialization" in the Brain*

▲ *Each hemisphere makes its own contribution to creative activities.*

are quite real and easy to demonstrate. However, it is important to keep in mind that the hemispheres work together in virtually everything we do (Hoptman & Davidson, 1994; Hellige, 1990). Also, even though certain kinds of mathematical reasoning and nonverbal artistic abilities are primarily right-hemisphere functions, the majority of mathematicians and artists, like everyone else, are right-handed.

 ## Pause for Thought

1. The cerbral cortex, which controls high-level thinking, can be divided into four lobes. What are the functions of each lobe? What's the difference between the sensory strip and the motor strip?
2. The cerebral cortex can also be divided into hemispheres. What connects the two hemispheres? What are the specialized functions of each side?

Critical Thinking
• •

3. One hemisphere is usually more dominant than the other. Given the tasks of each hemisphere, which hemisphere is probably the most dominant for you? Explain.

The Lower Brain

No matter how fantastic the cerebral cortex is, it will not keep the body running. For that, we need a "lower" brain. Deep inside the skull lies the **lower brain,** with the cerebral cortex fitting over and around it. The word *cortex* means "bark," as on a tree. Hence, the cerebral cortex covers the lower brain like a layer of bark. Use Figure 3.4 as we talk about the different parts of the lower brain. For most human responses (except automatic behaviors such as withdrawing a hand from a hot object), the cortex influences the lower units; they, in turn, influence the cortex.

The Thalamus

The **thalamus** (THAL-ah-mus) is an oval mass of nerve cells. It acts as a relay station to send incoming and outgoing messages to and from various parts of the brain. So if you want to move your big toe, the brain sends a message to the thalamus, which then sends it to the correct place on the motor strip. Otherwise, you might wind up blinking your eye.

Focus Questions

* What is the lower brain and what does it do?
* What are the major parts of the lower brain?

lower brain part of the brain common to animals and humans that regulates basic functions such as breathing

thalamus part of the lower brain that functions primarily as a central relay station for incoming and outgoing messages from the body to the brain and the brain to the body

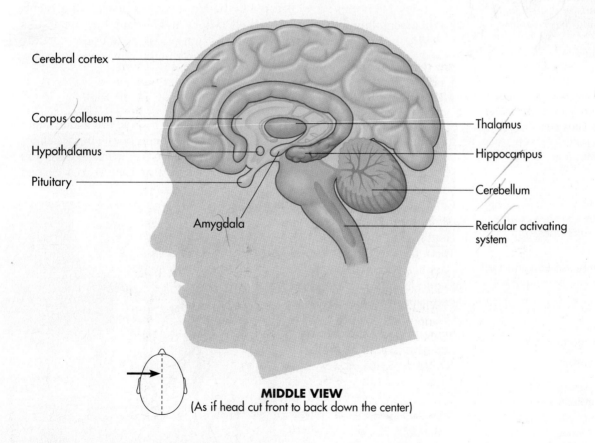

MIDDLE VIEW
(As if head cut front to back down the center)

▲ *Figure 3.4* *The Parts of the Lower Brain (left side of cortex removed)*

The Hypothalamus

The **hypothalamus** (*hypo* means "below") sits below the thalamus. While only the size of a large pea, it helps control rage, pleasure, hunger, thirst, and sexual desire. Thus, if its rage center is electrically stimulated, it can cause a person to go wild and start smashing things. We will discuss the hypothalamus further in Chapter 5 when we talk about motivation and emotion.

The Limbic System

The **limbic system** contains structures involved in basic emotions and, to some extent, memory. Scientists do not completely agree on what areas and functions should be considered part of the limbic system (Restak, 1995). For our purposes, however, two structures are especially important, the amygdala and the hippocampus. The **amygdala** (ah-MIG-duh-la) is primarily responsible for emotional responses, especially aggression. Animals with damage to the amygdala are not capable of aggressive behavior. The **hippocampus** (hippo-CAM-pus) enables us to form memories. Memories are not stored in the hippocampus itself, but it is critical to assembling information from elsewhere in the brain. Damage to this structure makes forming new memories impossible. Memories already stored are not forgotten, but the person cannot make new ones.

▲ *Whether it's his amygdala or his hypothalamus in operation, this man is obviously very angry!*

hypothalamus part of the lower brain that regulates basic needs (hunger, thirst) and emotions such as pleasure, fear, rage, and sexuality

limbic system lower brain area whose structures are involved in basic emotions and memory

amygdala limbic system structure involved in emotion, especially aggression

hippocampus limbic system structure involved in forming memories

cerebellum part of the lower brain that coordinates and organizes bodily movements for balance and accuracy

The Cerebellum

The **cerebellum** (sarah-BELL-um) looks like a ball of yarn a little larger than a golf ball, and it hooks onto the base of the brain below the visual, or occipital, lobe. Its job is complex. Whenever you move, it makes sure you stay in balance, remain coordinated, and get where you want to go. It helped you get your finger into your ear in the experiment at the beginning of this chapter. Here's another example: Think back to the first day of class this year. You had to go to rooms different from the ones you went to the previous year, and all was chaos trying to remember the right ones. But within a week, the cerebellum and cortex had programmed themselves to take you to every class in sequence, and you no longer had to pay attention to where you were going. In fact, often you now go from one class to the other, turning right, left, right, and so forth, while

▲ *The cerebellum helps us keep our balance.*

you are talking to someone—and you "magically" arrive at the right place. The cerebellum also contains thousands of nerve cells that are lined up in rows like the spokes of half a wheel, with the cerebellum core as the center. When someone throws a basketball to you, your eyes cause cerebellum cells to fire one after the other as the ball is tracked on its path toward you. The cerebellum calculates speed and direction as the cells fire, and it signals through the thalamus to the motor strip. Then your hands automatically go to the correct place to catch the ball.

Focus

The Cerebral Cortex and the Lower Brain

The brain could be compared to an office building in which executives at the top of the building (in the cerebral cortex penthouse) make the complex decisions about company goals and policies, while the custodians in the basement (the lower brain) regulate temperature, collect and deliver mail, and so on.

The executives (in the cerebral cortex) and the custodians (in the lower brain) obviously have a great deal of influence on each other's performance. It should be obvious that we couldn't live without the custodians. Could we live without the executives?

▲ *Alcohol would impair the ability of the RAS to react efficiently.*

reticular activating system (RAS) the alertness control center of the brain that regulates the activity level of the body; also called the reticular formation

The Reticular Activating System

The **reticular** (reh-TICK-you-ler) **activating system (RAS)** is part of the *reticular formation.* It sits right at the base of the brain inside the spinal cord. Here is a good way to get a feel for what it is like: Cut a two-inch square out of a woman's stocking and look at it. It looks just like a net. Insert it an inch or so into the end of a garden hose (the spinal column). Pretend that you insert the hose into the base of the brain, and you now have some idea of where the RAS is and a *very* rough idea of what it looks like. In fact, the word *reticular* actually means "net," and the RAS *is* a kind of net that "catches" nerve impulses. Nerve impulses from the brain to the body and from the body to the brain pass through the RAS so that it can take a reading of the level of activity throughout the whole system.

The RAS regulates how alert or how sleepy we are. If a lot of things are going on, many impulses arrive from the body and brain, and alertness increases. If everything is quiet, this system heads us toward sleep. It is quite sensitive to steady sounds. Thus, if you go listen to a lecture somewhere and the speaker talks very slowly and dully, little change is noted by the RAS, so it starts to put you to sleep. If you are trying to get to sleep at night and count sheep passing by, that endless rhythm makes you drowsy. Drugs used for surgery dramatically slow down the RAS so it "doesn't care" about pain signals and thus won't alert the brain about them. A major blow to the head causes such an overload of the RAS circuits that they shut off completely for a time, causing unconsciousness. A change in rhythm in the surroundings, an emergency, or emotional thoughts stir up the reticular activating system.

 Pause for Thought

1. How does the lower brain differ from the cerebral cortex?
2. What are the main parts of the lower brain, and what is the function of each part?

Critical Thinking
....

3. Jenny's basketball coach gets kicked out of the game. Jenny, the captain, must take over. Describe the various duties of the different parts of the lower brain in this situation.

Brain Communication

Focus Questions
• • • • • • • • • • • • • • • • • • • •

- What is a nerve cell?
- How does a nerve cell carry communication between the brain and the body?

We have discussed a number of units of the brain. It is obvious that all these parts have to communicate with one another, as well as with the rest of the body. Thus, the eye must send information to the occipital lobe, the foot to the sensory strip, the cerebellum to and from the muscles, and so forth. We have already noted that there is electricity in the nerve cells, but now the question is: How do we get the parts to "talk" to one another? One way might be to string nerves directly from one part to another. In the 1700s, scientists believed this was the case, but they were very wrong (Bergland, 1985). Why won't this work? Think about it for a minute. If you connected all the parts together and turned on a "switch," *everything* would go on at the same time, which would be a hopeless mess. So that can't be the answer.

Another problem is that the brain has to be able to join different ideas. But even using separate nerves for each unit still won't work. For instance, the brain stores the idea of *red*. If we connected a nerve from *red* to the idea of *rose,* that connection would work, but then how could we get the idea of *red* to the idea of *car* without triggering *rose* at the same time? Or how would we get the hypothalamus to signal rage without also sending out a signal for thirst, which would cause us to drink instead of yell? To solve these problems, we need many nerve cells that are separate but still able to alternate signals from one circuit to another. We certainly have more than enough nerve cells—as mentioned, about 100 billion. And each of them has thousands of connections to the others.

The Neuron

Each nerve cell, then, is separate, one from the other. A nerve cell is called a **neuron** (NYOOR-ron or NOOR-on). As you can see in Figures 3.5 and 3.6 on the next page, the body of the neuron has a number of fibers sticking out from it. The shorter ones contain receptors (receivers) for neuronal messages. These short fibers are called **dendrites,** a word meaning "tree," since they look like branches. Dendrites receive information from other nerve cells and send it through the cell body to the **axon.** (The axon is the very long fiber shown in Figures 3.5 and 3.6.) The axon carries the message from the cell to other neurons. At the end of the axon are thousands of terminals, each sitting opposite a

neuron a nerve cell; neurons transmit electrical and chemical information (via neurotransmitters) throughout the body

dendrites parts of neurons that receive information from the axons of other neurons

axon part of the neuron that carries messages away from the cell to the dendrites on another neuron

◀ *Lots of neurons are hard at work in both of these men.*

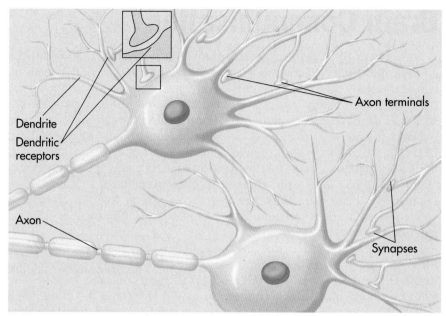

▲ *Figure 3.5*   *This artist's diagram shows how parts of the nerve cells look and connect.*

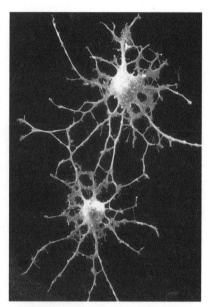

▲ *Figure 3.6*   *Electron Microscope Image of Two Nerve Cells*

synapse the junction point of two or more neurons; a connection is made by neurotransmitters

vesicles bubblelike containers of neurotransmitters, located at the ends of axons

neurotransmitters chemicals in the endings of neurons that send information across synapses

receptor for another neuron. So the message comes to a receptor on a dendrite, goes through the cell, and then goes out the cell's axon to another neuron.

The Synapse

If you look carefully at Figure 3.5, you'll see that there is a space between the endings of the axon and the waiting dendrites. This space is called the **synapse** (SIN-apse), which means "junction point." Since the neurons work by electricity, we now have another problem: Electricity will not go over a space, so it stops. And we have yet another problem: All electricity is the same. If you cut your finger and an electrical impulse goes up to the brain, how is the brain supposed to know it is a "pain message" and not a message to kick your foot?

Neurotransmitters

The solution to these problems lies in an amazing system of communication. The area where the axon ends, just before the synapse, is filled with small containers that look like bubbles. These containers are called **vesicles.** Inside each of them sit thousands of chemical "messengers." Since chemical molecules can be any size or shape, they are not like electricity—you can identify them. So if a circuit is for pain, the molecules inside that container will have a unique shape or makeup that means only "pain message" to the brain. If the circuit is for moving your arm, the container holds different-shaped molecules that will be used to signal only the movement circuit. These molecules are called **neurotransmitters** because they send (transmit) nerve *(neuro)* information from the end of the axon over the synapse to the dendrite receptor. Each circuit contains a different specific molecule for each activity that circuit controls: movement circuit, pain circuit, pleasure circuit, and so forth.

Use Figures 3.7 and 3.8 to follow what happens: You think, "Move my arm." The electrical impulse in the circuit for movement goes down the axon to a nerve ending (a terminal). The electrical impulse stops at the synapse. When it arrives close to that area, however, the chemical containers (vesicles) holding molecules for "movement" are designed to float toward the synapse, where they lock onto a terminal and open up, flooding the open space with neurotransmitters for "movement." Once in the open space, the chemicals then float to the appropriate dendritic receptors for movement. In other words, each receptor is designed to accept only a specific type of chemical molecule (the "movement" molecules, in this case). Once accepted by a movement circuit, these molecules excite the dendrites there, which starts an electrical impulse through the new cell as the process repeats. The process continues until finally the impulse ends at muscle receptors, and your arm moves. Since these impulses go at about 120 yards a second, none of us is so tall that this presents a time problem. The response is almost instantaneous.

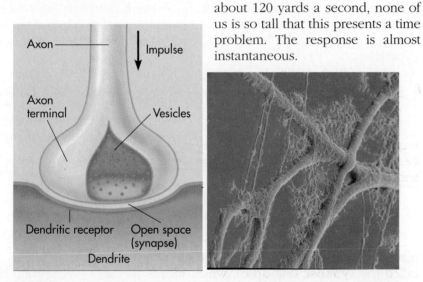

▲ **Figure 3.7** *An artist's illustration shows the inside of a synapse, and an electron microscope scan shows the startling complexity of a single nerve cell.*

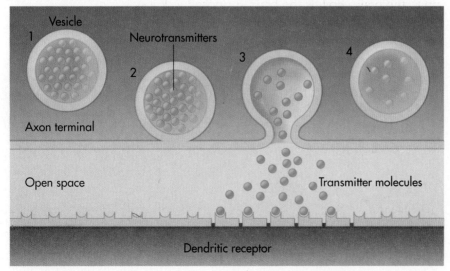

▲ **Figure 3.8** *The movement of a single container (vesicle) is shown (1–4 is the same one) as the neurotransmitter is deposited into the receptor.*

73

▲ *Everyday movements require the action of dopamine, a neurotransmitter.*

acetylcholine neurotransmitter that regulates basic bodily processes such as movement

dopamine neurotransmitter involved in the control of bodily movements

endorphins neurotransmitters that relieve pain and increase our sense of well-being

The same thing happens with the neurotransmitter for pain. Messages travel from a cut through a cell and down an axon to dendrites that will receive its pain molecules, through the cell to the next axon, and so forth until it reaches the brain, where it is interpreted as pain. We now know of 60 different neurotransmitters, but we will probably eventually find hundreds of them (Restak, 1994; Snyder, 1986, 1984).

The most common and well-studied neurotransmitter is called **acetylcholine** (a-SEE-til-KOH-leen), or Ach (A-C-H) for short. One of its uses is to send information from one nerve cell to another whenever we get ready to move some part of the body. Thus, if you are going to move your arm (as we've just described), the acetylcholine will *very* rapidly fire every nerve cell in sequence as your arm moves toward something. It will cause all the muscles in the arm to expand and contract, as necessary, so you can get the job done swiftly and accurately. Certain kinds of food poisoning, such as botulism, shut off the release of Ach. The result is paralysis.

Ach is also involved in memory. In many cases of Alzheimer's disease, an area of the brain that produces Ach is not working properly. Thus, less of this neurotransmitter is available to the person (Restak, 1994). This is one reason memory is so seriously affected in this disease. However, other neurotransmitters and physical problems in the brain are involved as well.

Another neurotransmitter that is involved in movement is called **dopamine.** A shortage of dopamine plays a central role in Parkinson's disease, which affects the body's ability to control movement. The symptoms include shaking and difficulty speaking. At present, Parkinson's is the only disease we know of that is caused by a shortage of a single neurotransmitter (Restak, 1994). What happens is that cells that make dopamine die off. Prescribing substances that produce dopamine often helps Parkinson's patients.

A newer technique holds some promise for Parkinson's and, to a lesser extent, Alzheimer's patients. In this technique, tissue from the adrenal glands that manufactures neurotransmitters is implanted in the patient's brain. This is a controversial procedure, and complete results are not yet in. However, it at least points to neurotransmitters as central to the problem and possibly central to its solution as well (Kimble, 1990).

Neurotransmitters also exist that relieve pain and increase our sense of well-being. They are called **endorphins.** The term refers to the facts that they are made by the body itself (*endo*) and that they act as a natural form of morphine (*orphin*).

One final thing might have occurred to you. If you were breathing in and had no way to turn off the muscles that inhale, you wouldn't be able to exhale. Similarly, since the reticular activating system has to slow down in order for you to sleep, there must be a way to turn some of its cells off. There is. Some dendritic receptors are designed so that when a neurotransmitter arrives, the cell turns *off.* An example of this occurs when people drink too much. The alcohol molecule resembles a neurotransmitter that the body uses to turn cells off. So when the alcohol gets into the system, cells begin to shut down. Cells turn off in the RAS, making the person sleepy; in the speech area, making him or her slur; in the cerebellum, causing him or her to eventually fall over; and so forth.

The Central and Peripheral Nervous Systems

Focus Questions

• Why is the spinal cord an essential part of the central nervous system?

• What other nervous systems aid in communication?

The complex overall structure of the body's system of nerves is divided into parts. These parts are based to a large extent on where the nerves are located and what areas of the body are involved. The two major divisions are the central and peripheral nervous systems. (See Figure 3.9.)

The Central Nervous System

The brain and spinal cord together make up the **central nervous system.** We have discussed the brain in some detail. Now we discuss its partner, the spinal cord. All the nerve impulses to the body from the brain and from the brain to the body must enter and leave the **spinal cord.**

Sometimes, for our survival, the spinal cord must activate the muscles long before we are even aware of it, a behavior called a **reflex.** In the first stages of an emergency, the brain does not act, but the spinal cord does. This happens in a close call when driving. You are about to hit another car, but "before you know it," you have swerved and missed it. The spinal neurons are short, direct, and very powerful in order to get us out of such close calls. They have very few synapses to slow them down. Just enough are available to send a quick message to the brain about what happened.

central nervous system the brain and spinal cord

spinal cord part of the body that functions as an automatic "brain" in its own right and as a relay station for impulses to and from the higher brain

reflex an automatic behavior of the body involving movement that is activated through the spinal cord without use of the higher brain

Brain

Spinal cord

Peripheral nerves

◀ **Figure 3.9** *The Central and Peripheral Nervous Systems*

▶ **Figure 3.10** *A Simple Sensory-Motor (reflex) Arc. A simple reflex is set in motion by a stimulus to the skin (or other part of the body). The nerve impulse travels to the spinal cord and then back out to a muscle, which contracts. Reflexes provide an "automatic" protective device for the body.*

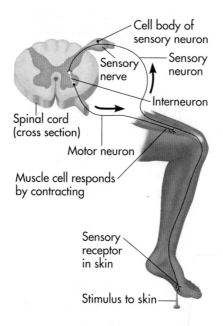

Cell body of
sensory neuron

Sensory
nerve

Sensory
neuron

Interneuron

Spinal cord
(cross section)

Motor neuron

Muscle cell responds
by contracting

Sensory
receptor
in skin

Stimulus to skin

In theory, the spinal cord could operate by itself. For example, a frog has a very small cerebral cortex. If the frog's head is cut off, some parts of its body still work. If the foot is pinched, what is left of the frog will still draw its leg up—for an hour or so. But can the head still work? In a really gory experiment in France many years ago, scientists tried talking to the heads of men who had just had them cut off in an execution. The heads did not answer (Von Frisch, 1963).

The Peripheral Nervous System

peripheral nervous system all the nerves outside the brain and spinal cord

The **peripheral nervous system** is made up of all the nerves other than those in the central nervous system. In other words, take away the central system—the brain and spinal cord—and what is left is the peripheral system. It includes the nerves in your foot or hand or stomach, for instance. The peripheral nervous system is further divided into two parts, the somatic and autonomic nervous systems.

somatic nervous system a division of the peripheral nervous system containing sensory and motor nerves

The Somatic Nervous System. The **somatic nervous system** is composed of sensory and motor nerves. The sensory nerves pick up information and relay it to the brain and spinal cord. For example, you touch something that has a rough texture, and sensory nerves send that information to the brain via the spinal cord. The motor nerves get instructions from the brain and spinal cord and put our muscles into action. Whenever we voluntarily move in some way, then, the somatic system is involved. (See Figure 3.10)

The Autonomic Nervous System. If you pay close attention to yourself, you will note that most bodily activities of the day are not under your voluntary control. You don't have to make yourself breathe in and out, you don't have to make your stomach digest food, and so on. So there is a system that runs much of the body all by itself. The portion of the peripheral nervous system that controls the glands, liver, stomach, heart, and so forth and the connecting neurons from the spinal cord make up the **autonomic nervous system,** which is shown in Figure 3.11 on page 77. The word *autonomic* means independent or functioning on its own, without conscious control. And that's what it does. If you look at Figure 3.11 you will note that almost everything on the list is automatically controlled in our daily lives.

autonomic nervous system the automatic control system of the body; regulates breathing, heart rate, digestion, and so on

The autonomic nervous system tries to stay in balance, but it can be overridden by the higher brain. This can happen when you face a difficult exam. The cortex in this case triggers an internal emotional response. Next, your heart speeds up; blood pressure increases; the liver becomes highly active to provide sugar for the muscles to handle this "emergency"; the stomach slows because the blood used to process food is dispatched to the outer portions of the body for the emergency (to give you muscle strength); and your pupils open up (dilate) to better take in the scene of the emergency. These reactions are designed to enable you to either fight or run from the situation. Such mechanisms provide for basic survival in a crisis. All these emergency behaviors are regulated by the first of two divisions of the autonomic system, called the **sympathetic nervous system.**

But once the sympathetic nervous system goes into action (causing, for example, the heartbeat to increase), how do we ever slow it down again? Why doesn't it just keep running at a tremendous speed? To avoid this problem, nature has devised a braking mechanism, a way to bring things back to normal. This countersystem, called the **parasympathetic nervous system,** is the second of the two divisions of the autonomic nervous system. You can remember this because *para* means "opposite of" (the sympathetic system). In general, then, the parasympathetic nervous system tries to conserve bodily energy and tries to get the system back into balance.

So we have an accelerator and a brake for emergency situations. When there is no emergency ("without arousal" in Figure 3.11), the two systems move more or less in balance throughout the day.

sympathetic nervous system a division of the autonomic nervous system that energizes and prepares for emergencies

parasympathetic nervous system a division of the autonomic nervous system that conserves bodily activity; works in opposition to the sympathetic system to calm us down

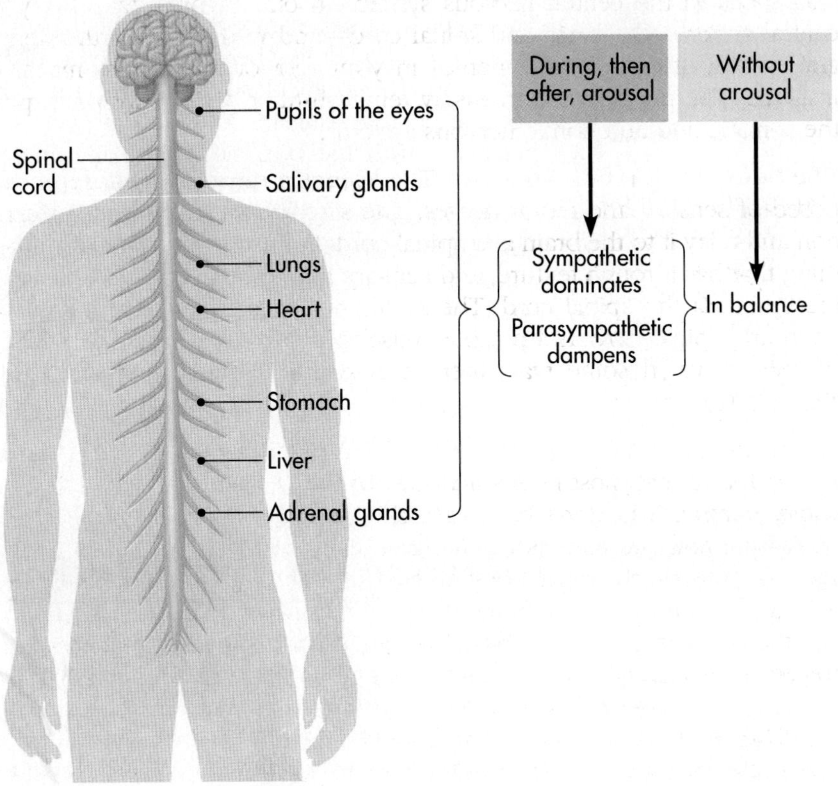

▲ *Figure 3.11* *The autonomic nervous system controls the vital organs and glands, and is kept in balance by its two divisions, the sympathetic nervous system and the parasympathetic nervous system.*

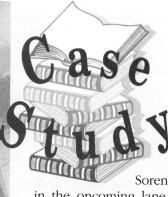

Phantom Limbs

Driving home from soccer practice one day, just months before his high school graduation, seventeen-year-old Tom Sorenson was struck by a car in the oncoming lane. The impact threw him from the car and tore off his left arm.

Weeks later Tom reported sensation in his missing arm: itching, pain, warmth. He felt he could move his fingers and reach for the phone and other objects. One of his physicians, neuroscientist V. S. Ramachandran (1998), author of *Phantoms in the Brain,* describes in his book how he studied Tom's phantom limb.

Ramachandran blindfolded Tom, tapped various parts of his body with a Q-tip, and asked Tom to report where he was being touched. When Ramachandran touched Tom's right shoulder, right leg, lower back, or most other areas, Tom reported those touches accurately. But then an unusual thing happened. When touched on the cheek, Tom felt the cotton not only on his cheek but on his missing thumb as well. Touched on the upper lip, Tom reported sensation in his missing index finger. Touched on the jaw, he felt his missing pinkie.

Ramachandran hypothesized that Tom's brain had reorganized itself in some small way, a remapping process that most scientists believe is impossible after a certain age. The arm and the face are not really close to each other anatomically speaking, but in the brain, these areas are neighbors. After the accident, the area in Tom's brain that had registered sensation from his left arm during his entire life until then, now had no job to do, so the region nearby, the region associated with the face, began to use that area—which could explain why Tom reported a single touch in two areas. Brain-imaging procedures later confirmed that remapping had indeed occurred—and the changes occurred in just four weeks! Whenever Tom smiled or moved his face in a certain way, this caused him to feel his phantom hand. If a drop of rain landed on his face, he felt the rain on the missing hand. Remarkably, the reverse occurred as well. Sometimes his phantom hand would itch, and to relieve that, Tom might scratch his cheek or jaw—and this worked!

You may find this hard to believe, but phantom limbs can even become paralyzed. In his mid-twenties, Phillip Martinez lost control of his motorcycle on a California freeway and suffered severe damage to his left arm. A year later, the arm had to be amputated. Complaining of intense pain and paralysis in his missing arm for ten years, he finally consulted Dr. Ramachandran who devised a simple plan. Ramachandran wondered if visual feedback would fool the brain into thinking that Phillip had two arms. He placed a mirror inside a box and punched out two holes in the side. When Phillip placed his right hand in the box, it would appear as if he had two hands. The result was instantaneous. With his hands in the box, Phillip felt like he could move his phantom hand. The moment he took it out, the hand became paralyzed again. After several weeks of practicing with the box, he was finally able to mentally amputate his missing limb. After ten years, to his great relief, Phillip's perception of his arm finally matched his reality. Ramachandran admits he can't explain why the mirror worked, but he offers one possibility: Phillip's eyes were telling him an arm existed, while his muscles reported the opposite. The brain, after a while, was forced to resolve the conflict in the most efficient way it knew how.

Review the Case Study

1. Can you think of any other examples in which one's perception does not match the reality of the situation?
2. What factors contribute to the false perception?

The Endocrine System

Communication by neurons is speedy and efficient, but it doesn't last very long. Some messages need to stay in the system longer. These messages come from chemicals called **hormones,** which are passed through the body in the bloodstream. *Hormone* comes from a word meaning "to activate," since that's what it does: Hormones can turn on other parts of the body. These chemicals are held inside **glands.** Glands that release hormones into the bloodstream and these hormones themselves make up what is called the **endocrine** (EN-doh-crin) **system.**

Hormones work like neurotransmitters in that they have a special molecular structure that must match the structure of a receptor. For example, there is a hormone-receptor pair designed only for a woman about to give birth. When the time comes, the hormone is sent through the blood to the proper area, where it locks onto its receptor and starts muscular contractions. If a woman never has a baby, this hormone is never used.

In the near-miss accident discussed previously, once the message gets to the brain about what is happening, it declares an emergency that will require the body to be active for a period of time. The hypothalamus uses neurotransmitters to signal the pituitary gland (discussed next). The pituitary then sends out hormones through the endocrine system. They arrive at the adrenal glands (also discussed later), which stir the body up for the emergency. When you get enough of the adrenal hormone in your body, you start to shake all over and feel sick—this is the worst part of a near-miss.

In the sections that follow, we look at the major parts of the endocrine system. Be sure to note that the brain, our inner selves, the body, and the environment all work together; not one of them ever works all by itself.

The Pituitary Gland

The **pituitary** (pi-TUE-i-ter-ee) **gland** is called the master gland of the body. In Figure 3.12, you will see that it is a small bean-shaped unit that is attached to and controlled by the hypothalamus. Physicians many centuries ago thought that mucus running from your nose came from this gland. *Pituita* was a taboo slang word used for this substance, and everyone who heard the word was disgusted. People were wrong about what the gland does, but the term stuck. The pituitary has two jobs: (1) to send messages that will start other glands going and (2) to determine how tall or short we will be (Bergland, 1985).

The pituitary makes a **growth hormone,** but it does it in fits and starts. Sometimes its action is delayed, causing people in the growth phase to worry that they will never reach an average height. On occasion, it seems to start too soon, creating youngsters who feel too tall and "not quite right."

Most of the time, these starts and stops in growth lead to an average height. But not always. When things are not working properly, there can be incredible growth. The tallest known person in history was 8 feet 11.1 inches tall. He died at the age of 22, partly as a result of this growth. The shortest known person was 23.2 inches tall

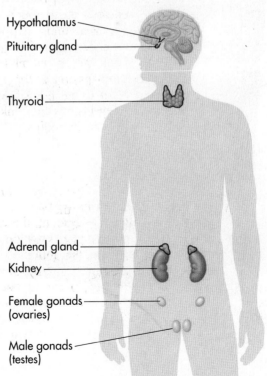

Hypothalamus
Pituitary gland
Thyroid
Adrenal gland
Kidney
Female gonads (ovaries)
Male gonads (testes)

▲ *Figure 3.12* *The Major Parts of the Endocrine System*

thyroid gland the gland that controls and regulates the speed of bodily processes, called metabolism

metabolism the speed at which the body operates or the speed at which it uses up energy

adrenal glands glands that cause excitement in order to prepare the body for an emergency or for some important activity

adrenaline chemical that prepares the body for emergency activity by increasing blood pressure, breathing rate, and energy level

▲ *Whether this is exciting or scary, you can be sure that her adrenaline is pumping.*

when she died at age 19. Today's medicine can handle most such situations if caught early enough, but these cases show what happens if the pituitary goes awry.

Like all body systems, the pituitary requires a normal environment. In one very sad case, a mother locked her growing child in a closet and allowed him out only to eat (from a dog-food bowl). As a result of the darkness and his poor treatment, he stopped growing. When freed by welfare workers, he began to grow again. Then, as a result of an error, he was sent back home. Locked in the closet once more, he stopped growing again. Fortunately, he was finally freed a second time and started growing again (Money, 1974).

Even diet can have a major effect on the pituitary. Poor nutrition can reduce the amount of growth hormone secreted. The Japanese as a group were short compared with most Americans 30 years ago. Then their economy picked up greatly, and food became more varied and accessible. Today, their average height is inches taller than it formerly was. Just the reverse was true for Brazil. For a time, more than a third of its population lived with a severe lack of food, and average height became shorter and shorter with each generation (Simons, 1987).

The Thyroid Gland

The **thyroid gland** and the parts connected to it look like a bow tie sitting inside the neck (look again at Figure 3.12). The pituitary signals the thyroid, whose job is to control **metabolism.** Metabolism is the speed with which the body operates. People with a very active thyroid can be jumping around all over the place, not able to sit still. People with a slow thyroid, on the other hand, tend to be sluggish. A *very* slow gland from birth can lead to mental retardation.

The thyroid gland may sometimes play a role in emotional state as well. An overactive thyroid gland can result in restlessness, nervousness, and anxiety. An underactive thyroid can result in a sad mood, or even depression in some cases. It's important to remember, though, that both anxiety and depression have many causes, and thyroid malfunction is only one of them.

The Adrenal Glands

The **adrenal** (a-DREE-nal) **glands** are located on the right and left sides of the body, slightly above the navel and to the back. When they operate at full force, they create an overexcited body, which none of us wants. But we don't go long without triggering them. In the near-accident example, the quick-acting spinal nerves make us swerve the car to avoid a collision. For a moment, we sigh with relief. But when all the activity gets to the reticular formation and then goes to the cerebral cortex, we begin to think about what *could* have happened. The cortex signals a major emergency to the hypothalamus, which tells the pituitary, which sends hormones to the adrenal glands. The adrenal glands then dump **adrenaline** (a-DREN-a-lin) into the bloodstream. Adrenaline prepares us for an emergency. We begin to breathe rapidly, blood pressure goes up, muscles tense, sugar is dumped into the body for energy, and we are so excited that our armpits and feet sweat. This system is amazing: It even sends out a chemical that will help the blood clot faster just in case we get cut! These reactions are not designed by nature to deal with traffic problems, but the body can't tell the difference between a real emergency (such as an accident we *don't* manage to avoid) and one we just think about. For instance, the whole emergency system is set into motion if we have to talk in front of a group or, for many of us, if we are about to take an examination. Hands tremble, armpits and feet perspire, we can hardly breathe, the heart is racing, all saliva is gone so that we feel like we are choking, and we know for sure we are going to die right in the middle of the talk or the test.

The Gonads

The **gonads** are the sex glands; they make the sperm or eggs used for reproduction. The male sex hormone is called **androgen,** and the female one is called **estrogen.** *Both* males and females have *both* hormones in their bodies; but for the male, there is more androgen, and for the female, more estrogen. These hormones make us look either male or female. For example, if a female is injected with extra androgen, she will grow body hair and a beard. Androgen also starts the sex drive for both males and females.

Earlier, we mentioned that brain and body affect one another. Nowhere is this clearer than in the case of sex hormones. If you neuter a dog, it will lose its desire to reproduce. This is *not* the case with an adult human. Even after an accident that removes the source of the hormones, the sex drive can remain for years. So even though our sex drive is at one time started by hormones, it is then taken over by the cerebral cortex, which makes it a social, symbolic behavior as well as a physical one. Many find this hard to believe, but because the cortex controls it, sex must actually be learned by humans. It is not like hunger or thirst. This fact is often a source of real confusion for adolescents, because it takes a long time to understand what sex is all about. To add to the problem, sometimes their friends of the same age *pretend* they already know all about it. The presence of the cortex does give humans the feelings of love, hope, warmth, respect, and care that can be attached to the sex act. But the presence of the cortex also means that the opposite feelings—fear, anxiety, and psychological pain—can likewise occur.

gonads the sex glands; they make sperm or eggs for reproduction

androgen the male sex hormore

estrogen the female sex hormore

 ## Pause for Thought

1. Describe how one neuron communicates with another neuron.
2. Describe the roles of the following neurotransmitters: acetylcholine, endorphins, and dopamine.
3. What is the difference between the central nervous system and the peripheral nervous system? Between the somatic nervous system and the autonomic nervous system? Between the sympathetic and parasympathetic nervous systems?
4. How is the endocrine system different from the nervous system?

Critical Thinking
. . . .
5. What might happen if the glands described in this section were too active or not active enough? Be specific.

APPLYING Psychology to life

Seeing the Brain in Action

The first genuine breakthrough in understanding the brain came in the early 1800s in a bizarre way. The person responsible was a medical student, Franz Gall. A vital ability in medical school is the ability to memorize, and he wasn't able to do this as well as others could. Rather than admit to a failing on his part, he began to look carefully at his fellow students. He convinced himself that the best memorizers had protruding eyes, which he did not have. He then made a direct connection between a physical feature and mental abilities. In this case, protruding eyes indicated a good memory (Krech, 1962).

Eventually, Gall expanded his ideas to include other features and mental abilities. His basic notion was that certain areas of the brain would be enlarged if a person possessed certain characteristics to a great extent. To Gall's way of thinking, it was logical that when an area of the brain is enlarged, it will create a corresponding bump in the skull. This theory is called *phrenology,* the study of bumps on the head as they relate to personality and mental abilities. According to his theory, if you have bumps near your temples, at the sides of the forehead, you enjoy destruction. A bump on the top of the head, just to the left of the middle, means you have a lot of faith, and so on.

Phrenology obviously doesn't work, and none of Gall's ideas have been supported by any evidence. However, phrenology did focus scientists' attention on the brain and on the idea that different areas of the brain are involved in different functions. Today, fortunately, we know much more about the brain than Franz Gall could ever have imagined possible.

Early work on brain functions had to rely heavily on observing the changes that occurred in people who had suffered brain injuries or had had some part removed by surgery.

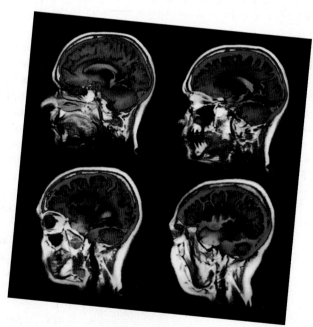

▲ *An MRI brain scan*

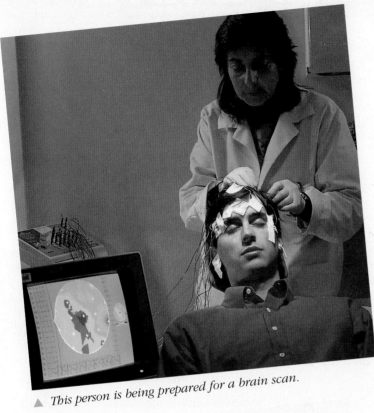

▲ *This person is being prepared for a brain scan.*

scans the brain and takes a picture of the levels of radioactivity. By reading the amount of radioactive glucose being used, we can determine what area of the brain is most active (Posner & Raichle, 1994). Originally, PET scans were used to diagnose various brain problems, such as tumors. Now, however, they can tell us what our brain actually does when we are performing specific tasks or experiencing certain sensations (Wheeler et al., 1997).

The MRI, like the PET scan, was originally given only for diagnostic purposes. It, too, however, can now be used in other ways. An injection is not required for an MRI, though. The MRI can detect smaller differences in the level and location of brain activity than is true for the PET scan. When having an MRI done, a person is placed on a short conveyor belt and moved inside a small oblong chamber that is part of a special machine. The person must remain motionless while the machine takes images of the brain's activity. By the way, if you have an MRI scheduled and suffer from claustrophobia, don't be embarrassed to tell your doctor or the technician beforehand. It's close quarters inside that chamber, and you may need a mild tranquilizer to reduce your anxiety. Some institutions are using newer, open machines for this very reason; but these new machines are not available everywhere.

That approach still has value and can provide us with useful information. However, recent years have seen dramatic improvements in our ability to "watch" the brain in action. Technology has made it possible for us to witness the brain's functions in remarkable detail. There are three major techniques in use today—the electroencephalogram, or EEG; positron emission tomography, or the PET scan; and magnetic resonance imaging, or the MRI.

The EEG uses electrical firing of the brain to graph brain waves. In this procedure, electrodes are attached to the head at various points (don't cringe—they are usually glued to the scalp, not nailed in place). A reading is taken of the electrical firing going on at those spots. Different patterns of brain waves indicate different functions. For example, as we discuss in Chapter 6, specific patterns show when a person is deeply asleep, dreaming, or relaxed but awake. Other patterns emerge when someone is suffering from a seizure.

To obtain a PET scan, glucose, a form of sugar, is specially treated to make it radioactive. This glucose is then injected into the bloodstream. When a part of the brain is highly active, it uses glucose at a high rate. Thus, the radioactivity will be higher in this part of the brain. A machine

Summary

1. The outermost layer of the brain is the cerebral cortex. The cerebral cortex is divided into two halves, called hemispheres.

2. The hemispheres are connected through the corpus callosum. The left half controls the right side of the body and vice versa.

3. The cortex is divided into sections, or lobes.

    a. The frontal lobe contains the motor strip, which controls movement; the prefrontal area, which is involved in personal memories; and the frontal association area, which integrates the environment and carries on complex analyses.

    b. The sensory strip, which controls sensation, is in the parietal lobe.

    c. Hearing and speech are functions of the temporal lobe.

    d. The occipital lobe organizes visual information.

4. The lower brain controls basic bodily activity.

    a. The thalamus is a relay station to and from the cortex and the lower brain.

    b. The hypothalamus is part of a system controlling rage, pleasure, hunger, thirst, and sexual desire.

    c. The limbic system controls emotion and, to some extent, memory.

    d. Within this system, the amygdala is responsible for emotions, especially aggression.

    e. The hippocampus is involved in forming memories.

    f. The cerebellum guides coordination and balance.

    g. The reticular activating system keeps us alert or puts us to sleep.

5. Parts of the brain are connected to one another through neurons. The brain is also connected to the body through neurons.

6. In the neurons, electricity runs from the dendrite through the cell to the axon and out to the synapse.

7. Communication through the synapses is actually handled by neurotransmitters, chemicals that regulate different systems, such as muscle movement and the recognition of pain.

8. The central nervous system consists of the brain and spinal cord.

9. All the nerves outside the brain and spinal cord make up the peripheral nervous system. It is divided into the somatic nervous system, which contains sensory and motor nerves, and the autonomic nervous system, which controls automatic bodily functions.

10. The autonomic nervous system is divided into the sympathetic nervous system, which readies us for emergencies, and the parasympathetic system, which operates to calm us down after the emergency is over.

11. The endocrine system uses hormones to provide a method of chemical communication longer lasting than that provided by neurons. The pituitary is the master gland.

    a. It guides growth.

    b. It also signals the thyroid for metabolism.

    c. It signals the adrenal glands for emergencies.

    d. It signals the gonads for sexual activity.

Vocabulary

cerebral cortex	lower brain	acetylcholine	parasympathetic
fissure	thalamus	dopamine	nervous system
hemisphere	hypothalamus	endorphins	hormones
corpus callosum	limbic system	central nervous	glands
lobes	amygdala	system	endocrine system
frontal lobe	hippocampus	spinal cord	pituitary gland
parietal lobe	cerebellum	reflex	growth hormone
motor strip	reticular activating	peripheral nervous	thyroid gland
sensory strip	system (RAS)	system	metabolism
occipital lobe	neuron	somatic nervous sys-	adrenal glands
temporal lobe	dendrites	tem	adrenaline
prefrontal area	axon	autonomic nervous	gonads
frontal association	synapse	system	androgen
area	vesicles	sympathetic nervous	estrogen
dominance	neurotransmitters	system	

Review Questions

Matching

Match the function with the proper part of the lower brain.

a. thalamus

b. RAS

c. cerebellum

d. hypothalamus

e. hippocampus

f. amygdala

g. synapse

h. axon

i. neuron

j. dendrite

k. neurotransmitter

l. vesicle

1. Controls balance
2. Controls hunger and thirst
3. Sends messages to various parts of the brain
4. "Catches" nerve impulses in order to register activity level
5. Triggers aggression in limbic system
6. Helps form memories
7. Receives electrical messages from other nerve cells
8. Space between nerve cells
9. Carries electrical messages to the end of the nerve cell
10. Chemical that sends messages from neuron to neuron
11. Nerve cell
12. Container for chemical messengers

For each of the following, answer T for thyroid gland, A for adrenal gland, P for pituitary gland, or G for gonads. Each answer will be used twice.

13. Regulates metabolism
14. Produces androgen and estrogen
15. Activated especially during emergencies
16. May cause general sluggishness
17. The master gland
18. Helps regulate blood pressure
19. Helps determine height
20. Sex glands

Discussion Questions

1. After learning about the specialized functions of the left and right hemispheres, which hemisphere do you think you rely on primarily when you take notes, study, and try to recall information for a test? Explain. How could you possibly make better use of both hemispheres? Be specific.

2. How do you suppose alcohol would affect each part of the lower brain (thalamus, hypothalamus, cerebellum, RAS, amygdala, hippocampus) and each part of the upper brain (frontal association area, occipital lobe, motor strip, sensory strip)? Explain.

3. Describe several situations in which you might want your neurotransmitters to operate very efficiently and quickly. Describe several situations in which you might wish your neurotransmitters to work inefficiently and slowly.

4. The "brain transplant" is a common science fiction theme. Just for fun, imagine that the procedure has just become possible, and you have been chosen as the first candidate. Discuss the following:

   a. Whose brain would you choose? Why?

   b. If you had to choose between a smart, somber brain and a simple, happy brain, which would you choose? Why?

   c. Regardless of your choices above, *who* would you be *after* the transplant? Would your identity be the same as it was before, because you would occupy the same body? Or would your identity be that of the new brain? Explain.

5. The chapter explains that our sex drive has both physical and social aspects and that sex must be learned by humans. Other than actual experience and heart-to-heart talks, how *do* we learn about sex? Through TV? Through the media in general? Who or what teaches us? And what is the message being taught?

Activities and Projects

1. This can be one of the most difficult chapters in the book because of the numerous terms you have to remember. We highly recommend this project, since the process of completing it will help you study, and you might even have some fun.

   Create a three-dimensional model of the brain that includes all the parts of the cerebral cortex and the lower brain described in the chapter. To avoid clutter, you may want one side to represent the cerebral cortex and the other side to illustrate the lower brain. For each part, include a simple visual that will help you recall the function of that part. For example, you could glue a piece of cereal next to the hypothalamus to indicate that the hypothalamus regulates hunger.

   The finished product should look polished and should reflect your hard work. Therefore, be creative with the materials you select. Sometimes, it's difficult for an audience to appreciate this sort of model without some insight from the creator, so present your creation to your class, pointing out why you used the visuals that you did.

2. You'll need to get a friend or two to help you with this project. Create a videotape that provides a glimpse into how the brain works. Have each person assume the role of one part of the brain, and then have the parts converse with each other. You might have each person wear a headband or hat to identify himself or herself. Here's a brief sample. The setting is a classroom during an exam.

   Occipital Lobe. That's right, Frank. Betty just sent me a bulletin from the eyes. The answers on that other answer sheet are B, C, D, C, A. . . .

   Frontal Lobe. Thanks, buddy. That could be helpful. Thanks to the hippocampus, we forgot to study for this test, you know. Tell you what, I'll see if I can get John down in motor strip to instruct the hand to fill in those bubbles.

Motor Strip. Yeah, Frank . . . uh-huh . . . whatever you say. (*Mumbles:* Always blaming the poor hippocampus.) But don't you think we should check with Conscience first?

Frontal Lobe. You're probably right. I always forget though . . . in what department can we find Conscience?

Motor Strip. Gee, Frank. That's you, isn't it?

Frontal Lobe. I guess. I'll have to consult with my colleagues up here. I'll get back to you in a millisecond or two. Don't fill in those bubbles quite yet.

Make sure your dialogue is essentially accurate in terms of brain functions so that the video is informative as well as entertaining. And you will probably want to describe a situation that includes some conflict the brain needs to resolve.

3. Several advertisers explicitly use the theory of left- and right-hemisphere dominance to promote their products. For example, they openly claim that their products appeal to the left hemisphere and then supply statistics. At the same time, they claim that their products appeal to the right hemisphere and then supply vivid, emotional pictures.

Other than these obvious examples, *do* advertisers direct their sales pitches to one hemisphere or another? To find out, collect 10 magazine ads that appeal primarily to the left hemisphere, 10 that appeal to the right hemisphere, and 10 that appeal to both hemispheres. Neatly tape each ad onto a sheet of paper, and provide captions explaining why you chose these ads.

4. Contact a local hospital and find someone there who knows about the latest techniques for studying the brain. Read the material at the end of the chapter on EEGs, PET scans, and MRIs, and write 10 to 15 questions you can ask this person. Try to avoid questions that require one-word responses. In fact, ask your interviewee to explain his or her answers; ask follow-up questions; and most important, listen carefully. If you can't arrange an interview at the hospital, conduct a phone interview. Write a report discussing not only the responses but also your reactions to the interview. You'd be surprised how many people are willing to share their expertise. After your interview, you might want to ask this

person to visit your class for a question-and-answer session.

5. What common expressions are hidden in the following puzzles?

a. NOON GOOD   b. HE'S HIMSELF

The answers are: (a) "Good afternoon" and (b) "He's beside himself." Although these particular puzzles are not extremely difficult, the skills of both hemispheres are needed to solve them. The left hemisphere needs to *read* the words, while the right hemisphere needs to determine the *spatial relationship* between the words (for example, the word *good* appears *after* the word *noon*).

Here's a more difficult example:

c.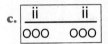

Why are some people better than others at solving these kinds of puzzles? One answer might be that some people have thicker and more efficient corpus callosums, allowing the two hemispheres to work together better. Another answer might be that, in some people, one hemisphere does not dominate over another; these people have developed an efficient "balance" between the hemispheres. In fact, there seems to be some evidence that left-handed people are more likely than right-handed people to have balanced brains. If this is true, it may be safe to assume that "lefties" would do better at solving the puzzles we've shown.

Conduct an experiment to find out if this assumption is correct. Put together a list of about 20 puzzles similar to those shown here. Either create your own or get them out of the comics section of a newspaper or *Games Magazine,* which regularly publishes these types of puzzles. Find 10 "righties" and 10 "lefties" to solve the puzzles (lefties are relatively rare, but you should be able to find 10). Allow each subject two minutes to solve the puzzles. Tally the correct answers. *Do* "lefties" perform better? What conclusions can you draw?

Incidentally, the answer to the last puzzle is "Circles under the eyes."

CHAPTER 4

S ensation and perception form our world. Without them we can make no sense of what is happening around us. Perception is controlled psychologically because we interpret the incoming stimulation (sensation) to fit our needs or desires. The basic information from such sensation is processed by remarkable physical receptors designed just for each task.

Sensation and Perception

Sensory Processes

We are so used to processing information from the senses that we take this ability for granted. Nonetheless, our ability to understand what is going on around us is truly remarkable. Our brains set up all kinds of methods for handling this complex information. If you receive information that is deliberately confusing—well, let's see what happens. We will give you a sentence, and you try to figure out what it says. We have put the "translation" of it somewhere in the next couple of paragraphs. Don't look for it until you have tried to figure the sentence out. Here it is:

ThEcOwgAvecOla.

This is really a sentence, but you have trouble processing it because the normal shapes and boundaries of the words and letters have been rearranged. Everyone must rely heavily on these shapes to be able to read as fast as we do. The eye skips and jumps from one part of the sentence to another. If a word is very common, like *and* or *the,* we take only a glimpse at it as the eye looks at clumps of words all at one time. The normal method for reading is to focus on the beginning letters of a sentence and determine what basic *shapes* the rest of the words in the sentence have. If everything looks familiar, we assume, after a very slight pause, that the words are known. If, as we read on, the sentence doesn't fit with what comes next, we stop and go back to find out what we missed. If you actually had to read every letter and word on this page, it would take you more than 20 minutes to read it and about eight hours to read this chapter—a fate no one deserves. So what is it we've done to make the example sentence so confusing? We've changed its physical structure. Here is the sentence written in something close to the normal structure; now you should have no trouble whatsoever with it: TheCowGaveCola.

All incoming sensation must be interpreted by the brain. As a result, quite often we see what we want to see and hear what we want to hear (or don't see or hear, according to what we really desire). So sensation is not merely a physical event—it can be very psychological. Here is a simple example of making something what it isn't. Read the following sentence from *right to left,* once, without stopping. *Don't* read it again yet.

.rat eht saw tac ehT

Most people read one of two versions: "The cat saw the rat" or "The cat was the rat." Both of these are wrong. You made this mistake because if you had read the sentence backward the way it really is written, it wouldn't have made sense to you. Read it again, this time very carefully, and you will see what we mean (Dunn-Rankin, 1978).

One more example: We assign a symbolic "top," "bottom," and "side" to most objects we know, and we keep them that way, regardless of their position. Cut out a piece of paper with four equal sides, put it up on the wall, and call it a "square." Tilt your head and view it. It is still a square. Move your head around some more. It is still a square. Now, cut out the same basic square and call it a "diamond" before you put it up on the wall with one corner at the top. Tilt your head to the point where it actually looks like a "square." Is it? No, it remains a diamond in your mind. In this

Focus Questions

• What is the difference between sensation and perception?

• What is the weakest light that can be seen? The lightest touch that can be felt?

89

▶ **Figure 4.1** *Absolute threshold refers to the minimum amount of energy needed for a sensation to occur. This chart shows the approximate absolute thresholds for the five main senses.*

absolute threshold the level of sensory stimulation necessary for sensation to occur

adaptation the gradual loss of attention to unneeded or unwanted sensory information

sensation the process of receiving information from the environment

perception the process of assembling and organizing sensory information to make it meaningful

Absolute Thresholds

Vision	Candle flame seen at 30 miles on a clear night
Hearing	Tick of a watch under quiet conditions at 20 feet
Touch	A bee's wing falling on your cheek from 1 centimeter (0.4 inch) above
Smell	1 drop of perfume diffused into a three-room apartment
Taste	1 teaspoon of sugar in 2 gallons of water

▲ *Being able to concentrate in a distracting environment is difficult at times. The process of adaptation helps us filter out meaningless sensory input.*

example, as well as the others, what started out as light energy coming into your eyes and going from there to the brain has been given a meaning not contained in the actual source of the light energy.

Before we can receive information from our senses, though, we must first pay attention to it. In order for that to happen, the incoming information must be strong enough to make us notice it. A very dim light will not be seen in the daytime and a very soft noise will not be heard, especially in the presence of other sounds. The level of sensory stimulation necessary for that stimulation to register is called the **absolute threshold.** (See Figure 4.1.) Standard absolute thresholds have been determined for each of our senses.

Once we are aware of some kind of sensory information—for instance, a sound—we do not necessarily continue to pay attention to it. If it is not particularly important, we will eventually ignore it or put it into the background. This process is called **adaptation,** the gradual loss of attention to unneeded or unwanted sensory information. Adaptation allows us to ignore meaningless sensory input. Without it, we would have to pay attention to every little thing going on in our environment. And that would make for a confusing situation indeed.

In this chapter, we will analyze some of our most incredible abilities: (1) **sensation**—the process of receiving information from the environment—and (2) **perception**—the process of organizing sensory information to make it meaningful. These two processes are intermixed. To make it easier to learn about them, however, we will divide the chapter into two sections, starting with sensation.

Sensation

In this section, we will look at the workings of each of the five human senses—vision, hearing, touch, smell, and taste.

Vision

Vision dominates the human senses. We always believe what we see first. Only secondarily do we accept information from taste, smell, hearing, or feeling. Thus, if you are brave enough to eat a green-colored steak, it will taste funny to you even if it has only been colored by a tasteless food dye. Despite the fact that your sense of smell says it is all right, that will make no difference in how it tastes.

Light. Light movement is based on the same principle as snapping a whip. In a whip snap, the energy starts at the wrist and is sent in the shape of a wave down to the end of the whip. Depending on how hard the whip is snapped, the waves can vary from long and slow to short and fast. Light starts out from the sun (or a light bulb) as **white light.** Color is seen only after the waves of white light hit objects and bounce back to us at different speeds or frequencies. There really is no such thing as "color." We simply give different light wavelengths certain names (see Figure 4.2). "Color" is seen because the eyes have different receptors for different wavelengths. Some frequencies (such as that of ultraviolet light waves) are too rapid for our eyes to be able to see the light, but these light waves can be used by other creatures. The bee seeks out flowers using ultraviolet light waves, for example. Frequencies that are too slow for us to see (such as infrared light waves) ... ...akes to see at night.

Focus Questions

• What happens after light that creates vision hits the eye?

• Is the eye really like a camera?

• How does the brain see color?

white light light as it originates from the sun or a bulb before it is broken into different frequencies

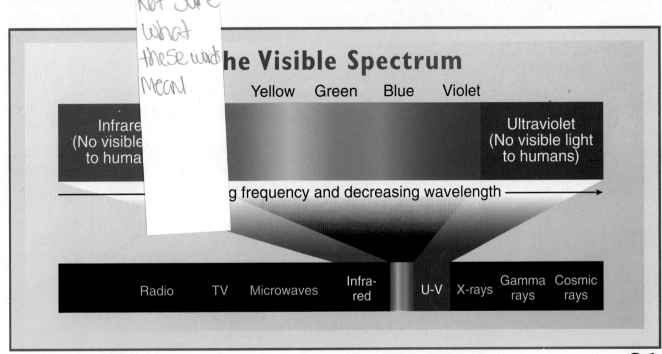

▲ **Figure 4.2** *Energy waves are represented here arranged by frequency and wavelength.*

The key to color, then, is white light waves hitting various objects in the environment and bouncing off at different wavelengths, which in turn hit receptors in our eyes. A good analogy is what happens if a shotgun is fired at the side of a hill: Some of the pellets hit dirt and are absorbed. Some hit leaves and are deflected. Some hit rock or other material and come back at us at different speeds. If these pellets were light waves, the ones that bounce back at us would be the ones we use for vision.

The speed of movement of light waves varies depending on the texture and solidity of what they hit. For instance, snowflakes are built like crystals, so they have many flat surfaces. Sunlight, which is white, hits the slick flat surfaces of the flakes and bounces off without breaking up, so we see the snowflakes as white. In the same way, a polished wood surface gives out almost-white streaks where the bright light hits the glossy spots (directly reflected light). If the end of a board is broken off, though, we can see a number of different colors. The light hitting the broken board breaks into different wavelengths, depending on which part of the board the light hits and how flat each part is. Water molecules are very strangely shaped and complex. Because of this, they absorb the energy at the red end of Figure 4.2 (the yellow and red light waves). This leaves two sets of rays that bounce back from water: green and blue. And this is why bodies of water look green or blue to us.

The Cornea and Iris. Figure 4.3 shows a top view of what the eye would look like if it were cut in half and the top taken off. The **cornea** (KOR-nee-ah) is a clear outer covering, behind which is a fluid. If you look at your eyes in a mirror, they seem shiny because you are seeing a reflection from the fluid behind the cornea. Next comes the portion of the eyes that lovers focus on. It is called the **iris** (EYE-ris) and is actually a colored circular muscle that opens and closes into larger or smaller circles in order to control the amount of light getting into the eye. To see it in operation, face a mirror, cover one eye, and turn on the light. Stand so that the light will hit the covered eye when you remove your hand. Remove

cornea the clear outer covering of the eye, behind which is a fluid

iris a colored circular muscle that opens and closes, forming larger and smaller circles to control the amount of light getting into the eye

▶ *Figure 4.3* *This cross section shows the eye as seen from the top.*

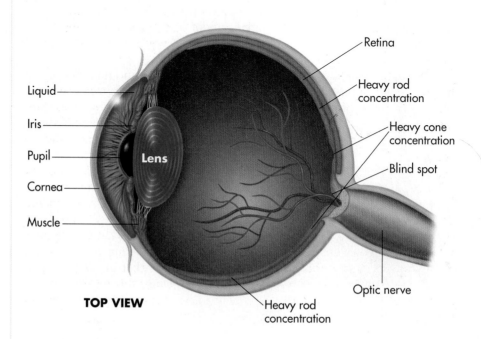

Liquid

Iris

Pupil

Lens

Cornea

Muscle

Retina

Heavy rod concentration

Heavy cone concentration

Blind spot

Optic nerve

TOP VIEW

Heavy rod concentration

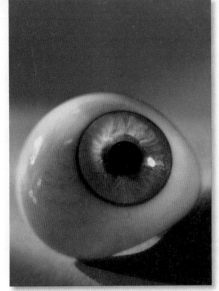

▲ *This model of the human eye clearly shows the cornea, iris, and pupil.*

your hand, and watch how the iris, which had opened because it was dark behind your hand, quickly closes until the circle at its center is very small. When you leave a movie matinee, your irises are wide open to catch the limited light in the darkened theater. As you walk out into the sun, the light seems blinding at first because the irises aren't able to close fast enough; they let in too much light to too many receptors.

The Lens. The **lens** of your eye is very much like a camera lens. It helps you to focus the objects you see onto the back of the eye, where there are receptors. If the lens is not shaped correctly, the image coming in will either overshoot or fall short of the receptors at the back of the eye, and this causes images to blur. Eyeglasses are designed to change the angle at which the light hits the lens, causing the incoming light waves to land properly on the receptors. The lens automatically adjusts to whatever object we want to see. As the muscles controlling the lens make the adjustment, they give the brain information about how much they have moved. This is one way we learn to judge how far away from us an object is.

lens the part of the eye that focuses an image on the retina

The Pupil. What is the black circle in the middle of your eye? Nothing. The **pupil,** as you can see in Figure 4.3, is just an opening that changes size as the iris muscles move to cover and uncover the lens. Since it is dark inside your eye, the opening of the pupil looks black; but if you flash a light inside, the colors coming back through the pupil can vary across the whole range, depending on how the light is bent and what it hits in there. This is what causes the "red eyes" effect you see in some flash color photographs.

▲ *You can find many parallels between the workings of the eye and the workings of a camera.*

pupil the opening in the eye

Psychological factors can control the iris muscles and thus the size of the pupil. The pupils of our eyes get smaller if we are disgusted. They get larger if we see something we really like (Millodot, 1982). Those who learn this think they might be onto something. Since the pupils enlarge if someone likes you a lot, checking out pupils may be a way to make sure. In fact, years and years ago about the only way most women could survive, socially and financially, was to marry someone. If a woman found a desirable male, she would put a few drops of medicine made from a poisonous plant called *belladonna* into her eyes, causing the pupils to widen. (*Belladonna* means "beautiful lady.") The woman couldn't see very well until it wore off; but long before science, nature knew what wide pupils meant, and the man began to fall in love, not quite knowing why. Lest you go off thinking this is foolproof, it's best to tell you that the pupils open up all the way when someone is *afraid* also, because this makes it possible to explore the threat in the environment better. Strong emotional arousal of any kind causes the pupils to widen.

▲ *Figure 4.4 Finding the Blind Spot. (a) With your right eye closed, stare at the upper right cross. Hold the book about one foot away from you and slowly move it back and forth. You should be able to find the position that causes the black spot to disappear. (b) Repeat this process, but stare instead at the lower cross. When the gap falls on the blind spot, the black line will appear to be continuous because your brain will fill in details for the place it can't find.*

retina the back of the eye, which contains millions of receptors for light

blind spot the portion of the retina through which the optic nerve exits and where there are no receptors for light waves

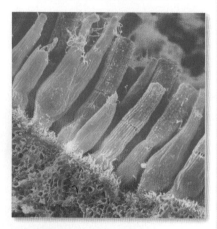

▲ *A portion of the retina, magnified to show individual rods and cones.*

▶ *Figure 4.5 Rods and cones transmit impulses through the optic nerve. On the right, the retina is enlarged to show the rods and cones.*

The Retina. When the light entering the eye gets to the back of the eyeball, it hits the **retina** (RET-in-ah). Millions upon millions of receptors are embedded in the retina. We will discuss them in a moment. Before leaving the overall structure of the eyeball, note in Figure 4.3 that there is a place where all the nerve cells leave the eye in what's called the optic nerve. Retinal receptors are to the right and left of this point, but there are none where this nerve bundle leaves. This is called the **blind spot.** We can't see anything when light waves hit that point. Still, the eyes dart back and forth so rapidly that we normally never notice it. If you want to find your blind spot, use Figure 4.4.

Rods and Cones. Go outside as twilight approaches. Take a chair, a blue object, and a red object (or go where there are some blue and some red flowers). Sit in the chair, put the objects down, and watch them as darkness approaches. The red objects will soon turn black and disappear, but the blue objects will not turn black until it is almost completely dark outside.

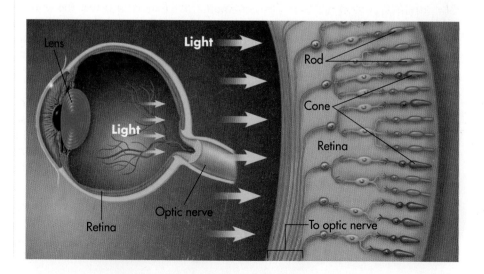

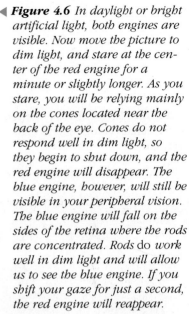

Figure 4.6 In daylight or bright artificial light, both engines are visible. Now move the picture to dim light, and stare at the center of the red engine for a minute or slightly longer. As you stare, you will be relying mainly on the cones located near the back of the eye. Cones do not respond well in dim light, so they begin to shut down, and the red engine will disappear. The blue engine, however, will still be visible in your peripheral vision. The blue engine will fall on the sides of the retina where the rods are concentrated. Rods do work well in dim light and will allow us to see the blue engine. If you shift your gaze for just a second, the red engine will reappear.

What you are experiencing is the fact that the retina is made up of two different kinds of receptors, as shown in Figure 4.5. The first type of receptor is called a **rod** because it is shaped like one. The second is called a **cone** because that's the shape it has. Rods are very sensitive to the violet-purple range of wavelengths, but we only "see" black and white with them. There are about 100 million rods in the retina, and they are used for night vision because they respond very well to low levels of light. Since the rods become more sensitive as it darkens, they keep the blue objects visible. The cones are shutting off, so the red objects disappear. Cones, on the other hand, are used for color and daylight vision and respond best to wavelengths in the red range. They shut off with little or no light. You can see color on a highway when you are driving through the city at night because the light level is almost as high as during the day. But if you watch carefully when you turn away from a populated area and drive down a dimly lit street, you will notice that the images you see are no longer sharp except where the headlights hit. This is because the cones, which provide sharpness of vision, have shut off, and rods by themselves only provide a rough outline of objects. Rods are very heavily packed into the sides of the retina. If you are trying to see something in a dark area, look slightly *away* from where you think it is, and the rods on the sides of your retina will pick up its shape. Or have a friend sneak up on you in the dark. Notice how you can spot him or her if you are approached from the side but have trouble if he or she moves toward the center of your line of sight. This is because the cones that have shut off are located mostly in the center of each retina. So when you enter a darkened movie theater, you can't see anything at first, since the cones can't handle darkness. In daylight, on the other hand, the rods shut off. (See Figure 4.6.)

rod a visual receptor most sensitive to the violet-purple wavelengths; very sensitive for night vision; "sees" only black and white

cone a visual receptor that responds during daylight; "sees" color

Color Vision. This is how color vision works: All the colors we see are red, blue, green, or a mixture of these three. You can understand the principle of mixture if you take red, blue, and green spotlights and shine them on a white wall. By mixing the lights, you will get every color possible. Throughout the center part of the retina are millions of cones connected together. Some receive red, some green, and some blue wavelengths. Depending on the texture of the object we are viewing, light from each part of the object will bounce back at different wavelengths, and the brain will mix these wavelengths, making the object appear a specific color.

color blindness inability to perceive certain colors, such as red and green

Color Defects. A number of people have a defect called **color blindness,** the inability to tell the difference between certain colors. The most common form of this problem is found in those who can see color only in the yellow-blue range an 'ㅤㅤred or green color. About 8 percent of males have this in ㅤㅤt; only 0.5 percent of ㅤㅤ For these people, the ㅤㅤen cone system does not work in terms of seeing color. The receptors *do* respond to the light-wave energy, but they *don't* see it as "colored." People with this condition do have a third color-receiving (cone) system that responds in the yellow-blue area (Mollon, 1982). In all other respects, their vision is completely normal. (See Figure 4.7.)

Truly "color blind" people are very rare. They respond to light waves only with rods. Even a moderately bright light can be very painful for them because all the rods are responding in unison to white light, something they are not designed to do.

People sometimes make unfounded assumptions and pass on the misinformation from one generation to another. You may hear that most animals see everything in gray because they have no color vision. This is simply not true. Many animals have very elaborate rod and cone systems, just as we do. And you will hear that bulls go crazy when they see a matador's red cape. Cattle do have full color vision, but the idea of red inflaming them doesn't make sense. The bull is responding to movement, not color (Grandin, 1995). If you don't believe us, try getting in a ring with one, waving a cape of another color, and see what happens!

Are You Color Blind?

No.	Normal eye	Color-blind eye	No.	Normal eye	Color-blind eye
1	12	12	6	nothing	45
2	8	3	7	26	2 or 6
3	29	70	8	45	nothing
4	5	2	9	5	nothing
5	74	21	10	nothing	5

▲ **Figure 4.7** *A Typical Test for Color Blindness*

Afterimages. All physical systems strive to stay in balance. If we are cold, we shiver to increase circulation; if hot, we sweat to cool down. The same principle applies to the cone network of the eyes. If ~~ colored object for a minute or so, the chemicals in the cones ~~ ou are seeing will be partially used up as changes in the ch~~ ~~ lectrical impulses (signals to the brain). The chemicals for ~~ u are *not* seeing are still intact. No message has been sent ~~ them because you haven't seen these colors. As a result, th~~ ~~s not in balance. If you look away from the object and star~~ ~~e of paper, you will see the object in opposite colors. This~~ ~~ults from the remaining "unused" cones firing so that all th~~ ~~ore themselves to equal chemical levels at the same time~~ ~~ss will occur if you stare at a television for a while and th~~ ~~all.

You do not see these afterimages during norma~~ ~~se you keep replacing one image with another, and each~~ ~~if-ferent set of cones. Figure 4.8 gives you the chance to ~~ ~~e principle in action.

didn't know that

afterimage image that remains after stimulation of the retina has ended. Cones not used fire to bring the visual system back in balance.

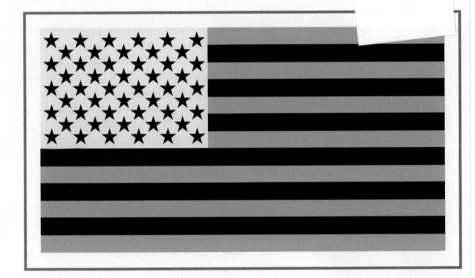

◄ *Figure 4.8 To demonstrate an afterimage for yourself, take a sheet of white typing paper or other flat white surface and put it aside. Focus your eyes on the last star of the flag (the one in the lower right-hand corner), and stare at it for one minute. Now quickly move your eyes to the white paper, and you should see the flag appear in red, white, and blue.*

 Pause for Thought

1. What's the difference between sensation and perception?
2. Why do some objects appear blue to us, while others appear red?
3. Describe the functions of each part of the eye. How do rods and cones contribute to vision? What does it mean to be truly color blind?

Critical Thinking
. . . .

4. Afterimages are fun to create and see, but the explanation for why they occur can be confusing. Imagine you have to teach this concept to a class of fifth-graders. What would you say?

Thinking Critically about Psychology

Do Subliminal Messages Really Work?

There are all kinds of audiotapes on the market today that claim to be able to reach your subconscious mind with wonderfully effective messages. Advertisers say that just by playing the tapes, you can control your weight, stop smoking, increase your self-esteem, or become more popular, more successful, or more of whatever they can dream up. The part of the tape you can hear usually contains easy-listening or classical music or some soothing sound such as ocean waves or a gentle rainfall. Supposedly hidden at a much lower volume is a repeated message, such as "You are a winner." Similar approaches have made use of videotapes. In these tapes, a message, such as "Don't eat chocolate," is flashed on the screen over and over, too fast to be clearly seen.

The idea behind all this is that even though we cannot consciously hear or see the message, it will still be registered at the subconscious level. The principle involved is called **subliminal** (sub-LIM-uh-null) **perception**—perception that takes place below our level of conscious awareness. (The word *subliminal* comes from the word *limen,* which means a line that marks off a boundary.)

What specifically is being claimed or stated? Messages that we are not consciously aware of can nevertheless greatly influence our behavior.

What is the objective evidence for and against this claim? A lot of attention was given to subliminal perception in the 1950s, when an advertiser very rapidly flashed the message "eat popcorn" on the movie screen at a theater. The advertiser claimed that popcorn sales increased 50 percent. Studies since then have not been able to repeat these results. Some experimenters have flashed words on a screen and offered a lot of money to students who could say what the words were. However highly motivated these students were, none of them was able to do the task (Moore, 1984; McConnell et al., 1958). Strangely enough, though, the lack of evidence that these tapes do any of the things they claim hasn't made much difference in their popularity. There has even been public concern over the possible effects of subliminal messages in rock music.

Businesses sometimes use subliminal messages to try to reduce shoplifting by customers and stealing by employees. Does this work? Occasionally, stores do see a drop in employee theft, but usually

subliminal perception stimulation presented below the level of consciousness

▲ *If subliminal messages were powerful, wouldn't they be used everywhere?*

▲ *Can subliminal messages flashed on a movie screen increase the sales of popcorn?*

that happens right after the program is put into place. As time goes on, the effects decrease greatly and eventually disappear.

What other interpretations might be made instead? If subliminal messages don't work, why do people keep buying these tapes and believe they really do help? Whenever people make a decision to improve themselves, or a new approach to an old problem is tried in the workplace, motivation increases. There is greater awareness of the issue at hand, and often that in itself is enough to change people's behavior. If the program itself is the reason for success, its effects will not fade away that much with time. Another possible interpretation is that expectation can bring about short-lived results. In other words, if we strongly expect our behavior to change because of these subliminal messages, we may in fact cause that to happen all by ourselves, regardless of the messages.

What are the most logical conclusions to draw? Despite all the furor, the best information we have is that subliminal perception is simply not an effective means for getting people to act in particular ways (McConnell, 1989; Pratkanis & Greenwald, 1988). The problem is a very basic one. The brain does not consider a faint message to be as important as one that shouts to be heard or is there for a while. So it just doesn't pay much attention.

Applying Critical Thinking Skills

Why do you think people continue to buy audiotapes with subliminal messages when evidence shows that these messages have no effect on perception or behavior?

See if *COOL* works for you....

Claim?

Objective evidence for and against claim?

Other interpretations?

Logical conclusions?

Focus Question

• What happens after sound waves hit the ear?

Hearing

Hearing, like vision, depends on energy. In hearing, or **audition** (aw-DISH-un), the energy form is sound waves. Sound waves have a much slower range of speed than light waves but move in roughly the same fashion.

Many animals use sound more than humans do. The dolphin, for instance, sends out clicks, and the echoes that come back tell it the size and shape of what the sound waves have hit—whether the object is food, something dangerous, or a place of refuge. Bats are amazing. They can find extremely small flying insects by bouncing sound waves off them. But nature has given their favorite food, the bat moth, a built-in detector for the sounds emitted by the bats, so the moths can try to escape.

The Characteristics of Sound. Sounds vary in **pitch,** which means how high or low a sound is. Another characteristic of sound is something called **timbre** (TAM-ber), which refers to the complexity of a tone. The differences in the sounds made by a piano, a flute, and a guitar are caused by variations in timbre.

Sounds vary in **intensity**— how loud they are. Intensity is measured in **decibels** (DES-uh-bells). When sounds reach a decibel level beyond 130 (see Figure 4.9), they can become painful. Continuous loud noises actually impair hearing by killing receptor cells in the ear. Sleep is disturbed by noise as loud as that made by a refrigerator (70 decibels) but is helped by a continuous sound of roughly 50 decibels (Gilbert, 1985).

The Structure of the Ear. "My, what big ears you have, Grandma!" said Little Red Riding Hood.

"The better to hear you with, my dear."

Actually, the wolf was wrong. Ear size makes very little difference, but the shape does have a purpose. The cupped design of the outer ear catches the sound waves and funnels them in toward the **eardrum** (see

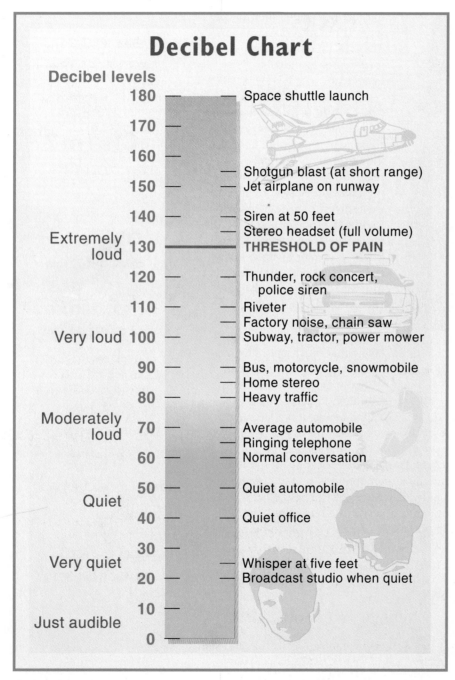

Decibel Chart

Decibel levels

Decibel level	Category	Sound
180		Space shuttle launch
170		
160		
150		Shotgun blast (at short range) — Jet airplane on runway
140		Siren at 50 feet — Stereo headset (full volume)
130	Extremely loud	THRESHOLD OF PAIN
120		Thunder, rock concert, police siren
110		Riveter — Factory noise, chain saw
100	Very loud	Subway, tractor, power mower
90		Bus, motorcycle, snowmobile — Home stereo
80		Heavy traffic
70	Moderately loud	Average automobile — Ringing telephone
60		Normal conversation
50	Quiet	Quiet automobile
40		Quiet office
30	Very quiet	
20		Whisper at five feet — Broadcast studio when quiet
10	Just audible	
0		

▲ **Figure 4.9** *Sound Levels of Various Objects and Events*

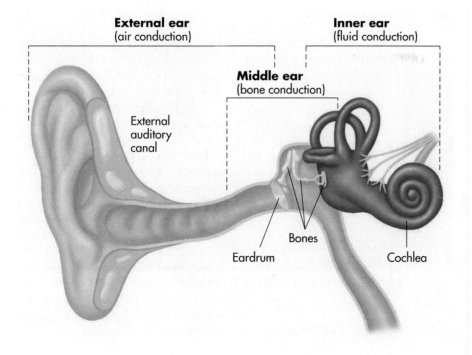

External ear
(air conduction)

Inner ear
(fluid conduction)

Middle ear
(bone conduction)

External
auditory
canal

Bones

Eardrum

Cochlea

◀ **Figure 4.10** *Structure of the Ear. Conduction means movement of sound, and it can occur through air, fluid, or bone vibration.*

audition the sense of hearing

pitch how high or low a sound is

timbre the complexity of a sound

intensity how loud a sound is

decibels a measure of how loud a sound is (its intensity)

eardrum a piece of skin stretched over the entrance to the ear; vibrates to sound

cochlea a snail-shaped part of the ear, filled with fluid and small hairs that vibrate to incoming sound

hair cells receptor cells for hearing found in the cochlea

cilia hairlike extensions on cells.

auditory nerve bundle of nerves carrying sound to the brain

Figure 4.10), a piece of skin stretched tightly—just like a drum—over the entrance to the rest of the ear. When the sound waves hit the drum, it vibrates. The vibration causes a small bone to vibrate. This bone is attached to another bone and acts as a lever, causing it, in turn, to vibrate. A third bone is attached to a snail-shaped unit called the **cochlea** (KOKE-lee-ah). The cochlea is filled with fluid and lined with special cells.

The key to hearing is the existence of these **hair cells.** The cells have hairlike extensions called **cilia** that are lined up in the cochlea and "tuned" to receive different frequencies, just as the strings are tuned on a musical instrument. They will respond to movement of only a *trillionth* of an inch, about the space between two atoms. As this movement occurs, it causes a flow of electrical particles in the nerve cell connected to each hair. The electrical impulse goes through the **auditory nerve** to the brain, where the sound pattern is interpreted. How strong a sound is and when it arrives at one ear is contrasted by the brain with the strength and arrival time at the other ear. The difference between them helps us locate where the sound is coming from.

Sound can have strong psychological implications. For instance, some cells specialize—that is, certain cells recognize specific important sound patterns. Thus, a mother bird makes sounds to her offspring inside the egg so she can be recognized later. The infant bird will then follow the mother's sounds as it moves about. Newborn human babies relax when hearing tapes of the mother's voice or heartbeat, so the psychological importance of sound must also be a human phenomenon.

▲ *Some animals can hear frequencies that humans cannot.*

▲ *Skin can register pressure as light as an insect or spider crawling up an arm.*

cutaneous receptors nerve receptors in the skin that respond to pressure, temperature, or pain

Cutaneous Senses (Touch)

Our skin contains three types of **cutaneous** (cue-TAIN-ee-us), or touch, **receptors.** Each sends a message to the brain, where it is recorded. One records pressure. It can register a pinprick, a bruise, or even an ant crawling up the arm. A second kind responds only to changes in temperature. A third kind remains active continuously to record an injury or poison. These last receptors cause the painful feelings we all dread, because they can fire for hours and hours after a burn or major cut. Figure 4.11 shows some of the cutaneous receptors.

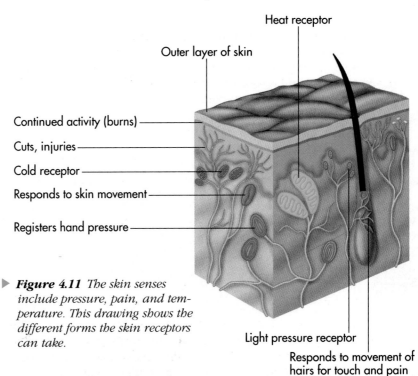

▶ *Figure 4.11 The skin senses include pressure, pain, and temperature. This drawing shows the different forms the skin receptors can take.*

In Focus

Three Types of Cutaneous Receptors

SOME RECEPTORS RESPOND TO PRESSURE.

SOME RECEPTORS RESPOND TO TEMPERATURE CHANGE.

SOME RECEPTORS RESPOND CONTINUOUSLY AFTER AN INJURY.

Your fingers are cold after handling ice or snow. You run your fingers under warm water, but the water seems hot. Can you think of a theory about cutaneous receptors to explain this?

Smell

The sense of smell, or **olfaction** (ol-FAC-shun), depends on the ability to detect chemicals. Once again, the human comes in a poor second to most animals. If you are upwind of a deer, it will take off before you ever see it because it is sensitive to your smell (no matter how often you bathe). A shark uses your odor molecules (among other things) in the water to decide if you are worth eating.

Smell is the most animal-like of the human senses. Odors are very hard to define using words, but when an odor is associated with an emotional event, we never forget it. If we ever happen to smell that odor again, it will recreate a very strong emotional memory (Engen, 1987).

Mechanisms of Smell.   Inside the nasal cavity (Figure 4.12 on the next page), embedded in a layer of mucus, are microscopic hairs, or cilia. They are similar in structure to the cilia found in the ear. However, they have a different function. These cilia collect molecules of odor. When the odor molecules attach themselves to the hairs, an electrical signal is sent to the **olfactory bulbs,** which generate a "code" that is sent to the brain for interpretation (Rivlin & Gravelle, 1984).

Smell Communication.   The most critical use for our sense of smell is information about food heading toward the mouth. In fact, smell is more important in eating than is taste. If you don't believe this, try holding your nose when you eat. The food will have almost no taste at all.

Focus Question

• How are smell and taste connected?

olfaction the sense of smell

olfactory bulbs units that receive odor molecules and communicate their nature to the brain

103

▶ **Figure 4.12** *Mechanisms of Smell*

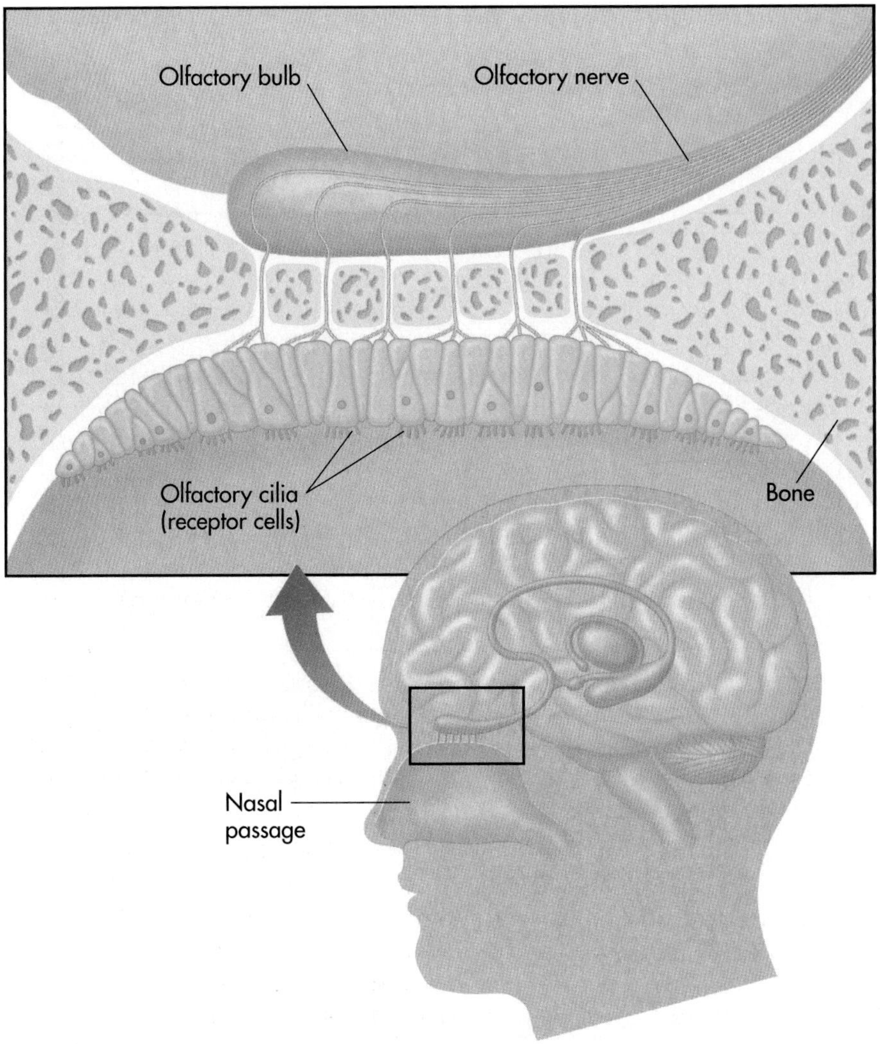

Olfactory bulb

Olfactory nerve

Olfactory cilia (receptor cells)

Bone

Nasal passage

pheromones odor chemicals that communicate a message

taste receptors chemical receptors on the tongue that decode molecules of food or drink to identify them

Animals use smell to communicate sexual interest. An animal's body sends out odor chemicals, called **pheromones** (FER-uh-moans), in order to reach a possible partner. Whether humans have such sexual communication is not clear. A few studies find some possible connection. Since almost all creatures communicate this way, it seems probable that the human would, too. This is difficult to study because human sexual interest is a complex mixture of things such as clothing, perfumes, fads about body shape, and so forth.

Taste

Taste receptors operate by chemical communication. The major receivers are the little red spots (because of their rich blood supply) on the tongue. These are called "taste buds" because they resemble flowers (see Figure 4.13). The mucus and saliva in the mouth cleanse the buds, but it takes a while to do so, as you may have learned on Thanksgiving if you have ever eaten some cranberries and followed them by a drink of milk—a horrible combination. There are four types of receptors—*salt, sweet, sour,* and *bitter* (see Figure 4.14). These combine sensations much as the cones in vision do to give us the subtle differences between, say, barbecued ribs and sweet-and-sour pork.

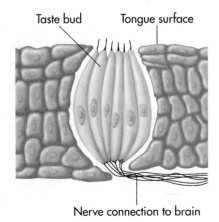

Taste bud

Tongue surface

Nerve connection to brain

▲ **Figure 4.13** *Taste Buds*

Salt Needs. Salt is necessary for survival. It operates nerve cells, helps keep body chemistry in balance, and is used for muscle contraction. A very low salt diet can make you dizzy and sick. In healthy people, excess salt is quickly and efficiently removed from the body in the urine with no ill effects. While some uses of salt may be learned (such as salting some cooked foods), the evidence suggests humans are born with a fixed sequence of need. The newborn does not like salt. But from the age of a few months onward, youngsters want salt. Until late childhood, this interest in salt remains high, while children dislike spicy, sour, or bitter food. This is why items on the children's menu at fast-food chains taste like cardboard with salt on it. That's all they want to eat (Cowart, 1981). The desire for salt gradually tapers off with age. But then, much later in life, it reappears. If their stomachs didn't rebel, older people would love chili dogs with mustard, onions, pepper, salt, and almost anything else around, because their taste receptors are not as sharp as they once were. Pregnant women seek an extra supply of salt for the fetus; you will hear of a pregnant woman suddenly needing a pickle in the middle of the night. One scientist mentions a woman who ate approximately 1,500 salted herring during her pregnancy—probably a record (Denton, 1983).

Sugar Needs. Most animals need sugar. Human newborns a day old can tell when something has sugar in it, and they will actively seek it. Sugar is vital for energy to run the body. Too little sugar makes a person tremble, and feel faint, and causes mental confusion. Hence, the desire for something sweet is built in, even if it presents problems for those on a diet.

Sourness and Bitterness Detectors. We have more than one type of bitterness detector on the tongue. These detectors are critical. Almost all poisons are bitter in one way or another. We need to process this information instantly while we are still only considering swallowing what was put in the mouth. Sourness detection also serves a protective function, but to a lesser degree. Food that has gone bad often has a sour taste to it. However, we can usually smell this problem before we put the food in our mouths. Bitter poisonous substances, on the other hand, frequently have no distinctive odor.

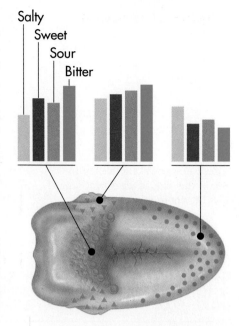

▲ **Figure 4.14** *The four types of taste receptors are located in various areas on the tongue.*

▲ *The sour detectors at full alert.*

 ## Pause for Thought

1. Describe several characteristics of sound. Describe the functions of each part of the ear.

2. What are three types of cutaneous receptors?

3. What is another name for the sense of smell? Describe how the brain receives information about smell.

Critical Thinking
....

4. You have to deliver a brief speech to your class on salt and sugar needs. What do you say?

- When we look at the world, why does it seem stable or constant?

Perception

The truly remarkable thing about the world "out there" is how stable and organized it seems. You go to the parking lot and put the key into the right car. You don't try to put it into a Honda if you own a Buick. At the supermarket, you buy three small grapefruit if that's what you need. You don't come back with three very large lemons. You go to another room to get a certain book. If the book is sideways, upside down, lying on the floor, whatever, you don't decide it is not the same book. But in every one of those positions, the book looks entirely different to the eye. What amazing creatures we are! Through a combination of inborn abilities and experience, we gradually are able to handle billions of bits of information correctly. We make the world make sense. This is *perception*. Perception is the process of assembling sensory information so that we can understand what the incoming energy means. Perception is always a matter of *interpretation* and *expectation*. Benjamin Franklin used to entertain his friends by hooking himself up to an electrical laboratory apparatus; then they all held hands, supposedly getting a wonderful sensation. Everyone laughed and thought it was delightful, but it was only a matter of suggestion (Oster, 1970).

size constancy the ability to retain the size of an object regardless of where it is located

In Their Own Words . . .

Oliver Sacks is a neurologist who is known for viewing his patients as individuals, and with great empathy and concern. Here, he talks about perception and sensation.

One does not see, or sense, or perceive, in isolation—perception is always linked to behavior and movement, to reaching out and exploring the world. It is insufficient to see; one must look as well. [One scientist] mentions the case of two children whose eyes had been bandaged from an early age, and who, when the bandages were removed at the age of five, showed no reaction to this, showed no looking, and seemed blind. One has the sense that these children, who had built up their worlds with other senses and behaviors, did not know how to use their eyes. Looking—as an orientation, as a behavior—may even vanish in those who become blind late in life, despite the fact that they have been "lookers" all their lives. (Sacks, 1995, pp. 117–118)

Sensation itself has no "markers" for size and distance; these have to be learned on the basis of experience. Thus it has been reported that if people who have lived their entire lives in a dense rain forest, with a far point no more than a few feet away, are brought into a wide, empty landscape, they may reach out and try to touch the mountaintops with their hands; they have no concept of how far the mountains are. (Sacks, 1995, p. 119)

Interpreting Primary Sources

Write a paragraph in response to this sentence by Dr. Sacks: "It is insufficient to see; one must look as well."

Perceptual Constancies

Our world is always in motion. So are we. Things change from one split second to another. The word *constancy* means holding steady. And this is what we must do to the world in order to maintain order and control, to make sense out of our environment.

Size Constancy. In the 1500s, Spanish explorers arrived at the Grand Canyon, the likes of which they had never seen before. According to their records, they stood atop the south rim and looked across at the other rim, in some places more than ten miles across. They looked down at the river and estimated its width to be six feet across. The Native Americans in the area knew better because they had been down to the bottom and had discovered that the river was about two miles wide (Hawgood, 1967). Thus, when the Native Americans stood on the rim of the canyon, they perceived a two-mile-wide river that looked smaller "because it was far away." They were using what is called **size constancy,** the ability to retain in memory the size of an object no matter where it is

In Focus

Size Constancy

If we stand on a railroad tie and look down the track, the railroad ties in the distance actually seem to get smaller. But because of size constancy, we're not fooled for a moment. The *eyes* record the railroad ties in the distance as tiny, but the *brain* STRETCHES them out to "normal" size.

Are we born with this ability to use size constancy? Does experience influence it?

---

located. This skill is so important that it appears in an infant only a couple of weeks old.

It is possible to trick the brain, and this allows us to see size constancy in operation. The average playing card is about three and one-half inches high. In a laboratory, a specially constructed playing card only two inches high is put in front of people. They are asked to judge how far it is from them. They will claim the card is much farther away than it is. Why? Because they know its usual size, and it appears smaller. Hence, their brains tell them that it *must* be more distant—things get smaller only with more distance.

Color Constancy. As discussed, we have three different color receptors (for red, blue, and green) that blend varying energy waves together to give an object color. But notice that if you take an apple from a bright kitchen into a darkened room with just the TV on, the apple still seems exactly the same color. It hasn't turned darker. The light being reflected from the apple cannot be the same in the two locations. So how do we hold the color constant? The visual network works all by itself once we have decided what color something is. It has the ability to increase or decrease *mentally* the internal firing of visual receptors to equal what the brain tells it the color is. This is called **color constancy,** but it only works—like size constancy in the Grand Canyon example—when we already know what color something is.

▲ *Size constancy allows us to perceive this picture fairly accurately.*

color constancy the ability to perceive an object as the same color regardless of the environment

▲ **Figure 4.15** *Depending on your assumptions regarding light direction, the brightness changes.*

Brightness Constancy. Possibly, color constancy can be better understood after we look at **brightness constancy,** which follows roughly the same principles. Find a familiar black object. Look at it indoors, and then take it outside on a very bright, sunny day. The level of brightness reflected from the object is extremely high outside, yet it looks to be about the same color as it did inside, rather than "bright black." The brain causes the rods and cones to compensate for the brightness. If the object seems too bright to match our concept of "black," some of the visual nerve cells shut off.

To see this aspect of perception in action, look at Figure 4.15. We assume the light is hitting the object from the left side. This makes the right side darker, as it would be in real life. But if you cover the "shadow" at the lower right, the picture no longer makes sense in terms of a belief that light is coming from the left. It now looks like an open book, one side of which could be dark regardless of light direction. Further, note that your visual system makes the "page" look much darker once you cover the shadow.

brightness constancy the ability to keep an object's brightness constant as the object is moved to various environments

shape constancy the ability to perceive an object as having the same shape regardless of the angle at which it is seen

Shape Constancy. Once we know an object's shape, we perceive it as always taking that form, a concept known as **shape constancy.** We will keep the shape the same even when the object appears at an angle that changes its actual image on the retina. You can demonstrate shape constancy for yourself. Look at a book lying flat on a table or desk. Now tip the book up on one corner. The image of the book is very different. However, the brain "knows" that its actual shape has not changed—the shape is held constant.

space constancy the ability to keep objects in the environment steady by perceiving *either* ourselves *or* outside objects as moving

Space Constancy. The most common type of auto accident is the "rear-ender." Despite many warnings, people don't take "not following too closely" to heart—because they don't understand perception. We have to keep objects in the environment steady in order to survive. This is called **space constancy.** But we must allow for some motion. There are two types of motion: *self-motion* and *object motion*. We must choose between allowing ourselves to move in reference to the environment and allowing the environment to move in reference to us. If we allow both at one time, severe dizziness results. For example, we can focus on telephone poles as we move along in a car (object motion), or we can focus on ourselves and the inside of the car (self-motion), letting the poles blur. Usually when we drive, we are aware of our own movement. When that is the case, we must hold the cars in front of us steady in our minds. As a result, only a *major* change in the speed of the cars will be noticed. A small change, such as occurs during a normal stop, will not be perceived well (Probst et al., 1984). This is why auto manufacturers were forced to put a third brake-warning light at eye level starting with 1986 cars.

◀ *Figure 4.16* *The "Visual Cliff."*
The baby would like to crawl to
the mother but is not about to
fall over a cliff to get to her.

depth perception the ability to
see the relation of objects in space

visual cliff an apparatus used to
demonstrate depth perception

Depth Perception

Depth perception is the ability to see
objects "out there" in space. It is built into a
baby from a very young age. This was shown
by an experimenter who was on a picnic one
day at the Grand Canyon. She wondered if
her baby would crawl over the canyon rim or
already "knew better." She sensibly decided
not to try it at the canyon itself in case the
baby failed to stop. So in a laboratory, she
constructed what is called the **visual cliff**
experiment (Figure 4.16 above). This experiment uses a large table with retaining walls of
wood on three sides. The fourth side is left
open. A piece of heavy, clear Plexiglas covers
the table and extends many feet beyond the
open edge. To the baby's eyes, it looks as if
anyone going beyond the end of the table
will fall into space. Babies from 6 to 14
months old were placed on the table and
enticed by their mothers to leave the table
and "fall" over the fake cliff. But the babies
wouldn't go beyond the edge onto the
Plexiglas. This showed that humans have
depth perception almost from the beginning.

In Their Own Words . . .

The researchers who designed and carried out the visual cliff
experiment described the reactions of the babies.

The behavior of the children in this situation gave clear evidence of their dependence on vision. Often they would
peer down through the glass on the deep side and then
back away. Others would pat the glass with their hands, yet
despite this tactual assurance of solidity would refuse to
cross. It was equally clear that their perception of depth had
matured more rapidly than had their locomotor abilities.
Many supported themselves on the glass over the deep side
as they maneuvered awkwardly on the board; some even
backed out onto the glass as
they started toward the mother
on the shallow side. Were it not
for the glass some of the children would have fallen off the
board. Evidently infants should
not be left close to a brink, no
matter how well they may discriminate depth. (Gibson &
Walk, 1997/1960, p. 94)

Interpreting Primary Sources

In this brief summary,
the authors make three
conclusions based on
their findings. State
these conclusions in
your own words.

▶ **Figure 4.17** *Notice that these pictures are not identical. When viewed together, they create a 3-D effect.*

retinal disparity the difference between the images provided by the two retinas. When the images are brought together in the brain, they provide a sense of depth.

texture gradient how rough or smooth objects appear; used in depth perception

▲ **Figure 4.18** *Visual texture helps with depth perception. Notice how the distant rows of flowers appear smoother than the front rows.*

Retinal Disparity. There are many cues for depth perception. Some of them require both eyes to work. They are called binocular cues ("bi" means two; "ocular" refers to vision). A very important binocular cue to distance is **retinal disparity.** There is a difference (disparity) between the images received by each of your retinas. To demonstrate, hold your finger steady in front of your eyes. First close one eye, then the other, and notice how the finger shifts. This is because each eye sees a slightly different image. We have to bring these images together in our brains in order to see them correctly. In the process of doing so, we judge and "see" distance and depth. See Figure 4.17.

We also use the actual angles of our eyeballs to gauge the distance of an object. The eyes turn inward toward the nose to focus on a near object and are straighter for far ones. Thus, the angle at which the eyeballs converge to focus on something is yet another clue to its distance from us.

Texture Gradient. Not all cues for depth perception are binocular. Some of them only need the use of one eye. They are called monocular cues ("mono" means one). For instance, we can see different levels of detail with only one eye. The amount of detail we can distinguish is referred to as the visual texture of objects, called the **texture gradient.** "Texture" refers to how smooth or rough something appears to be—that is, how clear its details are. "Gradient" means the different levels of texture we can see at different distances. Note in Figure 4.18 that we gauge the distance of flowers in each row by how clearly we can see them. Since we can see the individual flowers at the bottom of the picture, we know they are close. As they become more distant, we see much less detail, and they appear "smooth," blending together, so we know these are "way out there." Another monocular cue to distance is the relative size of similar objects we are looking at. The smaller the object, the farther away it is generally seen to be. Another monocular cue is how much figures overlap with one another. Looking at a group photograph, for instance, we see the complete forms of the people in front, the ones closest to us. Parts of the people behind them, however, will be covered up by the bodies of those in front and will be blocked out of our vision. Because of this overlap, we judge the ones in back to be farther away.

The importance of the visual sense in understanding distance and space is clear. As a result, blind children's spatial abilities are not as good

Case Study

Unraveling Sight

In 1991, a 50-year-old Kentucky man named Virgil underwent two surgical procedures that would restore sight to first his right eye and then his left. Virgil had been blind since he was five years old, and not even his doctors knew what to expect. Most people assumed that Virgil would unravel the bandages from his eyes, and if the operation worked, he'd walk around and act as any other sighted person would, which turned out to be far from the truth. In his book, *An Anthropologist on Mars*, Oliver Sacks (1995) describes Virgil's ordeal as a seeing person.

The first day after the operation, Virgil could not make out any distinct images. Light hit his eye and reached his brain, but he couldn't interpret what he saw. In the next few weeks, large shapes and objects began to take form, but Virgil still had difficulty focusing on objects directly in front of him. And although he could see now, he didn't always know what he was seeing. He was "mentally blind," explains Sacks. One time in a grocery store he was overwhelmed by the long rows of products lining the aisles, a troubling blur to Virgil, and he had to leave and shut his eyes for awhile. His own shadow startled him at times and he'd stumble or try to walk over it. Stairs looked to Virgil like a mesh of horizontal and vertical lines lacking depth. Blind, Virgil had moved effortlessly through his house, and now, every step became a challenge.

Virgil encountered other perceptual puzzles. He became fascinated with the visual changes resulting from moving objects closer and farther away. He needed to handle and move objects around repeatedly, and in effect, learned about size constancy. He also had a difficult time matching objects he knew by touch to what they actually looked like. By playing with a children's toy where he had to determine whether a square piece fit into a square slot, he learned about shape constancy. Things that moved also caused problems with constancy. If a cat, for example, moves from one end of the room to the other, the image of that cat on the retina changes. Virgil wasn't always sure if these varying images represented the same cat.

Virgil's view of the world eventually became more stable, but he did suffer relapses. While eating, for example, he might easily use his fork for a few minutes, then begin to miss his food entirely and finally resort to using his hands. Or, while shaving, his movements might become so disjointed that he'd need to turn off the lights and shave in the dark by touch. These relapses back to blindness could have been caused by biological defense mechanisms, explains Sacks. When the brain is overloaded with stimulation, it temporarily shuts down. Or Virgil could have simply been retreating to the thing he felt most comfortable with—touch.

Less than a year after the surgeries on his eyes, Virgil was hospitalized with a severe case of pneumonia. The reduction of oxygen to his brain caused damage to the visual area, and Virgil became blind again. Reluctantly, he returned once more to the sensory world he knew best.

▲ *The film* At First Sight *explores the concept of "mental blindness."*

Review the Case Study

How do you think Virgil's brief encounter with vision affected his identity?

Moving Cubes

This illustration offers no cues for depth, so the brain can view it in a variety of ways. Stare at the plus sign in the middle, and the front of the cubes will either appear to shoot out at you or to cave in away from you. You might even get one cube to shift toward you while the other shifts away.

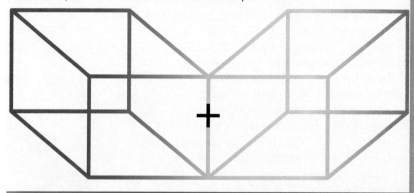

What types of cues could you add to help you perceive depth in this picture?

or as complete as those of sighted children, unless they develop specific strategies using their other senses (Thinus-Blanc & Gaunet, 1997).

Animals of many kinds also demonstrate this early depth perception, including kittens, chicks, lambs, baby goats, and rats. One striking difference the researchers noted, however, was that these animal babies did not make mistakes moving around on the equipment as the human babies did. Water turtles, though, didn't do so well; a fair number of them crawled right over the "cliff."

Perceptual Organization

When given incomplete perceptual information, we tend to organize it so that it makes sense. We interpret things the way we think they *should* be, not the way they actually are. For instance, look at Figure 4.19 on page 113. Part A is actually two rows, each one made up of three white stars followed by three white circles. But that is not what we tend to perceive. Instead, we tend to see three squares, one made up of white stars, one of circles, and one of stars and circles. We have organized this information and constructed something more complete from it. In the language of perception, this is called common region or **gestalt** (gesh-TAHLT), meaning an organized whole, shape, or form.

Early researchers who studied how we go about making these interpretations were called Gestalt psychologists, and they found that we use certain perceptual cues to make sense of things. One such cue is **similarity,** in which we group like things together. We used this cue

gestalt an organized whole, shape, or form

similarity a perceptual cue that involves grouping like things together

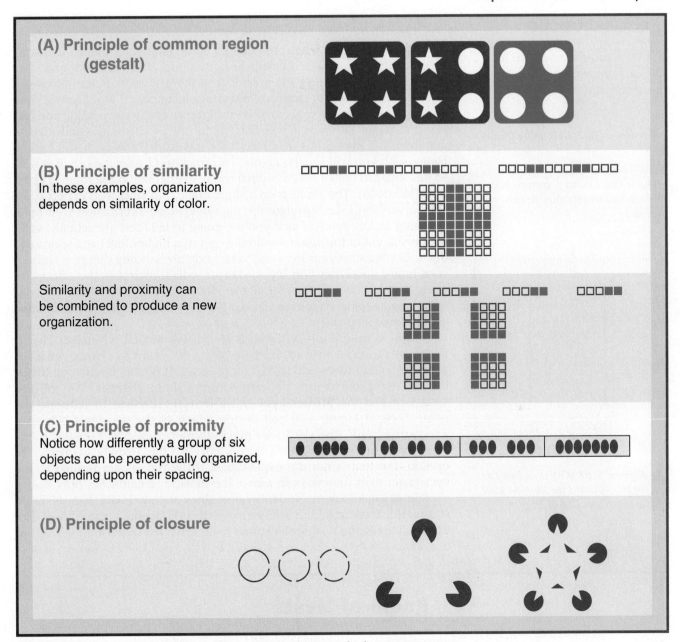

▲ Figure 4.19 *This diagram shows four common ways in which we organize what we see.*

in part B of Figure 4.19 when we grouped squares of the same color together to form a cross.

Using the perceptual cue of **proximity,** we group things together that are near one another. Figure 4.19, part C shows how this works. Here, groups of six ovals are perceived differently depending on the closeness to each other.

Another process is called **closure.** Here, we fill in (close) the details that aren't there to complete the picture. An example is shown in part D, Figure 4.19. When we can see only parts of things, we make them into whole objects. Using edges and other cues, we fill in what's missing and estimate the third dimension, depth (Kellman, 1997).

proximity a perceptual cue that involves grouping together things that are near one another

closure the process of filling in the missing details of what is viewed

113

Focus Question

....

• How can our tendency to view the world as a stable place lead to illusions?

illusions inaccurate perceptions

Müller-Lyer illusion illusion in which one line in a picture with two equal-length lines seems longer

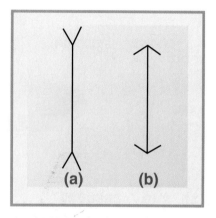

▲ **Figure 4.20** Why does line (a) in the Müller-Lyer illusion look longer than line (b)?

Illusions

Illusions occur when we perceive something inaccurately. In a way, they are misperceptions. Nonetheless, they are important, because they show how we construct the world. A striking illusion is the "Room of Mystery" often found at carnivals and amusement parks. When you go into one of these rooms, you seem to be walking at a very steep angle and feel like you might fall over if you don't hold onto something. Guides claim that there is a mysterious magnetic force involved. Actually, if you look at Figure 4.21, you will see the unique construction of such a room. It is built so that you can't tell it isn't a normal room; everything in the room is glued or nailed down. The room *is* on a slight angle, but since you expect to be able to walk and stand straight up, the unexpected information your brain is getting makes you feel as if you are going to fall. You are actually walking only at about the angle required to get to a higher level at a sports stadium. But because your eyes and your body are sending different clues to your brain, it decides you are in danger, which increases the effect. Try going through one of these or similar distorted rooms with a friend (you trust) and keeping your eyes closed. Now it's simple, because you aren't getting mixed signals.

Most people think of illusions as "mistakes" that we make. That is not really the case. Instead, over the years, we learn to change what we perceive so that the world makes more sense. It is truly fascinating to see the eye-brain mechanism perform some of these changes. We will use what is called the **Müller-Lyer** (MUE-ler-Liar) **illusion** to illustrate the point. Look at Figure 4.20 and decide which of the two lines is longer. The "arrowhead" line (b) looks much shorter. It is not; measure them. Some have thought the effect occurs because the arrowheads draw the eyes in, but that is not the explanation. If the figures are flashed to the eyes faster than the eyes can move, the illusion remains. So, how do we explain it? Let's look at the Müller-Lyer lines as they might appear in the real world. Look at Figure 4.22 on page 115. Notice that one of the highlighted lines in the wall looks farther away than the other. Because of our

▲ **Figure 4.21** In this tilted room, objects are glued to the walls and floor. Mixed signals cause the eye-brain mechanism to think the room is on a really steep angle, rather than a relatively slight one.

experience with size constancy, we tend to mentally stretch the far line, which makes it seem longer to us.

Many illusions come from the need for us to make sense of our surroundings. We make guesses in the context of what we think should be the case. For instance, suppose you see a small dot far away on the opposite side of the highway coming toward you. You assume this is a regular-sized car. Next, suppose you are in a field with no roads anywhere. Across the field, you see a round object the same size as the one you saw on the highway. This object is moving at the same speed as the other, just at eye level, coming right toward you. Can you imagine your panic? Since it can't be a car, it must be—what? An enormous bee? A hawk?

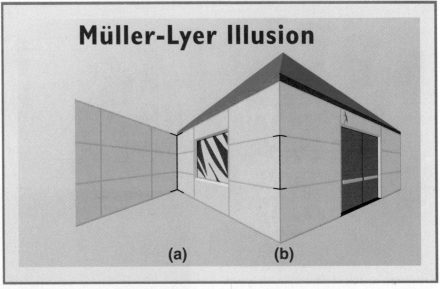

▲ *Figure 4.22* *Here's an example of the Müller-Lyer illusion in real life. Which line is longer? The line (a) looks more like a distant corner than a nearer one. Since the vertical lines form images of the same length, the more "distant" line must be perceived as longer.*

In any case, you form opinions about the nature of objects, and then they look that way to you—at least for a while. This is the case with what is called a **reversible figure.** Such a figure appears in Figure 4.23. Since the shape of the object in the figure is such that it can be more than one thing, the eye-brain mechanism keeps "changing its mind." First you assume that it is a vase. Then, all of a sudden, the faces of two people nose to nose appear. Then it looks like a vase again, and so forth. Obviously, something that appears to be an illusion is really the brain doing the best it can with an ambiguous figure, wanting to make certain it doesn't miss something important.

reversible figure illusion in which the same object is seen as two alternating figures—first one, then the other

 ## Pause for Thought

1. Describe the five constancies that help us view the world as a stable place.
2. What did the visual cliff experiment teach us about depth perception? How do retinal disparity and visual texture help us perceive depth?
3. This section describes two classic illusions: "The Room of Mystery" and the Müller-Lyer illusion. Why do these illusions fool us?

Critical Thinking
....
4. Draw an original example for each of the following principles of perceptual organization: similarity, closure, proximity, and reversible figure.

▲ *Figure 4.23* *This vase creates the reversible figure illusion.*

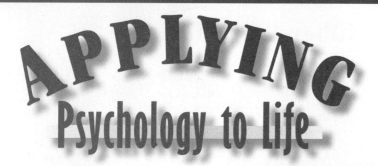

APPLYING
Psychology to Life

Do You Have ESP?

Most people you meet, possibly even you, have had an experience similar to this one: You feel as if you have gotten a message that a friend is sick or lonely and needs you. You call and check—and it turns out to be the case. Was this mental telepathy? That is, did the two of you actually communicate in some special way?

Most psychologists don't believe in the phenomenon of *extrasensory perception,* or ESP (receiving information without the aid of our "normal" senses—vision, hearing and so on—hence, *extra* sensory or even beyond normal awareness) (Alcock, 1990).

▲ *Some people disregard logic and believe psychic claims.*

Problems in Proving ESP

Here is where the difficulty lies: Many scientists say that the biggest problem with the existence of ESP is that there isn't any way to get the message from one person to another. For example, suppose you wanted to send a message to someone who is now in New York or California (that is, across the country, depending on where you live). How can it get to that person? Even if you get the message to the proper state, how do you guide it to the right street address?

The brain is run by electricity, and today's sensitive measuring devices can pick up electrical impulses about three or four inches from the skull. Beyond that, they pick up nothing. So electrical impulses don't seem to be the answer.

Another problem is that the ESP ability seems to come and go; it is not consistent. Those who claim to have it on one day may not have it on another. That makes it difficult to study.

Yet another problem is that most ESP demonstrations are fake. Stage shows in which someone "reads" another's mind are preplanned and use a confederate or stooge. Popular acts, such as bending a key with psychic forces, are magic tricks, not ESP.

History of Research

The history of research on this topic is filled with cases of fakery and wishful thinking. For example, back in the 1920s, several male university professors certified a woman named Mina Crandon as having extrasensory powers. She really didn't, but she did wear a loose-fitting robe at her seances, which very effectively misdirected the men's attention. It was the magician Harry Houdini who demonstrated that she was in fact a fraud (Gresham,

▲ *This is not exactly a scientific approach to predicting the future.*

1959). In that same period, one of the biggest names in ESP research, J. B. Rhine, supported the mind-reading abilities of a horse named Clever Hans. Later, it turned out that Hans's trainer was giving cues to the animal by slight nodding of the head, tensing of the body, and the like. By following these cues, Clever Hans was able to do arithmetic problems. Mental telepathy had nothing to do with it, and Rhine's reputation suffered a serious blow. (See the Case Study on page 44 for more on this.) Strangely enough, this kind of act came back on the scene many years later. In 1980, a supposedly telepathic pony appeared on a television show called "Those Amazing Animals." And in

that same decade, the 1980s, a major midwestern university found itself seriously embarrassed after some of its researchers were fooled by a couple of magicians. What the researchers thought was extrasensory perception turned out to be nothing more than an elaborate magic trick.

Claims of Special Powers

Even though scientists do not accept ESP as a genuine phenomenon, there are people who keep claiming they have these special powers. For instance, how do we explain those strange premonitions we sometimes get—those feelings that something is going to happen—that turn out to be true? If it isn't ESP, what is it?

Probably it's nothing more than coincidence. Most people fail to consider all the times those premonitions are false. We often don't even remember them. But the ones that come true? Those are engraved on our brains. What we end up with, then, is an exaggerated idea about how accurate our premonitions really are.

Many of us have heard of cases where someone had an uneasy feeling, changed his or her regular routine in some way, and because of that avoided some terrible disaster. Surely that's ESP, isn't it? Well, before you decide, try this tale on for size. A couple of psychologists boarded a flight for a business trip. Neither had a history of psychic experiences or any fear of flying, and both had taken the same flight before. This time, though, without warning, each of them, independent of the other, got an overwhelming feeling that something terrible was going to happen. After trying to talk themselves and each other out of this unexplainable dread, they decided they simply could not ignore it—it was just too strong. So they got off the plane. They both felt very foolish but also pretty relieved. Later that same day, they found out that the plane they were scheduled to take . . . arrived at its destination on time and without incident. True story.

Summary

1. Sensation is the process of receiving information from the environment.

2. Vision is our most powerful sense. It uses light waves from the environment, which go through a lens in the eye and hit the retina. Information is then forwarded to the brain. The receptors in the retina are rods for night vision and cones for daylight color vision.

3. Audition uses sound waves to stimulate the eardrum. Sound varies in pitch, timbre, and intensity. The intensity is measured using decibels. Hair cells in the cochlea are tuned to receive the information and forward it to the brain.

4. Cutaneous senses respond to three basic types of stimulation: pressure, temperature, and pain.

5. In olfaction, the olfactory bulbs receive information from cilia in the nose and send this information to the brain.

6. Taste receptors respond to sweet, sour, bitter, and salt. Sugar and salty substances are necessary for human survival. Sourness and bitterness receptors are used to detect bad food and poisons.

7. Perception is based on interpretation and expectation. To organize the world in order to understand it, our perception holds it steady by using size, color, brightness, shape, and space constancies.

8. Depth perception arises from retinal disparity, visual texture, relative size, and overlap. We also organize the world by using similarity, closure, and proximity.

9. Illusions are, in a way, misperceptions, but they show how we organize the world. The Müller-Lyer illusion is an example of how we evaluate objects to determine their shape and size.

10. Subliminal perception does not work, according to most studies. Still, some people continue to believe in it.

Vocabulary

absolute threshold	cone	cilia	depth perception
adaptation	color blindness	auditory nerve	visual cliff
sensation	afterimage	cutaneous receptors	retinal disparity
perception	subliminal perception	olfaction	texture gradient
white light	audition	olfactory bulbs	gestalt
cornea	pitch	pheromones	similarity
iris	timbre	taste receptors	proximity
lens	intensity	size constancy	closure
pupil	decibels	color constancy	illusions
retina	eardrum	brightness constancy	Müller-Lyer illusion
blind spot	cochlea	shape constancy	reversible figure
rod	hair cells	space constancy	

Review Questions

Matching

On a sheet of paper, match each term with the phrase on the right that best describes it.

1. pupil
2. lens
3. retina
4. cornea
5. iris
6. audition
7. decibels
8. intensity
9. pitch
10. timbre
11. cochlea

a. responsible for focusing
b. muscle that controls the amount of light that hits the eye
c. located at the back of the eye
d. black circle in the middle of the eye
e. outer covering of the eye
f. loudness
g. how high or low a sound is
h. measurement of loudness
i. hearing
j. unit in ear
k. complexity of sound

On a sheet of paper, for each of the following, answer R if rod applies, C if cone applies.

12. used for night vision
13. responds best to red wavelengths
14. more sensitive to violet-purple range of wavelengths
15. used for color and daylight vision

Multiple Choice

On a sheet of paper, write the letter of the answer that best completes each statement.

16. If someone is said to be color blind, it usually means that ▓▓▓▓▓
    a. he or she can see no color at all.
    b. some part of his or her cone system is not working.
    c. his or her system of rods is not working.

17. For people who are truly color-blind ▓▓▓▓▓
    a. none of their cone systems are working.
    b. none of the rods are working.
    c. neither cones nor rods are working.

18. Cutaneous refers to the ▓▓▓▓▓
    a. nose.   c. skin.
    b. ears.   d. eyes.

19. The hairs inside the nasal cavity are called ▓▓▓▓▓
    a. pheromones.
    b. bulbs.
    c. cilia.
    d. bulb cells.

20. Smell chemicals are called ▓▓▓▓▓
    a. pheromones.
    b. bulbs.
    c. cilia.
    d. nasalines.

Fill in the Blank

On a sheet of paper, write the vocabulary term that best completes each sentence.

21. Sally kisses John in a dark room. Although his face looks dark, she knows it's really a bright red. This is an example of ▓▓▓▓▓.

22. Ballet dancers who spin a lot in circles don't get dizzy because of ▓▓▓▓▓.

23. Flying in an airplane, you look down at the "tiny" cars, but you don't perceive them as tiny because of ▓▓▓▓▓.

24. The fact that one of our eyes actually sees something different from what the other sees is called ▓▓▓▓▓.

25. Visual texture helps one to perceive ▓▓▓▓▓.

Discussion Questions

1. Briefly define *ultraviolet* and *infrared* wavelengths. Describe how the world might be different if humans had receptors for these wavelengths. Be specific.

2. Which of your senses is most important to you? Explain. If you had to give up one sense, which one would you give up? Why? What if you had to choose between giving up hearing and giving up seeing?

3. What if you could magically improve the performance of one of your senses? Which sense would you choose to improve? Why? Could you improve the performance of this one sense without magic? How? Be specific.

4. Sometimes it's difficult to apply some of the perceptual principles discussed in this chapter to everyday life. Having said that, we'd like you to try. Take any three perceptual principles and explain how they play a role in our everyday planning, decision making, attitudes, and so on. For example, cars viewed from an airplane look like toys, yet because of size constancy, we perceive them as normal cars.

5. Each day, our senses are bombarded with stimulation from the environment. What do you suppose would happen if we were *completely* deprived of this stimulation for two or three days? List several possible side effects. *Hint:* Try finding someone who has driven alone on the highway at night. How did the person feel once fatigue set in?

6. Other than the five main senses highlighted in the chapter, do you think humans have any other senses? (Don't discuss ESP.) To answer this question, you mght look up kinesthesia, synesthesia, and equilibrium.

7. Mr. L reads the section on subliminal perception, concludes that tapes with subliminal messages have no effect on behavior, yet still goes out and buys several of these tapes. What are possible reasons for Mr. L's decision? Does his behavior seem fairly typical of most people, or not? Explain.

Activities and Projects

1. Pretend that you have been asked by the publisher of this textbook to add an illustration to highlight one of the concepts from the chapter: afterimage, constancy, illusion, reversible figure, and so on. Create this illustration, complete with directions to the viewer and a detailed caption that explains your picture and concept. You might draw, for instance, a red and yellow globe that only seems normal as an afterimage. Make your final product large enough to post in the classroom.

2. Create a board game that teaches players about sensation and perception. Keep in mind that some of the best board games have simple rules with simple objectives. Focus most of your energy on writing challenging questions and drawing game board panels that will teach lessons on seeing, hearing, and so on. One panel could read: "Sorry, your red and green cone systems do not work. You're somewhat color blind. Go back 2 spaces." Another panel could expand on this: "Whoa! None of your cone systems work. You are truly color blind. Move back 4 spaces." Ask your teacher if you can play the game in class as a review for the test.

3. Conduct a taste test on 10 to 15 people (your "subjects") to demonstrate how smell con-

tributes to taste. *Procedure:* Blindfold a subject and place four pieces of food in front of her or him. Don't tell the subject what foods you're using. The pieces can be taken from: (1) an apple, (2) a potato, (3) a pear, and (4) a carrot—or choose your own food groups. Guide the subject's hand to the first piece of food. Tell the subject to hold her or his nose with the other hand while eating the food and to continue holding it until she or he has guessed what the food is. Repeat this for each piece. Repeat the entire procedure for each subject.

Predict beforehand which kinds of foods the subjects will most often guess correctly. Which will they most often guess incorrectly?

After conducting the test, consider this: Since your subjects could not use smell to guess what they were eating, they had to rely on other cues or hints. What were some of these cues? Explain.

4. Look in a phone book to find a center for the vision impaired. Find out if there are any speakers who would like to talk to a high school psychology class. If this is inconvenient, conduct your own interview with a blind person, and report what you learn to your class. Possible questions: Have your other senses become stronger? (This question wouldn't apply to someone blind from birth.) Do you dream in sounds, smells, or images? What's the most difficult part about being vision impaired?

5. Create your own illusion. Take a small sheet of paper. Make three cuts in it, as shown in the diagram to the right. Hold the paper in your hand. With your left hand at the top of the left (shaded) side of the paper, turn this side over by pulling it toward you, so that your left hand ends up at the bottom, still on the left side of the paper. Put the paper down. The "flap" should now be sticking straight up. You can help to straighten it by folding it up and down. A top view of the finished illusion should look like the small drawing to the right. The illusion may not seem like an illusion to you, since you have created it. But try it on your friends and family. They'll insist that you used glue or two pieces of paper. In other words, what you have made *seems* impossible to make with a single sheet of paper.

Without offering your friends any instructions, give them a sheet of paper and let them try to create the illusion. What steps do they take? What problem-solving strategies do they use? Refer back to the chapter that discussed brain hemispheres (Chapter 3). Which hemisphere *should* play a greater role in solving the illusion? Why? Which hemisphere do you think your friends primarily used? Explain.

6. When you walk through a grocery store, do you avoid the generic sections? Do you perceive generic products as being inferior to brand-name products?

Conduct a test to see if people, because of their perceptions of labels, prefer brand-name products over generic products. *Procedure:* Buy a jar of peanuts (or another snack item). Empty half the peanuts into a brand-name jar. Empty the other half into a jar labeled "generic." Have people taste a peanut from both and decide which tastes better. Don't tell them you are conducting a psychology experiment, or they will figure out that the peanuts are identical.

Analyze your results. Did people's perceptions affect their preferences? Discuss. To help with your discussion, you might look up some *Consumer Reports* issues on food products.

7. Using the keywords "Visual Illusions" find 4 or 5 Internet sites that highlight illusions. Universities or colleges that teach psychology are usually good sources. If your classroom has an Internet connection, present the sites to your class, explaining why each illusion works. If a classroom computer is not available, write a report on what you learned while navigating these sites.

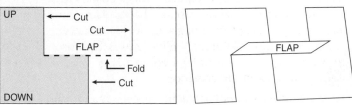

CHAPTER 5

Motivations and emotions are intricately guided by physical processes. Even so, human needs, desires, and feelings can become quite complex, because we are also guided by symbols and rituals.

Motivation and Emotion

Symbolism, Motivation, and Emotion

At first glance, both motivation and emotion seem reasonably straightforward, but nothing could be further from the truth. We will define and explore each of them shortly. But first, to illustrate how complex things can become, we will focus on hunger (a motivator) for a few moments. Satisfying hunger can be a mixture of social, psychological, and physical factors.

Visitors to the birthplace of William Shakespeare—Stratford-upon-Avon, England—are fascinated by some of the items on display. In an old tavern, there is a dining table from Shakespeare's era, the late 1500s and early 1600s. The table surface looks like it was worked on by a chain saw. It looks that way because thousands of travelers in those days gouged and stabbed at food they placed directly on the table after they had removed it from community bowls. Some people carried with them their own wooden plates, but others just attacked bread and meat on the table. At upper–social-class functions, soup was served in individual bowls, but in places like this one, the same bowl was passed from person to person so that each could eat a spoonful as it continued its circular trip around the table. The fork was forbidden because it was considered an instrument of the devil (it did not come into general use until the mid-1700s). The French king Louis XIV prided himself on being the best in his kingdom in one respect: He was able to eat chicken stew with his fingers without spilling a drop. The famous French author of the time, Michel de Montaigne, complained that he often found himself eating so fast he was constantly biting his fingers. Two customs of that era survive today: (1) the napkin—a real necessity then—and (2) hand-washing between courses, which now takes place only at fancy restaurants (Braudel, 1981).

▲ *The artist Botticelli lived from 1445 to 1510. In his painting,* The Wedding Feast, *notice that there are no eating utensils on the table.*

Knowing proper table etiquette can be important for getting ahead in business.

Note how, as you read this discussion, you had emotional responses—mostly negative—to the different behaviors mentioned. Why? Because satisfying hunger is not just a basic motivation. We attach rules and regulations to the process. What appears to be a basic "animal" behavior—eating—is filled with all kinds of symbolism. Eating is a special ritual. If we have something to celebrate or if we desire companionship, we go to a special place and are served food in a formal way.

The human higher brain operates largely in terms of complex symbolism and ritual. We even have "uniforms" to wear while satisfying hunger. The higher brain thinks that such symbols are real, not imaginary. Here is a good experiment to demonstrate this point. Ask an adult why it isn't acceptable to wear a clean pair of jeans to a formal dinner party. The answer you get will probably resemble, "It just isn't done," or "It would be embarrassing." There is no real answer that makes sense. It is a rule based on symbolism. Ask some friends who aren't taking this class why—*really why*—it would be weird for someone to wear a fancy dress or a suit when the group plans on getting pizza and spending the evening talking. They will come up with similar reasons, especially the circular one, "Well, it's just weird, that's all," which only proves our point and doesn't answer the question.

Finally, eating behavior in one of its most symbolic forms consists of *not* eating. People with important causes go on hunger strikes to call attention to things they believe need correcting. Eating is so important that they are able to attract attention by not doing it.

Focus Question

• How do different regions of the brain affect motivation and emotion?

motivation the drive to seek a goal, such as food, water, or friends

emotion a state of the body causing feelings, such as of hope, fear, or love

hypothalamus part of the lower brain that controls such basic needs and desires as pleasure, pain, fear, rage, hunger, thirst, and sex

Motivation and Emotion: Physical Factors

Motivation is what drives us to seek a specific goal. Hence, we are motivated to drink, eat, make friends, and so forth. **Emotion** is a state of the body that causes feelings, which vary according to how we view a situation—with fear, hope, love, and so forth. Motivation and emotion involve both physiological and psychological factors. We will start with the parts of the body that are involved. Use Figure 5.1 so you get an image of what we are talking about. In that figure, the head has been sliced down the middle vertically so you can see the inner structure of the brain.

The Hypothalamus

Attaining pleasure and avoiding pain are often cited as primary motivators in human behavior. Scientists have located the centers for both pain and pleasure in an area called the **hypothalamus** (high-po-THAL-ah-mus). Humans and animals alike have such centers. This unit also contains fear, rage, hunger, thirst, and sex centers.

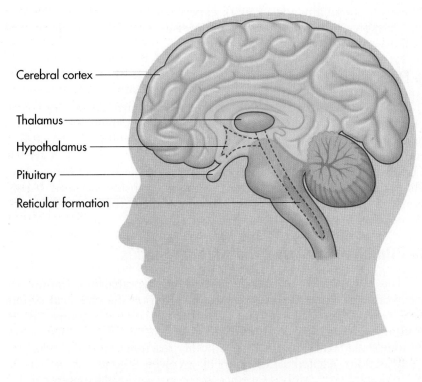

Cerebral cortex

Thalamus

Hypothalamus

Pituitary

Reticular formation

MID VIEW (As if head is cut down the center from front to back)

▲ *Figure 5.1*   *Major Brain Areas in Motivation and Emotion*

Sending electrical stimulation through a small wire to the hypothalamus can produce any of these motivators or emotions, depending on which part is touched. Animals receiving stimulation to the pleasure center if they push a lever have been known to stimulate themselves for up to 20 days at 20 responses per minute for a total of 576,000 pushes. Some of them preferred this to eating or drinking and died as a result (Valenstein, 1973; Olds, 1956).

Studies of the fear-rage portion of the hypothalamus have had their wilder moments. One experimenter connected a miniature radio receiver to the fear area of a bull's hypothalamus, and then he got into the ring with the bull. The experimenter was armed only with a radio transmitter. When the bull charged, he pushed a button, sending an impulse to the bull's fear center. Fortunately, the bull came to a screeching halt (Delgado, 1969). The experimenter was taking quite a chance. Right next to the fear area is an area for rage, which could well have been activated if the receiving wire had been off by a millimeter or so.

The Amygdala

The **amygdala** (ah-MIG-duh-la) is another brain structure involved in emotional responses, particularly aggression and fear. In fact, it can register fear and cause us to feel afraid all by itself, without involving our higher brain centers. Destroy the amygdala, and you also destroy fear.

▲ *Damage to the hypothalamus has resulted in this extraordinarily heavy rat, which has lost the ability to know when to stop eating.*

amygdala brain structure responsible for emotional responses of aggression and fear

125

An emotionally charged emergency situation will affect the reticular formation.

Persons without an amygdala cannot experience this emotion and cannot read the expression of fear on someone else's face (Behavioral Science Task Force, 1995; Goleman, 1995).

The Reticular Formation

Almost any emotional or motivational state involves taking some kind of action. Whether we run, fight, or seek something we need, we require an increase in activity level. Anyone who sits through a sporting event with no change in heart rate, blood pressure, or speech level has not been very involved in it. The **reticular** (re-TICK-you-ler) **formation,** as shown in Figure 5.1, is at the base of the brain inside the neck. It controls not only sleep but also how high or low the level of activity in the body is.

The Pituitary Gland and the Adrenal Glands

The reticular formation, amygdala, and hypothalamus cannot do their work all alone. They all frequently call upon the chemical system of the body to get us going. The controller of chemical responses is the **pituitary** (pi-TUE-i-ter-ee) **gland,** a small structure located just below the hypothalamus (Figure 5.2). The bodily reaction when a person gets highly anxious, excited, or emotionally involved is controlled at least in part by the pituitary. Suppose we see someone we love so intensely that he or she seems to be gradually killing us. The hypothalamus tells the pituitary, which uses chemicals to signal the **adrenal** (a-DREE-nal)

reticular formation unit in the brain that registers and controls activity level, increases excitement, and helps generate sleep

pituitary gland gland that controls other glands and hormones, as well as producing its own hormone that regulates growth

adrenal glands glands that secrete adrenaline, which stirs up the body, changing breathing, perspiration, heart rate, and so on

▶ *Figure 5.2* *Glands are significant physiological areas in emotion and motivation.*

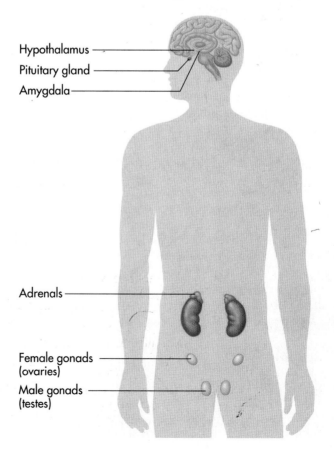

Hypothalamus
Pituitary gland
Amygdala

Adrenals

Female gonads
(ovaries)

Male gonads
(testes)

glands—there are two of them, one on each side of and about even with the belly button. These glands secrete the chemical *adrenaline* (a-DREN-a-lin), which makes the heart beat faster, breathing increase, and perspiration break out when we see the object of our love—or when we are faced with an emergency.

The Gonads

The sex glands, called **gonads,** are of two types: the **testes** in the male and the **ovaries** in the female. They produce sperm and eggs, respectively, as well as sex hormones. The hypothalamus signals the pituitary, which in turn causes the gonads to produce the sex hormones that will make a fetus into either a male or a female. Prior to birth, just a slight error can change the amount of sex hormone released. The result, on occasion, is an infant who has both male and female sexual organs. This problem is usually handled well today with surgery and hormone supplements. When the physician discovers it, a decision is made regarding which sex the child should be. Most infants with this abnormality have physical parts that belong more to one sex than the other. So hormones for the desired sex are administered, and eventually surgery is performed to make the child look and feel like a natural member of the assigned sex. It appears that most such children turn out well both physically and psychologically (Money, 1980). However, timing is critical. For this procedure to work, it must begin prior to 18 months of age. If it doesn't, serious problems and confusion can result (Hyde, 1994).

Sexual interest is controlled by the male hormones, called **androgens.** The female hormone, **estrogen,** seems to have the primary goal of regulating the reproductive cycles of the body. There is some indication that estrogen plays a limited role in sexual interest for women, but the androgens are the key to starting sexual interest in both males and females. Thus, both sexes have both male and female hormones. Obviously, the male hormone dominates in the male, and the female hormone dominates in the female.

Once someone starts to experience sexual interest, usually at the beginning of adolescence, all the symbolism of the higher brain enters into the picture. For humans, sexuality is mostly mental and symbolic, with the physical part playing a secondary role. This is why individuals can choose to give up sex and lead a celibate life. In contrast, people cannot choose to go without eating or drinking for long. The average person can go about three days without water and 60 to 70 days without food. You may have heard that if a person does not use the sex organs, the organs will gradually waste away. Or that each time they are used, people lose a little more of their "life energy." Neither of these myths is true.

gonads the sex glands

testes the male sex glands; they make sperm

ovaries the female sex glands; they make eggs

androgens male hormones; they control sexual interest in both males and females

estrogen the hormone that controls the female reproductive cycle

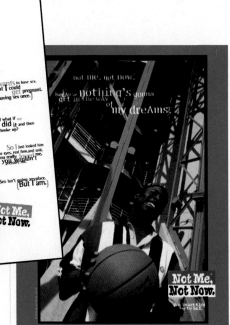

▲ *"Not Me, Not Now" is the motto of an educational TV campaign for and by teenagers in Monroe County, New York. These teens support the idea that sex and pregnancy interfere with future plans.*

127

Focus Questions

• What are drives?

• What causes hunger and thirst?

drives forces that push an organism into action to reach a goal

goal the target of a set of behaviors

homeostasis bodily process of maintaining a balanced internal state

Motivational Forces

Motivation is thought to result from **drives**—that is, forces that push the organism into action in order to reach goals. A **goal** is what our behavior is aimed toward. It is the target we are trying to reach. For example, if you are thirsty, you have a need for water and are driven by the body to seek it.

The body's drives operate in cycles designed to maintain balance over the long run. A period of high activity, for instance, is followed by a period of rest. This process of establishing physical equilibrium, or balance, is called **homeostasis,** literally translated as "standing (or staying) the same." (See Figure 5.3.) Thus, we are driven by hunger to eat. Once satisfied, though, we stop eating and go on to other things. These "start-stop" or "on-off" mechanisms help keep the body on an even keel. Homeostasis operates in all our basic drives. Next, we examine some of those basic drives in detail.

Homeostasis

Temperature too high: Expansion of blood vessels in skin. Sweating

Optimal range 98.6°

Temperature too low: Constriction of blood vessels in skin. Shivering

▲ *Figure 5.3* *Homeostasis keeps body temperature within an optimum range. When temperature becomes either too high or too low, the body reacts in ways that help it to revert to the desired temperature range.*

Hunger

In the middle 1800s, a man had part of his stomach left exposed after a shotgun accident. Experimenters talked him into becoming a guinea pig for their research on how the stomach works. A see-through covering was placed over the wound so the effects of various foods and other activities in the stomach could be viewed. After a while, the man got fed up with all this and fled to Canada, where he hid out. Later, when word came that he had died there, a doctor in the United States planned to try to get his body for a medical museum. The family heard about it and warned the doctor with a classic in telegrams. It read, "DON'T COME FOR AUTOPSY. YOU WILL BE KILLED" (Rosenzweig, 1962). As an extra caution, the family kept the body exposed a long time so it decomposed and became useless to any museum. Because of the stench, it had to remain outside during the funeral.

During the time the man was studied, however, his stomach provided much information on how the digestive system functions. For example, when people feel depressed, the amount of acid in the stomach drops noticeably, and salivation slows. Both stomach acid and saliva are needed for digestion. This may be one of the physical reasons why many depressed people don't want to eat. In contrast, when we are angry, the stomach's mucous membranes become red and engorged with blood, acid production more than doubles, and the stomach begins violent contractions. You may have experienced this from trying to eat during a family argument at the dinner table. Aside from the possibility of choking, the increased acid causes nausea. Either extreme—that is, too much or too little stomach acid—will affect our appetites.

What Causes Hunger?   Researchers are still trying to understand fully how we know it is time to eat or why we feel satisfied after a meal. The earliest suggestion was that the stomach growled and contracted when it was empty. To see if this was the case, in the early 1900s, experimenters had people swallow deflated balloons that were attached to a recording device. Then the balloons were inflated to touch the stomach walls, so each stomach contraction was recorded (see Figure 5.4). The experimenters found that when a person is hungry, the stomach does indeed contract, *but* it also contracts at other times (Cannon, 1939). So contractions might be part of the answer but are certainly not the complete one.

A problem with the contraction theory arose when it was discovered that people who had operations in which the stomach was removed still experienced hunger. How were they getting signals of hunger? In the 1960s, it occurred to some researchers that the hypothalamus might be involved. Following up on this hypothesis, the researchers discovered that electrical stimulation of the side part of the hypothalamus would cause eating behavior even in animals that were full. Similarly, damage to a lower portion of the hypothalamus would cause the animal to stop eating (Margules & Olds, 1962).

Still, knowing that the hypothalamus is involved doesn't explain *how* it works. A clue appeared years ago but was not understood for a while. You may have noticed that if you skip a number of meals, you begin to feel weak and sometimes dizzy. This is caused by a low **blood-sugar level,** a term referring to the amount of sugar (called **glucose**) in your blood. You can correct this situation for a short while by eating a

▲ *Getting a quick fix for low blood sugar can be a tasty temptation.*

blood-sugar level the amount of sugar contained in the blood, which indicates the level of hunger

glucose another name for sugar in the blood

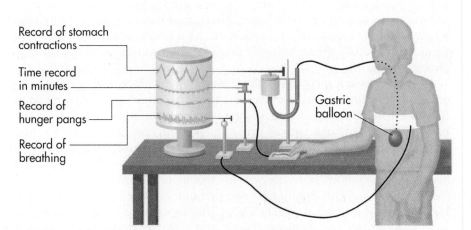

Record of stomach contractions

Time record in minutes

Record of hunger pangs

Record of breathing

Gastric balloon

▲ *Figure 5.4* *The subject pushes a key to indicate when stomach sensations are felt. This is then compared with actual stomach contractions.*

Feeling Hungry?

Here are four possible reasons why:

1. Your stomach is contracting.
2. Your blood-sugar level is low.
3. Your taste receptors are "on."
4. You've lost weight, and shrunken cells are signaling you.

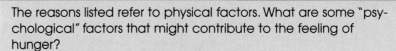

The reasons listed refer to physical factors. What are some "psychological" factors that might contribute to the feeling of hunger?

candy bar or drinking a soft drink, because either will flood the body with straight sugar. But then your blood sugar will zoom downward again. Eating something like meat, chicken, or pasta is a better solution, because your body will convert part of it into a steady source of glucose. In any case, researchers found that the hypothalamus contains *glucose monitors*, which determine the level of blood sugar. If the level starts to fall too low, these monitors send out signals that make you feel hungry (Arkes & Garske, 1982). If you skip a meal, your hunger disappears after an hour or so because the body dumps some of its stored glucose into the system to tide you over until the next meal.

There are other factors involved as well. The next time you eat, stop after five minutes or so and examine how you feel. Notice that you are already less hungry. But there hasn't been time for all you have eaten to get to your stomach, let alone to change your blood-sugar level. How can this be? The tongue, learning, and chemical responses all seem to play a role. From experience, we discover that food on the tongue means we will be satisfied. That is the learning part—previous association. When food hits the tongue, it communicates to the brain that you are eating. What if you stopped eating at that point? You will not be hungry for a while. In the intestines and stomach, however, there are other receptors that release a chemical to say when *they* are satisfied. As a result, since what you have eaten won't satisfy them, you will begin to feel hungry again (Whalen & Simon, 1984).

Taste is also a most important factor. It is critical to eating, a fact discovered in another unlucky event. A 10-year-old drank some boiling soup that fused his esophagus shut so he could not swallow. This was in the early 1940s when surgery was primitive. Nothing could be done for him except to insert a feeding tube through the area above the belly button into the stomach. The man lived a full life this way, but he found he didn't feel satisfied without taste. Hence, he would put a small amount of his (liquid) meals into his mouth first, spit that out, and then pour the rest into his feeding tube (Wolf & Wolff, 1947). The importance of taste, however, is short-lived. As we continue to eat, the taste receptors begin to shut down so that we will stop eating. Notice toward the end of a meal how tasteless your food becomes.

Factors Controlling Weight.   Because obesity is so often a topic of concern, there has been quite a bit of research on the problem. One of the most prominent theories suggests that the very heavy person is not able to read accurately the internal cues provided by the hypothalamus, blood sugar, and stomach—cues that would help him or her decide when and how much to eat. Instead, such people operate on external cues. In other words, if an item *looks* interesting or tasty, some obese people pay little attention to whether they need food at the moment but are carried away by its availability. There is a reasonable amount of evidence that this is the case in *some* obesity problems.

Overweight people also tend to eat whenever they are under stress, something that normal-weight and thin people generally do not do. In addition, in stressful situations, overweight women are more likely than men to eat sweet foods or foods high in fat. Thus, they consume more calories and run a greater risk of gaining weight (Greeno & Wing, 1994).

We all know people who can eat enormous quantities of food and never gain an ounce, while others seem to enlarge after eating a single cookie. One explanation for this is that people differ in their set points. A **set point** is a regulating mechanism in the body that determines what an individual's weight should be. If you have a high set point, your body will keep moving upward in weight to that point; if you have a low set point, your weight will move downward if necessary to reach it.

Set points, as we mentioned, vary from one individual to another. You may have noticed if you ever try to gain or lose weight that there is a specific weight that is very difficult for you to get above or below. That is your set point. A set point *can* be changed, but only with considerable work. A regular program of exercise will gradually change the set point to a limited degree in the case of those who are too heavy, and it will add muscle to those who are too thin (Horn & Anderson, 1993; Serdula et al., 1993). Your set point is to some extent determined by your fat cells. Fat

set point the body-regulating mechanism that determines a person's typical weight

▲ *Relying on internal cues for hunger, rather than external cues, can help people maintain a healthy weight.*

cells vary in both size and number from one person to another. Some people have trouble losing weight because as they start dieting, the fat cells shrink, which sends hunger signals to the body (Brown & Rodin, 1994).

It is risky to give an excuse to those people who want one for overeating, because overeating is almost always unhealthful. Still, the evidence is that a fair number of people are overweight based partly on their heredity and their metabolism—the speed at which the body uses up energy. Some people store fat more readily than others and have a slower metabolism than is needed to use it up.

What we eat seems also to have some hereditary basis. Taste receptors can vary from one person to another as the result of inheritance. One inherited factor that can arise if both the mother and father have a dominant gene for it is a horrible, bitter taste from eating green, leafy vegetables (Rodin, 1984). This may help explain why some children have such an aversion to certain types of vegetables; many are just being "difficult," but a handful actually experience a horrible taste from them.

Several researchers have reviewed more than a hundred studies on obesity and find that no single factor shows up consistently. Obese people seem to be quite variable in physical structure, psychological motivation, and eating behavior. Exceptions are those who are *very* obese—100 percent or more over their normal weight (Friedman & Brownell, 1995). These people probably have something wrong physically, as well as a tendency to respond to most food items, even a picture of a sandwich. In one extreme case, a girl was injured, damaging her hypothalamus. On her first day up and around in the hospital, her physician went with her to the cafeteria. On the way, he asked her if she was hungry, and she said no. But when she got there, she ran behind the counter and started grabbing handfuls of food, pushing them into her mouth (Pribram, 1971).

We have also learned that children must never be given food as a reward for doing something good, or food will take on an abnormal interest that can, over time, become a dominant one for the child. This behavior can carry into adulthood. Best to give the child some other reward whose power as a motivator is not as likely to increase as the drive to eat is. We should add, however, that infants are supposed to be chubby and should not be put on a diet except in the case of medical crisis or a disease.

▲ *You never hear parents say, "If you eat all your ice cream, you may have some spinach."*

Thirst

The human body is made up of roughly 65 to 70 percent water. As mentioned earlier, we can't go long without water. Whereas we have storage units for excess fat in case of an emergency, there is no place to store water, and we always need a ready supply. The amount of water we need is determined by units that "count" the number of water molecules in certain body cells surrounding the hypothalamus. When the count gets low, the desire for water increases.

While a dry tongue and the need to make it moist are important in thirst, there are also receptors in the intestine to make certain that this vital fluid actually gets into the body. Most animals have such receptors on the

▲ *Water cools the body as well as satisfying thirst.*

tongue, but we don't (Maddison et al., 1980). Instead, humans respond to temperature receptors on the tongue, which trigger a desire for cold drinks in summer and hot ones in winter (Kapatos & Gold, 1972). Dryness of tongue, temperature of water, and balance of water in the body cells are all registered by the hypothalamus.

For most of us, water intake is controlled by learning rather than by a physical signal. Over time, we learn the amount of water we need and the amount we tend to drink on a fairly regular basis. For example, studies show that right after playing tennis—before the bodily signals have been activated—the tennis player gulps just the right amount of water to compensate for the loss that will be signaled shortly (Pribram, 1971).

 ## Pause for Thought

1. Motivation and emotion are affected by several physical factors. Describe the role of each of the following: hypothalamus, amygdala, reticular formation, pituitary and adrenal glands, and gonads.
2. How does homeostasis affect hunger, taste, and thirst?

Critical Thinking
....
3. How can psychological factors affect the physical factors that control motivation and emotion?

Focus Question

• How can nonsurvival needs motivate people?

Nonsurvival Needs

We humans do a good job of taking basic needs and making them symbolic. The brain never seems content with leaving things alone. For example, we have a psychological need for change. There is always something "new" that we want to do, such as rearranging our rooms, changing the decorations or the colors, and so forth. This constant need for cerebral (brain) changes is a strong need, even though it is not critical to survival.

▲ *This monkey may not know what a train is, but it will work hard to see one in operation.*

curiosity motive a drive that moves a person to seek new and different things

manipulation motive a drive that moves a person to handle and use objects in the environment

Curiosity Motive. The strong psychological need to see new, odd, or different things is not confined to humans but is also found on a limited basis in "lower" animals. We used to have a German shepherd, for example, that drove us crazy with this **curiosity motive.** Naming it doesn't help. He learned to open closet doors to find out what was new in there. We might as well not even have had doors on the closets, because he would open them every time he was in the house. Discipline was not a solution; he would have had to be beaten into submission to obey, and we were too softhearted to do that.

In humans, one of the most noticeable bits of evidence of the curiosity motive is the fact that even in rush-hour traffic, people will slow down and jam things up hopelessly in order to view even the most minor accident. Curiosity is sometimes seen as a basic human response to the need to solve problems. The more we know about a particular subject, the better able we will be to solve problems in that area. Oddly enough, though, the more we know about something, the more our curiosity increases. The curiosity motive seems to come into play whenever there is a noticeable gap in our knowledge. And the greater our knowledge, the more likely we are to be aware of just how much more there is to learn (Loewenstein, 1994).

Manipulation Motive. When we move up the scale from dogs or cats to *primates* (such as monkeys, chimps, and humans), we find what is called a **manipulation motive.** This motive involves a drive to handle and use objects in the environment. Monkeys, for instance, love complicated mechanical puzzles of hooks, latches, and sliding bolts—just to have something to play with or examine. They will manipulate such things for hours with no other reward (such as encouragement or petting). Monkeys will work especially hard to be able to open a door and see a toy train going around in a circle, satisfying both

▲ *Curiosity and manipulation motives often work together.*

curiosity and manipulation needs (Harlow et al., 1956). Monkeys and other higher primates also love new human inventions, such as video players. When a foot switch is rigged to turn on a video player, monkeys will hold it down 60 percent or more of every hour merely to be able to enjoy the show. This is especially true of males, who will watch tapes of female monkeys about 75 percent of every hour if they are given the chance (Swartz & Rosenblum, 1980).

The important factor in these findings seems to be that these animals feel a desire for some type of change. Animals that are in very elaborate cages, such as brilliantly colored and decorated ones, eventually prefer simple cages, and the reverse is true for those in simple cages. Apparently, change, in and of itself, helps meet some need of the brain and possibly of the body as well.

Intrinsic versus Extrinsic Motivation. As mentioned, monkeys will play with latches and hooks endlessly if left on their own. But what happens if you start giving them a reward, such as a banana, for doing so? Something unexpected occurs: They lose their incentive to play and start to focus on the reward instead. If it doesn't arrive, they quit playing. We explain this situation in terms of the relation between **intrinsic motivation** and **extrinsic motivation.** *Intrinsic* means coming from within the organism. *Extrinsic* means coming from outside.

The importance of intrinsic motivation can be seen in many different areas. For example, higher intrinsic motivation leads to better performance at school and work and better overall psychological adjustment. It is related to greater creativity and general life satisfaction. In contrast, concentrating

intrinsic motivation motivation that comes from within the individual

extrinsic motivation motivation that comes from outside the individual

▲ *There may be no outside rewards involved, but these students are, nevertheless, highly motivated to learn.*

on the extrinsic rewards of an activity is associated with being less involved in what you are doing and having negative feelings about it (Behavioral Science Task Force, 1995).

You may remember how, as a child, you were curious about almost everything. Often, now, the reverse is true. This is one of the heavy prices we pay for organizing and structuring things into a formal school system. When we give people external rewards (such as grades and praise), we are using extrinsic motivation and to some extent removing intrinsic motivation. Thus, too many students begin to act like the monkeys, no longer able to get really deeply involved in what they're learning. But give these same students a problem outside the classroom, and they will work for hours on it (because of intrinsic motivation). So what is the solution? The school structure is so big and so formalized that it won't work to take away grades (extrinsic motivation). We need to find a way to add intrinsic motivation for students. If all of us were stuck on a desert island, it wouldn't be long before we were actually begging for a chance to learn something new.

▲ **Figure 5.5** *Contact comfort in Harlow's lab consisted of having a terry cloth "mother."*

contact comfort the satisfaction obtained from pleasant, soft physical stimulation

Need for Stimulation. All animals must have physical stimulation in order to develop properly. Monkeys that are not handled while they are growing up become cold, aloof, and unfriendly not only to others but also to their own offspring. Such monkeys can be partially "repaired" over a period of about six months if placed with other monkeys, but the fact that it takes so long shows the devastating effects of having no stimulation (Suomi, 1983).

Psychologist **Harry Harlow** showed the need for **contact comfort** dramatically in a series of studies with monkey babies. Monkeys were placed in a cage with two fake mothers. One of the "mothers" was made of wire and had a bottle attached to it where the monkeys could feed. The other mother was covered with terry cloth but provided no food (see Figure 5.5). Once the animals had adjusted to having the two mothers, a fear test was performed.

While a mechanical windup teddy bear may be fascinating to a child, it is very frightening to a monkey, so it formed the basis for the test. The mechanical teddy bear was put into the cage. The monkeys panicked. Here is the key point: Even though the monkeys were fed by the wire mother, they consistently ran to the cloth mother for protection and comfort when faced with the teddy bear. This indicates the importance of contact comfort in development. While we would expect the

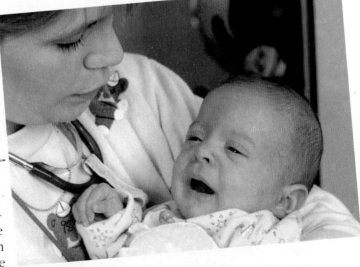

▲ *Contact comfort in the real world.*

monkeys to go to the mother that fed them, the pleasant physical contact of the cloth made them feel far more secure (Harlow, 1959).

There are parallel situations in humans. In one study during World War II, infants who were reared in an institution where there was almost no personal attention in the form of touching or holding were compared with infants who were reared in a prison nursery where they had contact with their mothers. The results were frightening: 37 percent of the institution-reared children died within a year, despite being fed and kept clean (Spitz, 1946).

There is even physical evidence of these needs. At the base of the brain is a unit called the *cerebellum,* which registers and controls bodily movement and sensation. (For more detail, see Chapter 3.) The cerebellum has a number of connections to emotional systems. Without enough rocking and touching, the cerebellum does not develop properly, which is likely to create permanent emotional and physical scars (Prescott, 1979). We suspect that nature sees to this need, giving mothers the desire, almost automatically, to rock their infants.

The Theory of Needs

Psychologist **Abraham Maslow** developed a theory called the **hierarchy of needs.** A hierarchy (HI-er-arc-ee) is a system that ranks items one above the other in importance. Maslow's goal was to put human needs into such an arrangement, as shown in the pyramid in Figure 5.6. The most obvious needs are at the base of the pyramid—the physiological, or physical, needs. These **physiological needs,** such as hunger and thirst, must be met first. When people are starving or thirsty, this will almost always dominate their thoughts and behavior.

Once the physiological needs are satisfied, however, we move upward. On the next level are the **safety needs.** Once we have food and water, we begin to experience less critical but still basic needs, such as trying to provide a little shelter and possibly a small nest egg of money so that we are "safe" over the long run.

When we are reasonably safe, we seek contact and love with another. These are called the **belongingness needs.** We cannot survive very

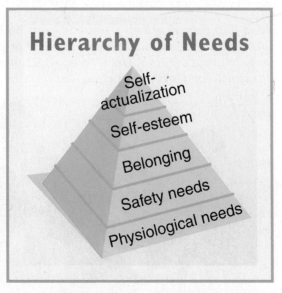

Hierarchy of Needs

Self-actualization
Self-esteem
Belonging
Safety needs
Physiological needs

▲ *Figure 5.6* *Maslow's Hierarchy of Needs. Learning and academic achievement are related to self-esteem. If you are hungry, feel physically threatened, or have relationship problems, you may regress to lower levels and not be able to concentrate on studying.*

Focus Question

• According to Abraham Maslow, what five types of needs motivate people?

hierarchy of needs a system that ranks human needs one above the other, with the most basic needs for physical survival at the bottom of the pyramid; proposed by the psychologist Abraham Maslow

physiological needs needs at the bottom of Maslow's hierarchy: hunger and thirst

safety needs needs at the second level of Maslow's hierarchy: shelter, nest egg of money

belongingness needs needs at the third level of Maslow's hierarchy: friendship, closeness with another

In Their Own Words . . .

Abraham Maslow (1908–1970) *was a humanistic psychologist. Humanists focus on fulfilling one's potential and believe that humans strive for personal growth. Here, in his own words, Maslow described part of his hierarchy of needs:*

Obviously a good way to obscure the "higher" motivations, and to get a lopsided view of human capacities and human nature, is to make the organism extremely and chronically hungry or thirsty. . . . It is quite true that man lives by bread alone—when there is no bread. But what happens to man's desires when there is plenty of bread and when his belly is chronically filled?

At once other (and "higher") needs emerge and these, rather than physiological hungers, dominate the organism. And when these in turn are satisfied, again new (and still "higher") needs emerge and so on. This is what we mean by saying that the basic human needs are organized into a hierarchy. (Maslow, 1943/1997, p. 189)

Interpreting Primary Sources

If you believed as Maslow did, what would you predict an individual's highest need might be?

well over time without friendship and closeness, so these needs appear after safety. It is very hard for anyone to feel important in the scheme of things unless at least one other person cares about him or her. So once we have satisfied the need to belong, we begin to feel acceptable.

Now we need to develop that self-acceptance into a sense of being more than a cog in the machinery—a sense of being a real person. These are the **self-esteem needs,** with self-esteem meaning liking and respecting yourself (in the positive sense, not in the sense of being "stuck-up").

Having attained the needs of the bottom four levels of the hierarchy, we are in a position to go on to even greater things—the need to establish meaningful goals and a purpose in life, called **self-actualization needs.** This term refers to our ability to put into practice (actualize) whatever skills and talents we possess. If you have carpentry skills, then these are used to make a fine product, the best you can—not something shoddy that barely hangs together. If you have musical talent, then you develop it so that you can sing or play an instrument beautifully and meaningfully (Maslow, 1954).

Maslow's theory has had an effect on our understanding of people who have trouble in life. They may lack a sense of purpose because they have failed to satisfy needs at one of the lower levels. For example, someone stuck at the belongingness level has a "hole which has to be filled, an emptiness into which love [needs to be] poured" (Maslow, 1968, p. 39).

self-esteem needs needs at the fourth level of Maslow's hierarchy: liking and respecting yourself, feeling important and useful

self-actualization needs needs at the top of Maslow's hierarchy: establishing meaningful goals and a purpose in life

▶ *Self-actualization needs and belongingness needs can be fulfilled in many ways. Both seem to be satisfied in this scene.*

In Focus

Unsatisfied Needs

Let's compare Maslow's hierarchy of five needs with a set of five building blocks. Once we arrange the first block to our satisfaction, we add the second block, and so on. A problem arises, however, when we can't arrange a particular block just the way we want.

For example, in the diagram shown here, someone has arranged the first two blocks pretty well. The third block, however, keeps falling off. This represents the fact that the person feels that he or she can develop no close or intimate relationships.

What's the solution? One obvious solution is to continue working on "block 3." If a relationship doesn't work out as well as expected, try again. As we all know, this is not always easy, but it is usually worthwhile. At the very least, don't believe that one or two failed relationships are a sign that all future relationships will fail.

Another "solution" is just to keep fiddling with and focusing on the first two blocks, thinking that this will take care of the falling block. This behavior is typical of some anorexics. They may feel that they're not loved, so they compensate by becoming obsessed with food (in other words, they keep rearranging the first block over and over again).

Still another "solution" is to forget the third block and put the fourth block on the stack. The person still has a difficult time developing close relationships, but the problem becomes less noticeable. This is typical of workaholics who try to attain self-esteem strictly through their jobs, at the expense of a meaningful private life.

To sum all this up: If a person cannot directly satisfy a need, he or she may compensate by becoming obsessed with some other, more accessible need. To *compensate* means to substitute one need for another.

What if a student is obsessed with becoming popular at school? How might this student be compensating for some need that hasn't been filled?

▲ *At the human level, motivation can be both symbolic and complex, as is demonstrated by affiliation and achievement needs.*

Some psychologists have been critical of the hierarchical nature of Maslow's theory, arguing that instead of following this system step-by-step, some people skip around. Take, for example, the "starving artist" who will sacrifice physical comfort in order to create works of art. In fairness, it should be noted that Maslow himself recognized this possibility.

Focus Question

• What psychological factors or needs influence motivation?

Psychological Motivation

The discussion so far strongly suggests that physiological needs are only part of the motivational picture. Since most of us are fortunate enough to get basic needs like hunger and thirst met on a regular basis, we don't have to spend a great deal of time dealing with them. Instead, we direct our energies toward more psychologically satisfying activities. The specific goals we choose will depend largely on what we have learned to seek out.

From time to time, psychologists have tried to make complete lists of such psychological motives—that is, needs human beings seem to have that lack any clear survival value. The lists are many, and the number of possibilities is nearly endless. For example, there are people who are "joiners," who seem to need to belong to every club and organization that comes along. People like this are said to have a high **need for affiliation.**

Some people seem willing to do almost anything to get other people to like them. They are even concerned about the opinions of people they don't know. These people have a high **need for approval.** Both of these groups have *learned* to value these goals and to associate them with good feelings or a sense of personal satisfaction.

Achievement Motivation.   One psychological motive stands out from the rest, probably because our culture values individual success so highly. The **need for achievement**—a strong desire for personal accomplishment and a high degree of competence—has long been a favorite subject for study. People who are high in achievement motivation tend to seek out challenges and to stick with tasks once they start. They also work harder and accomplish more than the average person.

As is true of other psychological motivation, the need for achievement seems to be learned. The parents of high achievers encourage and reward this kind of behavior. So do the schools and society at large. There is also evidence that firstborn children are more often high achievers than later-born children (Falbo & Polit, 1986). One explanation of this finding is that parents are more involved with their firstborn because their attention is not so scattered.

While a high need for achievement is generally seen as a positive thing, it *can* be taken too far. People sometimes feel terrible pressure to constantly do more and more, better and better. When this is the case, they often have trouble relaxing and suffer more than most of us from the effects of stress. And since we are on the subject of motivation, another problem is worth mentioning: People who develop eating disorders (see the Applying Psychology to Life feature at the end of this chapter) often come from families that emphasize very high levels of achievement (Yates, 1989).

need for affiliation psychological need to belong to and identify with groups

need for approval psychological need to have other people think highly of oneself

need for achievement psychological need for personal accomplishment

▲ *Our need for achievement is not always met.*

Pause for Thought

1. What is a nonsurvival need? Explain how the following nonsurvival needs motivate us: curiosity motive, manipulation motive, and extrinsic motivation.

2. What is contact comfort? Is contact comfort an example of intrinsic or extrinsic motivation?

3. What does Maslow mean by a hierarchy of needs? Which two needs must be met first? Which needs can then be satisfied?

Critical Thinking

4. How might a person's attitude affect the way he or she achieves certain needs in Maslow's hierarchy?

Thinking Critically about Psychology

Does Birth Order Matter?

Psychologists know that firstborns tend to be higher achievers than later-born children, in the general sense of life accomplishments. Many studies have examined the importance of birth order in school performance or scholastic achievement. What we want to consider in this critical thinking feature is whether birth order is an important factor in academic achievement.

What specifically is being claimed or stated? Firstborn children tend to do better in school and on scholastic achievement tests than later-born children.

What is the objective evidence for and against this claim? The evidence here is mixed, especially when individual cases are examined. Some studies have not found birth order to be a significant influence (Kessler, 1991; Retherford & Sewell, 1991). Other studies, perhaps greater in number, have found a connection (Zajonc & Mullaly, 1997; Zajonc & Bargh, 1980; Belmont & Marolla, 1973). In the many studies that have found a difference, firstborn children seem to have the advantage.

What other interpretations might be made instead? If we grant that firstborn children do achieve more academically, why might this be so? Well, it appears that it is not simply the fact of being born first that is critical—other, related factors are involved. For example, you might expect only children to be similar to firstborns, since they always have their parents' undivided attention. However, they are actually more similar to lastborn children. It seems that one relevant factor in academic achievement is having the opportunity to teach others—younger brothers and sisters—at an early age. Being the firstborn often makes that possible. The overall size of the family may also play a part here—the larger the family, the greater the effect. The age difference between children is another factor that must be taken into account. If the firstborn is only a year or two older than the next child in the family, the effect is extremely small. Furthermore, the advantage that firstborns seem to have doesn't appear until around the age of

▲ *The age differences between children in a family have an impact on the effects of birth order.*

▲ *Firstborns often help teach their younger siblings.*

See if *COOL* works for you....

Claim?

Objective evidence for and against claim?

Other interpretations?

Logical conclusions?

10 or so. Finally, the differences between firstborn and later-born children in scholastic achievement, while fairly consistent, are quite small, ranging from the equivalent of only 1.5 to 4 IQ points (Zajonc & Mullaly, 1997).

What are the most logical conclusions to draw? It seems fair to say that firstborns do enjoy a slight advantage over later-born children in academic achievement. However, we must also take into account the overall size of the family and the age differences between children in the family. And we must keep in mind that this advantage is clearly not large enough to have a serious impact in everyday life.

Applying Critical Thinking Skills

Apply the information in this section to your own family. Do the researchers' conclusions seem to accurately describe your family?

Emotions

Emotions are part of our physical survival system. Without anger and fear, for instance, we could not protect ourselves. In this sense, we are very much like animals. Again, however, humans often express themselves in a social and symbolic context. Thus, rioters have been known to destroy police cars because the cars are a symbol of authority, not because the cars pose an immediate life-threatening danger to the rioters.

Scientists have been arguing for centuries about how many human emotions there are and how they differ. The issue still has not been settled. (Try sometime to come up with a clear distinction between anger and frustration, and you will see what the problem is.) People the world over do seem to share certain basic emotions, such as joy, fear, anger, and sadness. Beyond this short list, though, we can't go very far. Significant cultural differences exist. For instance, what events produce which emotion? How and under what circumstances are emotions expressed? Each culture will have its own answers to these questions. It's usually a mistake, then, to assume that everyone everywhere responds and feels the same way (Mesquita & Frijda, 1992).

Facial Expressions and Emotion

We mentioned above that people around the world share certain basic emotions: joy, fear, anger, surprise, disgust, and sadness. There are distinctive facial expressions for each of these emotions (Behavioral Science Task Force, 1995). Further, it appears that these expressions are universal. That is, people from different cultures across the world use the same expressions and recognize them in others as well (Ekman, 1994; Izard, 1994). This does not mean that we cannot fake a smile or that the same thing triggers the same emotional response for every person in every culture. What it does mean is that we seem to be born with a set of facial expressions that can communicate what we are feeling without the need for language.

Opponent-Process Theory

Generally, when we experience an intense feeling of some kind, we don't just come back to normal or neutral once that feeling has passed. Instead, we often go beyond that middle ground. In other words,

In Their Own Words . . .

The **Basic Behavior Science Task Force** is part of the National Institute of Mental Health. It is a group of experts who were asked to provide guidance for the Institute's basic research programs. An excerpt from one of their reports follows:

The human face is a remarkable system consisting of 44 separate muscles; 4 are devoted to chewing and 40 to facial expression. No other species has such capacity for making faces! Why would nature devote such substantial resources to facial expression?

One function is to communicate feelings to others often in ways that powerfully influence their behavior. Facial expression also helps us experience emotion. Indeed, some theorists have suggested that without it we could not feel emotions. . . .

A depressed woman participating in a research study was filmed telling a doctor how much better she was feeling in therapy. Days later she attempted suicide. Slow-motion study of her facial expressions while talking to the doctor revealed hidden among her smiles the fleeting, almost invisible signs of intense distress. If warning expressions such as these could be detected on a routine basis in patients with severe mental disorders, suicide might claim far fewer lives each year. This example merely hints at the potential of research exploring the emotional and motivational wellsprings of our behavior. (Basic Behavioral Science Research For Mental Health, 1995.)

Interpreting Primary Sources

In what other situation would studies that use facial expressions to gain information about a person's emotional state be helpful?

▲ *No matter where you come from or where you live, a smile is still a smile.*

opponent-process theory theory that the presence of one emotion triggers its opposite, which then emerges somewhat later

the presence of one emotion triggers its opposite, which then eventually emerges. This phenomenon is described by the **opponent-process theory** (Solomon, 1980). For example, if you have just finished a lengthy final exam, one you have dreaded for weeks, you don't simply feel okay once it's over. Instead, for a while, you feel wonderful, elated, ecstatic. Similarly, it is not unusual to feel slightly depressed after a period of joy or high excitement. It doesn't mean there's something wrong with you. It's just part of our complicated emotional makeup.

Cognition and Emotion

cognition higher-order thought processes, such as reasoning and problem solving

Cognition includes higher-order thought processes, such as reasoning and problem solving. It is intimately involved in the emotions we feel. Thus, in laboratory experiments, when people in one group are led to believe they will experience pain, they become far more anxious than people in another group, who are told they will not be hurt. If members of the first group receive a minor shock, they overestimate how agonizing it is—just from the expectation of pain. Or take the sensation of starting to fall forward or backward. All of us immediately panic as we try to correct for it. But if we label the sensation as *fun,* then we don't react that way to the same sensations. Example? A roller coaster ride. Imagine how you would respond if all those sensations were present while you were sitting in class. As you can see, how something feels can be a matter of interpretation.

▲ *Fun or terror? You decide.*

In many cases, specific situations trigger particular emotions. We use these *situational cues* to determine what emotion we should be feeling. For example, when we're trying to get somewhere or do something and obstacles are put in our way, we tend to become angry, at least temporarily. When facing a threat, we may become angry or fearful or both, depending on the circumstances and how serious the threat actually is. Fear is more likely to result when we are uncertain about our chances of coming out okay or very certain that we cannot succeed in fending off this threat. It's the old fight-or-flight situation. A smart-mouthed little kid yelling insults and an attacking grizzly bear will not produce the same emotional response.

Often, physical arousal cannot be identified as a specific emotion until we label it. For example, two people meet face to face, about to get into a fight. One is seven feet tall and weighs 275 pounds; the other is five feet tall and weighs 75 pounds. Both are fully aroused physically, and devices that measure bodily responses wouldn't show a difference between them. Even so, aren't they feeling different emotions?

On the other side of the coin, our emotional state can affect how we view ourselves and our world. When we are in a good mood, we tend to see more of the positive things around us and ignore the negative. We also tend to view other people as happy, and our self-concept benefits as well. Unfortunately, the same process operates when we are depressed or unhappy—the whole world seems full of gloom and doom, and we see ourselves as being much worse off than we really are (Forgas, 1995).

Emotional Intelligence: Optimism

Case Study

One of the most powerful tools we can use to manage emotions is optimism. To understand the difference between optimism and its opposite, pessimism, consider the following cases from a book by psychologist Martin Seligman (1995), probably the world's foremost authority on optimism.

Luke is a fifth-grader whose parents have been fighting lately. One Saturday morning Luke asks his mom to drive him to baseball practice. Too busy to help, his mom asks his dad who is also busy, and the parents begin to fight. As he walks away, Luke thinks, "I did it again! I'm always making them fight. When am I going to learn to keep my mouth shut. Mom and Dad have been fighting so much lately. It's always because of me. I'm spoiling everything. If they get divorced, it's going to be my fault. I'm the world's worst kid. I'm always ruining everything!" (p. 61).

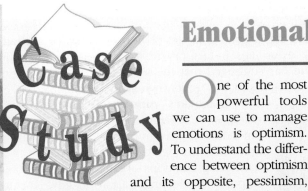

▲ *Can a pessimistic person learn to be optimistic?*

Rodney finds himself in a similar situation. He will celebrate his twelfth birthday soon and asks his mom about a party. His stepfather suggests a theme party: his friends can wear army clothes and play capture-the-flag with plastic guns and watch Schwarzenegger movies. Rodney becomes excited and they begin to discuss details about the party. Rodney's mom can't believe what she's hearing, and she and Rodney's stepfather begin to fight. Rodney thinks, "That was dumb of me. I know how much mom hates all that war stuff and she really hates those kinds of movies. She hardly ever lets me watch them. The two of them fight about these kinds of things a lot. I should have told Steve that I didn't want that kind of party, then they wouldn't be fighting now. It's my fault!" (p. 61–62).

At first glance, neither boy seems particularly optimistic—they both blame themselves for their parents' fighting—but in fact, their thinking is vastly different. Luke's conclusions about the situation are what Seligman describes as "permanent" and "global." Luke believes he spoiled *everything* and that he's the world's worst kid. Rodney's conclusions are more temporary and specific. He believes he simply should have told his stepdad "No." He doesn't feel he's a bad kid; he just made a mistake.

As you can see by these examples, optimists do not ignore the negative. They do, however, assess the events in their lives in a particular way. Optimists view most negative events as temporary; they don't blow negative events out of proportion; and they don't personalize every negative event—they accept blame when they are at fault but recognize when others are guilty. On the other hand, optimists do view positive events as permanent and global: *I'm a good student; people like me; I made the team because I'm a good athlete.*

If your pattern of thinking more closely resembles Luke's than Rodney's, here's some good news: optimism can be learned. Seligman has devoted entire books just to this learning process, so we can't even begin to offer tips in this short space. But numerous studies show that the effort to learn optimism is well worth it. Optimistic people achieve more and remain physically and mentally healthier than people who are not optimistic.

Review the Case Study

Hank gets a low grade on a test. What would be optimistic and pessimistic responses to this grade?

Emotional Intelligence

emotional intelligence the ability to properly feel, deal with, and recognize emotions

Clearly, emotions are a central aspect of human behavior and affect many different areas of our lives. In fact, psychologist Daniel Goleman finds them so important he has suggested that the ability to properly feel, deal with, and recognize emotions makes up its own kind of "intelligence."

Goleman's **emotional intelligence** is made up of several emotional skills. The first is emotional self-awareness—knowing what we are feeling and why. Next comes managing and harnessing emotions—being able to control and respond to feelings appropriately. Included here are controlling our impulses, tolerating frustration, and expressing our anger effectively. Another part of emotional intelligence is empathy—the ability to read what another is feeling, to take that person's perspective and be sensitive to his or her emotions. It is noteworthy that people who are antisocial, or people who commit crimes against other people, are usually unable to empathize with someone else.

Emotional intelligence helps us handle relationships better because it allows us to interact with others more effectively and sensitively. It can also help protect us from becoming depressed or overly anxious. From Goleman's perspective, simply having a high IQ, in the usual sense of the term, is not enough to guarantee success in the real world. We also need emotional intelligence (Goleman, 1995).

In Their Own Words . . .

*Psychologist **Daniel Goleman** believes that it is the people with high emotional intelligence, not high IQs, who really succeed in life. He also believes that this intelligence is not fixed at birth but can be learned. Here are some of his ideas, in his own words:*

Emotions that simmer beneath the threshold of awareness can have a powerful impact on how we perceive and react, even though we have no idea they are at work. Take someone who is annoyed by a rude encounter early in the day, and then is peevish for hours afterward, taking affront where none is intended and snapping at people for no reason. He may well be oblivious to his continuing irritability and will be surprised if someone calls attention to it. . . . But once that reaction is brought to his awareness—once it registers in the cortex—he can evaluate things anew, decide to shrug off the feelings felt earlier in the day, and change his outlook and mood. In this way emotional self-awareness is the building block of the next fundamental of emotional intelligence: being able to shake off a bad mood. (Goleman, 1995, p. 55)

The design of the brain means that we very often have little or no control over *when* we are swept by emotion, nor over *what* emotion it will be. But we have some say *in how long* an emotion will last. (Goleman, 1995, p. 57)

Interpreting Primary Sources

What does Goleman mean by the phrase beneath the *threshold of awareness?* What might be another way to say this?

Theories of Emotion

We will discuss three more theories of emotion in the sections that follow. At present, our understanding of emotion is incomplete, so all three theories can stand side by side as possible "answers," even though they are different. And one theory might fit a particular set of circumstances to which another one doesn't even apply.

The James-Lange Theory. The **James-Lange** (Lang) **theory,** named after the two men who proposed it, is simple. But it can be confusing unless you pay close attention. The theory suggests that emotions operate in reverse of the way most of us assume. In general, people think that we see a snake, feel an emotion, then run. These two men claimed that we see a snake, our bodies respond, we run, and *only then* do we feel an emotion because the body is so keyed up. They arrived at this theory because they believed that just thinking about or seeing a snake has no real effect until *after* the body has responded. So our physical feelings *are* the emotions.

James-Lange theory theory of emotion proposing that first the body responds and *then* one feels the emotion

Goleman's Emotional Intelligence

	Low Emotional Intelligence	High Emotional Intelligence
Emotional Awareness		
Managing Emotions		
Identifying and Understanding Others' Emotions (Empathy)		

Your parents are pressuring you to attend a certain college. How would you express your frustration over this in an emotionally intelligent manner?

Cannon-Bard theory theory of emotion proposing that the bodily reaction and the emotional response to an event occur at the same time

cognitive theory theory of emotion proposed by Stanley Schachter; it holds that people label a bodily response by giving it the name of the emotion they think they are feeling

The Cannon-Bard Theory. The **Cannon-Bard theory** of emotion is also named after two scientists. Their theory arose after the discovery of the thalamus as a physical unit of the brain that can instantly transmit messages (see Chapter 3). They claim that when an emergency is perceived, the bodily reaction and the emotional system respond at the same time. So the body responds first in the James-Lange theory; but in the Cannon-Bard theory, both responses occur together.

The Cannon-Bard theory might fit many cases, but for some the James-Lange theory fits better. For instance, in a near accident, we respond physically first, by reflex. Then, later, we start feeling panic. In this situation, the brain takes roughly two seconds to respond, a *long* time in an emergency. Hence, what we are feeling over the near accident comes after the body responds.

Schachter's Cognitive Theory. The psychologist **Stanley Schachter** (SHACK-ter) performed experiments to support his **cognitive theory**—the belief that we label our bodily responses as being certain emotions. His subjects were injected with adrenaline, which speeds up the body's processes. Subjects in one group were told that the drug would make them feel "high" or on top of the world. Subjects in the other group, who got exactly the same drug injection, were told the drug would make them feel angry. Subjects were then put in a room with stooges who were to act in a way that would support what the subjects had been told about the drug's effect. Thus, the subjects who were told they would feel high were surrounded by very happy stooges playing games and laughing. The "angry" subjects were placed in a room with stooges who complained, moaned,

▲ *Before he had a chance to feel panic, the driver of this automobile reacted instantly to try to avoid hitting other vehicles.*

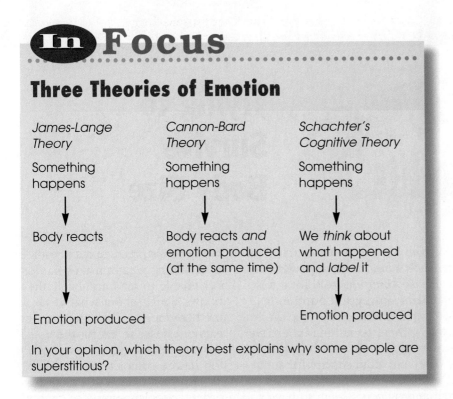

In Focus

Three Theories of Emotion

James-Lange Theory	*Cannon-Bard Theory*	*Schachter's Cognitive Theory*
Something happens	Something happens	Something happens
↓	↓	↓
Body reacts	Body reacts *and* emotion produced (at the same time)	We *think* about what happened and *label* it
↓		↓
Emotion produced		Emotion produced

In your opinion, which theory best explains why some people are superstitious?

and groaned about almost everything. The experiment showed that the subjects, once the drug had taken effect and stirred up the body, began to feel and act the way they had been prompted to—either high or angry. In these results, Schachter found support for his theory that we tend to label (cognitively) our behavior and control our feelings in terms of the atmosphere or environment around us and how others are acting (Schachter & Singer, 1962).

 ## Pause for Thought

1. Explain how people meet the following needs: need for affiliation, need for approval, need for achievement.
2. What is one conclusion we can make about birth order?
3. How can our thinking affect our emotions?
4. Your sadness finally passes. What happens next, according to the opponent-process theory?

Critical Thinking

5. Which of the three theories of emotions best explains why people develop phobias? Explain.

APPLYING
Psychology to life

Trying to Survive Body Size

The average wolf weighs about 80 pounds. It is not unusual for it to eat up to 18 pounds of meat at one sitting (Lopez, 1978). Yet it is rare to find an obese wolf, even in areas of plenty. Humans, on the other hand, have made the process of eating and not eating so complex that it often involves nothing but chaos, anxiety, and a great deal of injury to both psyche and body. For example, Inuit natives used to put a premium on obesity in both male and female marriage partners, while every decade or so, people in the other states try to turn themselves into walking sticks with a cell or two hanging onto them. We want to outline here some of the things that seem to be pretty well established with the hope that at least a few partially reasonable facts will be available to you.

Variety of Foods Necessary

Most rats know better than to keep eating the same thing over and over and over. Some variety of foods seems necessary for humans, too. Certain types of food groups provide vitamins and minerals people need. These are listed, with no preaching or discussion, in one of the half-

dozen annual almanacs (such as *World Almanac* or *Information Please Almanac)* sold for a few dollars at drugstores and in supermarkets.

There is nothing inherently wrong with fat, salt, or sugar. They are all necessary for survival. On the other hand, we humans do not seem to have very good detectors for telling us when we are overdoing any of the three. Consequently, we must remain skeptical of something like a "craving" for a hot dog.

Food can act in a fashion similar to a narcotic in that it can relieve tension by making a person groggy. Hence, many can fall prey to using food much as someone would use alcohol or drugs.

Eating Disorders

One of the toughest decisions many slightly heavy people have to make is what to do if the fashion of the moment is to be skinny. Set points are just plain higher for some people than for others. But there can be so much social pressure that it is hard to know how to handle it. One of the most serious dangers is the possibility of developing an *eating disorder.* In eating disorders,

the person's preoccupation with food and/or weight makes him or her unable to read accurately the body's signals about what food the body needs. Thus, the person eats or refuses to eat for the wrong reasons. (See Chapter 11 for a more complete discussion.)

In some kinds of eating disorders, people become so obsessed with dieting that they become dangerously underweight. Still, they refuse to eat. Over time, the body gradually adapts to lower and lower weights until eventually it is impossible to eat much of anything. Some people die of starvation because they simply can't hold down any food. In another kind of eating disorder, the person eats a great deal of food and then throws it up or takes heavy doses of laxatives in order to avoid gaining weight.

Fad Diets

If you want to make money, write a diet book, because there is always one on the best-seller list. These books often suggest dangerous paths to follow. Some fad diets can kill you by depriving you of absolutely necessary nutrients. Most people who go on one of these diets get off it within about six months anyway. A fad diet is not worth the risk. About the only consistent and safe way to lower weight is by exercising and eating less food (and, of course, not gorging on fats and sugars). If you are *actually* overweight, try eating only at mealtimes for a while and see what happens. Or try eating a little less on a consistent basis.

A Positive Approach

A couple of final ideas to make life a little better for everyone: Try to look at your body in a positive way. We *all* have our good points and bad points. If your weight is honestly out of control—if you are either too thin or too heavy—you are not alone. But something needs to be done. One of the most comfortable ways to handle it is to join a group of other people who are working together on the same problem. You'll get plenty of support from the group as you work to improve your health.

▲ *Ideal body size is a cultural concept. To the average Inuit male, the heavier Inuit woman is far more appealing than the skinny Anglo woman.*

Summary

1. Motivation consists of drives that make us seek specific goals. Emotion involves various states of the body that cause feelings. These feelings vary in terms of how we view a situation.

2. The hypothalamus contains centers for pleasure, pain, rage, sex, hunger, thirst, and fear. It controls other units of the body as we seek satisfaction or respond to certain feelings. The amygdala also triggers emotional responses.

3. The reticular formation controls the level of bodily activation. Given a need, it increases the body's activity noticeably.

4. The pituitary gland works under instructions from the hypothalamus and secretes chemicals that stir up the body.

5. The gonads control which sex the fetus will be. Later in life, they trigger sexual responses.

6. Hunger is signaled by the hypothalamus in response to stomach contractions, intestinal receptors, taste, and blood-sugar level.

7. A set point is the body's determination of what weight the individual should be.

8. Thirst is also controlled by the hypothalamus. Here, the dryness of the tongue and the amount of water in body cells are registered to determine if water is necessary.

9. Curiosity and manipulation motives seem to be needs of the brain. The evidence is clear that physically we also need stimulation and contact comfort.

10. Abraham Maslow's hierarchy of needs ranks our needs in a pyramid of importance. Most basic are physiological and safety needs, followed by needs for belongingness and self-esteem. At the top is the need for self-actualization.

11. Psychological motivation involves learned needs. These include a need for affiliation, a need for approval, and a need for achievement.

12. Firstborn children enjoy a very slight edge over later-born children in academic achievement, although other factors are also involved.

13. People around the world share certain basic emotions, which are communicated through specific facial expressions, but cultural variations exist as well.

14. According to opponent-process theory, the presence of one emotion triggers the later appearance of its opposite.

15. Thought processes and emotions affect each other. Emotional intelligence is the ability to properly feel, deal with, and recognize emotions.

16. The James-Lange theory of emotion claims that the body is stirred up first and then the emotion is felt. The Cannon-Bard theory says that the thalamus causes both the body and the emotion to be stirred up at the same time. Schachter's cognitive theory suggests that we label a particular excited state of the body with a certain name, so emotion is actually a cognitive process.

Vocabulary

motivation	goal	belongingness needs
emotion	homeostasis	self-esteem needs
hypothalamus	blood-sugar level	self-actualization needs
amygdala	glucose	need for affiliation
reticular formation	set point	need for approval
pituitary gland	curiosity motive	need for achievement
adrenal glands	manipulation motive	opponent-process theory
gonads	intrinsic motivation	cognition
testes	extrinsic motivation	emotional intelligence
ovaries	contact comfort	James-Lange theory
androgens	hierarchy of needs	Cannon-Bard theory
estrogen	physiological needs	cognitive theory
drives	safety needs	

Review Questions

For each of the following, answer R *for reticular formation,* P *for pituitary gland, or* A *for adrenal gland.*

1. Helps us react in emergencies
2. Regulates level of activity in the body
3. Signals other glands to release chemicals
4. Located just below the hypothalamus
5. Releases chemicals that affect heart rate
6. Controls sleep

Fill in the Blank

On a sheet of paper write the word or words that best complete each statement.

7. The female hormone is called ▨▨▨.
8. Sex glands are called ▨▨▨.
9. ▨▨▨ regulates the female reproductive cycle.
10. Male hormones are called ▨▨▨.
11. The part of the brain that controls aggression and fear is called ▨▨▨.

True/False

On a sheet of paper answer each statement true *or* false. *If false, rewrite to make it true.*

12. Stomach contractions cause hunger.
13. Low blood-sugar level causes hunger.
14. High blood-sugar level causes hunger.
15. Humans can store excess water for up to 48 hours.
16. We are born with certain body-weight set points, and they do not change with age.
17. A person's set point is partly determined by fat cells.
18. Inherited factors may lead to weight problems.
19. The hypothalamus regulates both hunger and thirst.
20. The James-Lange theory assumes that the body reacts first and then an emotion is produced.

155

Discussion Questions

1. The chapter mentions that eating involves special rituals. Analyze your own family's meals, taking into account both past and present gatherings. What "rituals" does your family seem to follow? What do these rituals say about your family? Have the rituals changed over the years?

2. Do you think that, in general, motivation changes as you get older? If so, in what ways does it change? Be specific. If not, provide examples to show that motivation does not change.

3. Imagine that someone gave you $100 for each "A" that you received on your report card. First, do you think that the money would motivate you? Why or why not? Second, assume that the money did motivate you. Would you actually learn more?

4. Besides money, what motivates adults you know to work every day? Which motivators are more important—money or the ones you've just listed?

5. Think about Maslow's hierarchy of needs in terms of your own life. Which needs have you adequately satisfied? Explain. (If you have indeed satisfied these needs, you don't spend much time thinking about them.) Which needs are you currently trying to satisfy? Explain. (These are needs that you do spend a great deal of time thinking about.)

6. According to Maslow, self-actualizers are people who strive to do their best, strive to reach their potential. If you look around, you'll probably agree that very few people consistently arrive at this level. Why not? Offer several reasons or explanations.

7. What is your birth order, and how do you think this order has affected your personality? If you don't believe birth order has much effect on people's personalities, explain your ideas.

8. If you had to assess your own emotional intelligence according to Goleman's ideas, what conclusions would you draw? In other words, how aware are you of your own emotions? Do you do a good job of reading others' emotions? How well do you manage your emotions? Be sure to offer examples.

9. Write down five or six fairly basic emotions. Think about your friends, family, and teachers. Do they express these emotions differently? Describe the similarities and differences in emotional expression. What types of events or situations produce which emotions?

Activities and Projects

1. Make a list of everything that you ate yesterday. Next to each food item, write I if the item was eaten primarily because of internal cues (for example, you were hungry), or write E if the item was eaten primarily because of external cues (it was time to eat, everyone else was eating, the food was there, and so on). For some items, both I and E may apply. In this case, pick the cue that seemed dominant, or stronger, at the time.

   Analyze your list. Is there a pattern? Do you eat for different reasons at different times of the day, for instance? Which cues seem to play a greater role in your eating habits? Explain.

   If there is a pattern, it may have something to do with your family life. To find out, conduct a brief survey. Interview the person who does the grocery shopping and/or cooking for your household. Have this person make a list of everything he or she ate the day before. After the list is made, explain to this person about internal and external cues, and then have the person mark each item I or E, just as you did for yourself.

   Did a pattern develop in your interviewee's answers? Compare these answers with your own answers. Can you draw any conclusions? Is there too much food in your house? The wrong kinds of food? Explain.

2. Conduct an experiment to find out the influence of visual external cues on eating. Buy a package of cookies or some other snack that your family likes. One day, leave the snack on the table, the kitchen counter, or somewhere else very visible, and see how many cookies are eaten by the end of the day. Wait a few days, and buy the same snack. This time, make sure somehow that everyone knows about the snack, but stick it in a drawer or in the refrigerator or somewhere else that is *not* very visible. But don't hide it; everyone should know where it is. Again, count how many cookies are eaten by the end of the day. Compare your results. Discuss your conclusions.

3. Some people feel that Maslow's theory has had an effect on the world of advertising. To understand how, collect 20 magazine ads, all for different products. Then take a sheet of paper, number it from 1 to 20, and divide it into three columns. Label the columns as follows: *Product; Need the Product Satisfies;* and *Needs* (notice plural) *the Ad Appeals to.* For example, the first entry might look like this:

Product	Need the Product Satisfies	Needs the Ad Appeals to
1. Brand X soda	physiological need	belongingness needs, self-esteem needs

In other words, soda satisfies a basic physiological need: thirst. Advertisers, however, in order to sell their products, appeal to our belongingness needs: They present images of friends having a good time. They also appeal to our self-esteem needs: They use slogans like "It'll make you feel better about yourself." Next, analyze your chart. How different are the second and third columns? Do any patterns develop in either column? If so, how do you account for this? Did your results turn out as expected, or were you surprised? Explain.

4. Write a personal essay in which you examine your needs for affiliation, approval, and achievement—and how those needs have changed over the last few years. Which need seems to motivate you the most? Essays of this kind usually turn out to be a process of self-discovery, and we hope that's the case for you. Here are a few writing tips to keep in mind: (a) Provide plenty of examples: "I joined wrestling because I wanted to feel part of a team." "I said no to get my friends' approval." "I worked hard to become captain." (b) Don't simply list what you've done to meet your needs. Develop each example. (c) Include concrete details in your descriptions. If you're describing the time you joined a band, describe how your band sounded, looked, and so on.

5. Ask one of your teachers if you can administer to the class a survey you've written. The main purpose of the survey is to see if firstborns really do enjoy greater success in school, but you can assess other factors as well. Before you administer your survey, show it to several people to make sure the questions are clear. Also, make sure your survey looks polished; if it seems like you haven't taken the survey seriously, neither will the people you select. You will probably want to avoid too many open-ended questions that require participants to fill in the blank. (Imagine trying to make sense of 60 different answers.) After collecting all your data, write a report on any patterns or absence of patterns you notice. Include a chart or two to summarize all your data.

Possible questions:

What is your sex? What is your age?

Do you have any brothers or sisters?

If you have brothers or sisters, list the sex and age of each one. Indicate if any of them are stepbrothers or stepsisters.

Have you joined a club or a sport in the last two years?

Do you consider yourself (a) very shy, (b) somewhat shy, (c) not usually shy, or (d) not shy at all?

Consciousness

In daily life, we continuously change from one state of consciousness to another. The unseen world of body chemistry controls our levels of awareness as well as our bodily processes as we go through the day. We never remain in the same state of consciousness for very long.

Defining Consciousness

Years ago, a teacher told one of us that we couldn't prove that a rock rolling down a hill didn't know where it was going. The whole class sat there and looked at him. We didn't know what to say. In a way, though, he had a point. Exactly what is consciousness? It is a lot harder to define than you might think at first; we can't touch it, find it, or pick it up. It is a **construct.** A construct is a concept that requires a belief in something that cannot be seen or touched but that, according to evidence, actually is present.

Some investigators in the 1500s came up with an idea for measuring consciousness. They took people who were obviously dying and put them on large scales. Researchers were stationed in front of the scales at all times. The moment the person died, they watched the dial in order to measure any weight difference when the "soul" or "consciousness" left the body. As you might have guessed, no change occurred. Consciousness must not weigh anything—or at least it is so light we don't have any way of recording it. Yet it seems obvious that it is there.

We will do the best we can with a definition: **Consciousness** is the organism's awareness of, or possibility of knowing, what is going on inside or outside itself. This definition fits the fact that we can receive stimulation, analyze it, and then take some action.

Consciousness: A Map of the Self in Relation to the World

Consciousness (for both humans and animals) is believed to involve our making a "map" of where we are in space and then more or less seeing ourselves on this map. Notice that when you think about something you did a while back, you actually seem to be watching yourself from the outside. Or if you want to, you can move inside the "you" that you are remembering and "look out" as you imagine doing what you did before. We think consciousness involves just such a series of stored and viewed images of ourselves. In other words, as we move about, different scenes—some from the environment, some from memory—flash before us, then fade and are instantly

◀ *The images in our conscious mind are constantly changing.*

Focus Questions
....

• What is consciousness?

• How do psychologists explain different levels of awareness?

construct a concept requiring a belief in something that cannot be seen or touched but that seems to exist

consciousness the organism's awareness of, or possibility of knowing, what is happening inside or outside itself

replaced by the next scene. Some of them are stored in memory for later use. This situation is a great deal like a motion picture at the theater. Movies are nothing more than a series of thousands of fixed images flashed one after the other on the screen so it looks to us as if the people are alive and moving. Thus, all day long, we combine millions of brief memory images of ourselves with our current images of the world, and we call this consciousness.

Levels of Consciousness

We are not necessarily conscious of everything we do. For example, experiments show that sometimes, when we are going to reach for something or get up and walk around, our brain circuits for these acts may fire *before* we consciously know we are going to do anything. Similarly, if a "forbidden" word is flashed on a screen in front of people very rapidly and then removed, the people's brains will respond electrically even if the people claim they didn't see the word. In such cases, it is likely that a kind of censoring has taken place, even though the people are not aware they are doing it (Loftus & Klinger, 1992). The level of awareness in these examples is called the **subconscious,** meaning consciousness just below our present awareness.

An example of subconscious thought would be a very vague feeling that for some unknown reason, the people around you at a party are acting strangely toward you. You don't put the feeling into words; and for the most part, you ignore it. Still, you feel vaguely uncomfortable or worried. You don't realize that you have *noticed* people's strange behavior toward you until you get home and start to wonder why you didn't have a very good time at the party. Then you remember what your subconscious picked up (and you wonder if maybe you had bad breath or something).

Some psychologists believe that we also have an even deeper level of awareness called the **unconscious.** The unconscious contains thoughts, information, or desires about which we have no true or direct knowledge (Greenwald, 1992). Unconscious thought is very easy to see in children. For example, a jealous brother keeps undoing the bolts on his brother's bicycle; but when caught, he really can't explain why he does it—even to himself.

The unconscious may not be as mysterious as it first appears to be. Some researchers believe that it provides us with what we refer to as *intuition*—thought that does not necessarily rely on logic and rational evaluation of events. A lot of information we take in is processed at an unconscious level (Epstein, 1994). For example, some of you may have worked the "jumbled words" puzzles in newspapers. In these puzzles, a meaningless series of letters can be turned into a word, if put in the proper order. If a puzzle is very difficult, we usually resort to a systematic approach. Often, though, we can come up with the answer almost instantly, without even being aware of exactly how we did it. For example, what does this spell?

DBRI

If you answered BIRD without going through it letter by letter, trying every possible combination, you probably processed this puzzle at an unconscious level. And you may have no idea how you came up with the right answer.

▲ *Are these people subconsciously aware that something strange is going on?*

subconscious consciousness just below our present awareness

unconscious thoughts or desires about which we have no direct knowledge

Unseen Forces

Focus Question

....

• What unseen forces control every living thing on Earth?

Many of us spend money to be scared out of our wits by a horror movie. If you stop and think about it, what makes the horror movie so exciting is that there are things hidden in the background—the unseen. We have a similar show going on around us all the time—and it's not only free but far more fascinating than the best of horror films. This is because it is real: All creatures are controlled by bodily rhythms and cycles, forces that none of us can see or feel. The most obvious effects are those involving night and day cycles: The rat, hamster, and beloved cockroach awaken and wander around during the night, while the squirrel, sparrow, chicken, and human come out during the day.

There are monthly cycles that can cause changes in feelings and moods. The best known of these is the female monthly cycle designed for reproduction, but females are not alone. While most males deny it, studies show that males also have a monthly cycle in which they become listless, slightly depressed, and "different from usual" for three or four days.

Finally, there are annual cycles in which people slow down and lose energy as summer approaches. And there are annual changes in weight, as well as in the chemical content of the body.

The most obvious annual rhythm in nature is bird migration. Birds don't fly south in order to be home for Thanksgiving; they are responding to a change in the light-dark cycle of the Earth as winter approaches. They perform this feat by using patterns of the stars as a guide during their flight. They are so accurate that some of them can go across country to the same 25-square-yard space they used the previous year. If the sky becomes overcast, built-in magnetic particles in their brains orient them to the Earth's magnetic field so they can stay on course. To date, no similar system has been found in humans, although some studies show that many people are able to orient themselves to north, south, east, and west.

◀ *Bird migration is triggered by changes in the light-dark cycle that signal a change in the season.*

Biological Clocks

biological clocks internal chemical units that control regular cycles in parts of the body

All creatures are under the control of **biological clocks.** These internal chemical units control parts of the body all by themselves and are programmed and regulated by nature. Even fetuses inside the mother have working biological clocks (Schwartz, 1984). Our internal temperature is run by one of these clocks, keeping us, when healthy, at plus or minus two degrees of the same temperature no matter what the weather outside of us is. The kidneys also operate independently. Their clock has to ignore the outside world because they must get rid of poisonous materials at regular intervals in order to protect us. Those clocks that ignore the environment use what are called **free-running cycles,** because they are under their own control.

free-running cycles cycles set up by biological clocks that are under their own control, ignoring the environment

Some clock systems can be changed. An example is the sleep-wake cycle. The sleep-wake cycle in humans is free running at birth. Babies start off driving everyone crazy because they want to eat and sleep at odd times during the day and night. After about 20 exhausting weeks, parents have usually trained the babies to fit the adults' schedule. This process of altering the free-running cycle is called **entrainment** (as in "training").

entrainment the process of altering the free-running cycle to fit a different rhythm

In Focus

Natural Cycles and Entrainment

The human body goes through a natural 25-hour sleep-wake cycle.

Earth, however, moves on a natural 24-hour light-dark cycle.

Through the process of entrainment, the human body adapts to this 24-hour cycle.

What factors tend to interfere with entrainment?

The human body has a natural rhythm that free-runs on a cycle of about 25 hours. If we lived in a cave (which some psychologists have done to prove the point), our body rhythms would go through a 25-hour cycle of sleep and wakefulness, of various chemical changes, and of the need for food or water. In other words, within 25 hours, each process would make a complete cycle of its own. This only works for a while, though. If the daily periods of light and darkness are not properly reproduced as part of the program, eventually these cycles no longer apply. In any event, away from the cave, each of us has to entrain to the Earth, which has a light-dark cycle of only 24 hours. The body can adjust to this one-hour change with little trouble, but some of you may spend the weekend doing everything you can to destroy this learned rhythm, putting it off by many hours. The result of changing your rhythm even by an hour or two can be a genuinely awful feeling come Monday morning.

You may have run across pamphlets, articles, and books that claim to be able to tell your personality and future based on "biorhythms." These have no scientific validity and are similar to fortune-telling.

Circadian Rhythms. Every living thing on Earth is controlled by the unseen forces that we call biological clocks. For example, there are plants that open up in the morning and close at night. Many think this happens so that the plants can get sunlight. Not so. If you take these plants into a lead-lined vault, they will open and close on schedule every 24 hours with no light at all. The plant is operating on what is called a **circadian rhythm.** *Circa* means "about" and *dian* means "a day," so the plant is changing its behavior twice in "about a day."

The human circadian rhythm is based on an entrained 24-hour cycle. Within that cycle, we have a high point and a low point. For most people, the lowest point (low temperature, low blood pressure, weakness, and so

circadian rhythm sequences of behavioral changes that occur every 24 hours

▲ *Morning-glories are aptly named—they open up at sunrise.*

▲ *Flying from the United States to Russia is guaranteed to give you jet lag.*

forth) is between 3 A.M. and 5 A.M. That is why, if you wake up at that time, even on a hot summer's night, you will feel cold and shiver. Although not everyone has the same rhythm, most of us come close. What happens if it is ignored?

Fighting the Clock. A Boeing 707 approached Los Angeles International Airport. The pilots had slept the previous day, but their home city—and basic rhythms—were set for a time that made it 3 A.M. for them when they arrived in the Los Angeles area. The people in the control tower watched in horror as the plane stayed at 32,000 feet instead of landing. It flew on out over the ocean. The staff in the control tower made noises through the radio to awaken the crew, all three of whom had fallen asleep while the plane was on automatic pilot. They awoke with just enough fuel to get back to the airport and land (Coleman, 1986).

A study of 30 pilots for Airline X found that the pilots started to fall asleep while flying on an average of 32 times a month. Fortunately, rarely do they all fall asleep at the same time. Some pilots keep a kitchen timer in the cockpit, and they set it in order to keep themselves awake (Winfree, 1987; Moore-Ede, 1986). These pilots are competent, but the airlines are asking them to fight nature, and that's hard to do at 3 A.M. with the steady sound and gentle rocking of the aircraft. Thus, the fact that you get some sleep is not always as important as *when* you get that sleep. A person can change his or her basic rhythm so that the low point comes during the day, but this takes months to do; and airlines, hospitals, police departments, and factories rarely let it happen, since they keep changing the workers' hours.

 ## Pause for Thought

1. Why is consciousness a construct?
2. What is the difference between the unconscious and the subconscious?
3. What is the length of the human circadian rhythm?

Critical Thinking
....
4. Pretend that you've been asked to speak to a company that uses workers around the clock. What kinds of suggestions would you offer to ensure alert and productive workers?

The Nature of Sleep and Dreams

Focus Questions

- What are some physiological changes that occur during sleep?
- Does REM sleep have stages?

It may seem that we simply get tired and go to sleep. But it's much more complicated than that. Sleep is far from just a time of peacefulness and relaxation. Only the first hour could be viewed this way, since it contains the deepest period of sleep. During this period, there is a dramatic fall in blood pressure, heart rate, and breathing. During the rest of the night, many unexpected events occur.

When we first lie down, electrical activity in the brain begins to slow. This is a period called the **twilight state,** with images and thoughts drifting in front of us, probably the one time during the day when we can totally relax and let the mind wander. Before you know it, you are heading for your deepest sleep.

There is no question that sleep helps restore the body. The making of new cells is at its maximum. Chemicals the brain has used up during the day are restored. This is also the time when body hair grows most rapidly.

twilight state relaxed state just before we fall asleep

REM Sleep

The most important purpose of sleep—dreaming—is something of a surprise. Let's look at what happens to each of us every single night—four or five times. The brain begins to fire furiously; blood pressure zooms upward; our eyes move rapidly from side to side and up and down; breathing and heartbeat are very rapid—all within a paralyzed body. This is called REM sleep.

Sleep is not a single state of consciousness involving only a single behavior. It can be divided roughly into two major types: The first is REM sleep, and the second is NREM sleep, which we'll discuss in just a bit.

REM (pronounced as one word, "rem") stands for *rapid eye movement;* and **REM sleep** is that period when our eyes are moving about in all directions within the eye sockets. You can watch this in action with dogs and cats. They have a REM period every 30 minutes or so after they first fall asleep. You can watch your friends or members of your family. You can actually see their eyeballs rotating in the sockets. They will have a REM period about every 90 minutes from the time they fall asleep until morning. If those you are watching are *really* in REM, you will not awaken them unless you call their names or make a *lot* of noise. In fact, as mentioned, they are paralyzed. Most likely, you have had a number of dreams in which you were trying to get away from an attacker but were unable to move your legs to run. That's because you *couldn't* move your legs—literally. Sleepwalking, which we will discuss later, does not occur during REM.

How long do REM periods or dreams last? You may have heard that dreams are over in about a second. That's not true. The actual dream lasts as long as it *seems* to take—around 5 to 40 minutes. Throughout the night, REM periods occur roughly every 90 minutes, with each REM lasting longer

REM sleep rapid eye movement sleep; the stage of sleep when dreams occur

▲ *Even dogs experience REM sleep.*

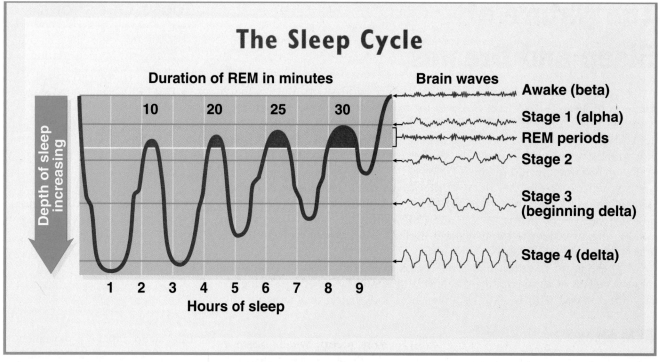

▲ Figure 6.1 *The Sleep Cycle*

than the previous one. Figure 6.1 shows the typical pattern of a night's sleep. Note that REM periods come during times when we are *not* in deep sleep. Also notice that as the night progresses, sleep gets lighter. The chances are that the dreams you remember are those coming closest to the morning. That's because they are the longest, they have occurred most recently, and you are the closest to being awake when you have them.

Brain Changes During Sleep

We need to pause here and give you an overview of the whole cycle of sleep, dreams, and the changes that occur during this time period. In addition to the waking state, there are five brain-wave patterns and corresponding stages of consciousness (REM and stages 1 through 4). These are shown in Figure 6.1, with the typical brain-wave pattern shown next to each stage of sleep.

Using the figure as a guide, first look at the brain waves running from the top to the bottom of the right-hand chart, comparing awake (**beta waves**) with relaxed (stage 1, called **alpha waves**), and with the deepest sleep (stage 4, **delta waves**). Notice that the deeper the sleep is, the slower the brain-wave pattern is. In fact, the delta waves in stage 4 are very slow and regular.

The graph shows the typical pattern of a night's sleep, starting at the top. Before bed we are awake (beta). We get into bed and relax (stage 1, alpha). As we begin to enter a twilight state, we are moving into stage 2, and the alpha waves disappear. Stage 3 is next as we drift into deeper sleep. Finally, we reach the deepest delta-wave sleep (stage 4). If you look to the left in Figure 6.1, you will note that by the time you reach stage 4, you are about one hour into sleep. At this point, you begin to go in reverse, heading from stage 4 back toward stage 1. Before the second hour, how-

beta waves rapid brain waves; appear when a person is awake

alpha waves fairly relaxed brain waves that occur in stage 1, just before we go to sleep

delta waves slow, lazy, deep-sleep brain waves

ever, when you would be arriving back at the regular stage 1 (relaxed alpha), something unusual happens. Instead of going into the regular stage 1, you enter stage 1 REM; this is rapid eye movement, or dream, sleep. The first dream of the night occurs, lasting about 10 minutes. You will not enter the stage 1 relaxed phase again until you awaken in the morning. Thus, the rest of the night, you will go from stage 1 REM to stage 4 and back again. Notice also that the length of dreams increases through the night, so that the last dream toward morning will be close to 30 minutes long.

Looking at Figure 6.1, you might assume that REM periods are similar to awake periods. The brain-wave patterns look very much alike. But a person in stage 1 REM is almost impossible to awaken. Not only that, but as mentioned, the person in this dream stage has periods of paralysis; it is very difficult even to get a reflex from him or her. The similarity of brain waves in the two stages probably reflects the fact that during dreams, the brain is very active, just as it would be if we were awake and looking around (beta). In any case, we clearly are not part of the waking world during REM sleep.

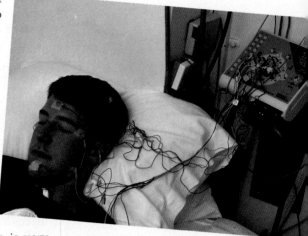

▲ *Believe it or not, this man can actually sleep with all those wires attached to his head as he snoozes in a sleep lab.*

NREM Sleep

The second type of sleep is called **NREM sleep,** which stands for *non–rapid eye movement sleep.* In Figure 6.1, all of the sleep below the white line is NREM sleep. During this "non REM sleep," the brain is still active, providing partial thoughts, images, and stories. But they do not have the organization of the "stories" found during REM activity.

When you are asleep, then, if you are not in REM, you are in NREM. NREM seems to be the time when the brain goes into "idle." Its operations are still going on, but they are neither at the level of wakefulness nor at that of REM dreaming. Some researchers think that this is the time when

NREM sleep non–rapid eye movement sleep; sleep involving partial thoughts, images, or stories that are poorly organized

In Focus

Comparing REM to NREM Periods of Sleep

REM	NREM
Rapid eye movement	Non–rapid eye movement
Increases in length as night's sleep progresses	Decreases in length as night's sleep progresses
Vivid dreams	Vague, partial images and stories
Nightmares	Night terrors
Paralyzed body	Sleepwalking and talking in sleep
Essential part of sleep	Less essential part of sleep

In your estimation, during which period would a child most likely wet the bed?

the body rests. Another process takes place during deep NREM sleep. For adolescents, deep sleep is especially important, because this is when the growth hormone is secreted. This is one reason why many adolescents sleep so much.

Focus Question

• What are three reasons psychologists offer for why we dream?

The Purpose of Dreaming

Some people claim they never dream, but that is probably not true. What is far more likely is that they do not remember their dreams. People do differ in how much of their dreams they recall (Rochlen, Ligiera, Hill, & Heaton, 1999). Dreaming seems to be necessary for our general well-being.

There are three major hypotheses about why we dream. Evidence supports all of them, so they can sit side by side at this stage of our knowledge.

The first hypothesis is that dreams are used to get the brain reorganized after a day's work of thinking and dealing with problems. This makes sense because we know that brain chemicals are used up during the day. Notice how hard it is to study on nights when you have done a lot of mental work during the day. To restore the chemicals, we have to cut off the outside world in order to keep new problems—which would require more work—from getting in. The brain, however, cannot remain inactive. So dreams keep the brain busy with old material while it is being recharged, so to speak.

The second hypothesis is that dreams are designed to help work out unsolved problems left over from the day. You can find evidence for this in something that has happened to almost everyone. You go to bed with a problem of some sort that you haven't been able to solve—maybe in math or history, or maybe a personal problem. When you wake up the

Focus

Three Major Theories about Why We Dream

To process information:

Brain chemicals are used up during the day. While the brain replenishes these chemicals, dreams process the past day or week or more.

To work out unsolved problems:

We go to bed with a problem. When we wake up, the problem is solved (or forgotten—which in itself may be a solution).

To make sense of random stimulation to the brain:

While we sleep, the brain flushes out the garbage we don't need. In the process, the brain is stimulated in a random or "crazy" way. So we dream to make sense of the random stimulation.

If you were an experimental psychologist, how might you test the validity of each theory?

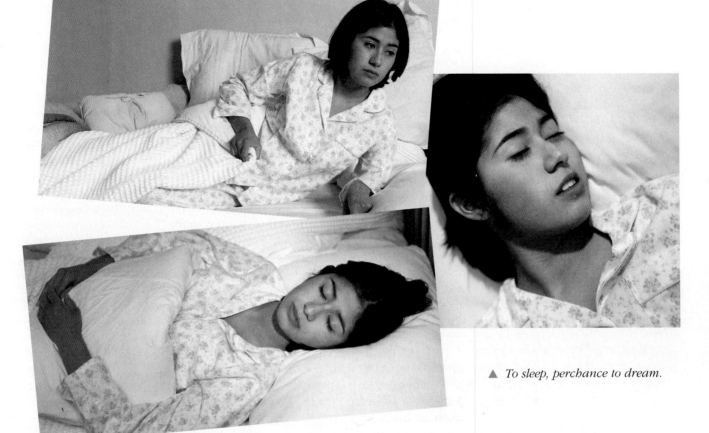

▲ *To sleep, perchance to dream*.

next morning, there's the solution, as obvious as can be. When we are under stress or depressed, we sleep longer, and the amount of time spent in REM increases. This fact strongly suggests that we are working on the things that are worrying us while we dream.

The third explanation comes from today's emphasis on the computer. It is possible that we get too much unnecessary material in our "files" from the day's tasks. Thus, dreams result from electrical realignments, revising, and updating going on in the brain. As various electrical circuits are being fired, different memory circuits are being triggered. The brain is trying to make sense of the bits and pieces of information that are appearing while we are cleaning out the material, so it makes up a "story" to fit them, and we have a dream. This would account for why we so often put odd things together in a dream.

There is one thing missing in our coverage to this point. What actually causes dreams, since there is no external stimulation? First, remember that all our memories, thoughts, and actions are controlled by electrical impulses within the brain. Add to this the fact that electrical bursts occur in cycles throughout the night. These bursts come from deep within the brain at regular intervals (90-minute cycles). Special brain cells turn them on and off. The electrical impulses move upward, hitting various portions of the upper brain, firing different memory circuits. The result is what we call dreams. These bursts also cause eye movements. We are not "watching" our dreams. Even people without sight from birth have rapid eye movements, but the content of their dreams centers on sound and touch (Coleman, 1986).

....

- What did Freud think about dreams?

- Do we dream in color or in black and white?

Psychology of Dreams

Throughout history, dreams have been considered mystical and, in some cases, able to predict the future. There is no scientific evidence to support such claims. Since we know that dreams are made when electrical impulses cause the firing of our own memory circuits, it is obvious that the material is coming directly from us. If coming from us, then we should be able to tell the future just as much when we're awake as during a dream—if the future can be known. It also seems unlikely that dreams tell us much more about ourselves than we already know. A dream *can* trigger a memory that we have forgotten or deal with something that we hadn't paid much attention to, but this is far different from receiving a special secret message.

Sigmund Freud analyzed dreams to find clues to his patients' inner thoughts and forbidden impulses. He believed that dreams were symbolic expressions of our unconscious conflicts. You may be surprised to learn that Freud sometimes did psychoanalysis by mail. In one of his most famous cases, he cured a boy of an irrational fear through correspondence.

Dream Content

Most dreams, most of the time, are about very ordinary events. We dream about things from a normal day: family, friends, and school. Dreams also contain a lot of material about worries, fears, or feeling inferior, because these are concerns we all have. And often, dreams involve an argument. The good part about these kinds of dreams is that in them, we almost always turn out to be right. That's not hard to understand, since we're usually convinced we're right in the waking state. Still, it's nice to have our dreams agree with us.

While 70 percent of our dreams are about people we actually know, there are also other unexpected common images in dreams. For example, 40 percent of females dream about the sea or bodies of water, while only 27 percent of males do. Falling or being chased in a dream is very common and occurs about equally for males and females. Sex and romance are likewise typical. And the following themes occur with some frequency among completely normal males and females: violence, talking to dead friends or relatives, shoplifting, finding yourself naked in public, and discovering the "secret of the

In Their Own Words . . .

Recently, letters have come to light in which **Sigmund Freud** *interpreted a woman's dream by mail (Benjamin & Dixon, 1996). The young woman wrote that she was in love with an Italian man her parents disliked. In her dream, the man's brother gave her a letter saying that her sweetheart had married someone else. Despairing, she stabbed herself in the heart but felt no pain. In fact, she felt wonderful. She awoke depressed and upset. Here is part of Freud's reply:*

Now for the little I can grasp of the hidden meaning of your dream. I see your emotions towards the young Italian are not undivided, not free from conflict. Besides the love you feel for him there is a trend of perhaps distrust, perhaps remorse. This antagonistic feeling is covered up during your wake life by the love-attraction you undergo and by another motive, your resistance against your parents. Perhaps if your parents did not dislike the boy, it would be much easier for you to become aware of the splitting in your feelings. So you are in a conflict about him and the dream is a way out of the maze. To be sure, you will not leave him and fulfill your parents' request. But if he drops you this is a solution. I guess that is the meaning of the dream and your emotional reaction is produced by the intensity of your love while the content of the dream is the result of the repressed antagonism which yet is active in your soul. (As quoted in Benjamin & Dixon, 1996, p. 465)

Interpreting Primary Sources

Freud wrote that besides love, the young woman probably felt distrust or remorse towards her sweetheart. What event in the woman's dream do you think led to his conclusion?

▲ *The first dream looks like a winner. As for the other two—well, both our wishes and our fears often appear in dreams.*

universe"—which unfortunately we forget by the time we wake up (Evans & Evans, 1983).

Bizarre dreams also occur. Usually the core of the dream is reasonable, but the story winds up happening in a strange place or with people you don't expect. Thus, ugly Uncle Harry is seen starring as the handsome leading man in a romantic movie. We suspect these strange combinations occur from the random nature of the electrical firing, putting things together we normally would not allow if we were awake and in control. Strange dreams do *not* mean something is wrong with you. The only time you should be concerned is if the same dream occurs over and over and really is bothersome. Then it's time to sit down with a friend and try to figure out what it means. It will probably then disappear, as long as you don't let it worry you.

The concept that dreams are symbolic or represent deep, hidden impulses, needs, or desires has been around forever. Even world leaders have been known to guide their movements by dreams. The story goes that Abraham Lincoln had dream warnings that it was dangerous for him to go to Ford's Theatre, where he was later assassinated. Most, but not all, researchers today believe that dream content of this sort is just a reflection of daytime, waking concerns that appear at night. They do not believe that dreams are the result of some special message from another world or from our own unconscious world.

Finally, something we don't understand at all: about 50 percent of our dreams are in color, and about 50 percent are in black and white. Despite numerous experiments, we can't figure out why this is so. No, we don't even have a guess. It's not related either to the scenes in the dream or to the amount of color we see when awake. Researchers have even put colored filters over people's eyes for a week to see if that makes a difference, but it doesn't change the proportion of color in their dreams.

Focus Question

• • • • • • • • • • • • • • • • • • • •

• What is the difference between nightmares and night terrors?

nightmare frightening dream that occurs during REM

REM rebound increase in the number of dreams after being deprived of REM sleep

night terror a horrible dream occurring during NREM, when the body is not prepared for it; also called an *incubus attack*

Nightmares

Two frightening experiences can occur during sleep. The first happens during REM and is called the **nightmare.** Fortunately, nightmares are infrequent; only about 5 percent of the population have them as often as once a week. The odds that all of us will have a nightmare on occasion are very high, though, since we all carry around bad memories that can be triggered. Nightmares are more likely when people have missed REM periods for a day or so from drinking too much alcohol or not getting enough sleep. The reason nightmares appear then is that if REM is blocked, **REM rebound** occurs. REM rebound refers to the fact that the first time we go to sleep after being deprived of REM, both the length and the number of dreams increase (rebound) dramatically to make up for the loss. Hence, the chances of having unpleasant dreams increase. In general, however, we have no evidence that nightmares indicate something is wrong with the person. They seem to be just part of dreaming. And despite the fact that you will hear the rumor frequently, nightmares are not caused by eating something strange.

Night Terrors

The second frightening experience during sleep is another kind of dream, one that you may have been lucky enough to avoid. It is called a **night terror,** a horrible dream that is quite vivid and real.

What makes night terrors so awful is that they occur during NREM, not REM. The body knows that a regular dream is coming every 90 minutes and prepares for it, but the body is caught completely unprepared by an unpleasant dream that is triggered during NREM. The physical overload it

In Focus

Comparing Nightmares to Night Terrors

Nightmares	Night Terrors
Occur during REM, usually during the second half of the night	Occur during NREM, usually during the first hour of sleep
Mild physiological changes	Drastic bodily changes: breathing and heart rate rise dramatically
Associated with vivid images	Associated with panic
Most likely to occur during REM rebound	Most likely to occur in children

Why do nightmares usually occur during the second half of the night?

◀ *Being a child is not always fun, especially when the monsters are after you.*

causes sets off major bodily changes. Breathing rate zooms upward, the person feels choked, and heart rate takes off to an unbelievable 170-plus beats a minute. These events create a feeling of panic and a fear of dying. The sleeper usually springs up in bed, sweating, nauseated, and afraid.

Night terrors are fairly common in very young children. For some unknown reason, these dreams seem to be connected with a maturing brain. Thus, in general, night terrors should probably *not* be treated by a professional, since all that would do is call attention to them and frighten the child even more. The child will most likely grow out of them. If night terrors occur with any frequency beyond middle adolescence, however, the chances are good that something physical is wrong, and this should not be ignored. A physical exam is clearly in order.

 ## Pause for Thought

1. Describe a typical sleep cycle for one night.
2. What are three hypotheses about why we dream?
3. What are some of Freud's main beliefs about dreaming?

Critical Thinking
. . . .
4. Neighbor A has a son who suffers night terrors. Neighbor B has a daughter who has been having nightmares. Explain how the two problems differ and why everything will probably be OK.

Case Study

Losing Sleep

Two famous cases highlight the dangers of staying awake for long stretches of time (Coren, 1996).

In 1959, New York disc jockey Peter Tripp announced he would raise money for charity by staying awake for 200 hours. He spent most of his time in an army recruiting booth so that people passing on the street could watch his progress. He ignored doctors' warnings about pursuing his goal but did agree to let them examine him every so often. As you might expect, Tripp's ordeal was a bumpy ride. He hit some deep lows, but he was also able to present his three-hour radio broadcast each day, which probably means he could adjust his biological clock to some extent, even under these circumstances. By the fourth day he had a difficult time completing even simple tasks like reciting the alphabet. He thought spots on the table were bugs and imagined spiders in his radio booth. Near the end of his marathon, he believed that one of his doctors wanted to bury him alive and ran away from him in terror. When he finally got to sleep, he dozed for thirteen hours, and his mood returned to normal.

In 1964, a young man from San Diego, Randy Gardner, decided he would stay awake for 264 hours for a school science fair. That's eleven days, if you're counting! Like Tripp, Gardner experienced wide-ranging highs and lows. The people who were with him during the more normal periods reported that Gardner suffered no ill effects from staying awake so long and, for years afterward, others were led to believe that maybe sleep isn't so crucial after all. In fact, Gardner experienced many of the same symptoms as Tripp. After only the second day, he had trouble focusing and wouldn't watch TV for the rest of his time awake. He couldn't concentrate well, and his memory was often terrible. One time, a psychologist who was monitoring Gardner asked him to begin at 100 and keep subtracting seven. After a few subtractions, Gardner stopped and seemed to be struggling for the next number, then couldn't even remember what he was supposed to be doing. His speech was often slurred; his thinking became confused. At various points in his experiment, he also suffered delusions, believing one time that he was a famous black football player and misinterpreting others' remarks as racist. When he finally reached his goal, he slept for almost fifteen hours and woke up feeling normal.

Although both men suffered no long-term damage, they were clearly setting themselves up for a host of potential problems. Rats deprived of sleep during laboratory experiments die after about three weeks. Curiously, autopsies fail to pinpoint an exact cause of death in these cases. So why is sleep so important? One possible answer may involve REM, or dream sleep. Maybe we sleep so we can dream; maybe dreams are that essential. If people are awakened, for example, every time they are about to have a dream, they feel as bad as if they had had no sleep at all. The importance of dreams is also shown by the fact that nearly all creatures—except for one species of bird—have what appear to be dream periods. Elephants, cows, rats, mice, cats, rabbits, and donkeys all have REM.

Review the Case Study

Describe several common symptoms you experience when you don't get enough sleep.

Practical Issues in Sleep

Focus Questions

• Does everyone need about the same amount of sleep?

• Are sleepwalkers really asleep?

• Is insomnia a common problem?

A person's patterns of sleep change as the years progress. Infants spend a good 75 percent of the time in REM sleep. The brain has so much building to do that chemicals are used up very quickly and need to be constantly restored. By adolescence, the brain is fully developed, but major physical and psychological changes are still going on. As a result, regular sleep is important—at least in theory. Adolescents usually have so many "social obligations" that their sleeping schedule is chaotic. Finally, toward old age, people require much less deep sleep, probably because of changes in the brain cells that control sleep. In this section, we deal with issues that apply to the teenage years through age 25.

Social Entrainment

Problems can arise from too much *social entrainment* of sleep cycles. Sometimes, for social purposes, we alter our rhythms—because, for example, we are going to too many parties, visiting too much, or "hanging out" too much. Just getting eight hours of sleep is not enough. Sleep has to come at the right point in the circadian cycle. Otherwise, the cycle gets off-balance, which in turn makes the person feel terrible and also leads to errors on the job or to trouble solving problems. If there is not enough REM, the body craves more. The longer this goes on, the harder it becomes to get back to a reasonable rhythm.

Length of Sleep

People differ in the amount of sleep they need each night. For most of us, though, the body tends to seek about seven to eight hours' worth. Some people need a little more and some a little less. You actually have to experiment to find out what the correct amount is. Almost no one can get by for any length of time with less than five hours of sleep a night. Teenagers need a little more sleep than adults do, between eight and nine hours a night. However, today teenagers average almost two hours less sleep than they did several decades ago (Holden, 1993). In fact, these days many people are sleeping less in order to do more. The effects of this trend are potentially quite harmful. Productivity suffers when people get too little sleep; it doesn't increase. And people are more prone to mental confusion and accidents when they are sleep deprived.

Although, on occasion, a normal person can sleep up to 17 hours a night, too much sleep doesn't work either (Winfree, 1987). After sleeping 11 hours, the brain is drowsy and we do poorly on tasks requiring alertness. Long sleepers (10 hours plus) also tend to die earlier than short sleepers (6 hours). But this is probably not related to sleep itself. For one thing, long sleepers are less active. Another factor centers on something we mentioned earlier: Those with problems need more REM, so they sleep more. If you worry a lot, your stress level is going to be much higher overall, and your body is more likely to give out earlier.

▲ *New mothers often have to catch a few hours' sleep whenever they can—not the most restful way to do it.*

▶ *Contrary to popular belief, it is not dangerous to waken a sleepwalker.*

Walking and Talking in Your Sleep

A fair number of people sleepwalk or talk in their sleep. Neither indicates something is wrong with them. On the side of the brain, there are specific areas that control body movements and speech (see Chapter 3). When random electrical impulses hit these areas, they cause walking or talking. Such behavior typically occurs during stage 4 sleep, a deep NREM sleep period, so the person is not really awake or making much sense. Trying to communicate is fruitless. You may have heard it is dangerous to awaken a sleepwalker. That's not true at all. Sleepwalkers are just asleep. Wake them up so they don't wander off and hurt themselves. Just be sure they're sitting or lying down first.

Sleep Disturbance

About 10 percent of adult Americans have trouble sleeping. Most such problems are self-created. Dogs and cats don't seem to have **insomnia** (in-SOM-nee-ah), the inability to get enough sleep.

insomnia the inability to get enough sleep

The two most common causes of insomnia are getting out of the normal circadian cycle and taking drugs or alcohol, especially before going to sleep. The irony is that these drugs (including "relaxers" or "sleeping pills") tend to block REM sleep. As a result, over a week or so, we are losing more and more REM sleep and feeling worse and less able to sleep. By the end of a week, we are starting to feel depressed. The more depressed we are, the more we need REM, and so forth. Really heavy alcohol use for an extended period of time can cause such severe REM rebound that dreams appear while the person is still awake—in a form like night terrors. Bugs seem to be attacking, snakes are crawling under the bed, and so forth. These are the result of continued heavy use of drugs or alcohol. On the other side, sometimes drugs can help bring on sleep for a very brief time after a trauma, such as a death in the family.

An infrequent problem that usually starts sometime in the teens or early twenties is **narcolepsy.** In this disorder, an individual can go into "instant" REM anywhere, anytime, even while driving a car or talking to someone. Thus, although rare, it is extremely dangerous, since the person immediately loses consciousness. Drugs are available that often help, so treatment is mandatory. We don't know the cause.

Another problem, usually with older people, is called **sleep apnea** (AP-nee-ah). The word *apnea* means "not breathing." Someone with this disorder literally stops breathing hundreds of times during sleep and keeps waking up. Normally, the person doesn't know this is happening.

narcolepsy disorder in which a person falls instantly into sleep no matter what is going on in the environment

sleep apnea condition in which a person's breathing often stops while the person is asleep

States of Consciousness

So far, we have discussed cycles everyone goes through in the normal course of events. We are all subject to biological rhythms that include deep sleep, dreams, and wakefulness. However, some states of consciousness do not occur naturally, such as hypnosis or meditation. They require effort or training. For this reason, they deserve a section of their own.

Hypnosis

Hypnosis has a colorful history. It involves being in a relaxed state with a heightened ability to focus on specific things while ignoring the usual distractions. Before we go on, it might help to give you a feel for why people think hypnosis is a strange and mysterious force. One of the words connected with "mystical" happenings that we still use is *mesmerize* (MEZ-mer-eyes), which means to put someone under your power. This term comes from Anton Mesmer, who worked in the late 1700s "curing" people of their ailments. Mesmer claimed that he had special magnetic powers and that people who needed help could have their body magnetism "realigned" if they came to him. He had an enormous bathtub filled with iron filings, water, and ground glass. Iron rods stuck out from the side of the tub, and the "sick" visitors were told to hold onto them. Mesmer then entered the room wearing colorful, flowing robes and touched the tub, claiming he was mixing his magnetism with theirs. Mesmer was clearly a quack, since for those who couldn't make it to his place, he sold bottles of his special magnetism for a "take-out" cure (Ellenberger, 1970).

The surprising thing is that many people were helped by this nonsense. We know today that such "cures" come from the power of suggestion. Suggestion is basic to hypnosis.

Focus Questions

• What are several facts and myths about hypnosis?

• Can people be hypnotized to do things against their wills?

hypnosis a state of relaxation in which attention is focused on certain objects, acts, or feelings

▲ *While hypnosis is real enough, much of the stage variety is just entertainment and its value is questionable.*

Thinking Critically about Psychology

Can We Relive Childhood?

O ccasionally, the media publicize claims that hypnosis is able to do extraordinary things. For instance, you will sometimes hear that witnesses to a crime can be hypnotized to better remember what happened. (As you will learn in Chapter 8, this is not the case.) A more outlandish notion is that through hypnosis we can gain access to previous lives. Such claims are usually fairly easily disproved. For instance, under hypnosis, a man reported that several hundred years ago he was a Japanese warrior. However, when questioned, he could not say who the Emperor of Japan was during that era. The fact is that every Japanese warrior would know his emperor's name as well as he knew his own. So we can conclude that this man's claim was not valid. Other reports of this kind can generally be dealt with in the same way.

Another intriguing area sounds a lot more reasonable and possible, however. This is the idea that under hypnosis people can be taken back to very early in life, something called **age regression.** Supposedly they can relive that period, remembering events from as far back as infancy.

age regression process of reliving one's very early childhood under hypnosis

▲ *A swinging watch is not necessary in hypnosis; it simply gives the person something to focus on.*

What specifically is being claimed or stated? In a hypnotized state, people can go back in their minds to a much earlier age and relive that time, remembering things that were previously forgotten.

What is the objective evidence for and against this claim? The evidence suggests that hypnotized people can appear to bring back very early memories and behave as if they were in fact much younger. Are they really reliving their early childhood? Well, probably not. For one thing, while they may act and sound as if they were, say, three years old, they do not solve problems as a three-year-old does. For another, they do not make the kind of grammatical errors that a child that young would typically make (Spanos, 1994). In addition, the memories such people recall are often not true. The events they supposedly remember simply never happened (McConkey, 1992).

What other interpretations might be made instead? It has been noted that when people are hypnotized, they are much more open to suggestion. It is quite possible that they are reacting "as if" they were much younger because it has been suggested to them that that is the truth of the matter. It has also been noted that hypnosis produces distortions in perception and memory. Thus, they may be "remembering" what they think might have happened instead of real events. Experiments have been done in which subjects were told, before they were hypnotized, that they were probably born in a hospital that placed colored mobiles over their cribs. This was made up by the experimenters. It didn't actually happen. Later on, under hypnotic age regression, about half of the subjects distinctly remembered seeing these colored mobiles, supposedly shortly after they were born (Loftus, 1997; Spanos, 1994).

What are the most logical conclusions to draw? The safest conclusion in this case is that age regression is not a valid process. More likely, people are behaving and remembering as they think they should, or as has been suggested to them, rather than actually reliving an earlier period in their lives.

See if COOL works for you....

Claim?

Objective evidence for and against claim?

Other interpretations?

Logical conclusions?

Applying Critical Thinking Skills

Given the various findings presented in this section, what general conclusions can you make about memory and about hypnosis?

The Nature of Hypnosis. Hypnosis is formally defined as a state that helps a person focus attention on certain objects, acts, or feelings. The best way to understand hypnosis is to think back to a time in the past few days when you were both studying and listening to music. You could not do both of them equally well at the same time. If you focused on the music, what you were reading faded. If you focused on what you were reading, the music faded. So it is obvious that we have the power to control how much attention we give to different things in the environment (Greenwald, 1992). And if we want, we can cut out some stimulation altogether. You have been doing that while reading this book. Here are some of the things you may have been blocking out: that you have shoes on your feet, that the room is light, that there is noise coming from an air conditioner or furnace, that your arms are connected to your body, and so forth. Once you are aware of these things, they come into focus, one by one, demonstrating our point. Memories are cut off as well. You may have "forgotten," for example, the sights, smells, sounds, and feelings of your first day in high school—until reading this sentence.

The brain is like a mammoth stereo system with billions of speakers, switches, and filters. You can turn on one, then another, blend them, mix them, or make most of them turn off completely. Some people get so good at controlling incoming stimulation that they can stick a needle right through their arms and not feel a thing. (Do not try this yourself!)

Depending on the goal, hypnotists use the power of suggestion to aid in focusing or blocking whatever system is desired. Thus, a person can be aided in forgetting something, remembering something, reducing pain, and so forth. All of us can do anything without hypnosis that we can do under hypnosis. Some people just don't have enough confidence in themselves to believe that this is the case, so they rely on an outsider—a hypnotist—to aid them.

A Special State? Some people think hypnosis is a form of sleep. This belief may have arisen because subjects can get so relaxed they are like rag dolls and they act semiconscious. Or it may be because some hypnotists say, "You are getting sleepy." But the hypnotic state is really not related to sleep. Hypnosis is an intense form of relaxation with the person fully conscious.

Does the hypnotist really have control over the person? Only if the person wants to be under control, since he or she is still conscious. If you tell someone in a deep trance to stay in the room and you'll be back in a couple of days, he or she may sit there for a while, relaxed, until what you've said fully registers. The person will then get up and leave. **Trance** is just another word for the state of relaxation that the person is in. The deeper the trance, the more likely the subject will be relaxed and will cooperate with the hypnotist's suggestions.

There is much arguing about whether someone can be made to do something "immoral" under hypnosis. This is very unlikely, unless the person really wants to do it and uses the hypnosis as an excuse. If, however, the subject is in a deep trance, he or she may trust what the hypnotist says far more than he or she normally would, so that is a problem. In this sense, hypnosis *can* be dangerous, since the subject lets down defenses while putting faith in the hypnotist. Thus, hypnotized people could say or do things that would embarrass them later on. The actual physical dangers are few, but some subjects get a headache afterward or feel a little anxious or confused.

trance another word for the state of deep relaxation that can occur during hypnosis

Uses of Hypnosis.   At one time or another, hypnosis has been said to cure almost everything. It *does* have some uses. It might help with reducing weight or with giving up smoking or drinking, but its effectiveness in these cases is only as great as the person's real *desire* to change (Wadden & Anderson, 1982). Hypnosis can help with minor pain, such as some dental work; it can help a woman through a *normal* childbirth; it can help reduce some headaches. Hypnosis cannot improve memory, but it can help you focus better on such things as study assignments, so it has been useful in education. While there is some disagreement about its use with major pain, most agree that in Western society, it is usually not very effective.

A great deal of "hype" is given to so-called posthypnotic suggestion, with people claiming that it can cause someone to do something that he or she can't control. This is quite an exaggeration. Since a person is suggestible under hypnosis but still quite conscious, he or she may later do what was suggested but doesn't *have* to do anything. The situation is roughly the same as the one in which you go to school and three people in a row say you don't look very well today. You don't have to believe them, but the repeated suggestion makes you wonder, and you actually start to feel not all that well, even if you were fine before they said anything. Or right now we can suggest that your neck feels a little stiff. Aren't you moving it a little to check? No hypnosis is involved, but you still check it because of the suggestion.

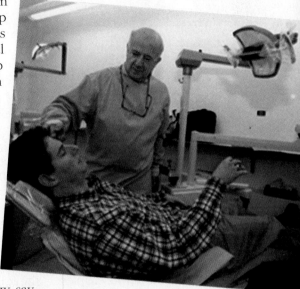

▲ *Although hypnosis can* help *reduce pain, a little anesthetic couldn't hurt.*

Meditation

Meditation is a form of self-control in which a person uses many of the "switches" and "filters" of the brain to cut off the outside world. He or she then focuses on some steady rhythm or sound, trying to put the brain more or less into "neutral" in order to feel peaceful and at ease. The steady sound can be a hum or a word or phrase that the person repeats, or even simply the ticking of a clock. Meditation can be very effective in lowering blood pressure or slowing heart rate. The techniques of meditation are actually tools to help us relax. Some people can do it without going through any ritual. And some people cannot relax, no matter what. When some try to relax, it makes them nervous!

meditation a form of self-control in which the outside world is cut off from consciousness

 ## Pause for Thought

1. What is social entrainment and what problems does it cause?
2. How much sleep do most people need? What are some differences between short sleepers and long sleepers?
3. Describe three main types of sleep problems.
4. List two myths and two accurate statements about hypnosis.

Critical Thinking
....
5. How can hypnosis actually make memory worse? Mention age regression in your answer.

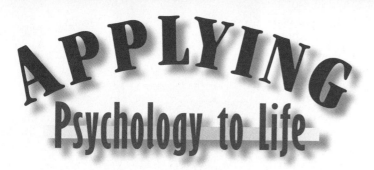

APPLYING Psychology to Life

The World of Consciousness

Here are some practical and, we hope, interesting applications of the material discussed in this chapter:

Problem Solving

Try using the dream state for problem solving. Look up a problem in a math book—a problem that you can solve but that will take some time. Look at it just before going to bed. You will probably have the solution by morning (or be very close), since your brain has been working on it.

Many people claim that the twilight state is the period when we are most creative. Let your mind wander during this time and see if you don't come up with an unusual idea. If it sounds quite good, get up and write it down before you sink into deep sleep. Of course, it may not seem so hot in the morning—but who knows?

Create a Dream

Try to *make* a dream. It can be done. Think about something very simple and not threatening, and tell yourself that you want it in the dream. It will probably appear in some form during the night. If you're lucky, it may

occur late, toward morning, and you will remember it. Sometimes, though, it will not appear until the following night.

If you see a horror movie that really scares you, it also might appear in a dream—something you *don't* want. The computer theory we discussed works pretty well in this case. Here's what you do: Just before getting into bed, go over the part that scared you and reassure yourself that it didn't—and won't—really happen. If you do this, the odds are great that you will have "cleared" that problem from your memory system, and it will not appear in a dream.

Memory and Daydreams

Find something you want to memorize. For example, pick a few lines of a poem or a saying. Read them over about five times while you sit on the bed. Then forget them and go to sleep. By morning, you will have most of the material stored, and it will require only a little more work for you to retain it permanently.

Night dreams are not the only dreams we have. Every 90 minutes during the day we have daydreams, unless something is really distracting us. Now that

you know this, think about a daydream *after* you've had one. (Don't try to "catch" it in midstream.) Notice how much more organized it is than a night dream. This is because you keep better control when you are awake.

Sleep Patterns

Set your own internal alarm clock. You have one. Pick a time you want to wake up, but make it real; in other words, plan on doing something at that time. Your internal clock will time the number of 90-minute cycles and shorten the later dreams as you approach your wake-up time. The odds are that you will not hit the time exactly but that you will awaken just before or after the REM closest to the time you set.

Notice how much easier it is to get to sleep if you go to bed an hour later than you did the night before, rather than an hour earlier. This is because when you go to bed an hour later, you are actually moving toward the body's free-running cycle of 25 hours. In contrast, if you go to bed an hour earlier, you are just adding another hour *against* your natural rhythm, which makes sleep more difficult to attain.

If you are up very late some night and do not sleep late the next morning, note that the following night you will feel like you had more dreams than usual. This is true. REM rebound will occur, especially after two such nights in a row.

Most of us know if we are "night" or "day" people. To "prove" it, take your temperature every hour for 18 hours or so. It will start to increase and reach its high point for the day (roughly 99.5 degrees) in either the evening or the late morning. This increase tells you that you are entering your best time of day. If you're really interested, and if you are a day person, get up sometime at 3 or 4 A.M. and notice how low your temperature is.

Forcing Sleep

It's not a good idea to *try* to get to sleep, no matter how important it is that you do. The brain will decide you are trying to do something critical and will signal an "emergency." This will change your body chemistry so that you will never get to sleep. Instead, count something like imaginary horses jumping a fence. Such rhythmic thoughts will distract the brain and lull you to sleep.

Some animals, such as cows, sleep with their eyes open. Observe your friends in a 2 P.M. class, and you will see behavior that resembles that of the cow. Chimpanzees, monkeys, and humans not only have a 3 A.M. dip in energy but also one at 2 P.M. This is a natural rhythm, not related to eating lunch. Recognizing this, many cultures allow for a nap in the early afternoon. Ours doesn't—hence, you and your classmates may have a tendency to doze in your afternoon classes.

▲ *He isn't bored, honest! It's just his body's natural rhythm taking over.*

CHAPTER 6 REVIEW & APPLY

Summary

1. Consciousness is our awareness of events inside and outside ourselves. Consciousness seems to be made up of a series of scenes put together into a whole as we move about. Levels of consciousness are the conscious, subconscious, and unconscious.

2. Different body rhythms are controlled by biological clocks that cause events to start or stop at certain times of the day, month, or year.

3. Sleeping and waking in humans follow an entrained 24-hour cycle called a circadian rhythm. Each of us follows this rhythm and has a high and low point every 24 hours.

4. Sleep is divided into REM and NREM periods. Most dreams occur during the REM period.

5. Dreams occur every 90 minutes throughout the night, with each dream longer than the previous one. The basic purpose of dreams seems to be to keep the brain active while the outside world is shut off. It is primarily during this time that the brain chemicals are restored.

6. Most dreams are about everyday events. Sometimes bizarre dreams can result from random firing of the memory circuits. Sleepwalking and talking in one's sleep result if an electrical impulse hits the areas of the brain controlling these activities during NREM.

7. Hypnosis involves being in a relaxed state with a heightened ability to focus attention. People under hypnosis can control memories, bring them back, or make them disappear. Hypnosis is of some use in reducing pain and may help a person lose weight or stop smoking—but only if the person already really wants to do this. Age regression under hypnosis doesn't work.

8. Meditation is a form of self-control in which outside stimulation is greatly reduced to create a peaceful state.

Vocabulary

construct	twilight state	night terror
consciousness	REM sleep	insomnia
subconscious	beta waves	narcolepsy
unconscious	alpha waves	sleep apnea
biological clocks	delta waves	hypnosis
free-running cycles	NREM sleep	age regression
entrainment	nightmare	trance
circadian rhythm	REM rebound	meditation

Review Questions

Fill in the Blank

On a sheet of paper write the word or words that best complete each statement.

1. If someone is mad at his or her uncle but is completely unaware of this, the anger is probably hidden in his or her ▒▒▒▒.

2. Bodily rythmns are controlled by ▒▒▒▒.

3. A concept that requires a belief in something that can't be seen or touched is called a ▒▒▒▒.

4. The free-running daily cycle of most humans is ▒▒▒▒ hours.

5. Most humans have altered their free-running cycle through ▒▒▒▒.

6. The human circadian rhythm is based on a ▒▒▒▒-hour cycle.

7. Another name for knowing, or awareness, is ▒▒▒▒.

8. REM stands for ▒▒▒▒.

9. If REM is blocked for several nights, ▒▒▒▒ may occur.

For each of the following states of consciousness, indicate A for alpha waves, B for beta waves, and D for delta waves.

10. Very relaxed
11. Awake
12. First 10 minutes of sleep
13. Deep sleep

For each of the following, answer REM *or* NREM.

14. When the brain is idle
15. Associated with vivid dreams
16. Paralyzed body
17. When night terrors occur
18. Gets longer as night progresses
19. Associated with narcolepsy

Matching

On a sheet of paper, match terms in the second list to definitions in the first list.

20. Episode of panic and fear
21. Can be caused by drinking alcohol
22. Breathing stops
23. Falling suddenly into sleep

   a. sleep apnea
   b. narcolepsy
   c. insomnia
   d. night terror

True/False

On a sheet of paper answer each statement true *or* false. *If false, rewrite to make it true.*

24. Hypnosis has been verified to improve memory.

25. Hypnosis is regarded as a special sleep stage.

26. It is unlikely that a person will do something immoral under hypnosis.

27. Most doctors in the United States agree that hypnosis can help reduce major pain.

28. Meditation helps us shut out the outside world.

29. Childhood night terrors in general should not be treated by a professional.

30. Most children outgrow night terrors.

Discussion Questions

1. Besides consciousness, can you think of any other constructs, or beliefs, that people have? Name one. (Remember, a construct can't be seen or touched.) What evidence would suggest that this construct actually exists?

2. Consciousness is an awareness of what is going on inside and outside the organism. Do you think that people who are highly intelligent experience this awareness at a greater level than people who are less intelligent? Explain.

3. The unconscious contains thoughts and desires about which we have no knowledge. If you could suddenly become aware of these "hidden" thoughts by simply pushing a button, would you do it? Why or why not?

4. Pretend that your principal reads this chapter and decides to make changes in the school schedule as a result. What changes might the principal propose, and why? Be specific.

5. The chapter offers three possible hypotheses on why we dream. Write a fourth hypothesis based on your own experiences or on material you've read in this text.

6. The chapter mentions that hypnosis occurs when a person focuses attention on a single thing—mainly on the suggestions of the hypnotist. What other factors could affect whether hypnosis will occur? You might mention characteristics of the person being hypnotized, characteristics of the hypnotist, and characteristics of the situation—for example, hypnosis is less likely to occur on a crowded subway than in a quiet office.

7. In what ways is hypnosis similar to meditation? Are they different in any way? Explain.

Activities and Projects

1. Prepare a list of questions for an interview with your grandfather or grandmother or someone about the same age. Find out how sleep patterns generally change as a person gets older. Avoid too many questions that simply require a yes-or-no response. If you do receive a simple answer, ask the person to elaborate.

Possible questions:

a. How has the quality of sleep changed as you've grown older? Is it more satisfying now than 20 years ago, or less satisfying?

b. Do you sleep more now than 20 years ago, or less? How does this affect your everyday routine?

c. What kinds of events in your life forced you to alter your sleep-wake cycle?

d. Are your dreams more vivid now than they were 20 years ago? Do you remember your dreams more today than you did then?

Write a detailed report of your interview. Be sure to include your questions. Also, include your general reactions to what you found out.

2. This chapter mentions that there seem to be some differences between long sleepers and short sleepers. Find out if the differences also involve personality. Use 20 subjects and ask each of them the following questions:

a. Do you consider yourself to be (1) highly imaginative, (2) somewhat imaginative, or (3) not very imaginative?

b. Are you (1) usually introverted or (2) usually extroverted?

c. When you are given an assignment, are you generally (1) a highly motivated worker, (2) a somewhat motivated worker, (3) a somewhat unmotivated worker, or (4) a highly unmotivated worker?

d. In general, do you consider yourself (1) a leader or (2) a follower?

e. How long do you usually sleep: (1) six hours or less, (2) seven hours, (3) eight hours, (4) nine hours, (5) ten hours or more?

Analyze your results. Does there seem to be some correlation between personality and length of sleep?

3. Keep a dream journal for several nights. Write down each dream exactly as you remember it. After about a week of jotting down dreams, analyze them. Were there any common themes or common objects in many of them? Did you dream in color? Which colors? Did the dreams tend to be bizarre or somewhat orderly?

What do the answers to all these questions say about your personality in general? Explain.

4. Sit-coms and cartoons and even some movies would have you believe that hypnosis is a mysterious, trancelike state in which the subject becomes a robot who will obey the hypnotist's every command. This project will give you the chance to find out if people really believe these myths. In the process, you can educate some of your friends.

Prepare a list of statements about hypnosis and present them to about 15 people. Some statements can ask for true-false answers. Others can ask for a level of agreement using the following statements: (1) strongly agree, (2) somewhat agree, (3) neither agree nor disagree, (4) somewhat disagree, (5) strongly disagree. Here are some sample statements—all myths:

Using a posthypnotic suggestion, a hypnotist can get someone to cluck like a chicken every time she hears a bell for a week.

People who are hypnotized do not later recall what happened during hypnosis.

If a person is truly hypnotized, the hypnotist can get that person to steal something from a store.

One's memory greatly improves under hypnosis.

People who are hypnotized are in a deep stage of sleep.

Studies show that 90 percent of smokers stop smoking after a single hypnosis session.

The best way to hypnotize someone is with a slow-moving pendulum.

Write a report analyzing your results. Which myths are most commonly believed? Maybe you can ask subjects to explain their answers so you can discuss why the myths persist. Another option is to develop a hypothesis before you administer your questions and then plan your study accordingly. For example, you might guess that older people believe fewer myths about hypnosis than younger people or that people who watch a lot of TV believe more myths.

5. Ask a close friend who can remember a recent dream to write down as many details of the dream as she or he can remember. Then have the friend write a paragraph on a separate sheet of paper analyzing and interpreting what she or he thinks the dream means. You'll have to find someone who's willing and able to complete such a task. Before reading the paragraph, write your own paragraph about what you think the dream means. Try to relate the dream to your friend's life. If the friend is extremely worried about a college application, for example, maybe this worry is reflected in the dream. Finally, compare and contrast the two paragraphs, and have your friend do the same. How do they match up?

Unit 3

In this Unit...

Cognitive
Processes

189

CHAPTER 7

Principles of Learning

Most often, when we think of learning, we think of the formal type that occurs in school. Learning, however, takes place continuously every day. In this chapter, we examine some of the mechanisms that aid in this process.

Four Types of Learning

In this chapter, we will discuss four types of learning. The first, called *classical conditioning,* involves making unavoidable physical association. The second involves learning caused by the consequences of actions we perform. For instance, we learn that pressing one's finger very hard on the edge of a sharp knife is not a good idea. This is called *operant conditioning.* The third type of learning results from observing others. If someone dives into a black lagoon and does not resurface, you know not to do that. This is called *social learning* (because it results from viewing other people). The fourth type emphasizes thought processes in learning. It is called the *cognitive approach.*

Classical Conditioning

The most primitive learning, classical conditioning, was first demonstrated by a physiologist and absentminded professor in the early 1900s, **Ivan Pavlov** (PAV-lov). He was a man with a very hot temper who blew up at assistants for the slightest mistake. He fined them for being late to work, even though they had to walk through an ongoing Russian Revolution to get there. When *he* was late, on the other hand, he did not dock his own pay (Windholz, 1987; Miller, 1962). Pavlov also became infuriated with the dogs used in his experiments because they kept falling asleep. Despite these problems, his early discoveries led to major advances in understanding how people and animals learn.

Pavlov's first love was physiology. It was with some reluctance that he began to study psychological processes. However, eventually he became quite enthusiastic about this new subject matter and investigated such areas as mental disorders, the process of aging, and personality types (Todes, 1997; Windholz, 1997). It was his research on conditioning, however, that laid the groundwork for certain types of behavior therapy that would become important decades later (Wolpe & Plaud, 1997).

◄ *Ivan Pavlov (center) and others observe a classical conditioning experiment.*

Importance of Association

Pavlov's original goal was to understand how the digestive system works. He wanted to discover how salivation and gastric juices aid in digestion. By today's standards, the experiments were both basic and simple, but such was not the case in the early 1900s. (In fact, Pavlov was awarded a Nobel Prize in 1904 for his work on the digestive system.) Pavlov surgically separated the stomach from the esophagus (which carries food from the mouth to the stomach) in dogs. This operation meant that: (1) food taken by mouth would never reach the stomach and (2) food could be put directly into the stomach without having to travel through the mouth.

Pavlov was quick to note three strange things. First, food put directly into the stomach did not generate all by itself enough gastric juices for digestion. Thus, salivation at the time of eating is critical to proper digestion. Second, even though *no* food was placed in the dog's mouth, the animal would still salivate copiously just at the *sight* of the food. But Pavlov's third finding was the most important one for our purposes: the sight of the *experimenter* who fed the animal would cause the dog to salivate even if that person was not carrying any food. This meant that receiving food could be conditioned to (associated with) the mere presence of the experimenter who did the feeding.

So far this is all clear and easy to understand, but from this point on, students almost always get confused. This is because classical conditioning involves a specific terminology, not because there is anything really complicated about the ideas.

▲ *Pavlov is famous for his experiments on conditioning dogs in the early 1900s.*

classical conditioning Ivan Pavlov's method of conditioning, in which associations are made between a natural stimulus and a learned, neutral stimulus

stimulus anything that elicits a response

response a reaction to a stimulus

unconditioned stimulus a stimulus that automatically elicits a response, as meat causes salivation

unconditioned response an automatic response to a particular natural stimulus, such as salivation to meat

Outline of Classical Conditioning

A Model T Ford is one of the first cars that Henry Ford produced. This makes it an item of first importance—a classic. Since Pavlov's experiments were the first in the learning area, they also are considered classical. This is how we get the term **classical conditioning.**

The following steps are involved in classical conditioning. You start with a reflexive, or "natural," stimulus-response pair. The word **stimulus** refers to anything that causes some kind of reaction. That reaction is termed the **response.** Thus, since meat makes a dog salivate, meat is the stimulus (S) for the response (R) of salivation. The behavior involved is completely automatic; the animal salivates when food is put into its mouth. Here is a diagram of this activity:

Receives food (S) → Salivates (R)

So food is a stimulus (S) and salivation is a response (R) to that stimulus.

Note that no special *conditions* are needed for meat to cause salivation; it is natural and automatic. Hence, Pavlov called the food an **unconditioned stimulus** (UCS) and salivation an **unconditioned response** (UCR). Replacing the diagram above with more accurate terminology, this is what we get:

Receives food (UCS) → Salivates (UCR)

Since seeing an experimenter will not elicit salivation all by itself, it is a *neutral* stimulus (NS) for salivation. It has no effect on this response. In order for the dog to salivate at seeing the experimenter, some specific conditions are necessary—namely, the animal must associate the experimenter with food. This would diagram as follows:

Sight of experimenter (NS) → Receives food (UCS) → Salivation (UCR)

When that association takes place over time, then "seeing the experimenter" becomes a **conditioned stimulus** (CS). In other words, the special condition of associating the experimenter with food has been met. A diagram of this process of association looks like this:

Sight of experimenter (CS) → Receives food (UCS) → Salivation (UCR)

Eventually, the animal responds to the conditioned stimulus alone, by salivating, much as it did to the unconditioned stimulus of food. Salivation at the sight of the experimenter, since it is now triggered by a CS, with no food present, becomes the **conditioned response** (CR) (even though it's the same type of salivation). This last step is:

Sight of experimenter (CS) → Salivation (CR)

Here is a quick review to help clarify. You hear someone mention that he or she desperately wants a juicy dill pickle. Note that just reading this is causing you to salivate. How is this possible? In the past:

Eating pickle (UCS) → Salivation (UCR)

Before you actually eat a pickle, you think or say to yourself, "Pickle."

Word pickle *(NS) → Eating pickle (UCS) → Salivation (UCR)*

Over time, the word *pickle,* which is only a sound and not a real object, becomes associated with a real pickle, which *does* cause salivation. So we now have:

Word pickle *(CS) → Salivation (CR)*

John B. Watson and Emotional Conditioning

Several years after Pavlov's early experiments, psychologist **John B. Watson** appeared on the scene. While he was working his way through school, one of his jobs was to take care of laboratory rats. Gradually, the rats became Watson's pets and friends. One of his favorite pastimes was to teach them all kinds of tricks. The rats were able to find their way through elaborate mazes he built, to solve problems such as the need to dig through obstacles he had put in their path, to act as construction workers in tunnels he started for them, and so forth. Based on his observations, Watson eventually

conditioned stimulus a previously neutral stimulus that has been associated with a natural (or unconditioned) stimulus

conditioned response a response to a stimulus that is brought about by learning—for example, salivating at the word *pickle*

Focus Questions

- What is emotional conditioning?
- According to John Watson, how are emotions learned?

◄ *Little Albert was the subject of one of John Watson's experiments on fear.*

193

In Focus

Classical Conditioning

Here's how we learn involuntary responses.

Before Conditioning	Unconditioned stimulus (UCS) → Unconditioned response (UCR) **This is automatic. No learning is involved.**
During Conditioning	Neutral S (N) → Unconditioned S (UCS) → Unconditioned R (UCR) **We pair the neutral stimulus with the unconditioned stimulus.**
After Conditioning	Conditioned S (CS) → Conditioned R (CR) **The neutral stimulus is no longer neutral, it is conditioned. It now produces a conditioned response, so we call the neutral stimulus a conditioned stimulus.**
Example	Lemon drop box (N) → Lemon drop (UCS) → Salivation (UCR) Lemon drop box (CS) → Salivation (CS)

Think of one behavior you've learned through classical conditioning and draw a diagram like the example above.

▲ *Children are automatically afraid of loud noises.*

decided that what seemed to be the rats' complex behavior actually resulted from little more than a series of stimuli and responses, rather than from some exotic concept such as "intelligence."

Watson went even further and suggested that at the human level, "deep emotions" are also just the result of association and learning. One of his most famous experiments involved trying to get a human to spread (or generalize) the emotion of fear from one object to another. This, he thought, would demonstrate that emotions can be mechanically induced (Cohen, 1979). Watson's work in this area has concerned many people because of the ethics involved in how he dealt with a child. His research would never be allowed today, but since he did it, we might as well discuss it.

A woman who worked at the same clinic as Watson would bring her child with her while she was working. Unknown to the mother, Watson started a series of conditioning experiments with the child. This 11-month-old is now famous in psychology and is known as "Little Albert."

Before describing what happened to Little Albert, we need to give you some background information on fear. An unexpected loud noise makes anyone's heart race. We don't have to *learn* to be startled or afraid. It happens automatically. So a sudden loud noise is an unconditioned stimulus for the unconditioned response of fear.

Watson put a white laboratory rat into the room with Albert. Albert loved the furry creature and played with it. While Albert played, Watson sneaked up behind him and banged a steel bar with a hammer, creating a horrible, startling noise. Albert fell forward, crying and burying his face in a mattress on the floor. The next time he reached for the rat, Watson repeated the crashing noises. Little Albert became terrified of the rat. Here is the situation:

Loud sound (UCS) → Fear (UCR)

followed by the association phase:

Rat (NS) → Loud sound (UCS) → Fear (UCR)

which then becomes:

Rat (CS) → Fear (CR)

Watson then went on to demonstrate what is called **stimulus generalization,** which means that a response can spread from one specific stimulus like the white rat to other stimuli resembling the original one in some way. To show this had occurred, Watson brought in a white rabbit, which also frightened Albert. Albert even showed some concern about a fur coat and a mild negative response to a Santa Claus mask, objects somewhat similar to the white rat.

Before the mother discovered these goings on and fled with Albert, Watson had shown two things: (1) conditioning of emotions to neutral objects is possible and (2) a conditioned emotion can generalize to other objects that have similar characteristics. All of this is helpful to know, but there still is a problem. Because no one ever located "Big" Albert after Watson's experiment and because no one since Watson has done a similar kind of experiment, we don't know how long such conditioned emotions last (Samuelson, 1980).

Most likely Albert's fear disappeared, since we do know from other studies (with adults) that if you stop pairing something like a frightening noise with an object, the original association will begin to disappear. This disappearance is called **extinction,** as in the verb "to extinguish." Thus, after a while, Pavlov's dogs would extinguish (stop) their salivation in the presence of the experimenter unless the experimenter continued to feed them occasionally.

Once extinction has occurred, however, it is not necessarily permanent. An extinguished response will sometimes suddenly reappear, for unknown reasons. This event is known as **spontaneous recovery.** In other words, the previously "lost" or "forgotten" response is recovered without anyone doing anything. It simply happens spontaneously, all on its own.

stimulus generalization process in which a response spreads from one specific stimulus to other stimuli that resemble the original

extinction the gradual loss of an association over time

spontaneous recovery the sudden reappearance of an extinguished response

In Their Own Words . . .

Early behaviorists, such as **John B. Watson,** *had to fight for acceptance of their approach to studying human behavior. In many ways, applying behavioral principles went against the more popular ideas of the time. Nowhere is this clearer than in the area of child rearing, a subject Watson wrote about in great detail.*

[M]any . . . educators have been insisting for the last twenty years upon a method of training which allows the child to develop from within. . . .

The behaviorists believe that there is nothing from within to develop. If you start with a healthy body, the right number of fingers and toes, eyes, and the few elementary movements that are present at birth, you do not need anything else in the way of raw material to make a man, be that man a genius, a cultured gentleman, a rowdy or a thug. (Watson, 1928, pp. 40–41)

Elsewhere, Watson summarized his views in the following way:

Give me a dozen healthy infants, well-formed, and my own specified world to bring them up in and I'll guarantee to take any one at random and train him to become any type of specialist I might select—a doctor, lawyer, artist, merchant-chief, and yes, even into beggar-man and thief, regardless of his talents, penchants, tendencies, abilities, vocations and race of his ancestors. (Watson, as quoted in Murchison, 1927, p. 10)

Interpreting Primary Sources

Do you think that Watson's view of human nature is accurate? Does his claim to be able to control the destiny of any child make you uncomfortable? Why or why not?

▲ *Mary Cover Jones developed a technique to rid children of some phobias.*

Removal of Fears

One very important discovery was made as a result of Watson's experiments, and it came from a student who worked for Watson, **Mary Cover Jones.** Aware of the effect that Watson's experiments had had on Little Albert, she wondered if she could reverse the procedure and *cure* a child of a terrible fear. She found a three-year-old, "Peter," who panicked at the sight of a rabbit. In an experiment, she brought a rabbit into the room with Peter, close enough for him to see it. She then gave the child some food he liked. She moved the rabbit closer and gave more food, and she continued this process, associating the pleasure of food with the feared object. It worked: Peter lost his fear of rabbits (Jones, 1924). Jones had found the key to removing all manner of fears, called *phobias,* that can make people's lives miserable—fears of elevators, snakes, dogs, and the like. Associating something pleasant with a feared object is still used quite successfully today to reduce or stop such fears.

As a sort of footnote: Mary Jones was a close friend of Watson, so she never said anything negative about him. Even so, she does note that one day, when he was visiting her at home, she left him in a room with her child, who was about the age of Little Albert. From the other room she heard a very loud banging noise, but when she hurried back, everything seemed normal (Jones, 1974). Was Watson trying to set up another "experiment"?

 ## Pause for Thought

1. What is classical conditioning?
2. What is the difference between a neutral stimulus and a conditioned stimulus?
3. What is the difference between an unconditioned response and a conditioned response?
4. What famous experiments did Ivan Pavlov, John B. Watson, and Mary Cover Jones conduct?

Critical Thinking
....

5. Pretend you have to speak to a class of third-graders about classical conditioning. You're afraid the terms—*unconditioned stimulus, unconditioned response,* and so on—are too confusing. What terms would you use instead, and how would you explain classical conditioning?

Operant Conditioning

Despite the importance of the studies just described, most learning does not occur in a classical stimulus-response sequence. It usually involves some voluntary action taken by the learner. This type of learning is called **operant conditioning,** in which a behavior is learned or avoided as a result of its consequences.

Classical Versus Operant Conditioning

In classical conditioning, learning takes place without any choice. In other words, meat on the tongue (or something that has been associated with meat) will automatically cause salivation without any choice by the organism. In operant conditioning, the organism plays some role in what happens. The theory of operant conditioning claims that humans and animals learn as an end product of performing certain actions (or *operations*).

The distinction between classical and operant conditioning is often hard to grasp when encountered for the first time. But the brain has a way of remembering unusual things better than it remembers the commonplace (we will discuss this in Chapter 8), and we want to take advantage of this fact now by giving you an example that is truly absurd, so you won't ever forget it. Here we go:

Someone in your household decides to condition you classically to hate a certain vegetable. At random times, this person, carrying a handful of the cold vegetable, sneaks up behind you and shoves it into your mouth while talking into your ear about something nauseating. After a few of these encounters, you will find the thought of that vegetable quite unpleasant. You have now been *classically* conditioned to dislike the vegetable, since you had no control whatsoever over what was happening.

Second scene: You find three different varieties of canned vegetables in the cupboard. You have never eaten any of them. You reach in, take one out, cook it, and eat it. You do the same thing with the other two later on. The one you like best you will probably reach for and cook again. In this case, you have been *operantly* conditioned by your actions (operations) and their consequences to prefer one vegetable over another.

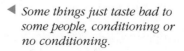
◀ *Some things just taste bad to some people, conditioning or no conditioning.*

Focus Questions
....
- What is operant conditioning?
- How is operant conditioning different from classical conditioning?

operant conditioning conditioning that results from the individual's actions and the consequences they cause

In Focus

Operant Conditioning

How We Learn Voluntary Responses

Voluntary response → Reinforcement → Voluntary response is repeated
If we receive reinforcement for a voluntary behavior, we're more likely to perform the behavior again in the future.
Sample **Work hard → Earn a raise → Continue to work hard**
Can you think of a behavior that you've done in the past 24 hours that has been formed through operant conditioning?

Focus Question

• How do reinforcements affect behavior?

B. F. Skinner

Psychologist **B. F. Skinner** is best known for his work with the operant conditioning theory. He believed that how we turn out in life is the result of what we learn from all the operations we make over the years (Skinner, 1990). If our actions result in people getting angry and disliking us, we are being operantly conditioned to believe that the world is a dangerous and threatening place. If the environment rewards us when we perform certain acts, then we tend to repeat them. Thus, if you study hard, do a good job on a paper, and get a note of praise, you will tend to study hard and do a good job again. If you get a nasty note on your paper even though you've done well, you will lose your desire to repeat these actions.

The seeds of Skinner's work were planted when he was a boy. He set up a pulley system in his bedroom closet that kept a large sign, "Hang up your pajamas," visible until he opened the door and placed the pajamas on a hook, at which point the sign moved out of view. He was operantly conditioning himself, and his action was probably reinforced by an absence of getting yelled at for being sloppy (Fancher, 1979).

Later, Skinner was so concerned about how our surroundings affect us that he reared his daughter in what he called an "air crib." In this crib, the environment—such as the temperature, humidity, and light—was carefully controlled at all times. The child was also not confined by diapers. The "diaper" consisted of a continuous roll of sheetlike material that was fed in one side of the air crib and pulled out the other. Skinner wanted the perfect environment for his little girl. She turned out just fine, but we'll never know whether she was really helped by the special crib.

Operant Conditioning Processes

Reinforcement is an important ingredient in operant conditioning. It is something that follows a response and strengthens our tendency to repeat that response in the future. The word means the same thing in learning as it does in construction work: When something is reinforced, it

reinforcement something that follows a response and strengthens the tendency to repeat that response

is made stronger. For example, say that there is a bar inside an animal cage, and each time the animal presses the bar, food appears. The behavior of bar pressing is reinforced by the arrival of the food. After a while, when the animal is hungry, it will walk right over to the bar and push it.

One type of reinforcement is called **primary reinforcement.** The word *primary* means "of first and greatest importance." A primary reinforcer is something that is unlearned and is absolutely necessary for survival, such as food or water. The possibility of obtaining one of these when you perform an action is the strongest incentive to learn.

Not all of our behavior involves primary reinforcers, however. For example, we engage in a truly weird activity that we take for granted: We work, struggle, fight, and wish for rectangular pieces of gray and green paper. People even commit crimes, lie, and cheat just to get these pieces of paper. Where's the reinforcement? We're talking about money, of course. Since you can't eat or drink it, it can't be a primary reinforcer, but it certainly does reinforce. Money is a secondary reinforcer. **Secondary reinforcement** is anything that comes to *represent* a primary reinforcer. Because money can buy food and drink, it represents these primary reinforcers. All secondary reinforcers are related to some primary one. For example, you work for a high grade because it is a formal way of receiving

primary reinforcement something necessary for psychological or physical survival that is used as a reward

secondary reinforcement anything that comes to represent a primary reinforcer, such as money

Positive and Negative Reinforcement

Positive Reinforcement   Negative Reinforcement

Angela picks up her jacket because she was praised the last time she did it.

Allison picks up her jacket to stop her father's nagging.

What are some positive and negative reinforcements for earning good grades in school?

praise. This praise represents the physical love (primary reinforcement) in the form of hugs that you got from caregivers when you did a good job as a child.

positive reinforcement reinforcement that involves strengthening the tendency to repeat a response by following it with the addition of something pleasant

negative reinforcement reinforcement that involves strengthening a response by following it with the removal of something unpleasant

We have been talking about **positive reinforcement** up to this point. Positive reinforcement occurs when something the organism wants (such as food) is added on (+, positive) after an action. Another type of reinforcement is called **negative reinforcement.** Negative reinforcement occurs when something unpleasant is stopped or taken away (–, negative) when the organism does something.

If the floor of a cage gives an animal a shock and the animal learns to push a bar in order to stop the electricity, this is negative reinforcement; it strengthens a response (pushing the bar). Say that someone wants you to take out the trash, which you keep forgetting to do. So the nagging starts, and it keeps on and on. You are being negatively reinforced: All you want to do is find a way to stop the endless whining about what a mess you are. You take out the trash and therefore are performing an act in order to stop something unpleasant.

In both positive and negative reinforcement, then, the consequences of an action are something the organism wants. In one, something pleasant is added; in the other, something unpleasant is stopped or avoided. Try to remember that reinforcement always strengthens a response, rather than weakening it, and this will be easier to understand.

punishment the process of weakening a response by following it with unpleasant consequences

Punishment.   Students often confuse negative reinforcement with punishment, but there is a very basic difference. **Punishment** is an attempt to *weaken* a response by following it with something unpleasant. There are two basic ways to punish someone. First, something desired can be taken away, as when someone is fined for a traffic violation. Second, something unwanted can be added, as when students in the "olden days" had to write "I shall not talk in class" 100 times on the blackboard. But in either case, the goal is to weaken the behavior, not to strengthen it.

▶ *Punishment in this case probably includes that awful feeling in the pit of your stomach.*

In Focus

Generalization, Discrimination, and Extinction

Joe makes a wisecrack in his first-period biology class, and everyone laughs, even the teacher. The following types of learning may occur:

Generalization:

He makes wisecracks in other classes, in front of other teachers.

Discrimination:

He makes wisecracks in other classes, but when no one laughs or when the teacher glares at him, he stops. He decides to tell jokes only during first period.

Extinction:

He continues to make wisecracks during first period, but when others tire of his jokes and stop laughing, he stops.

Generalization, discrimination, and extinction occur during both classical and operant conditioning. Are the above situations examples of classical or operant conditioning?

Generalization and Discrimination. As mentioned earlier, a classically conditioned response can spread, or generalize, to similar stimuli. **Generalization** can also occur in operantly conditioned behavior. For instance, suppose a small boy who pats a dog and gets a wagging tail approaches the next dog he sees in the same fashion. That dog also wags its tail, and the boy's action generalizes to all dogs, for the boy assumes they are all friendly. Suppose, however, that the third dog the boy pats bites him. In such a case, generalization has been instantly halted and replaced by **discrimination learning.** In other words, the child learns to tell the difference (discriminate) between dogs or between situations that are not all the same.

Babies often embarrass adults because of their generalizations. For instance, a baby girl hugs her father and says, "Dada." Daddy gets so excited about this that he praises her and runs to tell the mother that she has called him by name. The little girl generalizes the response, sensibly in her own mind, by calling every man she meets "Dada." When the other men don't give her the same positive reinforcement, she gradually discriminates between who is really "Dada" and who isn't—even though she doesn't actually know what that sound means.

Extinction. Often, when a response is no longer followed by reinforcement, a person will gradually stop making that response. This situation is called *extinction,* the same term used earlier with classical conditioning. In both classical and operant conditioning, then, extinction can occur. In both cases, an association has been weakened—in classical conditioning, because the unconditioned stimulus is no longer present, and in operant

generalization a behavior that spreads from one situation to a similar one

discrimination learning learning to tell the difference between one event or object and another; the reverse of generalization

► *This Seeing Eye dog is capable of complex sequences of behavior, many of them learned through shaping and chaining techniques.*

conditioning, because reinforcement is no longer present. Spontaneous recovery, the sudden reappearance of an extinguished response, can also occur in operant conditioning as well as in classical conditioning.

Shaping and Chaining.   So far, we have been talking about fairly simple one-step behaviors. Is operant conditioning limited to behaviors of this kind? The answer is no. Two major techniques can be used to teach more complex or complicated responses.

shaping the process of gradually refining a response by successively reinforcing closer approximations of it

The first such technique is called **shaping,** the "method of successive approximations." What does this mean? In shaping, increasingly closer versions (approximations) of the desired response are reinforced in turn (successively). We start out reinforcing a rough version of the response we're after. Once that rough version has been learned, the standard goes up. Now, a smoother or more accurate attempt is required before reinforcement will be given, and so on. Thus, a dog being trained to jump through a hoop will first be reinforced by praise or food for approaching a hoop that lies on the ground. Next, the dog is reinforced for walking through the hoop as it is held vertically touching the ground. Then the dog is shaped to jump through the hoop held a few inches off the ground, and so forth. The same process is followed when someone is learning how to play a tune on the piano or how to swim.

When we want a complete sequence done in order, we usually have to start by reinforcing each part of that sequence. Then each part or link is connected to the others by reinforcement. This process is called **chaining,** as in "connecting together." In learning a new dance, for instance, people learn the different steps or parts of the dance first. Then they put the parts together like links in a chain.

chaining reinforcing the connection between the parts of a sequence

Seeing Eye dogs for the blind are highly intelligent and remarkable examples of what shaping and chaining can produce. They can read stoplights and traffic patterns, find curbs and doors, discover dangerous holes that might trip their owners, or find things the owners drop. They will even resist dangerous commands from sightless persons. All these behaviors occur as a smooth, ongoing process that looks completely effortless—and is, after being done hundreds and hundreds of times. Since these animals are capable of forming close psychological bonds, only occasionally during training is a reinforcer such as food used. The dog wants to please the trainer to such a degree that a pat on the head or some other form of approval or praise is more than enough and is generally even preferred.

The Coast Guard Search and Rescue teams tested an unusual use for pigeons. A pigeon's vision is much sharper than a human's. Pigeons were trained to search for an orange disk and, when it was located, to push a button with their beaks as a signal. After training, they went on helicopter rescue missions to watch for orange "disks"—life jackets attached to people in the water. Pilots have trouble seeing them, but pigeons don't. Pigeons have a 90 percent success rate, whereas pilots are stuck at 35 percent. As you can imagine, the victims were thankful when the pigeons spotted their life jackets and pecked signals to the rescuers (Fox, 1980).

Schedules of Reinforcement

There are different methods of providing reinforcement during operant conditioning. So far, we have focused on **continuous reinforcement.** Here, each time a desired behavior occurs, it is reinforced. In many cases, this is not a good method, because the creature gets used to having the reinforcer and will quit responding if it doesn't show up every time. This problem can be avoided by using different **schedules of reinforcement**—that is, different techniques. When the organism is not being continuously reinforced—when it does not get a reward each time it performs a desired act—it is on a **partial reinforcement schedule.** There are four types of partial reinforcement schedules.

Variable Ratio. A pigeon quickly learns to peck at a button for food. But if you use continuous reinforcement, the pigeon will quit unless it is really hungry. In contrast, suppose the pigeon gets food after five pecks, then after seven pecks, then after three, or whatever variable numbers you want to use. Once you stop the reinforcement, the pigeon will peck over 10,000 times before finally giving up (Skinner, 1957). This is the **variable ratio schedule.** (See Figure 7.1.) *Ratio* refers to numbers. Thus, with the pigeons, you vary the number of pecks required before reinforcement occurs. Humans can really get hooked on this type of schedule, which is how slot machines work. Since players don't know exactly when the money will fall through the chute, they work hard at it, just like the pigeons. Usually, the machines are set to give a few coins as reinforcement every now and then but to give a jackpot only infrequently.

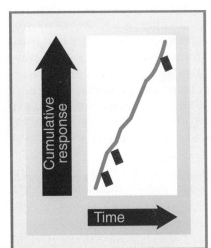

▲ *Figure 7.1 Steep slope indicates rapid, steady response rate (reinforcement indicated by blips).*

Focus Question

• Why is it more effective to use schedules of reinforcement to affect behavior than continuous reinforcement?

continuous reinforcement reinforcement given each time a behavior occurs.

schedules of reinforcement different methods of reinforcing

partial reinforcement schedule reinforcement not given each time an act is performed

variable ratio schedule schedule in which reinforcement occurs after a desired act is performed a specific but variable number of times

fixed ratio schedule schedule in which reinforcement occurs after a desired act is performed a fixed number of times

Fixed Ratio. What happens if you keep the ratio the same, so there is one reinforcement every time the creature performs a *certain number* of acts? For example, what if the pigeon is rewarded after every five pecks? This is called a **fixed ratio schedule,** since the relationship between the number of pecks and the number of reinforcements is always the same. With this method, the pigeons will peck as rapidly as possible because they know that the faster they go, the greater the number of reinforcements they will receive.

▲ *Modern working conditions do not always encourage the greatest productivity.*

At first, this seems like it might be a good way to squeeze every drop of work possible out of factory workers—but there are major pitfalls. Suppose that an electronics company decides to put the workers on a fixed ratio schedule in which they are paid by the number of components they produce. As workers are forced to speed up, they will put screws in halfway and leave out parts in order to save time and produce more pieces. Some workers may decide to try to outproduce the others, which might seem to be a benefit; but even then, pressure from the group as a whole will force a quick end to this competition. On occasion, though, the fixed ratio schedule may work, as with individual farmhands who are paid by the bushel.

variable interval schedule schedule in which reinforcement occurs after a desired act is performed following a variable amount of time

Variable Interval. A third type of partial reinforcement schedule is called a **variable interval schedule.** Here, the creature never knows (in terms of time, or interval) when the reinforcement will arrive. It may come at the end of three minutes, then two minutes, then five minutes, and so forth. A real-life example can be found in that baffling activity called fishing, in which a person sits hour after hour holding a pole up in the air staring into space while apparently nothing happens. Actually, variable interval reinforcement is going on and keeps the person moving the boat or adjusting the line. The line is attached to a bobber that floats on the water. At unpredictable intervals (from the current or a small wave most often, but on occasion from a fish), the bobber will disappear below water level, causing considerable excitement and keeping hope alive (Kary, 1984). With variable interval reinforcement, animals will keep working at a steady, sluggish pace, just to be sure they are performing the right act when the prize comes. But they don't overdo it in terms of speed.

fixed interval schedule schedule in which reinforcement occurs after a desired act is performed following a fixed amount of time

Fixed Interval. A fourth type of schedule, called a **fixed interval schedule,** gives a reward when a specific, fixed amount of time has passed. It has an interesting effect on the behavior of animals. Pigeons that learn they are going to be rewarded every five minutes no matter how fast they peck become very casual about it all. They walk over to the pecking button, hit it once, saunter away for a while, and then return, hitting it again. They mope about until just before the five-minute interval is over. Then they move to the button and peck rapidly.

 **Focus**

Schedules of Reinforcement

Variable Ratio

Reinforcement is given after a variable number of behaviors.

Fixed Ratio

Reinforcement is given after a fixed number of behaviors.

Variable Interval

Reinforcement is given after a variable amount of time.

Fixed Interval

Reinforcement is given after a fixed amount of time.

Which two schedules of reinforcement would produce behaviors that are difficult to extinguish?

 ## Pause for Thought

1. What is the main difference between classical and operant conditioning?
2. What are some examples of primary and secondary reinforcers?
3. How does reinforcement affect behavior? How do positive reinforcement, negative reinforcement, and punishment differ?

Critical Thinking

4. Think of an original example for each of the following: generalization, discrimination, extinction, shaping, variable ratio, fixed ratio, variable interval, fixed interval.

Thinking Critically about Psychology

Do Rewards Really Work?

What if your teachers handed out free movie passes to students who scored 85% or higher on tests? Would this motivate you to study harder? B. F. Skinner and most other behaviorists would guess that you would, provided you enjoy movies. But would you really learn the material better than if no reward were given? Some recent research suggests that outside rewards affect only short-term learning habits.

What specifically is being claimed or stated? Typical rewards used in school, such as gold stars, stickers, privileges, and even praise and grades, do not create lasting, effective learning habits.

What is the objective evidence for and against this claim? Much of the evidence against this claim is presented throughout the chapter, so we'll emphasize the evidence supporting the claim. Numerous studies have shown that subjects who expect a reward for completing some school task do not perform as well as other subjects who expect nothing (Kohn, 1993). This seems to hold true regardless of the age or sex of the subjects and regardless of the tasks performed, which range from memorizing facts to creating art projects. In fact, these results become even more pronounced when the tasks are challenging. Other studies have focused on the effects of using grades to motivate learning. Several researchers conclude that grades actually interfere with an interest in learning (Grolnick & Ryan, 1987; Butler & Nisan, 1986). Psychologist Martin Seligman goes as far as to suggest that some kinds of praise meant to bolster self-esteem can actually be detrimental. He argues that our society values self-esteem so highly that we often use praise inappropriately—meaning that the praise is not connected to any particular behavior (Seligman, 1995). In fairness, however, it must be pointed out that research clearly supports the usefulness of rewards, especially verbal rewards, in most types of learning (Eisenberg & Cameron, 1996).

What other interpretations might be made instead? Sometimes it's difficult to define and measure learning. A student who expects a reward for completing an art project may not produce as interesting a final product as someone who does not expect a reward, but maybe this rewarded student still benefits. Maybe he or she, after receiving a string of rewards for various projects, eventually learns to enjoy the process of creating art and becomes better at doing so. The same could apply to someone who receives high grades for completing assignments. As for praise, most of us know how it feels to receive an empty compliment, but this false praise probably needs to happen persistently for damage to occur; for some this persistence unfortunately happens frequently (Seligman, 1995).

One recent study at Columbia University offers a slightly different glimpse at this issue (Mueller & Dweck, 1998). Researchers asked young stu-

▲ *Recognition and praise for a hard-won accomplishment can mean a great deal.*

dents to solve increasingly difficult math problems. Some students were praised for their effort; others were praised for their intelligence (getting the right results). When the "intelligent" students were faced with the more challenging problems, they were less determined and enthusiastic than subjects who had been praised for their efforts. The "good effort" students also reported greater interest in the material to be learned.

What are the most logical conclusions to draw? This is a tough call to make since learning is such an individualized process. If you've ever crammed for a test, you know that the reward of a good grade can keep you studying. But do you really learn the material when you cram? Do you adopt lasting and effective learning habits? The most logical conclusion is that both sides are correct. Rewards can interfere with true learning, but eliminating rewards completely would not serve anyone well. Instead, some middle ground might work best. Schools should encourage students to think for themselves, provide interesting lessons that students can apply to their own lives, and allow students many options in the learning process. At the same time, schools should think long and hard about the ways they use rewards to motivate learning.

Applying Critical Thinking Skills

Would free movie passes for high test scores motivate you in any way? Explain.

See if COOL works for you....

Claim?

Objective evidence for and against claim?

Other interpretations?

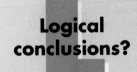
Logical conclusions?

Extinguishing Bad Habits

1.   Remove, avoid, or delay reinforcement.
Jim has a bad habit of snacking while doing homework. Snacks are obviously the reinforcement, so Jim might try doing his homework in a place where snacks are unavailable. If that's impossible, he could delay the reinforcement: no snacks until he finishes 30 minutes of homework. Another way to avoid this reinforcement is to place the snacks out of sight or in inconvenient places.

2.   Do not remove reinforcement, but find a new behavior to get that reinforcement.
Sally's jokes in class are reinforced by the laughter and attention she receives. Sometimes her jokes are disruptive, though. Her teacher realizes how much this reinforcement means to Sally and uses attention to reinforce other, less disruptive behaviors.

3.   Narrow or avoid the stimuli (or cues) that precede the habit.
Gina buys too many unnecessary items at the grocery store. One of the cues that precede this behavior is hunger. If she eats before shopping, she can easily avoid this one cue. The items themselves are also cues to buy. Gina might avoid these cues by making a list of items beforehand.

Focus Question

• What kind of learning do social learning theorists emphasize?

social learning learning from the behavior of others

observational learning a form of social learning in which the organism observes and imitates the behavior of others

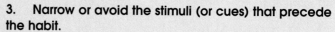

Social Learning

In present-day psychology, most research has moved away from classical and operant conditioning. While both play a role in learning, they fall short of explaining complex learning processes. One current theory about learning involves what is called **social learning,** and its most prominent theorist is psychologist **Albert Bandura** (ban-DUR-ah). He claims that the most important aspect of learning was missed by Pavlov, Watson, and Skinner, for he feels that between the stimulus and the response is the complex "inner person" who is able to analyze events and make decisions before a response is given. (In case it slipped by you, the learning theorists we discussed earlier more or less ignored the individual and focused on robotlike patterns of stimulus and response or action and reinforcement.) Bandura believes that we need a more complex explanation for behavior when we analyze group, or social, living. According to Bandura, in order to survive, we imitate directly the activities of those around us. Imitation, then, is one type of social learning.

Much of our behavior is acquired by **observational learning,** meaning that we learn patterns of behavior by watching others and deciding what to imitate. From the parent, a child learns speech patterns, personal

▲ *Social learning theorist, Albert Bandura.*

4. Break the chain.

Determined, Lisa walks to the exercise room after school to ride the stationary bike. On her way there, she stops at her locker, talks with a few friends, decides which books she'll need to bring home later, sees some other friends, and takes care of a few minor chores. She gradually talks herself out of exercising: 10 minutes have already gone by, she's busy, by the time she gets there it will be 3:30, and so on. If she walks straight to the exercise room after her last class, she can break the chain of behaviors that interfere with her exercising.

5. Monitor the bad habit.

Jerry spends too much money. If you were to ask him how much he actually spends in a week, however, he couldn't even guess. If he wrote down what he spent each day, he could monitor his behavior and set a specific goal for himself. Jerry also has a bad habit of saying *like* too often—but the problem is that he's usually unaware of this. He asks a friend to give him a subtle signal every time he says *like*. Eventually, this awareness helps him, you know, like, curb his habit.

Describe one of your bad habits and decide which method would be most effective in breaking that habit.

habits, and how to react to other people. In other words, the child observes and then patterns behavior after the behavior of the important people in his or her life (Bandura & Walters, 1963). Just in case you feel a little confused about the terminology: *Social learning* refers to *all* learning in a social situation. *Observational learning* is *one* of the processes used for social learning; in this process, we (and many animals) watch events, persons, and situations for cues on how to behave.

In a now-famous experiment, Bandura demonstrated that children who observe aggressive adult models become aggressive themselves as a result. The children watched adults slugging plastic stand-up dolls. When the children were left alone, they imitated this behavior.

We once had a neighbor who was so afraid of germs that she would disinfect her house every 48 hours. She would not enter any neighbor's house, preferring to stay outside where she thought the air would be fresher and more germ free. We were very surprised, however, when her daughter began to wear gloves while riding her tricycle—surprised, that is, until we were invited over to the woman's house for the first time. During the whole time we were there, the woman wore thin, latex, surgical gloves (true story).

▲ *This child is observing and copying his father's behavior.*

▲ *These laboratory film clips show an adult modeling aggression and children imitating it.*

Don't miss the important point that Bandura is making: The child does not require a *specific* reinforcement such as food for learning to occur. Social learning can occur by exposure and imitation alone. Bandura felt that earlier explanations of learning were too simplified.

Focus Question

....

• What kind of learning do cognitive theorists emphasize?

cognitive approach an approach to the study of learning that emphasizes abstract mental processes and previous knowledge

Cognitive Psychology and Learning

Bandura's pioneering approach to social learning is clearly more complex than older theories. Today psychologists are finding that even his early version doesn't completely account for the elaborate task of learning. Bandura himself more fully includes thought processes in his research and general approach, referring to it as social *cognitive* theory (Bandura, Barbaranelli, Caprara, & Pastorelli, 1996; Bandura, 1991). In fact, much of the present research looks at learning through the **cognitive approach.** The word *cognitive* here means "knowledge-using," with "knowledge" meaning far more than just a stimulus and response or imitation. Psychologists who follow the cognitive approach emphasize that we are able to learn very abstract and subtle things that could not be learned simply through conditioning or social learning. For instance, some people have learned through the stories of others that it is bad luck to walk under a ladder or to break a mirror. This kind of belief is very abstract and hence could not be learned by any method other than the cognitive one. When psychologists study cognition, then, they focus on how complex knowledge is obtained, processed, and organized.

Complexities of Conditioning

The conditioning process can be far more complex than it at first appears. Clearly, rewards have different effects on different people in different situations, partly because of how people interpret events in their lives. The cognitive learning theorists would certainly not find that surprising. They believe that to omit mental processes from the conditioning equation is to ignore the most interesting and meaningful aspects of human behavior (Thompson, 1994). They support their position by pointing out that even the "simple" conditioning of animals is not really so simple after all.

For example, the type of cage an experimenter keeps an animal in will affect the animal's learning ability, as will the amount of time the animal has previously spent in the cage. If an animal is in unfamiliar surroundings, it gets preoccupied with its new environment and doesn't pay attention to the experiment (Hall, 1980). If the cue that food is coming is a sound, a rat startles. If the cue is something visual above the animal's head, it stands on its hind legs (Hollis, 1997). And as in the case of Pavlov's dogs falling asleep, animals vary in the degree to which they are interested in the experiment itself. Additionally, animals condition more easily to pictures of rats or spiders than they do to pictures of flowers and mushrooms (Marks, 1979).

Individual differences also exist among animals in operant conditioning. For example, pigeons tend to peck at lighted keys even without reinforcement, and they peck differently if they are trying to get water as compared to their efforts to get food (Miller, 1983).

For humans, it is not always necessary to have something actually happen for classical conditioning to occur. You can use mental images for both the unconditioned and conditioned stimuli (Dadds, Bovbjerg, Redd, and Cutmore, 1997).

All of these findings make it clear that the conditioning process is more complex than just stimuli, responses, and consequences. To see how complicated it can become, think about how the results might have changed if Little Albert had been a bit older and had *known* that Watson was standing behind him banging the bar.

Under the cognitive theory, complexities Watson didn't know about take on a new light. For instance, at first it seems reasonable to assume that Watson's work with Little Albert can explain such human problems as phobias—in other words, that fears of closed spaces, heights, snakes,

In Focus

Four Types of Learning

Classical Conditioning: Learning by association
Operant Conditioning: Learning through reinforcement
Social Learning: Learning by observing and imitating
Cognitive Learning: Learning through mental processing

Allison becomes extremely fearful around dogs. She could have learned this fear through *any* of these types of learning. Can you explain each possible way?

Case Study

Conditioning: A Matter of Life and Death

A 9-month-old baby lay in a hospital crib starving to death, his weight less than 12 pounds. The baby was so thin that his ribs stuck out and the skin hung from the bones of his arms. His eyes were wide and dull; he spent most of his time staring into space. Death seemed inevitable because each time he swallowed food, it would reach a certain point in its downward movement and then his muscles would contract in the opposite direction, causing him to throw up.

Some central part of the child's brain was sending a signal to "throw it into reverse" when the food reached a certain spot. All available forms of medical and surgical treatment were tried, and there seemed to be no hope. Finally someone hit on the idea of using a basic psychological principle—conditioning. When you *condition* a response, you form a connection or association between the response and something else.

Doctors had to find the exact location in the digestive tract at which the reversal of the food movement took place. Once they located this precise area, the process of conditioning began. A wire that could carry an electric shock was attached to the infant's leg. Each time food

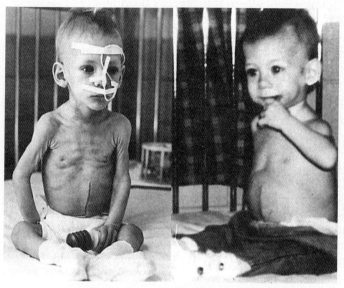

▲ *The power of conditioning is demonstrated in these two photos of the 9-month-old baby.*

arrived at the "reversal spot," a light shock was sent to the leg at one-second intervals until the vomiting was over. At first there seemed to be no significant change, but his doctors persisted. At the end of two weeks of treatment, his normal food reversing had been thoroughly associated with something very unpleasant for the infant. His brain decided to stop the reversal process in order to avoid the shock. Soon afterward, the infant began to gain significant weight—26 percent in just two weeks—and he was discharged, well and happy. When he was tested again a year and two years later, he was psychologically and physically healthy (Lang & Melamed, 1969). In less extreme cases, when the baby is not starving, sometimes a milder punishment is effective, such as squirting something bitter or sour into the baby's mouth.

Review the Case Study

Pick a simple behavior of yours and explain how that behavior may have been conditioned.

open places, or germs arise from straight association. But this is not necessarily the case. Psychologists have discovered a strange quirk about phobias. While many of them may indeed come from association, there is clearly a cognitive (or knowledge-based) aspect to them, because phobias usually develop in relation to some kind of *natural* danger. Thus, if you are in a closed space, you really may be trapped; if you are up high, you may fall; some snakes are indeed poisonous; if you are out in the open, you may be more vulnerable; germs can kill you. All of these are known phobias; in contrast, phobias for neutral or "unnatural" things, such as umbrellas, trees, light switches, or automobile tires, generally do not occur. It is possible to condition animals and people to fear these kinds of neutral objects, but it isn't easy, and it takes a long time (Behavioral Science Task Force, 1995). As you can see, the conditioning of fears seems to develop through a sophisticated cognitive process.

Another complication arises when we look at the difference between learning how to do something and actually doing it. Sometimes learning is not all that obvious. For instance, if an experimenter does not put any food in a maze, but just lets some rats wander around in it, they still learn something about the maze. If food is then made available, these rats will learn the correct route through the maze much faster than rats who have never seen the maze before. Learning like this that is not obvious at first, but takes place under the surface, so to speak, is called **latent learning.**

As we have seen, simply being exposed to something may result in a small amount of learning. However, we generally learn much more when we are motivated or reinforced for doing so. And thought processes play a large part in whether we are motivated and what is most reinforcing to us. Motivation to perform some action will be determined in part by what are called **expectancies.** Expectancies are our beliefs about our chances of successfully performing this action and of getting the desired reward (Ryckman, 1997; Rotter, 1982). If we think we won't be able to do it, we probably won't try. If we think we will be able to do it, but won't get a reward anyway, we probably won't try. Here's a real-life example. Let's assume that your social skills are okay, but nothing to shout about. You have met someone that you want to ask to a concert or for coffee or to go to the mall with you. Two questions must be answered before you decide whether to act or remain silent: (1) Can you say the right things and present yourself well enough that your invitation will have a chance? (2) If you can, is the person likely to accept your invitation? A "no" answer to either question makes it pretty unlikely that you will go ahead and take the risk.

Our thought processes also influence how desirable a particular reinforcement is. Assume, for example, that you have an equal chance of getting a snowmobile, an all-terrain vehicle, or a jet ski. Which one would you rather have? The preference for certain items or events over others refers to their **reinforcement value.** Thus, some of us will work very hard to have a day off to lie around and relax, while others will work just as hard in order to go biking or skydiving. The reinforcement value of any particular object or event, then, is highly individualized.

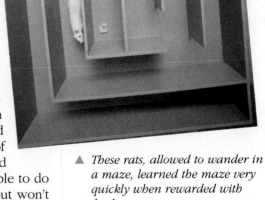

▲ *These rats, allowed to wander in a maze, learned the maze very quickly when rewarded with food.*

latent learning learning that is not obvious but goes on under the surface

expectancies beliefs about our ability to perform an action and to get the desired reward

reinforcement value the preference for certain types of reinforcement over other types

Focus Question

- How did Tolman explain the ability of humans and animals to learn about location?

cognitive map a mental image of where one is located in space

strategies methods for solving problems

Cognitive Maps

In the 1930s, psychologist **E. C. Tolman** was already arguing that the mechanical stimulus-response view was too shallow an explanation for all learning. But only with the emergence of cognitive psychology has his early claim been taken seriously and studied extensively. Tolman claimed that even rats in a maze were able to form what he called a **cognitive map.** This term refers to the ability of humans and animals to form mental images of where they are located in the environment. Thus, when a maze is changed, a rat is able to visualize the change after going through it once and then to run the maze to seek food using the new mental image (Tolman et al., 1946).

We now know that Tolman was right—that there is no such thing as a simple organism. Rats in mazes, for example, not only form some kind of cognitive map but also use **strategies** (techniques for solving problems) to explore carefully the alleyways of a maze without going over the same territory more than once. Chimpanzees in a maze are remarkable. An experimenter can carry a baby chimp through a complicated maze and deposit bananas in 18 different places in the alleyway while the chimp watches. When freed, the chimp can find an average of 12 of the 18 bananas quickly without duplicating any routes (Olton, 1979, 1978). Birds that store pine seeds in the ground for months at a time have the same excellent record. In fact, they even pass by storage places of other birds and pick up only their own seeds (Kamil & Roitblat, 1985).

One of the most amusing experiments in this area involved bees who use a "scout" to find food (Gould, 1985, 1984). After finding the food, the scout flies back to the hive to tell the others where the food is. The location is indicated by an elaborate scout-bee "dance" that shows the direction and distance of the food location by the length of its up-down movement and the general pattern

▲ *Fellow bees, pay attention! I know where the food is!*

of its flying. One researcher took a scout bee out into the middle of a lake in a boat and exposed it to food. When it flew back to the hive, it dutifully reported the direction and distance of the food to the others. Since the other bees also have cognitive maps, they presumably thought the scout was mentally disturbed. (Food in the middle of the lake? He's got to be kidding!) Not one bee moved. In the next step of the experiment, a scout bee was taken by boat to the shore at the other side of the lake, exposed to food, and let go. When it reported back to the same hive, all the bees came flying posthaste!

Here is an experiment for you to do; we will discuss the results below. Get a large piece of *unlined* paper. In the center, put where you live. Try to draw your map to scale, but don't use a ruler. Pick two places approximately the same distance away from your home, one to the right and one to the left of it. One should be a place you don't like for some reason; the other, a place you have good feelings about. Draw a map of the streets from your home to each of these two places.

The Map. Don't read this section if you haven't finished your cognitive map yet.

This experiment shows how psychological factors enter into a cognitive map. Note that you have probably made the distance to the unpleasant place greater than the distance to the pleasant place because you don't want to go to the unpleasant one. You have created a symbolic map that tries to move you closer to the pleasant place. In line with this symbolism, you have also straightened out the curves and bends in the road and generally altered the map to fit your own desires rather than strict reality. If the places are not actually equidistant from your home, you can check with a ruler how much you "psychologically" changed the two distances.

 Pause for Thought

1. How is social learning different from conditioning? Explain one method of social learning.
2. The cognitive approach and conditioning emphasize different sorts of learning. Explain.
3. How do cognitive maps and strategies affect learning? Explain how reinforcement values affect behavior.

Critical Thinking

4. Describe a task that requires both social learning and cognitive strategies.
5. Provide original examples of latent learning and expectancies.

APPLYING
Psychology to Life

Learning How to Learn

There are courses as well as many excellent books on how to study. How far you want to go into the subject is a matter of personal choice. Here, however, are a handful of firmly established facts about studying that have stood the tests of time and of many experiments. We hope you will take them to heart. The more of them you use, the better off you will be. Some of them require no pain whatsoever.

Learn to Be a Speedy Reader?

First, two "don'ts": There are many courses in speed reading, but speed reading doesn't work for studying. As your speed increases, comprehension decreases. If you are a very slow reader (less than 70 words per minute on a novel or newspaper article), you might benefit from extra training just to get your speed up to 100 or so words per minute. But speed reading reduces learning when you read faster than 250 words per minute. Learning "in your sleep," by using a tape recorder or other such device, doesn't work either. You learn only in proportion to how awake you are. All the

machine will do is disturb your sleep (Evans & Evans, 1983).

Rewrite and Review

The single most effective thing you can do to help you learn is to write a synopsis in your own words of every two or three paragraphs of the chapter you are studying. Stop reading when an idea seems to be completed and write it out in your own words. You should wind up with your own "minichapter" when you are done. Review your synopsis, note anything that isn't clear, and go back to the text to clarify that point, revising your notes. Keep your minichapters in a separate notebook so you can use them for review later.

Yes, Take a Break!

Here is a technique you will like. The brain demands rest in order to bring together material properly. This might explain why, when you have tried to solve a problem and have finally given up and gone to bed, the solution will suddenly be there when you wake up. The brain has been working on the problem without all the clutter that normally distracts it during the day.

While such a system won't work for regular studying, its principle can be applied. The human attention span is usually about 30 minutes. So quit studying after 25 or 30 minutes—eat or drink

▲ *A familiar method of learning.*

something, talk to someone, do anything different for about 5 minutes. Then go back to studying for another 25 to 30 minutes.

Also, you should change subject matter with each new study cycle (30-minute period), coming back later, if necessary, to the earlier ones. Keep away from similar material from one cycle to another. Put math between history and English, put English between math and chemistry, and so forth.

Finally, at the end of the study period for each subject, try to establish some principle that brings the material together. Ask yourself, "What exactly is the *issue* involved in what I've just studied?" Then review your summaries and leave them alone. If you have *really* studied, your brain will keep working.

Study Skills

A. Things **NOT** to do
   1. Don't read too fast
   2. Don't try to learn in your sleep

B. Things **TO DO**
   1. After a few paragraphs, write down the information in your own words. Make sure that you understand the material. You have a better chance of remembering what you really understand.
   2. Keep the summaries in separate places for later review.
   3. Study in 30-minute blocks. Take a short break. Give yourself a little reward.
   4. Change subject matter between study periods to give the brain a rest.
   5. Review for the main ideas and to make connections meaningful.

▲ *Some tips on effective studying.*

Summary

1. Classical conditioning occurs when a neutral stimulus is associated with a natural stimulus until both bring the same response.

2. Operant conditioning requires some action on the part of the organism. These actions can be positively or negatively reinforced, or they can be punished.

3. Schedules of reinforcement include fixed interval, fixed ratio, variable interval, and variable ratio schedules.

4. Social learning centers on observation of other people. We learn appropriate behaviors by watching others and imitating them.

5. The cognitive approach emphasizes the role of thought processes in learning. Our beliefs about our ability to perform an action and get a reward are an important factor. Also, we prefer some types of reinforcement over others.

Vocabulary

classical conditioning	primary reinforcement	variable ratio schedule
stimulus	secondary reinforcement	fixed ratio schedule
response	positive reinforcement	variable interval schedule
unconditioned stimulus	negative reinforcement	fixed interval schedule
unconditioned response	punishment	social learning
conditioned stimulus	generalization	observational learning
conditioned response	discrimination learning	cognitive approach
stimulus generalization	shaping	latent learning
extinction	chaining	expectancies
spontaneous recovery	continuous reinforcement	reinforcement value
operant conditioning	schedules of reinforcement	cognitive map
reinforcement	partial reinforcement schedule	strategies

Review Questions

For each of the following, indicate whether the capitalized behavior is learned primarily through classical conditioning (CC), operant conditioning (OP), or social learning (SL). Write your answers on a sheet of paper.

1. Nino *EATS* at Lou's Pizza for the first time. Since he enjoys the food, he returns there every Saturday for dinner.
2. The main reason that Nino *EATS* at Lou's Pizza is because all his friends eat there.
3. Every time Nino drives into Lou's parking lot, his *MOUTH WATERS* because he knows he will eat soon.
4. Little Lauren *WEARS* her mom's clothes simply because she wants to imitate her mom.
5. Little Lauren's *HEART RACES* every time she wears her mom's clothes.
6. Little Lauren *WEARS* her mom's clothes often because she knows she will always get a laugh.

Read the following example of a behavior learned through classical conditioning: "The first time that Sarah went to the DENTIST, he stuck a long NEEDLE in her mouth, which naturally caused her to experience FEAR. After a few visits, she experienced FEAR not only when the needle was stuck in her mouth but also when the DENTIST appeared to call her into the office." Using this example, identify the following concepts (possible answers are capitalized above): Write your answers on a sheet of paper.

7. The unconditioned stimulus (UCS)
8. The unconditioned response (UCR)
9. The conditioned stimulus (CS)
10. The conditioned response (CR)
11. The stimulus that started out as neutral (N)

On a sheet of paper, indicate for each statement if it is an example of positive reinforcement or negative reinforcement.

12. Tom hangs up his coat in order to get a dollar.
13. Tom hangs up his coat in order to stop his mom's yelling.
14. Mary stays at home every weekend so she won't run into her old boyfriend.
15. Mary stays at home every weekend because her new boyfriend always comes over.

Matching

On a sheet of paper, match the terms in the right column with the statements in the left column.

16. Phil loves to talk, but when he discovers that no one really listens to him, he stops talking.
17. Phil learns that it's all right to talk during class discussions but not during tests.
18. Phil talks to a person in class wearing green shoes who actually listens to him. As a result, he tries talking to other people wearing green shoes in other classes.
19. Gamblers never know how many times they need to bet in order to win.
20. Factory workers get a break every three hours.
21. Whenever you kick a vending machine three times, candy bars fall out.
22. Every once in a while, candy bars fall out of the vending machine.

a. generalization
b. extinction
c. discrimination
d. fixed ratio
e. variable ratio
f. variable interval
g. fixed interval

Discussion Questions

1. One day, little Theodore is extremely startled when he hears the doorbell, and he begins to cry uncontrollably. In the days that follow, stimulus generalization occurs. Describe what might happen during the following days. How would you extinguish his fear?

2. Describe a fear that you once had that is pretty much extinguished today. Why or how was the fear extinguished?

3. According to operant conditioning, people continue to perform certain behaviors mainly because of the reinforcement they receive. Pick three or four common behaviors you see every day, and identify the reinforcers for each. For example, why do you come to school each day, wear the clothes you do, talk to your friends, and so on? Each behavior may have several reinforcements.

4. Bad habits also persist because of reinforcements. Pick two of your own bad habits, and identify the reinforcers for each. How would you remove or change these reinforcements and possibly extinguish the bad habits?

5. Every time you pass a certain classroom at school, you become anxious. What kind of conditioning probably caused this, and how would you extinguish your anxiety?

6. How might a behaviorist explain superstitious behavior like wearing a lucky necklace or tapping home plate three times before standing in the batter's box? Which schedule of reinforcement would probably best apply?

7. Describe two behaviors that you probably acquired through observational learning. Did the models you observed guide you in any way? Could you have learned these behaviors in any other way? Though you mainly learned these behaviors through observation, what role did conditioning play? For instance, did you eventually receive reinforcement for these behaviors?

8. Your grades have been slipping lately, and your parents have become concerned. They decide to use some of the principles of learning discussed in this chapter to motivate you. One month, they try positive reinforcement; another month, negative reinforcement; and finally, punishment. Explain in practical terms what they might do each month, and explain what method would best motivate you.

Activities and Projects

1. Imagine that you are a consultant hired by your principal to create and implement a program at your school to improve discipline and/or student morale (you can define *morale* any way you want). Using some of the principles of learning outlined in this chapter, create such a program. First, you'll have to decide which behaviors you want to create or change. Do you want students to show up on time to class? Cheer louder at basketball games? Stop throwing food at each other? Once you decide on a specific behavior or two, what kind of reinforcement or punishment will best create that behavior? A high school version of gold stars? Free lunches? Recognition? Days off?

Schools are sometimes slow to change, so you may want to select moderate goals and simple, straightforward plans to achieve them. Consider actually submitting your proposal to your principal.

2. The following activity is for the lover of household pets. Take a cat or a dog, and train the animal to perform a simple behavior like rolling over or pushing open a door. The best way to produce this simple behavior is through shaping: Every time the animal comes even close to performing the behavior you want, reinforce it with food. (Do the shaping when the animal is hungry.) Once the animal knows what it needs to do to get the food, put it on a fixed ratio schedule for a few days and then on a variable ratio schedule for a few days. (If it's at all possible, use two different animals, and train each on a different schedule.)

Which schedule seems to be most effective? Explain. Would it be more difficult to extinguish behavior learned through one schedule than behavior learned through the other? Explain. Finally, jot down any general problems you have in training the animal(s).

3. Interview two parents from two different families about the kinds of discipline and motivation they use in raising their children. All parents have used at least some of the learning principles discussed in the chapter. Your job is to find out which ones these parents use and how they use them. You may need to teach the parents some of the terminology from the chapter. Here are some sample questions:

Are there any consistent reinforcements you offer your children, regardless of age?

How do you motivate your children to complete chores?

How do you find the right reinforcement for each child? Or do you use the same reinforcement for all your children?

Your five-year-old insists she wants a certain toy while you're walking through a toy store. She begins to insist loudly. What do you do?

Do you have any system for punishment? Do you use time-outs? Removal of privileges?

4. Get a friend to participate in an experiment on shaping. Conduct the experiment where there will be few distractions. Sit across from the friend, and read the following directions:

Imagine you're applying for a job and I'm the boss. I'm going to ask you a series of simple questions that will determine whether I'll hire you. My decision to hire will be based not on the content of your answers but on the behaviors that you happen to perform in the next few minutes. So just pay attention and try to produce as many positive responses from me as possible after each question. The more positive responses you receive, the better your chances will be of getting hired.

Have ready a list of 25 to 30 simple questions, such as name, address, and so on. Before you begin asking the questions, decide on a simple behavior you want to shape. For example, if you

notice that your friend is slouching back in the chair, try to get him or her to lean forward and fold his or her hands.

Slowly read the list of questions. The answers, of course, are meaningless. But whenever the friend comes progressively closer to the behavior you want, nod and say, "OK." Your friend should interpret this as a positive response. If the friend continues to slouch, shake your head disapprovingly and say, "Uh-oh" (or something similar). *Note:* Your first few responses will be negative, since the friend has no idea what you're reinforcing. This whole process of shaping is similar to the "hot and cold" game that most of us played as kids. Whenever the person gets "hot," or close to doing what you want, you positively reinforce him or her. Whenever he or she gets "cold," you offer no reinforcement.

Repeat this entire procedure with two other friends, and compare the results. Discuss whether the shaping was generally successful. On the average, how long did it take for your friends to figure out the behavior you wanted? (*Note:* If your friends did not figure out the behavior but still *did* the behavior by the end of your questioning, shaping can be considered successful.) Finally, what were some of the obstacles that interfered with the shaping process? Explain.

5. Find out who some of the top-ranked students in your school are. Interview two of them to find out about their study habits. Ask them this: "It's the night before an important test. What steps do you take to study? Be specific. How long do you study?"

Once you accumulate a list of specific studying behaviors, conduct an informal survey around the school, asking people whether they use any of the strategies on your list. Ask them how often they use the strategies: very often? once in a while? never? Finally, ask them their grade point averages.

Compare the grade point averages with the answers on your survey. Do you find that these are related in any way? Explain.

An alternative to conducting a survey might be to convince two teachers to poll their classes about study habits. One class could be an advanced class, and the other could be a regular class.

Information Processing and Memory

To acquire information, we must control what comes in and what is blocked out from the environment. Material that we retain is sent through a short-term memory, where it is processed, and then moved to a long-term storage area, where physical changes occur in the nerve cells.

Acquiring Information

Focus Question
....
• Why is it easier to learn something that "grabs" your attention?

All day long, we talk, read, listen, discuss, fight, hope, believe, wish, despair, and analyze. All of these behaviors are taken for granted. But none of them is possible without our learning and storing the information that we use in each case. We sit and mumble to ourselves, but we are mumbling *something,* and the something comes from things we have stored in memory. So no issue is more critical to psychology than how we acquire and retain information.

To start off, we have listed four passages for you to read. Read them only once. In order for us to make the points we need to make, *please* don't reread these passages until we refer to them later.

1. In 1925, lawyer William Jennings Bryan prosecuted John Scopes for teaching evolution and won the case. In 1919, many states were won over to the cause of the Eighteenth Amendment, which prohibited the sale of liquor. Fourteen years later, the Twenty-First Amendment repealed the Eighteenth.

2. Raoult's Law states that the depression of the freezing points and the elevation of the vapor pressures of liquids that are dissolved are in proportion to the number of molecules of substance dissolved.

3. If you are attacked by a dog, hit its nose hard and fast. Put your forearm in front of you and jam it into the dog's open mouth. Bring your other arm around behind the dog and press it against the dog's neck. Force the dog's head backward and over your arm, snapping the neck.

4. The following is a poem about outlaw John Wesley Hardin, who roamed the West in the late 1800s. He had killed five people by the time he was 15 years old. Later he became a sheriff!

   John Wesley Hardin, meanest outlaw of the West,
   Killed over 40 men, and his reasons weren't the best.
   From a hotel room next to his, a snoring man disturbed his rest.
   So he simply fired through the wall and shot the man to death.

Learning Curves

Learning processes can be plotted out visually using graphs. For example, graphs can be used to study the influence of attention on learning.

Influence of Attention. **Attention** refers to a person's alert focusing on material. When we attend to something, we become physically aroused, and this activates chemicals in the brain that aid our ability to learn. Even accidental learning requires a minimum amount of attention (Seger, 1994).

The item about John Wesley Hardin is a real attention grabber. Probably every one of you can repeat a good portion of its content without having to check back. A graphic view of learning the whole poem would look something like Figure 8.1 (see page 224). The figure shows that, although a person would probably make errors on the first few trials, learning would take place rapidly until the person reached 100 percent mastery.

▲ *Accidental learning in this situation could be deadly.*

attention alert focusing on material

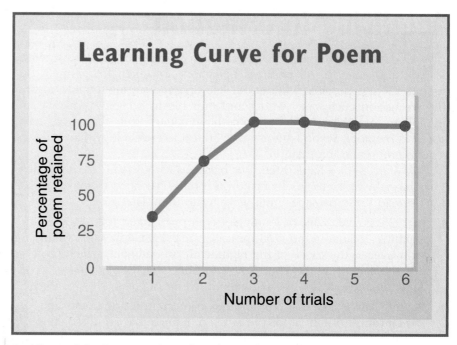

▲ *Figure 8.1*   *Learning Curve for John Wesley Hardin Poem*

(The term *trial* refers to each attempt to recite the material after a session of memorizing.)

Conventional Learning.   Compare the John Wesley Hardin poem with item 2, Raoult's Law. Because the material is not an attention grabber for the average person, it involves a slower learning process. Motivation and attention are moderate, so learning is more of a struggle. Over a period of

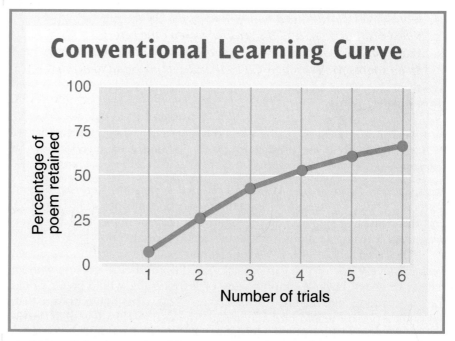

▲ *Figure 8.2*   *Conventional Learning Curve for Raoult's Law*

time and through a number of trials, the graph of learning this information will look like Figure 8.2. Note that here the curve moves gradually upward with practice as learning progresses, but it shows nothing close to the dramatic upward movement of learning the John Wesley Hardin poem. The curve in Figure 8.2 is the conventional (or usual) one that applies to most learning. It is simply called the **learning curve.**

Chemical Influences on Learning

Many chemicals influence learning. These chemicals fall into two broad categories: stimulants and depressants.

Stimulants, such as the caffeine in coffee, tea, and some soft drinks, can actually increase learning. They stir up the body's activity level, which in turn increases memory. To have this effect, a soft drink must have sugar in it, too, not an artificial sweetener. Artificial sweeteners alter the normal firing pattern of brain cells, canceling the benefit of caffeine. In any case, stimulants increase the level of brain chemicals that allow for more rapid learning. Strong stimulants, however, such as amphetamines (speed), can overstimulate the brain and cause the reverse—loss of learning.

Overall, the best of all worlds is to be naturally excited about what you are learning, because then your body will produce its own chemicals to assist in the task. Anxiety about taking a test, at reasonable levels, acts just as caffeine does to stimulate the person. Some students "come apart," though, and drive the anxiety level so high that it acts like the amphetamines, blocking learning.

Any depressant drug—such as a tranquilizer or alcohol—will block the firing of brain nerve cells and reduce learning. So will hot dogs or cold-cut meats. They contain a preservative that in low concentrations tends to depress learning ability. But you have to eat three hot dogs or cold-cut sandwiches to get the effect, which is pretty hard to do without feeling horrible. Someone once said that "we are what we eat," which doesn't make much sense; but what we eat or drink *can* sometimes influence our behavior.

The fact is that taking in *any* chemical will alter a person's bodily condition, or state. If someone learns something while in that altered state, the material learned will be easier to remember later on if the same state is reproduced. At the extreme, people who have drunk too much will not remember what happened once they are sober, but the odds are that the memory will return if they get in that condition again. The same principles apply to someone who studies after drinking three cups of coffee. This is called **state-dependent learning,** meaning that the learning and reproduction of the material are reliant (dependent) on the condition (state) of the body at the time of learning.

Emotional Factors in Learning

The most important learning is that centering on survival. Animals whose existence depends on remembering who or what is dangerous are in an excited state when a crisis arises, and this excited state increases the

learning curve a gradual upward slope representing increased retention of material as the result of learning

Focus Question
• • • • • • • • • • • • • • • • • • • •
• What foods will affect rates of learning?

▲ *Can caffeine increase learning?*

state-dependent learning learning that occurs in one chemical state and is best reproduced when the same state occurs again

Focus Question
• • • • • • • • • • • • • • • • • • • •
• Why is it important for teachers to make learning fun or interesting?

225

brain chemicals for learning; hence, the animals have increased memory potential. Similarly, a place that provides food is a good place to remember, and animals' brains seem to become primed for learning at the discovery of such a source.

For humans, the principle is the same but more complicated. Here are the results of an experiment called "Nancy's Visit to the Doctor": Researchers gave subjects a long, tedious, and involved story about Nancy's visit. As you might have guessed, the subjects remembered little when they were tested later. In contrast, when the story was given to a different group and was altered to start off with the possibility of a major change or crisis in Nancy's life (an emotion generator), subjects remembered the details of the visit quite well (Owens et al., 1979).

So emotional involvement increases learning. Another good example is the use of humor in the classroom. In moderation, it increases the level of brain activity. Too much humor, though, will wind up making humor itself the subject matter and will detract from learning. In some cases, the fact that a teacher is unpleasant can increase learning for a while, because even though the emotion created is negative, it still *is* an emotion. After a while, however, the teacher's nastiness or ridicule becomes the major focus of attention, and learning decreases.

Transfer of Training

transfer of training learning process in which learning is carried over from one task to another based on similarities between the tasks

positive transfer transfer of learning that results from similarities between two tasks

One major learning process is called **transfer of training.** Its principle is relatively simple: Learning task A will carry over (transfer) to learning task B if there are similarities between them.

Positive Transfer. Police officers who shoot on a range at targets that dart, hide, and suddenly reappear will be better able to shoot at real-life targets because of the similarity of the tasks. Hence, the learning in one situation *transfers* to that in a similar situation. This is called a **positive transfer.** The same technique is used by airlines when they have pilots fly in simulators that recreate precisely the feel and movement of a genuine aircraft.

If you are interested in chemistry, you may already have been exposed to some of the elements found in Raoult's Law (item 2 at the beginning of the chapter), and you probably remember at least part of what it said. This involves a transfer of training from your exposure to similar material. If you have never studied chemistry, though, chances are that Raoult's Law is already long gone from your memory storage area—or never even made it into your memory at all, as we'll discuss later.

▲ *The cockpits of flight simulators look like the real thing—a necessity for positive transfer.*

So positive transfer takes place when some useful similarity exists between what you have learned in the past and the new material. For example, a person who has taken courses in Latin will have an edge over others when taking Spanish, since many Spanish words are similar to Latin words.

negative transfer interference with learning that results from differences between two otherwise similar tasks

Negative Transfer. Sometimes transfer is not a useful thing. On these occasions, **negative transfer** occurs. If you learned to drive a car with an automatic transmission and then changed to a car that uses manual shifting, requiring a clutch, odds are that you stalled frequently, ground the gears a lot, and felt quite uncomfortable. If you learned how to drive with a manual transmission and then drove an automatic, you probably kept pushing an imaginary clutch to the floor and felt very foolish. The previously learned task is interfering with the present one.

Exercising the Mind?   Latin was picked merely as an example above. Still, for a while, educators believed that if you took very difficult and obscure courses like Latin, even if you didn't want or need to, somehow the pain and struggle involved in doing so "exercised" your mind so you would be smarter for most other courses. That has proved not to be the case. Some courses are considered a necessity for a proper education; and for many people, they are not easy. Such courses include chemistry, physics, and advanced mathematics. But although they are difficult, they don't "exercise the mind" in the sense of making it "stronger" for other courses. Chemistry and physics will transfer to one another because of some similarities, but there will be no transfer between, say, chemistry and history, physics and literature, or mathematics and Spanish.

Information Processing

Learning and reproducing what we have learned is referred to as **information processing.** In other words, information processing is another term for the methods by which we take in, analyze, store, and bring back the various things we learn. Next, we discuss studies of these various processes.

Using a Schema

Suppose we were to ask Little Red Riding Hood how to get to Grandma's house. She would not come out with the answer automatically but would go through a series of steps to figure it out. She would have to bring various bits of stored mental information together in an ordered sequence before she could give an answer. Here are the steps:

1. Process words in the question asked.
2. Match the question to rough categories of information she knows in order to find the correct area where the information might be.
3. Within the area chosen, search to find a representation of Grandma in her house.
4. Hold that representation in her own consciousness while she locates the brain representation of where she herself is when the question is asked.
5. Find all the connections (streets and directions) between where she is now and where Grandma is located.
6. Answer the question step by step, from where she is to Grandma's house, all the time blocking out incorrect connections that might appear (such as where Uncle Harry's house is) (Anderson, 1983).

This organized and systematic approach to answering questions or solving problems is called a **schema** (SKEE-ma). The word *schema* comes

information processing the methods by which we take in, analyze, store, and retrieve material

Focus Questions

- What is a schema?
- Why are schemas useful in organizing information?

schema an organized and systematic approach to answering questions or solving problems from the Greek, meaning an "outline or pattern." In other words, each of us has a plan for solving problems.

An organized search is required because of the complexity and amount of material stored in the brain. In fact, it truly leaves one in awe to think that any of us can *ever* come up with an answer to any question, much less do so in a matter of a few hundredths of a second.

▶ **Figure 8.3** *Finding Grandma's House*

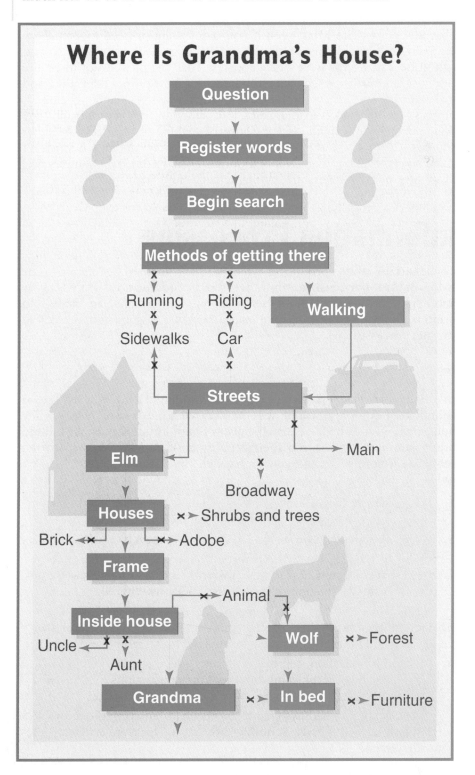

Figure 8.3 shows a small part of the schema used to find Grandma's house. As you can see in the figure, the original information, given in the form of a question, has to be processed through the correct sensory register (visual, auditory, smell, touch, taste)—in this case, auditory, since Little Red Riding Hood *heard* the question asked. Creating the answer requires, among other things, remembering how she got there (walking, running, riding), deciding whose house she is going to (aunt's, uncle's, grandmother's), and analyzing the types of houses possible (wood, brick, adobe, or gingerbread).

Importance of Organizing Information

The importance of organization is demonstrated in the following experiment: Pictures of rooms containing various objects were given to subjects to see how many objects they could recall when the pictures were removed. If a picture contained an unnatural scene—for example, if the picture showed a kitchen knife on the coffee table, pots and pans on the dining table, and flowers on the stove burner—the picture was very hard to remember. This experiment suggests that in everyday activity, we form an organized, coherent, structured "map" of our world. If what we see doesn't "match" our existing memory (that pans belong on the stove), we have to stop and overcome confusion (Mandler & Ritchey, 1977).

Many of our memory sequences have been thoroughly learned. If the brain fires the information memory of "capital" for "United States," for example, the hookup is so well established that very quickly the answer will arrive: "Washington, D.C." Of course, there are always a few who will say, "Bowlegs, Oklahoma," but that's the way life is!

You should note that an important aspect of learning is the ability to eliminate or block out the *incorrect* areas we run across during the search for an answer. If you remember the story of Little Red Riding Hood, you'll recall that on one occasion, instead of meeting her Grandma, Little Red met a wolf with his snout sticking out over the bedcovers. So as she tries to answer the question, she runs into a chain of information connected to wolves—forests, other animals, snouts, nose size, and so forth—most of which must be blocked out in order to get the right answer to where Grandma's house is. The X's in Figure 8.3 show some of the areas that must be blocked.

Finally, when we learn something new, it must be stored in the correct area. If information about a car is stored where flowers and bushes are located, the chances of ever retrieving that information are remote. There is some suspicion today that a fair part of what we call "intelligence" may be the ability to store and block information properly.

▲ *Who made it to Grandma's house first, Little Red or the big, bad wolf?*

Pause for Thought

1. List several chemical influences and emotional factors in learning.
2. What is meant by transfer of learning?
3. What is the difference between positive and negative transfer?

Critical Thinking
....
4. Describe one schema you've used in the past 24 hours.

Focus Questions

• What are four special processes for improving learning?

• How do each of these processes improve your ability to remember?

elaboration the process of attaching a maximum number of associations to an item to be learned so that it can be retrieved more easily

Special Learning Processes

Using a flashlight in the dark, you can find an octopus in an aquarium more easily than you can find another kind of fish because the octopus has so many tentacles sticking out. If you find one of the tentacles, it is easy to locate the octopus's body. The same is true when we are trying to locate something we have learned. The more elaborate we make it, the greater the chance that one of the side branches will be spotted in a brain search and that we can then get to the main memory.

So, now the question is, do you remember item 1 at the beginning of the chapter, about William Jennings Bryan and about Prohibition? No? There is a reason for this. First, you didn't give it your full attention because it wasn't that interesting. Second, it was too factual, meaning it had few associations, or branches, and no emotional color to help you hook onto the basics. Go back and read it again. Then read this version:

In 1925, lawyer William Jennings Bryan prosecuted a young high school teacher named John Scopes who wanted to give students information about evolution. The trial took on the atmosphere of a circus. It became a free-for-all, with shouting by "liberated" (for that time) college students and young reporters who reflected antireligious feeling that was then erupting in the country. The teacher was found guilty, so Bryan won the case, but he was mocked so much during the trial that some people believe that this led to his death five days later.

In the late 1800s, a group of women, tired of having drunken, abusive husbands arrive home only after they had spent all of the family money at the local bars, organized the Anti-Saloon League to abolish alcohol. They rejoiced when the Eighteenth Amendment, which made the sale or manufacture of liquor illegal nationwide, went into effect in 1919. Fourteen years later, it became clear that mobsters were reaping enormous profits from the sale of illegal alcohol and were using those profits in other crimes. Violations of the Eighteenth Amendment were rampant among all classes of people. Congress eventually gave in and passed the Twenty-First Amendment, which repealed prohibition.

The Elaboration Process. This revised passage should help you understand the process psychologists call **elaboration.** Elaboration is an effective method for storing learned material by using a maximum number of associations—as long as the associations make sense. Especially useful are colorful associations—such as the circus and the Anti-Saloon League women in the example just given—that grab your attention and help tie all the information together.

The moral is that if you have to read something dull, try associating it with something important in your life. Parts that are especially difficult to remember can be treated with the device for learning isolated facts that we will talk about in the next paragraph. Here's an example of elaboration: The Twenty-First Amendment is for those *21* or older and not *for teens* (passed *fourteen* years after Prohibition started).

▲ *Among the Anti-Saloon League's concerns was not only alcohol, but also domestic violence.*

230

Focus

Elaboration

Material to be learned:	Associate this new material with "old" material:	The new material is effectively stored:
Rapid eye movement (REM) is associated with vivid dreaming.	New = REM Old = DREAM The new term, REM, is made up of nearly the same letters as DREAM, a word that's very familiar.	REM = DREAM
The cerebellum controls balance and coordination.	Associate the word CEREBEL-LUM with something else that represents balance or a lack of balance. Actually draw this in your notes:	An acrobat has excellent balance. An acrobat has a well-developed cerebellum.

How would you use elaboration to remember the definition of state-dependent learning (which can be found on page 225)?

Mnemonic Devices. Somewhat similar to elaboration are **mnemonic** (nee-MON-ick) **devices,** named after the Greek goddess of memory, Mnemosyne. She held an important position because memory was vital in the days before books or photocopy machines existed. Even though a type of paper had been developed in 3000 B.C., everything was written on long scrolls that had no pages. If a scroll was unrolled a few times, the words on it would disappear. It is hard to imagine, but early English common law (part of the basis of our present legal system) was normally guided by memory, too, rather than by written record (Boorstin, 1983).

Mnemonic devices are unusual associations made to material in order to aid memory. They are not logical, but they can help you remember information. They can replace unthinking, rote memorization, which is the most difficult learning process because it lacks associations with material you already know. If you can already make sense of whatever you are trying to remember, don't use mnemonic devices.

mnemonic devices unusual associations made to aid memory

Focus

Common Mnemonic Devices

Material to be learned:	Mnemonic device:	How information is stored:
Grocery list: milk, eggs, celery, and so on	**Method of Locations** Imagine a familiar location (like your house) and place the items to be remembered in various areas of that location. It's usually effective to enlarge the items in a bizarre way.	The sink is filled with milk that overflows onto the floor. Giant eggs roll along the tabletop. On the chairs, sitting at attention, are giant celery stalks; they prevent the eggs from falling.
Voluntary = Operant conditioning Involuntary = Classical conditioning	**Acronym** Take the first letter of each item on a list and make a word.	**VOICE** V = voluntary O = operant I = involuntary C = classical E is thrown in to make a word.
A part of the brain: the cerebellum, which controls balance	**Narrative chaining** Tie together the material to be learned into a story.	He hit me in the cerebellum with a brick, and I was thrown off balance. . . .

As you can see, some of these methods overlap one another. With practice, we all develop our own personal mnemonic devices.

What mnemonic devices or "tricks" do you use while studying?

In this regard, it is interesting to note a special use for mnemonics. Students who are slightly mentally retarded usually have trouble organizing material and making elaborations and meaningful associations. When mnemonics are used extensively in teaching them, they both learn better and remember better (Scruggs & Mastropieri, 1992).

Sometimes, mnemonics are helpful to all of us. For example, say you are at a party with mostly unfamiliar people. In the midst of them, you meet someone you like and want to remember, Harriet. Making a weird association with her name can keep you from forgetting it. If you are lucky, there will be something unusual about her hair (very long, bright green, shaved head, etc.). You keep saying to yourself "Hairy-et"; you have formed a mnemonic device. Here's another great use of mnemonics. Most of us, at one time or another, are asked to give someone the license number of our car. Unless you have a special license plate, you probably have trouble remembering the number. Mnemonics can solve this problem. For example, PWC-303 becomes "Put on a Warm Coat, or you'll FREEZE-OH-FREEZE." No, it doesn't make much sense, but it *is* hard to forget. (One of your authors still has several old, expired license-plate numbers rattling around in her head, taking up space.)

There are serious limitations to this system if used excessively or with images that are too bizarre, because then you won't remember the associations, much less the original information. Still, it is a useful technique for certain important things that you just keep forgetting. We hope you can see that mnemonics come down to little more than a type of elaboration in which you use the unusual to try to call attention to something later on during a mental search.

We should warn you about a couple of things before we leave this topic. First, mnemonics will *not* work unless you use them from the beginning with whatever you are trying to remember. Attempting to attach them later won't help you remember. Second, you should start using them while you're still young. Elderly people aren't very good at this, even with practice. So keep your imagination active (Baltes & Kliegl, 1992).

Principle Learning. A very useful learning technique is called **principle learning,** which means you focus on the basic idea behind what is to be learned. See if you can still recite the basic principle behind dog defense that you read about at the beginning of the chapter (item 3). You should be able to. If not, one more reading and you won't forget it, because the method of defense is based on a principle of physics: Pressure exerted at one point and at a counterpoint will snap something.

Another brief example: When learning a segment of history, tie it to a principle, and you can more easily make sense out of what the characters are doing. If you are studying the westward expansion of settlement in the United States, you can use a mental map as your principle. Then you will know that most of the pioneers wound up at the left of the map, most of the urban people were at the far right, the gold rush was to the left, and so forth. While this is a rather primitive example, it should demonstrate the basics of forming some kind of principle to guide learning. Evidence suggests that learning a principle and an example or two of that principle increases the amount of positive transfer that takes place (Reeves & Weisberg, 1994).

▲ *Mnemonics can help you remember the names of people you meet at a party.*

principle learning a method of learning in which an overall view (principle) of the material to be learned is developed so that the material is better organized

In Focus

Principle Learning

New material to be learned:	Tie the new material to the general principle:
Infants sleep 12–22 hours a day and spend 20 percent of that time in REM. Children sleep 10–12 hours a day and spend 15 percent of that time in REM. Young adults sleep 8–10 hours a day and spend 10–15 percent of that time in REM. Old people sleep 6–8 hours a day and spend about 5 percent of that time in REM.	The older you get, the less sleep you need, and the less time you spend in REM. 

Which mnemonic device will you use to remember what principle learning means? Explain.

chunking putting items into clusters or "chunks" so that the items are learned in groups rather than separately

▲ *Expert chess players chunk sets of moves to outwit their opponents.*

Chunking. It is not a good idea to treat items separately if they can be united in some sensible fashion. We learn better if things are clustered together. **Chunking,** at its simplest, means putting things into "chunks," such as organizing information by "either/or" descriptions (good/bad, bright/dim, alive/dead). On a more complex level, chunking relies on putting, say, all trees together as trees, even though they don't always resemble one another that much. In other words, when we call both oaks and evergreens "trees," we are *chunking* on the basis of bark, leaves (counting a pine needle as a leaf), trunk, and so forth in order to form the concept of "tree."

How confused the world would be without chunking! Every single item would have to be learned separately. In one study, children who were blind until about 12 years of age and thus could not store information visually by chunking were extremely confused when finally able to see. For a while, their world was chaos. A rooster and a horse were confused because they both had tails. One boy who gained his sight at age 11 thought a fish was a camel because its fins looked like a hump (Delgado, 1969).

Both authors of textbooks and teachers have to have some basic organizational structure in their approach to their subject matter. This structure consists of units, or groupings within the subject. For example, in chemistry, first you learn basic principles about how molecules behave. Later on, you learn basic principles about how water molecules interact with acid (not necessarily very well). In each subject, you can use the teacher's or author's units to form your own chunks of information that will tie together the separate facts you need to learn.

In Focus

Chunking

Without chunking		Number of items to be remembered	With chunking	Number of chunks to be remembered
Phone number: 5558424		7	555-8424	2
Social Security number: 092353979		9	092-35-3979	3
Driver's license N34688521948		12	N346-8852-1948	3
New zip codes: 930651220		9	93065-1220	2

What are some other common examples of chunking?

Retaining Information

Learning material is not of much use unless we can hold onto it. In this section, we discuss the methods and systems by which we remember and the factors that go into causing us to forget what we have learned.

Principles of Forgetting

Forgetting does not necessarily mean losing what we have learned. Often, it involves only an inability to bring back certain material. In other words, sometimes a memory is still in the brain, but because other things interfere with it, it is hard to find. For example, suppose your home phone number, which you have used for years, is 555-2678. Chances are you won't be able to retrieve easily a phone number of a recent acquaintance that is 555-2786 because the older learning will keep interfering.

Viewed in this way, **forgetting** is an increase in errors that we experience while trying to bring material back. But we are assuming here that there has been sufficient time to learn the material and that it has been stored. What happens when there isn't time for enough practice?

The Forgetting Curve. Forgetting occurs very rapidly. If you look at Figure 8.4 on page 236, you will see what happens if we learn something only to the point of being able to recite it one time and then don't practice it. By the end of one hour, roughly 50 percent of a poem is gone. Retention falls to 35 percent by the end of two hours, and so forth.

The only way that we can permanently store something of average interest (unlike the John Wesley Hardin poem or the phone number of a special friend) is by **overlearning.** This term sounds strange at first, but as you can see from the figure, if you just learn something to the point of one recitation, you aren't going to retain it. Hence, you have to *over*learn it, meaning that you rehearse it over and over beyond the one perfect recitation. After many rehearsals, the **forgetting curve** shown in Figure 8.4 will not apply. Such is the case with "I pledge allegiance to the _____ _____ _____" and so forth. Note that your brain keeps going on and on for a while, filling in blanks, because the material has been learned so well, or overlearned.

Recall and Recognition. In tests of how much we have forgotten (or the reverse, how well we can remember), psychologists identify two types: **recall** and **recognition**. Both are tests of memory, but recognition is easier than recall. Recall requires bringing back and integrating many specific learned details—as in an essay test, for example. Recognition, on the other hand, is used in the familiar multiple-choice tests, in which you must *recognize* the right answer ("Which one is correct, a, b, c, or d?").

Here is an example of the difference between the two. You see someone a couple of times a week who wears a uniform (someone at a burger place, a worker at the school cafeteria, someone who pumps gas, or the like). You don't know this person as a friend, but you see him or her regularly. Then one day you are shopping, and you see this person out of uniform. You know that you remember his or her face from *somewhere,* but you can't quite get it. You are trying to *recall* who the person is, and you start a long search through all the possibilities, which can be innumerable. Eventually you might get it. Suppose, however, that you

Focus Questions

- What are four special processes for improving learning?
- How do each of these processes improve your ability to remember?

forgetting an increase in errors in bringing material back from memory

overlearning learning something beyond one perfect recitation so that the forgetting curve will have no effect; the development of perfect retention

forgetting curve graphic representation of the rate and amount of forgetting that occurs

recall the ability to bring back and integrate many specific learned details

recognition the ability to pick the correct object or event from a list of choices

235

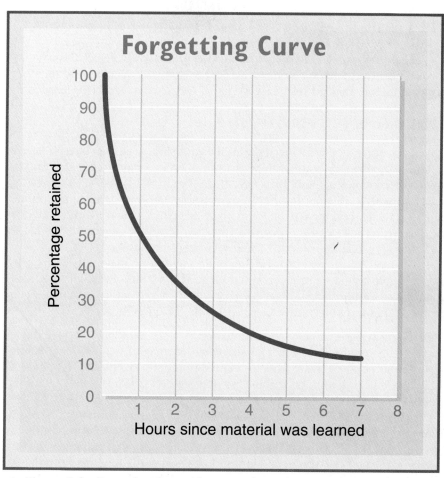

▲ Figure 8.4 *Forgetting Curve. The curve shows the amount retained of material learned to the point of one perfect recitation.*

were given a *recognition* test and one of the items to choose from was something like "Woman who works at the Taco Palace." You would get it immediately. Why? Because a recognition test lists the memory storage areas for you to search; you need only to go to each storage area to see if there is a correct match.

How Little We Forget.   Here are some rather startling findings that show how much we actually store and how little we really forget. Subjects in one study had the capacity to recognize roughly 90 percent of 2,560 slides they had viewed. Two of the subjects who scored in this range had seen 1,280 slides in just one day (Haber, 1970). Persons 35 years out of high school can *recognize* about 90 percent of their classmates' faces in the yearbook, although they can recall the names of only about 25 percent of them (Bahrick et al., 1974).

Interference Theory.   No one doubts that many of the things we start to learn are not practiced enough and merely disappear forever without being permanently stored. And some material that we do store just decays for one reason or another, never to be seen again. But the major theory that explains forgetting is called the **interference theory.** Interference causes us to forget because there is a conflict between new and old material in the memory system.

interference theory the idea that we forget because new and old material conflict (interfere) with one another

236

The theory goes this way: Bringing in new material can cause processing difficulties if we already have somewhat similar material stored. This can be the case if you are trying to learn a new telephone number. Or suppose you are trying to remember a sound, such as a musical note. You hear tone A and are in the process of storing it. Then, shortly afterward, tone B is introduced. The result is considerable interference, confusion, and difficulty in remembering A. The new tone, B, requires processing and interferes with your remembering tone A much more than would a blank space of time after the introduction of tone A.

▲ *"I recognized your face, but I couldn't recall your name."*

The problem is that two memory systems for similar material operating at the same time cause confusion. Also, if new material is very much like old material, the brain has some trouble figuring out where it should go, since the two pieces of material compete for the same space, so to speak, in the memory storage system. In either of these cases, the new material can fail to be stored properly or at all.

Of course, some forgetting is intentional, rather than resulting from interference. Assume, for instance, that you always park your car in the same lot. You need to forget where you parked it yesterday and the day before if you're going to be able to find it quickly and easily today. Similarly, when you have learned incorrect information about someone or something and now have the right information, you may deliberately remove the inaccurate material from your memory (Johnson, 1994).

Pause for Thought

1. How do elaboration, principle learning, and chunking help us remember something?
2. What are mnemonic devices, and how can we best use them?
3. How can overlearning help prevent forgetting?

Critical Thinking
. . . .

4. Write two test questions for this chapter. One question should require recall; the other should require recognition.

Focus Question

• How much data can your brain store?

• How are memories stored?

Mechanisms of Memory

People buy computers with a certain amount of storage capacity, so many gigabytes (billion bytes) of information. Since you are familiar with this, it should help you to understand how much we can store in our own memory banks. For starters, very primitive organisms can store 200 billion bytes of information using only thousands of nerve cells (Benner, 1984). Humans have billions of nerve cells, each one with millions of connections, so our capacity is just about limitless.

Suppose that you were to write out everything you have stored in your brain right this minute until the brain is empty. You would be writing a very long time, to put it mildly. If you are average, your present storage is the equivalent of 35 million pages the size of those in the book you are now reading!

This is very hard to believe, but stop and think: You have stored so much that has happened to you—your first bed, your first room, the size and color of the seat on your first bicycle, the shape of the sidewalk in front of your home, and on and on. (You may have heard that people use only 10 percent of their "brain power." There is no evidence at all to support or disprove this claim. Someone just made it up decades ago, and it is still passed from one generation to another as a fact.)

Encoding. When we remember something, it seems that we are "seeing" or "hearing" it. But that is not how the brain itself works. Memory is stored in some kind of physical chemical code, the nature of which we don't fully understand yet. This process is called *encoding*. We can grasp the principle but not the physical details. An analogy is computer code made up of strings of numbers, such as 0-1-1-0 and 1-0-1-0, each standing for something different. Thus, a long string of 0-1-1-0-1-0 and so forth might stand for "horse." We believe today that nerve cells fire in certain sequences, just like the combinations of 0's and 1's, and in this way they reproduce any memory desired. As they fire in sequence, they produce what we call "thought."

Theories of Memory. The brain contains about 100 billion nerve cells. They are separated one from the other but communicate by means of electrical and chemical information that goes from one nerve cell to the other. Each nerve cell junction is called a *synapse* (SIN-naps), as discussed in Chapter 3.

In Their Own Words . . .

Elizabeth Loftus, *a professor of psychology at the University of Washington, is an expert on repressed memory. In 1994, she published* The Myth of Repressed Memory, *in which she explores this topic. In the following excerpt from the book, Loftus presents a compassionate explanation for false memories:*

But perhaps the most compelling reason to believe these stories of recovered memories is that not believing is edged with painful complexities and ambiguities. We want to believe—in fact we need to believe— . . . because the belief . . . affirms that our own minds work in an orderly, efficient way, taking in information, sorting it, filing it, and calling it back later in full and vivid detail. In a chaotic world, where so much is out of control, we need to believe that our minds, at least, are under our command.

If our minds are capable of feeding us tall tales from the past with such intense, hallucinatory detail that it never occurs to us to question them, where is the boundary between truth and lie, reality and fantasy, sanity and madness?

The boundary, I believe, is permeable and unguarded, and we cross it all the time in our dreams, desires, and imaginations. Memory is the vehicle by which we transport ourselves from reality to fantasy and back again, as many times as it takes to spin coherent and colorful stories from the dry straw of real life. Our memories tell us stories, and we listen, enthralled. We want to know what happened in our past, we need our questions answered, we seek to resolve our uncertainty and ambiguity. Memory, our most loyal and faithful servant, complies with our wishes. (Loftus & Ketcham, 1994)

Interpreting Primary Sources

Write a brief paragraph explaining what you think Loftus meant when she wrote, "Memory, our most loyal and faithful servant, complies with our wishes."

One basic theory of memory holds that as we learn something, the physical structure of the synapses changes shape, a possibility suggested by microscopic studies of synapses after learning. These physical changes seem to alter which nerves will connect with which other nerves via synapses, how easily a set of synapses will fire, and what the sequence of firing will be.

Thus, the memory becomes like a toy train with a series of switches turned on or off. As you learn something, you increase the chances that the same sequence of nerve firings will occur for each memory. The more often you repeat the material, the more solid becomes the "track" over which the memory train will travel. Similar theories suggest that the chemicals used to make the connections across the synapses increase with each learning, making certain connections faster and easier (Squire, 1987).

A second theory centers on the idea that the synapses grow once a pattern is established. In other words, we make certain memories; and as they are stored, the synapses grow to hold them. Such growth is very obvious as a child develops. Learning, then, becomes a matter of using newly grown nerve cells in the synapses to form a map. If the memory is no longer useful, growth slows down. Later, new growth starts for a new memory or for a modified memory (Rosenzweig, 1984). There is support for both this system and the one we just discussed. We don't know enough yet to bring it all together into a clear pattern.

While performing brain surgery, neurosurgeons have discovered that it is possible to touch parts of the brain with an electrically activated wire and cause the patient to relive, as if in a "movie" dream, a sequence from some earlier time in life, like a birthday party in childhood (Penfield, 1959). Such events certainly suggest that memories are stored in certain areas of the brain and that a whole sequence of nerve firings can occur from one stimulation.

More recent research suggests that special types of memories are stored in the frontmost part of the brain. These are memories of specific personal events or episodes in which we are very much aware of ourselves. These memories are not just an objective listing of things that have happened to us; they have emotional aspects as well (Wheeler et al., 1997).

▲ *Nerve cells switch on or off in sequence when memory is in operation.*

Short-Term and Long-Term Memory

A common plot on television involves a man or woman who is struck on the head while witnessing a murder and forgets "everything." Fearful of exposure, the murderer follows this person around, waiting for a chance to do him or her in, not knowing that the memory of the murder is "gone."

Although this situation is exaggerated (as usual), a good solid blow to the head, a major trauma, or an electric shock can produce **amnesia,** the blocking of older memories or the loss of more recent ones. The term *blocked* is used because most of the material will return after a period, unless the person has suffered a severe injury or the amnesia resulted from a disease (Graf et al., 1984). In some cases, however, once amnesia has started, people don't *want* to bring back certain memories, so they block them from returning even though physically they could be available.

Strangely enough, the material that disappears in amnesia is fairly selective. People rarely forget how to tie a shoe or brush their teeth. The most likely explanation for this is that these acts have been performed so

Focus Questions

- How would your life be different without short-term memory?
- What physical changes occur during the storing and retrieving of memories?
- How do short-term memories become long-term memories?

amnesia the blocking of older memories and/or the loss of new ones

239

▲ *The woman in the middle is suffering from amnesia.*

often for so long that only massive brain damage would erase them, since they are so permanently fixed in memory. Also, we have somewhat different memory systems for activities or tasks and for information.

Explaining Amnesia.   There are two possible explanations for the phenomenon of amnesia: (1) Amnesia could result from a temporary reduction of blood supply from an injury. This will disrupt the proper nourishment of the cells and reduce their chemicals, which, in turn, will alter the firing of the nerve cells to produce a memory. (2) A blow to the head will cause major electrical changes that will disrupt the transmission across the synapses and temporarily dislodge older memory systems, meanwhile just about wiping out most newer memories that haven't been thoroughly stored.

You may hear that if a person has amnesia, another blow to the head will bring back the memories. As you can see, this is a ridiculous notion. The only possible results of another blow are further confusion and more disruption of the memory systems. It is truly hard to imagine how people can come up with such strange ideas.

Sequence of Memory Loss.   Most people with amnesia can recall events from the distant past but nothing recent. And when memory returns, it starts with older memories and moves up to the present. This was our first clue to the fact that we have both a **short-term memory** system and a **long-term memory** system. Thus, the memories immediately preceding an accident are gone forever because they never made it from the short-term storage system to permanent, long-term storage.

The two memory storage systems seem to be at least partially independent (Graesser, Singer, & Trabasso, 1994). In cases of injury to different parts of the brain, some people lose only short-term memory (STM), while others lose only large portions of long-term memory (LTM).

short-term memory memory system that retains information for a few seconds to a few minutes

long-term memory memory system that retains information for hours, days, weeks, months, or decades

STM lasts from a few seconds to half a minute. LTM can last from hours to days to a lifetime, depending on the amount of time a memory spends in the storage system, where it becomes more and more solidified.

All incoming material goes first to the STM, where it is "processed"—that is, we make a decision about whether to keep it or not. Next, the material is either eliminated or moved to the LTM storage area. A principle that applies in long-term memory is something called **consolidation.** Consolidation is a process by which, over time, a memory solidifies until it becomes permanent. The term itself refers to the fact that the memory is brought together (consolidated) into a clear and organized whole.

Under normal circumstances, the STM will hold only seven (on occasion up to nine) items before the material has to be moved on to the LTM. The only reason we can learn anything is that this memory system doesn't care how *long* each of the seven items is. This means we can group, or chunk, items together.

Here are 13 items to learn: moon, cow, the, jumped, ate, over, the, hamburger, lunch, at, in, barn, the. The STM can't hold these 13 items. How do we do it? We chunk. The cow//jumped over moon//ate the hamburger at lunch//in the barn (Tulving & Partay, 1962). We now have only four items, which are easily put into STM.

So far, we have left out a slight technicality to simplify our discussion of the STM and LTM systems. There *is* one additional system that comes just before STM, called the **sensory memory system,** which includes direct receivers of information from the environment. One set of receivers is called **iconic** (eye-KON-ick) **memory.** The word *icon* means "image"; so we see and hold an image in front of us. The iconic system is probably an electrical trace left over from firing the visual network, because it lasts only a few seconds. During that time, we make a decision about whether to send the image to the STM or eliminate it (Cowan, 1984). A similar system for sound is the **acoustic** (ah-KOO-stik) **memory,** in which we can hold words for a few seconds while again we decide if we want to move them to STM or forget them (see Figure 8.5).

consolidation process by which a memory solidifies over time, eventually becoming permanent

sensory memory system system that includes direct receivers of information from the environment—for example, iconic, acoustic

iconic memory a very brief visual memory that can be sent to the short-term memory

acoustic memory a very brief sound memory that can be sent to the short-term memory

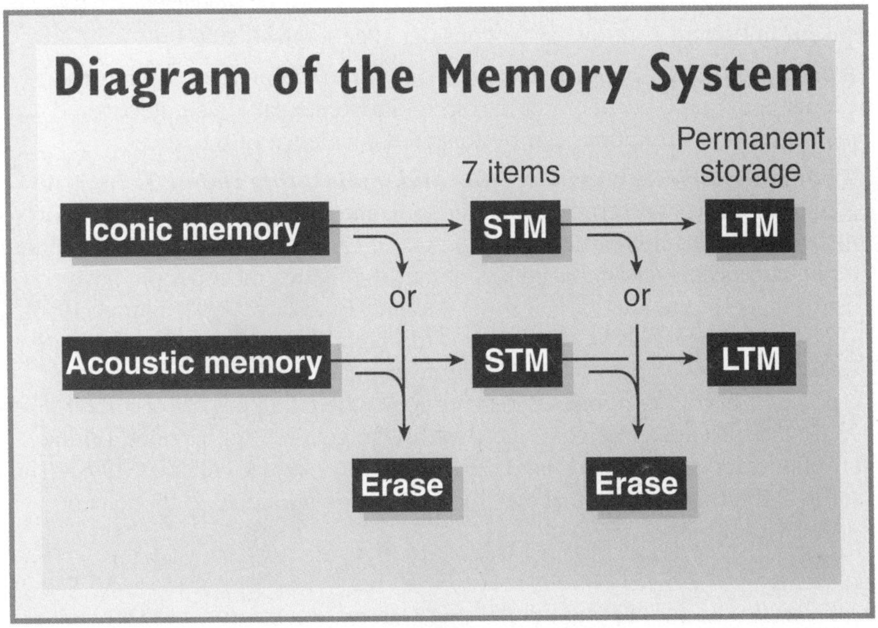

◀ **Figure 8.5** *Diagram of the Memory System*

Diagram of the Memory System

Thinking Critically about Psychology

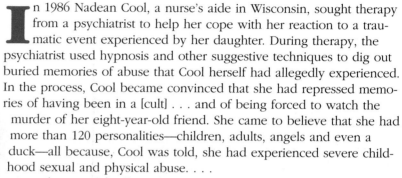

Repressed Memories

In 1986 Nadean Cool, a nurse's aide in Wisconsin, sought therapy from a psychiatrist to help her cope with her reaction to a traumatic event experienced by her daughter. During therapy, the psychiatrist used hypnosis and other suggestive techniques to dig out buried memories of abuse that Cool herself had allegedly experienced. In the process, Cool became convinced that she had repressed memories of having been in a [cult] . . . and of being forced to watch the murder of her eight-year-old friend. She came to believe that she had more than 120 personalities—children, adults, angels and even a duck—all because, Cool was told, she had experienced severe childhood sexual and physical abuse. . . .

When Cool finally realized that false memories had been planted, she sued the psychiatrist for malpractice. In March 1997, after five weeks of trial, her case was settled out of court for $2.4 million (Loftus, 1997, p. 71).

When stories about repression and recovered memories were first publicized, they were generally accepted as scientifically supported phenomena. It was thought that repression occurs in most cases of child sexual abuse and that recovered memories of abuse must be true. Critics were not so sure, however. They argued that most people who have endured terrible events in their childhoods do not repress them but in fact remember them in some detail. They further argued that it is possible to "remember" events that never actually occurred, as in the case cited above. According to recent estimates, there are a million cases a year of recovered memory of sexual abuse. Clearly, this is an important controversy to consider (Pendergrast, 1997).

▲ *Most people remember traumatic events rather than repress them.*

What specifically is being claimed or stated? Repression of traumatic events commonly occurs in cases of childhood sexual abuse. Recovered memories of such trauma can be trusted as evidence of the abuse.

What is the objective evidence for and against this claim? There is no way to objectively determine whether someone has forgotten something or not. And there is no reason to assume that it cannot happen. As to how often repression occurs among victims of abuse, the figures most people have heard range in the area of half to 60 percent (Bradshaw, 1992; Blume, 1990). Other researchers believe this figure is too high, that a more accurate figure would be considerably lower. One study found that of the women who reported a history of abuse, 81 percent remembered all or part of it their entire lives. Nineteen percent said they had forgotten it for a period of time, but the memory came back later on (Loftus, Polonsky, & Fullilove, 1994). This study and others suggest that the frequency is more like 20 to 25 percent.

The second part of the claim involves accuracy. Is it possible to "remember" something terrible that never happened? Obviously, given the case quoted above and others as well, it is possible in some instances. But are these instances rare or common? Furthermore, can memories of upsetting events be deliberately planted in someone's mind? Again, the answer seems to be yes. For example, researchers have been able to plant false memories in subjects by having the subjects' family members tell the subjects about things that never happened: that as young children the subjects got lost in a shopping mall, were briefly hospitalized with an infection, or spilled a punch bowl on some people at a wedding and were horribly embarrassed. Generally speaking, between 20 and 25 percent of the subjects eventually recalled these false memories (Loftus, 1997; Loftus & Ketcham, 1994).

You can argue, of course, that while these incidents do contain unpleasant emotional content, they do not begin to approach the seriousness of sexual abuse. That seems to be a valid point. Furthermore, how can we prove that any memory of sexual abuse is true or false? After all, the person who supposedly committed it is not likely to come right out and admit it. In light of these issues, some researchers argue that the critics have gone too far—that the critics are exaggerating the extent to which recovered memories are false (Pope, 1996).

What other interpretations might be made instead? Let's assume that at least some cases involve false memories. If these memories are not true, how can we account for them? To begin with, in most cases, the people were in psychotherapy. People in psychotherapy are often especially open to their therapists' suggestions and usually want to do what the therapists ask. Consequently, they may "remember" what they think the therapists want to hear.

Another possibility is that some therapists actively suggest past abuse to their clients because they believe that the clients actually were abused. They believed that it was important for clients to recall the abuse and used techniques to help them remember (Poole, Lindsay, Memon, & Bull, 1997, 1995).

What are the most logical conclusions to draw? Considering all the evidence, it seems that repression of childhood sexual trauma can and does occur, but the idea that most victims of sexual abuse repress their memories does not seem to be valid. It also seems likely that some "recovered" memories are false. Thus, while repression of childhood sexual abuse can occur, it probably occurs less frequently than we've been led to believe.

See if COOL works for you....

Claim?

Objective evidence for and against claim?

Other interpretations?

Logical conclusions?

Applying Critical Thinking Skills

Fact: Studies show that false memories can be deliberately planted. Fact: One recent survey reports that 25 percent of therapists focus on repressed memories. Given these two facts, what safeguards should therapists observe during therapy?

Focus Questions

- What are several unusual types of memory?
- Are eyewitness reports reliable?

eidetic imagery an iconic memory lasting a minute or so that keeps images "in front of" the viewer so objects can be counted or analyzed; also called *photographic memory*

Special Issues in Memory

You have no doubt heard stories of startling feats of memory. Usually these are tricks. When they are not, they may be caused by a defect in the memory system, such as occurred with the man called S.

Photographic Memory. One commonly claimed feat is photographic memory, called **eidetic** (eye-DET-ick) **imagery.** Supposedly, people can look at a picture of something like a chain. Then, when the picture is taken away, they can count the links in front of them even though the picture is gone. Some people *do* have longer iconic memories than others, possibly lasting a minute or so; these are usually children. But in all of the psychological literature, only one or two people might have had eidetic imagery. So, for all practical purposes, it doesn't exist. Try it out for yourself on Figure 8.6.

Eyewitness Memory. Memory is vitally important in eyewitness testimony; but unfortunately, it is often wrong. For example, descriptions frequently fit a stereotypical image of a "bad guy" rather than the actual criminal. Further, under extreme stress, perception can be faulty, and witnesses often either speculate or use their LTM banks to fill in details that never existed (Poole & White, 1991; Kassin, Ellsworth, & Smith, 1989; Loftus, 1984).

Eyewitness testimony is so unreliable because our brains are never content to let incoming information stand on its own. We process it, reprocess it, and keep working on it so that it makes *complete* sense in terms of everything we know, even though the facts in real life—that is, what we saw—seldom fit together completely. Consequently, so-called eyewitness testimony often includes information obtained after the fact, rather than being limited to what the person actually saw and remembers.

▶ ***Figure 8.6*** *Look at this picture for 30 seconds, then look at a blank wall and try to reproduce it in as much detail as possible.*

The Man Who Couldn't Forget

Case Study

If you've ever wished you had a better memory, consider the case of a Moscow man known as "S." Russian psychologist Alaksandr Luria (1968) studied S for many years. He claimed that S's ability to store information was unlimited. Most people can easily store seven to nine items in short-term memory. S, however, could hear a long list of meaningless numbers or letters and recall them perfectly. If asked to recite the list backwards or to report every fifth item on the list, S could perform this task flawlessly—not only during the test, but decades later!

Most people would probably view this ability as a gift rather than as a defect, but S had trouble filtering incoming material he didn't need. His life was a misery because he could not forget *anything*. When people talked, he could block out nothing. The words he heard became images that collided with one another, got mixed up, and triggered endless confusion. The more people talked, the less he could make sense of anything. Even a neutral word like *something* could provoke vivid images.

Unlike the rest of us, S could never discard items from his memory. Imagine all the useless information he retained in a lifetime: old phone numbers, old bank account balances, one long list after another. Eventually, after a career as a reporter and then as a financial analyst, S became a stage performer, one of the few jobs in which he could be successful.

A young man from Connecticut known as H. M. experienced the opposite problem. He'd been suffering from severe seizures, and doctors hoped that removing parts of his temporal lobes would stop the seizures (Restak, 1984). The operation worked, but it also damaged H. M.'s hippocampus, the part of the brain that helps form memories. As a result, H. M. could meet someone, a barber for example, talk to him, and within a matter of minutes, he might forget not only what he talked about but that he'd even met the man! He could meet the same barber every day for a week and still not recall the barber's face. After his uncle died, H. M. responded emotionally, but when he was later reminded that his uncle was dead, he had no recollection of this news and responded as if for the first time.

When tested by his doctors, H. M. could sometimes recall a list of six or seven items, provided there was no delay between hearing and reporting the items. Also, he could learn how to solve a maze, and if he practiced tracing the maze over and over again, he could even recall the solution days later. He couldn't recall, however, actually being tested. Why the discrepancy? Note that tracing a maze involves motor skills which are processed and stored in a particular way. H. M. remembered how to walk and turn and bend down to tie his shoe, but he didn't necessarily know where he was, even while in his own neighborhood.

These two extraordinary cases help reveal that many areas of the brain are involved in the process we call memory. With S, one sense spontaneously sparked another, which could have led to a richness of life had he been able to harness the many images racing through his head. With H. M., his ability to store some new materials but not others shows the sophisticated pathways the brain uses to form a memory.

Review the Case Study

Would you say that your short-term memory is more like S's or H. M.'s? Explain.

▲ *Unfortunately, eyewitnesses frequently get it wrong.*

During class one day, a teacher staged a fake assault on himself. Later, during the "lineup," over 60 percent of the student eyewitnesses were wrong in their choice of who did it (Buckhout et al., 1972). In another (real) case, 17 eyewitnesses identified a man as the one who shot a police officer, but clear evidence later emerged that the man was not even near the scene at the time of the crime (McCloskey & Zaragoza, 1985).

Just to show you how easily memory can change, here is part of a laboratory study on eyewitness identification. In an accident case in which there was *no* broken headlight at all, two sets of witnesses were asked slightly different questions by the experimenter:

First group of witnesses: "Did you see *a* broken headlight?"
Second group of witnesses: "Did you see *the* broken headlight?"

The experimenter found that the use of the word *a* leaves the issue of whether or not there was a broken headlight in doubt. Only 7 percent in the first group answered "yes." But when the word *a* was changed to *the,* the witnesses assumed the presence of a broken headlight. Agreement doubled based on just this one word change; 15 percent in the second group said they had seen a broken headlight. Note how easily we are swayed by suggestion. So the precise wording of questions is extremely important (Kassin et al., 1989).

Hypnosis doesn't make eyewitness accounts more accurate, because under hypnosis, people are more suggestible than at almost any other time. Hence, the accuracy of identification can be even worse, depending on how the questions are formed.

Identifying Faces and Seeing Through Disguises. Much of what we have been talking about in this chapter suggests that people would be very inaccurate at identifying faces seen during a crisis. And this turns out to be the case. For example, a crime is likely to take place quickly, so a person witnessing the crime has very little opportunity for elaboration (developing associations). Without time to make associations, the eyewitness has little chance of picking the right person later. In addition, identification across racial lines is especially poor, particularly when white people are doing the identifying (Kassin et al., 1989).

Even after being warned in an experiment, subjects have problems remembering faces. One researcher gave subjects a set of pictures of people's faces and told them that they were later going to identify one of these pictures as part of a second set. They were given a long time to analyze the first set. Later, one of the faces was put with a second set of pictures, and subjects were asked to locate it. Most of the people failed the task, even though there was none of the pressure in this experiment that would be involved in a real-life crisis (Harmon, 1973).

▲ *Faces are not hard to disguise—a mustache and dark glasses may be enough.*

Our perception of others is quite faulty. This is clearly demonstrated by the effect of using disguises. If a person changes his or her hairstyle or, for men, adds a beard, accurate identification drops 25 percent. With both a new hairstyle and a beard, or with a change of hair color for a woman, it drops 52 percent. And if the person to be identified is seen only in profile, accuracy of identification falls a full 61 percent (Patterson & Baddeley, 1977).

Pause for Thought

1. According to interference theory, why do we forget?
2. What role do nerve cells and synapses play in memory? Describe two theories.
3. Explain how short-term memory, long-term memory, sensory memory, iconic memory, and acoustic memory differ.

Critical Thinking
. . . .
4. Eyewitness memory is often influenced by the way the investigator asks questions. Devise an original study in which you test this assumption.

APPLYING
Psychology to Life

Testing Your Memory

E arlier in this chapter, we discussed an established principle of learning and memory called *consolidation*— the solidification of a memory over time. Here's a chance for you to test this concept. You will need a partner to do so.

Test Your Short-Term Memory

The first experiment involves short-term memory, which allows for no consolidation. Take the phone book and put it on a table about 25 feet from the telephone. Have your partner stand by the phone book. Find a number at random and circle it. Read it once. Now, try to get to the phone to dial the number. All the time you are on your way, your partner is to shout random numbers out loud to you (5, 29, 3, 12, 8, whatever).

You don't stand a chance of making it to the phone with the circled phone number intact in your brain. Each new number that your friend calls out is fighting for a position among the magic quantity of seven items that can be stored in the STM. One "old" number is knocked out as a new one comes in. You can try talking or humming to

▲ *Short-term memory can hold about seven items, exactly as many as are in your telephone number.*

yourself as you run to the phone, but that won't work. Now the STM is trying to store the words you are making or the humming sound (and you are still picking up some numbers from your shouting partner).

Sleep on It

The second experiment centers on partial consolidation. This time, put a pad and pencil next to the phone so that, instead of dialing, you can write down what you would have dialed. That way, you can see what we're talking about.

First, remember that sleep is an excellent consolidator. All night, the brain will be working on material you give it. The night before this experiment, pick a number from the phone book, and write it down. As you sit on the side of the bed before going to sleep, rehearse it two or three times. Wait five minutes. Rehearse it again a few times. Then turn the piece of paper over so you can't see the number, and go to sleep.

Next day, don't look at that piece of paper next to your bed! When your partner arrives, look at the piece of paper, and review the number twice. Then head for the phone while your partner is shouting numbers. Write what you would have dialed on the pad you've placed next to the phone. The odds are overwhelming that you will have most of the correct numbers. You may not yet have them in exactly the right order, but it will be obvious that they have been at least partially stored.

▲ *Family photos trigger many memories—some true, some not.*

Written in Stone?

For the third part of the experiment, your partner—at random—picks a number you know very well and says it to you ("Amy's number"). You head for the phone as your partner keeps shouting numbers. This time you will be frustrated because you will have to keep fighting STM storage as you bring back LTM (Amy's number). You'll be able to do it, though, because the number is permanently stored, or *consolidated*.

The final experiment involves being an "eyewitness." Somewhere in your home is a box of family photos. There's at least one photo you know very well but haven't seen for a month or so. Tell your partner which one it is, and he or she can get it for you. Don't look at it. Next, write out everything you think is going on in the photo—who is where, what they are wearing, and so forth.

When you are done, compare what you have written down with the real photo. Note how many details you have added that are not in the actual photo—usually things that you wish were there or that you think would logically be there.

To sum up, one psychologist has said "You could think of consolidation as being somewhat like writing your name in wet concrete. Once the concrete has set, the information is fairly lasting, but while it is setting, it can be wiped out (amnesia) or scribbled over (interference)" (Coon, 1998).

CHAPTER 8 REVIEW & APPLY

Summary

1. High levels of emotion and attention promote learning.

2. In positive transfer, learning of one task is carried over to a new task that is similar. Negative transfer interferes with learning; it occurs when you are learning two tasks that are similar in many regards but that have some significant differences.

3. A schema is an organized pattern for analyzing information in memory.

4. Memory is greatly aided by elaboration.

5. When material to be remembered is not easily organized, mnemonic devices can aid in retention. In addition, if items can be put together under a general principle, retention is greatly increased.

6. We can learn better if we are able to organize information according to some pattern, a process known as chunking.

7. Recognition is easier than recall because it involves the matching of memories rather than a detailed search for one. Recognition demonstrates just how much we actually are able to retain.

8. Memory is the result of learning that has altered the chemistry and/or structure of the nerve cell endings, called synapses. Memory is divided into three parts: the very brief sensory memory system, the slightly longer short-term memory, and finally the long-term memory.

9. Memories of childhood sexual abuse may sometimes be repressed and then recovered, but this does not seem to occur in most cases; and recovered memories are not necessarily accurate.

10. Photographic memory seems to exist in only a few people. It is probably the result of an ability to hold images iconically longer than normal.

11. Eyewitness memory is quite defective because it is based on what people think and want rather than on what they actually observe.

Vocabulary

attention
learning curve
state-dependent learning
transfer of training
positive transfer
negative transfer
information processing
schema
elaboration

mnemonic devices
principle learning
chunking
forgetting
overlearning
forgetting curve
recall
recognition
interference theory

amnesia
short-term memory
long-term memory
consolidation
sensory memory system
iconic memory
acoustic memory
eidetic imagery

Review Questions

Fill in the Blank

On a sheet of paper, write the word or words that best complete each statement.

1. Tracy knows Italian, so learning Spanish is easy for her. This is called ▨▨▨▨ transfer.

2. Stacy knows Italian, so learning Spanish is difficult, because she confuses the two. This is called ▨▨▨▨ transfer.

3. A basketball player learns something at practice while sweating, forgets it at home, then remembers it again the next day at practice. This kind of learning is called ▨▨▨▨.

4. The mental outline we use to solve problems is called a ▨▨▨▨.

5. Taking in, storing, and bringing back the things we learn is called ▨▨▨▨.

6. ▨▨▨▨ is the process of associating new material in some way with something important in your life.

7. Focusing on the basic idea behind a concept is called ▨▨▨▨.

True/False

On a sheet of paper, answer each statement true or false. *If false, rewrite to make it true.*

8. Mnemonic devices often make use of weird images.

9. Chunking leads to negative transfer and should usually be avoided.

10. If we forget something from long-term memory, this usually means it is gone from the brain.

11. Overlearning will help to prevent forgetting.

12. The interference theory suggests that interference of ideas causes us to forget.

On a sheet of paper, answer each of the following with the term recall, recognition, or both.

13. Essay tests

14. Matching tests

15. Fill-in-the-blank tests

16. True/false tests

Matching

On a sheet of paper, match the term in the right column with the description in the left column. Answers may be used more than once.

17. Holds sounds for only a few seconds

18. Usually lasts for up to a few hours

19. Visual electrical trace that lasts a few seconds

20. Photographic memory

21. Permanent memories stored here

22. Holds about seven to nine items

23. Probably doesn't even exist

24. Chunking helps overcome its limitations

25. Memories are consolidated here.

26. Means "image"

a. iconic memory

b. short-term memory

c. long-term memory

d. acoustic memory

e. eidetic imagery

Discussion Questions

1. As explained in the chapter, attention certainly affects learning. Describe a teacher who does a good job of holding your attention. What techniques does this teacher use? Review the section on emotional factors in learning. What kinds of emotions does this teacher generate, and what effect do these emotions have on learning?

2. In a few sentences, describe a time when you've experienced positive transfer and a time when you've experienced negative transfer.

3. Which schema do you think would be more elaborate: (a) deciding to buy and actually buying a pair of shoes or (b) deciding to go to a party? Explain.

4. Most of us develop our own mnemonic devices for studying for exams. Briefly describe one of your methods and a time when you used it.

5. Teachers often use both recall and recognition in their tests. In your opinion, which method more accurately measures how much you actually know? (Be honest.) Explain.

6. The chapter explains that patient S's life became a private hell because he couldn't forget anything. This may be true, but S's ability might serve him well in certain occupations. Which ones? Explain. What problems would he have even in the occupations that you have listed? Explain.

7. Imagine someone with a problem that is the opposite of S's problem—that is, he or she *does* eliminate *all* incoming information. Describe a typical experience this person might have.

8. Research has actually been done to find out which drugs will promote quick, solid consolidation and which drugs will tend to block consolidation. If these drugs were proved to be safe, what practical applications would each of the drugs have? In other words, when would you want quick consolidation, and when would you want to block consolidation? Explain.

9. You are investigating a case in which a young person allegedly has recovered memories of abuse. The accused abuser denies the charges. What kinds of questions would you ask these two to help you determine who is right?

Activities and Projects

1. Take a close look at the chart of a schema in Figure 8.3 on page 228. Using this chart as a model, design your own schema. First, pick a possible question or problem that needs to be solved—for example, "Should I quit my job?" Second, jot down a rough draft of your schema. Be creative. Perhaps brainstorm with a friend or two. Third, decide on a final version of the schema and transfer it onto a poster. Use arrows, different colors, and boxes to clarify and highlight the entire process. Also include a key that will explain what your arrows and other symbols mean.

2. The chapter explains that we form organized "maps" of the world. Objects that don't "fit" on a map are more difficult to remember. Test whether this is true.

Take a photograph of your kitchen. Include in this photograph common kitchen objects. Take another photograph of your kitchen. This time, include objects that don't belong in a kitchen. Be subtle; for example, put a toothbrush on the table.

With these photographs, test six subjects, repeating the following procedure for each subject: (1) Present photo number 1; allow the subject 30 seconds to memorize it. (2) Have the subject start at 50 and count down aloud to zero by fours (50, 46, 42, and so on). (3) Allow the subject as much time as necessary to write down all the information he or she can remember from the photograph. (4) Repeat these three steps for the other photo.

Analyze your results. Which objects were best remembered? Least remembered? Which photo elicited the most mistakes? Are there any other conclusions that you can draw? Explain.

3. Test the effectiveness of mnemonic devices on 10 subjects. Write up a typical 20-item grocery list and *slowly* read the list aloud to each subject, explaining first that he or she will have to memorize the list. Once you finish, have each subject start at 50 and count down aloud to zero by fours (50, 46, 42, and so on). Then have each subject write down as many grocery items as possible without any time limit.

For half the subjects, instruct them beforehand to picture a room in their house. As each item is read, have the subject picture the item in some location in the room. In addition, have the person enlarge the item in a weird manner. For example, for "Milk," have the subject picture milk overflowing in the kitchen sink.

For the other half of the subjects, tell them to memorize the words.

Compare your results. Were the "mnemonic subjects" able to learn and use the mnemonic technique easily and effectively? Why or why not? What conclusions can you draw in general? Explain. (Subjects using the mnemonic device will often remember the list even a week or two later!)

4. The chapter points out that eyewitness testimony is not always reliable. See how well your friends do at picking out faces. Find an *old, useless* yearbook. Cut out 60 pictures (all males or all females) and put them into two equal piles. Have a friend study pile A for five minutes. Then, before giving him or her pile B, slip a picture from pile A into pile B. Tell your friend that he or she needs to identify the picture that you slipped in. Repeat this entire procedure on seven other friends.

How well did they do? Ask them what cues they used to help them or what interfered with their remembering the face. Explain their answers and any conclusions you can draw.

5. Create a videotape that teaches viewers—probably your class—about memory. The tape should be both entertaining and educational. Here are some ideas:
a. Show nine items on the screen. Ask the audience to study the items for about 15 seconds and then write down all they can recall. Repeat the procedure for 16 items. This should demonstrate the limits of short-term memory.

b. Show a picture of 10 U.S. quarters, only one of them accurate. Ask the audience to pick the right one. This can show that memory is not perfect—that attention is important.

c. Show a chessboard with several pieces on it. The position of the pieces should reflect what could really occur in a game. Ask your audience to study the board and later draw what they recall. Next, show a chessboard with the same number of pieces. This time the pieces should be placed on the board randomly. Chess players will probably have better recall of the first chessboard because it fits their "map" of the world.

6. Conduct the last experiment described in the Applying Psychology to Life feature at the end of the chapter using two or three family members as subjects. Find an *old* photograph and briefly describe the photo so your "subject" knows which one it is. Have the subject write down everything he or she can remember about the photo.

During this time, ask a few leading questions, like "What color is my sweater in the picture?" or "What time is it on the clock?" Be as subtle as possible. In actuality, there will be no sweater or clock in the photo. You're simply testing whether they will fill in details or reconstruct the scene according to what they think *should* be there. Repeat this entire procedure for five other old photos.

How influential were the leading questions? Explain. Did subjects fill in details that weren't there even before you started asking the questions? Explain your results.

Intelligence and Creativity

Most of us can recognize the end product of intelligence or creativity. Scientists, however, are not sure exactly what intelligence and creativity are. A number of tests have been devised to try to measure these characteristics. This chapter looks at the nature of these tests as well as some pros and cons of using them.

Understanding Intelligence

In this chapter, we tackle one of the oldest and most researched areas of psychology: intelligence. In a way, it seems that the more we study the topic, the more complex it becomes. So we will deal with considerable controversy and disagreement as we proceed.

Defining Intelligence

The word *intelligence* seems perfectly clear when we hear it, but on close examination it becomes quite vague. Just what does the term really refer to? A formal definition might help a little: **Intelligence** is the ability to understand and adapt to the environment by using a combination of inherited abilities and learning experiences.

Psychologists first tried to measure intelligence in a mechanical way. In the late 1800s, researchers assumed that since mind and body are so difficult to separate, it might be possible to measure intelligence with a series of physical tests. Some of these measures seem outlandish today. For instance, one test item involved pressing a pointed rubber plug against the subject's forehead with increasing pressure until it caused pain. The idea was to measure many supposedly "bright" and "dull" people, find out which group was better able to stand the pain, and then use these "test" results in order to measure other people with the plug and classify them as either dull or bright.

As you might have guessed, this approach did not work very well for measuring intelligence. However, it was not a total failure. One type of response that was part of this early attempt has reemerged in recent research. The early psychologists believed that how quickly a person could react to a stimulus indicated how bright that person was. More recent studies have found that the speed with which someone can take in information and respond to it is indeed related to that person's level of intelligence (Deary & Stough, 1996).

The Stanford-Binet Intelligence Scale

The first workable intelligence test was constructed in the early 1900s. In France, the minister of public instruction wanted to find some way of locating students who were not bright enough to be in the regular school system. His goal was to provide them with special instruction. He appointed a man named **Alfred Binet** (be-NAY) to solve the problem. The updated version of Binet's test is still used today, nearly 100 years later. It is called the **Stanford-Binet Intelligence Scale** because it was refined at Stanford University in California.

Binet was not sure what an intelligence test should include. He, like everyone else, had trouble defining the term. Eventually, he came up with four elements that he believed were important for intelligence:

1. *Direction* is the ability to set up a goal and work toward it.
2. *Adaptability* means that when faced with a problem, the person can make the adjustments needed to solve it.
3. *Comprehension* means having a basic understanding of exactly what the problem is.

Focus Question

....

• How do psychologists define intelligence?

intelligence the ability to understand and adapt to the environment by using a combination of inherited abilities and learning experiences

▲ *Although not a high achiever as a young student, Albert Einstein became known as a true genius.*

Focus Questions

....

• What four elements did Binet use to measure intelligence?

• What does IQ mean?

Stanford-Binet Intelligence Scale intelligence test developed by Alfred Binet and later refined at Stanford University

▲ *Binet's goal in developing an intelligence test was to find those children who needed special help in school.*

4. Finally, the person working on the problem should have some idea of whether he or she has been able to solve it correctly. "Solving" the problem is worthless if the solution is wrong. Hence, Binet called the last item *self-evaluation*.

It's interesting to note that the same general abilities are tested by the Stanford-Binet today. However, the latest edition of this test places more emphasis on several types of reasoning processes, such as critical thinking and analysis (Daniel, 1997).

Binet's ideas may seem obvious today, but that is because we're used to them. At the time, they were very innovative. He developed test items that measured each of these areas; then he put the items in order of increasing difficulty. As the items got progressively more difficult, they applied to higher age groups. In this way, he could test both older and younger students.

Test-Item Construction. At the simplest level, typical Binet test items included naming major parts of the body (arms, legs, and so on) or selecting specific objects from a pile (pick up the toy train, pick up the ball) when asked to do so by the examiner. More difficult items appeared for older children: "Indicate which number is not in its correct position: 12, 9, 6, 3, 15." At a higher level of abstraction, we have this one: "Bill Jones's feet are so big that he has to pull his trousers on over his head. What is foolish about that?"

Before the test was finished, items were administered to large groups of children of varying ages. The items were then put in order of increasing difficulty. For example, if all five-year-old children could solve a particular item, it was considered too easy for that group, so it would be tried with four-year-olds. If it was too hard for five-year-olds, it would be tried at the age-six level. The goal was to get items that most, but not all, of the children of a given age could answer. The final test was designed to measure mental ability from ages 3 to 15 years.

Mental Age. We expect the average five-year-old to pass most items at the five-year-old level, since that is how the test was designed. Thus, the child who is chronologically five years old (age based on birthdays), if average, should also have a **mental age** of roughly five years.

But what if a certain five-year-old is brighter than the average five-year-old? This would mean that his or her mental age must be higher than that of the average five-year-old. Suppose this particular child answers all the items for five-year-olds as well as most of those at the six-year-old level. When the test is scored, the child's mental age has gone beyond age five into the six-year-old area. So, his or her mental age would be six.

> **mental age** the level of intellectual functioning in years, which is compared with chronological age to derive IQ

In Focus

Binet's Definition of Intelligence

Direction: Set goal.
Adaptability: Adjust goal.
Comprehension: Understand problem.
Self-Evaluation: Assess solution.

Mighty Stacy walks up to the plate. Annette, on the pitcher's mound, decides she's going to strike her out, but she can't give her any easy pitches *(direction).* She throws three pitches inside, and the count is three balls and no strikes. She decides to give up speed for accuracy *(adaptability)* and throws the ball over the middle of the plate. Mighty Stacy swings and misses. Annette now understands the problem *(comprehension):* Mighty Stacy can't hit slow pitches. Annette throws another slow pitch over the middle. Mighty Stacy swings and misses. The count is three balls and two strikes. Annette winds up and lobs the ball over the plate. Mighty Stacy swings and launches the ball over the outfielders' heads. Annette sits on the mound and wonders whether slow pitches were the answer *(self-evaluation).*

If you were to evaluate your own intelligence using Binet's four elements, what would be your conclusion? How well do you apply each element?

intelligence quotient (IQ) a measure of intelligence originally obtained by comparing mental age, as determined by testing, with chronological age

IQ. A term you hear all the time is *IQ*. The IQ, or **intelligence quotient,** is a measure of intelligence obtained by comparing mental age with physical age. A quotient is a number obtained by dividing one number by another. To make calculation easy, the number 100 was chosen as the center, or perfectly average, point. An IQ of 100 is a perfectly average IQ.

Notice how we get this IQ of 100: Take the mental age, divide it by the chronological age, and multiply by 100 (to get rid of any decimals).

$$\frac{\text{Mental age}}{\text{Chronological age}} \times 100 = IQ$$

Thus, the IQ of our perfectly average five-year-old is calculated this way:

$$5/5 \times 100 = 100 \text{ IQ}$$

The child we've described as having a mental age of six must have a higher IQ score:

$$6/5 \times 100 = 120 \text{ IQ}$$

We hope this formula helps you understand what an IQ means and where it comes from. However, you should be aware that the formula is no longer used today. For a number of reasons, it was replaced by statistical tables many years ago.

There is a wide range of possible IQs. Categories of IQs are shown in Figure 9.1, along with the percentage of people falling into a given category as well as the label attached to each category. Note that most people do not have very high or very low intelligence quotients. The largest group (49 percent) falls within the average range.

Wechsler Intelligence Tests

The Binet test certainly served its purpose of locating children who would have trouble in school, since the Binet test deals almost exclusively

Focus Question

••••••••••••••••••••••••••••••••

- How did Wechsler's test improve upon Binet's for testing IQ?

▶ *Figure 9.1* *Classifications of Intelligence Quotients for Wechsler*

Classifications of Intelligence Quotients

IQ	Category	Percentage of people
130 or above	Very superior	2.6
120—129	Superior	6.9
110—119	High average	16.6
90—109	Average	49.1
80—89	Low average	16.1
70—79	Borderline	6.4
69 or below	Mentally retarded	2.3

with words, and they are the core of schoolwork. Almost all the items require some kind of searching for a word answer, as in the question, "Brother is a boy; sister is a _____."

There were problems with the Binet test, though. One psychologist, **David Wechsler** (WEX-ler), worked at New York's Bellevue Hospital, where he handled derelicts from skid row who were brought there by the police. Most of these people had had little formal education, and school-related material was not usually part of their lives.

Wechsler wanted to develop a program to help these people find jobs and get out of the mess they were in, and so he needed some measure of how bright they were in real-world intelligence rather than in school-work. The highly verbal Binet test just didn't do the job. Wechsler hit on the idea of a two-part intelligence test. The first part contained verbal items like the Binet **(verbal scale),** but a second part was a *non*verbal IQ test, called a **performance scale.**

▲ *Wechsler's performance scale includes nonverbal tasks similar to the one this boy is doing.*

Wechsler's performance scale relies minimally on the use of words, but it still requires the ability to reason. Here are a few of the types of performance items he used in his original test, which came out in the 1930s: In *picture completion,* the test taker was shown a series of pictures from which some important part had been removed. For example, at the simplest level, a picture of a pig with no tail was shown, and the test taker was to indicate what was missing. In another type of item, the *object assembly,* a picture of a familiar figure or object (for instance, an elephant) was cut up like a jigsaw puzzle. The test taker first had to recognize what the parts made when they were fitted together and then had to assemble them. (See an example of a performance scale test in the Applying Psychology to Life feature on page 278.)

Eventually Wechsler constructed different forms of his intelligence test for use with different age groups. They all provide three IQs. One is verbal, another is performance, and the third combines these two to give a full-scale IQ. The **Wechsler Adult Intelligence Scale (WAIS)** is used with adults, people aged 16 and older. The **Wechsler Intelligence Scale for Children (WISC)** is for children aged 6 to 16. There is also a test for preschoolers four to six years old.

Wechsler's idea worked well. Interestingly, studies over the years have shown that the Wechsler performance scale measures roughly the same abilities as the verbal scale (Daniel, 1997). This probably results from the fact that to solve the performance items, a person must call on symbolic skills ("This is an elephant; an elephant has a trunk over here"). Symbolic skills are very much involved with verbal problems, since words are symbols.

So all of our IQ tests seem to be measuring the same general thing. This "same thing" may or may not be identical with a person's *real* intelligence.

verbal scale IQ test items that rely heavily on word comprehension and usage

performance scale IQ test items that try to bypass verbal material and focus on problem solving without words

Wechsler Adult Intelligence Scale (WAIS) an intelligence test for adults that provides three IQs: verbal, performance, and full-scale (total)

Wechsler Intelligence Scale for Children (WISC) an intelligence test for children aged 6 to 16 that provides three IQs: verbal, performance, and full-scale

The Wechsler Tests

Two frequently used intelligence tests are the Wechsler Intelligence Scale for Children, or WISC, and the Wechsler Adult Intelligence Scale, or WAIS. The Wechsler tests place more emphasis on performance tasks (such as doing puzzles) than does the Stanford-Binet. As a result, individuals who are not particularly skilled in the use of words will not be as likely to receive low IQ scores on the Wechsler tests.

In addition to providing one overall score, the Wechsler tests yield scores in several areas—vocabulary, information, arithmetic, picture arrangement, and so on. It is therefore possible to compute separate IQ scores for verbal and performance abilities. This type of scoring provides a more detailed picture of the individual's strengths and weaknesses than a single score does.

Below is a sample of questions similar to those on five of the verbal subtests on the Wechsler. (Test items courtesy of The Psychological Corporation, New York.)

General Information

1. How many wings does a bird have?
2. How many nickels make a dime?
3. What is steam made of?
4. Who wrote *Tom Sawyer*?
5. What is pepper?

General Comprehension

1. What should you do if you see someone forget his book when he leaves his seat in a restaurant?
2. What is the advantage of keeping money in a bank?
3. Why is copper often used in electrical wires?

Arithmetic

1. Sam had three pieces of candy and Joe gave him four more. How many pieces of candy did Sam have altogether?
2. Three men divided 18 golf balls equally among themselves. How many golf balls did each man receive?
3. If two apples cost 15 cents, what will be the cost of a dozen apples?

Similarities

1. In what way are a lion and a tiger alike?
2. In what way are a saw and a hammer alike?
3. In what way are an hour and a week alike?
4. In what way are a circle and a triangle alike?

Vocabulary

1. "What is a puzzle?"
2. "What does 'addition' mean?"

What is the major difference between the Wechsler tests and the Binet test?

What Is Intelligence?

Focus Questions

• •

- Intelligence traditionally refers to "book smarts." Are there other kinds of intelligence?

- Should IQ tests be used to assign grade levels to young children?

Haven't we just spent a lot of time discussing that very topic? Actually, we have not, and this is very important: For the most part, we have been discussing intelligence *testing,* especially IQ tests, which is quite a different matter.

Think about this for a few seconds: Since we are not certain exactly what intelligence is, but we do depend on intelligence tests, what we *call* intelligence is, in fact, whatever the intelligence tests measure. That sounds absurd at first, but note the predicament we are in. We have these tests that can tell the difference between people's school abilities in a general sort of way. We use the tests all the time to try to estimate how bright a person is. Hence, we are constantly using the test results themselves as the equivalent of intelligence.

There are some serious flaws in this system. For instance, all of us know people who score very high on these tests but can act foolishly in most areas of life. We also know people who score low average but who are great problem solvers and really handle everyday life effectively. Clearly, the IQ test measures something important, but it certainly is not the final word on intelligence.

◀ *Problem solving in real life takes many forms.*

Gardner's Theory of Multiple Intelligences

theory of multiple intelligences
Howard Gardner's theory that intelligence is made up of seven abilities—language, logical/mathematical, visual/spatial, musical, bodily movement, intrapersonal, and interpersonal

Many psychologists have been dissatisfied with the fairly narrow definition of intelligence that has been accepted for such a long time. They feel that to concentrate so much on academic, or school-oriented, tasks is to lose a great deal of what can and should be considered intelligent behavior (Sternberg, 1997). One of these psychologists, Howard Gardner, has proposed a view of intelligence that incorporates many nonacademic abilities.

According to Gardner's **theory of multiple intelligences,** there are seven fairly broad basic components to what we should define as intelligence. Only two of these are school related: language abilities and logical/mathematical abilities. The other five are things you probably do not usually think of as "intelligence" but more likely consider special talents. The remaining five are visual/spatial thinking, musical ability, bodily movement ability, intrapersonal skills, and interpersonal skills. Visual/spatial thinking is what artists and engineers emphasize as they create paintings and blueprints. Music is just what you think it is and includes composing as well as performing. Bodily movement is the ability that dancers and athletes possess to a much higher degree than the rest of us. Intrapersonal skills relate to how well we know ourselves, while interpersonal skills relate to our ability to interact well with other people—our social skills.

We do not yet have well-established tests to measure these abilities, as we do for traditionally defined intelligence, but alternative tests are being examined for accuracy and usefulness (Neisser, 1997). Existing intel-

In Focus

Seven of Gardner's Multiple Intelligences

Which intelligence do you believe is strongest in you?

▲ *Psychologist Howard Gardner*

▲ *Musical ability is one of Gardner's multiple intelligences.*

ligence tests do provide us with information and likely will continue to be used for a long time. However, new approaches such as Gardner's have a great deal to offer in terms of drawing a more complete picture of what intelligent behavior really consists of.

Influence of Society on Definition of Intelligence

Wechsler cautioned that our definitions (and tests) always reflect the culture within which we live—in other words, they reflect whatever society at the moment views as worthwhile, meaningful, and valuable (Wechsler, 1975). In some times and places, for example, the skills needed to be an excellent farmer are far more important than the skills needed to be a lawyer.

One study compared the definition of *intelligence* used by Australians with that used by Malaysians. The researchers found that the latter group defines *intelligence* as the ability to get along well with other people and to do so in a socially efficient way. The Australians, on the other hand, are quite industrialized and emphasize academic skills, just as we do (Brislin, 1983; Gill & Keats, 1980).

While this situation makes the definition of intelligence that we use rather questionable in many cases, we can't throw intelligence tests out just because they *do* reflect our culture. After all, we have to succeed somehow within the limits of our society. Also, some kind of test is better than none, and we don't know what to replace these tests with. Still, almost everyone knows that if you judge people's abilities just by the results of their IQ tests, you're going to miss some potentially very capable people who don't do all that well on the tests.

Thinking Critically about Psychology

Intelligence and Real-Life Success

We have suggested that intelligence is related to success in life. We have also suggested that other factors are equally important to success. We expand on this issue here. Because mental retardation brings with it so many other limitations, we will deal here only with intelligence that is average or higher.

What specifically is being claimed or stated? Within the range from average to the highest levels, intelligence is related to success in the real world, especially job performance.

What is the objective evidence for and against this claim? Interestingly enough, supporters of both sides generally agree on the numbers provided by research findings. Studies have shown that intelligence accounts for between 4 and 29 percent of the variation in how well people do on the job (Ceci & Williams, 1997; R. Wagner, 1997; Sternberg, Wagner, Williams, & Horvath, 1995). The major difference between the two sides on this issue has to do with what these percentages mean. Some point out that intelligence is the single best predictor of how well people will succeed on the job (Brody, 1997; Ceci & Williams, 1997). Others, though—not denying this fact—go on to argue that it leaves a substantial amount of job-success variation unaccounted for: between 71 and 96 percent. Their point is that other factors might predict job success as well as or better than intelligence does (R. Wagner, 1997; Sternberg et al., 1995; Gardner, 1993).

What other interpretations might be made instead? One research area has focused on "practical intelligence," the skills we need to solve everyday problems—what we usually call common sense. There are indications that practical intelligence may indeed be related to how well we deal with our lives in the real world, including demands and problems on the job (Sternberg, 1997; Sternberg et al., 1995). Another finding is that IQ is related to academic success, which in turn is related to how much education one gets. Education level, in turn, is related to occupational opportunities. Clearly, occupation is related to how well we do financially, which is one measure of job success. Thus, while intelligence is related, it is an indirect relationship (Brody, 1997).

▲ *Intelligence and academic success are related.*

▲ *Some useful problem-solving skills are hands-on and do not involve academic subject matter.*

See if COOL works for you....

Claim?

Objective evidence for and against claim?

Other interpretations?

Logical conclusions?

What are the most logical conclusions to draw? Given the fact that experts in this area seriously disagree, you could clearly argue that either side is right—that it is simply a matter of interpretation. In this light, we offer a compromise. We believe that the most reasonable conclusion is that while intelligence scores provide a fairly strong prediction of real-life success, it is highly likely that other factors are at least as important as IQ. Considering the direction recent research has taken, quite possibly these factors will eventually be identified.

Applying Critical Thinking Skills

As suggested above, factors other than intelligence probably play a significant role in real-life success. In your opinion, what are those factors?

Focus Question

• Why are twins good subjects for intelligence studies?

Is Intelligence Inherited?

Most of the evidence indicates that heredity plays an important part in basic intellectual potential. The majority of investigators in this area have concluded that roughly 50 percent of what we call intelligence is the result of some kind of hereditary influence. The other 50 percent comes from all kinds of things—education, social class, environment, nutrition, amount of stimulation, and the like (Plomin & DeFries, 1998; Neisser et al., 1996).

These conclusions are based on studies of the IQs of twins. Some twins come from the same fertilized egg. These *identical twins,* therefore, have exactly the same heredity. If they have the same heredity, and IQs are to some extent inherited, their IQs should be very close to one another, even if they are reared apart. And indeed that turns out to be the case (Neisser, 1997).

Other twins are called *fraternal.* These twins have the same environment inside the mother and will share many of the same characteristics, but they come from two separate eggs. Hence, their heredity is not identical. Their IQs should be close, but not as close as those of the identical twins. Again, this turns out to be the case.

Finally, to round out the analysis, a comparison is made between the IQs for nontwin brothers and sisters. They are as close in heredity as fraternal twins but experience greater environmental differences because they are not the same age. Hence, their IQs should be closer to one another than to the IQs of other children down the block but not as close as the twins' IQs. That also turns out to be true (Kamin, 1978; Munsinger, 1975). Note, though, that environment *is* important. A brother and sister who live together are usually much closer in IQ than those who are reared apart.

▲ *Identical twins are usually very similar in intelligence.*

The Effects of Environment

Inheritance clearly plays a role in what a person can become. But it only sets up certain limits. Within these limits, the environment plays its role (Turkheimer, 1991). For instance, say a person wants to become a runner. The person has inherited a basic body structure, a certain lung capacity, and a specific leg structure. What he or she does with these inherited traits is the result of effort and environment. His or her parents may or may not have provided, through heredity, the equipment for this person to become an Olympic candidate. But what they have given are the physical limits for a maximum and minimum running ability; this is what their child has to work with.

In the intelligence area, intriguing studies show that brain changes can occur in animals depending on the type of environment in which they are raised. Rats that live in a stimulating, enriched environment with plenty of activities to perform *literally* grow a thicker, heavier brain than other rats. The brain's nerve cells actually branch out and weigh more if the rats have developed in a stimulating environment. Other studies show that if an animal's visual system is given very high levels of stimulation—rather than, say, its hearing or smell—the visual portion of the brain becomes much heavier than these other parts (Greenough, 1985).

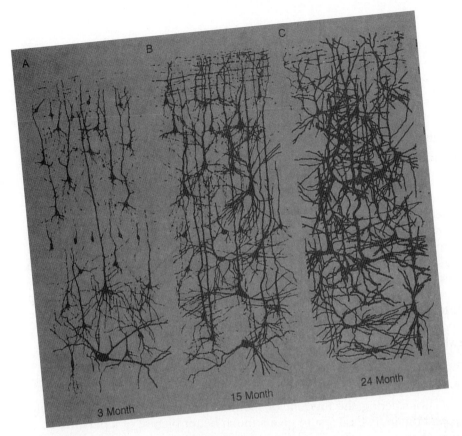

◀ ***Figure 9.2*** *Sections from the Cerebral Cortex of Children Aged 3, 15, and 24 Months. Note the increased branching and thickening of dendrites. From the work of Conel (A) 1947, (B) 1955, (C) 1959. From* Language of the Brain *by K. Pribram, Prentice-Hall, Inc., 1971. Reprinted by permission.*

Researchers believe that exactly the same types of changes take place in the human brain (Neisser et al., 1996). Figure 9.2 is very interesting in this regard. It shows the brain cell development of the normal child from 3 to 24 months of age (Pribram, 1971). What these studies demonstrate is the importance of environment. They do not suggest that a child can progress faster than nature allows. As we discuss in Chapter 10, on child development, nature has built in a sequence of mental development that the child follows, with one stage leading into another. Training or stimulation *cannot* speed up the sequence of development. Nevertheless, it is critical that the child be given a stimulating environment. As the brain develops, it can take in more and more from the environment, so the environment must contain stimulating objects and events.

 ## Pause for Thought

1. How does Binet's definition of intelligence differ from Wechsler's? What motivated each man to study intelligence?
2. Explain how IQ is calculated.
3. According to Gardner, what areas have traditional intelligence tests ignored?

Critical Thinking

4. What personal characteristic or characteristics other than intelligence might affect real-life success? Prepare an argument supporting the view that this characteristic is more important to success in life than is intelligence.

Issues in Intelligence Testing

Next, we want to discuss some of the issues surrounding IQ scores. You will find that this area of study is far from peaceful and quiet.

Individual Versus Group Testing

Both the Binet and the Wechsler tests are administered individually. A psychologist sits at a table with a student, asking the test questions and demonstrating the problems contained in the test. These **individual intelligence tests** take an hour or so to administer, plus additional time for scoring. Such a lengthy process provides more opportunity for the test administrator to see the person in action and to understand some of the reasoning behind his or her answers. The biggest problem, though, is the cost. An individual test administration is expensive.

Other tests cost as little as 10 to 20 cents per person. These **group intelligence tests** are given to large numbers of people at the same time and scored by computer. Hence, they are done entirely on paper. Here are two group IQ test items:

1. A hat is to: (a) smell (b) look through (c) wear (d) smoke.

2. *Ear* is to *hear* as *eye* is to: (a) tear (b) see (c) spectacles (d) eyelash.

Considering the amount of money and time involved, you would expect the individual test to give a much better picture of a person's abilities. It does, and this is particularly important in testing a person who has serious problems or who will use the results in making a specific, important decision. Overall, however, group tests can be reasonably accurate in predicting school potential. They do, though, present the problem of being completely verbal and offering no opportunity to measure performance.

Uses and Limits of IQ Scores

In general, things like achievement in history, reading comprehension, and biology are all related to how well one does on the IQ test.

But test results must be viewed cautiously, especially if school performance is better than IQ score. The test can be a poor predictor, most often failing to predict things like how well a person actually does a certain task in the real world. And the person scoring the IQ test *can* make errors, sometimes enormous ones, as great as 30 points. Errors are usually not that large, though, and on average vary about seven points from what the correct IQ is supposed to be. Still, people should never be content to let one low score stand as is. In such a case, it is very important to administer another IQ test to be certain the first one was not in error.

Court Cases.   In recent years, federal and state courts have more and more been ruling that IQ test results alone cannot be used to make judgments about which classes or schools to place children in if the children haven't done well on the test (Matarazzo, 1990). There are good reasons for many of these rulings.

IQ tests are constructed by and contain material from the white middle-class group. As a result, these tests label six times more nonwhites than whites as "mentally retarded" (discussed later in this chapter). This difference is so high that the test, rather than the basic abilities of the non-

individual intelligence tests IQ tests administered on a one-to-one basis—one examiner to one test taker

group intelligence tests IQ tests administered to many people at one time; tests are highly verbal and use paper and pencil

whites, immediately becomes suspect. When a test unfairly measures the abilities of different cultural groups, it is said to suffer from **cultural bias.**

The problem is that certain concepts, words, thoughts, phrases, and ideas vary from one subgroup to another in our mixed society. Chinese Americans, Japanese Americans, Hispanics, African Americans, Irish Americans, and Italian Americans all come from cultures that are not identical to middle-class white America. The differences are a valuable and important part of the American way of life. Nonetheless, these differences can influence test results in an often subtle but unfair fashion. What seems to be an identical question for all groups can turn out not to be.

Thus, for some reason, African American children have trouble with the instruction, "Mark the apple that is whole." But they have no trouble with "Mark the apple that is still all there" (Wright & Isenstein, 1975). Since this is the same instruction, it becomes clear that how a question or instruction is worded—which is the result of the test maker's own race and social class—can alter test results.

Larger cultural issues are also involved. For instance, it has been argued that African Americans tend to value and emphasize thought processes (such as problem solving and classifying) and approaches to test taking that are different from those valued and emphasized by whites (Helms, 1992). Such differences could obviously have a negative effect on one's IQ score.

Here is another example: In Brazil and some other Latin American countries, most people pay little attention to time. One study showed that almost all the clocks (even the official ones) and watches in Brazil are set incorrectly. If you arrive late for an appointment, nobody pays any attention (Levine et al., 1980). In contrast, in the United States, people run around all the time clocking themselves to the vibrations of quartz watches, splitting the second down into little bits. Now, suppose we are comparing the IQ test results of someone from a Latin American culture with those of someone from a typical North American culture. A cultural difference of this sort can have a major impact, since many items on an IQ test are carefully timed. If you run out of time, you lose IQ points!

cultural bias the unfair measurement of cultural groups' abilities

▲ *Whether scoring tests or relating to other people in general, we should take into consideration any cultural differences.*

In Focus

Potential Problems with Intelligence Tests

- Tests may unintentionally reflect a cultural bias.
- Tests may unintentionally reflect a middle-class bias.
- Individually administered tests are costly.
- Tests are sometimes a poor predictor of "success" in the real world—that is, outside school.
- Test scores might be inaccurate.
- Tests measure only a limited range of abilities.

Can you think of a question that would include a subtle cultural or middle-class bias?

Superior Intelligence

The heading of this section may seem offensive at first. However, if you reread Figure 9.1, you will see that the word *superior* is just one of the technical classifications at the upper end of the IQ range. The term *genius* is no longer used. Whichever term is applied, though, certain images are frequently associated with very high intelligence. Extremely bright people are often depicted as eccentric and strange, sickly and frail, isolated from the rest of society. Is this an accurate picture? Stay tuned, and you will find out.

Personal Characteristics

In the early 1920s, most people believed that high intelligence was linked to insanity and a number of other problems. But no one had ever carefully studied the issue. A man named Lewis Terman decided to find out what bright children were really like. He selected 1,528 children to participate in his study. Their average IQ was 150, a higher score than 99.9 percent of children. He found these children to be extremely successful in school, which was certainly no surprise. However, he also found that they were psychologically well adjusted, were physically quite healthy, and interacted well with other people.

These people have been studied at regular intervals since 1921. In fact, Terman died before the study could be completed. The person who took over for him was one of the original subjects who, along the way, became a prominent psychologist. As adults and into old age, the subjects remained healthier and more successful than average. They also had lower rates of divorce, alcoholism, and suicide (Goleman, 1980). At last look, about half of the people in the original group were still alive (Friedman et al., 1995). Finally, we offer a piece of psychological trivia: In honor of Lewis Terman, the man who designed this study, his subjects are affectionately referred to as "Termites."

It is true that extremely gifted children can be bored in school and teased by other kids. They need special programs to keep them interested and challenged (Winner, 1997). Most very bright children, though, do fine in school and don't have these kinds of problems.

Other studies have found that highly intelligent people tend to have greater self-esteem. They are also less gullible than most—that is, harder to hoodwink and influence or persuade of something they find difficult to believe (Rhodes & Wood, 1992). It would seem, then, that the popular image of extremely bright people is not very accurate.

▶ *A remarkable example of superior intelligence, Marilyn vos Savant has one of the highest IQs ever officially recorded. When she was only 7 years and 9 months old, she could answer questions that the average 13-year-old can answer. At ages 8, 9, and 10, she got perfect scores on the Stanford-Binet test (Lemley, 1986).*

Does intelligence alone account for these differences? Probably not, although it plays a major role. Most likely, several related factors have some input. For instance, early success in school may build confidence, which has a positive effect on self-esteem. In addition, we tend to like what we are good at, so those who do well in school are more likely to stay in school and get professional training. A good job means fewer worries, better access to medical care, less stress on a marriage, and so on.

None of this guarantees that everyone with a high IQ will succeed in life. It does mean that as a group, these people have a somewhat better shot at making it. Please remember, though, that the reverse of all this does not doom someone to failure. We know too many people who have changed direction at various points in their lives to say that anything so complicated as one's happiness or success is set in concrete early on.

Mental Retardation

Mental retardation affects quite a large number of people. There are about 5 million people with notable retardation in the United States. **Mental retardation** is defined as below-average intellectual functioning in which an individual is unable to handle tasks appropriate to his or her physical age. Learning ability and social adjustment are impaired. The condition is usually present at birth and discovered at an early age.

Basic Classifications

The basic classifications of mental retardation follow, along with some of the things the people in each category generally can and cannot do.

IQ 70–79: Borderline Mental Retardation. Those labeled borderline score just below the "low average" group in IQ (see Figure 9.1). They are slow learners, and most fail to complete high school. Generally, these people are employed in "nonintellectual" occupations and are not legally retarded in the sense that they would be entitled to disability benefits. (This is the classification of individuals about whom the courts are concerned when they restrict the use of the IQ test, as discussed earlier.)

IQ 52–69: Mild Mental Retardation. Most people legally termed "retarded" fall into this category, and most require special help in school. The behavior of people in this group varies considerably depending on whether the IQ is toward the higher or lower end of the range. Someone with a 69 IQ can function pretty well on his or her own, can usually marry, and can maintain a family. At the lower end of the range, some supervision is required, since these people have trouble with abstract reasoning and problem solving.

IQ 36–51: Moderate Mental Retardation. People in this group have physical problems, often stemming from a serious disease. They are trained in how to take care of themselves and can live at home, but with supervision. When fully grown, most have the skills of a four- to seven-year-old and can read, write, and speak at that age level.

IQ 20–35: Severe Mental Retardation. People in this group usually require constant supervision. About 75 percent have a physical defect or have had a major disease and cannot benefit from school (Cleland et al., 1980).

IQ 19 or Below: Profound Mental Retardation. The smallest group of people, about 1 percent of the mentally retarded population, fall into this

mental retardation below-average intellectual functioning that prevents a person from being able to perform at the level appropriate for his or her age

▲ *Mental retardation is not an automatic barrier to living a good life.*

271

category. Rarely do they mature mentally beyond age two; and even as adults, they can engage in only limited communication. They are unable to dress or care for themselves without considerable training (Robinson & Robinson, 1970).

Physical Factors

Retardation results from known physical defects in only about 20 percent of cases. Most of these cases fall into the categories of severe or profound retardation, although a few are in the moderate group. The physical problems usually come from an injury or disease that has affected brain growth and development. The more common causes are lack of oxygen at birth, extreme malnutrition, and exposure to toxic chemicals. Defects can also be inherited from the parents.

Most people who are mentally retarded, then, do not have any obvious physical brain problem. You might expect that if autopsies were performed on the brains of a very bright person, an average person, and a mentally retarded person, there would be a clear difference among these brains. That is not the case. All three brains would look approximately the same. It is true that there are differences in the way the brains *work*, but with our present state of knowledge, we can't *see* what those differences might be.

Environmental Factors

Is it possible that some factors in the environment can lead to retardation? One thing we do know is that proper nutrition is absolutely critical to brain development. This is one of the reasons school lunch programs are so important. If vital nutrients are absent during critical periods of brain growth, development is permanently slowed. Poor health and infection can have similar effects. Alcohol or drug abuse by pregnant women can also damage the unborn child. Finally, a lack of stimulation, as discussed earlier, won't actually damage the brain but can slow the growth of vital nerve cells. Any or all of these factors can be involved in mental retardation. Since the majority of people with this problem come

▶ *The mother's condition during pregnancy can have serious consequences for her newborn child's intellectual functioning.*

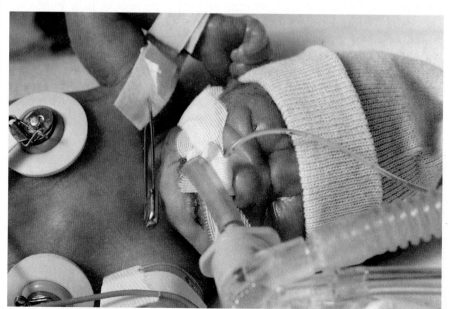

from areas of poverty, we suspect that in many cases the environment is a major factor.

We have a lot to learn about mental retardation. There are puzzling cases in which the parents have done everything possible, the environment is reasonable, there is no *apparent* physical defect, yet the child is still retarded.

Methods of Treatment

Medicine is making great strides in dealing with physical causes of mental retardation. For those suffering from environmental problems, many programs are available to provide intellectual stimulation. In the past, this generally meant sending virtually all such children to special education classes. For some, this is still the best alternative. For others, though, special education classes do not provide enough challenge, and the students feel isolated from other children. It is important, too, that where special education is provided, it is made to fit the particular abilities of individual children (Detterman & Thompson, 1997). There is a great deal of variation in patterns of abilities and disabilities among mentally retarded children.

Recently, efforts have been made to keep mentally retarded children in regular classes as much as possible. This approach is called **inclusion.** How well it works depends on many factors, but it can be remarkably successful. When both parents and teachers are truly committed to making it work and the child is not severely impaired, the results can be startling indeed. Many children learn much more than anyone thought they were capable of. And a number go on to become completely self-sufficient adults.

For seriously mentally retarded children and adults, there are also programs that include training in motor coordination, practical social skills, and self-care. So even though we don't completely understand the causes of retardation, large numbers of those who a few years ago would have been left in institutions are now able, at least partly, to take care of themselves.

Special Cases—Savant Syndrome

So far, we have covered a number of characteristics associated with high and low intellectual functioning. However, one intriguing phenomenon

In Their Own Words . . .

Darold A. Treffert *has worked extensively with savants. In the following excerpts, the psychiatrist summarizes the serious dysfunctions and amazing abilities of several such persons.*

Jeremy can stand at the side of the railroad tracks and give you the cumulative total of the numbers on the boxcars, however many, as the end of the train rolls by. But he is severely autistic* and cannot count.

George and his identical twin brother Charles can tell you all the years in which your birthday fell on a Thursday. They can also tell you, within a span of 40,000 years backward or forward, the day of the week on which any date you choose fell or will fall. . . . Yet they cannot add simple figures or even tell you what a formula is, let alone write one out.

Leslie has never had any formal musical training. Yet upon hearing Tchaikovsky's Piano Concerto No. 1 on the piano for the first time in his teen years, he played it back flawlessly and without hesitation. He can do the same with any other piece of music, no matter how long or complex. Yet he cannot hold a utensil to eat and merely repeats in monotone fashion that which is spoken to him. Leslie is blind, is severely mentally handicapped and has cerebral palsy. . . .

Alonzo has an IQ of 50 and a vocabulary of about that many words. Like Leslie, he only parrots back what is said to him and rarely initiates speech. But his animal sculptures are magnificent. He can complete a horse and colt in absolutely perfect anatomic detail in less than an hour. One fleeting glance at a picture is all he requires for a model that he will then reproduce in three-dimensional detail. (Treffert, 1989, p. xii)

*Autism is a severe developmental disorder, and below-normal mental functioning is one of its symptoms.

Interpreting Primary Sources

Dr. Treffert has described savant syndrome as a condition with "islands of mental ability in a sea of mental handicap and disability." Do you think this is an accurate description of the passage above?

inclusion the practice of keeping children with disabilities in regular academic classrooms

savant syndrome condition in which a person with below-normal mental capacity possesses a special talent or mental ability to an extremely high degree

has thus far has escaped explanation. In **savant** (saw-VAHNT) **syndrome,** a person with below-normal mental capacity possesses a particular talent or mental ability to an unusually high degree (Ericsson & Charness, 1994). Such people, called *savants,* are very rare, and more males than females exhibit these symptoms. Savants are most often born with the condition. On occasion, though, it is acquired later because of disease or injury (Treffert, 1989). We don't know what causes savant syndrome, but it is a fascinating example of the complexities of our mental makeup (Gardner, 1993). For some interesting cases of savant syndrome, see In Their Own Words on page 273.

Focus Questions

- Can creativity be defined and measured?
- Can creativity be taught?

creativity the mental processes that result in original, workable ideas

Creativity

While intelligence tests have been the focus of much interest for generations, many psychologists have pointed out that these tests do not detect the "spark" that motivates a person to do an exceptional job in finding better ways of handling problems or in inventing something new. In other words, being creative. As a result, there is now a great deal of interest in trying to find a way to measure this dimension of the person. The IQ test doesn't tap whatever it takes to produce original, workable ideas—that is, it doesn't measure **creativity** (Helms, 1992; Getzels & Jackson, 1962).

Tests of Creativity

Suppose two people are shown a picture of a man sitting in an airplane and are asked to write a story about what he is doing. They produce the following:

1. Mr. Jones is flying home after a week away from the family. He will be happy to see his family again. The plane is only about an hour away from landing. He is hoping that soon he will have some good news about a promotion that he and his family have been waiting for. He decides to take a nap and dream about how well things have been going.

2. Mr. Jones is sitting in an aisle seat, looking toward the closed door leading to the cockpit at the far end of the plane. He wants to put on a leather flight jacket and goggles and burst into the cockpit, his scarf hanging from his neck and shimmering in the light as he takes over. He opens the windows and feels the cold air hit his face, invigorating him. He is going to show the pilots how a real aviator can do the job. He will take them all for a sightseeing trip over the North Pole.

Based on the same stimulus—a picture of a man in an airplane—these two stories show a striking difference. The first one is a standard, straightforward, dull account of a businessman flying home. The second is unexpected, novel, and humorous, showing a flair for the unusual—what some psychologists call "creativity," or at least an important aspect of it.

These psychologists believe that a person must deviate from the expected in order to come up with creative products; invention is the result of unusual thinking. How many times have we all said, after seeing the solution to a problem, "Why didn't I think of that?" The answer was right before our eyes, but we didn't see it. Instead, we kept trying to solve problems in the old way. We were too conventional. We had what is called a **set,** a tendency to try to use the same old solution over and over again—even when it doesn't work.

Invention—and, we assume, creativity—is an ever-present necessity. Take the movie scene in a Wild West saloon where a man breaks off the neck of a whiskey bottle and pours himself (and the barmaid) a drink. In real life, this procedure was often an actual necessity, rather than just a dramatic gesture, since sometimes a cork could be wedged so tightly into a bottle that 300 pounds of pressure would have been needed to remove it. The problem was solved when someone took a piece of metal, twisted it into a spiral, put a sharp point on it, added a handle to push down on the top—and there it was, the corkscrew.

Breaking Set

Creativity is in all of us. When we (your authors) were young, there was no such thing as a "pop-top" soft-drink can. A special pointed can opener was needed to open a can of soda. If the opener was lost on a picnic, our ability to **break set**—think imaginatively by using different objects—was remarkable. We used rocks, nails, fingernail clippers, hairpins (a failure), and tire irons to try to open the cans.

Psychologists have come up with a definition of creativity as the ability to break set—to get out of the traditional mold and find a novel solution to a problem. But breaking set should result in something that works properly. An architect can break set and produce a bridge like no bridge anyone has ever seen before. But if it falls into the river, he or she wasn't demonstrating creativity. Truly creative people can move away from the expected but still keep enough of a hold on reality to make the solution workable (Barron & Harrington, 1981).

Tests of creativity, then, try to measure originality. One creativity test asks the test taker to give some uses for everyday objects such as a tin can and a brick. Creativity is measured by the kinds of responses given. If they deviate from the expected, then this counts toward a higher score. But "You can eat a brick," though unusual, is not creative, since it is not tied

set a tendency to solve problems in the same way over and over

break set come up with unusual, unexpected ideas; use something in a way different from the way in which it is normally used

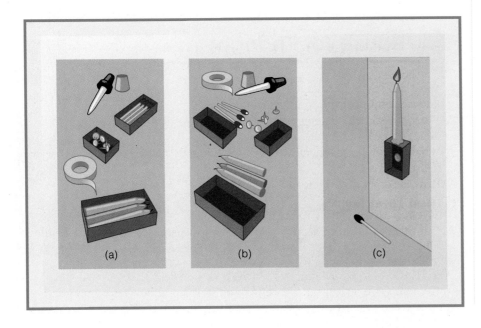

◄ *If you have practical intelligence you should be able to solve the problem of how you would mount a candle on the wall using only the items in (a). One solution is illustrated in (c). (When presented with the same items as they appear in (b), most people found it easier to break set and solve the problem.)*

(a)   (b)   (c)

to reality and shows no cleverness of thought. On the other hand, "Grind it up and put it in an enemy's red-pepper jar" has some merit in the creative sense. Tests of creativity, then, try to measure the unexpected but possible.

Creative Students

Evidence continues to mount that those who are creative are often different from the "very bright" as defined by the IQ test. Creative students are frequently unpredictable and disruptive. They may act a bit silly and have a tendency to contradict their teachers. Often, they have trouble fitting well into the standard educational system, which focuses on straight academic achievement rather than on innovative approaches to problems (Helms, 1992).

Rarely could truly creative students be called "teacher's pets," but they actually do learn the material in the classroom. They seem to be on some side road to accomplishment that is parallel but not identical to that of the "bright" students. While they do very well on standard achievement tests, their grades may be a different story.

Generally, creative students have IQs that are slightly above average but not necessarily extremely high. Beyond that, there seems to be no relationship between IQ and creativity. In other words, to be truly productively creative, you need an IQ of about 110 or so. However, having a higher IQ is no guarantee of being more inventive. So, as we've already stated, the IQ test is measuring something different from creativity or innovation. If we look for creativity only among the top 20 percent of IQs, we miss 70 percent of the creative people (Barron & Harrington, 1981; Torrance, 1980). While a few students do get extremely high scores on both IQ and creativity tests, they are definitely the exception.

▶ *One person's junk becomes someone else's masterpiece.*

Pause for Thought

1. What are some advantages and disadvantages of individual intelligence tests over group intelligence tests?
2. What are some problems with applying the results from intelligence tests?
3. What are some treatment methods for people who are mentally retarded?
4. How is set related to creativity?

Critical Thinking

5. Is it possible or even worthwhile to try to measure creativity?

Mahatma Gandhi: A Different Kind of Intelligence

Case Study

If we had met Mahatma Gandhi when he was a young student, he probably would not have struck us as particularly intelligent. He certainly didn't stand out as a leader: his grades were average; he barely made it into college. If we broaden our definition of *intelligence,* however, as Howard Gardner urges, we would recognize that Gandhi, even at a young age, excelled in a different kind of intelligence: interpersonal relationships. In his book, *Creating Minds,* Gardner (1994) describes Gandhi's extraordinary skills.

Gandhi began his career practicing law in South Africa. After a humiliating experience in which his rights were violated because he was Indian, Gandhi spent the next 20 years working to gain equal rights for Indians in South Africa.

It was in South Africa that Gandhi began to discover and develop his ability to mobilize people for a cause. He organized meetings, argued legal cases, and led petition drives. Ridiculed, beaten, and even jailed, he never let obstacles slow him down. When the South African government declared that all Indian marriages were illegitimate, Gandhi objected and led a nationwide strike by Indian workers. As a result, some of the government's racist laws were eventually overturned. Keep in mind that Gandhi held no government office. He didn't have great reserves of money or important contacts in politics who could grant him favors. He simply knew how to bring people together. And this is how he did it.

Rather than attacking the entire government as being unjust, he would focus on a specific injustice such as an unfair tax and publicize that issue. Then he would provide people with concrete ways to protest that injustice, insisting always on nonviolent methods, mainly petitioning, picketing, and marching. Gandhi himself would often fast, a remarkably effective way for him to direct attention to an issue. Finally, he would offer the opposition numerous opportunities to give in.

When he returned to India, he continued to use these tactics to battle injustice. In Gandhi's eyes, British rule over India constituted the ultimate injustice. After Britain ordered a tax on all salt and ruled that Indians could not make their own salt, Gandhi organized a monumental march that spanned over 200 miles in 24 days. Unfortunately, violence erupted amongst a small group of marchers, and the British military had to be called in to control the crowd. They overreacted and began beating innocent marchers who remained determined in their refusal to fight back. To many, this marked the beginning of the end of British rule over India. Prior to this march, the British had presumed they were superior; they had a right to impose their rule on another people, they thought. But their actions during the Salt March clearly demonstrated otherwise.

While it's true that Gandhi's interpersonal brilliance and creativity brought about social changes in both South Africa and in India, his relationship with his own family was distant. He could speak to millions and move them, but he couldn't be intimate with those closest to him. Gardner acknowledges that it is possible to be both brilliant and deficient in the same general category of intelligence.

Review the Case Study

Do you agree that interpersonal skills should be regarded as a type of intelligence? Explain.

APPLYING
Psychology to Life

What IQ Testing *Can* Do

We have covered some of the problems with IQ testing in this chapter, and they are important considerations. On the other hand, sometimes not enough attention is paid to the good that IQ testing can do. We feel that a large part of the controversy about IQ has come about because too often these tests are misused. When intelligence testing is done properly, the benefits usually outweigh the disadvantages.

The Wechsler scales measure several different abilities. The pattern of how well and how poorly someone does on the different parts or subtests can provide highly useful information. For example, some subtests are particularly sensitive to anxiety—that is, a person who tends to become very anxious under pressure will do poorly on them. Others measure abstract reasoning without being affected much by the amount of schooling a person has had. Still others depend fairly heavily on one's formal education. And of course, there is the overall division into verbal and performance tasks.

If a tester is well trained, she or he can analyze these subtests and come up with a great deal more than just an IQ score. This

information can be extremely helpful in trying to determine the type of program in which an individual should be placed. To support our point, we will discuss two real-life examples of the usefulness of IQ testing as a diagnostic tool.

In the first case, a young man was found wandering the streets. He was unable to tell the police or a social worker much about his situation. His speech was slow and halting, and he gave the

impression of being mentally retarded. Later on, it was learned that the uncle with whom he had been living had died recently. Now the young man had no relatives, no home, only an eighth-grade education, and no means of making a living.

An intelligence test was given to this young man. A careful analysis of the results showed that he was not mentally retarded. In fact, he was highly intelligent, as

▲ *Formal education affects the results of some IQ tests, but not others.*

long as he didn't have to deal very much with words. He appeared to have a physical problem that interfered with his ability to understand and use language. Instead of being institutionalized, he was placed in a training program and learned to repair a variety of electrical appliances. Eventually, he became completely self-supporting as a repairperson.

The second case involves an adolescent girl who had recently transferred from a rural district to a new school in the suburbs. Her grades were a disaster, and school officials needed to know if she was capable of doing the work. Could she benefit from remedial classes, or was special education the answer?

Test results showed that, indeed, she did have a low IQ—when only the overall score was used. Further analysis, however, revealed that her low score was due mostly to her nervousness about taking the test and her poor educational background. Her reasoning ability was actually slightly above average. So she was placed in remedial reading classes and made excellent progress. Within a year, she had rejoined her classmates and was maintaining a C+ average in school.

Not every case turns out so well, of course. However, with all the criticism of IQ testing, it seems only fair to offer some balance on the issue. The important points to keep in mind in judging a test's usefulness are the type of test given, the purpose for giving it in the first place, and the qualifications of the person administering the test.

Wechsler Performance Scale Subtests

Coding

Shown: Fill in:

1   2   3   4   1   4   3   2

○   □   △   ⊙   __   __   __   __

Block design
Assemble blocks to match this design.

Picture completion
Tell me what is missing.

Picture arrangement
Put the pictures in the right order.

Object assembly
Assemble the pieces into a complete object.

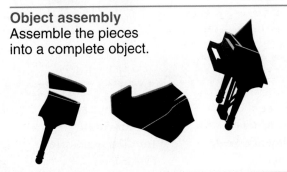

▲ *Examples shown here are similar to items from the Wechsler Performance Scale subtests.*

CHAPTER 9 REVIEW & APPLY

Summary

1. Alfred Binet originally designed an intelligence test to identify students who needed special training. Direction, adaptability, comprehension, and self-evaluation were the aspects of intelligence for which Binet developed test items. The version of that test used today is the Stanford-Binet Intelligence Scale.

2. Originally, IQ scores came from dividing mental age by chronological age and multiplying the result by 100.

3. Since the Binet test is so verbal, the Wechsler test was developed. It includes both a verbal scale and a performance scale. The performance scale measures approximately the same thing as the verbal scales do—but we are not sure exactly what that is.

4. Gardner's theory of multiple intelligences proposes that intelligence is made up of seven abilities—language, logical/mathematical, visual/spatial, musical, bodily movement, intrapersonal, and interpersonal.

5. Intelligence is currently the single most predictive factor for real-life job performance; but other factors are probably as important, if not more so.

6. Roughly 50 percent of intelligence is inherited; 50 percent is environmental. Heredity sets certain limits, and the environment fills in within these limits.

7. IQ scores can vary as much as 30 points in error. Normally, though, scores vary from the correct IQ by only about seven points.

8. IQ tests show some cultural bias. For that reason, many courts have ruled that IQ tests alone cannot be used to make decisions about the classes or schools in which children will be placed.

9. Mental stimulation can increase the size and thickness of brain nerve cells.

10. Most mental retardation does not result from known physical defects. Many environmental factors may influence retardation, especially poor nutrition and lack of stimulation.

11. Savant syndrome is a rare condition in which a person with below-normal mental capacity possesses a particular talent or mental ability to an extremely high degree.

12. Creativity is defined as the ability to break set. Those who do well on creativity tests need not have extremely high IQ scores, so we believe this ability is a dimension of the person not tapped by the IQ test.

Vocabulary

intelligence	performance scale	theory of multiple	mental retardation
Stanford-Binet	Wechsler Adult	intelligences	inclusion
Intelligence Scale	Intelligence Scale	individual intelligence	savant syndrome
mental age	(WAIS)	tests	creativity
intelligence quotient	Wechsler Intelligence	group intelligence	set
(IQ)	Scale for Children	tests	break set
verbal scale	(WISC)	cultural bias	

Review Questions

Matching

On a sheet of paper, match terms in the right column with the descriptions in the left column. Answers may be used more than once.

1. Deals mainly with verbal skills
2. Includes both verbal and performance scales
3. Uses picture completion
4. One of the first intelligence tests ever used

   a. Wechsler Intelligence Test

   b. Stanford-Binet Intelligence Test

Multiple Choice

On a sheet of paper, write the letter of the choice that best completes each statement.

5. The original purpose of the Binet Intelligence Test was to pinpoint
   a. above-average students.
   b. below-average students.
   c. students with brain damage.
   d. hyperactive students.

6. Which of the following best describes what Binet meant by "self-evaluation"?
   a. relating an IQ score to your personality
   b. feeling good about your IQ score
   c. knowing that a solution to an IQ problem is correct
   d. adding up your IQ score

7. Little Alfred is given a jigsaw puzzle, but he isn't able even to begin putting it together until he turns all the pieces over. This needed mental adjustment is what Binet called
   a. adaptability.
   b. comprehension.
   c. direction.
   d. self-evaluation.

8. Mental age refers to a person's
   a. chronological age.
   b. attitude toward problem solving.
   c. intellectual ability level.
   d. performance ability.

9. The Stanford-Binet IQ compares
   a. school grades with mental age.
   b. school grades with chronological age.
   c. performance with chronological age.
   d. mental age with chronological age.

10. Creativity is often increased through
    a. set.
    b. breaking set.
    c. heredity.

11. *Set* refers to
    a. brainstorming.
    b. the first step in problem solving.
    c. looking at a problem in only one way.
    d. flexibility in thinking.

True/False

On a sheet of paper, answer each statement true *or* false. *If false, rewrite to make it true.*

12. Wechsler's performance scale measures basically the same thing as his verbal scale.
13. All countries define intelligence in about the same way.
14. Heredity seems to play some role in intelligence.
15. The Binet and Wechsler tests are usually given to groups.
16. A stimulating environment may cause the brain to grow thicker and heavier.
17. Sociocultural factors may influence an IQ score.
18. Highly intelligent people tend to have more psychological problems than the average person.
19. Inclusion of mentally retarded children hardly ever works.
20. Mental retardation can be caused by a lack of oxygen at birth.

281

Discussion Questions

1. Your friend Jorge believes that studying intelligence is a waste of time. All it does is allow others to discriminate against people who have low "intelligence." Besides, you can never measure it accurately anyway. Your friend Maureen disagrees. She believes that intelligence testing can single out people of low intelligence and help those people through special programs. With whom do you tend to agree? Why? Explain.

2. The chapter suggests that real-life success, while related to IQ, depends on other factors as well. Examine some of the part-time jobs you've had, and describe several factors that contributed to success in those jobs. Define *success* in any way you want. If you haven't had a job, ask a friend or family member about factors that have contributed to job success for him or her.

3. If colleges were to view intelligence as Gardner does, how might the application process for admission be changed? Do you think this new process would more accurately predict success in college than ACT and SAT scores do?

4. Fascinating research is currently being conducted on ways to increase the efficiency of the brain (despite its already remarkable efficiency). If you could increase the "intelligence" of your future children by taking certain "safe" drugs, would you do it? Why? (This may seem like an impossibility today, but it may not seem that incredible by the time you're a grandparent.)

5. Imagine you could speak to a savant who was able to explain the nature of both his or her disability and his or her special talents. What type of savant would you talk to—one with extraordinary musical abilities? artistic abilities? other abilities? What kinds of questions would you ask? And what answers do you think you'd get?

6. See how creative you can be: write down *chalkboard eraser* at the top of a sheet of paper, and list 15 original uses for the eraser. Did you notice any pattern in your answers? Did you follow set or create new uses? Was it easier to think of the first few items or the last few? Why?

7. Some argue that creativity becomes stifled once children begin school. Do you agree? What are some ways in which your own school promotes or blocks creativity?

8. In the book *Flowers for Algernon,* the main character, Charly, is retarded but seemingly happy, in spite of others' ridiculing him. He sees the ridicule as friendship. Later, he is the subject of an experiment that increases his intelligence dramatically. His happiness, however, is threatened, because now he understands the ridicule. Which extreme would you find preferable: to know and be miserable or to not know and be happy? Explain.

Activities and Projects

1. The chances are great that the person in your school who knows the most about intelligence testing is your school psychologist. Prepare a list of questions beforehand, and then interview this person. Possible questions:

   What kinds of intelligence tests do you use?

   How do these tests differ from one another?

   How have recent intelligence tests overcome the possibility of cultural bias?

   Do you ever encounter students who purposely do poorly on the tests so they won't be moved out of a special program?

   Write a report on the interview and your reactions to what you learned.

2. Many people argue that the creative process is intuitive. They believe that if people are pressured into

being creative, creativity will decrease. Find out if this is true.

Take a sheet of paper and write down these four terms across the top of it: *paper clip, can of hair spray, automobile tire, scissors*. Find six friends to participate in your experiment. Tell three of them (one at a time) the following: "You have to help me with this experiment. You see these four terms? You need to think of as many uses as possible for these objects. And you only get five minutes. This is really important to me—I need to get a good grade—so concentrate." You can use your own words, of course, but the idea is to create pressure. Tell the remaining three friends something like this: "Could you help me with an experiment? It's fun. You get five minutes to write down as many uses as possible for these four objects. Just do your best."

Once you get all six lists, go through the uses listed and circle the ones that you think break set. Breaking set will be your way of defining creativity. The more items you circle, the more creative the person has been (according to this limited definition). How will you know which ones to circle? A good guide to use is this: If someone writes that scissors can be used to poke a hole in paper, and if in your lifetime you have actually seen someone doing this, then this is *not* an example of breaking set. If someone writes that scissors can be eaten, this should not be circled, either, since it is entirely unrealistic. If someone suggests that scissors can be used as a paperweight, this probably can be accepted as creative.

Compare the results of the "pressured" group with the results of the "nonpressured" group. Who performed more creatively? Was pressure a factor? Were there any other factors that may have influenced your results?

3. Write a personal essay in which you examine your own intelligence. Here are some questions you might want to address: Would you like to know your IQ score? How do you react toward people who seem more intelligent or less intelligent than you? Do you think your friends are about as intelligent as you are? Do you think this is one way friendships are established? Do you agree with Gardner that intelligence should be measured in a variety of areas? In which of these areas are you intelligent?

4. This project will give you a chance to express one of your multiple intelligences while exploring the world of the savant. Complete one of the following choices:

a. Write a poem about savant syndrome. The speaker of the poem can be an observer, a family member, or the savant.

b. Write a song, with or without words, about savant syndrome. For example, imagine a piano piece in which one section is fluid yet frenzied, representing the extraordinary skills of the savant, and another section is full of dissonance and unusual rhythms to reflect impairment.

c. Create a dance that reflects the world of the savant. If you select choice c, try to find someone who is completing choice b, and work together.

5. Find a copy of the book *Flowers for Algernon* and read (or reread) it. It's fast and fascinating reading. Write a report comparing and contrasting the main character's happiness level with his intelligence level. When does he seem happiest? Saddest? Why? Is Charly, the main character, the same at the end of the novel as he was at the beginning, or has he grown in any way? Explain.

6. Visit or call a center in your area for people with mental disabilities and ask about the advantages and disadvantages of (a) special education classes and (b) inclusion. Maybe someone at the center can recount a few "success" stories. If the center treats people with physical impairments, ask about special training programs in motor skills, social skills, self-care, or any other special needs. Write a report on your visit, and be sure to include your reactions.

Many of the centers welcome volunteers. If this interests you, it could be a good opportunity to do homework and help someone else at the same time.

A love story that begins with an incredible experiment!

A less than ordinary man is turned into a genius. He Awakens to an exquisite love experience, but at an impossible price for

CHARLY

Unit 4

Human Development

CHAPTER 10

Infancy and Childhood

Throughout our childhood, everything that happens to us arises from and is controlled by developmental processes that follow a fixed plan or sequence. Mental, moral, and physical growth must evolve at their own speed with the aid of a suitable environment.

The World of the Child

Focus Question
....

• Is an infant's fear of loud noises a factor of nature or nurture?

Here is a conversation between a researcher and a four-year-old boy (Phillips, 1969):

"Do you have a brother?"
"Yes."
"What's his name?"
"Jim."
"Does Jim have a brother?"
"No."

Is there something wrong with this child? No. As we start this chapter, we enter a foreign world—that of the developing child. While children partially resemble the rest of us, their thought processes can be quite foreign to our everyday thinking. The "problem" Jim's brother has is that he is not able to look at something from any point of view but his own—not yet. We will discuss a possible explanation for this a little later.

Heredity Versus Environment

For as long as scientists have studied animals and people, they have asked questions about what is caused by **heredity**—that is, what is actually contained in the genes themselves—and what is caused by the **environment**—which is what goes on in the world around us. The issue of which is responsible is called the **nature/nurture controversy.**

Things that do not depend primarily on learning are due to physical factors, or *nature;* things that are learned are due to the environment, or *nurture*. Before we can understand how children develop, we need to know which abilities and characteristics are mostly due to their physical nature. We already know that the environment, or nurture, plays a large part in the development of most skills. Nearly always, though, the source of these skills is some combination of nature and nurture. Only recently have scientists begun to study the processes by which this interaction might take place (Bronfenbrenner & Ceci, 1994).

Let's consider an example. Not that long ago, most people, including so-called experts, claimed that the world of the infant was chaos and confusion. How very wrong this view turned out to be! The interaction between environment and heredity can be seen clearly in some experiments that show just how alert and intelligent the seemingly mindless infant really is. To understand one study in this area, you have to know first of all that infants can vary their sucking patterns on nipples or pacifiers.

heredity characteristics obtained directly from the genes

environment a person's surroundings, which influence the person's characteristics and development

nature/nurture controversy contrasting views of how we gain certain characteristics: *nature* refers to heredity, *nurture* to environment

◀ *These twins were separated at birth, one living in the United States, the other in Japan. They were reunited after 43 years.*

Specifically constructed nipples that would register when the baby sucked were put in the infants' mouths, and earphones were put over their ears so they could hear voices. The infants had a choice of hearing their own mother's voice or that of a different mother. In order to hear their own mother's voice, the babies had to learn to slow down their sucking and to leave a fixed amount of time between suckings. If they speeded up, they got a different mother's voice.

Amazingly, these infants were able to vary their sucking so they could hear their own mothers, and that became their favored pattern of sucking. This means that infants are able to learn from the environment, that they can make discriminations among different voices, that they have a memory system that can hold the voices, and that they can understand something as complex as an association between sucking and hearing a voice. This is a beautiful example of the importance of the environment and the use of already inherited skills on the environment (Stillings et al., 1987; DeCasper & Fifer, 1980). Oh, yes, we forgot to tell you—all the infants were under 72 hours old!

genes the basic units of heredity

chromosomes structures containing genes; all human cells contain 46 chromosomes, except reproductive cells, which contain 23

zygote fertilized egg

The Role of Heredity

Genes are the basic units of heredity. They contain directions for many characteristics, such as eye color and shape, hair color and texture, adult height, general body build, and so on. Except for the effects that the prenatal environment can have (the pregnant woman's nutrition, injury to the fetus, and so on), everything babies are born with is determined by their genes.

Genes are carried on larger units, the **chromosomes.** Every kind of body cell contains 23 pairs of chromosomes, for a total of 46—every kind but one, that is. The reproductive cells, the egg and the sperm, each contain only 23 chromosomes, one half of each pair. When they unite at conception, the fertilized egg, or **zygote** (ZYE-goat), then has the necessary number, 46, for proper development.

▲ *Genetic traits pass from the grandparents to the parents to the children.*

While the environment is also critical to proper development, psychology in recent years has focused more and more on the influence that heredity has on many of our abilities and behaviors. The influence of heredity on intelligence is considerable, as we discussed in Chapter 9. And genes can clearly influence a child's activity level, how easily soothed an infant is, his or her emotional responsiveness, and how a child reacts to new or novel things in the environment. There are even indications that tolerance for alcohol may have a genetic background.

Note, though, that if something is inherited, this doesn't mean it can't be changed by the environment. A person may inherit the potential to be a great runner, but only with environmental training will he or she actually perfect this skill.

Twin Studies

As we mentioned in Chapter 9, there are two types of twins. With one type, twins develop from two different eggs fertilized by two different sperm. They are called **dizygotic** (dye-zye-GOT-ick) **twins,** or fraternal twins, because they come from two *(di)* fertilized eggs *(zygotes)*. Thus, they are no more alike in their heredity, or genetic structure, than any other sibling pair.

With the second type, twins develop from only one fertilized egg that for unknown reasons divides in two. These **monozygotic** (mah-no-zye-GOT-ick) **twins,** or identical twins, have the same (identical) genes or heredity. Psychologists study them to see how they are alike—especially when they have not been reared together but have grown up in different homes. If they are reared apart and have similar characteristics, the environment probably has had little influence on this fact, while heredity has played a major role.

A careful study of hundreds of pairs of grown monozygotic twins separated from birth has shown some startling similarities. For instance, these twins' basic temperaments, occupational interests, hobbies, preferences for art and music, and athletic interests were quite similar, even though they had never met each other. At approximately the same age, the twins developed the same fears and nightmares, stuttering, bed-wetting, and bouts of depression (Bouchard, 1997; Bouchard et al., 1990). In one case, one twin was raised as a German Nazi while the other was raised as a Jew in the Caribbean. When they were first united in their late 40s, they both sported the same type of mustache, wore the same type of wire-rimmed glasses, liked the same foods, liked to scare people by sneezing loudly, stored rubber bands on their wrists, read magazines from back to front, and enjoyed eating alone in restaurants—something few men like to do (Bouchard, 1983; Holden, 1980).

While not all monozygotic twins are this much alike, there is little doubt that heredity plays a very important role in development. Most researchers today estimate that roughly 50 percent of our personality traits and intelligence are the result of genetic factors (Neisser et al., 1996; Turkheimer, 1991; Bouchard, 1983).

▲ *Dizygotic twins, like those on the left, are no more similar genetically than any other pair of siblings. Monozygotic twins, like those on the right, are as genetically identical as any two people can be.*

dizygotic twins twins who develop from different eggs fertilized by different sperm; they are not identical in their genetic makeup

monozygotic twins twins who develop from one fertilized egg; they are identical in their genetic makeup

Focus Questions

- Do all species follow the same developmental patterns?
- What creature has the longest development period?

Developmental Patterns

An early study in psychology took a very unusual look at the process of development. A husband-and-wife team adopted a chimpanzee, a lovable seven-month-old female. They decided to rear this chimp along with their other new (human) child to see what happened.

Both were treated identically—or as identically as possible, taking their physical differences into account. At first, this "experiment" looked like a disaster. In fact, the parents felt some panic for a while when the chimpanzee progressed faster than their son. For example, the chimp learned to feed herself, drink from a cup, and obey her "parents" much earlier and faster than the boy did. By the time both "children" had reached the age of two, however, the boy had overtaken and passed the chimpanzee in every respect except physical strength and amount of body hair (Kellogg & Kellogg, 1933).

This dramatic study makes a point of major importance: Development within a species (whether people, elephants, dogs, or some other species) is orderly and specific. It has its own timetable and pattern. The pattern is related to how complex the mature organism ultimately will be. At first, the boy living with the chimp developed slowly in comparison. Later, though, he went beyond the chimp's abilities, because human beings reach a higher level of intelligence and other skills than chimpanzees do. The human has the longest developmental period of all creatures. The fact that developing humans are weak and helpless for so long is probably the reason we have an elaborate social structure of closely knit families who can protect and care for the helpless young ones (Bjorklund, 1997).

Much of our development is a process of integrating our extraordinary brains with our bodies. Thus, the baby starts out with a series of reflexes, or automatic reactions. These reflexes will occur with the proper stimulation, and the baby does not have any control over them—not at first. For instance, if you touch a baby's cheek, it will turn its head and start sucking. If you place your finger in the palm of an infant's hand, it will grasp it tightly—just as a chimp does, incidentally. And if a baby is startled, its arms

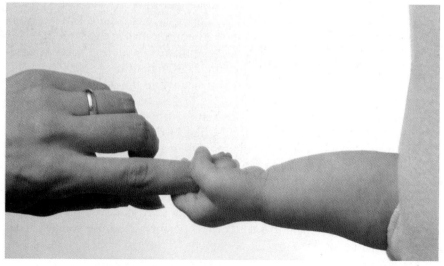

▲ *A sweet example of a baby's grasping reflex.*

and legs suddenly shoot out, away from its body. The sucking, grasping, and startle reflexes are some of the building blocks for later, more complicated behavior.

With age, most of these reflexes disappear, and the activities can be regulated by the higher brain. In other words, they stop happening automatically and become actions that we choose to do or not do. Interestingly, the sucking and grasping reflexes may reappear in people who have suffered certain kinds of damage to the brain. Such people find themselves automatically and unwillingly sucking when the cheek is touched and unable to let go of objects placed in their hands. For these people, the higher brain has, for want of a better term, been "disconnected."

Maturational Processes

A child is preprogrammed for certain activities, such as walking, a natural skill that begins to develop sometime between 9 and 15 months after birth. To the casual observer, this process seems to be "learned," but it is not. As uncoordinated as babies seem to be during the process of starting to walk, they will be able to walk on their own with no training at all.

Some parents work and work with their children, thinking that somehow they are *teaching* them to walk. All this training does, at best, is to help the child walk about a month earlier than he or she normally would have, by roughly 15 months, which is an average. Walking at an earlier or later age (within the normal range) is *not* a sign of future intelligence or of being "slow" but is just a reflection of individual differences. Nature must take its course.

For some reason, many people have trouble believing that developing the ability to walk is automatic. But in some Native American cultures a mother would strap her infant onto her back so she could go about her chores, thus preventing the baby from "practicing" walking. When these children were finally freed, they very quickly walked quite well on their own. This kind of skill, which develops automatically as the child becomes more mature, is part of the process called **maturation**—the automatic, orderly, and sequential process of physical (and mental) development. The same rules apply to other skills, such as speech and reasoning, which we will discuss shortly.

Many toys on the market claim to speed up the development of a child's intelligence, but these claims should not be taken too seriously. There is no question that children need stimulation from their surroundings, and play is one of the best ways for that to occur. It is important for parents to spend time playing and "talking" with their babies, because this is a good way to stimulate the infants' brains. But it simply takes time for all the nerve cells to grow, develop, and branch out. No toy in the world can make that happen any earlier than it normally would.

Every child needs good nutrition, stimulation, and safety. A good environment is necessary for proper development, but it won't *speed up* the

▲ *Babies who have no chance to "practice" walking still walk quite well when they are old enough.*

maturation the automatic, orderly, sequential process of physical and mental development

291

process. What we're saying here may require a moment's careful thought in order to be grasped: Without a stimulating environment, the child's mental growth can be slowed. With a stimulating environment, it will proceed at its own internal pace, not exceed it. Many parents are too impatient; they can't accept what nature dictates.

Patterns (sequences) of maturation are essentially the same for all children. The *timing* of development, however, varies from one child to another. Only notable extremes are important. A child who develops very, very slowly and walks, for instance, at a much later age than the average child may have something wrong physically. The timing of a child's development would have to be quite a bit slower than the average, though, before parents should be concerned.

Growth Cycles

growth cycles orderly patterns of development

Our various parts do not develop at one uniform rate. There are different **growth cycles** for different aspects of human development. In other words, some areas develop more rapidly, some develop more slowly, and some develop in spurts or increase dramatically in a short time. For instance, at age eight, 95 percent of the basic structure of the brain has been completed, but the body has 55 percent left to go, and the reproductive system more than 90 percent.

There are also differences between the sexes in these cycles. Girls are more orderly and stable in their growth cycles. From infancy, they show a continuous movement forward in babbling, word making, and bone and muscle development. Boys grow in spurts and mature more slowly, although eventually they reach the same level.

imprinting a biological process in which the young of certain species follow and become attached to their mothers

Critical Periods

We can get insight into humans by studying animal behavior. Ducks and some other birds, for example, are programmed to accept a mother at a specific time in development. If there is no "real" mother around, some strange things can happen. One researcher, Konrad Lorenz, found that ducklings whose mother wasn't available would follow *him* around if he quacked and walked in a squatting position (Lorenz, 1952). They assumed that he was their mother.

Ducklings acted this way only if they were confronted with a false "mother" shortly after hatching. As it turns out, ducklings are programmed to accept almost anything as a mother at this time. The term for this attachment is **imprinting.** The animal's

◀ *Naturalist Konrad Lorenz and friends*

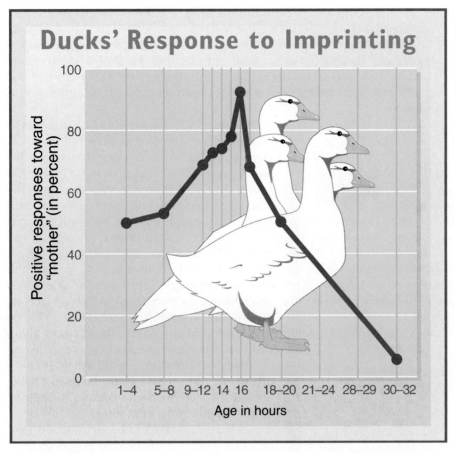

Ducks' Response to Imprinting

Positive responses toward "mother" (in percent)

Age in hours: 1–4 5–8 9–12 14 16 18–20 21–24 28–29 30–32

▲ *Figure 10.1* *Ducks' Response to Imprinting. Note the critical period peaks at 16 hours.*

brain is ready to be engraved (or imprinted) with a mother image at this time. The "mother figure" must move around for imprinting to occur. One of the most unusual studies of this sort involved imprinting ducklings on a tin can that was pulled around a pond in circles.

Imprinting occurs during a **critical period**. A critical period is a specific time period in an animal's maturation when a particular skill may be learned or an association made; the learning or the associating can occur *only* during this period if it is to occur at all. Notice in Figure 10.1 that ducks' acceptance of a fake mother peaks at about 16 hours after birth and then rapidly declines. Imprinting seems to be the result of a chemical released by the body at a certain time. If an animal's chemistry is deliberately altered, the critical period can be extended or even eliminated (Colombo, 1982).

Critical periods must be part of all species, because they show up in so many places. Dogs, for instance, form solid attachments with humans only up to 12 weeks of age. After that time, they can be unpredictable. Because of this, you want to get a dog that has been around humans quite a bit during that 12-week period, especially if the dog is a large and possibly dangerous one. Dogs from pet stores should always be bought before they are 12 weeks old, because they are frequently isolated behind glass and have limited social experience.

Just as a dog automatically wags its tail, a baby will start to smile during its first month, even if no one is around. By the second month, smiling

critical period a specific period of development that is the only time when a particular skill can begin to develop or a particular association can occur

occurs in response to a pleasant sound or a caress. This happens with blind infants as well, so it can't be a matter of imitation.

Smiling becomes associated with certain events through learning at about three to four months. Both animals and humans need frequent touching, holding, and rubbing from birth onward, or the results are disastrous. (The Case Study feature about Genie on page 311 provides details about this.)

feral children children supposedly reared by animals

In Their Own Words . . .

Konrad Lorenz *(1903–1989) let many of his research animals have free run of the house. A lot of funny things happened as a result. In one instance, one of the birds, a cockatoo, bit all the buttons off shirts hanging on the clothesline, and a tame rat repeatedly gnawed out little circular pieces of sheets to line her nests. Lorenz's work with ducklings resulted in this episode:*

The ducklings . . . were most demanding and tiring charges, for, imagine a two-hour walk with such children, all the time squatting low and quacking without interruption! In the interests of science I submitted myself literally for hours on end to this ordeal. So it came about, on a certain . . . Sunday, that, in company with my ducklings, I was wandering about, squatting and quacking, in a May-green meadow at the upper part of our garden. I was congratulating myself on the obedience . . . with which my ducklings came waddling after me, when I suddenly looked up and saw the garden fence framed by a row of . . . faces: a group of tourists was standing at the fence and staring horrified in my direction. Forgivable! For all they could see was a big man with a beard dragging himself, crouching, round the meadow, in figures of eight, glancing constantly over his shoulder and quacking—but the ducklings, the all-revealing and all-explaining ducklings were hidden in the tall spring grass from the view of the astonished crowd. (Lorenz, 1952, pp. 42–43)

Interpreting Primary Sources

While amusing (or amazing) the watching tourists, Lorenz was actually conducting research. Instead of bringing animals into the laboratory, he usually observed animals in nature. What advantages does this approach have over laboratory research? What advantages does conducting animal research in laboratories provide?

Finally, a most intriguing critical period occurs for humans: If you want to learn a foreign language with a correct and natural accent, you should start learning it before the age of 12. After that age, you can learn the language, but you will never have speech sounds that match those of the native speakers. There is an exception, though. Some people have a special ability to imitate sounds; these people are said to have an "ear" for languages. They will be able to get much closer to matching the correct accent, but the rule applies for most of us.

You probably have heard tales about children who supposedly have been reared by animals. They are called **feral** (FER-al) **children,** the term *feral* meaning "wild, untamed." Such children supposedly walk on all fours and swing from trees.

There has been one documented case of a boy who was discovered at age 11 or 12 after living in the woods by himself for five or six years. His rescuer named him Victor. The young man could not speak. He did bite, as any human child will, but he didn't growl or swing from trees. The importance of critical periods and maturation within a social setting did show up. Since they were bypassed, he had almost no "human" skills. Victor eventually did learn the ways of society, in that he cleaned himself and ate the way we do. He also learned primitive speech and could print a few words, but he was never able to come close to what others his age could do in either area (Itard, 1932). The authors of a journal article summarized the situation this way:

His life showed that the biological blueprint does not provide all that is essential for normal human development; human contact is needed as well. Denied this contact, Victor was physically, socially, and emotionally stunted. (Basic Behavioral Science Task Force, 1996a, p. 622)

When you read about cases of children being brought up by animals, be careful not to accept them as fact before asking yourself some questions. For instance, chimpanzees will almost automatically "adopt" an orphaned infant chimpanzee if its mother belonged to their group. They have even been known to take in an orphan whose mother was not a member of their group, but that is very, very rare. Chimpanzees are more likely either to kill or ignore such an infant (Goodall, 1971). If they are this reluctant to take in a "foreign" baby of their own species, wouldn't they be much more reluctant to care for a human baby?

Also, remember how long human infants are almost completely helpless, unable to do much of anything for themselves, including eating. Unless an adult human is around to take care of them for at least the first year of life, and probably longer, they will die. Without that kind of care, abandoned infants could not survive long enough to be taken in by animals (Graber, 1988). As for stories about children reared by packs of wolves, human babies would probably be considered food by the wolves, not welcome additions to their group.

▲ *Naturalist Jane Goodall with some orphaned chimpanzees. Apparently, no adult chimps in their group took them in.*

Pause for Thought

1. To what do the terms *nature* and *nurture* refer?
2. What do genes and chromosomes have to do with inherited traits?
3. How do fraternal and identical twins differ?

Critical Thinking
....
4. Rachel is a new mom who wants to use some of the information from this chapter to help raise her daughter. What advice can you give her on maturation, growth cycles, and critical periods?

Focus Questions

- What happens to children when their mothers work outside the home?

- Does family structure affect a child's development?

nuclear family parents and their children

extended family nuclear family plus other relatives

The Family and Child Development

Many children in our society grow up in a **nuclear family,** made up only of parents and their children. An **extended family** includes other relatives, such as aunts, uncles, or grandparents. Most people think that the majority of Americans lived in extended families until very recent times. This is not actually true. On farms, grandparents and other relatives often lived on the family's land, but they usually had separate houses some distance apart. One estimate is that since our nation began, no more than one-fifth of the American people have ever lived in extended-family households (Degler, 1980). The typical American family of today, however, is different in some important ways from the family of 30 or 40 years ago.

Changing Family Structures

One change has to do with divorce. Between the 1950s and the 1980s, the divorce rate climbed steadily. By the 1980s, about half of all marriages were ending in divorce. The rate has now stabilized, but it hasn't gone down much. This means that about half of today's children will spend some time in a single-parent family before they reach the age of 18 (Davies & Cummings, 1994; Barber & Eccles, 1992).

The mother usually heads the single-parent family, since in 90 percent of divorces, she is given full custody of the children. Unfortunately, the mother is also more likely than the father to suffer financially. Women's income goes down further than men's and stays lower for a longer period of time after a divorce. Consequently, children of divorce often suffer not only from the divorce itself but also from its economic aftermath (Basic Behavioral Science Task Force, 1996a; Silverstein, 1996).

The divorce rate is unquestionably something to be concerned about, but it is important to remind ourselves that marital conflict brings with it

▶ *Today, parents share many child-rearing tasks.*

its own dangers, in terms of the effects on children. While it is not possible or even desirable to avoid disagreements entirely, a great deal of arguing and fighting between parents tends to threaten their children's sense of emotional security. It also fails to teach the children good ways to solve problems that arise between people. Consequently, they often do not know how to deal effectively with their own conflicts (Goodman et al., 1999). High levels of marital conflict lead to more adjustment problems in the children. Interestingly, this is true after a divorce, as well as beforehand (Davies & Cummings, 1994).

For some children, then, a divorce that actually brings an end to the conflict may be preferable to continued arguments between parents.

When a single parent gets married again, the children usually are not sure what the "new" parent means to their lives. Often, children resent stepparents and are afraid that they will try to take the place of the absent parent. When other children also come into the picture, confusion and jealousy are bound to occur. The best thing stepparents can do is go slowly. It takes time for everyone to get used to this new arrangement, and rushing things makes it worse. It is also important for the parent-couple to talk about problems ahead of time and agree to back each other up. To do that, they must have similar ideas about what children should and should not be allowed to do. When the adults are prepared for confusion and are careful to treat everyone fairly, the new family has a much better chance of making the situation work.

▲ *Children from previous marriages can both enrich and complicate remarriage.*

Another recent change has to do with the roles family members play. Most families today need more than one income in order to have a decent standard of living. Nearly half of married women with infants now have jobs outside the home, and nearly two-thirds of all mothers do. While it is true that household chores are shared more among parents and children, such changes are not as big as you may think. Women still do almost all the housework, especially the cooking and shopping (90 percent) and most of the child rearing, too (Ozer, 1995; Phares, 1992; Burros, 1988).

The goal of having both parents share in child care is an important one for the children and parents alike. When mothers feel overwhelmed by these responsibilities, they experience higher levels of anxiety and stress and may become depressed. This is especially true when the father is present in the home but does not become involved or respond to the mother's need to have him take over for a while. On the up side, when both parents are involved in caring for the children, not only do the children benefit, but both mothers and fathers are happier and more satisfied with their lives (Silverstein, 1996; Ozer, 1995).

When Mothers Work Outside the Home

Mothers play an important part in their children's lives and are typically the first persons babies become attached to. Many people today have asked what happens to children when their mothers work outside the home. Two important issues are (1) whether the amount of time children spend with their parents decreases and (2) whether the children's attachment to the mother is weaker.

Mothers who work outside the home obviously don't have as much time for their children as full-time homemakers do. In fact, full-time homemakers spend twice as much time with their children, playing with them, taking care of them, disciplining them, and so on. The issue is whether this difference in amount of time has a negative effect on the children of mothers who work outside the home.

For some time, the answer was not entirely clear. However, a very substantial recent study looking at thousands of subjects over a period of several years seems to have answered the question quite definitely. The researcher found that there is no harm done to the children by the mother's outside employment. Even when mothers work outside the home during the first three years of their children's lives, no negative effects were discovered (Harvey, 1999). The most important thing is not the amount of time itself but whether the children feel loved and cared for.

Apparently, this is possible, regardless of the amount of time spent, if the children are given warm affection and if guidelines about which behaviors are acceptable and which are unacceptable are enforced (Barber & Eccles, 1992).

Children's attachment to the employed mother seems to be the same as to the homemaker mother, given a general sense from the mother of love and acceptance. Children who spend half their time in day-care centers develop just as strong an attachment to their mothers as the children of full-time homemakers (Belsky, 1990). Whether the mother is satisfied with what she is doing and whether she has her husband's support seem to be more important for everyone's welfare than whether she works outside the home or not (Levanthel-Belfer, Cowan, & Cowan, 1992).

Fathers and Children

While mothers generally do more of the child rearing, fathers are still important to children's development. Fathers tend to spend less time with their children, but they do the same kinds of things as mothers do—playing with the children, taking care of them, disciplining and teaching them (Silverstein, 1996). Having a warm, affectionate father or father-figure around helps children become independent and better able to do things for themselves. Fathers also help children develop a feeling of being worthwhile and useful (Phares, 1992).

When there is no father in the home, however, the effects are not always as bad as you might expect. Many problems found in homes where only the mother is present are caused by too little money and too much stress on the mother, rather than by the father's absence in itself. Boys from such homes are usually just as masculine as other boys, and neither girls nor boys necessarily get into more trouble at school. The important point is for children to feel loved and cared for. This is easier to do when two parents share the load, but it is not impossible with only one (Barber & Eccles, 1992).

▲ *Fathers make an important contribution to their children's sense of well-being.*

Parenting Styles

Psychologists have identifed three basic styles of parenting: permissive; authoritarian, or dictatorial; and authoritative. Generally, each one has fairly predictable effects on the children.

Permissive parents tend to let their children do whatever they want. These parents don't make many rules, and they fail to consistently enforce the few rules they do make. As a result, their children don't learn much about unacceptable behavior and its consequences. Children raised in this kind of atmosphere are usually impulsive and irresponsible. As you might expect, they don't have much self-discipline. They also tend to lack self-confidence and to have trouble making decisions and doing things for themselves. Because of these characteristics, they frequently don't get along very well with other children.

The **authoritarian,** or **dictatorial,** style of parenting is one in which the parents approach their children as tyrants approach their subjects. Dictatorial parents are rigid and inflexible. They set down the rules and demand compliance, often administering harsh punishment for disobedience. The children have very little, if any, input into how their lives are governed. Dictatorial parents don't trust their children to make decisions for themselves. Consequently, their children usually are not very good at making decisions. These children tend to be moody, have poor self-esteem, and often have trouble getting along with others.

The **authoritative** style puts parents in the role of authority figure but not dictator. Authoritative parents do make rules and enforce them. However, they are both caring and flexible, interested in their children's views. These parents try to help their children grow as individuals. They try to help them learn to make their own decisions and solve their own problems. Unlike permissive parents, they don't ignore or cover up an important issue. Unlike dictatorial parents, they don't simply hand down a solution that must be accepted by the child. Instead, authoritative parents listen and offer suggestions and support.

Children raised in this kind of atmosphere tend to be self-reliant, friendly, and self-confident. They take responsibility for themselves and their behavior and usually have stable relationships with others. They have a generally positive image of themselves and of other people as well. We should note that these characteristics are related to being well adjusted and psychologically healthy.

Other Influences

Before leaving the topic of parenting, we should make a few points. Parents are not all-powerful. They can and do have a lot of influence, but they are not completely responsible for everything a child does or fails to do. To make any sense of this complicated matter, you have to look at the importance of other children, brothers and sisters, school, teachers, and the rest of the outside world (Kagan, 1996). Also, children are born individuals. A parenting approach that works well with one child may fail with another child.

Today, we hear a lot about parents "teaching" foreign languages or an appreciation of classical music to their child before it is even born, while it

permissive parenting style parenting style in which parents let children do as they wish; few rules are made or enforced

authoritarian (dictatorial) parenting style parenting style in which parents rigidly set the rules and demand obedience

dictatorial parenting style (see **authoritarian parenting style**)

authoritative parenting style parenting style in which parents seek input from children; parents are consistent but flexible in enforcing rules

▲ *Whatever one's parenting style may be, a small child can make an incredible racket!*

is still in the womb! (No, it doesn't work.) And some parents are so worried about their child's success that they spend day after day trying to find the right preschool. Many psychologists are seriously concerned that the expectations placed on parents have gone too far. Psychologists are afraid that this pressure to be perfect parents may work against children, not for them. For example, when we put too much emphasis on parents' mistakes, we end up making the parents so insecure that they actually do a worse job, not a better one. Love, affection, guidelines, listening, encouragement—these are the most important things for a child's healthy development, and they are what most parents try hard to provide.

Child Abuse

We have mentioned that discipline and guidelines help a child to grow psychologically. But the type of disciplining techniques or punishment that parents use is equally important. Physical punishment—hitting, slapping, and so on—is not a good way to handle problems. It doesn't help the child learn very much about right and wrong, and it can also get out of control fairly easily. When physical punishment is too harsh, it becomes child abuse. Clearly, a child can be abused psychologically, too. But because that problem is much harder to define, most of the information we have focuses on physical abuse.

In this country, two and a half million cases of child abuse and serious child neglect are reported each year. In one million of these cases, the abuse has been verified by an official agency (Stokols, 1995; Thompson & Wilcox, 1995). Such cases include broken bones, bruises all over the body, severe burns, and extreme psychological trauma. The mistreatment of children results in the death of 1,400 children each year. As tragic and alarming as these figures are, they are thought to be much lower than the actual occurrences of child abuse, since many cases are never reported. There is reason to believe that even the number of child deaths from abuse has been underestimated (Peterson & Brown, 1994). When a large number of parents were asked whether they had been violent enough with their children that they could have injured them, 1.5 million said yes. That figure is probably low, too, since it includes only parents who were willing to admit to such violent punishment (Phares & Compas, 1992; Starr, 1979).

Whether a parent will abuse a child depends on a lot of different things. We don't know them all, but we do know some conditions that make abuse more likely to happen. For example, most child abusers don't know much about children. They don't know how old a baby must be before it can be toilet trained or before it will sleep through the night. Such parents are usually not very mature themselves and often are looking for love *from* a baby, rather than understanding how much work and responsibility are involved in being a parent.

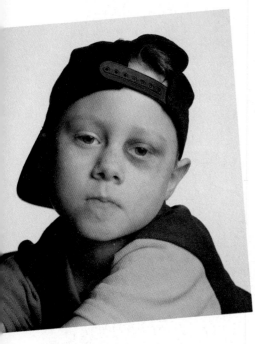

▲ *Child abuse paints a sad picture.*

Often, abusive parents come from violent backgrounds themselves. We should note, though, that while abused children run a higher risk of becoming child abusers themselves, the majority of child abusers don't fit this mold. (See Thinking Critically about Psychology in Chapter 1, pp. 14-15.) Other factors that lead to child abuse are financial problems, unemployment, too much stress on the parents, alcoholism, psychological problems, and isolation or being far away from friends and family (Phares & Compas, 1992). For many of these reasons, teenaged parents are more likely to abuse their children than people who become parents at a later age.

Sequences of Development

Focus Questions
....
- Is a child's fear of the dark the result of poor parenting?
- How did Piaget explain how children learn to think and reason?

One of the most important advances in understanding children has been the discovery that we develop in the physical, moral, and intellectual areas in a sequential fashion. This finding is important to both parent and child. Nature requires that the brain and nervous system grow and mature before certain events occur.

Here is an example of this sequential development. Until about 9 to 12 months after birth, most babies are happy to go from person to person and even to be left alone with a stranger. But at that point, the brain has developed enough that the child is very much aware of the mother or father and is beginning to grasp the fact that parents can disappear and that in their place appears a "foreigner," the baby-sitter. So, from this time until about 18 months, the child panics when left with someone else. This is a normal phenomenon called **separation anxiety.**

separation anxiety the baby's fear of being away from the parent

Separation anxiety can be seen in every culture and every normal baby. Obviously, then, it does not mean the parents are doing a bad job or that there is something wrong with the baby. All it does mean is that the brain has reached a certain level of development. Just as separation anxiety seems to appear out of nowhere, it will eventually disappear, and it has nothing to do with how the parents are rearing the child.

By about the child's fourth year, the brain is mature enough to grasp the concept of monsters and the possibility that a monster is sitting there in the dark next to the child. Comedian Bill Cosby used to do a routine in which a child smears Jell-O on the floor so the monster will slip on its way in. While this is funny to us, it certainly isn't to the youngster.

It is helpful to know that the child is not a "sissy," that a fear of the dark and of monsters is normal, and that the child shouldn't be punished because he or she is afraid. Often it helps to get children to say over and over, "I am brave—I can take care of myself," as they are exposed to longer periods of time in the dark.

Some children simply can't adjust to the dark. All the commotion about whether to let them have a night-light is not sensible. What possible harm is it going to do? (None.) Fears and nightmares about creatures disappear by about age eight when the brain begins to deal with more complex concerns, such as bodily injury and physical danger.

Because understanding these patterns of development is so important, the next two sections will cover some core theories about how we develop mentally and morally.

▲ *Stand by me—please!*

301

Piaget's Theory of Cognitive Development

cognitive development the ways in which thinking and reasoning grow and change

Jean Piaget (ZHAN Pea-ah-ZHAY) (1896–1980) was a Swiss psychologist who studied **cognitive development,** the ways in which a child's thinking and reasoning change and grow. Piaget divided this development into four basic stages. While not everyone agrees with every detail of his theory, it clearly has stood the test of time. In its outline, it seems to apply to most children and to explain why they see the world the way they do. The stages and ages listed can overlap, and not all children follow the *exact* pattern, but in general, the system is valid (Beilin, 1992; Piaget, 1929).

Sensorimotor Stage (Birth to Two Years).   During the **sensorimotor stage,** the child spends time on two activities: sensation (*sensory*) and movement (*motor* responses, meaning arm, leg, and trunk movements). Thus, the baby sees, studies, and grasps a bottle; the milk provides a pleasurable sensation. So learning requires the motor response and a connection with sensation. The two will later be tied together by symbols (the word *bottle*). The child also reaches for other objects that bring either pleasure or pain. A connection is made between these objects and the effects they create, and words are eventually attached to each. Thus, the mental image becomes associated with a symbol. This is the basic unit of thought.

sensorimotor stage Piaget's first stage of child development, from birth to about two years of age, in which knowledge is tied to movements and objects in the environment

Objects are not "permanent" during this learning process. From about three to five months of age, if an experiment is set up in which the child is playing with a toy and the toy disappears through a trap door, the child doesn't show any concern—doesn't even look for the toy. How could this be? Apparently, children this age are so self-centered that they view everything in the world from their own reference point. Since the toy is no longer in their line of vision, it no longer exists. The concept of things moving somewhere else is not possible yet.

Children can see quite well. In the very beginning, babies' eyes focus most comfortably at a distance of somewhat less than a foot so they can focus on the breast for feeding. But their vision is sharp from the first few weeks. Even as adults, we are all programmed to respond to movement anywhere in our line of vision because it may signal danger. Since the child is still in training, so to speak, he or she will be most interested in the movement itself, not associating it yet with anything else (like danger). Thus, if you move a small white elephant toy along, pass it behind a screen, and bring out on the other side a red lion, a child younger than five months old will show no concern about the strange thing that has happened but will be fascinated by the movement alone.

▲ *Developmental theorist, Jean Piaget*

In other words, the child has not as yet formed the concept of what is called **object permanence**—that is, specific objects do not exist all by themselves. They exist only as the child perceives them. The concept of permanent objects first appears at about 10 months. Note that this is just about the time that separation anxiety appears. Probably, the presence and absence of the parent helps the child form this concept, since when the parent leaves, an "object" of great importance is gone.

object permanence Piaget's term for the awareness that specific objects are real and exist all by themselves

Toward the end of the sensorimotor period, the child begins to name real things in a real world. Thus, there are endless requests for a bottle. The brain has replaced reaching for a bottle (motor) and getting it (sensation) with a symbol—that is, the word representing that object. The sensorimotor stage is over.

In Focus

Piaget's Stages of Cognitive Development

Approximate Age	Stages and Related Abilities
	Sensorimotor (birth to 2 years)
Birth	Raw sensation! Lights . . . sounds . . . smells . . . tastes.
3 months	Significant movement. Reaches for objects.
5–8 months	No object permanence yet—if object leaves view, it no longer exists.
9–12 months	Object permanence appears. Separation anxiety.
2 years	Begins to move from world of all sensations and movements to world of thought.
	Preoperational (2 to 7 years)
2 years	Object permanence well established.
	No reversibility or conservation skills.
	Self-involved—unable to view world from another's point of view.
3–7 years	Growing awareness of reversibility and conservation.
	Concrete operations (7 to 11 years)
7 years	Reversibility well established.
8 years	Some conservation skills well established.
9–11 years	Able to view world more and more from another's point of view.
	Formal operations (11 and on)
11 and on	Growing ability to think abstractly and symbolically.

If you were a parent and wanted to informally test some of these developmental abilities during the next several years as your child grows, how would you do so?

Preoperational Stage (Two to Seven Years). In the **preoperational stage,** children know that things can be permanent. The child is not yet able *(pre)* to operate effectively on and within the world, however.

Children at this age are not logical creatures. They think that rocks have the same feelings they do, and they have long discussions with them. In fact, they have long discussions with just about everything and everyone. Language develops at an extremely fast rate during this stage, and the child's vocabulary expands enormously. Many symbols, or words, are used to represent actions and objects. The child's point of reference, however, is still the child: The world only exists in terms of himself or herself.

During this stage, the child is unable to change places with someone else and see things from another point of view. The child cannot under-

preoperational stage Piaget's second stage of child development, from about two to seven years of age, in which children acquire language and the ability to use symbols but are still not capable of logical thought

303

reversibility Piaget's term for the idea that a relationship that goes in one direction can go in the other direction also

conservation Piaget's term for the idea that some of an object's characteristics can be changed while others remain the same; for example, changing shape does not change volume

concrete operations stage Piaget's third stage of child development, from about 7 to 11 years of age, in which the child understands that there is a real world with real objects, which exist apart from the child and which can be manipulated

stand the principle of **reversibility,** which means that if a relationship goes in one direction, it can be turned around and go the opposite direction, too. Thus, the little boy at the beginning of this chapter could understand the relationship he had to his brother but not the reverse, the relationship his brother had to him.

Another interesting point is that children at this age cannot grasp something called **conservation,** the idea that you can change some of an object's characteristics while keeping others the same, or *conserving* them. For instance, the mass (amount) of an object stays the same (is conserved) no matter what you do to its shape. A ball of clay has the same mass if you stretch it out to look like a hot dog.

But suppose you have a five-year-old watch you take a glass of Kool-Aid and pour it into a taller, thinner glass (so the column of the drink is higher). If you ask the child which glass holds more Kool-Aid, she will insist that the taller one does, even though the pouring took place right in front of her. By six years of age, the child will go back and forth on this issue. She will say that possibly the taller one has the same amount, but she will not be certain.

The important point is that even though the child is still self-centered, he or she is beginning to notice differences between people and objects in the environment. These will finally become clear in the next stage.

Concrete Operations Stage (7 to 11 Years). The third stage of Piaget's system is called the **concrete operations stage.** The world has become fixed and real (that is, *concrete*), with separate objects that are different and that lie outside the child in the world. Seeing things from someone else's viewpoint is no longer a problem. Thus, the child's ability to reason in a logical way has gone up a rung on the ladder.

Children at this stage are still limited, however. While they can see objects as permanent and complete, they have some trouble seeing objects as having more than one dimension at the same time. So a child at the beginning of this period will say about some pencils: "This pencil is long; this one is thin; this one is fat." By the end of the seventh

▶ *Children seven years and older can compare objects using more than one dimension.*

year, children can compare pencils: "This pencil is longer and thinner than that one."

Conservation is much less of a problem, too. By age eight, children have no trouble at all insisting that the two glasses of different shapes hold the same amount of Kool-Aid. From ages 8 through 11, the child seems to be bringing together all the principles we have just discussed. While doing this, however, he or she is forming rules and regulations that must be followed to the letter. It is hard for children at this stage to look at things in any way other than either black or white—gray areas are still a little too difficult to understand.

Formal Operations Stage (11 Years On). Piaget's fourth stage of development, called the **formal operations stage,** appears sometime after 11 years of age and can become more elaborate and complex into young adulthood. The term *formal operations* refers to the ability to deal with highly symbolic thoughts, such as those found in mathematics, logic, and philosophy. According to Piaget the formal operations stage is the highest level of cognitive development.

While some people never make it to this stage no matter what, you can spot it developing in those who suddenly become concerned about issues such as truth and justice, fairness, and personal rights. Such concerns peak in most adolescents. Unfortunately too many people become callous and begin to lose these concerns along the way into adulthood.

Formal operations is Piaget's most controversial stage in terms of the possible effects of cultural differences. Reaching it depends largely on becoming familiar with the type of scientific and critical thinking most often taught at the high school level in industrialized countries. Children who are not exposed to this kind of thinking will not engage in it. Thus, people in societies without such school systems generally do not reach the formal operations stage of cognitive development. These findings led Piaget himself to eventually conclude that the formal operations stage is not free of cultural influences (Rogoff & Chavajay, 1995).

formal operations stage Piaget's fourth stage of child development, beginning at about 11 years of age, in which the ability to deal with the highly symbolic and abstract thoughts found in logic, math, philosophy, and ethics begins to appear

 ## Pause for Thought

1. What is the difference between a nuclear family and an extended family?
2. What kinds of developmental problems does divorce create?
3. What occurs when both parents are highly involved in caring for their children?
4. What are the main qualities of the permissive, authoritarian, and authoritative styles of parenting?

Critical Thinking
. . . .
5. Suppose you work with children and you wish to use some activities to identify their level of cognitive development. What kinds of activities could you try?

Focus Questions

• When do children first know the difference between right and wrong?

• What are Kohlberg's three main stages of moral development?

▶ *This boy is old enough to reason fairly abstractly, but he is a cookie thief nevertheless.*

A General Principle

A basic principle of cognitive development is that it advances from the simpler to the more complex. This principle is true outside Piaget's theory as well as within it. As children mature, their thinking becomes increasingly complex and more sophisticated. Simple concepts are gradually replaced by more complicated ones. For instance, a very young child sees a dog and says, "doggie." Everyone around agrees and smiles. That same child then sees a cow and says, "doggie." This time, the results are different. People around the child now say, "No, that's not a doggie; that's a cow." This is how children come up with categories that help make sense out of the world. So, at some point in time, this child will arrive at a category of "animal," which in turn is made up of many slightly different concepts—one for "doggie," another for "cow," and so on. Eventually, this system will expand even further and may include such classes as mammals and reptiles.

When we have sound, logical categories, our thinking becomes more efficient, and our understanding is more complete. Thus our ability to deal with information from our environment is better as well.

Kohlberg's Theory of Moral Development

Moral development, the development of ideas about right and wrong, also seems to follow a maturational sequence, or series of stages. As in Piaget's system, there is not necessarily a fixed pattern of development that fits every single person, and there can at times be a mixture of stages (Snarey, 1985). But there is a major difference between stages of moral reasoning and Piaget's cognitive stages. A person may be capable of a high level of moral reasoning but still not be inclined to "be good." In other words, we have a choice regarding moral issues but not regarding mental development.

The theory of moral development we consider here was developed by psychologist **Lawrence Kohlberg.** Kohlberg's system has many subcategories. For our purposes, however, the three main levels or stages should be enough to suggest the general principle.

Preconventional Level (Younger Than Six Years). At the early **preconventional level,** morality is determined by the sheer power of outside authority. Adults impose their own wills on children. At these ages, it is impossible for the child to grasp the complexities of right and wrong. Instead, the child focuses on whether he or she is being punished or rewarded. If you are punished, you are "bad." If you are not punished, or if you are praised, you must be "good."

Toward the end of this stage, children do begin to grasp that if people do something for you, you should do something for them. But the resulting behavior is not all that strongly related to "morals." Children are in it for what they can get at this time because they are still so self-centered.

Conventional Level (7 to 11 Years). The **conventional level** of moral reasoning focuses on the expectations of others as the major motivation for doing what is right or wrong. At first, children are seeking the approval of others. But gradually, there emerges the idea of social order, or behaving in a certain way because society expects it.

In time, the *intentions* of a person's actions become an important consideration in whether the child judges these actions to be right or wrong. In other words, whether or not someone meant to do something is taken into account, just as the legal system makes a distinction between involuntary manslaughter and deliberate murder.

The majority of older people, whether adolescents or adults, don't go much beyond this conventional level of moral reasoning. But some do make it to the final stage.

Postconventional Level (11 Years On). A relatively small proportion of the population reaches what is called the **postconventional level** of moral reasoning. If this development occurs, it does so at about age 11 or 12. Now that the brain and experience have primed the person for dealing with them, issues like personal ethics and human rights come to the foreground (Snarey, 1985; Kohlberg, 1963). Here is a comparison of answers to a moral problem given by people at the preconventional level and by people at the postconventional level:

> *Problem:* After a shipwreck, 11 men are in a lifeboat, one wealthy and powerful, 10 poor. You can save either the one rich man or the 10 poor men. Which would you save?
> *Preconventional answer:* The rich man, because he will give you a big reward.
> *Postconventional answer:* The 10 poor men, because human life has value regardless of wealth or status.

You probably will take the second answer for granted, but that has required quite a bit of maturing. When you were very young, you probably would have given the first answer.

A complication with this system of moral development is that behavior differs depending on what kind of situation you are caught up in. Sometimes we let morality go out the window for our own convenience. With the intellectual development discussed by Piaget, we can't go backward; but with morality, sometimes we "know better" and still don't care. Some psychologists believe that establishing right and wrong might actually arise from biological changes in the brain, despite the fact that the rules vary from one culture to another (Kagan, 1984).

preconventional level. Kohlberg's early stage of moral development, in which morality is determined by the sheer power of outside authority

conventional level Kohlberg's middle stage of moral development, in which moral reasoning is based on the expectations of others regarding what is right or wrong

postconventional level Kohlberg's last stage of moral development, in which personal ethics and human rights come into play

Thinking Critically about Psychology

Solving Moral Dilemmas: Masculine and Feminine Reasoning

In the early 1980s, psychologist Carol Gilligan published criticisms of Kohlberg's theory (Gilligan, 1982). In particular, Gilligan criticized Kohlberg's ideas about the highest level, postconventional reasoning. She noted that his original subjects were all males and proposed that his system emphasized male moral values in the form of abstract moral principles, such as justice. This emphasis, she believed, placed women at a disadvantage. She further noted that in her own research, women as a group tended to score lower on moral reasoning tests than men. The reason for this, she suggested, is that women focus more on caring for others and on a sense of connectedness than on abstract notions of justice. (She did state, though, that males *and* females use both care and justice in their moral reasoning.) Gilligan's comments appealed to many people, and her approach was fairly quickly accepted by a number of psychologists. Let's examine this issue further.

▲ *Both males and females use the same strategies for reaching moral decisions.*

What specifically is being claimed or stated?

Lawrence Kohlberg's theory of moral development contains a gender bias. It emphasizes abstract principles, such as justice, instead of concern for others, which is more important to women.

What is the objective evidence for and against this claim?

Aside from Gilligan's own research into this area, there is not much support for gender differences in moral reasoning (Martin & Ruble, 1997). Other researchers simply have not found such differences. In fact, they have found that men are as likely as women to use care for others as the basis for a moral decision (Helwig, 1997; Hurd & Brabeck, 1997). Some have even gone so far as to suggest that Gilligan herself is guilty of gender bias. In their view, her proposal is based on a stereotype—namely, the assumption that women are more nurturing and concerned with others' welfare than men are.

What other interpretations might be made instead?

Rarely in psychology do all the research findings agree completely. It is possible that Gilligan's research is simply an example of that. Another factor to keep in mind is that the study of gender is a relatively new area in psychology. Regarding the rapid acceptance of Gilligan's findings, some suggest that at the time there was a kind of "bandwagon" approach to the topic. People were eager to jump on it and emphasize the differences between men and women, as opposed to their similarities (Hurd & Brabeck, 1997). Psychologists do try hard to be objective, but we are human, too, after all.

What are the most logical conclusions to draw? We believe that Gilligan's added emphasis on care as a basis for moral judgment is important to our understanding of human development. However, the original claim does not hold up. Males and females use the same approaches to solving moral dilemmas. There is little or no evidence of gender differences in the highest level of moral reasoning.

Gilligan used the following story with 11- to 15-year-old American children.

The Porcupine and the Moles

Seeking refuge from the cold, a porcupine asked to share a cave for the winter with a family of moles. The moles agreed. But because the cave was small, they soon found they were being scratched each time the porcupine moved about. Finally, they asked the porcupine to leave. But the porcupine refused, saying, "If you moles are not satisfied, I suggest that you leave." (Gilligan, 1982)

Gilligan found that boys who read this story tend to opt for justice in resolving the dilemma: "It's the moles' house. It's a deal. The porcupine leaves." In contrast, girls tend to look for solutions that would keep all parties happy and comfortable, such as "Cover the porcupine with a blanket."

Applying Critical Thinking Skills

An absent-minded cashier gives back too much change to Anthony and, later, to Lauren. According to the conclusions presented above, Anthony and Lauren will use similar reasoning when deciding whether to return the money. Do you agree? Explain.

See if **COOL** works for you....

Claim?

Objective evidence for and against claim?

Other interpretations?

Logical conclusions?

Focus Questions
....
- Do animals use language to communicate?
- What are major factors affecting language development?

The Development of Language Skills

Psychologists study communication in any form, even communication among and by animals. Some claims have been outlandish, though. In 1852, it was said that a captain captured a pirate ship and found a dog that could sing and dance. In 1600, supposedly there was a beautiful white horse that could dance and count and one day just climbed straight up the side of a church steeple to talk to the people (Thomas, 1983). Although we aren't likely to accept these claims, we do know that dogs, cats, birds, and most other animals can communicate by sound or action. So before getting into the issue of human language, we want to set the stage with some other types of "language."

Chimpanzees can be taught to communicate symbolically using sign language somewhat similar to that used by humans, and some chimps have learned as many as 1,000 different sign-language words. The ability to use sign language clearly shows that chimpanzees can engage in a form of speech. They don't, however, have the necessary vocal apparatus to talk, nor do they show the level of language skills found in humans.

▲ *This chimpanzee can communicate using sign language.*

And, after all, how well would we do on tests of tree-swinging and mutual maintenance (such as cleaning and grooming one another)—tasks chimps perform with great expertise? The point is that we are asking them to perform unnatural acts, and they do themselves proud even though they are not destined to become as proficient in word language as we are.

Despite the chimpanzees' remarkable feats, it appears that only humans are destined to speak, to communicate through a verbal language, the use of meaningful symbols and sounds. We are the only creatures with both the physical structures needed to make all the sounds and the brains to make rules of grammar and invent new words.

Processes of Language

Babbling is a natural activity for babies, even deaf ones who cannot hear their own or others' voices. Buried in all this noise-making are the sounds used in *any* human language. A basic blueprint of all speech sounds is programmed in the infant from birth. The environment, by providing examples to imitate, then guides each infant to the correct speech pattern for the society within which that infant lives. From this vast array of sounds, children pick and choose the ones that fit the language of those around them. This is why older foreigners have trouble learning a new language. For instance, English speakers use a *th* sound frequently, but it doesn't appear in German, so German children early on drop it from their supply of sounds unless they are also learning English.

Psychologists believe that language patterns develop because certain sounds are reinforced or rewarded whenever they occur. Thus, the sounds

Case Study

Genie

In 1970 a near-blind woman in Los Angeles walked into a welfare office with her 13-year-old daughter to seek assistance for her blindness. A worker there noticed the sorry condition of the young girl, "Genie," and reported the case to her boss. Soon after, the awful truth began to unravel.

Authorities discovered that Genie, weighing less than 60 pounds, had been locked in her bedroom and strapped to a potty chair day after day for nearly her entire life. At night she was wrapped in a tight-fitting sleeping bag and placed in a crib, the sides of which were lined with wire mesh. Believing she was retarded, her father rarely spoke to her and wouldn't allow others to make contact with her either. There was no television or radio in the house, and any talk was softly spoken because of the father's intolerance for noise. Except for bathroom noises and a neighbor's occasional piano playing, Genie heard virtually nothing.

Barely able to see and fearing for her own life, Genie's mother felt trapped as well. After Genie turned 13, however, her mother finally worked up the nerve to leave her husband and to take her daughter with her.

When she was found, Genie could understand fewer than 20 words and could utter only two or three. About a year later, Genie had the language skills of a two-year-old. Though her vocabulary had increased, she could still only string together two- and three-word sentences. This stage in language development is usually followed by a great burst of progress in most children, but that never occurred in Genie. She could communicate with others, especially through her nonverbal behavior, but she could not master certain rules of grammar.

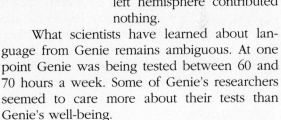

▲ *Critical steps must be followed for language skills to develop.*

She could not distinguish between *you* and *me,* for example. She couldn't phrase a question properly, to move words around to form a normal pattern (Rymer, 1993). She might say, "You where is chair in kitchen?" Genie's speech level never progressed beyond that of a child of four or five years old.

Susan Curtiss (1977), one of the many researchers who spent countless hours with Genie and who became close to her, reported that Genie did have a good sense of humor. She scored well on tests measuring spatial skills. And she even learned to lie, a sure sign of cognitive development. But her language skills—skills requiring the use of the left hemisphere—remained poor. And brain-wave tests confirmed this. When processing a language task, Genie's left hemisphere contributed nothing.

What scientists have learned about language from Genie remains ambiguous. At one point Genie was being tested between 60 and 70 hours a week. Some of Genie's researchers seemed to care more about their tests than Genie's well-being.

In the end, Genie's well-being was not given much of a chance either. She did spend four stable years in the homes of two of her researchers, but she was then sent to one foster home after another and was apparently mistreated in some of them. She lived again with her mother for a short while, and then in an adult care group home. She now resides in a more caring foster home and still visits her mother.

Review the Case Study

Genie had to learn to communicate with nonverbal methods. What ways do you think Genie used?

In Focus

Kohlberg's Dilemmas

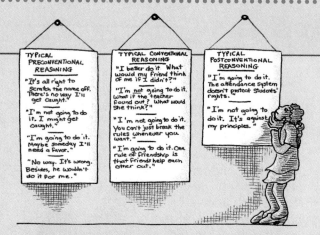

Kohlberg collected much of his information about morality through interviews with hundreds and hundreds of subjects. He would present these subjects with numerous moral dilemmas, similar to this one:

"Every day at the end of class, your teacher tells you to take down the attendance slip. One day a good friend runs into you before you reach the attendance office and begs you to take his name off the sheet. He says he can't tell you the reason why he cut class, but that it was important. Would *you* scratch off the name?"

For this example, Kohlberg would not be concerned so much with whether you would or would not remove the name from the attendance sheet. He was more concerned with the *reasoning* behind the decision. Kohlberg believed that this reasoning would reveal your level of moral development.

Typical Preconventional Reasoning

"It's all right to scratch the name off. There's no way I'll get caught."

"I'm *not* going to do it. I might get caught."

"I'm going to do it. Maybe someday I'll need a favor."

"No way. It's wrong. Besides, he wouldn't do it for me."

Typical Conventional Reasoning

"I better do it—what would my friend think of me if I didn't?"

"I'm *not* going to do it. What if the teacher found out? What would she think?"

"I'm not going to do it—you can't just break the rules whenever you want."

"I'm going to do it. One rule of friendship is that friends help each other out."

Typical Postconventional Reasoning

"I'm going to do it. The attendance system doesn't protect students' rights."

"I'm not going to do it. It's against my principles."

If you had to summarize each of these three types of reasoning in a word or two, which words would you use?

for *Da-da* and *Ma-ma* are among the first to be learned because they bring such joy to the parents.

Language does not simply express our thoughts. It also influences how we think about and perceive the world. For instance, people who live in areas where it is nearly always cold and snowy may have words for many different kinds of snow. We do not. Consequently, we don't pay much attention to these differences or even see them, for that matter.

Rules of Language

In the process of learning to speak, children follow rigid, fixed rules. For example, a child in an early Kohlberg stage will say that someone who breaks three cups accidentally is "badder" than someone who breaks one cup on purpose. Adding the *er* is a "rule" they learn and apply to almost any word to indicate a greater degree of something. Words like *doggie* are made plural by adding *s*, so the rule is followed for all other words: "Those mans feeding corns to the sheeps." Correcting children does not affect their loyalty to these rules. They keep right on making the same mistakes, even though no one else speaks this way.

The most important thing at this stage is the location of the word. A child knows the difference between "Doggie eat" and "Eat doggie." Thus, grammar involving plurals and other rules are artificial and learned only from reinforcement at a later stage of development. Communication is the child's goal at the beginning.

Biology and Language

Since sounds, words, word arrangements, and accents all vary from one culture to another and even from one section of a country to another, it is obvious that environment plays a critical role in speech development. Some experts feel, however, that many basic ideas or ways of organizing our world might be inborn rather than learned. This might explain why all known societies have a concept of something being "in here" or "out there" or of something being "big" or "little." Their belief is that from the beginning we have a biological program for language development but that it needs an environment for fine-tuning (Bickerton, 1984; Chomsky, 1980).

While controversy about inheriting "ideas" still exists, almost everyone now agrees that we do inherit the *potential* for speech sounds and that this is not environmental. It also seems obvious that sounds and words have to be stored over time, and this process in the normal child depends on brain development. By age two, the average child knows about 300 words; by age three, roughly 1,000 words. By age six, the average child can correctly use 5,000 words and understands almost twice that number. The average adult has a vocabulary of about 10,000 words but can grasp the meaning of at least 50,000 words, probably partly from context. There seems to be no doubt about it: Humans are born to talk, and we will spend most of our lives in the world of words.

 Pause for Thought

1. Describe some differences in how children reason at the preconventional, conventional, and postconventional levels of moral development.
2. Do males and females seem to show different patterns of reasoning when solving moral dilemmas? Explain.

Critical Thinking
....

3. As noted in the chapter, environment plays a key role in speech development. How has your environment—both in your home and in your community—shaped your speech?

APPLYING Psychology to Life

The Child Within

Centuries ago, it was believed that a child was a miniature adult. As a result, few, if any, provisions were made for the child's need to develop and mature. Later, some philosophers and psychologists went to the other extreme, claiming that children were so unformed that they could be made into anything adults desired.

Sigmund Freud, the founder of psychoanalysis, insisted that the first five years of life were the critical ones and that by the end of the fifth year, we had become what we were going to be—at least in terms of our abnormalities. It is hard, even today, to avoid hearing that someone who acts strangely probably does so as the result of something that happened in childhood. Few psychologists embrace this point of view any longer, but it continues nonetheless. Similarly, we still hear what a terrible disservice mothers who work outside the home are doing to their children— another belief that is not supported by the evidence.

While it is possible that what we write here today will not bear the scrutiny of time, at least today's views are far more balanced, have quite a bit of experimental support, and *seem* to make sense. Here are a few very important discoveries:

(1) Parents don't simply control whatever happens to the child. The child also influences parents by his or her behavior.
(2) Childhood friends have a striking impact on how we develop. In fact, their influence often outstrips that of parents.

▲ *Nowadays psychologists realize that children are not just miniature adults.*

(3) Genetic factors play an important role in what we are.

Although what we have inherited is very important, the evidence is strong that we have within us the ability to determine much of our fate. For example, not all children who were abused or who grew up under horrible circumstances become delinquents or criminals. We hear and read about only a selected few.

You might want to try a little private research on yourself to see what you come up with. Sit down sometime and just think for a while about the course of your own development. For example, what childhood memories are the strongest? List a few. Did these events have a major impact on what you are today? What interactions with your parents when you were a child do you remember? How much influence did they have on what you are today? In terms of your basic personality (dependent, independent, adventuresome, shy, and so forth—don't lie to yourself), how similar are you today to what you were like as a child? What was the worst thing that ever happened to you, and did it really influence the course of your life up to the present? How similar or dissimilar are your real views on morality, the world, your friends, and so forth to those you think your parents had when you were growing up? And how much influence did your very good (or bad) childhood friends have on you?

It is very hard to come to any final conclusion from such an exercise, but it will shed a great deal of light on your course of development, and a picture of yourself should emerge. There is no reason why your conclusions should be any less accurate than those of the "experts." In all probability, you will be *more* accurate, if you're being honest with yourself, since it has been *your* life, after all.

▲ *Friends can have tremendous influence on a child's development—sometimes even more than parents have.*

Summary

1. The nature/nurture controversy assumes that both heredity and environment are important; but one side emphasizes the genes (nature), and the other side emphasizes the surroundings in which the child lives (nurture).

2. Developmental patterns show that each species has a fixed rate at which development proceeds and which seems to be related to the potential and complexity of the species.

3. Maturation is an automatic, orderly, and sequential process of physical and mental development. Training has little effect on the speed or outcome of the process, although growth cycles are involved that vary the speed and timing of a child's development.

4. Critical periods are specific time periods in an animal's maturation when a particular skill is learned or an association made. Imprinting is the accepting of a mother, and must occur within a specific time after birth.

5. The nuclear family is the most common family unit in the United States today. Different approaches to parenting have different effects on the child. The three major parenting styles are permissive, authoritarian (or dictatorial), and authoritative.

6. Child abuse results from several factors, including a parent's lack of knowledge regarding developmental sequences, which causes the parent to have unrealistic expectations of the child, and pressure on a parent from unemployment, financial problems, and the like.

7. Separation anxiety occurs at about nine months of age and is a fear of being away from either parent.

8. Jean Piaget developed a four-stage theory of mental development that follows a sequence based on age and brain maturation. Lawrence Kohlberg has a similar three-stage system for the development of moral reasoning.

9. Language involves a maturational process based on inborn capabilities. Over time, the child learns to conform more and more with the grammatical rules of his or her specific language.

Vocabulary

heredity	critical period	object permanence
environment	feral children	preoperational stage
nature/nurture controversy	nuclear family	reversibility
genes	extended family	conservation
chromosomes	permissive parenting style	concrete operations stage
zygote	authoritarian (dictatorial)	formal operations stage
dizygotic twins	parenting style	preconventional level
monozygotic twins	authoritative parenting style	conventional level
maturation	separation anxiety	postconventional level
growth cycles	cognitive development	
imprinting	sensorimotor stage	

Review Questions

Multiple Choice

On a sheet of paper, write the letter of the choice that best completes each statement.

1. If we agree that violence is caused mainly by nurture, we are agreeing that violence
   a. is mainly inborn. b. is mainly learned.
   c. cannot be studied. d. is hereditary.

2. Which of the following statements about developmental patterns is *not* true?
   a. Development within a species is orderly.
   b. The human has a longer developmental period than animals.
   c. It's usually possible through training to speed up the developmental timetable of any species by quite a bit.
   d. The development process integrates the brain and the body.

3. Which of the following statements about growth cycles is *not* true?
   a. There are differences between the sexes.
   b. The brain develops sooner than the body.
   c. Girls develop in a more orderly and stable way than boys do.
   d. The reproductive system develops faster than the brain.

4. Authoritarian parents
   a. supply reasons for punishment.
   b. tend to be inflexible.
   c. are usually good listeners.
   d. were troublemakers themselves as children.

5. Authoritative parents
   a. are flexible.
   b. usually raise self-reliant children.
   c. encourage their children to make their own decisions.
   d. do all of the above.

True/False

On a sheet of paper, answer each statement true *or* false. *If false, rewrite to make it true.*

6. Monozygotic twins have exactly the same heredity.

7. Imprinting is affected by chemical changes in the body.

8. Critical periods apply to all animals except humans.

9. In time, a feral child will usually catch up to the ability level of others his or her age.

10. Extended families are more common today than in the past.

11. Studies show that children of mothers who work outside the home form attachments to their mothers that are just as strong as the ones formed by children whose mothers don't work.

12. Separation anxiety seems to have more to do with nurture than nature.

Matching

On a sheet of paper, match the terms in the right-hand column with the description in the left-hand column. Answers may be used more than once.

13. Fertilized egg
14. Basic units of heredity
15. Most body cells contain 46 of them
16. Reproductive cells contain 23 of them
17. Conservation skills are not quite established.
18. The world becomes fixed.
19. Objects are not permanent.
20. This is the highest level of cognitive development.
21. Others' approval helps us determine right and wrong.
22. People's rights are given great consideration.
23. A person is extremely self-centered at this level.

a. genes
b. chromosomes
c. zygote
d. sensorimotor stage
e. preoperational stage
f. concrete operations stage
g. formal operations stage
h. preconventional
i. conventional
j. postconventional

317

Discussion Questions

1. As noted in the chapter, a stimulating environment is crucial to maturation. In what ways was your early childhood stimulating? Do you remember any particular toys? Did your parents or grandparents read or sing to you? How do you think this stimulation affected you?

2. Alisha is a mother who works outside the home. She argues that she spends at least two to three hours of "quality time" with her child every evening. Her friend Tonya is a mother who is not employed outside the house. She argues that these two to three hours may be quality time for Alisha but not necessarily for her child. Maybe morning or afternoon is the time when the *child* is most open to quality interaction. In other words, *maybe* the two to three hours in the evening are a crabby time for the child, and the child benefits little from the interaction. With whom do you tend to agree? Explain.

3. The chapter mentions that all normal children experience separation anxiety. Not all parents, however, deal with the anxiety in the same way. For example, let's say that a stranger picks up the child, and the child begins to cry. Some parents tend to take the baby away almost immediately to soothe the child. They let the child gradually decide when he or she is ready to approach the stranger. Other parents let the stranger hold the child, hoping that the child will get used to the stranger, despite the child's continuing anxiety. In your opinion, which approach would promote a stronger and longer-lasting sense of security for the child? Explain.

4. Briefly describe your childhood household. Did the person who raised you work outside the home? Were you ever in day care? Describe the effect these arrangements may have had on your personality.

5. Which parenting style do your parents usually use? Is it effective? If so, why? If not, what changes would you like to see?

6. Think of some decisions you've made recently that have been based on preconventional, conventional, and postconventional moral reasoning. For ideas, see the In Focus feature on Kohlberg's dilemmas.

7. Do you agree that there are no gender differences in moral reasoning? Can you think of *any* moral issues on which males and females are divided? To answer these questions, focus on a particular issue, and explain how males and females seem to view the issue. You might focus on moral issues concerning friendship, dating, raising children, or marriage. For example, how do males and females view spanking? How do they view "rules" of friendship we should follow?

Activities and Projects

1. To learn about the effects of environment and heredity, interview a set of identical twins. Write a report on your interview, and include a reaction to what you learned. Possible questions:

   What are some of your common personality traits, interests, and values?

   Which of these similarities do you think are influenced by heredity, and which are probably influenced more by environment?

   In what ways are you different?

   How do you account for these differences?

   Do other people sometimes fail to recognize your uniqueness?

2. This activity will help you examine how much your personality is influenced by your heredity and how much by your environment. Make a list of 20 characteristics that you have in common with your parents. The characteristics can be physical, mental, behavioral—just about any similarity that you can think of. After each item, write down whether the characteristic, in your opinion, is influenced mainly through heredity or mainly through environment.

My Characteristics

heredity	environment

Parents' Characteristics

heredity	environment

The characteristics are most likely influenced by both, but choose the influence that you perceive to be slightly dominant.

Next, have one of your parents make the same list, following the same instructions—but don't let him or her see your list.

Compare the two lists. Were the characteristics listed pretty much the same? Were your conclusions about heredity and environment about the same? What general conclusions can you draw from this? For example, which kinds of characteristics (physical, mental, behavioral, and so forth) seemed to be most influenced by heredity? Least influenced by heredity? Explain.

3. We can all think of memorable childhood experiences that have helped to shape our personalities. Pick one of these memorable experiences and describe it in a couple of pages. Include all the rich and vivid detail that made the experience memorable for you. Write the description not as an essay but as if you were telling a story to a good friend.

4. Probably one of the most successful educational television programs for children is *Sesame Street*. Watch about an hour of the program, and take notes on the various teaching techniques used: length of skits, music, repetition, and any other techniques that you notice.

Next, watch about 10 to 15 television commercials (don't rely on memory), and take notes on techniques that advertisers use to sell their products: length of commercials, music, repetition, and so on.

Notice any similarities? Write a detailed report comparing and contrasting *Sesame Street* and the television commercials. If possible, talk to parents whose children watch *Sesame Street* and ask them about the effectiveness of the techniques used.

5. Contact three teachers. One should be a first- or second-grade teacher (whose students will probably be preoperational). Another should be a third- or fourth-grade teacher (whose students will probably be concrete operational). The third should be a fifth- or sixth-grade teacher (whose students will probably be formal operational). Ask the teachers if they would be willing to participate in a 15- to 20-minute experiment. All they'll have to do is allow their students to draw pictures after reading to the students the following instructions: "Draw a picture of a typical day at your home." Try to get all the teachers to use the same size paper and the same writing utensils—crayons, for example.

Analyze the three groups of drawings. You might look at some of the following aspects of the drawings: the size and proportions of objects drawn, the colors used, and the number of people drawn versus the number of objects. (Note: Artistic ability should probably not be given much weight in your analyses.) Try to relate these observations to Piaget's theory. Do the drawings reveal in any way the artists' stages of cognitive development? Explain.

Don't feel limited by these suggestions about your analyses. Although many therapists are trained in analyzing such pictures, most agree that there are no simple or set answers. They admit that their analyses depend on intuition and creativity to some extent. So be creative. Perhaps get a friend or two to help you brainstorm.

6. Conduct your own survey to find out if males and females differ in their moral reasoning. Your survey might include yes-no questions, statements that ask respondents how much they agree or disagree, or multiple-choice questions. You probably should focus on a single area, such as friendship or dating. If several people in your class complete this project, it might be interesting to compare the results of the surveys. Males and females may differ in one area but not another. After you compile your data, create a chart or two to summarize your findings, and write a report analyzing your results.

CHAPTER 11

Adolescence

T hroughout adolescence, significant growth and changes occur. Adolescents are different from other age groups in their physical, psychological, social, intellectual, and moral concerns and processes.

320

Defining Adolescence

The years between childhood and adulthood make up the period of development called **adolescence**. This period starts at age 11 or 12 and generally is considered over by 18 or 19. Pinpointing exactly when adolescence ends and adulthood begins, though, is not an easy task in our society. People can vote and join the military at 18. In most states, they can marry without their parents' permission at that age. But a person must be 21 to have all the legal rights that adults enjoy. And even reaching that age does not automatically grant full adult status. Many people 21 and older are still single, still in school, and still dependent on their parents for financial support. They are adults in the eyes of the law but are not yet self-sufficient or living on their own. In any case, since the physical and psychological changes of adolescence are fairly complete by age 19, that is a reasonable end point.

The range of ages from 11 to 19 is further divided based on physical and psychological similarities within these smaller age groups. Early adolescence goes from 11 to 14. Middle adolescence runs from 14 to 16. Late adolescence ranges from 16 to 19. As we discuss these periods in greater detail, differences among the age groups will become clear.

adolescence the period of development between childhood and adulthood

Physical Changes

Throughout adolescence, the most startling developments are physical. Sudden changes take place in sexual maturation and physical growth. Changes in height and weight are dramatic and troublesome. The biggest problem, however, is that while these changes in physiology remove from the adolescent the label *child,* adolescents are not yet adults. They may feel for a while that they are "nowhere," neither adults nor children.

Focus Questions
· ·
- What physical changes occur during adolescence?
- Do girls mature earlier than boys?

▲ *Major physical changes are just around the corner for these kids.*

puberty the time of sexual maturation

hormones chemical regulators that control bodily processes such as emotional responses, growth, and sexuality

pituitary gland the master gland of the body; it activates other glands and controls the growth hormone

adrenal glands glands that cause excitement in order to prepare the body for an emergency or for some important activity; also involved in sexual maturation

gonads the sex glands

▲ *Alfalfa's pants are a good indication he's had a recent growth spurt.*

growth spurt a rapid increase in growth during puberty

Sexual Development

Puberty, or the period of sexual maturation, is a notable feature of adolescence. **Hormones,** chemicals that control body growth, emotional responses, and physical changes, are responsible for sexual maturation. Several hormones are extremely active in adolescence. The **pituitary** (pi-TUE-i-ter-ee) **gland** secretes growth hormones and increases the production in other glands of other hormones. Two systems under the pituitary's control are the **adrenal** (a-DREE-nal) **glands** and the **gonads** (GO-nads), or sex glands. Adrenaline from the adrenal glands and sex hormones from the gonads work with the pituitary to bring about sexual maturation.

During puberty, breast development and the start of menstruation occur in females. Noticeable voice changes and the development of facial hair and thicker body hair occur in males. Both sexes begin the process of sex-organ maturation, which is accompanied by the growth of pubic hair. Many people think sexual development is gradual from childhood through adolescence, but this is not so. Amazingly, 90 percent of sexual maturity occurs after puberty starts, which accounts for the concern and preoccupation with sexuality common for people in this period of their lives. Other effects of hormones include skin problems, like acne, and increased perspiration. While these are natural outcomes of the bodily changes taking place, they are also sources of embarrassment and concern for many adolescents.

It may surprise you to learn that the impact of hormones on an adolescent's emotional state is not clear-cut. It is true that adolescents generally are moodier than adults, but so are children, and children are not being bombarded with all these chemicals. The many intense changes taking place in adolescence probably have as much to do with emotional response as the hormones themselves. In any case, emotional ups and downs are more evident early on and largely disappear by late adolescence (Buchanan, Eccles, & Becker, 1992).

Physical Growth

During adolescence, the body is moving upward and outward rapidly in what is called the **growth spurt.** When growth spurts occur, development is not orderly. Arms and hands may grow at a different rate from legs, for instance, while other parts of the body develop at yet another rate.

Although they may look gangly, teenagers have exceptionally good coordination. It is because growth is so rapid and uneven that adolescents may *feel* awkward and "not quite right." Most teenagers, however, handle puberty much better than people think. In fact, only a small number of adolescents, roughly 15 percent, have any real trouble adjusting to these dramatic changes (Petersen, 1987).

Growth spurts come earlier for girls than boys, but for both sexes, early adolescence is the time of maximum physical development. Between the ages of 9 and 12, girls may grow as much as three inches taller in one year. For boys, this growth occurs between 11 and 15, when they may gain as much as four inches in height in a year. The average height of Americans in general has increased notably over the years, partly because of better nutrition and less hard physical labor at young ages. This is the case for adolescents as well as adults. On average, teenagers are a full six inches taller today than they were 100 years ago (Bronfenbrenner & Ceci, 1994).

Rates of Maturation

Differences between boys and girls in the level of physical maturation are greatest and most obvious in early adolescence. By age 14, most girls have matured fairly completely, while most boys lag behind by two to three years. This difference between the sexes creates problems in how they relate to one another, especially where dating and dancing are involved. Most males are shorter than females their own age during early adolescence, making the situation even more awkward. When girls start dating, many go out with older boys, largely because of these differences. By middle adolescence, the maturity gap between the sexes has narrowed considerably; and for most, by late adolescence, it has disappeared altogether.

Besides overall gender differences in the rate and timing of physical maturation, individual differences exist as well. Small differences do not have much impact on the individual. When physical development occurs substantially earlier or later than average, however, there are psychological effects. The particular kinds of effects that occur depend on two factors: (1) whether the adolescent is an **early maturer** (one and one-half years or more ahead of the average) or a **late maturer** (one and one-half years or more behind the average) and (2) whether the individual is male or female.

Early maturation is more of an advantage for boys than girls. Boys who develop ahead of schedule have higher self-esteem and feel better about how they look. Early-maturing girls feel awkward about being different from their friends. They are more self-conscious and dissatisfied with their weight and general appearance.

Development that starts later than average is worse for boys than girls. Boys who are late maturers, like early-maturing girls, feel awkward about their bodies. They are more self-conscious, less self-confident, and express greater dissatisfaction with their overall appearance than other adolescent males. Late-maturing girls, however, do not seem to suffer many negative effects. Generally, they have high self-esteem and are satisfied with their physical appearance. They also have the advantage of being similar to boys their own age in height and overall maturation (Peterson, 1987).

One problem that seems to go along with both early and late maturation is increased conflict with one's parents (Laursen & Collins, 1994).

▲ *Most of these girls have already reached their adult heights. The boys probably still have some growing to do.*

early maturer someone whose physical development is one and one-half years or more ahead of average development

late maturer someone whose physical development is one and one-half years or more behind average development

InFocus

Maturation Timetables

Early Maturers		Late Maturers	
Boys	**Girls**	**Boys**	**Girls**
High self-esteem	Generally low self-esteem	Generally low self-esteem	High self-esteem
Satisfied with physical appearance	Dissatisfied with physical appearance	Dissatisfied with overall appearance	Satisfied with physical appearance
	Highly self-conscious	Highly self-conscious	

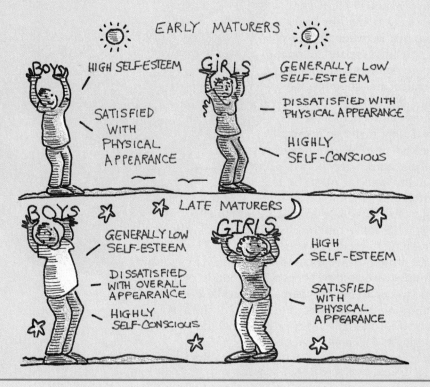

The feelings listed here are based on appearance. What other factors affect self-esteem during early adolescence?

Trouble often comes from the parents' excessive concerns about an early-maturing child. The parents of a late maturer may not be able to understand that late physical maturation does not mean delayed psychological maturity as well, so they may treat the young adolescent as if he or she were still a child.

Maturation that occurs later or earlier than average can create either pluses or minuses. Either way, though, the impact is felt primarily during adolescence. For most early or late maturers, neither the problems nor the advantages appear to last into adult life.

▲ *Is our current notion of ideal beauty unhealthy?*

Weight: Too Much or Too Little?

Along with rapid growth and sexual maturation come fluctuations in weight. Concern about weight is a common problem for adolescents. Being underweight or overweight can result from hormonal imbalances, physical changes, psychological difficulties, genetics, or some combination of these factors. For instance, some males try to compensate for a temporary "string-bean look" by eating too much. In addition, food can act as a sedative to relieve loneliness. When dealing with issues of weight, patience is probably called for, as difficult as that may be. Some physical changes *are* drastic during adolescence, but, even so, people in their early twenties are the leanest of all age groups.

Weight and body image are more often problems for females than for males. Society places more importance on physical appearance for women than for men. The "ideal beauty," that unrealistic picture of what the perfect woman should look like, has become thinner and thinner over the years. As two psychologists have noted, in the 1950s, a typical winner of the Miss Sweden title was five feet seven inches tall and weighed 151 pounds. Thirty-some years later, that title winner was five feet nine inches tall (two inches taller) and weighed only 109 pounds (over 40 pounds less) (Wade & Tavris, 1993). A height-to-weight ratio like that borders on being seriously hazardous to one's health.

The damage done by social pressure to conform to such an impossible ideal is hard to overstate. At a minimum, it makes most women dissatisfied with their appearance. As many as three-fourths of American women think they are "fat" or at least should lose a few pounds. In reality, many of these women are not even slightly overweight. At a more troublesome level, such social pressure can result in constant unhealthful dieting. When the pressure is echoed by friends and family, the potential for problems is very high indeed (Pike, 1995).

Focus Question

• Why is body image often more of a problem for females than males?

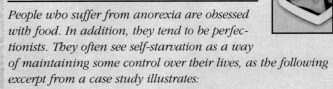

In Their Own Words . . .

People who suffer from anorexia are obsessed with food. In addition, they tend to be perfectionists. They often see self-starvation as a way of maintaining some control over their lives, as the following excerpt from a case study illustrates:

Although she did not allow herself to eat, Joan still felt hungry; in fact she was starving most of the time. She thought about food constantly, spent all of her time reading recipe and health books, and cooked elaborate meals for the family.

Although she weighed less than 100 pounds, Joan still felt overweight and believed that she would look better if she lost more weight. She had an overwhelming fear of getting fat, because she believed that gaining weight would mean that she was not perfect. She tried to be a model young adult and struggled to be what she imagined everybody else wanted. She gave little thought to what she would want for herself. It seemed to Joan that everything in her life was out of control and that her weight and body were the only things over which she could be in charge. The demonstration of strict self-control with regard to eating was a source of pride and accomplishment to Joan. (1995, pp. 251–252)

Interpreting Primary Sources

In what ways did Joan demonstrate her obsession with food?

eating disorders conditions in which a person cannot read the body's nutritional signals and eats or refuses to eat for the wrong reasons

bulimia nervosa an eating disorder that involves binging on food and purging by vomiting or using laxatives

The evidence is absolutely clear that being somewhat overweight is nowhere near as risky as attempting to become too thin. Also, excessive dieting can lead to **eating disorders.** A person with an eating disorder is unable to correctly read the body's signals about its nutritional needs. The person eats (or refuses to eat) for the wrong reasons. Whatever the specific disorder may be, the person is obsessed with food.

In the condition known as **bulimia nervosa** (bul-LEE-mee-uh ner-VOE-suh), people go on binges, eating large amounts of rich, calorie-laden foods. They then try to keep the food from causing any weight gain by either forcing themselves to vomit or taking excessive doses of laxatives. Thus, bulimia is sometimes called the binge-and-purge syndrome. As you might suspect, such people often develop problems in their digestive systems. Another side effect is severe irritation of the mouth and throat, as well as erosion of tooth enamel from all that stomach acid.

Most bulimics are adolescent or young adult females. However, as many as 15 to 20 percent are young men. Males who become bulimic often are trying to maintain or qualify for a particular weight class in athletic competition. The motivation for females, though, is usually that same old sad story—they are trying to achieve an "ideal" weight that is unrealistic. Their self-esteem depends so much on how they look that they are sacrificing their health in the quest for unreachable perfection. In fact, among females, low self-esteem is a major factor in predicting who is most likely to develop an eating disorder of some kind (Joiner & Kashubeck, 1996; Martz, Handley, & Eisler, 1995).

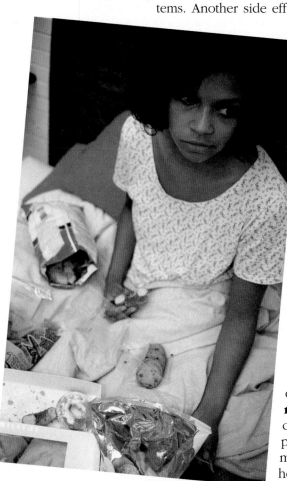

▲ *Bulimics often binge on junk food.*

An even more serious eating disorder is **anorexia** (an-oh-REX-ee-uh) **nervosa.** In anorexia, the person basically has stopped eating and is at least 25 percent underweight. (Say that the normal weight for a particular woman's height and age is 130 pounds. If she is anorexic, she will weigh less than 98 pounds.) This condition is physically extremely harmful, even potentially fatal, because food intake decreases to the point of starvation.

anorexia nervosa an eating disorder that involves severe loss of weight from excessive dieting.

Nearly every system of the body can be damaged by the effects of anorexia. An additional problem is that as the body adjusts to an extremely low food intake, it becomes unable to handle nourishment except in very, very small amounts. People with anorexia usually have to be fed intravenously to stay alive. Their body images have become so dis-

▲ *Anorexia is a life-threatening disorder.*

torted that even when they are little more than skeletons, they still see themselves as fat.

Anorexia is almost exclusively a problem for women. It has been estimated that 95 percent of anorexics are adolescent or young adult females. Their motivation is similar to that of female bulimics. In addition, they often have gotten substantial praise in the past for dieting and losing weight. Over time, they learn that not eating continues to bring praise. Eventually they become so thin that they begin to get attention for being sick. As is true for bulimics, their feelings of self-worth are excessively tied to their appearance.

 ## Pause for Thought

1. List the major physical changes that occur during adolescence.
2. How do early and late maturers differ?
3. Describe two eating disorders that adolescents sometimes develop.

Critical Thinking

4. If you had to create a poster that highlights the advice about dieting in this section, what information would you include? Remember, a poster needs to grab your attention and communicate its message in concise phrases.

Thinking Critically about Psychology

Dieting and Health

For a long time, when people wanted to lose weight, they went on a temporary diet. It was the accepted way to take off unwanted pounds. And for many people, it still is. About 25 percent of all men and 40 percent of all women in America are on a diet right now (Horm & Anderson, 1993; Serdula et al., 1993). More recently, though, we have learned of the so-called yo-yo effect of dieting—that is, what comes off goes back on again, plus a little extra besides. Also, there are concerns that repeated dieting can damage people's overall health. Let's look at this issue more closely.

What specifically is being claimed or stated? Repeated dieting in the long run is not good for weight control or general health.

What is the objective evidence for and against this claim? The first question we should ask is whether diets work. Generally, the answer is yes and no. There is a very high relapse rate among dieters—that is, they tend to gain back the weight they lost. One extremely large survey found that about a fourth of dieters lost weight and kept it off (Consumers Union, 1993), but that is a much higher percentage than most studies have shown. More often, it is estimated that diets only work for about 5 percent of the people who go on them. It seems that, for most people, diets don't do what they are supposed to do—get weight off and keep it off. But is the yo-yo effect of dieting harmful to people's overall health? Although not all studies agree, the evidence is overwhelming that the answer to this question is yes. Weight fluctuation clearly has negative health effects on many bodily systems, such as metabolism, hormone levels, digestion, and cardiovascular functions (Brown & Rodin, 1994).

What other interpretations might be made instead? Is being overweight unhealthier than repeated dieting? Well, there is one factor we haven't taken into account. That factor is whether the people dieting were really overweight to begin with. True obesity means having an excessive amount of fat tissue in the body and being at least 25 to 30 percent over the normal weight limit for one's age and gender (Friedman & Brownell, 1995). There are serious health consequences to being seriously overweight. So, what's the answer? Are

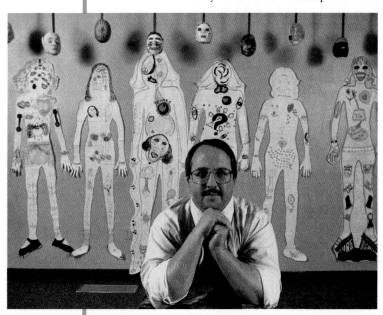

▲ *Behind this psychologist are self-portraits and life masks made by some of the clients at his eating disorders clinic.*

the risks of repeated dieting greater than the risks associated with obesity? We really don't know. The results are definitely mixed (Brown & Rodin, 1994). A basic problem here is that many people are trying to reach an unattainable goal. Our current definition of attractiveness requires a much thinner body than most people can acquire and still stay healthy.

What are the most logical conclusions to draw? It seems reasonable to conclude that the original statement holds up, especially for people who are not actually overweight to begin with. Those people who are constantly losing and gaining back 10 pounds or so would be better off to adjust their expectations instead. As boring as it seems, mak-

▲ *Constantly thinking about your weight can be self-defeating.*

ing moderate but permanent changes in lifestyle that include eating sensibly and increasing daily activity is the best and healthiest way to lose weight and keep it off—that, plus having more realistic goals in the first place.

Applying Critical Thinking Skills

What is the difference between dieting and permanently changing one's lifestyle?

See if COOL works for you....

Claim?

Objective evidence for and against claim?

Other interpretations?

Logical conclusions?

- Why do teens often join cliques or gangs?
- Why is gaining a sense of identity critical?

rite of passage a socially recognized and ritualized change in status, such as the passage to adulthood

Psychological Issues

Adolescence is often painted as a time of great difficulty and confusion. While the trials of this period vary from one culture to another, there is little indication that it is actually that bad for most adolescents. But many problems leave a number of teenagers in a type of limbo.

One of the hardest issues to deal with is trying to find an identity. Until adolescence, there is no pressure to find out about yourself. Now it becomes necessary to try out different roles to see which ones fit. The problem is made worse in our society because the adolescent is normally not expected to take on adult responsibilities but, at the same time, *is* expected to show more maturity and a sense of commitment.

Other societies, especially some in nonindustrialized nations, handle the transition from childhood to adulthood more simply. This transition is made through some kind of initiation, or **rite of passage,** meaning that a change in status is recognized by a formal ritual. Adulthood rituals often involve cutting oneself, being decorated in some specific way, or drinking a foul-tasting potion as part of an elaborate ceremony. After the ceremony is over, the whole community is aware of the person's official adult status.

We have no such ceremonies, so adolescents by and large find themselves somewhat cut off from the mainstream of society. They need to form their own subculture in order to avoid complete isolation. Subcultures invariably have all kinds of rules, regulations, and dress codes so that members can take pride in belonging and can be distinguished from "outsiders." Forming groups and achieving a sense of identity are two crucial psychological issues during adolescence. And they are related to each other in some interesting ways.

Conformity and Group Identity

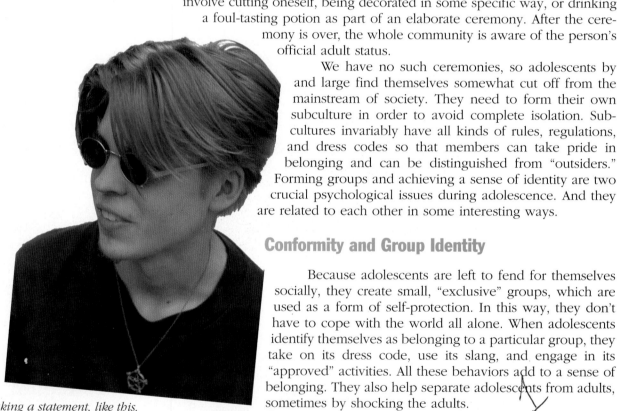

▲ *Making a statement, like this, is often part of defining who you are.*

Because adolescents are left to fend for themselves socially, they create small, "exclusive" groups, which are used as a form of self-protection. In this way, they don't have to cope with the world all alone. When adolescents identify themselves as belonging to a particular group, they take on its dress code, use its slang, and engage in its "approved" activities. All these behaviors add to a sense of belonging. They also help separate adolescents from adults, sometimes by shocking the adults.

Thus, adolescents may shave their heads, wear their hair long and shaggy, dye it green or purple, wear deliberately scuffed boots, or leave the laces untied on their tennis shoes—whatever happens to be in vogue at any given time. For example, when we were adolescents, anyone who wore green on Thursday was considered "weird" and was in for a very rough day, and this "rule" controlled adolescents from coast to coast for several years! Such conformity to the group is understandable: Nobody wants to be alone.

Groups differ in terms of their size, how strictly defined they are, and how closely their rules must be followed. Fairly large groups with loose rules and relatively changeable memberships are called **crowds.** Crowds usually have shared interests, and the members dress similarly; but the structure of crowds is looser than that of more clearly differentiated groups.

Both the **clique** (KLEEK or KLICK) and the **gang** are very tightly knit, with a limited membership and strict rules for admission and proper behavior (Conger and Peterson, 1984). Major differences between the two are that cliques are usually based on common school-related interests, such as athletics or other types of activities. Gangs, on the other hand, have a rebellious or antisocial outlook.

Many adolescents who join gangs do so for the same reasons they might belong to any other group. Membership provides a sense of belonging and status, the security that comes from knowing you have friends to back you up. The problem, of course, is that by definition, gangs engage in antisocial behavior. Thus, it is obviously much better if teenagers can get these needs met in a more constructive way.

Friendships are important throughout life, of course, but they seem to be even more important during adolescence. Most teenagers have at least a couple of good ones, and nearly a third of their waking time is spent with their friends (Hartrup & Stevens, 1997).

The need to conform to the group in dress and language is strongest in early adolescence, between ages 11 and 14. By the end of middle adolescence, around age 16, it has begun a sharp decline. This rapid decline continues through late adolescence, so that rigid conformity has almost disappeared at age 18.

An expert in personality development, **Erik Erikson** (1902–1994), saw support from social groups as necessary for exploring individual identity (Erikson, 1968). Others have expanded on his idea by referring to early adolescence as a time of **group identity versus alienation.** In other words, an adolescent who fails to get a sense of belonging by identifying with a group will feel like a foreigner, alienated from others of his or her age. This adolescent will also have more trouble forming a sense of individual identity toward the end of middle adolescence and through late adolescence (Newman & Newman, 1984).

Individual Identity and Erik Erikson

Personal background often plays a key role in determining what a person emphasizes in both personal and professional life. Such was the case with personality theorist Erik Erikson. He never met his Danish biological father, who deserted his mother before Erikson was born; he never even knew his name. His mother was Jewish and married a Jewish physician named Homburger when Erikson was a very small boy. For years, Erikson thought Dr. Homburger was his biological father. Until he was an adult, he used that last name. (His middle initial, H, stands for Homburger.)

To protect young Erik from being confused and hurt, his mother and stepfather decided not to tell him about his father's abandonment. From a fairly young age, however, Erik felt that something wasn't right. For instance, his mother and stepfather were rather small, with dark hair and eyes, but he was tall, blond, and blue-eyed—obviously Scandinavian. He also felt out of place with his schoolmates. Those who were Jewish did not accept him because of his physical appearance. Those who were

crowds large groups with loose rules and changeable memberships

clique a very tightly knit group with limited membership and strict rules of behavior; normally tied to school activities

gang a rebellious, antisocial group with strict rules; not connected with accepted school or social organizations

group identity versus alienation Erikson's idea that early adolescents either belong to a group or feel lost (alienated)

▲ *Young people join gangs for the same reasons they join other groups.*

Focus Question

• What choices about identity do adolescents make?

331

▲ *Belonging to a group is the first step in forming an individual identity.*

identity a sense of oneself as a unique person.

identity confusion Erikson's term for uncertainty about who one is and where one is going

moratorium a term used by both Erikson and Marcia to describe the adolescent's delay in making the commitments normally expected of adults

Christian considered him Jewish because of his parents' religious beliefs.

From childhood on, he was confused about his own identity, unsure where he fit in the scheme of things. Eventually, he learned the truth about his father, which added to his feelings of insecurity. When he graduated from high school, he had no idea what to do or be. For several years, he wandered around Europe as an artist, painting and sketching, but with no real goals.

He was 25 years old before he decided what he wanted to do with his life. It was then that he met Anna Freud, Sigmund Freud's daughter, and began to study psychoanalysis and child development. As if to free himself completely from his crisis of identity, he took Erikson as his last name, reducing his stepfather's name to an initial (Hopkins, 1995).

Because of Erikson's circumstances at birth and his experiences in childhood and adolescence through young adulthood, his sense of self was poorly defined. It took many years and a lot of trial and error before he understood who he was and knew which roads he wished to travel (Hall et al., 1985).

It should come as no surprise, then, that Erik Erikson emphasized the importance of forming an individual identity in his theory of personality development. According to his theory, from approximately age 12 until at least the end of the teenage years, accurately defining the self is our major psychological task. Belonging to a group is the first step. The next step is seeing how you are different from that group, how you are a unique person. Developing a sense of yourself as an individual means achieving **identity.** Never reaching this goal results in **identity confusion**—uncertainty about who you are and what direction you should take.

For Erikson, adolescence represents a crossroads, a time of upheaval, of selecting from many possibilities the ones that fit. This is not easy to do. As a result, adolescence is not an easy time. Too many decisions are forced on the adolescent too quickly. He or she must not only define the self and learn how to relate to the other sex but also make plans about occupations to pursue (Erikson, 1968). Because these decisions have long-range consequences, they create a lot of anxiety and insecurity.

It is natural for youth to flounder around, going back and forth before completing this task. Most adolescents experiment with a variety of roles, discarding one to try out another. In their search, some will identify with a public figure, perhaps an actor, actress, or rock star, taking on his or her mannerisms and style of dress, at least for a while.

Delaying the usual commitments of adulthood to find one's identity is called a **moratorium** (meaning a period of "time out"). In our society, this means that adolescents can engage in behaviors that are not allowed for adults. For example, think of how your community would react to a group of adults who dressed like teenagers and roamed around the local mall, teasing and jostling each other and shouting and waving at people they know. More broadly, teenagers are not expected to marry, start a family, or support themselves. Moratorium is definitely reserved for adolescence.

Achieving an identity takes a long time, and some youths try to make decisions about their identity too soon. Because they do not give themselves enough time to sort everything out, they decide on an identity that does not really fit. Such adolescents may end up living a life that is not right for them. They may also marry the wrong person. During adolescence, falling in love is part of the identity process. Adolescents help confirm their own identity by gaining someone else's acceptance. As far as Erikson is concerned, real love between two people cannot exist until each knows himself or herself.

Gaining a sense of identity involves a number of specific tasks. The first is developing a clear and unique definition of self, plus acceptance of that self-concept. Others include making a commitment to goals and values, actively planning for or working toward those goals, and feeling confidence in the future, in the ability to achieve those goals.

When people have a sense of identity, they also have an understanding of **fidelity.** Fidelity is Erikson's term for being faithful to one's ideals and values as well as being loyal to others we care about, even if they don't always live up to our expectations.

▲ *Psychologist Erik Erikson*

Individual Identity and James Marcia

James Marcia (1980) expanded on Erikson's work and divided the identity crisis into four states. These are not stages but rather processes that adolescents go through. All adolescents will occupy one (or more) of these states, at least temporarily. Because these are not stages, however, people do not progress from one step to the next in a fixed sequence, nor must everyone go through each and every state.

Identity Foreclosure.   Adolescents who simply accept the identity and values they were given in childhood are in a state of **foreclosure.** This means they are not giving themselves a chance to explore alternatives. They have not experimented with other possibilities before deciding who they are. Instead, their self-concept has been defined by other people. For some adolescents, a **negative identity** results from foreclosure. These are the kids who were labeled *bad* or *troublemakers* in childhood and who have come to accept that label. Whether the identity is negative or not, foreclosure means blocking off certain possibilities for growth and individuality.

Identity Diffusion.   Adolescents who don't have a clear idea of their identity *and* who are not trying to find one are in a state of **diffusion.** These adolescents may have struggled with the issue of identity in the past, but they never resolved it, and they seem to have stopped trying. The outcome is a lack of self-identity and no real commitment to values or personal goals.

Moratorium.   Adolescents who are trying to achieve an identity through experimentation and trial and error are in a state of *moratorium,* discussed earlier. Adolescents remaining in moratorium, or time out, may or may not achieve a sense of identity. Some give up the struggle and wind up in a state of diffusion.

fidelity Erikson's term for faithfulness to one's ideals and values; loyalty

foreclosure Marcia's term for the state in which the adolescent accepts the identity and values he or she was given in childhood

negative identity Marcia's term for an identity that results from defining oneself as bad or as a troublemaker

diffusion Marcia's term for the state in which the adolescent has no clear idea of his or her identity and is not attempting to find that identity

James Marcia's Identity States

Foreclosure	Diffusion	Moratorium	Achievement
Individual makes *definite commitment...*	Individual makes *no commitment...*	Individual *delays commitment...*	Individual makes a *firm commitment...*
but commitment is *not* based on any internal "*soul searching*"...	and does *no* "*soul searching*"...	and struggles a great deal with internal "*soul searching*"...	after experiencing meaningful "*soul searching*"...
thus, individual *conforms:*	thus, individual *wanders:*	thus, individual *searches:*	thus, individual *finds* identity:
"I think I'm going to be a plumber because my dad and his dad were plumbers."	"I think I'll do some traveling after graduation . . . or maybe I'll get a job . . . or . . ."	"I don't know what I want to do, but I don't want to rush into anything either. I want to find something that's right for me."	"It took me a while to find what I want out of life, but now I think I have a good idea."
In summary— Commitment: Yes Searching: No	In summary— Commitment: No Searching: No	In summary— Commitment: No Searching: Yes	In summary— Commitment: Yes Searching: Yes

Is it possible to be foreclosed or diffused and still be happy?

identity achievement Marcia's term for the state in which the adolescent has developed well-defined personal values and self-concepts

Identity Achievement. Adolescents who have gone through the identity crisis and come out with a well-defined self-concept—who are committed to a set of personal values, beliefs, and goals—have reached the state of **identity achievement.** Their identities may well be expanded and further defined in adulthood, but the basics are there, and such adolescents are well prepared to make meaningful lives for themselves.

Pause for Thought

1. What is a rite of passage, and what role does it play in our society?
2. How do crowds, cliques, and gangs affect conformity?
3. Describe the major tasks that adolescents face, according to Erik Erikson.

Critical Thinking

4. Describe a person who might, in terms of identity, be foreclosed in some ways and in a state of moratorium in other ways.

Intellectual and Moral Changes

Since adolescents must deal with such a staggering number of issues, it is fortunate that their thought processes and moral reasoning have reached their highest level. Agreement that general reasoning abilities reach their peak in adolescence is easily demonstrated. The most popular individual intelligence test for adults starts at age 16 (Wechsler, 1981). Also, as discussed in Chapter 10, Jean Piaget devised a theory of how thought processes progress as we mature. The last stage in Piaget's theory of cognitive development—formal operations—begins at age 11 or 12.

Piaget's Formal Operations Stage of Cognitive Development

In Piaget's theory of cognitive development, the **formal operations** stage includes the ability to reason in abstract ways—to consider the possibilities instead of thinking only in terms of concrete realities. Adolescents are capable of thinking in this way, of testing hypotheses. When asked such questions as "*If* such-and-such takes place, *then* what will happen?" most adolescents think through the outcomes in systematic, logical ways that were not possible before.

formal operations Piaget's term for the ability to reason in abstract ways and use complex thought processes

The ability to think abstractly helps the future become more real. Something that potentially exists is just as likely to be true as something that already does exist. With formal operations, we can deal with what might be, what could be, *if* certain things took place. Without formal operations, we are limited to the concrete, to the existing order of things.

Before reaching this level of abstract thinking, then, children see the world in concrete terms. Thus, if Mary got some extra money, so should Max—period. At the formal operations stage, however, the situation is seen differently. Suppose that Mary had been deprived while Max had had certain advantages earlier. The adolescent realizes that making up for past inequalities between the two is fair. Max does not need to get any money because justice demands that their situations be made more equal.

▲ *Adolescents are usually idealistic about the possibilities life has to offer.*

This high level of reasoning ability helps adolescents consider how the world could be a better place and why personal principles are sometimes more important than external rules and laws. Consequently, it is almost impossible to separate general cognitive abilities or thought processes from moral reasoning.

Kohlberg's Postconventional Level of Moral Reasoning

As explained in Chapter 10, Lawrence Kohlberg believed that moral development follows a maturational sequence. Individuals who have reached the **postconventional level** of moral reasoning make decisions about right and wrong according to basic principles. This holds true even if their actions must go beyond society's laws or authority's rules and regulations. Generally, this level of moral reasoning is not reached before middle or late adolescence.

postconventional level Kohlberg's last stage of moral development, in which personal ethics and human rights come into play

335

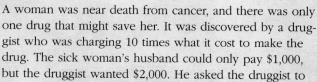

In Their Own Words . . .

*To study moral dilemmas, **Lawrence Kohlberg** asked children of different ages about made-up situations. The following is an example of one he used:*

A woman was near death from cancer, and there was only one drug that might save her. It was discovered by a druggist who was charging 10 times what it cost to make the drug. The sick woman's husband could only pay $1,000, but the druggist wanted $2,000. He asked the druggist to sell it cheaper or to let him pay later. The druggist said no. So the husband became desperate and broke into the store to steal the drug for his wife. Should he have done that? Was it wrong or right? Why? (Quoted in Coon, 1998.)

Interpreting Primary Sources

How would you answer the questions ending the selection above?

social contracts Kohlberg's term for agreements based on what's "best for everyone"

universal ethical principles Kohlberg's term for concepts such as justice and honor

Focus Question
....

- How does family structure affect adolescence?

Postconventional moral reasoning is subdivided into two stages. The first emphasizes **social contracts.** When people agree to something because they believe it is best for everyone involved, they are bound by this mutual agreement, or social contract.

The second stage operates according to **universal ethical principles.** Here, concepts like justice and honor are guidelines for right and wrong. This stage is the most complex and also the one least often reached by people.

Lawrence Kohlberg tested his theory by presenting moral dilemmas to people and asking them not only what they would do in the situation but why they would do it. It is the "why" that shows one's level of moral reasoning, not the "what." For instance, in the example in Chapter 10, a person could either save one rich man in a lifeboat or 10 poor men, but not both. The postconventional answer given was to save 10 poor men, because human life has value regardless of wealth.

It would be possible, though, to give another answer from the postconventional viewpoint. Suppose a person said the rich man should be saved because he could do more to improve the world through the proper use of his wealth than all the poor men put together. The final justification for this choice is that human life has value beyond the lives of the people in the lifeboat. This answer is also an example of postconventional moral reasoning.

The same principle is involved in both answers—the value of human life. It is the interpretation of how to apply the principle that differs. But the fact that complex interpretation is going on is the key to this level of moral development.

The Family's Influence on Adolescence

What Generation Gap?   We tend to take the existence of a serious "generation gap" for granted in this country. But does such a gap actually exist? And if so, is it as serious as we are led to believe? The topic of how parents and teenagers relate to one another raises a number of questions. As before, the answers are slightly different for early, middle, and late adolescence.

Adolescents have been said to live in an "intense present." As a result, death seems quite foreign, and it is not a part of their thoughts very often. The distant future is also excluded from this daily living process. These feelings can be explained by the fact that the majority of adolescents are not tied to major lifelong responsibilities. Without these concerns, only the immediate past and present remain in focus most of the time, particularly in early and middle adolescence. By late adolescence, the future takes on greater importance as high school graduation nears.

Close scrutiny of the adolescent value system shows that what has been absorbed to this point is thoroughly locked in. Goals, such as trying to make life more moral, saner, and more humane—all improvements badly needed—reflect basically the same ideals that are held by most adults. More often than not, parents and teenagers are on the same wavelength. Most parents, at one point in their own past, were aiming for the same thing, and those ideals are still there. For many adults, though, actually working toward those goals has become a less urgent priority over time.

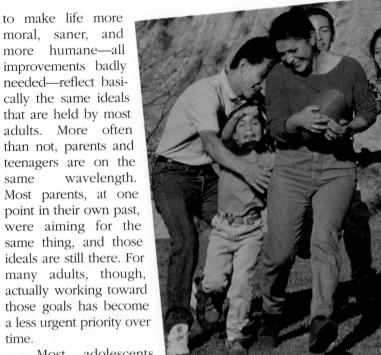

Overall, teenagers and their parents generally get along well together.

Most adolescents have a good and loving relationship with their parents. They share feelings of closeness and generally get along well together. As both parents and adolescents know, however, things do not always run smoothly at home. Research has shown that when children become teenagers, their parents, especially their mothers, experience greater stress, unhappiness, and dissatisfaction than at any other time.

Are Family Conflicts Necessary? Although the press has exaggerated the "generation gap," it is true that increased conflicts (arguing, nagging, and so forth) occur during a child's teenage years. This squabbling and bickering is at its worst in early adolescence—roughly between ages 11 and 14. During middle adolescence, it starts to decrease; and it usually is over for the most part by age 16. Late adolescence brings with it greater harmony with parents (Paikoff & Brooks-Gunn, 1991).

Conflicts occur even when teenagers and parents love each other and get along most of the time. Why is there so much arguing and bickering between them? Some researchers see conflicts between parents and their teenage children as both unavoidable and *necessary*.

Adolescence as a separate time given special emphasis is a fairly new idea. Many experts believe that it has only existed since the 1920s at the earliest. A century ago, many children left home when they hit puberty, and they began to work as apprentices for adults other than their parents. This was particularly true for boys. Among girls, sexual maturity occurred several years later than it does today. For most girls, sexual maturity meant marriage. And marriage meant leaving home (Degler, 1980).

It is only in the recent past that adolescents have remained at home, financially dependent on their parents, for several years beyond puberty. Many agree this is an economic necessity. Others suggest this situation may be an unnatural or artificial arrangement. Those who take this position point to animal behavior for support.

▲ *Some conflicts between teenagers and their parents are unavoidable.*

Among many primates who live in groups, the offspring leave their group when they are old enough to start their own families. If they don't, they are forced out by the adults. A similar situation occurs even among solitary animals like the cougar. Cougars are "loners." Adult cougars stay together long enough to reproduce, and then they go their separate ways. The female rears her young alone. When they start to mature, she makes them go out on their own. A young cougar who doesn't want to leave home will be attacked by its own mother until it finally gives up and goes away.

Do Conflicts Make Separation Easier? There is clearly a connection for various animals between sexual maturity, or puberty, and a "natural" desire to become independent of the family unit. Is there a similar connection for humans? Quite possibly there is. It has been noted, for instance, that tension between parents and teenagers is highest during puberty (Paikoff & Brooks-Gunn, 1991). It is to the advantage of the species for its young to establish homes and families of their own. Consequently, it may be that puberty in some way triggers conflicts in order to make the separation easier for both sides.

To see how this might work, consider one more example from animals that live in groups, wolves and chimpanzees. The increase in strength and size plus the additional adrenaline and sex hormones of puberty give young male wolves and chimpanzees a push to challenge the older, more senior males. By winning such a fight, a younger male can improve his standing in the group. "Adolescent" female chimpanzees seem to provoke irritation in their mothers and are competitors for the males' attentions. In other words, the physical changes of puberty create different attitudes in young animals *and* differences in how they are perceived by their elders (Goodall, 1971).

Most cultures with rituals that mark entrance into adulthood (rites of passage, discussed earlier) are very clear about this issue. Once puberty starts, the children leave home. In some, even before puberty, older children no longer sleep in the family home. They see their families during the day, but at night they are with other adults or in "dormitories" constructed just for this age group. When they reach puberty, they marry and establish their own households. The separation from the original family is complete.

These studies suggest that making children and parents live together beyond the point of "natural" separation means that conflicts are bound to occur. In the words of one expert: "If teenagers didn't argue with their parents, they might never leave home at all" (Steinberg, 1987, p. 39).

Case Study

Cliques

Two high school seniors discuss their experiences with cliques at school and how those experiences helped shape their identities.

In my school, the word *clique* has a very negative connotation, so I've tried to stay independent of them. Consequently, I have friends from many different groups. I can hang out with various crowds, remain neutral during fights within the groups, and start hanging out with new people at any time. Those are definitely benefits. On the flip side though, I am not immediately included in group activities for weekends and dances. I don't think it's that people don't want my company; it's just that they don't automatically think to invite me. In that respect, being independent can be rather lonely. The only time I feel connected and have a sense of belonging is during the run of a play when the cast and crew become really tight. My friends who are involved in sports say the same thing about their various sports seasons. During those few weeks the people involved in the same activity build a deep friendship if only for the duration of the activity.

Other than that, I am a bit of a chameleon. On my low days, it seems like this is a flashback from my early adolescence when I was a self-described "nerd." Mostly though, I realize that I chose this social situation. Each of my groups of friends fulfills a different need in my personality. When I see the groups around me, most all of the kids have known each other since junior high. I moved to my current high school during sophomore year when many of the groups were well established. I had no chance of creating the same comfort level and history that already existed amongst them.

—Kat Banakis

I'll admit it: freshman year went by without me having any real friends. I had several acquaintances, but in a school full of cliques, I was alone. I just didn't seem to fit in. However, as the years went by, I slowly developed several groups of friends. By senior year, I finally fit in. These strong groups helped me to understand exactly who I was by seeing the differences between myself and the others. Although I had a slow beginning, I was able to develop these tight bonds and a group identity which led to the realization of my self-identity.

While I've been able to identify myself socially, I am still searching for what I want to accomplish in my life. I've put down economics on those college applications as an intended major, but I'm still not sure if that is what I want. I suppose I'm in a state of searching and exploration. That worried me at first. I wanted to immediately decide what to become as an adult. But now I understand what a long process this is, and I am ready to continue to seek my niche in life in terms of my future job. So my advice to myself is not to worry. These things will come in time.

—Jeff Tsan

Review the Case Study

What are some of the advantages and disadvantages of belonging to a clique? What are the advantages and disadvantages of *not* belonging to a clique?

Focus Questions
....
- Why do some adolescents become juvenile delinquents, and others don't?
- Can delinquency be prevented?

juvenile delinquency repeated violations of the law by those aged 17 and younger

▲ *Gang members attending a "truce rally" in Los Angeles are searched before entering a high school gymnasium.*

Juvenile Delinquency

There is no question that our country today is a terribly violent one. Our homicide rate has doubled since 1950. In some urban areas, violence has become so common that most children living there have witnessed at least one violent crime within the past year (Osofsky, 1995).

Young people have played a role in this increased violence. Between 1981 and 1990, the number of adolescents arrested increased at a rate nearly 12 times higher than that for people over the age of 18. And the types of crimes committed by teenagers are more serious and more violent now than ever before (Yoshikawa, 1994).

Juvenile delinquency, the repeated violation of the law by those aged 17 and younger, is a serious problem in our society. In addition, juveniles who commit violent crimes or are substance abusers usually continue on this path well into their twenties (Buchanan, Eccles, & Becker, 1992). The cost, in human suffering and dollars, is staggering. Before looking for solutions, however, let us first consider what might influence such behavior.

Factors Associated with Delinquency

Psychologists have collected a great deal of information on juvenile delinquency. Before discussing their findings, though, we want to issue a word of warning. A number of characteristics are related to delinquency; these are factors that put adolescents at higher risk for getting into trouble. This does *not* mean that everyone with these characteristics is or will become a juvenile delinquent. Many, in fact, will overcome these obstacles and go on to lead productive lives. Furthermore, sometimes delinquency shows up where no risk factors are present. Thus, in some cases, the parents seem to be doing everything right, but the child has been difficult from the start and is always in trouble. In short, there are no perfect predictions in this area.

Many people believe that adolescents from low-income families are more likely to break the law. However, research shows that this is simply not the case. Income alone is not a factor (Hinshaw, 1992; Zigler et al., 1992). People also tend to believe that kids whose mothers work outside the home are more likely to get into trouble. Again, research shows this to be a myth. Interestingly, it appears that the father contributes more to his children's antisocial behavior than the mother does. A father who is aggressive, irresponsible, detached, and unaffectionate increases the risk of antisocial behavior in his children. When he has a history of criminal activity or substance abuse, the risk increases even more (Phares & Compas, 1992).

Delinquency, especially aggressive behavior, seems to grow best in an atmosphere of chaos, conflict, and discord far beyond the normal tensions that occur in most families. Poor communication, abusive relationships in the family, and little affection or support from the parents make the situation worse. Also, when parents fail to provide and enforce reasonable rules and guidelines, when they are not involved in their children's lives, the risk is greater still. All these factors increase the likelihood that an adolescent will both do poorly in school *and* get into trouble with the law (Hinsaw, 1992; Phares & Compas, 1992). And, like it or not, underachievement in school and delinquent behavior are related.

Preventive Programs

Many programs have been developed to deal with delinquency. Too many of them, though, are put into place after a delinquent behavior pattern has already been established. While some of these programs can still help adolescents turn themselves around, it is more difficult to produce change at such a late date.

Oddly enough, the most successful programs were not designed to deal with juvenile delinquency. They were set up to teach expectant mothers how to be better parents or to help troubled preschool children do better in school. Many years later, researchers discovered that these programs had an impact on the probability of future juvenile delinquency.

The families in these original programs were at high risk for trouble. At the time, psychologists were not sure exactly what factors were involved in delinquency. However, looking back, we can see that these families had many of the problem characteristics we just talked about.

The successful programs did several things. They provided parenting classes and group meetings for the parents. They included in-home visits to the families in which the families were taught how to solve problems. They helped find high-quality daycare services. They encouraged parents to participate in school activities and generally to become more involved in what their children were doing. Thus, nearly all the family issues associated with juvenile delinquency were dealt with, even though that was not the original goal.

▲ *Early parenting classes can help prevent delinquency later on.*

Years later, when these children had reached late adolescence or early adulthood, they were compared with a similar group that had not taken part in any preventive program. The results were clear and consistent. The children in the program were more likely to graduate from high school, go on to college, and have a stable job. Police records showed that there were far fewer arrests in this group, from one-fourth to one-half as many as in the comparison group. In addition, the arrests that did occur involved less serious offenses (Zigler et al., 1992).

 ## Pause for Thought

1. What cognitive changes occur during adolescence?
2. What kinds of moral reasoning become possible during adolescence?
3. In what ways is the term *generation gap* accurate? In what ways is it inaccurate?

Critical Thinking
....
4. This section describes what community programs have done to prevent juvenile delinquency. Using this information, describe what one household can do to prevent juvenile delinquency in that home.

APPLYING
Psychology to Life

Good Communication

The level of tension and conflict in any home comes from many different sources. One major cause of trouble is poor communication between teenagers and their parents. Most parents will never see this book, so we cannot deal directly with them. But since adolescents can change the way discussions take place, too, a few rules of good communication follow. Some of them may seem too obvious to bother with, yet very few people follow them, which causes no end of unnecessary problems.

Guide for Good Communication

1. Pick a convenient time and place to talk for *both* parties. An example of *not* following this rule is "Bob, get in here right now! I want to talk to you!" A different example: Bob tells his father he wants to talk to him. His father says, "Sure, I'll be finished with this in a couple of minutes." Bob gets mad and shouts, "Oh, never mind! You're always too busy to talk to me anyway, so just forget it, okay?" A better approach is "When you have a few minutes, there's some-

thing I want to talk about. How's right after dinner in the living room?" Be sure to set a specific time and place instead of leaving it open.

2. Be direct and clear when you speak, but also be polite rather than rude. If you're too subtle, your message won't get through; most people can't read minds. On the other hand, insults slam the door on communication. Amy tells her mother, "Your hair looks awful like that!" Laura says to her mother, "I saw a hairstyle

the other day that would look great on you. Here, take a look at this picture I cut out of a magazine. Isn't that terrific? It's made for you, I can tell." Which one would you rather listen to—and maybe even cooperate with?

3. Take responsibility for your own feelings and accept what the other person feels. Saying, "*You* make me so mad when . . ." puts the responsibility for your anger on the other person. Saying,

▲ *Mealtimes provide opportunities to practice good communication.*

"*I* get so mad when . . ." puts the responsibility where it belongs. An example of acceptance is "My doing that really bothers you, huh?" Nonacceptance is shown by "Well, I don't see why you're upset! What's the matter with you, anyway?" or "It's dumb to get so mad when it's not that big a deal." Try to understand that not everyone responds the same way to a particular situation.

4. Stick with the subject. This rule sounds so easy, but it is broken all the time. For instance: "Oh, yeah? Well, what about the time you . . .?" or "I just knew that's what you'd say. You always say that. I'm sick and tired of hearing it," or "I don't see why I can't have my friends over when I want to. What about Aunt Esther? You let *her* stay here for three weeks, *in my bedroom!*" It's impossible to avoid emotional reactions to a sensitive subject completely. The goal is to be alert and get the discussion back on track quickly.

5. Don't play the "blame game." Trying to decide who's at fault is very tempting. But it usually doesn't solve anything. Eventually, it may be important to figure out how (not how much) each person contributes to the problem so that changes can be made.

For the most part, though, it really doesn't matter who is more to blame. (Trust us!) The real point is that a problem needs to be solved. Looking at what needs changing rather than who is more responsible brings you closer to finding a workable solution.

6. Listen to what is being said. There are several parts to this rule. First, wait until the other person has finished speaking before you start thinking about your own reply. Second, never interrupt unless you honestly don't understand; if you don't understand, ask direct questions. Third, try to rephrase in your own mind what the other person is saying. Fourth, open your mind to the possibility that you may not have "heard it all before."

Practice Helps

Remember that following these rules will not solve every

problem. Sometimes, even with excellent communication, people still find themselves disagreeing.

After you have a basic understanding of these rules, try them out with a couple of friends or classmates. Everyone takes a turn at playing each of three parts: the speaker, the listener, and the referee (the "official" who decides when a rule has been broken). The subject you choose to talk about is up to you. However, the more strongly you feel about a topic, the more likely you are to break the rules of good communication.

Guidelines for Good Communication

1. Choose a time and place convenient and appropriate for both parties.

2. Be direct but polite. Rudeness cuts off communication.

3. Acknowledge your feelings and the feelings of the other person. Use "I" messages.

4. Keep the discussion focused on the issue at hand. Don't bring in past history.

5. Name calling and placing blame prevent problem solving. Look for how you can contribute to the solution.

6. Listen carefully to what is being said. Don't interrupt. State in your own words what you think the other person is saying.

Summary

1. Physical growth in adolescence includes sexual development during puberty, which is controlled by the pituitary gland and hormones from the adrenal glands and gonads. Changes during puberty include maturation of the reproductive system, voice changes, breast development, and changes in facial and body hair.

2. During the adolescent growth spurt, girls may grow as much as three inches in one year; boys, as much as four inches. Growth spurts happen earlier in girls. In general, early maturation is an advantage for boys but not for girls, while late maturation is a problem for boys but not for girls.

3. Excessive concern about weight can lead to eating disorders, especially among female adolescents. In bulimia nervosa, the person binges on food and then purges the food from the system. In anorexia nervosa, the person stops eating and maintains a dangerously low weight.

4. Belonging to a group helps adolescents feel less alone and is a first step toward developing a sense of identity. Conformity to groups is highest in early adolescence. By the end of middle adolescence, it has begun to fall rapidly.

5. Crowds are fairly loose in structure and membership. Cliques are small, rigidly defined groups whose members share school-related interests. Gangs are small, rigidly defined groups with a rebellious or antisocial outlook; members share similar out-of-school interests. Those who do not have a group identity feel alienated from others.

6. Erik Erikson viewed adolescence as a time for developing a sense of identity. This means not only deciding who you are but also becoming committed to personal goals and values. During identity formation, a moratorium occurs, delaying adult commitments so that adolescents have the opportunity to experiment with different roles. Achieving an identity includes developing fidelity, or loyalty to one's values and beliefs as well as to people one cares about. Failure to achieve an identity results in identity confusion.

7. James Marcia described four identity states. Foreclosure occurs when adolescents make identity decisions based on the identity and values given them in childhood by other people. Identity diffusion exists when adolescents have an unclear sense of self and have stopped trying to find themselves. Moratorium involves trying out a number of possibilities. Identity achievement includes a clear definition of self and a commitment to the future.

8. During the formal operations stage, abstract thinking and logic are developed. Reasoning is systematic, and possibilities as well as realities can be carefully considered. Postconventional moral reasoning involves the application of social contracts or universal ethical principles to determine right and wrong.

9. Most adolescents have a good relationship with their parents. Nevertheless, tension and conflict between parents and children are highest when the children are adolescents. Some researchers believe this is part of a natural separation process that occurs among animals and in more primitive cultures. The greatest conflict arises when the adolescent reaches puberty.

10. Juvenile delinquency is a serious problem in our society. Among the factors contributing to juvenile delinquency are a chaotic and conflict-laden family life, poor communication, and abuse, as well as lack of support, affection, and involvement from the parents. Preventive programs attempt to educate and encourage parents while the children are still small.

Vocabulary

adolescence	late maturer	group identity versus	diffusion
puberty	eating disorders	alienation	identity achievement
hormones	bulimia nervosa	identity	formal operations
pituitary gland	anorexia nervosa	identity confusion	postconventional level
adrenal glands	rite of passage	moratorium	social contracts
gonads	crowds	fidelity	universal ethical
growth spurt	clique	foreclosure	principles
early maturer	gang	negative identity	juvenile delinquency

Review Questions

On a sheet of paper, answer E for early adolescence, M for middle adolescence, and L for late adolescence for each statement.

1. Don't care about what others wear
2. Highest level of arguing with parents
3. Females much more mature than males
4. A 15-year-old
5. Females slightly more mature than males
6. Less fighting, more harmony between adolescents and parents

True/False

On a sheet of paper, answer true or false for each statement. If false, rewrite to make it true.

7. Nearly 10 percent of our sexual maturation occurs during puberty.
8. Early adolescence is a time of maximum physical growth for females but not for males.
9. An early-maturing boy generally has a higher self-concept than an early-maturing girl.
10. Both the clique and the gang have strict rules for how to behave.
11. Statistics show that adolescents from low-income families are more likely to break the law.

Fill in the Blank

On a sheet of paper, write the word or words that best complete each statement.

12. A ceremony or ritual marking the entry into adulthood is called a ▓▓▓.
13. According to some psychologists, the main issue in early adolescence is group identity versus ▓▓▓.
14. Erik Erikson sees the main issue in adolescence as identity versus ▓▓▓.
15. Sticking with your beliefs is called ▓▓▓.
16. Delaying commitments to beliefs and values is called ▓▓▓.

Matching

On a sheet of paper, match the term from the list in the right column with the description in the left column.

17. Has no identity and has stopped trying to find one
18. Makes decisions about identity too soon
19. Trial-and-error period
20. Has a well-defined self-concept

a. foreclosure
b. identity achievement
c. diffusion
d. moratorium

345

Discussion Questions

1. The chapter explains that in our society, it's difficult to determine exactly when adolescence ends. Do you think you'd rather have the end of adolescence more clearly defined, or do you prefer it loosely defined as it is now? Why?

2. If you could be considered, as of this moment, a full-fledged, 100 percent, certified adult, would you want that? Discuss.

3. Consider a 15-year-old from a primitive society who becomes an adult after an elaborate ceremony or ritual (rite of passage). Does this 15-year-old, since he is considered an adult and since he considers himself an adult, experience the same conflicts and frustrations that most adolescents in industrialized society experience? Explain.

4. Most of us at one time or another have been a part of a clique, whether we realized it or not. Why do people form cliques? Explain. Do cliques serve any positive or worthwhile functions? Explain.

5. Marcia acknowledges that part of an individual's identity may be foreclosed, another part achieved, and so on. For example, an individual may make a firm and personally meaningful commitment to career and achieve identity in this area; but this same individual may wander and be diffused in matters of religion. Pick three of the four identity states and explain how you might fit into each category at this stage in your life.

6. Surveys have shown that teenagers and adults agree on important issues such as education, work, politics, and drugs. If you and your parents were surveyed on these four areas, what would the results be? Where would agreement be high? Where would it be not so high?

7. Most experts agree that adolescence is longer today than it was 50 or 60 years ago. One reason is that young people remain home longer than they once did. Can you think of any other factors contributing to the lengthening of adolescence?

8. No matter how well we get along with our parents as adolescents, there comes a time when we need to break away and assert our own independence. There are several ways in which we do this, some of them deliberate and intentional and some of them not so intentional. Describe several ways you use or have used to break away from your parents. Briefly describe your parents' reactions.

9. Read through the rules of communication listed at the end of the chapter. Which ones seem to be hardest for you to follow? Which rules are you good at? Explain.

Activities and Projects

1. Find several songs that focus on a single adolescent issue or concern, such as identity, friendship, confusion, relationships with parents, or the like. The audience for a particular song may very well be adults, but if you believe the song relates to adolescents for some reason, then use it. Take portions of the songs and weave them into a medley that focuses on a single theme. This probably goes without saying, but be creative. Let's say you find five songs that all include the line, "I need." Taping all these back to back might be effective. Or include your own voice between songs. Or include some of your own lyrics. Hand in your tape, the lyrics, and a paragraph explaining what all this means to you.

2. Create a public service announcement that teaches an audience of parents about some issue concerning adolescents. The final product can be a poster with colorful illustrations and captions or a brief video segment. You can teach parents why it's so important to respect your privacy, or how to talk to you, or why you need your independence. If several classmates complete this project, maybe you

can arrange for parents to visit class one day so you can present these public service announcements to a real audience. Imagine the lively discussion that could result from this activity!

3. Write a short scene, about 50 lines or so, between a parent and an adolescent. The scene should focus on some conflict the two of them are trying to resolve. Don't feel you need to explain the entire situation to your audience right from the beginning. A little suspense is OK; the audience will catch up with you. The conflict can involve something relatively simple, like a curfew, or a more serious issue, such as leaving home. Recruit a classmate to help you perform your scene for the rest of the class. Or recruit two classmates and direct.

4. James Marcia insists that actively searching for values, beliefs, and goals is essential to forming a meaningful identity. We want you to do some of your own searching. To do this, we want you to answer three main questions:

   a. "Who am I?"
   What are some of your major beliefs and values today? What are some of your strengths and weaknesses?

   b. "Where do I come from?"
   Describe several experiences from your past that have helped shape your personality. Describe the important people who have had an impact on your life.

   c. "Where am I going?"
   What are some of your career goals? Personal growth goals? What are some of your fears about the future?

   The questions listed under the three main questions are merely suggestions. You need not address every one of them. This is one of those assignments that, if taken seriously, you can refer back to in years to come and really appreciate. (Trust us!)

5. Often, cliques acquire stereotypical names: jocks, burnouts, brains, and so on. List the names of the cliques at your school and copy this list onto five other sheets of paper. Next, find five "strangers" or acquaintances at school (not close friends), and

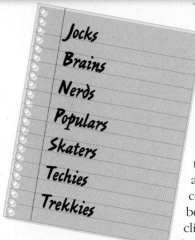

Jocks
Brains
Nerds
Populars
Skaters
Techies
Trekkies

show each of them your list. After each clique, have them write down the following: (a) what a person needs to do in order to be admitted to the clique and (b) what is considered proper behavior within the clique. Without looking at their answers, follow the same procedure yourself.

Finally, compare the lists. We don't want you to use friends for this activity because your friends' perceptions of the cliques will most likely be similar to yours. We want to discover whether "strangers" have the same perception of certain cliques as you do. Do they? Explain.

If you want to be bold, show your list to a member of one of the cliques you described on your sheet. Does this person feel your perceptions are accurate?

6. This activity will give your parents a chance to reminisce about their own adolescence. (If your parents are unavailable, find someone who would be about the same age as your parents.) Have your parents think back on their adolescent years, and have them make a list of things that an adolescent needed to do in order to be "cool" (or what it meant to be "uncool"). Ask them to include at least 10 to 15 items. Without looking at their list, write your own list of things an adolescent needs to do today in order to be "cool." Again, try to think of at least 10 to 15 items.

   Compare and contrast the two lists. What are some similarities and differences? Based on the lists, would you say that the period called adolescence has changed much in the past 20 or 30 years? Explain. Finally, show the two lists to your parents and discuss their reactions to the lists.

347

T he mental and social skills developed during childhood and adolescence have been more or less a training ground for what is to follow. Many problems have not been fully resolved. In adulthood, the time comes to try to bring everything together into a whole.

Adulthood and Aging

Defining Adulthood

In our society, once people over the age of 18 become self-sufficient and self-supporting, they are usually considered adults. However, adulthood is not just one time of life but many. For example, a 21-year-old and a 45-year-old have very different concerns, abilities, needs, and goals. Adulthood, then, can be divided into different periods. Officially, there is no real agreement regarding when these periods occur. For convenience, we will call the ages from 20 through 39 early adulthood, from 40 through 59 middle adulthood, and from 60 on late adulthood.

As we discuss age ranges, remember that they are arbitrary. A person's actual age may well be less important than that person's experiences and outlook on life. The problems and activities that belong to one age group or another are only generalizations, and not everyone will fit into these neat categories. This is especially true in our present society, since people live longer and healthier lives. As time goes on, the categories of "middle age" and "old age" apply to later and later periods of life.

Focus Question
....
• For most young adults, what are the main concerns?

Early Adulthood: 20–39

Although some start earlier and others later, sometime during their 20s and 30s, most people take on the adult responsibilities of marriage, career, and children. A sense of identity is gained through these duties, and this makes young adults more stable and less insecure than adolescents. They are more emotionally invested in the welfare of other people, particularly their spouses and children. They take responsibility seriously, and they can make personal decisions about their own lives—something they have wanted to do for years.

Marriage and Divorce

Despite the somewhat shaky image of the institution of marriage, most people marry and expect the marriage to last. For about half of these couples, that expectation will be realized. No one knows exactly what it is that makes any particular marriage work. Sometimes, the most unlikely combinations are wonderful successes. And in this brief space, there is little we can say on the subject.

However, we do want to mention one critical ingredient—mutual respect, a term that encompasses a great deal. *Respect* means that you view others as important people, paying attention to them and seeing their ideas, abilities, needs, and wants as meaningful and worthwhile. *Mutual respect* means that two people both give *and* receive respect. It means that you treat the other person with consideration, not demeaning or insulting him or her. This quality does not guarantee success. However, without mutual respect, a marriage simply cannot work.

The days of *The Donna Reed Show, Leave It to Beaver,* and *Father Knows Best* are definitely over. Less than 10 percent of the American population is made up of married couples with children, with only the father employed. Among the majority of couples today, both work outside the home.

▲ *Being middle-aged now doesn't mean what it did decades ago.*

For those who divorce, the odds are overwhelming that the mother will have custody of the children. Roughly 90 percent of single-parent families are made up of mothers and their children. Customarily, the fathers have visitation rights and the obligation of child support. Only about half the time, though, do the children actually receive all the support the courts have ordered. In too many cases, both the amount of support paid and the frequency of visitation start to decrease two or three years after the divorce (Silverstein, 1996; Levant, 1992).

The effects on the children, both financially and psychologically, are not good. They often feel abandoned or rejected by their father if he is no longer involved in their lives. Perhaps these fathers do not realize how important they really are. In any event, divorcing parents can ease the heartache immensely by focusing on the children instead of each other, and by refusing to allow visitation, child support, or the children themselves to be used as pawns.

Family Life

While their careers may also be important, most young adult women, according to statistics, focus more on their families. Whatever changes may have occurred in our society, it is still true that most women are distressed by the prospect of reaching the age of 30 *un*married (Kaslow, 1992). In a marriage, women take care of more family obligations than men do, and they make more personal adjustments to the needs of their husbands than vice versa. Women do most of the child care as well (Denmark, 1992). Young women today face conflicts and stressors that simply did not exist a few decades ago. Because most married women work outside the home, they are often torn between their obligations to their jobs and their obligations to their families (Ozer, 1995; McWilliams, 1992).

So where is the man all this time? Well, he is doing more than men formerly did. In early adulthood, men still tend to focus mostly on their careers, but they are also more involved in their family lives than used to

▶ *Most single-parent families are headed by women.*

be the case. They spend more time with their children and are less likely to always let the job come first. For instance, a few years ago, it would have been almost unthinkable for a man to ask for special consideration at work in order to take care of a fairly routine family matter. Now such a request is not unusual. Lest we get too carried away, though, the changes have not been great. In the 1960s, men whose wives were employed did about 20 percent of the work around the house, including taking care of the children. By the early 1990s, that figure had moved up to around 25 percent—not exactly an astounding increase (Ozer, 1995; Levant, 1992).

There is no question that young families experience high levels of stress trying to "do it all." While that stress is felt more keenly by women, men feel it, too. This stress affects not only the family, but also the job as well. In fact, this work-family conflict is sufficiently great that many experts now strongly recommend that employers provide more support and help for their employees (Adams & Jex, 1999).

It seems that our society is somewhat hypocritical in its attitude toward parenting. On the one hand, it urges parents to devote themselves to their children. On the other hand, it provides few rewards for doing so and makes few allowances for the difficulties involved in raising a family. In many European countries, businesses routinely provide family leave and day care to their employees. Here, however, that is the exception rather than the rule.

▲ *Men today are more involved in family life than ever before.*

Midlife Transition

Young adults eventually enter middle adulthood, but the progression is not always smooth. Serious questions about the real meaning of life arise. The ups and downs that can occur indicate that a person has entered the midlife transition.

In the United States, the age of 40 signals the true beginning of "middle age." At some point in their late 30s or early 40s, then, most people begin to reexamine their lives. They look closely at the direction their lives have taken and make decisions about where they want to be in the future. Of course, this happens at other ages as well. However, in midlife, there is often a sense of urgency involved.

As people realize that they are no longer young, they begin to think in terms of how many years they have left. They start to focus on signs of physical decline and an awareness of aging. There is no question that things are not as they used to be. Their parents are becoming truly old. Their children may be almost grown. Perhaps a few friends have had heart attacks. The days of a wide-open future, with endless possibilities, are over. All of these facts contribute to feelings of vulnerability and uncertainty.

In Their Own Words . . .

Daniel J. Levinson *is an American researcher who studied men's development in adulthood. He describes the male midlife transition below:*

A number of changes commonly occurring at around 40 intensify the sense of aging. A man experiences some of these changes as minor and takes them in stride, but others strike with great impact, arousing his anxieties about getting old and confronting him with his own mortality.

One important change . . . is the decline in bodily and psychological powers. In his late thirties and early forties, a man falls well below his earlier peak levels of functioning. He cannot run as fast, lift as much, do with as little sleep as before. His vision and hearing are less acute, he remembers less well and finds it harder to learn masses of specific information. He is more prone to aches and pains and may undergo a serious illness that threatens him with permanent impairment or even death. These changes vary widely in their severity and their effects on a man's life. Reduced strength and agility may be less distressing to an accountant than to a professional athlete (or a fierce competitor at tennis who cannot bear to lose his standing on the local ladder).

The decline is normally quite moderate and leaves a man with ample capacities for living in middle age. But it is often experienced as catastrophic. A man fears that he will soon lose all the youthful qualities that make life worthwhile. When youth is totally lost, all that is left is to be totally old. (Levinson, 1978, pp. 213–214)

Interpreting Primary Sources

Some men compensate for bodily decline by remaining active in less strenuous activities. For example, a baseball player may take up golf. What are some other ways men may compensate for the decline in bodily and psychological powers?

Focus Question

* What physical and psychological issues do people face during middle adulthood?

As bad as this may sound to you, not everyone becomes miserable and depressed. For some people, this is a time for reassessing life's goals and refocusing energies on new interests and activities. For others, though, it is a time of terrible upheaval and loss of purpose, when they seriously question many of the values by which they have lived. Many people do experience some confusion, insecurity, and dissatisfaction during this transition, but a so-called midlife *crisis* is not inevitable.

Middle Adulthood: 40–59

Up to middle adulthood, most women have been primarily involved with their families and most men with their careers. During this middle period, however, priorities seem to shift, and men and women reverse their focus. Perhaps because midlife is a time of reassessment and taking stock, they discover aspects of themselves that have been neglected, and they seek to give these aspects expression. This is potentially one of the best times of life.

In general, men begin to appreciate their more "feminine" characteristics and women their more "masculine" ones (McGrath, 1992). Beginning sometime in their mid-40s, men become more emotionally expressive and warm, more giving of themselves than before. Relationships begin to be more important than career or money. At the same time, women are growing more independent and assertive, more determined to go out on their own and do what they want to do instead of making so many compromises for the family.

For a while, this situation can create conflicts. As the husband turns to his family to develop his more tender side, the wife is out pursuing her own interests. The children, nearly grown, often have little need or desire for closer contact. Thus, the man may feel betrayed and unnecessary. The woman, on the other hand, may resent his demands coming at a time when she is finally free to accomplish what she wants on her own.

For many people in their 40s, marital satisfaction is at an all-time low. For some couples, these conflicts will be serious enough to end the marriage. It is true that most divorces take place relatively early in the marriage, usually in the first six or seven years. However, about one-sixth of divorces occur among those age 45 or older (Wainrib, 1992a).

If people can be patient and tolerant, they will get a breather, so to speak. Marital conflicts don't have to last or cause real harm. The late 40s and 50s are a time when people become calmer and more accepting both of the changes in their lives and of each other. In fact, by their mid-50s (and beyond), men tend to see women as more powerful and dominant than men, a reversal of what was true in their youth (Belsky, 1992; Gutmann, 1987).

Some have called this decade the "mellow 50s," the prime of life. Friends and earlier values become increasingly important; the dreams and goals of earlier years mellow into more realistic hopes. People generally are more satisfied with life. There is often a sense of relief that the struggle to achieve is less urgent. Marriages grow more settled, and people begin to sense a greater mastery over their personal world. Feelings of increased freedom and self-worth are common.

In Focus

"Typical" Early and Middle Adulthood Tasks

	"Typical" Male		"Typical" Female
EARLY ADULTHOOD (20–39)	Focuses on career but more involved with family than in past Still does only about 25 percent of housework		Takes care of more family obligations Does most of the child care
MIDLIFE TRANSITION	Feels a sense of urgency Focuses on physical decline Appreciates his feminine side		Feels a sense of urgency Focuses on physical decline Appreciates her masculine side
MIDDLE ADULTHOOD (40–59)	Becomes more emotionally expressive, warm, and giving During 40s, marital satisfaction at all-time low During 50s, mellowing occurs		Becomes more assertive and independent During 40s, marital satisfaction at all-time low During 50s, mellowing occurs

During middle adulthood, why do men tend to become more emotionally expressive, and why do women tend to become more assertive?

▲ *The "empty nest" can be a happy place to be.*

empty-nest period the time of life when one's children have grown and moved away from home

menopause the "change of life" period for women, when menstruation and ovulation stop; physical symptoms include dizziness and "hot flashes"

The Empty-Nest Period

At the beginning of this century, most women were widowed within two years of the marriage of their last child; thus, virtually all of their married life was spent rearing children. Now, most women who are finished with active motherhood still have 40 percent of their lives left to live, and most couples will be together another 10 to 20 years (Wainrib, 1992a; Degler, 1980).

The **empty-nest period** is the time of life after the children leave home. It has been suggested that some parents, mothers especially, feel useless and depressed when the children leave and the "nest" is empty. While this period does bring major changes, the concept that such feelings are inevitable has been discarded. Most studies now show that the majority of women do not have these feelings. In fact, most marriages improve and most parents are happier once the children are gone.

Nonetheless, some women do suffer from the problem. Most often, they are people who have led rather restricted lives, lack intimate contacts outside the home, and have few interests or activities of their own. In addition, their marriages tend to be not all that great, so they have little to fall back on.

Menopause

At some time in their late 40s to early 50s, women go through a period commonly called the "change of life," or **menopause.** Menstruation and ovulation gradually stop as the result of a dramatic decline in the production of female hormones. Physical symptoms include "hot flashes," dizziness, insomnia, perspiring or "night sweats," and occasional heart palpitations. Some women experience menopausal acne. In addition, postmenopausal women are at higher risk of developing heart disease and/or brittle bones.

Medically replacing the lost female hormone can alleviate these symptoms, but this procedure is still considered controversial by many. Some argue that all women as a matter of course should receive this hormonal therapy. Others believe that caution is called for because we do not yet have enough information about the therapy's long-term effects.

Much has been made of the psychological problems associated with menopause, but again they are exaggerated. Only a small number of women find it necessary to seek psychological help. Contrary to earlier beliefs, studies show that the likelihood of depression actually goes down, not up; the rate of depression among women in this age group is lower than that for younger women.

It seems that more problems arise from society's ideas about what menopause is like than from the transition itself. Traditionally, women's value to society has declined when they are no longer able to bear children. Fortunately, however, there are clear signs that this attitude is changing.

Late Adulthood: 60 and Older

As we grow older, we become more philosophical. We attempt to bring the pieces of our lives together, to reflect on all that we have done, and to see ourselves as part of the cycle of life on Earth. Some of the major tasks we face include adjusting to an increased number of deaths among friends, accepting what we have not been able to do, and preparing for our own eventual death. Most older people take comfort in what they have accomplished and appreciate the fact that they will leave something of themselves behind.

According to 1990 census data, there are approximately 32 million people aged 65 and older in this country, and the percentage of the population in that age range is increasing steadily. In the mid-1980s, people over 60 outnumbered teenagers for the first time in our history. It is projected that by the year 2030, one in five people will be at least 65 years of age. Average life expectancy at birth is about 75 years, or nearly 30 years longer than it was in the early 1900s. However, women who have already made it into their 50s can expect to live another 30 years. Women live roughly six years longer than men, and the majority of women over 65 are widows. By age 80, there are three women for every man; 36 percent of men this age are married, but only 6 percent of the women are (Wainrib, 1992a).

Along with the great increase in the number of older people has come a major expansion in a branch of psychology called **gerontology** (jer-un-TALL-uh-jee), which is the study of aging and older people. Gerontologists study the aging process and the psychological difficulties associated with it. The following sections describe some of the findings of their research.

▲ *Advanced age is no barrier to having a good time.*

gerontology the branch of psychology that studies the aging process and the problems of older people

Pause for Thought

1. What are some ingredients that help keep a marriage together?
2. How do men and women differ in their roles in the family?
3. What ranges of responses do people have during the midlife transition?

Critical Thinking
....

4. One family friend has become depressed during middle adulthood; another is fine. Offer possible explanations.

Thinking Critically about Psychology

Stereotypes of the Elderly

I t has been noted that we have more stereotypes about old people than about any other age group. For instance, we tend to assume that the elderly are stuck in the past (which is not true) and that they are much less competent in every way than younger people.

The stereotype of growing old in our country includes an image of becoming forgetful and absent-minded. Mental functions, according to this image, inevitably undergo a serious decline in old age. This all seems to imply that the aging process actually causes such declines. Is this true?

What specifically is being claimed or stated? The aging process causes mental abilities to decline.

What is the objective evidence for and against this claim? Just as bodily processes slow down with age, certain mental processes seem to slow slightly. But we have to be careful about assuming that all older people automatically lose significant cognitive ability. Most evidence suggests that this is not the case. In animals and human beings, substantial memory deficits occur only in a minority. The decline is most evident in tasks that are learned under pressure within a certain time limit and in things recently learned. Thus, older people do seem to take longer to process information and may have more trouble holding information in short-term memory (Verhaeghen & Salthouse, 1997). However, long-term memory tends to remain intact. Further, the decline generally does not begin to appear until about age 70.

What other interpretations might be made instead? If aging doesn't automatically cause declines in mental ability, what might cause the problems that we do sometimes see in older people? Health is an important factor. For example, medical conditions such as diabetes and high blood pressure frequently interfere with cognitive functions (Zelinski et al., 1998), and mental abilities show a sharp decline when death is not far away (Small & Baeckman, 1997). Old people in

▲ *John Glenn, former astronaut and current United States Senator, does not fit our stereotypes of older people.*

good health do about as well on learning tasks as younger people, as long as no time limit is imposed. In addition, some older people have experienced ministrokes without even knowing it; and this kind of injury can have effects on learning and memory. Usually, then, when serious memory problems occur in older people, they are more often due to disease or injury than to the effects of aging itself.

See if COOL works for you....

Claim?

What are the most logical conclusions to draw? The original statement is partially true. Speed of information processing and short-term memory do tend to decline somewhat with aging. However, serious declines in mental ability among older people are usually caused by factors other than aging.

Remaining active and involved with others is a key ingredient to successful aging.

Objective evidence for and against claim?

Other interpretations?

Logical conclusions?

Applying Critical Thinking Skills

Think about four or five people over the age of 60 who are in good health. They might be relatives of yours or the grandparents of close friends. Do any of them fit the stereotype of the "forgetful oldster"?

The Aging Process

Aging in our country is a real challenge because as a culture we put a premium on youthfulness—to a ridiculous degree. We spend a lot of money on products designed to help us deny or hide the fact that we are getting older. While ours is not the first civilization to struggle with the facts of aging, we may deserve an award for being the most blatant about it. People in other countries fight aging, but most recognize that older people may have grown wiser from their vast experience and should be valued and sought out for this wisdom. Many Americans do not share this attitude.

Cellular Time Clocks

The life span for each species is preprogrammed. Within a given species—horse, elephant, human, mosquito—each creature seems to have a fixed length of time on Earth.

We mentioned earlier that average life expectancy for people in the United States is greater today than in the past. However, individual people are not really living *longer* than people in the past did. Instead, *more* people are living into old age.

In other words, a person who was able to avoid serious disease or injury in the 1800s had roughly the same chance of living to about age 70 as a person today. The big difference is that today fewer people die at young ages from disease or during childbirth. Unless we can figure out a method for controlling age by some manipulation of genes, humans will still die at sometime around 110 to 115 years, even if all diseases are eradicated (Papalia, Camp, & Feldman, 1996).

As we age, our bodily functions slow down, problems with vision and hearing are likely to get worse, and we are more prone to disease and injury. Indications are that this occurs because body cells have internal "time clocks" that dictate how long each particular type of cell will continue to function and replace itself. Toward the end of the life span of a member of any species, the cells have notably deteriorated.

In a fascinating study, researchers found that individual cells have a strict limit on the number of times they will divide through the course of a creature's life. In fact, if cells are allowed to divide a few times and then are frozen for a period, when they are thawed, they will continue dividing up to the same fixed number of times—no more, no less (Hayflick, 1994). This built-in limit on cell division also limits how much we can increase the life span by eliminating diseases. But a new line of research has emerged. Researchers are now trying to find a way to extend the life of cells themselves by changing their time clocks. If this could be done, not only would people live longer, but many physical effects of aging would simply disappear. So far this approach hasn't gotten anywhere, but who knows what the future will bring?

▲ *Different species have different internal "time clocks." The adult mayfly's cells are pre-set to last for only a few hours; the Giant Galapagos Tortoise can live nearly 200 years.*

Mental Ability of Older People

As the Critical Thinking in Psychology feature points out, declines in mental functions, such as memory, are by no means an inevitable part of old age. However, when older people *do* experience trouble with memory, it is very distressing and frustrating for them, it has a strong negative effect on their self-concepts, and it causes anxiety and depression (Hulicka, 1978).

There are hints that in time we may be able to correct many memory problems of this sort. We know that the number of nerve cells in the brain decreases with age, but this may not be the real source of the trouble, since we have so many of them to begin with. In fact, for the typical older person, the brain has shrunk only about 8 percent from its original size by the age of 75.

Instead, studies with aged animals and humans show that the more important loss involves chemicals that are used to communicate from one cell to another. The first "brain transplants" performed involved taking tissue from the adrenal glands, which produce this nerve cell chemical, and placing it inside the brain. While this is probably not the final answer, a number of people gained improved memory from the process.

One often-neglected consideration is nutrition. Many older people get so fed up with fixing meals for three-quarters of a century or so that they don't eat as well as they should in their later years. In other chapters of the book, we have mentioned how disastrous poor nutrition is for the mental development of children and adolescents. The same is true for older people, only here we are not dealing with development as much as with preservation of the brain cells.

▲ *Good nutrition is critically important for good mental ability.*

Intelligence and Aging. Old age does not *automatically* bring a decline in intellectual ability or achievement. In many cases, when standard IQ tests are used, older people do not score as high as younger people do, but the reasons may not have to do with intelligence itself.

For one thing, those who take such tests may be trying too hard to succeed and may be highly anxious. For another, the test items are usually in a format too small for many older people to see and to handle with comfort. The test is not supposed to be a measure of a person's vision. But most of all, the IQ test is designed to measure school potential, and that clearly is not relevant to older people.

Most experiments aimed specifically at older people show it is incorrect to assume that intelligence declines with age. As we've already mentioned, an older person's memory is intact for the most part. Individuals who were bright and active in youth tend to be the same in old age. Most of the time, when you run into an older person who is irritable, stubborn, and rigid, you will find that he or she was also this way when young. Such behavior is usually not the result of aging itself.

Senile Dementia. Many older people are labeled *senile,* a term that is not very flattering. But it doesn't mean what most people think it means. *Senility* simply refers to the state of being old. The proper diagnosis for diminished mental faculties resulting from aging is **senile dementia** (deh-MEN-sha). It is the word *dementia* that refers to the loss of mental capacity, not the word *senile.*

senile dementia loss of mental faculties in old age

359

cerebral arteriosclerosis blockage of blood vessels to the brain; it can result in loss of mental faculties

Alzheimer's disease a disease involving loss of chemical nerve cell transmitters and other damage to nerve transmission that results in mental deterioration

Many believe that senile dementia is inevitable with age. This is not the case. Only disease can result in changes sufficiently dramatic to have such an effect. *Genuine* senile dementia occurs in only 23 percent of the aged population. Of that 23 percent, only 3 percent are affected by age 70. To account for the remaining 20 percent, you must go all the way to 100 years of age.

Substantial brain changes can and do result from a blockage of the blood vessels going to the brain—a condition called **cerebral arteriosclerosis** (ar-teer-ee-oh-skluh-ROH-sis). The major cause of senile dementia, though, is **Alzheimer's** (ALTS-high-mers) **disease.**

Alzheimer's results from a loss of the chemicals used to fire the brain cells. This, in turn, can cause debris to form in the brain. The disease most often seems to arise from a genetic defect. Over time, it leads to disruption of speech, personality, memory, and body control. The risk of Alzheimer's increases greatly with advanced age, and most people with the condition are over 80 years old. There are drugs that can help with the symptoms and slow the progressive deterioration somewhat, but at present there is no cure (Papalia, Camp, & Feldman, 1996).

There is a tendency in too many cases to label older people as having senile dementia even when there is no evidence of brain damage. Brain damage is *very* hard to diagnose without evidence of disease or injury. The tragic aspect of all this is that a number of quite treatable ailments can produce the same symptoms.

Somewhere between 15 and 30 percent of those diagnosed as having senile dementia in reality are suffering from other problems. Among them are depression, alcoholism, vitamin deficiencies, and the misuse of prescription medicines. Far too often, when the patient is old, no one bothers to make a thorough examination. This neglect is probably a reflection of our youth-oriented culture, at least in part.

▲ *Alzheimer's disease, like many other diseases, has received much more public attention and research funding after a famous person is known to have the problem.*

 Pause for Thought

1. What do gerontologists study? What have gerontologists discovered about cellular time clocks?
2. In what ways do cognitive abilities decline in old age, and in what ways do these abilities remain stable?

Critical Thinking
....
3. Pretend you know someone in late adulthood who has been a little forgetful lately. This person asks you about senility and Alzheimer's disease. What could you say that might reassure the person that he or she is probably fine?

Concerns in Late Adulthood

Research shows that survival in old age is clearly related to having minimal physical and economic dependence on others. In other words, complete reliance on others is the worst thing that can happen to old people. When this occurs, they feel trapped because they can no longer make the changes they want; they no longer have *choice*. Most older people desire self-sufficiency, as well as some degree of freedom and activity. Their needs are clearly tied to the most basic fears they have: (1) poor health; (2) social isolation; and (3) a loss of feeling meaningful to society (Wainrib, 1992a, 1992b).

Retirement

Most people look forward to retirement, and most retired people like their new lives. For a long time, it was believed that those who retired were a miserable lot. Some clearly are. For example, some men seem so lost that they follow their wives around the house, driving them crazy. They wind up doing such things as alphabetizing all the soup and canned goods in the cupboard. After that, they don't know what to do with themselves. These men, though, are the exception. We know less about women in retirement. Fewer women have been in the work force long enough to have retired, and most research in this area has looked only at men. From what we do know, however, it appears that the majority of men and women adapt well to this change in status and enjoy the freedom that retirement brings (Belsky, 1992).

You may think that the older someone is, the less active that person will be after retiring, but actually, age is not a very good predictor. Those people who have emphasized independence and personal involvement in life tend to stay active and to look forward to each new day, regardless of how old they are.

Isolation and Bereavement

Social isolation is a fear that old people have, but it is a fear rather than a reality for most of them, according to the statistics. Those most vulnerable to isolation are in poor health or do not have a reasonable amount of money. Although overall our society leaves a great deal to be desired in terms of its approach to the aging, individual families do a pretty good job. The majority of old people are not isolated, withdrawn, or lonesome.

There are exceptions to this generalization. The death of a close friend or spouse at any time changes one's life considerably, and this is far more likely to happen in late adulthood. We used to believe that the death of a spouse was always an extremely traumatic event for older people and that it was harder on men than on women. The upheaval in the survivor's life supposedly went on for years and years. Now it appears that these conclusions are only partly true.

There is no question that the death of a spouse involves a major loss and dramatic changes in a person's life. Research in recent years, however, reveals that most old people, women *and* men, do adapt. In fact, they usually have adjusted quite well within a year or so. In addition, there seem

▲ *While most older people are socially active, isolation is devastating for some.*

to be few differences between men and women concerning how well and how soon they recover (Belsky, 1992). Perhaps because loss is part and parcel of being old, people eventually develop ways to cope with it.

Women face greater burdens in this regard than men do. Since the average age of widowhood is 65, most married women will spend one-third of their lives without their spouse. And they will probably spend those years by themselves. Two-thirds of all widows live alone (Wainrib, 1992a).

As you might expect, older women are more likely to be put in the position of caring for a seriously ill spouse than older men are. However, you might be surprised to learn that this situation seems to be more stressful for women than for men. Since women have often spent most of their lives taking care of others, why would this be so?

Some possible answers are that society provides less support and reinforcement for women in this position and that women are more reluctant to ask for help with the task. Women's traditional identity includes the role of caregiver. Thus, the work they are doing is not seen as anything special. For men, though, it is. So men generally get more praise and recognition for taking on this role. In addition, a woman may feel that asking for help seems like admitting failure. Men do not experience the same constraint (Belsky, 1992).

Institutionalization

Everywhere we look, we see images of old people in institutions. But only about 5 percent of older people live in nursing homes. Most older people still have active ties with their families and friends, which is very good for them and for their families.

Even though most older people are not in institutions, those who are may be encouraged to remain dependent. Institutional staff frequently do

▼ *People known to be successful and productive in their later years include (from left to right) Grandma Moses, artist; George Burns, entertainer; India's Prime Minister Indira Gandhi; Physicist Albert Einstein; Rosa Parks, civil rights activist; and South African leader, Nelson Mandela.*

too much for older people, keeping them in a subservient role. While their intentions are good, they are making these people feel even more helpless.

Even so, being in an institution is not *necessarily* a bad thing. Whether it is good or bad depends on whether institutionalization is intended to "remove" a person from society, as well as on the quality of life in the institution. If institutional life includes the opportunity to visit with family and friends and to take part in such activities as study groups and field trips, then life can be quite pleasant. If the institution is not well run, however, its residents risk experiencing isolation because they have no meaningful activities, no chance to be around children, and no opportunity to use any of their skills. These circumstances can quickly lead to depression, serious physical illness, and even death.

Achievement

When discussing late adulthood, it is impossible to avoid such topics as poor health, senile dementia, widowhood, and so on. But we don't want you to leave this section discouraged or depressed. Aging is not simply an inevitable decline into disability; all is not gloom and despair. For instance, older couples experience less conflict and more pleasure in their marriages than young couples do. They are more affectionate with each other, too (Carstensen, Isaacowitz, & Charles, 1999). In addition, many elderly people remain productive throughout their lives.

Providing a complete list of people who continued to make important contributions well into old age would fill a book all by itself. However, we can point out a few examples: Pablo Picasso, Michelangelo, Eleanor Roosevelt, Albert Einstein, Georgia O'Keeffe, George Burns, and Katharine Hepburn, not to mention psychologists Erik Erikson, B.F. Skinner, and Jean Piaget.

A President Speaks on Aging

At the age of 56, and upon losing his bid for reelection, Jimmy Carter suddenly had to reassess his attitude on aging and retirement.

He discovered he was about a million dollars in debt because he'd neglected his farm supply business while president. He had no job prospects, and he wondered if he could be productive and happy during this next stage in his life. In his most recent book, *The Virtues of Aging* (1998), Carter shares his ideas on how to grow old gracefully, ideas that ultimately can be beneficial to people of all ages.

Carter writes, "Each of us is old when we *think* we are" (p. 11). If we sit in front of a television day in and day out, we will feel old, regardless of our age. If we engage instead in more active pursuits, we can remain physically healthy and mentally sharp well into our retirement years. Carter insists, in fact, that our health does not inevitably decline as we get older. If we eat right and exercise regularly, we can maintain an active lifestyle for many years. He adds, "It's better to use recreation to *preserve* health rather than to use medicines and treatment to *regain* health" (p. 63).

Jimmy Carter practices what he preaches. He began mountain climbing when he was 60; ten years later, he was still climbing. Now in his 70s, he enjoys a variety of activities, including fly-fishing, skiing, tennis, woodworking, and jogging. Along with these recreational activities, Carter also spends a great deal of time assisting others. He helped organize the Friendship

▲ *President Jimmy Carter working for Habitat for Humanity.*

Force, a foreign-exchange program for older people. He helps raise funds for Habitat for Humanity, an organization that builds homes for needy families. Not only does he promote and publicize the program, he shows up with hammer and nails and helps build the homes.

What if a person's health does decline with age? Carter argues that we must learn to accept the decline and not be shamed by it. For example, if we have trouble keeping our balance, there's no shame in using a cane or wheelchair. There's no shame in wearing a hearing aid if that's necessary. And if a disability keeps us from more active pursuits, we can still explore new interests, such as writing or painting. We can still touch others. Even in retirement and in less than perfect health, we can contribute.

And we don't have to run for president to make a difference, explains Carter: "All of us have adequate talent, intelligence, education, social status, and opportunity to be completely successful in life" (p. 131). All we need to do is make ourselves aware of our immediate world and pay attention to what we can do to make a difference outside our very doors. Carter is not speaking, of course, about financial success, or fame or power. He's speaking about living a full and enriching life, regardless of age.

Review the Case Study

Can you think of an individual who already seems to be following Carter's advice?

Thanatology

Thanatology (than-uh-TALL-uh-gee) is the study of death (*thanatos*, "death"; *logy,* "study of"). It is a relatively new area of study that came into its own in the 1970s. Until that time, the general attitude of psychology was that death was a "nontopic"—something to be ignored. This has changed noticeably.

Hiding from Death

One of the most common complaints from thanatologists is that our society refuses to admit that death exists. We do everything in our power to hide from it and to shield others from its existence. The reality of death is denied by the sentimental or sensational deaths so often seen in the movies and on television. The portrayal of death as glorious and uplifting or at least sudden and dramatic ignores the reality of it all.

We even hide the grossness and agony of killing in wartime by making it the action of patriots and heroes. Patriotism and heroism are not bad in themselves, of course. But in this case, they are part of an attempt to escape from the basic fact of death and the decomposition of the body.

Check out the sympathy cards sometime: Many such cards contain *no* reference to the fact that a life has ended. Although flowers are a popular picture on the cards, generally these flowers are not alive and growing, nor are they shown in some kind of container, like a vase (McGee, 1980). Apparently, card manufacturers don't want to suggest anything resembling an urn.

Issues Regarding Death

One theme occurs continually in studies about those who are dying, and it is so basic that we usually don't pay any attention to it: Death has never happened to any of us before. We may have read about it, come close to it, or seen someone else's death, but we ourselves have never experienced it. Thus, we face the ultimate unknown; and the fact that our society refuses to admit that death is a natural process gives the unknown an added dimension of terror.

We must, however, be careful about assuming that every normal person is afraid to die. In cases of terminal illness, a number of studies have shown that most old or dying people eventually come to accept death as a natural process. They are more concerned about making preparations for the end than about the end itself. They may well have periods of being anxious and scared, but they benefit greatly from a chance to talk about their feelings.

What are terminally ill people most afraid of? They have three basic fears: (1) loss of mastery over themselves, (2) separation from loved ones, and (3) the gnawing fear of being replaced by another (Kavanaugh, 1974). Their major concern is about being left alone in an unpredictable situation where they are also faced with the frustration of not being able to do anything about it. A dying person, then, needs reduced conflict, time to assemble inner resources, and a continued relationship with a loved one up to the end.

Focus Questions

- What insights have psychologists given us about the process of dying?
- What are dying people most afraid of?

thanatology the study of death and of methods for coping with it

▲ *The funeral of a loved one forces us all to examine our feelings and attitudes toward death.*

365

Stages of Dying

A well-known researcher on death, Elisabeth Kübler-Ross, proposed that people who are terminally ill go through a series of stages as they approach death. She suggested that first they *deny* that they are dying. Then they feel *anger* or resentment that it is happening to them. Third, they try to *bargain* with God for a little more time. Fourth, they become *depressed*. Finally, they adopt a more or less *peaceful acceptance* of the whole event, trying to tie up loose ends for themselves and their loved ones (Kübler-Ross, 1969).

In many ways, Kübler-Ross created a double-edged sword with her suggestion. On the one hand, her system holds up in a general sort of way and helps explain many of the behaviors of people who are terminally ill. On the other hand, critics of her system feel that it takes away from the individuality and personal responses each of us may have if we face this crisis.

For example, suppose someone in this situation is angry about something. He or she may indeed have a legitimate cause other than the illness, but too many people will say, "Oh, he's going through the anger stage; that's all." Today there is a movement toward acceptance of the fact that although emotions of the dying person may follow a rough pattern, these emotions are still real and valid. They are more than a stage, and he or she should be recognized as an individual until death.

In Focus

Kübler-Ross's Stages of Dying

The Monologue of the Terminally Ill

Denial   "There must be some mistake with the test results. Are you sure you're looking at *my* results? This is nonsense. I'll just have to get another opinion—from a doctor who knows what he or she is talking about."

Anger   "Why me? I exercise every day. I don't smoke. I do all those crazy things you're supposed to do to live longer. It's not fair."

Bargaining   "Please, God, let me live another year and I promise I'll go to church every Sunday. It's just that there are a couple of things I want to accomplish. Just another year."

Depression   "I become sad thinking about all the friends I'll miss. I grieve when I think of losing my family."

Peaceful Acceptance   "I'm not afraid to die anymore. I know now that death is part of life. I still feel sad at times, but I've come to accept death, and I'm at peace about it."

If someone close to you had a terminal illness, how would knowing about these stages help you talk with this person? How might this knowledge interfere?

Help for the Dying

Thanatologists point to the fact that dying away from home is a relatively new phenomenon and is primarily an outgrowth of our mechanized society. In many parts of the world, death is prepared for by the family unit, with everyone participating, including the person who is dying. One of the most frightening experiences is being alone when dying. At home, the person feels considerably less alone. In fact, most funeral rituals used today started out as something done within the home. Thus, washing and preparing the body were previously done by the family. The "wake"—in which family and friends stay with the body—was common before mortuaries existed.

The Amish (AH-mish) society has managed to hold onto many of its traditions separate from the hectic modern world and is a model for handling death. Amish people still make a living by farming, using horses instead of tractors, and in general have resisted so-called scientific advances. When someone dies, the immediate family is relieved of all work except for making a list of people to be notified. The family assumes responsibility for dressing the body in special funeral clothing. (Each person in the community has his or her own set of white garments to wear only when he or she dies.) Everyone is prepared for death, and the attitude is one of acceptance. Most Amish people die at home in the presence of their families. This is in stark contrast to the rest of our country, in which most deaths take place in institutions.

One emerging trend is the use of **hospice care,** which focuses on managing pain, promoting comfort, and improving the quality of life for people who are terminally ill. Hospice care can take place in the person's home, in a special facility, or even in some hospitals. The goal is to provide a warm, supportive environment in which death is accepted but life is valued until its final moment. A variety of professionals tend to the needs and fears of the person who is ill and help family members deal with the situation (Papalia, Camp, & Feldman, 1996).

▲ *Amish families provide strong support for family members who are dying.*

hospice care care for terminally ill people that emphasizes pain management, comfort, and quality of life

 ## Pause for Thought

1. What are some common fears of people in old age?
2. What are three fears of people who are terminally ill?
3. What is the purpose of hospice care?

Critical Thinking
. . . .
4. Dave is a professional baseball player who realizes that because of his age he can no longer compete. He goes through a series of stages similar to what Kübler-Ross suggests that terminally ill people experience. Describe what Dave might be feeling.

APPLYING Psychology to Life

Cross-Cultural Attitudes toward Aging

A very negative attitude toward aging exists in this country. Instead of seeing it as a natural process and part of the life cycle, we tend to view growing old as an abnormal state, something to hide from or try to deny (Daniel, 1996/1994). While everybody wants to live a long life, no one wants to get old. That's a neat trick, if you can do it. But the simple fact is that we're either going to grow old or die prematurely—there aren't any other alternatives. One very sad side effect of our negative attitude is that many older people themselves have accepted it, and they wind up viewing themselves as a burden. In fact, surveys show that older people devalue old age *more* than younger people do.

Complex Attitudes

Other cultures react differently to both the aging process and their older citizens. But it's still a complicated picture. For instance, in certain African and Central American tribes, elders are revered for their wisdom. They are also feared, though, because of the belief that they live so long by taking the lives of young people. Thus, old men are often suspected of having special or even demonic powers and may be unfairly blamed for the deaths of younger people in their communities. In some African tribes, old women enjoy increased status because they have authority over their daughters and daughters-in-law and are greatly respected by their sons, who often have stronger ties to their mothers than to their fathers. In addition, being a grandmother automatically demands a high level of respect (Gutmann, 1997). On the other hand, in some other tribes there is a tendency to see old women as witches (Gardiner, Mutter, & Kosmitzki, 1998).

Roles Change

In some Native American tribes, as older men with-

▲ *In some cultures, the passing down of knowledge is a respected task assigned to the older generation.*

draw from other roles they have had, they increase their involvement in the community's spiritual life. Younger members of many tribes have been showing more interest in tribal rites and traditions in recent years. This renewed interest has led to an increased interest in tribal elders and what they can tell younger members about the tribe's history and religious practices (Gutmann, 1997). In addition, it is common among American Indians for everyone to share in the responsibility for taking care of all family members, including older ones. Many Hispanics in this country follow similar practices (Gardiner, et al., 1998).

Family Care Systems

Among the Chinese, in many Muslim countries, and on an Israeli kibbutz, putting an old person in some kind of nursing home is virtually unthinkable. Old people in these societies live in a family member's home, where they are taken care of until they die (Gardiner, et al., 1998; van der Gaag, 1996/1995). Here too, however, strains can be felt. Many of these societies are just beginning to experience increases in the number of older people. Furthermore, most of the responsibility for care falls on the younger women, and worldwide more and more women are employed outside the home (van der Gaag, 1996/1995). It seems safe to predict that as the older

▲ *Among many American Indian tribes, there is renewed interest in what tribal elders can contribute.*

populations continue to grow in these countries and women continue to be employed in greater numbers, the family care system will become seriously stretched, perhaps to the breaking point.

A More Positive View.

In this country, positive changes are occurring. Young people are viewing aging in a better light, probably because older people today are so much more active than used to be the case. If the shift in attitudes is real and continues in the same direction, future generations of older people will have a more positive view of themselves. When that happens, we will have achieved a reasonable view of the life cycle in its entirety.

Summary

1. During late adolescence and early adulthood, most people start their families and careers. In very general terms, the male devotes most of his time to career and the female to family, even if the woman works outside the home.

2. At some point around the age of 40, most people go through a midlife transition. This is a time for reexamining one's life.

3. In middle adulthood, people's priorities shift. Men become more giving and emotionally expressive while women become more independent and assertive. The 50s are usually a time of mellowing.

4. Two major changes that occur in middle adulthood are the empty-nest period and menopause.

5. Late adulthood begins in the 60s. In the United States, more people are living longer, so this group is increasing in size.

6. Aging may occur because of internal "time clocks" that dictate how long cells will continue to function and replace themselves.

7. Mental ability for most older people is quite good, although a little slower than before. Senile dementia occurs in a minority of older people. The major cause is Alzheimer's disease, which involves a loss of chemicals that fire brain cells.

8. Older people are concerned about poor health, social isolation, and a loss of feeling meaningful to society. In reality, neither isolation nor institutionalization is common for older people, and many continue to make important contributions.

9. Thanatology is the study of death; it emphasizes making death a natural part of the life cycle. Terminally ill people should be an active part of the family as much as possible. There is much criticism of how we handle death in this country.

Vocabulary

empty-nest period	senile dementia	thanatology
menopause	cerebral arteriosclerosis	hospice care
gerontology	Alzheimer's disease	

Review Questions

True/False

On a sheet of paper, answer each statement true or false. If false, rewrite to make it true.

1. The midlife transition, though not as tragic as everyone used to think, is inevitable.
2. Marital satisfaction is typically at a low point during the midlife period.
3. Most divorces take place during midlife.
4. Men and women tend to adopt each other's characteristics during middle adulthood.
5. Studies show that the majority of women never experience feelings of uselessness and depression during the empty-nest period.
6. The onset of menopause tends to create significant psychological problems for the majority of women.
7. Studies show that most old people are isolated, withdrawn, and lonesome.

Fill in the blank

On a sheet of paper, write the word or words that best complete each statement.

8. The study of death is called ▒▒▒▒.
9. The study of older people is called ▒▒▒▒.
10. Women live roughly ▒▒▒▒ years longer than men.
11. The blockage of blood vessels going to the brain is called ▒▒▒▒.
12. Menstruation gradually stops during ▒▒▒▒.
13. The loss of mental faculties due to disease is called ▒▒▒▒.
14. A major cause of senile dementia is ▒▒▒▒.
15. About ▒▒▒▒ percent of older people live in nursing homes.
16. The final stage of Kubler-Ross's stages is called ▒▒▒▒.

Multiple Choice

On a sheet of paper, write the letter of the answer that best completes the statement.

17. Alzheimer's disease disrupts
    a. speech.
    b. body control.
    c. personality.
    d. all of the above.
    e. a and b only.
18. Which of the following is *not* a myth about senility but is true?
    a. Senility is caused by disease.
    b. Senility occurs in a majority of older people by the age of 70.
    c. Loss of brain cells during aging leads to mental impairment.
    d. Senility is inevitable with age.
19. People who were highly active in youth usually
    a. slow down in old age.
    b. remain active in old age.
    c. live very long lives.
    d. experience fewer worries about old age.
20. If a person living in the 1800s avoided serious injury and disease, the chances that the person would live to be 70 were
    a. still worse than today.
    b. about the same as today.
    c. better than today.

Discussion Questions

1. Other than mutual respect, what ingredients are important for a successful marriage? To answer this question, consider your own successful relationships and what makes them last.

2. Do you think your parents will experience an empty-nest period when you leave home? Why or why not?

3. If you're a male, would it bother you if your wife's career was more "significant" than yours and if she made much more money than you? Why or why not? Be honest. If you're a female, would it bother you if you made more money than your husband? Why or why not?

4. When you hear about research on manipulation of genes to prolong the life span, do you tend to become excited about the prospect, or do you think the life span is something that really shouldn't be toyed with and manipulated by science? Argue for one of these points of view.

5. The number of people over age 65 has increased dramatically and will probably continue to increase. Let's assume that many of these people choose *not* to retire; consequently, the unemployment rate among young people rises sharply. Should the older people be forced to retire? Why or why not? Explain.

6. If you were about 75 years old and were unable to live independently, do you think you'd prefer to live in a well-run nursing home so you could associate with others your age, or do you think you'd rather live with your own children (assuming they welcome you!)? Explain.

7. The chapter describes several ways in which our society tends to ignore the reality of death. For example, even sympathy cards avoid mentioning words like *death* and *dying*. What are some other ways in which we ignore death? Explain. Consider language, hospital procedures, and funeral rituals.

8. If you found out that you had only a year to live, would you continue to live life as usual, or would you drastically alter your lifestyle? Explain. If you *were* to change your life drastically, what would you do differently? Be specific.

Activities and Projects

1. This may be the chapter that relates to you least, since you haven't yet been through the changes described. What might really bring the chapter to life for you is talking to a variety of adults on a variety of issues. Find three or four adults who wouldn't mind being interviewed on videotape. Then create a video journal about adulthood and aging. Since your subjects are the highlights of this project, try to keep yourself out of the video as much as possible. For example, you might ask a question off camera and then have all the adults address the same question—which may require some editing on your part. If it's OK with your teacher, show the video to your class.

2. Imagine yourself at the ages of 30, 40, 50, and 60. Then write four journal entries, one for each age, taking the point of view of your future self at that age. *Note:* The ages are approximate. If it makes more sense to you, for example, to use the age 33 instead of 30, go ahead. You might save this journal for the future to see how accurate your predictions turn out to be.

3. If we summarize some of the findings discussed in the chapter, we might say that adults in early adulthood (20–39) tend to be stressed and anxious, while adults in middle adulthood (40–59) tend to become more compassionate and mellow. This is obviously a generalization and not true for everyone, but we want you to use it as a basis for the next activity. Conduct an experiment to determine whether "middle" adults, being more relaxed, will be more likely than "early" adults to help a stranger.

General procedure: Walk through a mall with a shopping bag that has a ripped bottom. Stuff the bag with prepurchased merchandise and some papers. As you approach someone in the mall, allow the contents of the bag to slip through the bottom of the bag, and then record whether the person helps. Repeat this procedure 20 times, half the time on "early" adults and half the time on "middle" adults. (You'll have to use your own judgment here as to ages.)

Specific points: (1) The reason you want to include papers in the bag is that papers will tend to cause a mess and will create a *need* for help. (2) You probably want to conduct this experiment with a friend. One person can drop; the other can record. (3) Record not only whether the person bent down to help you but also what the person said or didn't say, and so on. In other words, record as much information as possible about each subject. (4) If possible, test only subjects who are alone. Being with others might influence a person's helping behavior, and that is not what you're testing here. (5) If possible, divide your subjects equally between men and women. If that is not possible, try to use all men or all women. Again, gender is not a factor that you're studying, and you are attempting to eliminate this factor at least to some extent.

Discuss your results. Can you draw any conclusions? Was our hypothesis about the characteristics of the two age groups supported by your findings? Explain. Be sure to include the specific reactions of each subject.

4. As mentioned in the chapter, our society is obsessed with youth, and many products on the market today reflect this obsession. In fact, many products seem to be designed to stall or deny the aging process. Collect several advertisements that promote these kinds of products and organize them in a creative way for a collage. *Note:* Some products that are not specifically designed to stall or deny the aging process may still reinforce the obsession with youth.

5. Write a dialogue between a husband and wife discussing whether they should invite one of their parents to live with them. The parent in question is not always able to move around easily. One person in the dialogue should support housing the parent; the other should be against it. End the dialogue with some kind of resolution. The dialogue will certainly be influenced by several factors: whether the husband and wife have children living at home, whether the husband and wife both work, and so on. You can fill in these details in any way you like.

You don't need to use quotation marks, but make it clear when a new speaker is talking—maybe by using different-colored pens, skipping lines, introducing each speaker with *H* or *W* (for husband and wife), or giving names to your characters.

6. Conduct research on Alzheimer's disease and organize your information into a report. Be sure to include your own reactions to the material and impressions about what should be done to help these people, increase public awareness, and so forth. Also answer some of the following questions: (1) What are the stages of the disease that an Alzheimer's patient experiences? (2) What are the possible causes? (3) What research is being conducted on "cures"? (4) Is there anything one can do to reduce the risks of getting Alzheimer's disease?

7. Visit one of the following three places and write a report on whether you would ever want to be a "customer" at the place—assuming you *needed* the services. Explain in detail why you would or would not want to be a customer.

   a. *Nursing home:* Talk to someone in charge who can inform you of the services and activities that the facility provides. Also find out the costs of the care. If possible, visit with a few of the residents to get their feedback on the facility.

   b. *Funeral home:* This may sound a bit morbid, but visiting such a place when you don't really *need* to can be fascinating. Again, find out about services and costs. Ask the director about the main functions of funeral homes in our society.

   c. *Hospice:* More and more hospitals are developing hospice programs as an option for terminally ill patients. The chances are good that you can find a hospice in your area. Find out about the services provided, how a hospice is different from a normal hospital setting.

CHAPTER 13

Gender Differences

There are all kinds of myths about differences between the sexes. In this chapter, we explore what science has learned about the differences between males and females. In general, the two sexes are quite similar. A few differences have been found, but the causes are usually not clear.

Male and Female—A Brief History of Myths

Before we can even begin to discuss similarities and differences between males and females, we run smack-dab into confusion about terms. Generally, *sex* refers simply to being male or female, while *gender* refers more to what society views as appropriate for males and females. However, many specialists in this area of study use the term *gender* to refer to the state of being male or female, and we have decided to follow their example (Hyde, 1994). For our purposes, then, the word **gender** refers to the sex of an individual.

Studying the similarities and differences between the sexes, as you might imagine, has had a rather colorful history. In the old days, males' desire for domination led to some bizarre "scientific" attempts to show that males are smarter than females. We might look at a few of them.

One of the claims made by males 100 years or so ago concerned brain size. Since women have smaller heads than men, their brains must be smaller, so the male scientists said that females were not as bright. This idea was finally given up when it was discovered that physical brain size is not related to intelligence.

▲ *Males and females are far more alike than different.*

gender the sex of an individual, male or female

In Focus

Gender Quiz

Complete this true/false quiz before reading the chapter. See project 5 on page 401 for answers.

1. Females have fewer genetic defects and greater endurance than men.
2. The front part of the brain is more highly developed in males than in females.
3. Female infants are more active than male infants.
4. Females have a special natural ability to take care of children—some might call it a maternal instinct.
5. Males have better natural ability than females to handle mathematics.
6. Males are more oriented toward achievement than females.
7. When couples break up, men are more likely to initiate the breakup.
8. When it comes to choosing a mate, men and women look for the same characteristics.
9. Only females experience monthly hormonal changes.
10. If parents are extremely strict, their children will tend to develop more masculine traits.

hormones chemical regulators that control bodily processes such as emotional responses, growth, and sexuality

androgen the male sex hormone

estrogen the female sex hormone; controls the female reproductive cycle

Focus Question
....
• Can sex hormones affect behavior as well as physical development?

▲ *The motherly behavior of this bear is probably largely due to the effects of hormones.*

Then the scientists decided that the front part of the brain was better developed in males. So that was the area showing that men were smarter! But they found this, too, to be false, since it was eventually shown that females were as well developed in this part of the brain as males.

The disputes became stranger when it was claimed that male hormones kept men's minds cool and "dry," leading them to have a clever, "dry" wit. Then it was said that females should not be educated because this drained vital fluids from their bodies. And so forth.

The point is that male/female relationships have been dominated even in science by mudslinging rather than by research. Today, the studies are much more scientific and accurate, and we hope we can shed some light on what differences, if any, really exist between the two sexes.

The Role of Hormones

Each of us, male or female, has both male and female hormones. **Hormones** are chemical agents that cause physical changes in the body. There are two types of sex hormones, **androgen** and **estrogen.** Males have more androgen, and females more estrogen.

Whether a fetus becomes male or female results from which hormone is present in the fetus in greater quantities. Until the second month of development, all fetuses are exactly the same. Which sex we become depends on genetics, which causes certain mechanisms to increase the amount of one hormone over the other.

Hormones have some interesting effects on male/female behavior. For instance, injection of androgen into a pregnant monkey can produce an offspring that by nature should be female but that also has some male physical characteristics. Androgen injected into a human adult female can increase her aggressiveness. And male monkeys with too little androgen show many patterns of behavior normally found in female monkeys.

Levels of sex hormones can be off slightly without producing serious abnormalities, yet they can result in slight changes in behavior. For example, some years ago, a number of pregnant women were given medication that had the side effect of making their bodies produce more androgen than normal. Their female offspring tended to be somewhat "tomboyish." In contrast, males who before birth had their androgen production reduced were a bit less rough and aggressive.

In both cases, it is important to remember that the children were not abnormal; they were behaving within the normal range for their sex. When the levels of hormones are genuinely defective, children with characteristics of both sexes can be born. For instance, they may have the internal equipment of males but the external parts of females, or vice versa.

In general, hormones play a lesser role in humans than they do in other animals. For the most part, we are able to limit their effect on our behavior and on how masculine or feminine we feel.

Male/Female Differences

Males are bulkier and stronger as a group than females, but females have fewer genetic defects, live longer, and have greater physical endurance. The other obvious, major male/female difference is that the female bears the offspring and provides the nourishment for the infant, which creates a very strong bond between the two.

The only activities, then, that clearly and absolutely belong to one sex or the other are those involved in reproduction. All other differences are simply a matter of degree or frequency of occurrence. In other words, there are certain trends for one gender or the other, but no rule holds hard and fast.

Focus Question
....
- What are some of the physical differences between males and females?

Nurturance

It is generally accepted as fact by the public at large that women are more nurturing than men are. That is, they are more inclined to take care of and show concern for other people and are better able to care for others. Is this "fact" really a fact? The best answer seems to be "sort of." Women generally do show more empathy for and intimate involvement with others of all ages (Cross & Madson, 1997; Feingold, 1994; Cohn, 1991; Maccoby, 1990). This finding is no longer really in dispute.

When it comes to helping others, though, the results are mixed. Whether men or women are more likely to offer their assistance to someone else seems to depend on the situation. In close relationships, women respond more quickly and more often to other people's needs. In unfamiliar settings, men can prove to be more willing to help someone (Baumeister & Sommer, 1997).

So, what can we conclude at this point? Well, it seems safe to say that, generally speaking, women are somewhat more nurturing than men are. But what is the underlying cause of this difference? The Critical Thinking feature on page 378 suggests one possible answer.

Focus Question
....
- Are females more nurturing than males?

▲ *Males can be nurturing, too.*

Aggression and Activity Level

We usually see aggression as primarily a masculine characteristic, and males do indeed generally show more aggression than females. In fact, the greater aggressiveness of males is the best-documented psychological gender difference of all (Baumeister & Sommer, 1997; Feingold, 1994; Maccoby, 1990). Most likely, hormones play a part in this difference.

Thinking Critically about Psychology

The Maternal Instinct

Very closely related to the issue of nurturance is the suggestion that women are better at it because they possess a maternal instinct. In other words, along with the ability to conceive and bear children, women have a built-in program for caring for those children.

What specifically is being claimed or stated? Women have an innate special concern for and ability to take care of children that men do not have.

What is the objective evidence for and against this claim? There is abundant evidence that women in fact do most of the child care (Basic Behavioral Science Task Force, 1996a; Silverstein, 1996; Ozer, 1995). There is also abundant evidence that they are the more nurturing sex, as we have already discussed. But are these differences based more on women's basic nature or on environmental factors—our familial and societal expectations about women and motherhood? There is no ready method for clearing this up. However, one way to determine whether females have an inborn "maternal instinct" that males do not have is to search the animal world, where creatures are not guided by social forces to the same extent we are.

As you would expect, chimpanzee mothers seem to automatically know how to care for their babies. Furthermore, when a new baby is born into a group, both the adolescent and adult females show a great deal of interest in it. In fact, the adolescent females are so intent on holding and playing with it they frequently get into trouble with the baby's mother. The adolescent males, on the other hand, exhibit a little curiosity at first but then are mostly indifferent (Goodall, 1986).

There are exceptions to the rule we're about to describe, and male lions and bears are among those exceptions. Both have been known to kill the young unless their mothers keep constant vigil. So we can give up on them. But in the animal world as a whole, the story is different if the male is forced to take care of the infants. For instance, male rhesus monkeys typically respond to their babies with either hostility or indifference. The close bond is between mother and infant.

Yet in a series of studies, researchers have taken away the mother, forcing the male in the family to be left alone with the infant. At first the father "complains" and "objects" violently, but within a short time, he begins

▲ *Maternal behavior in humans comes from many sources, some physical and some psychological.*

to groom, care for, and show a strong attachment toward his infant. Male rats exhibit the same sequence of behavior (Suomi, 1983). Thus, it appears that if the maternal instinct does exist, it is not limited to the female of the species.

Further arguing against a strong maternal instinct in humans is the fact that a human mother with her first baby usually doesn't have the faintest idea what to do. This is particularly so when she has not had much experience with babies. For one thing, the baby's head is so wobbly it looks like it's going to fall off at any moment. The task of caring for this tiny, helpless infant seems absolutely overwhelming. First-time mothers must call on other women with experience or frantically read baby-care books to find out what to do.

Even animal mothers do not always behave maternally. Among chimpanzee mothers, some are especially good and caring, while others are less so. In one case, an adult female took her daughter with her on horrible raids within their own group. The two would forcibly wrench babies from their mothers' arms, then take them off and kill them (Goodall, 1986). Wild animals that give birth in captivity sometimes reject or mistreat their offspring, and attendants are quick to remove the infant if its mother does not respond favorably soon after its birth. These are not normal circumstances and consequently do not prove anything. However, they should lead us to wonder just how universal the maternal instinct might be.

What other interpretations might be made instead? The influence of the environment cannot be discounted. Even female animals are not always maternal, and male animals can "learn" to care for their young. Female animals that live in groups are exposed from the day they are born to other females caring for babies. This is probably most relevant among chimpanzees and other primates because they are so similar to us. Among humans, certainly, experience counts. Perhaps because we are such complicated creatures, we must learn how to take proper care of children, especially infants.

What are the most logical conclusions to draw? It seems unlikely that women have a clear-cut maternal instinct that automatically makes them superior caretakers. Obviously, men can do an equally good job of it. We do know that babies elicit a protective response from us. Perhaps it is this protective response that is built on by the mother through learning and day-to-day experience.

See if **COOL** works for you....

Claim?

Objective evidence for and against claim?

Other interpretations?

Logical conclusions?

Applying Critical Thinking Skills

Maternal instinct *refers to mothering, of course. Describe one study that shows that males may have a similar instinct.*

Does this mean that females are not aggressive? Absolutely not. Given the right circumstances, females may not only equal males in aggressive behavior but exceed them. What it does mean is that more males than females are more likely to behave this way in more situations. For instance, when packed together in a big crowd, men tend to get aggressive, but women tend to get nervous.

Gender differences in *activity level* appear in infants as early as 45 hours after birth, with males more active. When asleep, male children twitch and jump, use their muscles more; females smile more. Male children engage in more physical activity than females. This difference also shows up in monkeys, suggesting a biological origin. From infancy, male monkeys are wrestling, pushing, and shoving one another, while females are relatively quiet (Caplan, 1984).

Such findings have, in the past, been interpreted to mean that the female wants to be dominated. *Very* few people now agree with that suggestion. In fact, when a male monkey gets a little too heavy-handed, the female will clobber him. This has been known to happen among humans, too.

We mentioned that differences in activity level may have a biological origin. We can't completely ignore the role of the environment, though. Boys not only engage in high levels of activity but are actively encouraged to do so (Rogoff, 1990). By adulthood, however, gender differences in activity level have virtually disappeared (Feingold, 1994).

In Their Own Words . . .

Deborah Tannen, *a professor at Georgetown University, is an expert on how men and women use language to communicate. The following excerpt is from* You Just Don't Understand *(1990):*

Sitting in the front seat of the car beside Harold, Sybil is fuming. They have been driving around for half an hour looking for a street he is sure is close by. Sybil is angry not because Harold does not know the way, but because he insists on trying to find it himself rather than stopping and asking someone. Her anger stems from viewing his behavior through the lens of her own: If she were driving, she would have asked directions as soon as she realized she didn't know which way to go, and they'd now be comfortably ensconced in their friends' living room instead of driving in circles, as the hour gets later and later. Since asking directions does not make Sybil uncomfortable, refusing to ask makes no sense to her. But in Harold's world, driving around until he finds his way is the reasonable thing to do, since asking for help makes him uncomfortable. He's avoiding that discomfort and trying to maintain his sense of himself as a self-sufficient person.

Interpreting Primary Sources

Why does Harold feel uncomfortable asking for directions? Do you think he represents most men? Explain.

Pause for Thought

1. What are some ways in which androgen and estrogen affect behavior?
2. What conclusions have researchers reached about activity level and aggression in males and females?

Critical Thinking

3. Explain what we know about the nurturance abilities of men and women. Given what we know, what changes could we make as a society in raising children?

Intelligence

In infancy, the basic intellectual processes of the male and female seem the same. Over time, however, differences develop in certain areas. Despite this, scientists believe that males and females are very close in overall intellectual abilities.

Spatial Skills

At about 11 years of age, boys begin to score better on tasks involving mathematics and spatial skills. The term **spatial skills** refers to the ability to imagine how something would look in space—for example, getting a three-dimensional image of the parking lot with the cars parked at right angles to the curb and then mentally rotating the cars so that they are parked parallel to the curb.

Video games involve considerable spatial skills. In general, boys are better at these games than girls, but there is a "trick" here in that girls don't get involved with these machines as often. When they do, they learn the skills quite well. (See Chapter 2, where we discuss a study comparing males and females on video games.)

There also are unexplained research findings such as this one: A study of 3,000 students found that 13-year-old girls scored better on spatial skills than boys the same age (Meece et al., 1982). Generally speaking, training does increase girls' spatial reasoning skills and their performance on most—but not all—such tests (Vasta, Knott, & Gage, 1996). At the moment, whatever differences exist are best explained as resulting from differences in social role, social class, ethnic background, and the type of test given, rather than from clear differences between the sexes.

Some people have suggested that the brains of males might be physically different from those of females. Indeed, the brains do differ: Certain areas in the brains of one sex have more cells than the same areas in the brains of the other sex and vice versa, but to date we have not been able to relate these facts to any differences in mental abilities.

Mathematical Ability

A study of 40,000 seventh-grade students showed that by age 13 males did better than females on the part of the Scholastic Aptitude Test (SAT) that measures mathematical reasoning. There were 13 boys to every girl scoring over 700 (95 percent) on the math portion of the test. Boys *seem* to have a wide lead in the area of mathematics (Benbow & Stanley, 1983). This difference is real, but explaining it is another issue.

A few have argued that because girls can have the same formal training as boys in mathematics if they want to, these tests must indicate some innate, basic difference between the sexes. But evidence for this claim is at best mixed.

Problems that contradict a theory of male superiority in math show up in other studies using the same group that took the Scholastic Aptitude

Focus Questions

- Are boys better at math than girls?
- Why do girls' grades drop in junior high school?

spatial skills skills involving the ability to imagine how an object would look if it was moved about in space

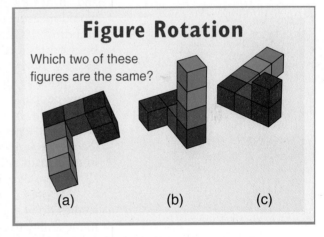

Figure Rotation

Which two of these figures are the same?

(a)   (b)   (c)

▲ *An example of spatial reasoning*

▶ *Are the female students at a disadvantage in this math class?*

Test. These studies show that girls did better than boys in math courses and in advanced placement math tests. It seems unlikely that the SAT would measure math skills while the math courses wouldn't (Beckwith & Woodruff, 1984). Other studies show no difference at all between girls and boys on tests of high-level reasoning, such as geometry proofs (Senk & Usiskin, 1984).

Possibly the answer lies in the fact that without even knowing it, many people have a bias against girls being involved in math, which has traditionally been part of the male domain. For example, some studies show that teachers call on boys more often than girls in math classes (Sadker & Sadker, 1985). Further, it has been shown that girls' confidence in their math ability actually goes down *before* their performance starts to slip (Orenstein, 1994).

At present, we can only come to this conclusion: Taken as a whole, studies do not show that there is some basic difference between the sexes in the ability to handle mathematics. A great number of things would have to be cleared away first before we could conclude that there *is* a difference. Here are some:

1. The test results would have to be more consistent from one study to another.

2. We would have to compensate for the fact that teachers and parents expect males to do better than females in this area.

3. We would have to look at the fact that more boys than girls claim they enjoy math. If it's really true that boys tend to like math more, then we have a serious problem comparing the sexes in math abilities (Meece et al., 1982).

4. In general, a lot of people don't want to struggle with math. It may well be that females take advantage of the social forces claiming they are not very skilled in this area in order to bypass it and avoid the hassle.

The fact that no conclusion can be reached is in itself very important, since this leaves the question wide open. This is certainly a critical area that should not be closed without very hard evidence.

Verbal Ability

Verbal ability refers to dealing with word problems, reading, writing, and so on. Generally speaking, school-age girls do better at these tasks than boys. They continue to hold a slight edge until adolescence. Over the years, though, the small advantage females seem to have in this area declines. By late adolescence, it has virtually disappeared. This finding, plus others we have covered, has led many researchers to believe that gender differences in mental abilities no longer exist (Hyde, 1994; Hyde & Linn, 1988; Feingold, 1988).

Environmental Influences

There is no way to remove environmental influences from the development of all kinds of skills. We have already noted that teachers call on boys more often in math classes. Actually, teachers call on boys more often, period. They give boys more of their attention and time and are more likely to ask boys than girls to expand on their answers and think things through (Hyde, 1994; Sadker & Sadker, 1994).

With spatial or mathematical abilities, environmental influences reach far beyond the classroom. For example, research has shown that more mathematical toys are given to boys. Also, boys more often play with toys such as footballs. Catching and throwing such toys require spatial orientation.

The real clincher has its sad side: Right at junior high school age, females as a group show a sudden and dramatic drop in grades and in intelligence test scores. Does female intelligence suddenly plummet like a rock at this age, so that girls know hardly anything anymore? Naturally, that idea is ridiculous.

Many females have been convinced by the "system" that they are supposed to be dumb to be appealing to males. Interestingly, females who refuse to go along with all this and assert themselves show no decline in intellectual ability (Maccoby & Jacklin, 1974). Also, when females are past that "dumb" period, they really soar, especially in college, where their grades are almost always better than those of males. And their accomplishments in college include high achievement in the areas of math and spatial skills. In fact, over one-third of mathematics professors are female.

 Pause for Thought

1. What probably accounts for males' higher scores on spatial skills tasks?
2. What are some differences between males and females in mathematical ability?
3. What are some factors that would need to be resolved before these differences could be validated?
4. Are there any differences between males and females in self-confidence or the drive for success? Explain.

Critical Thinking

5. Given what researchers have found out about friendships and communication between males and females, offer some practical advice to both men and women.

Focus Questions

• Is one sex more confident or more oriented toward achievement than the other?

• Are women better communicators?

Social Factors

Social factors play an important part in how we view the sexes. They also play an important part in how we view ourselves as members of one sex or the other.

Self-Confidence

Researchers have found no clear differences in how readily males and females are influenced by others' suggestions. Some studies show males are more likely than females to go along with the group (Eagly, 1978). Other studies show the opposite, and many find no differences at all (Baumeister & Sommer, 1997; Feingold, 1994).

Females consistently rate themselves as high on self-confidence as males do, at least through childhood. Both are about equal in their tendencies to explore novel environments, engage in unusual activities, and refuse to be stepped on by others. Also, girls feel as important as boys—at least until high school.

Adolescence often brings with it a decline in girls' self-confidence. Much of the problem can be traced to their concerns about how boys will react. Thus, they are unsure how they should behave. Interestingly, girls who attend all-girl schools suffer less in this regard. In addition, the loss of confidence is greatest among whites and Hispanics. African American girls tend to hold on to their self-confidence throughout adolescence (Orenstein, 1994). Once in adulthood, women and men are fairly equal in self-confidence (Feingold, 1994).

In some studies, girls *claim* that in their daily lives, they are more anxious and fearful than boys. But we can't put much scientific faith in this finding, because girls may be feigning weakness as part of a social role. When faced with something frightening, boys sweat and swallow a lot and girls screech, but privately they admit to being equally terrified.

So what conclusion can be reached about self-confidence? No notable difference exists.

▲ *In adulthood, men and women overall are equally self-confident.*

Friendships

Humans are clearly social animals. Whatever our age or gender, we seem to need the company of other people, at least some of the time. Throughout the life span, friends are an important source of emotional support, sharing our experiences and just having fun with us. Both males and females seek and value close relationships in which they can feel accepted for who they are. While gender differences do exist, they do not override this basic desire for meaningful social interaction.

One gender difference is apparent in how groups of children behave. Boys' groups usually have a leader, even if it's an informal arrangement. Girls' groups are much less likely to be structured in this way. More often, the girls all have fairly equal status within the group. When deciding what

▲ *Friendships are important to both genders.*

the group is going to do, boys more often issue orders or make demands, while girls tend to make suggestions (Maccoby, 1990).

Among adults, several trends have been noted. Women more often have a best friend of the same sex than men do. Generally speaking, women have a few close female friends, while men have a larger number of male acquaintances (Cross & Madson, 1997; Archer, 1996).

Interestingly, when it comes to really close sharing of emotions, disappointments, and concerns, a man is more likely to talk with a woman than with another man. Why might this be so? The answers are not conclusive. However, it appears that men may be reluctant to appear weak around other men. They may worry that admitting to failings and showing emotions such as fear could damage their status. Another possibility is that women may be seen as less judgmental (Baumeister & Sommer, 1997).

This next finding is something that our female readers will probably find hard to accept. But it has been demonstrated over and over again. Believe it or not, when couples break up, women more often initiate the breakup than men do. Not only that, but following this unhappy event, men suffer more and for a longer period of time (Baumeister & Sommer, 1997).

Drive for Success

Achievement has often been considered a masculine goal. But research indicates that females are, in fact, just as oriented toward achievement as males. Large numbers of studies find no overall sex differences in this regard (Zuckerman & Wheeler, 1975). Why, then, do so many people think of men as being more driven to achieve?

The evidence points to societal beliefs that suggest there is something wrong with a woman who seeks success. Girls are told not to be "too important" or they won't appeal to boys. Stop and think for a minute: Isn't there at least a hint of this belief even in your own group?

The causes are all around us. Watch TV ads carefully sometime, and note how, even now, women are often connected somehow with soap or food products that need cooking. Men tend to be the focus in ads involving something mechanical, such as a product that would be used with a car or lawn mower. In this way, then, both sexes are subtly indoctrinated.

Some earlier studies suggested that this propaganda had a clear effect. Even at the college level, when female students got higher grades than males—which is the norm—they still anticipated doing poorly in the future. The males, including those who had not done well in school, expected future success (Dweck et al., 1980). More recent research, however, disputes that finding. Even in high school, females by and large are now aware that they don't have to restrict themselves to "female" occupations. They believe they can become involved in the wide spectrum of occupations available to all (Rubenstein, 1992). Once in those occupations, women do quite well. Despite the questions raised in former times about women's ability to lead others, for instance, research shows that in leadership roles they are just as effective as men (Eagly, Karau, & Makhijani, 1995).

Communication

Do men or women talk more? Are men—or women—more likely to touch someone they're talking to? In both cases, the answer is women, right? Wrong! Men not only talk more than women, they also interrupt other people's conversations more often. And it is men who tend to touch people while they are talking; women more often are the ones being touched (Hyde, 1994).

Let's try another question. Do men or women reveal more about themselves in a conversation? In this case, the answer *is* women. Many studies show that women engage in more self-disclosure than men, especially when they are talking with special friends or family members. This situation has been of some concern to psychologists because it can sometimes create problems for men in several areas. For instance, self-disclosure is necessary in counseling and in close relationships. It is hard to express your feelings, find emotional support, or get your needs met if you cannot talk about what is going on inside. The magnitude of this problem, though, seems to have been exaggerated. Recent evidence shows that gender differences in the amount of self-disclosure are actually quite small, only about 10 percent (Dindia & Allen, 1992).

Focus Question

• Are there any differences in the way males and females interact with other people?

▶ *What does this picture reveal about masculine and feminine modes of communication?*

In Focus

Male and Female Communication

What differences do you notice in these conversations?

Still, when it comes to understanding each other and being understood, it almost seems as if men and women come from separate countries. We don't exactly speak different languages, but we do place very different interpretations on what is said to us. A book by Deborah Tannen (1990) sheds a great deal of light on this subject. Deborah Tannen is a specialist in the use of language, and the following material is derived from her work.

Before going any further, we need to explain that men and women seem to operate from very different overall views of the world. Men tend to see the world in terms of a hierarchy, where keeping or improving your status and independence is critical. Women, on the other hand, tend to see it as a cooperative network, where being more closely connected to others is what matters most.

These basic differences in approach can account for the vast majority of problems the sexes have in understanding each other. For instance, when a woman checks with her husband before making plans, this supports her feeling of connectedness. On the other hand, a husband's checking with his wife may threaten his image of control and self-reliance, especially if other people are around.

▲ *Books on how to communicate with the other gender are big sellers.*

Even in childhood, males and females communicate differently. Boys tend to sit beside each other to talk. To boys, this is less confrontational than sitting face-to-face, or head-to-head, as it were. Girls sit facing each other to talk. This allows for more direct interaction and clearer observation of facial expressions and gestures.

There is not enough space here to delve fully into the subject of communication differences. But there is room for one example. Suppose someone says to a friend, "I'm having a terrible time getting along with my boss," and then briefly describes the situation. How does the friend respond?

Women are likely to empathize or tell about a similar problem they have. Men are likely to offer a solution or minimize the magnitude of the problem. In both cases, the friend is showing interest and concern.

By minimizing how bad the problem is, the man is offering reassurance. By offering a solution, he is trying to help. After all, it doesn't do your status any good to have a big problem with someone more powerful than you. Negating the problem will improve your standing. Solving it will let you avoid a confrontation and add to the friend's status as well.

When another man gets these responses, he will probably react positively. A woman, though, is likely to feel insulted or ignored. Why? When she expresses her feelings and those feelings are accepted by another person, she feels closer. But when a solution is given instead, the woman feels cut off. And to her, negating or minimizing her problems implies a lack of concern. She is seeking connectedness, which she will get from discussing the problem further or hearing that someone else has had the same experience.

How does a man react to receiving an empathetic response or being told about a similar problem? He is likely to feel challenged or insulted. To him, saying that you've had a similar problem may mean you are trying to upstage him, and telling him you know how he feels may be interpreted as condescension. Is it any wonder that men and women so often seem to be at cross-purposes?

Selecting a Mate

Psychologists have been studying the characteristics that people want and value in a potential mate for decades. Gender differences are clear-cut and consistent. They hold true across generations and across cultures. They have resulted in complaints from women that men are superficial and interested only in a woman's looks. They have resulted in complaints from men that women are materialistic and interested only in a man's income. So who is right? It appears that both are, to some extent.

A massive analysis of research done in this area over the last 25 years or so provides some interesting insights. The characteristics most often studied are social and economic status (middle class, working class, and so on), physical attractiveness, personality, intelligence, ambition, character (honesty and sincerity), and sense of humor. Women give more weight to socioeconomic status, ambition, character, and intelligence in mate selection. Both sexes value physical attractiveness in a mate, but men give this characteristic more weight than women do (Buss, 1994). The sexes are equal in the importance they attach to personality and sense of humor.

As to why these differences are so far reaching, the answer probably has less to do with ego than with concern for the next generation. In other words, the situation is probably best explained in terms of the welfare of the (potential) children. For instance, general physical appearance to some extent reflects a person's genetic makeup. This will be passed on to the offspring. Thus, people look for physical characteristics that will benefit their children. Furthermore, in our society, children's survival depends on having access to good housing, medical care, education, nutrition, and so on. Look at the characteristics that women emphasize. They are all related to the ability to survive with some degree of comfort (Feingold, 1992).

The reasons we have just given for these gender differences may be arguable, although some psychologists believe this explanation fits the facts quite well. The differences themselves, though, are not in dispute. The differences are real.

In our society, the man's status is also important for part of his family's identity. When a woman marries, she usually takes her husband's name. Children are usually given their father's last name. We tend to trace our ancestry more through our father's family line than our mother's.

It is tempting to believe that because our culture does things a certain way, everybody else does it that way, too. Usually, though, this is not the case; and it is not the case here. Among the Sioux, for instance, this tradition was reversed. Wives kept their own names, and the children belonged to the mother's clan, not the father's. Family property was held by the mother, and a child's lineage was traced through the mother's ancestry (Kelton, 1993).

Selecting a Mate

Men look for . . .

- Physical attractiveness
- Character
- Intelligence
- Personality and
   Sense of humor
- Socioeconomic status

Women look for . . .

- Socioeconomic status
- Ambition
- Character
- Intelligence
- Personality and
   Sense of humor
- Physical attractiveness

▲ *Men and women tend to emphasize different desired qualities in a potential mate.*

Focus Question

....

- How severe are hormonal effects on most people?

menstrual cycles monthly cycles that revolve around the elimination of the lining of the uterus when the egg has not been fertilized

Hormonal Cycles

With large numbers of women now employed in very responsible positions, some discussion has focused on what effect **menstrual cycles** have on women's behavior. Menstruation occurs approximately once a month when the lining of the woman's uterus, which could have been used to hold a fertilized egg, is discharged because it is not needed. The lining comes out as a harmless bloody fluid. The lining will build anew the following month to complete the cycle.

Because there are so many hormonal changes that go along with this process, many females suffer physical discomfort and moderate changes in mood. From these facts arises the common belief that females will act strangely once a month. This belief has sparked comments concerning whether a woman, in light of these hormonal changes, would be able to handle the office of president of the United States.

As recently as the 1950s, women were expected to come apart at "that time of the month." They literally would not swim or play games, and it was considered dangerous for them to take a bath. (Quick showers were okay, though, in case you wondered.) In the 1980s, some female defendants claimed they were under the influence of menstrual symptoms when they murdered their husbands. This defense was used fairly successfully in England.

As usual, we must try to get a little perspective on the issue. In extreme cases, the menstrual cycle can have severe physical and psychological effects. But this happens so very rarely that it is not something for the average female to worry about. The Case Study on page 391 describes common misconceptions and gives you accurate information about this topic.

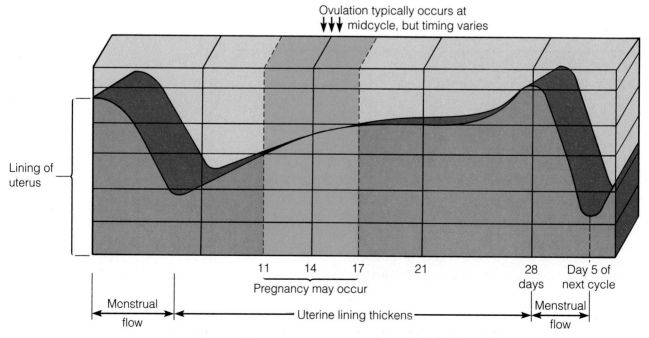

▲ *Figure 13.1*   *Typical pattern of the menstrual cycle*

PMS—Fact or Fiction?

Case Study

In the 1870s, advertising headlines screamed "A FEARFUL TRAGEDY" over the story of a clergyman murdered by his wife who "had become insane from 16 years of suffering with female complaints." Supposedly she would have been free of these complaints if she had taken the popular Lydia E. Pinkham's Vegetable Compound, a liquid mixture of exotic ingredients which included a notable amount of alcohol (Jackson, 1984).

Because so many hormonal changes accompany the menstrual cycle, many females experience physical discomfort and moderate mood changes. Extreme cases of severe physical and psychological effects resulting from the menstrual cycle are rare. There is a condition called **premenstrual syndrome (PMS)** that afflicts about 5 percent of women (Gise, 1991). PMS usually occurs three to seven days prior to menstruation itself and causes anxiety, irritability, and mental confusion. Most women do not have severe symptoms, but when they do occur, they are very unpleasant. Medical treatment to reduce the severity of the symptoms is available.

So why do people believe that PMS is more widespread? Psychologist Carol Tavris argues that women *learn*—mistakenly—that hormones control them once a month. If they are experiencing a bad mood, they are likely to blame it on PMS. When Tavris presented a checklist of PMS symptoms to men—back pain, sleeplessness, headaches—the men were just as likely to report PMS symptoms as the women, as long as the checklist was not labeled, "A PMS Symptoms Checklist" (Tavris, 1992).

As you may have read in Chapter 6, we are all controlled by unseen forces, especially bodily rhythms. The female's monthly cycle is one of these. You may be surprised to hear that males also follow a monthly cycle. Males have a monthly hormonal change that is not as major as the female one, but it does cause mild depression, lethargy, and moodiness about once every 28 to 30 days (Luce, 1971). When a husband and wife live together for a long time, their cycles tend to become synchronized—that is, they happen at the same time, which is not necessarily a blessing (Nicholson, 1984).

▲ *Today we have a better understanding of hormonal changes than we did in the past.*

premenstrual syndrome (PMS) anxiety, irritability, and mental confusion resulting from monthly female hormonal changes

Review the Case Study

As you can see, myths about PMS have been generated for many years. From your observations, what is the status of the myths today? Do teens today, for example, still attribute many bad moods to PMS?

• Are gender behaviors innate, or learned?

• Why is it harmful to society to strictly define gender roles?

gender role behavior acts that reflect society's view of what is appropriate for males and what is appropriate for females

identification the process of modeling behavior patterns after (usually) a member of the same sex

▶ *Strictly defined and traditional gender roles would likely exclude this behavior for a little boy.*

392

Gender Role Behavior

Many of our ideas about gender role behavior come from society, and we start picking up these ideas at a very young age. For instance, the color blue is used for baby boys. This comes from an old superstition that evil spirits threatened boys in the nursery and that blue, borrowed from the "heavenly blue" of the sky, would ward off these spirits. Later, legend suggested that baby boys were often found under cabbages (which are often blue in Europe). Girls were supposedly born inside pink roses, so that is their color (Brasch, 1967).

Identification and Gender Role

Gender role behavior involves acts that reflect society's view of what is appropriate for males and what is appropriate for females. A simple example is society's idea of who should play with dolls and who should play with soldiers.

Gender role behavior is thought to arise from **identification.** Identification is the process of modeling one's behavior after the behavior patterns of another person, usually one of the same sex. Even though the mother tends to have more influence than the father on children of both sexes, a child will most often actually *imitate* the parent (or another adult) of the same sex.

But it is a little more complicated than that. Fathers who are very warm and affectionate toward their daughters tend to produce a *mild* tomboyishness in them. Extreme strictness, severe control of the child, or unusual physical punishment tend to dispirit both male and female children. These children become docile, at least externally, and they submit to others. This submissiveness can be deceptive, though, because a time may come when such a child will "explode."

Boys whose fathers were not present during the preschool years—that is, up to the age of five—tend to be less aggressive and not quite as active in sports. This finding, even though it is only a statistic and does not apply to all males, deserves a little elaboration.

The assumption that males should be football players and females powder puffs in order to be "normal" turns out not to be the case. The most normal people in terms of mental health are those who lean slightly away from excessive masculinity or femininity. This is an important finding because many single mothers panic unnecessarily, afraid that something is going to go wrong with their fatherless children. Most boys in such a position tend to find a role model outside the home very quickly and imitate some older male, perhaps a teacher or an uncle.

And there are still more complications. In families where either the mother or the father is unusually dominant, the children tend to identify with that dominant parent, even across sex lines. If there is no striking dominance, some daughters identify with the father, some sons with the mother, and some children with both. In addition, children can identify with brothers and sisters. Boys who have only brothers and girls who have only sisters tend to adopt more traditional gender roles than those in families with a mixture. And girls who grow up without an older brother are more competitive than those who have one (Stewart & Winter, 1974).

Psychologically Generated Gender Roles

As far as we can tell, animals of all kinds are very aware of gender. Monkey mothers carefully examine their newborn babies' genitals and treat babies differently depending on the offsprings' gender. For instance, they do not allow as much fighting and bickering among females (Money, 1980). Among humans, parents strongly encourage activities that are socially defined as appropriate for the child's gender, especially when the children are quite young and especially for boys (Martin & Ruble, 1997). Fathers, though, are somewhat more determined about this than mothers are (Lytton & Romney, 1991).

As mentioned, playthings for boys contrast noticeably with those for girls. There is no reason at all, for example, why boys would not want to play with doll furniture, since they usually spend considerable time with miniature action figures. In fact, when families send their children to nontraditional nursery schools where fixed gender roles are not taught, the children do not show the usual tools-only-for-boys and teacups-only-for-girls interests. So we know that much of gender role behavior is the result of social training.

Research shows that adults treat a baby differently depending on whether they think they are dealing with a boy or a girl. Even with a baby only a few months old, adults will offer a female or male toy, depending on whether they are told the baby is a girl or a boy. In one study, subjects were introduced to a baby (who was actually a boy) and later asked to describe the infant's characteristics. Those who were told that the baby was a girl described him in "female" terms as being soft and smiling (Sidorowicz & Lunney, 1980).

▲ *When fixed gender roles are not emphasized, children play with whatever they think is fun.*

▲ *This character on a TV comedy show was so androgynous that no one could tell whether "Pat" (on the left) was a woman or a man.*

Mixing Gender Roles.   By strictly defining gender roles and emphasizing differences when they don't exist, we tend to restrict the full range of possibilities for both men and women. "Masculine" men, for instance, have difficulty enjoying and showing affection toward babies, playing with small animals, or even listening to someone's personal problems. "Feminine" females often can't assert themselves or make independent judgments. Thus, it would seem that a mixture of so-called feminine and masculine behaviors makes for the richest life, and we restrict this potential when we stress gender differences.

It is difficult to describe what is strictly masculine or strictly feminine. In our culture, masculinity tends to be associated with dominance, assertiveness, achievement, and leadership, while femininity is associated with compassion, sociability, and tenderness.

The problem is that people who fall into the more extreme gender roles are more rigid and have fewer options open to them in different situations. Nothing says that people can't be in between these extremes. For this reason, psychologist Sandra Bem (1975) developed a concept she called **androgyny** (an-DRAH-ja-nee). An androgynous person is relatively high in both masculine (*andro*) and feminine (*gyn*) characteristics. The ideal androgynous person would be both an achiever and a social creature, capable of expressing emotion *and* taking action.

Bem found that androgynous people are in better psychological health than those with very strong gender identities. This makes sense when you think about it, because the broader the base of one's activities, the more varied and exciting life can be.

There are serious pitfalls, though. A woman who adopts what society considers to be too many masculine characteristics is not going to fit

androgyny the quality of having both masculine and feminine characteristics

in very well. Worse in society's view, however, is the man who adopts too many feminine traits—he's in for even more trouble. To complicate Bem's proposal, society values masculine traits more highly than feminine ones. According to society, then, both men and women are better off with masculine characteristics.

Despite these problems, Bem's work is important because it focuses on the extremes that too many people adopt. Her basic idea about androgyny is useful because it leads the way to more flexibility and a greater willingness to share the characteristics of members of the opposite sex. Even changing one's view moderately and realizing that not every boy has to play ball nor every girl play with dolls can make life more rewarding all around.

Current Views of Gender Roles. Traditional gender roles assigned specific activities to males and quite different ones to females. To oversimplify, males were considered the heads of the household and were primarily responsible for financial support of the family. Females were expected to devote their time to caring for the home and children. Although there is still a lot of heated controversy about the value of this division of labor, current views of gender roles are clearly more egalitarian—that is, they allow both men and women more equal access to a variety of activities and responsibilities. Usually, this means that it has become acceptable for men to be more involved in child care and household chores and for women to have greater freedom, especially in the areas of education and occupation.

This change can be seen across a wide range of cultures, and we are not the most liberal one—not at all. On the other hand, we are not the most conservative, either. In a survey of attitudes in 14 different countries, the most egalitarian views were found in the Netherlands, Germany, and Finland. The most traditional views were found in India, Pakistan, and Nigeria. The United States and Canada fell in just about the middle (Williams & Best, 1994).

Within the United States, a shift away from the traditional view of gender roles has been going on for decades. From the 1970s through the mid-1990s, there has been a steady trend toward adopting a more egalitarian approach. Men are somewhat more conservative than women in this regard, although their views are more liberal now than in the past. And even though the trend holds true across the nation, of all areas of the country, the South is still the most traditional (Spence & Hahn, 1997; Twenge, 1997).

 ## Pause for Thought

1. What factors do men and women consider when selecting a mate?
2. Explain some hormonal changes that both men and women experience monthly.

Critical Thinking

3. John grows up in a household with traditional gender role models. Jerry sees androgynous models. Both men become teachers. How might these two men be different at work?

APPLYING Psychology to Life

Searching for Gender Differences

Next, we're going to look at some differences in the behaviors of the sexes. As far as we know, there have been no formal psychological studies of any of them, but they do seem to be real differences— at least in the sense that society apparently encourages them.

Observe them for yourself, and see if we aren't correct. You might want to try to figure out why they occur. We have our own ideas for each, but they're just guesses, so try to come up with your own.

Social Differences

Note the difference in how males and females talk to members of their own gender when they are close friends. Males are very rude and aggressive to those they like best ("Hi there, ugly!"). Apparently, the ruder the men are to one another, the closer the relationship. Females don't usually express affection in this fashion.

Note that females hug one another, put an arm around the other's shoulders, and touch one another's hands. Males, on the other hand, will hit each other in the shoulder with a fist, shove each other, or, in sports, pat one another on the posterior.

When a group goes out to a restaurant, note how females tend to get up and go to the rest room together. Men go to the rest room separately, usually not getting up en masse to exit as the females do.

Academic Differences

Male readers may have balked at an earlier statement about females doing better in school than males do. Try this out: Ask 10 males and 10 females their grade point averages. For each sex, take the numbers, add them up, divide by the number of people, and you have the average. Note that the female grade point average is probably higher than the male one.

Test for Differences

In the next paragraphs, we have constructed a "quiz" of sorts, which might be fun to try

▲ *Males are likely to show friendship in a somewhat aggressive way.*

▲ *Females do more hugging and touching than males to show they care.*

out the next time a group is together. You'll be surprised at the major differences in responses between the sexes, and we hope it helps you gain some insight into the opposite one. If you actually reach the point where you can explain the opposite sex, you will have done something nobody has done before.

1. (a) Think about the pluses and minuses of being a male in America today; of being a female. In your opinion, do males or females have it better? Why?

   (b) Imagine that you are a member of the opposite sex. How would you be better off? What would the problems be?

2. (a) If you were married, would you want your mate's income to be above, below, or equal to yours? (Think about it, and answer truthfully!) How important is this to you, and why? Ask yourself the same questions about intelligence and looks.

   (b) Suppose you had to choose between your mate's having a job with more prestige and status than yours and your mate's having a job that pays more than yours. (It must be one or the other; it can't be both or neither one.) Which would you choose,

and why? Compare your answers with those of the opposite sex.

3. If you could decide your baby's gender, would you? If so, would you prefer a boy or a girl? Would your answer be different if you already had a child of that sex? If you could decide what your baby would become as an adult, including talents, personality, and occupation, would you? If not, why not? If so, what would your decision be? Do females and males differ in how they answer these questions?

4. (a) A millionaire will give you, absolutely free, a brand-new car of your choosing if you agree not to speak to any of your friends for a month. During that time, if you tell anyone why you are doing this, the deal is off. Would you accept the offer?

   (b) The same millionaire will give you $25,000 if you agree not to take a bath or shower, not to change your clothes, and not to wash your hair or comb it for two months, while keeping the reason secret. Would you accept this offer? Do more males or more females answer "yes" to either offer?

5. If you had all the money you wanted to spend on entertainment, what would you plan for one 24-hour period for yourself and no more than three friends of the same sex? (No dates allowed, please.) How do females and males differ in their answers?

Summary

1. Hormones control the basics of physical gender development. Both sexes have both male and female hormones; but in each sex, one kind of hormone dominates over the other.

2. The major difference between males and females is the fact that females bear children. Other differences that show up in humans and animals are that males tend to be more aggressive and to have a higher activity level, while females tend to be more nurturing.

3. When taken together, studies show no clear-cut differences between the sexes in intelligence, self-confidence, or drive for success.

4. Males and females differ somewhat in their social relationships. For example, women have a few close friends, while men have more acquaintances.

5. Males and females communicate somewhat differently. They also differ somewhat in the characteristics they seek in a mate.

6. Menstrual cycles can cause emotional upset and physical distress, but normally these difficulties are not severe.

7. Identification can be quite complex, and a person can identify with a brother or sister as well as with either parent or another adult. In general, males identify with older males and females with older females—usually the parents, if they are available.

8. Androgyny seems to be a goal worth working for, but there is a risk of social disapproval if a person goes too far in mixing gender role behavior.

9. Current views of gender roles are more egalitarian than older views.

Vocabulary

gender	spatial skills	gender role behavior
hormones	menstrual cycles	identification
androgen	premenstrual syndrome (PMS)	androgyny
estrogen		

Review Questions

Multiple Choice

On a sheet of paper, write the letter of the answer that best completes each statement.

1. Injecting an animal with androgen would probably increase
   a. breast size.
   c. moodiness.
   b. brain size.
   d. aggressiveness.

2. The female hormone is called
   a. estrogen.   b. androgen.   c. androgyny.

3. Which of the following characteristics apply to females?
   a. greater endurance
   b. live longer than the opposite sex
   c. fewer genetic defects
   d. all of the above

4. Evidence indicates that male infants are naturally
   a. more active than females.
   b. less active than females.
   c. just as active as females.

5. Which gender *performs* better on tests of spatial skills?
   a. males   b. females   c. neither

6. Androgynous people on the average are
   a. less healthy than people with strong gender identities.
   b. more healthy than people with strong gender identities.
   c. just as healthy as people with strong gender identities.

7. Which of the following reasons might discourage a person from becoming androgynous?
   a. Society values masculine traits over feminine traits—so why be feminine?
   b. Women who are masculine may not be accepted by society.
   c. Men who are feminine may not be accepted by society.
   d. all of the above

True/False

On a sheet of paper answer each statement true *or* false. *If false, rewrite to make it true.*

8. The brains of males are different from the brains of females.

9. Evidence indicates that males are naturally better than females at math.

10. Surveys consistently show that males have higher self-confidence than females.

11. Females are as oriented toward achievement as males.

12. Studying animal behavior helps us realize that the maternal "instinct" is present only in females.

13. Premenstrual syndrome afflicts a majority of women.

14. Males experience their own hormonal cycles that start and end every three months.

15. Overly strict parents will tend to feminize their children.

16. Children tend to identify with the dominant parent.

For each of the following descriptions of communication skills, answer M *for males or* F *for females.*

17. Interrupt conversations more often

18. Self-disclose more often

19. Concerned about improving status

20. Sit beside each other rather than face-to-face

21. More likely to empathize than to try to solve another's problem

Discussion Questions

1. Imagine you are a parent. Would you ever buy your daughter a truck or a football? Would you ever buy your son a doll or a toy kitchen set? Why or why not?

2. Do you find that girls are drawn more to baby-sitting jobs than boys are? If so, how do you account for this? Are girls encouraged to be more nurturing, or is this natural?

3. Though gender roles have leveled out some, it seems that males, for the most part, are primarily responsible for asking females out for a first date. If you disagree that this is true, explain. If you agree, explain why females usually do not initiate first dates.

4. Which characteristics of male and female communication apply to you? Males, you might recall, tend to offer solutions to their friends' problems. Females tend to empathize. Offer examples in your answer.

5. If it's true that males and females communicate differently, maybe we can all use some advice from the opposite sex. What advice about communication would you offer to the opposite sex?

6. How do your friendships or the friendships you know about match up with what researchers have found? Do boys' groups have a leader? Do girls' groups place less emphasis on status? Are boys

more likely to confide in a girl than in another boy?

7. Researchers have found that when couples break up, women are more likely to initiate the breakup. Are there also differences in the *methods* men and women use to break up?

8. Analyze the gender roles of your family members. Do they follow more traditional or egalitarian gender roles? What effect do you think this has had on you?

9. Describe several advantages in being a member of the opposite sex. Be nice.

Activities and Projects

1. Neatly print the following information onto two index cards:

   The reason I want to be an engineer is that I've always done well in math and I enjoy it. For example, in third grade, I won first place in a math test in the area and, ever since, I've always been excited about math classes. I know that my other grades are just average, but I've always gotten an A or B in math.

At the top of one of the cards, print "Georgia Roanoke." At the top of the other, print "George Roanoke." Take another index card and print the following information on it:

   How would you rate this person's chances of succeeding in a career in engineering?

0	1	2	3	4	5	6	7	8
Dismal	Very poor	Poor	Below average	Average	Above average	High	Very high	Out-standing

Are you beginning to get the idea? Find 32 high school subjects, 16 males and 16 females. Eight of the males and eight of the females will see the "Georgia" card. The other eight males and eight females will see the "George" card. Record their ratings onto some kind of data sheet.

In order to get accurate and honest ratings, you must make sure that your subjects don't find out the purpose of the experiment—which is to see if the male, because of males' supposedly "superior" math skills, will be rated higher, despite *identical* qualifications. To make sure your subjects don't know your purpose, you might say something like this: "In English class, we're learning about how to write résumés and how to fill out job applications. We all had to write a paragraph and exchange the paragraph with someone in class. Then that person goes around and collects ratings. We thought the ratings would be more accurate if we exchanged paragraphs rather than collecting our own ratings. So be completely honest."

Analyze your results. What was the overall average rating for Georgia? For George? What was the female average rating for both cards? What was the male average rating for both cards?

Draw a simple chart and list all these ratings. Discuss your results. Did the hypothesis seem to be supported by your findings: Is there a sex bias against females involved in math? Were you surprised by your results? Why or why not?

2. This next activity is a variation on the previous one. Follow the same procedure, but this time use middle-aged adults as your subjects to see if people with more traditional backgrounds will, in fact, be "traditional" in their ratings. Discuss your results.

If you're conducting this experiment *and* the previous one, compare and contrast the results. Maybe you can conduct one activity while a friend conducts the other, and then you can compare and contrast each other's results.

3. Most libraries save back issues of the most popular magazines for years and years. Sift through them to find several magazine ads from 1960, 1970, 1980, 1990, and the present. As you look through these ads, jot down information about the ones that seem to promote traditional gender role behavior and the ones that seem to defy it.

Organize your notes into a report. Which products and brand names are most commonly linked to gender roles? How have ads changed from 1960 to the present? Do you notice any patterns? Are ads today still sexist? Explain.

4. It seems that everyone has some opinion on gender differences. Men are better drivers. Women have a more sophisticated sense of humor. And on and on. Write a personal essay in which you discuss some of your own opinions about gender differences. Some areas you may want to address: sports, work, school, emotions, romance.

5. Take another look at the gender quiz in the In Focus feature at the beginning of the chapter. As you found out while reading the chapter, all but question number 1 are false. Show the quiz to eight males and eight females and record their answers. Then go back to the person who got the highest score and the one who got the lowest score, and interview these two people. If there is a tie for highest or lowest, randomly pick one of the people who tied. For your interview, you can use the questions listed in Applying Psychology to Life on page 396, or you can write your own—as long as both people are asked identical questions.

This will be your hypothesis: The person who scored lowest on the quiz probably knows less about gender differences and similarities than the one who scored highest. The one who scored lowest then should also exhibit more traditional attitudes about sex roles—simply because this person doesn't know any better. In other words, you're testing whether ignorance breeds sexist attitudes.

Analyze and compare the two interviews in detail to determine if this hypothesis seems to be true. The most difficult part of this analysis is trying to decide objectively whether the answers are, in fact, traditional and sexist—or not so traditional. You'll have to use your judgment. Just make sure you can support your judgment in some way. Also, try to be fair. The answers to questions 1, 2, and 3 in the Applying Psychology to Life quiz will probably be the most revealing.

Unit 5

In this Unit...

Personality, Adjustment, and Conflict

CHAPTER 14

Theories of Personality

Personality is a term referring to long-lasting patterns of behavior. This chapter discusses several theories of personality, each with its own view of what motivates human beings. Some suggest we are the products of unconscious forces, some that we are what we learn, and some that we inherit our personalities.

Difficulties in Understanding Personality

In this chapter, we try to get a handle on personality. And what a difficult task that is. People aren't always what they seem. For instance, many professional comedians are very quiet at home, and some of the better ones suffer from serious bouts of depression. Classmates and teachers often misunderstand what you are really like and what you really feel. They may think you are aggressive when you are really shy. They may think you are outgoing when in fact you look forward to being alone. They may see you as a loner when you actually need company.

And as if this isn't complicated enough, we all behave differently at different times. When we are eating alone at home, our manners may be disgusting. When we are out for dinner, no one would suspect how sloppy we can be.

You can see, then, that trying to pin down personality is a tough assignment. We won't succeed completely. Still, it is worthwhile going over some of the theories about how our personalities develop. These theories attempt to bring together in an organized, coherent way a set of beliefs about how we become who we are.

The Usefulness of Theories

What is the purpose of having theories? There are a couple of answers to this.

First, part of a theory may turn out to be correct. Thus, eventually we might be able to explain how we got the way we are by combining the most workable parts of a number of theories of personality.

Second, a theory gives us a framework in which to study people. Then we can either accept or reject the claims of the theory based on what studies show to be the case. For instance, at one point it was said that those who abuse and beat their children had parents who beat *them* when they were children. As it turns out, in reality this may or may not be the case. But the hypothesis was useful because it gave us something to study, to either accept or reject.

Defining Personality

Some people are cheats and liars on one day and super-moral on the next. But most of us most of the time respond roughly the same way in many situations. In fact, this is the definition of "personality."

Personality consists of broad and long-lasting patterns of behavior. These patterns are fairly consistent from one day to the next. Thus, the odds are that a person who is afraid of canoe trips, hiking, swimming, and heights will also be afraid of roller coasters. In contrast, those who constantly take chances, drive like fools, and will bet on anything will ride a roller coaster that has all the support bolts loosened. Once we assume that some aspects of personality are fairly stable, we can look at theories that try to explain their origin.

personality a person's broad, long-lasting patterns of behavior

Psychoanalytic Theory

psychoanalytic theory a theory that personality is based on impulses and needs in the unconscious

Psychoanalytic theory is a personality theory based on the assumption that how we develop and behave result from impulses or needs that are unknown to us. In other words, what we are comes from hidden forces. The theory arose from a belief that people with psychological problems were unable to see the origin of their difficulties. To view these forces requires a trained professional who will *analyze* one's thoughts, feelings, and history to reveal what is going on beneath the surface. That's how we got the term psycho*analysis*.

Sigmund Freud

The most famous psychoanalyst is **Sigmund Freud** (FROID) (1856–1939). His theory of how we develop and what controls us dominated psychology from the early 1900s through the late 1940s. Freud believed that the core of one's personality appears within the first five or six years of life and is more or less fixed by that age. For him, individual development has its source in the family and the conflicts that every family has. Our feelings about ourselves come from jealousies, anxieties, and guilt regarding how we relate to other family members and how they view us.

This emphasis is not hard to understand, since Freud's own family life was chaotic. His father was 20 years older than his mother, had a couple of children by a previous marriage, and had a mistress as well. Freud's mother had eight children after marrying Freud's father. At one point, there were the eight children, a half-brother the age of Freud's mother, the father, and a nephew all living in the same cramped 30-foot-by-30-foot room (Clark, 1980). It makes sense that the family friction and unwanted intimacy this brought about would lead to many of Freud's beliefs.

Freud studied to become a physician and for a while actually practiced medicine in the traditional sense. But two things changed the course of his life: (1) As he listened to patients, he became more and more convinced that the problems they were having came from psychological forces rather than physical ones, and (2) he couldn't stand the sight of blood. At one point, Freud tried to treat his patients by giving them cocaine. Eventually, he became addicted himself and just about ruined a very meaningful career before overcoming the problem (Reisman, 1966).

▲ *Sigmund Freud, the father of psychoanalysis, and friend*

An early case that Freud consulted on involved a woman who couldn't drink water but who stayed alive by eating only fruit, such as melons. This clearly wasn't a "normal" sickness, and Freud couldn't make sense of it at first. A physician friend of Freud's told him that he had been successful in using hypnosis with patients with strange symptoms in order to find out what was going on. So Freud thought it should be tried. Under hypnosis, the woman recalled that when she was a child, she one day found a hated servant's dog drinking out of a water glass in the kitchen. Thus, it seemed that hypnosis helped get to parts of the patient's mind that were unknown to her normally (Freud, 1938). (This case is covered in detail in the Case Study on page 411.)

Freud began to believe that we are guided by impulses and needs that don't show up on the surface. From this belief arose his famous concept, the unconscious.

The Unconscious

Freud believed that childhood conflicts within the family are removed from conscious memory but are still "in us." These events are held in the **unconscious,** the part of us we are not aware of. As far as Freud was concerned, the conscious mind is like the tip of an iceberg. The far larger part, the unconscious, is below the surface (Epstein, 1994). Our true feelings sometimes appear in dreams or in mistakes we make when speaking. Freud claimed that if he talked to a patient long enough, he found some of the material that was causing the trouble buried. So he gave up hypnosis as not needed and used his "talking cure."

Freud reached the unconscious by using **free association,** a process in which the patient says *everything* that appears in his or her mind, even if seemingly not connected. In other words, no "censoring" is allowed. The basis for this method of treatment was Freud's assumption that the unconscious always seeks expression in one way or another. If the patient talked

unconscious according to psychoanalytic belief, the part of the mind that is beyond consciousness. Although we are unaware of its contents, they strongly affect our behavior.

free association Freudian process in which a person says everything that appears in his or her mind, even if the ideas or images seem unconnected

▲ *Free association occurs when this patient says whatever comes to his mind.*

long enough, more and more of the unconscious would appear in what was being said. The analyst could then put it all together into a coherent picture and thus explain problem-causing behavior. For example, if you have a deep-seated anger toward a friend, the more you talk about this person, the more likely it is that some unconscious material about what caused the anger will appear.

Freud was quite taken by the theory and writings of Charles Darwin. Darwin's work suggested that the human is basically an animal, even though we have higher mental abilities as well as the ability to make moral decisions. As a result, Freud focused mostly on animal-like aspects of our behavior. In other words, he focused on our very strong drives to satisfy bodily needs—food, comfort, sex, self-preservation. All human societies in one way or another try to block expression of too much animal-like behavior, so we can't always satisfy these needs—or even admit we have them. Since they won't go away, we try to hide from them by putting them into our unconscious.

If everything we wanted to do was good, there would be no problem. But all of us have desires that we would just as soon no one else knew about, so we make them "disappear." This disappearance is called **repression.** According to Freud's theory, from childhood on, needs and desires that are forbidden cause guilt. As a result, they are pushed out of consciousness (repressed) into the unconscious, where they live. They do not remain quiet, however. They reappear as conflicts and anxieties that interfere with daily life and normal functioning.

repression the process of pushing the needs and desires that cause guilt into the unconscious

The Libido

Freud's theory emphasizes an interaction between conscious and unconscious forces. Freud developed his theory during a time of great scientific discovery in the fields of chemistry and physics about electricity, magnetism, and energy forces. He absorbed some of these ideas and assumed that the human had *real* (biological, not symbolic) energy inside, which controlled behavior. This energy he called **libido** (luh-BEE-doe).

libido Freudian term for internal energy forces that continuously seek discharge

The libidinal energy constantly seeks some kind of discharge, just as lightning discharges into the ground when it finds a high tree. In the process of seeking discharge, this energy creates tension. If the tension is not released in real life, the desires appear as dreams or fantasies. An attempt at release can also appear as psychological disturbance.

Focus Question

• What are the three parts of a person's inner world?

Freud's Map of the Mind

Freud divided the individual's inner world into three parts. One is responsible for survival needs; another, for society's rules of behavior. The third part deals with the real world and tries to keep the demands of the other two in balance.

id Freudian psychological unit containing basic needs and drives

Id. All of our basic needs and drives make up the **id.** Therefore, the id contains our major energy force (libido), which is constantly seeking expression. We cannot know, directly, what goes on in the id, because it is unconscious. It is also completely unconcerned about any reality except its own desires. Because of its emphasis on sexual and aggressive impulses, the id can cause many psychological problems. Without it, however, we would not eat when hungry or defend ourselves if attacked. Without it, we could not survive.

Superego. Although the id is necessary, if we acted out every impulse we had any time we wanted, society would fall apart. To hold the id in check, we each have, according to Freud, a **superego.** The term *superego* is an approximate synonym for "conscience." The superego causes us to feel guilt for being bad and pride for doing the right things. It develops out of the punishments and rewards we get from our parents, the first representatives of society's laws and customs. We need a superego, but like the id, the superego exists only for what it wants. If allowed to operate unchecked, it would block all our drives and instincts, letting us die rather than break a rule.

Ego. The third portion of the individual is called the **ego.** The ego is roughly the same as the *self.* The job of the ego is really to allow the id to express itself in some safety. In other words, the ego pays attention to reality and monitors what is going on in the environment as well as listening to what the superego has to say. If the id wants to steal wallets at a police station, the ego will listen to the superego and examine reality, saying, "That's not a very clever idea." So the ego acts as a controller, attempting to balance our desires with the demands of reality.

Our personalities show how good a balancing act we have developed. For instance, if the id takes over because the superego is not strong enough, we will develop personalities that are more and more demanding in terms of animal needs. On the one hand, if the ego loses its ability to strike a balance, we become pouty, whining individuals who are never satisfied. On the other hand, if the superego dominates as the result of endless control of our every desire, we become guilt ridden, shy, fearful, and withdrawn.

Stages of Development

Freud's five stages of personality development go from birth through adolescence. As mentioned earlier, Freud believed that personality is basically formed by the age of five or six. Consequently, all the major conflicts and psychological tasks we must deal with take place in the first three of his stages. The two later stages are necessary for completeness, but neither one presents any important new crises or demands.

According to Freud, adults' psychological problems have their roots in early childhood and can be traced to unresolved conflicts that originated during that time. When a conflict is not adequately resolved, some libidinal energy gets stuck, or *fixated,* at that stage. Such energy fixations create psychological trouble eventually. In fact, many behaviors that indicate trouble in one of Freud's first three stages appear later on in life, not in childhood. Examples of this include such problems as alcoholism, eating disorders, and severe depression. We give more examples of these behaviors in the following paragraphs.

Oral Stage: Birth to Age One and One-Half. In the **oral stage** of development, feeding is the main source of infants' pleasure, and weaning

▲ *In psychoanalysis, the mind has three parts: the id, ego, and superego.*

superego Freudian psychological unit roughly synonymous with the conscience

ego Freudian psychological unit that is based in reality; the "self" that allows controlled id expression within the boundaries set by the superego

Focus Question

• According to Freud, how does personality develop?

oral stage Freudian stage of development during which feeding and weaning are the child's main issues

409

is the task to be dealt with. When a child is weaned too early or too late, personality problems develop. Examples of oral-stage behaviors include depending too much on other people, rejecting others or being very sarcastic, and either overeating or self-starvation.

anal stage Freudian stage of development during which toilet training is the child's major concern

Anal Stage: Ages One and One-Half to Two and One-Half. The psychological task during the **anal stage** is toilet training. Toilet training that is either too lenient or too harsh will cause psychological problems. Anal-stage behaviors include such things as being excessively stingy or overly generous as well as sticking very rigidly to rules and regulations or being irresponsible and rebellious.

phallic stage Freudian stage of development during which the child experiences romantic interest in the opposite-sex parent and hostility toward the same-sex parent

Phallic Stage: Ages Two and One-Half to Five or Six. During the **phallic stage,** children experience the "Oedipus complex" (or Oedipus conflict), named for a character in a Greek play who killed his father and married his mother—without knowing it at the time. The Oedipus conflict, then, involves a desire to marry the opposite-sex parent, along with jealous and hostile feelings toward the same-sex parent. Because parents are bigger and more powerful than children, there is also a fear of punishment involved. In turn, the possibility of being punished causes guilt because, in the child's mind, one is punished only for being bad. A complicated set of emotions must be dealt with during this stage.

The only way to cope with all of these romantic, jealous, aggressive, anxious, and guilty feelings is to "identify" with the parent of the same sex, which means taking on as many of his or her characteristics as possible. Failure to resolve this conflict through identification can result in a wide range of psychological disorders. Freud believed that unreasonable anxiety, extreme guilt, phobias, and depression, for example, originate in the phallic stage of development.

latency stage Freudian stage of development during which the child's earlier conflicts are hidden or go below the surface

Latency Stage: Ages Six to Preadolescence. When something is latent, it is below the surface, hidden, not obvious. In the **latency stage,** conflicts and problems from the earlier stages remain subdued, or latent. No new conflicts arrive on the scene during this period.

genital stage Freudian stage of development during which the individual seeks an appropriate marital partner and earlier conflicts reappear

Genital Stage: Adolescence Onward. As people seek an appropriate marriage partner and prepare for adult life, the conflicts of early childhood reappear. No new conflicts arise during this **genital stage,** but all of the old ones resurface. Although the ways in which they are expressed may have changed, their content is left over from the first five years of life.

Focus Question

....

- How does Carl Jung's view of personality differ from Freud's?

Carl Jung

Carl Jung (YOONG) (1875–1961) was a friend and follower of Freud. The two men became quite close, so that when their relationship later got rocky, strange things happened. For example, Jung one day told Freud that he (Jung) had had a dream about corpses in coffins. Freud thought this meant that Jung wanted him dead, and as a result he fell over in a faint. Then they started calling one another names fitting to their profession, such as "crazy" and "neurotic" (Brome, 1967).

In any case, Jung began to doubt the Freudian theory's emphasis on animal functions. Eventually, he went off on his own, emphasizing what

Psychoanalysis is Born

Case Study

In 1880, a friend and colleague of Freud, Josef Breuer, began treating a 21-year-old woman he named Anna O. The treatment lasted about a year and a half, but the case would ultimately split the two friends apart and mark the beginning of psychoanalysis.

Anna O. had been a healthy and energetic young woman, devoted to her family and to helping others. She was especially close to her father who was strict, but he spoiled her at the same time. When he became gravely ill, she stayed at his side and nursed him as best as she could. Her efforts caused her to become ill herself.

She began complaining of a general tiredness and a loss of appetite. She suffered from frequent headaches, and her right arm became numb and paralyzed at times. Mostly, she walked around as if she were sleeping. She couldn't always talk in her native German. She could, however, speak the other languages she knew, such as English or Italian. She even hallucinated at times, imagining black snakes and skeletons.

▲ *Josef Breuer*

After her father died, these symptoms intensified. At times, Anna would spontaneously talk, which seemed to relieve her symptoms for a while. Anna later called this the "talking cure" (Freud, 1938). Dr. Breuer encouraged this talking. He concluded that talking allowed his patient to dredge up important memories. Once these memories were brought to the surface, he theorized, the symptoms associated with the memories would disappear.

Anna went through a time, for example, when she couldn't drink, even though she was extremely thirsty. During psychoanalysis, Anna recalled that when she was a child, she had seen a servant that she hated letting a dog drink from a water glass in the kitchen. After she recalled this incident and expressed her disgust openly, she could drink again. Another time, she recalled how her right arm had gone numb while helping her sick father. She had dozed off and dreamt of snakes crawling toward her, and in her dream, she was unable to move her arm to brush away the snakes. Again, once she discovered the source of her symptoms—after many sessions and through great effort—the symptoms eventually disappeared; her right arm no longer became paralyzed!

One day Breuer found Anna in a fetal position, moaning in pain. She said, "Now comes Dr. B.'s child" (Gay, 1988). Anna was experiencing what is known as a hysterical pregnancy. The word *hysteria* refers to physical symptoms that come from a psychological problem. In hysterical pregnancies, the patient has all the symptoms and pains that go along with pregnancy and even a major swelling of the abdomen (from body water), but there's no baby (Schultz, 1969). A few such cases still occur every year, even on occasion to males.

Breuer was shocked by Anna's statement and felt so uncomfortable about pursuing the source of her fantasies that he stopped treating her and asked a colleague to step in. Anna O. became a housemother in an orphanage for a while, and then ran a shelter for unwed mothers. Freud criticized Breuer for not exploring Anna's feelings, and this disagreement led to a strained relationship between the two. Freud moved on to other cases, of course, never shy about digging for the truth—regardless of the content—and revolutionized therapy in the process.

Review the Case Study

Why is talking such a powerful tool in this type of situation?

In Their Own Words . . .

Carl Jung *described his concept of archetypes in an interview given when he was in his eighties:*

You see, the archetype is a force. It has an autonomy, and it can suddenly seize you. It is like a seizure. So, for instance, falling in love at first sight, that is such a case. You have a certain image in yourself, without knowing it, of the woman—of any woman. You see that girl, or at least a good imitation of your type, and instantly you get the seizure; you are caught. And afterward you may discover that it was a . . . mistake. You see, a man is quite capable, or is intelligent enough to see that the woman of his choice was no choice; he has been captured! He sees that she is no good at all, . . . and he tells me so. He says, "For God's sake, doctor, help me to get rid of that woman." He can't, though, and he is like clay in her fingers. That is the archetype. (Evans, 1964, pp. 51–52)

Interpreting Primary Sources

In what way is an archetype different from a stereotype?

he really believed: that the unconscious is a well of mystical and religious beliefs that controls our behavior.

Pursuing his belief, Jung studied very old paintings, statues, relics, and books about myths and religion. No matter what civilization he studied—ancient, old, or new—he kept finding certain themes. For example, there were stories about and pictures of great heroes and concepts of "mothers" as strong and supportive, especially "Mother Earth" as something that provides us with food and care. And the idea of God in one form or another kept repeating itself (Jung, 1933, 1958).

Jung believed these basic ideas must be inherited, and he called them **archetypes.** An archetype is a universal human concept. It is like a master recording that is then used to manufacture large numbers of CDs or tapes. Jung figured that if such concepts appear everywhere throughout history in separate civilizations that have had no contact with one another, they must be part of all humans from the very beginning of each life.

archetypes Jung's term for inherited universal human concepts

▶ *The story of Cinderella, pictured here as a play, contains several archetypes. How many can you identify?*

Instead of being guided by an unconscious that seeks bodily pleasure, then, all humans must be controlled by certain beliefs we inherit, such as our image of the ideal woman or man. All these archetypes together make up the **collective unconscious.** It is called *collective* (meaning "everyone together") because the ideas are shared by the entire human race. Jung felt that it was "unconscious" because we are not fully aware we are part of these forces.

Each generation inherits beliefs in certain ideas or roles that are connected with certain behaviors—for instance, all civilizations have beliefs about mother, hero, wise old man, and so forth. Without even knowing it, we imitate the fixed images about these concepts and develop personalities to fit them.

Thus, despite the fact that a new mother may be unsure about what her baby needs, she *pretends* to know all and be all for the child. A skinny, weak, and hopelessly shy male will actually feel guilty if he doesn't stand up to another male who is over six feet tall and weighs 240 pounds. The man feels he should be a "hero." While both the man and the woman are being unrealistic, it would seem they are trying to fit into the myths of the collective unconscious.

At least one part of Jung's theory seems true of all of us. He claimed that in the process of trying to become like these mythical people, we hide our real feelings and our real personalities. The fake personality that we then develop is called a **persona** (per-SONE-ah), which comes from Latin and refers to the frowning or smiling masks that were worn by players in Greek and Roman stage plays. We use psychological masks to fit what we think we are supposed to be, rather than let ourselves be what we actually are. How many times, for instance, have you smiled and been pleasant around someone who is irritating you?

◄ *The persona is the social mask we wear.*

collective unconscious Jung's term for the portion of a person that contains ideas or archetypes (such as hero, mother, and so on) shared by the whole human race

persona Jung's term for a "mask" people wear to hide what they really are or feel

Pause for Thought

1. How did Freud study the unconscious? Why do we call his theory *psychoanalysis?*
2. Why do we repress desires, according to Freud, and what happens once the desires are repressed?
3. Describe Freud's map of the mind.
4. According to Carl Jung, what makes up the unconscious?

Critical Thinking

5. Mrs. Z reads about Freud's stages of development and decides to raise her children in a manner that will get them through the stages successfully. What does she do at each stage?

Thinking Critically about Psychology

How Powerful Is the Unconscious?

Freud's influence on psychological thought has been enormous. Jung's approach has been less influential. However, since both their theories emphasize the importance of unconscious forces, claims about this emphasis apply to both. The issue we want to consider here, then, is whether or how much humans are ruled by unconscious forces within them.

What specifically is being claimed or stated? Our behavior is largely determined by urges and desires of which we are unaware—urges and desires that reside in the unconscious realm of the mind.

What is the objective evidence for and against this claim? Looking for objective evidence where this topic is concerned is not going to be very fruitful. The fact of the matter is that we have no *direct* evidence that the unconscious even exists. Of course, we have no *direct* evidence that a particular thought exists, either, but we do not doubt humans' ability to think and reason. What we have to rely on is indirect evidence, which is usually more subjective than we might wish.

▲ *The power of the unconscious was the subject of the classic 1950s science fiction film* Forbidden Planet.

So where do we begin? Well, we all know there are things we want to do that we shouldn't do, but the mere fact that we do know about them makes them conscious, not unconscious. We certainly have things stored in our brains that we can't remember for the time being. And often we do things we shouldn't do that are obvious to others but that we deny. But this seems to be shaky proof at best that an active unconscious is controlling our behavior.

One researcher has noted that Freud places little emphasis on rational thought and that this is a serious flaw in his theory. After all, if people thought irrationally most of the time, they would not do a very good job of responding adaptively to the environment. In other words, life is a series of problems to be solved, and the only way to solve them well is by reasoning them through. However, the most important psychological function from Freud's perspective has to do with fantasizing and dreams, not real-life adaptation (Epstein, 1994). This may be a legitimate criticism, but does this criticism constitute proof that Freud's theory is incorrect? Not really. However, it does present a serious logical question. How could humans have survived so long without relying heavily on their reasoning abilities?

On the other side of the coin, developmental psychologists have long noted that little children frequently say they are going to marry their mommy or daddy when they grow up. Is this evidence of an unconscious Oedipus conflict? And what are we to do with the fact that human mythology across the world and across the ages has consistently contained so many of the images Jung referred to as archetypes? If simple animals like birds can have an innate sense of how to build a complicated nest, why couldn't humans have an innate sense of the human condition?

What other interpretations might be made instead? The other interpretations are as plentiful as the psychologists who make them. For instance, rather than exhibiting an Oedipus conflict, children may be trying on social roles when they say they are going to marry a parent. Inability to remember something could be a problem in memory retrieval, rather than an unconscious desire not to know it. Human mythology contains certain themes because human capacities and experiences are similar, regardless of culture and time. We deny having done something unacceptable because to admit it would damage our self-concepts. And so on.

What are the most logical conclusions to draw? Many of Freud's and Jung's concepts do not hold up very well in the real world. For reasons we have noted, though, we really have no concrete answers for you. Rather than finding this frustrating, we think it is one of the most exciting aspects of the study of psychology—few things are absolute.

We *can* say that today's psychology does not emphasize the influence of an unconscious. It focuses far more on a person's ability to control current behavior, rather than dwelling on childhood influences and unconscious impulses. Freud hoped that someday the id, ego, and superego would be located—that they would be shown to have a definite biological basis. This has not happened. Maybe someday there will be an easy answer to whether the unconscious controls our behavior. So far, though, this has not happened, either.

See if COOL works for you....

Claim?

Objective evidence for and against claim?

Other interpretations?

Logical conclusions?

Applying Critical Thinking Skills

Freud believed that slips of the tongue revealed the unconscious. For example, if a patient told him, "I'll play you later," Freud assumed he had no intention of paying—the patient, in fact, was playing with him. Do you think these Freudian slips actually reveal the unconscious, or are they merely slips of the tongue? Explain.

neo-Freudians those psychoanalysts who broke away from Freud to emphasize social forces in the unconscious

▲ *Psychoanalyst Karen Horney*

Social Psychoanalytic Theories

Both Freud and Jung dealt with an unconscious that they thought was biological. In other words, they thought that inborn needs or mythological beliefs control people, with little influence from what happens in the environment. A number of psychoanalysts agreed with the concept of an unconscious but objected to the fact that the early theories ignored the impact of social forces.

These psychoanalysts believed that the unconscious also holds all our worries and concerns about how well we get along with others. Think about how sweaty and anxious you got the last time you met someone you wanted very much to like you. While a reaction like this might start off biologically, it quickly becomes a social issue. Given their different focus, this splinter group of psychoanalysts came to be known as social psychoanalysts, or **neo-Freudians,** the latter term meaning "new" (revised) Freudians.

Karen Horney

Psychoanalyst **Karen Horney** (HORN-eye) (1885–1952) was outspoken about breaking with the Freudian tradition. She strongly disagreed with Freud's focus on biological drives. Horney felt that dealing with impulses from an id is less important for personality than coping with the stress of social needs. Hence, she was a neo-Freudian.

Horney claimed that the human feels most helpless, anxious, and lost in life around the issues of getting enough love. All of us need love badly, so we are constantly afraid that important people (like our parents when we are very young) will not like us. Our basic anxiety, then, comes from "the feeling a child has of being isolated and helpless in a potentially hostile world" (Horney, 1945, p. 41). This is so threatening that we build our personalities around fighting rejection. As a result, we go along with people when we don't want to.

A person who does not receive love is one who is always anxious and afraid (Horney, 1950). For this person, anxiety gradually builds up in the unconscious because of confused or inadequate social relationships. The person's behavior will then be dominated by social concerns because of the constant pressure from the unconscious.

Alfred Adler

Alfred Adler (1870–1937) was a follower of Freud who also had trouble with Freud's heavy emphasis on biological needs. He believed, like Horney, that social interaction is the key to proper development. He said that one of the biggest problems people face is trying to feel important and worthwhile around others.

Those who are insecure struggle to make themselves look better. They spend their lives trying to dominate and control others in order to avoid their own inner feelings of inferiority. School bullies are perfect examples of this type of behavior. When one gets beneath the surface to the unconscious, one finds that these people doubt themselves and are afraid and weak. Hence, they take off after those who are physically weaker in order to try to make themselves feel important and strong. In Adler's words, "children who have a great feeling of inferiority want to exclude stronger children and play with weaker children whom they can rule and domineer" (1969/1929, p. 25).

Erik Erikson

As mentioned, Freud felt that personality is pretty well set in the early years. Very few psychologists believe this anymore. As we'll talk about later, some aspects of personality tend to remain the same, but there are many things about us that change throughout life.

One theorist who supported the idea of change is **Erik Erikson** (1902–1994). His theory divides life up into eight stages. Like Horney and Adler, Erikson believed that social forces are most important. It is the types of relationships a person has during each of the stages that form his or her personality. Erikson's theory is appealing because it implies that we can "rescue" ourselves from problems almost anytime in life, all the way up to old age.

Stage one is in infancy. Erikson stressed the importance of warm relationships with the mother during feeding. Depending on how the mother and child get along, the child either relaxes and feels trusting or is tense and mistrusting of others. Erikson, therefore, called this stage *trust versus mistrust.*

Stage two comes at year two of the child's life. During this time, the child tries to become an individual—of sorts. Clearly, he or she is pretty helpless but nonetheless is seeking a feeling of being a separate person. If the parents don't allow this, the ego is injured, and the child feels shame. If the parents allow some freedom, a feeling of independence arises. This feeling is called *autonomy* (aw-TAWN-oh-mee). Erikson called stage two *autonomy versus shame.*

Even in *stage three,* from ages three through five, children are still very dependent on their parents. But this is the time when children try to take control of their environment—within limits. Thus, making a pile of rocks of their own design is important. Pretending to be a teacher or police officer or parent begins, and children make up their own rules about how these tasks are performed. They are taking the initiative in developing the behavior and rules of their pretend work. If not allowed this chance, children begin to feel bad and guilty for having failed. This stage is called *initiative versus guilt.*

In *stage four* (ages 6 to 12 years), children begin to develop all kinds of skills and to get rewards for what they do. These can range from stars pasted on the forehead (for the younger ones, we hope) to extra TV privileges. The children are being molded to do more and better things (that is, to be "industrious"). If the skills or rewards are not forthcoming, they feel inadequate. This stage, then, is called *industry versus inferiority.*

Erikson saw *stage five,* adolescence (also discussed in Chapter 11), as very important. One tries to get a hold on the inner self by seeking an answer to the question, "Who am I?" Finding self-identity requires the safety of a group. For this reason, adolescents form tightly knit groups to keep the self free from adult or "outsider" influence. The groups even have uniforms of sorts, which adults can't seem to handle without coming unglued. Certain types of shoes, clothing, special language, hairdos, and the like all help to keep the group together for this important process and exclude both older and younger people.

This is also the time for falling in love so the person can find out the answer to "Will someone love who I am?" (Muuss, 1975). (Fortunately, for

Focus Question

- According to Erik Erikson, what stages do people encounter throughout life?

▼ *In adolescence, falling in love is often part of establishing an identity.*

almost all of us, there usually is *someone* somewhere who will see us as a little more than merely adequate.) Finally, this is the time when young people start a search for solutions to religious, vocational, and personal issues (finding a "role" in life) (Erikson, 1968). Stage five is called *identity versus identity confusion.* In other words, failure to develop a strong sense of self results in uncertainty about what one is supposed to be and do.

Stage six occurs during adulthood, starting in the late teens and running until about age 30. This is a time of forming permanent relationships and sharing on an intimate level. This intimacy provides a true feeling of satisfaction because you are important to at least one special person. There is a sharing of a special closeness with another, a true process of give and take. Without it, there is loneliness. Hence, this stage is called *intimacy versus isolation.*

Middle adulthood is *stage seven,* from age 30 to 65. During this time, either a person expands and gives (generates) something important to the world in the way of a family or job, or he or she psychologically stands still and produces nothing (stagnates). This stage is called *generativity versus stagnation.*

In late adulthood, *stage eight,* from age 65 on, that which has gone before should, with a little luck, make some sense. One should be able to accept that the end is coming and find that life has been a worthwhile event—that something good was accomplished from living (Erikson et al., 1986). The self (ego) should feel reasonably complete when viewing what has happened, despite all the problems along the way. If a person doesn't feel this, he or she despairs, feeling life has been meaningless. Thus, this stage is called *ego integrity versus ego despair. (Integrity,* in this context, means a feeling of wholeness or completion.)

Assessment of the Neo-Freudians

The neo-Freudians brought an important new dimension to psychoanalysis: the influence of social forces. Clearly, they provided more to work with in analysis than simply biological drives. Erikson's theory is especially helpful in suggesting the possibility that we all have a chance to "repair" ourselves as we go along in life and are not stuck with something from childhood. Despite these alterations, however, the problem of whether we have an unconscious or not still exists.

 ## Pause for Thought

1. How do Horney's and Adler's ideas differ from Freud's?
2. For each of Erikson's eight stages, think of two or three key words that might help you remember the stage. For example, for stage one, you might list *caring* and *touch.*
3. Many aspects of one's personality might change over the course of a lifetime. According to Erikson, what is most important in bringing about these changes?

Critical Thinking
....
4. Jill tries on her mom's dresses, and John tries on his dad's suits. Are they expressing unconscious desires to be like their parents, or are there more concrete reasons for their behavior?

 **Focus**

Erikson's Eight Stages

Trust
Infant is totally dependent on others and learns to trust these others.

versus

mistrust (birth to 2 years)
Infant learns to distrust others.

Autonomy
Child tries to become a separate individual and is allowed some independence by parents.

versus

shame (ages 2 to 3 years)
If not allowed to develop a feeling of independence, the child feels shame.

Initiative
Child tries to take control of environment and is allowed some control.

versus

guilt (ages 3 to 5 years)
If not allowed to take any initiative, the child feels guilty for having failed.

Industry
Child wants to do more and better things—to be industrious—and develops skills for which he or she receives rewards.

versus

inferiority (ages 6 to 12 years)
If the child does not develop skills or is not rewarded, he or she feels inferior.

Identity
Adolescent searches for a role or identity in life and develops a sense of self.

versus

identity confusion (ages 13 to 18 years)
Adolescent feels confused if no role is found.

Intimacy
Young adult shares special or intimate feelings with one special person.

versus

isolation (ages 18 to 30 years)
When the young adult does not experience this sharing, loneliness and isolation prevail.

Generativity
Adult feels the need to generate or contribute something important to the world and is able to do so.

versus

stagnation (middle adulthood)
If unable to contribute anything important, the adult deteriorates or stagnates.

Ego Integrity
Person looks to the past and feels a sense of accomplishment or integrity.

versus

ego despair (late adulthood)
If the person looks back and feels no sense of accomplishment, he or she feels empty and despairing.

As a parent, what kinds of things will you do with your child to promote trust, autonomy, initiative, and industry?

Focus Question

• How does behaviorism contrast with psychoanalysis?

behaviorism a personality theory that focuses on overt acts or behaviors

Behaviorism

Not all personality theories deal with the unconscious. In fact, in **behaviorism,** the unconscious is ignored altogether. Early theories in this area focused on our acts, or behaviors, as if we were robots. According to these theories, our personalities evolve from a series of rewards or punishments. For example, those who drop out of school to work will, in the long run, lose a great deal of money. But for the short term, each week or so they get a lot more money than their friends who are still in school. According to behaviorists, these people are getting a continued series of rewards that shape their behavior. In contrast, psychoanalysts might claim that dropping out has deep-seated causes in the personality.

John B. Watson

John B. Watson (1878–1958) was an early behaviorist. He believed that if he had complete control of a person's environment from infancy, he could make that person become absolutely anything at all—doctor, lawyer, beggar, or thief. His best-known research was on learned fears (see the "Little Albert" study in Chapter 7). According to Watson, we are afraid of objects or situations because of frightening associations we have made to them in the past.

B. F. Skinner

Perhaps the best-known behaviorist is **B. F. Skinner** (1904–1990). Skinner had a very strict religious upbringing. His grandmother used to hold his face over a stove of hot coals to show him "what hell was like." Later, when he was in school, he chose to withdraw from social activities, and he spent his time reading science books instead of going to movies or dating much (Skinner, 1967). He was fairly unhappy as a young man, and throughout his life he was neither very good at dealing with other people nor very charitable toward them (Mills, 1997). Of some interest, as he entered old age (Erikson's eighth stage) he mellowed a bit and viewed the human being in somewhat less mechanical terms.

In any case, for the early Skinner, everything we do is the result of a mechanical association of events with their consequences. For example, say you plan to go over to a friend's house tonight for dinner. But then, later in the day, you decide to find a different friend with whom to go get something to eat. This was *not* a voluntary decision on your part, according to Skinner. Instead, you added up the number of pleasant experiences you had had with friend number one and those you had had with friend number two, and you chose the second friend because you had more positive associations with that person. While you *think* you had a choice, you really didn't. Thus, all our behaviors result from a series of **reinforcements** (see Chapter 7).

▲ *Sharing positive experiences with a friend reinforces the friendship.*

reinforcements events that follow responses and strengthen the tendency to repeat those responses

Those who make clothing know that there are certain parts of a shirt that take more of a beating than others. If you haven't bought something really cheap, the manufacturer will have used extra stitches or material to *reinforce* these parts—make them stronger. A similar thing happens to humans, according to Skinner's system. Each time you laugh or share with friend A versus friend B, you reinforce the odds that you'll want to see friend A again. The same thing applies throughout all personality development. If studying is reinforced by good grades, you will study more often. If the reinforcement you get from skipping school is greater than the guilt it creates, you will continue to skip school.

Albert Bandura

Note again the last sentence. A person might base behavior on feelings of guilt. Guilt obviously is a broad, internal concept that doesn't fit very well with Skinner's mechanical view of behaviorism. To many, Skinner's system is flawed because it doesn't give a person enough credit for being a thinking creature.

▲ *Enjoying the company of others makes us more likely to want to see them again.*

This was the complaint of **Albert Bandura** (b. 1925), a behaviorist who has elaborated on Skinner's system. He does not deny that we learn a great number of things by straight association. If you're bitten by a dog, a cat, a raccoon, and a snake when you are growing up, there's no question that your personality will include a clear-cut fear of animals. But we also learn many things by using our ability to think, analyze, and interpret.

Bandura feels that much of our personality comes from observing others and **modeling** ourselves after them. This process can be very complicated, rather than just mechanical. If you observe an alcoholic uncle in the family who is very friendly and outgoing and an aunt who is a teetotaler but nasty and aggressive, your feelings for or against alcohol are going to be very complex—something Skinner's system doesn't allow for.

modeling Bandura's term for learning by imitating others

Bandura still is behavioristic, because he believes learning is a process of association. But the organism interprets and chooses between associations rather than just "counting" them and responding automatically to the one that for the moment has the most positive reinforcements. In other words, the organism performs an internal analysis.

Bandura's studies on modeling have been very important. They have shown that if children observe someone beating up a plastic doll, these children will act aggressively themselves (see Chapter 7). Perhaps more important, Bandura showed that, for instance, if someone is seriously afraid of snakes he or she can lose that fear over time by seeing another person handling snakes comfortably. The person with the fear of snakes can model his or her behavior on that of the other person. The important point is that we can relearn or retrain ourselves by deliberately developing a new set of associations (snakes are harmless) to replace the old.

Assessment of Behaviorism

We have mentioned most of the problems with behaviorism as we've gone along. The biggest one, especially for Skinner, is that it shortchanges the human's ability to think. On the positive side, though, the theory does show that we learn many behaviors just because they have been reinforced by positive consequences and associations.

Focus Question

• What are some of the main ideas of humanists?

humanism a personality theory that emphasizes the positive potential of the person

ideal self Rogers's term for the goal of each person's development; the self each person would like to be

Humanistic Theories

As you might have guessed, some people eventually objected to what they saw as a rather depressing picture of the individual either as a bubbling id trying to express itself or as a robot. These people considered Freud's idea of an unconscious filled with id impulses unacceptable and the behaviorists' failure to acknowledge the importance of personal experience unworkable.

In reaction to these theories, some psychologists developed the theory of **humanism,** which emphasizes the whole person with his or her positive potential and which accepts the person as an individual human with all kinds of good qualities. So the focus is on *human* qualities, which explains how the name of this theory came about.

Carl Rogers

The leading humanist, **Carl Rogers** (1902–1987), studied to be a minister for a while, but he had trouble with the idea that people are sinful. Instead, he believed that we are basically good. The biggest problem we have, he said, is living up to what he called the **ideal self.** The ideal self is as close to perfection as one can get. Each of us comes into the world ready to become this ideal self, but at times we fall by the wayside while trying to get there.

In Focus

Rogers's Fully Functioning Individual

Both individuals have the power to be fully functioning, but only the second individual realizes this potential, through the help of that individual's environment.

If the person on the left went to three psychologists—a psychoanalyst, a behaviorist, and a humanist—how might each psychologist describe the person's problem?

We are like flowers in our potential. If the environment is halfway decent, we will grow into humans who can be proud and internally beautiful. This can be accomplished by almost anyone who has the acceptance and warmth of love that comes from parents in the early stages, from friends in the next stage, and from an intimate, personal relationship with someone as an adult. When we have united what we *should* be with what we *are,* we have become what Rogers called **fully functioning individuals** (Rogers, 1951).

fully functioning individual
Rogers's term for someone who has become what he or she should be

Abraham Maslow

Psychologist **Abraham Maslow** (1908–1970) followed in Rogers's footsteps. He saw the human as having deep needs for beauty, goodness,

In Focus

The Big Picture: Major Personality Theories

	Early Psychoanalysis	Social Psychoanalysis	Behaviorism	Humanism
Major Theorists	Freud Jung	Horney Adler Erikson	Skinner Bandura	Rogers Maslow
Main Beliefs	Personality and behavior determined by hidden, unconscious forces	Personality influenced by the unconscious, but this unconscious is not all biological—social factors help shape the unconscious	Personality shaped by rewards and punishments and by modeling—forget the unconscious	Personality influenced by the unique potential within each of us
Role of the Environment	Plays big role during first five years of life—but after this, inner forces are more important	Plays big role in supplying love and making person feel important	Is all-important—it makes us who we are	Decent environment needed to nurture inner potential
Definition of Healthy Personality	One that adequately balances conflicts between conscious and unconscious forces	One that recognizes the social forces of the unconscious and that tries to repair itself by resolving conflicts	One that receives effective rewards and punishments—the individual has little choice in this	One that is fully functioning and self-actualized

Which personality theory seems most applicable or accurate in today's world?

justice, and a feeling of completeness—all the hopeful and positive things about human beings. Each of us has inherited something unique, and *if* the environment will cooperate a little, we have the opportunity to become great (Maslow, 1970).

self-actualized Maslow's term for the state of having brought to life the full potential of our skills

Maslow does not mean "great" in the sense of "famous." Rather, being great means *actualizing* (bringing to life) our personal skills. Thus, the fulfilled person is **self-actualized.** We can accomplish this despite personal problems. For instance, he saw Abraham Lincoln as self-actualized, even though the man suffered endless bouts of deep depression (Maslow, 1968). A truly self-actualized person might be a student who comes from a terrible environment but who propels himself or herself to a level of outstanding achievement. (Maslow is discussed more thoroughly in Chapter 5.)

Assessment of Humanism

Humanism is very upbeat; it makes us feel good. It also positively encourages a person to take charge of his or her own fate in a reasonable fashion. Unlike other theories, it emphasizes what goes right rather than what goes wrong in personality development—a welcome change. Critics argue that it goes too far in a positive direction. However, a fair amount of research backs up the basic ideas that humanism supports. The major problem, perhaps, is that this theory is too simple and vague to fully account for the great variety we see in the human personality.

Focus Questions

- What are common personality traits?
- What is a cardinal trait?

personality traits more or less permanent personality characteristics

Trait Theories

Personality traits are the more or less permanent characteristics each of us has. Taken together, they make up our personalities. Aggressiveness is a personality trait; so is shyness. These traits influence how we perceive the world and respond to it. For example, if you are easygoing, you will most likely see the world as a friendly place, rather than a threatening one. And you will probably react to problems or conflicts without becoming extremely upset or anxious.

Trait theorists generally agree on what a personality trait is. They differ on what specific traits are the most important ones and how those traits can be observed. For the most part, trait theories are more concerned with describing what personality is than where personality comes from.

Gordon Allport

cardinal traits Allport's term for very strong personality characteristics that affect most of what a person does

Gordon Allport's (1897–1967) theory starts out with the common terms that people use to describe one another. They include such adjectives as honest, dominant, outgoing, and many others. Allport then divided these into three major categories of traits—cardinal, central, and secondary. The categories go from the strongest and most often expressed traits to the weaker ones that are seen only on occasion.

Cardinal traits are extremely strong personality characteristics that are expressed in almost everything a person does. They have been described as a person's ruling passion. They are also quite rare. Very few people have a cardinal trait. When they do, it affects their daily life in many ways. Adolf Hitler probably had a cardinal trait relating to power and control. On the other side of the coin, Mother Teresa may have had

424

a cardinal trait relating to concern for other people.

Central traits are highly characteristic of people and will apply across many situations. Most people can be fairly well described by five to ten of them. This category contains the items most of us think of when we use the term "trait." Central traits include being optimistic, shy, suspicious, sociable, decisive, deceitful, and many other attributes.

Secondary traits are the weakest and least characteristic group of all. These are traits that appear only in certain situations. They usually do not describe the individual very well. For example, a person could be generally easygoing and calm but become highly aggressive when a loved one is threatened.

◀ *Mother Teresa's cardinal trait was probably her deep concern for other people.*

central traits Allport's term for personality traits that are highly characteristic of a person

secondary traits Allport's term for weak personality traits that appear only on occasion

Raymond Cattell

Raymond Cattell (1905–1998) divided personality traits into two major categories, surface traits and source traits. **Surface traits** are used to describe behavior that we see a person engaging in on a fairly regular basis. For instance, we might notice that a friend gives in to what other people want, is reluctant to take a stand on anything, and never offers an opinion. Each of these descriptions is a surface trait because it can be easily and directly observed. These separate descriptions, though, tend to cluster together. According to Cattell, they cluster together because of an underlying personality trait. It is this underlying **source trait** that produces the behaviors we can see. In our example, the source trait is being submissive. Cattell came up with 16 source traits that he believed adequately describe most people. (See Fig. 14.1 for a list of Cattell's source traits.)

surface traits Cattell's term for characteristics that can be easily observed by others

source traits Cattell's term for personality traits that underlie surface behavior

Hans Eysenck

Hans Eysenck's (1916–1997) system is a little different from the others we have discussed. In Eysenck's view, there are only two major dimensions necessary to describe most people's personalities. These dimensions are extraversion (plus its opposite, introversion) and emotional stability (plus its opposite, emotional instability). **Extraversion** refers to where one fits on a scale from very outgoing to very quiet and reserved. **Emotional stability** refers to how much a person is affected by feelings. It includes such traits as how calm or anxious, depressed or upbeat, controlled or impulsive a person is. Eysenck believed that by combining these dimensions, most people's personality structures would be covered fairly well.

extraversion Eysenck's term for the personality dimension of being outgoing and sociable

emotional stability Eysenck's term for the personality dimension that concerns how much a person is affected by feelings

425

Cattell's Primary Source Traits

Reserved	Outgoing
Less intelligent	More intelligent
Affected by feelings	Emotionally stable
Submissive	Dominant
Serious	Happy-go-lucky
Expedient	Conscientious
Timid	Venturesome
Tough-minded	Sensitive
Trusting	Suspicious
Practical	Imaginative
Forthright	Shrewd
Self-assured	Apprehensive
Conservative	Experimenting
Group dependent	Self-sufficient
Uncontrolled	Controlled
Relaxed	Tense

▲ *Figure 14.1* *Cattell theorized that our surface personality traits are caused by 16 underlying traits, which he called source traits. He believed that through psychological measurement of these traits, we can predict people's behavior in various situations.*

Examining Personality Traits

In this section, we cover recent studies on personality traits, discussing what is known about them and where they might come from. A great deal has been learned from major research being conducted at the University of Minnesota, where 350 pairs of twins are being studied (Bouchard, et al., 1990). Since identical, or monozygotic, twins have exactly the same heredity (they come from the same fertilized egg in the mother), they can be compared with fraternal, or dizygotic, twins (who do not have as much heredity in common, since they are from different fertilized eggs) or with nontwin brothers and sisters. If the same trait often shows up in identical twins but not in other pairs, then the odds are good that it is an inherited trait.

Major Permanent Traits: The Five-Factor Model

The most recent evidence from twin studies and other research suggests that five personality factors seem in large part to be inherited or at least appear at an early age (Nigg & Goldsmith, 1994; Bouchard et al., 1990). These five factors are: (1) extraversion, or how sociable and outgoing people are; (2) agreeableness, the opposite of which is being antagonistic; (3) conscientiousness, which involves self-discipline and the will to achieve; (4) emotional stability, as opposed to being anxious, hostile, overly impulsive, or depressed; and (5) openness to experience, which includes curiosity and the willingness to consider other points of view (Ackerman & Heggestad, 1997). These five factors are found across cultures, at least among highly industrialized countries (McCrae & Costa, 1997). And how much or how little an individual has of each of the traits seems to be fairly enduring (Hogan, Hogan, & Roberts, 1996).

One type of study followed 10,000 people—ages 25 to 74—for nine years to see how they changed over this period. Three characteristics tended to remain the same regardless of age. These three are very close to the five factors just mentioned: (1) degree of friendliness, (2) how eager people are to do different or novel things, and (3) how comfortable or anxious they feel (Costa et al., 1987; Costa & McCrae, 1986).

People *do* change throughout life in terms of how satisfied they feel, how high their morale is, and how active they are. To this point in time, however, only the five factors just discussed seem pretty well set, maybe in "plaster," by the early 20s. These traits appear from birth and later are reinforced or not as other people respond to them. Thus, learning does have an influence, but only after certain tendencies have already been inherited (Nigg & Goldsmith, 1994). We all know of families in which two children were very different from birth; one was aggressive and cried a lot while the other was quiet and smiled. Parents and others respond in a certain way to these differences, and thus they continue to add to whatever inherited tendencies are already there.

Effects of the Environment

Most scientists who study personality today believe that roughly 50 percent of the total personality is controlled by heredity. Obviously, the environment has an effect, but we seem to lean toward certain types of behavior from birth, as we've just discussed.

An environment, however, is not simply "good" or "bad." One of the more interesting recent findings is that even what seems to be exactly the same environment for the children in a family is, in fact, different for each child. Since each has a different personality from the beginning, they react differently to the same thing. If two children in a family are taken to a movie together, for example, it will have a different effect on each child. Such findings suggest that parents cannot control how children will respond; parents can only provide the best possible environment.

You will sometimes hear that birth order (whether one is the first, second, or third child, for example) is very important in how a child turns out. But after thousands of studies in this area, there seems to be very little support for any lasting effect. Parents in normal families tend to treat the children as equally as possible, and for the most part, they succeed. But each child sees what is going on from a different point of view.

Finally, current studies are showing that interactions with a brother or sister or with playmates or school groups carry far heavier weight over time than do the parents. Of course, this assumes that the parents are not causing the children to live in a house of horrors but are providing an acceptable environment.

▲ *Cain and Abel are classic examples of sibling rivalry.*

Pause for Thought

1. Explain what motivates behavior, according to John B. Watson and B. F. Skinner.
2. How is Albert Bandura's theory both similar to and different from Skinner's?
3. How do we become fully functioning, according to Carl Rogers, and self-actualized, according to Abraham Maslow?
4. How do Allport, Cattell, and Eysenck view personality?

Critical Thinking
....
5. Five personality traits appear early and tend to endure. Identify those traits. Imagine a 20-year-old who is deficient in one of these traits. For example, this person is not very self-disciplined or open to new experiences. What are some steps he or she can take to overcome this "deficit"?

APPLYING
Psychology to Life

Theorizing About Your Own Personality

▲ *Is her id or her superego in control at this moment?*

As we mentioned at the beginning of this chapter, we don't have enough information yet on how accurate different personality theories are. Still, it might be interesting for you to explore some things about yourself to see if you can find support for the theories discussed. Don't take it all too seriously; we're just doing an "experiment," so to speak.

Start with the Freudian theory. Go back in your mind to the last time you had a secret desire to do something you didn't think proper or moral. Note that you didn't merely go out and do it without caring. Instead, what probably happened was that you felt a very strong internal "push" to go ahead and do it. Next you began to feel concerned and guilty, and you had a sinking feeling in your stomach that you might actually do it. Then you weighed the pros and cons, the rights and wrongs of the situation. Finally, you did or didn't do it. Note how very close this comes to your ego (your *self*) trying to let the id have its way but also balancing the reality and

▲ *Anxiety can be the source of bad habits, like nail biting.*

morality of the situation by listening to the superego. It certainly seems like Freud might have been partly right, doesn't it?

Now the behavioral theory. Pick a habit you have that you're not necessarily happy with: biting your fingernails, humming, doing funny things with your fingers, tugging at your socks, or who knows what. Go back in your mind to the last couple of times you did this behavior. You didn't want to do it, but it came automatically. Such habits are

very hard to trace in some cases, but here is how they probably get started: Sometime in the past you felt a lot of stress and strain. The way the body is constructed, when stress occurs, we prepare to take some kind of action, like running away. That's natural. But often we can't actually run away—society won't allow it. So, rather than run, you started doing something—anything— with your body to relieve the tension. Having done *something,* your body relaxed a little. This made you feel better, which reinforced the behavior (even though what you did wasn't *really* helpful). Thus, you tend to repeat this something—humming, nail biting, and so on— year after year. Each time, the reinforcement adds up, so that the drive to do it gets stronger and stronger. The behavior becomes part of you. As you can see, this is the behavioral explanation for how we gradually develop patterns of activities that come to represent our personalities.

For the third example, the humanistic theories, you have to use your "Freudian superego" and not cheat. At a certain point, we will tell you not to read any further. Please don't, or you'll spoil the experiment. Don't even peek a line ahead. Here we go: In private, write down the three things that you most admire about yourself. Beneath that, write the three things about yourself that you find most obnoxious, gross, or unpleasant. Be *very* honest. Don't read any

further until you have finished writing.

Now you need to examine your inner feelings very carefully. Notice how much stress and strain you felt, how physically uncomfortable you were, when you wrote the bad part. Note how you avoided and wanted to get away from it. Why? Could it be that you are basically a good person seeking self-actualization and fulfillment and that you are destined to be good? That these negative things just don't seem to belong to you and should go away? That's what the humanists would say. (Just remember that defects are part of all of us, and you're not alone at all in feeling bad about certain aspects of yourself.)

▲ *Assessing your own personality for strengths and weaknesses can also produce stress.*

Summary

1. Freud's system focuses on unconscious impulses that are constantly seeking expression. The id contains our animal needs and tries to do what it wants. It is controlled by the ego, or self, which balances the desires of the id with the restraints and judgments of the superego, or conscience.

2. In the view of Carl Jung, we are guided by a collective unconscious, which holds myths about certain concepts (such as "mother" and "hero") and passes them on from one generation to another. He believed we also make up "fake" personalities, or masks, called personas.

3. Karen Horney considered social influences most important in personality development. We live from birth with a dread that we will not be accepted by others, and this concern colors our personalities. Alfred Adler agreed about the importance of social factors and stressed that we feel inadequate and spend our energies trying to be important to offset such feelings.

4. Erik Erikson developed an elaborate theory in which life is divided up into a series of eight stages. In each of these stages, we have to deal with others. How we turn out depends on how good these relationships are during each stage.

5. Behaviorism sees personality as arising from learning and association. B. F. Skinner claimed that we act strictly in terms of the kinds of reinforcements we get, rather than in terms of conscious choices. Albert Bandura also focused on learning but claimed that we are more than just robots—that we can accept or reject certain kinds of behavior that we have learned by a process called modeling.

6. Humanistic theories stress that we are basically good and are aiming to fulfill our potential if the environment cooperates even a little bit. Carl Rogers saw us as destined to become fully functioning individuals. Abraham Maslow called people who found a place in life and did their jobs with excellence "self-actualized."

7. Gordon Allport's theory divides personality traits into cardinal, central, and secondary traits. Raymond Cattell's theory looks at clusters of surface traits that make up the underlying source traits. Hans Eysenck's theory focuses on the personality dimensions of extraversion and emotional stability.

8. The five personality factors that seem to be inherited (or, at least, that are with us from a very early age) are extraversion, agreeableness, conscientiousness, emotional stability, and openness to experience.

9. Aside from our parents, the most important influences from the environment on our personalities seem to come from brothers, sisters, playmates, and school groups.

Vocabulary

personality	phallic stage	ideal self
psychoanalytic theory	latency stage	fully functioning individual
unconscious	genital stage	self-actualized
free association	archetypes	personality traits
repression	collective unconscious	cardinal traits
libido	persona	central traits
id	neo-Freudians	secondary traits
superego	behaviorism	surface traits
ego	reinforcements	source traits
oral stage	modeling	extraversion
anal stage	humanism	emotional stability

Review Questions

Matching

On a sheet of paper, match the terms in the right column with the statements in the left column. Answers may be used more than once.

1. The unconscious is biological and remains basically unaffected by the environment.

2. Free will does not really exist.

3. Observing others helps shape our personalities.

4. The whole person is emphasized.

5. Humans have a powerful potential for good.

6. The unconscious is concerned about how we get along with others.

  a. humanism

  b. behaviorism

  c. early psycho-analysis

  d. social psycho-analysis (neo-Freudians)

Fill in the blank

On a sheet of paper, write the word or words that best complete each statement.

7. According to Freud, the part of the personality that makes us feel guilty is called the ▒▒▒▒.

8. Freud's method for studying the unconscious is called ▒▒▒▒.

9. One's psychological mask, or ▒▒▒▒, hides one's real personality.

10. Those psychologists who broke away from Freud to emphasize social forces are sometimes referred to as ▒▒▒▒.

11. ▒▒▒▒ argued that love is an essential ingredient for a healthy personality.

12. Erikson's term for sharing a special closeness with another is called ▒▒▒▒.

13. According to Maslow, a person who strives to fulfill his or her potential is becoming ▒▒▒▒.

Discussion Questions

1. There was a time when it was very fashionable to be psychoanalyzed. Why do you suppose it was popular? Also, do you think you would ever want to be psychoanalyzed? Why or why not?

2. Sharon suffers from a severe bout of depression. How might Horney's explanation of her depression differ from Adler's?

3. Freud was probably correct to some extent in saying that much of our personality remains unchanged as we grow. Erikson was also probably correct to some extent in saying that much of our personality *does* change. Think back on your junior high school years. Describe aspects of your personality that have changed and aspects that have remained essentially the same.

4. Edie is unhappy with her job as a salesperson. How would a humanist and a behaviorist explain Edie's unhappiness?

5. Describe one or two behaviors that you're fairly certain you learned through modeling. Do you think the models knew you were watching? Explain.

6. In the 1960s, some attempts were made to implement humanism in the classroom. These attempts turned out to be a disaster. Despite this, some people might argue that there's nothing wrong with applying humanistic ideas in the classroom, as long as certain guidelines are set. Propose a humanistic change you'd like to see adopted at your school. Make the proposal practical and somewhat detailed. (A "humanistic" change would be one that would encourage students to handle their own fates.)

7. If you could magically change one aspect of your personality—right now—would you choose to change something? If so, what would you change, and why? If not, why not? Also, what is one aspect of your personality that you would never change? Explain.

8. The chapter explains that five personality traits seem not to change with age: extraversion, agreeableness, conscientiousness, emotional stability, and openness to experience. Does this conclusion accurately describe your own life? Why or why not?

Activities and Projects

1. Write five unemotional statements about yourself on an index card. Make one of these statements a complete lie. Write the statements before reading any further.

   Now, find 15 males and 15 females who do not know whether these statements are true or false. Tell each subject that one of the statements is a lie, and ask the subject to try to pick out the lie. Record their responses and the reasons for their responses.

   As the chapter mentions, there is no clear scientific evidence that the unconscious exists, but this project may be an informal way of testing its existence. You may have unconsciously given yourself away when you wrote the lie—maybe by the size of the words, the spacing between words, the phrasing, and so on.

   Analyze your results. How many picked the lie? Which sex did better? If one sex did better, can you draw any conclusions about this? Based on your results, what conclusions can you make regarding the unconscious? Is it possible to scientifically study the unconscious? Explain.

2. When we think of modeling, we usually think of the long-term effects that our families as models have on us. It might be fun to examine whether modeling is a factor at all between strangers. You'll need to go to a mall (or a similar setting) with a friend to conduct this experiment. The hypothesis

will be this: People are more likely to be influenced by a model who resembles them than by a model who is vastly different.

General Procedure: Either you or your friend should dress in a "traditional" manner. *You* decide what might be considered traditional for your area. The other person should dress in a more "radical" manner. Again, you decide what radical means. Your task will be to find 20 people who fit your "traditional" definition.

Specific Procedure: The traditionally dressed person—the *model* in this case—will sit next to a subject. After about a minute or so, the radically dressed person will approach the model and say, "I'm doing a report for school on shoppers in malls. Would you mind filling out a survey?" Repeat this procedure 10 times. Half the time, the model will say, "Yes, I love filling out surveys." The other half of the time, the model will say something like this: "Nothing personal—but it seems that every time I come here I fill out 10 surveys. I'd rather not right now." After each "yes" or "no" from the model, the survey person will ask the subject, who has been overhearing all this, the same question. Record whether the subjects agree to take the survey and if the subjects' responses match the model's. Finally, repeat this entire procedure, using the "radical" person as the model this time.

The survey mentioned is mainly camouflage, but if the subject agrees to take the survey, you need to have something ready. So just write a quick survey with questions like, "How often do you shop?" and "Do you usually shop with friends or by yourself?" Make 20 copies of the survey. If you want, you can include one or two "meaningful" questions that you *will* analyze, which might relate to your modeling hypothesis. For example, "Should male store clerks be required to wear ties? Should female store clerks be required to wear dresses?"

Analyze your results. It might be helpful to draw a simple chart summarizing your results for each model. *Did* the traditional model have a greater effect on responses than the radical model? Make several guesses as to why or why not. What other conclusions can you draw from your results? Discuss.

3. As explained in the chapter, we all have some notion of our ideal selves—how we would ideally like to be. Pretend that you have, at this moment, become this ideal self. Don't make this ideal so perfect that you could never possibly achieve it. Simply envision how you would like to be in the near future. With this notion of your ideal self in mind, consider the following categories and describe your attitudes toward these categories from the point of view of your ideal self: (a) school, (b) money, (c) gender roles, (d) family, (e) friends.

Remember, you should describe your ideal attitudes—not your material ambitions. For example, for the money category, you wouldn't describe how much money you'd make as your ideal self; you'd describe your attitude toward money in general. Here's a sample (remember, the ideal self is writing): "I used to think that I wanted to be rich, but it's not that important to me now." You might write something like this, for example, if you presently seem too preoccupied with money. Write approximately a paragraph for each category. (If writing from the ideal point of view is awkward, write it in any way you like, as long as you still describe your ideal attitudes.) Write your descriptions before reading further.

Now, list all five categories on four separate sheets of paper. Hand two of the sheets to two friends and the other two sheets to two family members. Instruct them to describe what they perceive to be your *real* attitudes today toward these categories. Have them write a few sentences on each category. In other words, these four people will describe your *real* self, as they see you. Tell them to be as specific as possible.

Compare your *ideal* descriptions with others' *real* descriptions in detail. Are they similar or dissimilar? Explain. According to your comparison, would you say that you're a "fully functioning individual"? Explain.

CHAPTER 35

Psychological tests are designed to measure facts about the individual objectively. The goals are to avoid bias of the type found in an interview and to compare individuals as factually as possible. The major tests are for personality, aptitude, achievement, and vocational interest. So far, such tests are the most accurate method we have to evaluate people in these areas.

Measuring Personality and Personal Abilities

Why Psychological Tests Are Used

The first thing we want to do is find out how many criminals and dangerous characters there are in your class. We can do this by using a book from 1911. According to its author, the really evil ones have the following four characteristics: (1) very low forehead, (2) strangely shaped head and jaw, (3) eyebrows growing together over the bridge of the nose, and (4) very protruding ears (like Mickey Mouse?) (Lombroso-Ferrero, 1911). You may find it hard to believe—or maybe not—but after the book came out, police frequently held people who looked this way on suspicion.

Next, let's divide up your classmates by body type. The very heavy ones are smiling, happy people, really good-natured. Those with muscular bodies love adventure and athletics and have muscles in the brain. Those who are skinny are extrasensitive to pain and read books all the time (Sheldon, 1936).

What do you think? The first theory you probably don't believe because it never became part of our culture. The second one, however, is a little harder to fight, since so many people accept it, even though studies over the years have shown it to be false. Although there are happy heavy people and brainy thin people, overall the body does not reflect a specific type of personality. For example, Sherlock Holmes, the brilliant fictional detective, fit the stereotype of thinness. However, his older *and even smarter* brother, Mycroft, was a very large man, quite overweight.

To try to find out what a person is really like and to avoid such wild speculation, psychologists use psychological tests. A **psychological test** is a systematic measure of what people know; how they act, think, or feel; or what their goals are or should be. A psychological test can measure personality, intelligence, occupational needs, or job skills. These tests try to be as factual and unbiased as possible and provide a picture of personality or personal skills.

psychological test systematic measure of what people know; how they act, think, and feel; or what their goals are

Making a Personality Test

Suppose you wanted to make a test to find out what Sally X is really like. One of the first things you might do is pick test items that could reflect personality. Here are some: Did you have nightmares about monsters as a child? Did you ever wet your bed? Do you sometimes hate school more than anything else in the world? Do you ever have trouble getting to sleep?

These sound like they might give us some useful information for exploring Sally's inner workings. But if you take these items and ask Sally to reply and she says "yes" to all of them, does she have a personality problem? The answer is *no*. All of us will answer "yes" to all these questions, if we are being truthful. So, we have a problem: if everyone answers "yes," we have no way of focusing on an individual personality.

Focus Question

- What are some ingredients of a personality test?

Standardization

How can we make up a test that will work? Before going any further, we must have clear directions for taking the test, scoring it, and interpreting it. These procedures make up what is called **standardization.** When a test is standardized, it is given and "graded" exactly the same way for every person who takes it.

standardization the process of developing clear directions for taking, scoring, and interpreting a test

Establishing Norms

For the next step, you have to come up with many items covering the relevant areas. Once you have done that, you must give the items to a large number of different people—older, younger, male, female, and so forth. You do this to find out how most people in each group answer the questions. The answers will vary, depending on the group. You want to know what the *normal,* expected, responses are for most people in a specific group. By doing this, you are finding what are called **norms.**

norms patterns of test answers from different types of people

Norms show you the pattern of answers for different types of people. Since, in a personality test, we are trying to find something *individual* about the person, we will focus on the answers that are *not* common to those of her group to get a clue about Sally. If she answers a question like "I feel very happy most of the time" or "I never lie down when I'm studying" differently from her norm group, we believe we are detecting something special about her. In this way, we try to form a personality picture of her as compared with others. (Note that for purposes of testing, we assume that if most people feel a certain thing, it must be "normal." While this is not necessarily a good idea, it's the only way we can do it.)

▲ *The typical responses of groups of people establish a test's norms.*

Establishing Validity

The test has been given to enough different types of people to establish some norms. Can we now give the test to Sally X? Suppose her answers differ from those of the norm group in that she finds things upsetting that others do not, she has trouble getting along with teachers, and she can't seem to accept the standards of society. Can we tell her she has a personality problem and needs help?

If we do, based on these findings, we are making the same error as the developer of the "criminal test" mentioned in the first paragraph. The fact that something sounds good and we *think* it is the case doesn't make it so. As a matter of fact, if these are Sally's "problems," they match the answers of a group of highly creative students who deviate from the norm about as much as those who have serious personal difficulties.

So how do we make certain a test is measuring what it is supposed to measure? For example, let's leave the area of personality for now and assume we want to develop a test that will predict how good an accountant you would be. What do we do?

Once the items have been chosen, we can give the test to a group of students about to enter an accounting class. We can score the test, wait until the students have finished the class, and compare the scores they made with how well they did in the course. If the high scorers did well in the course and the low scorers did poorly, we have a good idea that the test works. This is called test **validity.** If a test is valid, it measures what it is supposed to measure. Validity, then, refers to the meaning we can attach to test scores (Messick, 1995).

Thus, before we can give the test to Sally, we first have to establish the validity of the test items we are using. We could do this by giving the personality items to large numbers of students and then finding out if those who answer certain items deviating from the norms drop out of school, are sent to the principal, get into fights, and so forth. If these people have all kinds of trouble, we have established validity. If not, the test is not valid—it doesn't measure what it is supposed to be measuring.

Establishing Reliability

One final thing must be done before we can have confidence in the test Sally will get. Test items can always be affected by what is going on around us. Most personality tests contain items such as "I feel depressed," or "I feel left out and don't have many friends." Suppose that Sally goes to a movie the night before the test. To her, it is a very sad, depressing movie that makes everything seem hopeless. But her companion doesn't agree and hence cannot share Sally's emotions regarding the film. If Sally takes the test the next day, the odds that she will say she feels depressed and left out by her friends are very high—even though this may not be her typical state. Answers to test questions should not be too influenced by such temporary changes. In other words, the test must have **reliability.**

Reliability means that the answers must be reasonably consistent. A friend who shows up one time for a date 20 minutes early, one time 3 minutes late, one time 50 minutes late, and so forth is clearly unreliable. So, too, with the test. It is unreliable if it is inconsistent.

One way to measure reliability is to give a test to group A on a given day and then give the same test to the same group two weeks later. If their answers are mostly the same both times, then the test is reliable. If many answers change from one time to the next, the test is unreliable. You can see what would happen with the accounting test if one week someone got a score of 98 percent and the next week the same person got a score of 34 percent on the same test. Obviously, the test couldn't be used to measure a person's accounting abilities or anything else.

In summary: A test must have a large number of items. It must be standardized, so everyone takes it the same way. It must be normed so that we know how different groups of people tend to answer the questions. It must be valid and measure what it claims to measure. And finally, it must measure reliably.

validity the extent to which a test measures what it is supposed to measure

reliability measure of a test's consistency

▲ *A useful test must be standardized, valid, and reliable.*

Focus Questions

- What is a personality inventory?
- How are personality inventories used?

personality inventory a list of items about a person's beliefs, habits, hopes, needs, and desires

MMPI-2 latest version of the Minnesota Multiphasic Personality Inventory, the most widely used personality inventory

Personality Inventories

A **personality inventory** is a list of statements about beliefs, habits, hopes, needs, and desires. The test is given using a test booklet and answer sheet. Its format is *objective*—that is, it consists of multiple-choice or true/false questions, and these tests are sometimes called *objective tests*. The questions are very similar to the ones we've been talking about: "I believe that people like me," "When I get bored, I stir things up," "I have a happy home," and so forth.

Probably the best-known and most widely used personality inventory today is the *MMPI,* or *Minnesota Multiphasic Personality Inventory*. The MMPI has been in use since the 1940s and underwent major updating and revision in 1989. The new version is called the **MMPI-2.** A number of other personality inventories are based in part on this test.

The original MMPI contained over 500 true/false items. Several more were added as part of the revision, and a special version was constructed for use with adolescents (Keller, Butcher, & Slutske, 1990). The items on the test are divided into scales, with cutoff points for the normal range of scores within each one. For example, there are scales for social shyness, depression, suspiciousness, and anxiety. In addition, there are scales that try to determine how well the person understood the questions and how much he or she lied or tried to put on a good act. Three more such scales were added to the revised edition.

In Focus

A Good Personality Test

A thousand seniors sit in a classroom taking a personality test. Their answers will form the **norm** for other seniors.

Suppose that, in response to one of the test questions, 96 percent of the seniors say they study for at least one hour every school night. (Hard to imagine, but just suppose . . . .) What would this information begin to tell us?

The test used most often in schools is the **California Psychological Inventory (CPI).** It has 480 items, which are scored in terms of categories like feelings of self-acceptance, self-control, desire to achieve, and how you get along with others (Gough, 1960). The test is one of the best of this type, but even given that, it is only *fairly* valid and reliable. Thus, it can be faulty for any given person, even though overall it is useful for quickly locating some people with difficulties. The trouble with these tests is that too often they also pick out people who *don't* have problems.

Another major problem with personality inventories is the meaning people attach to the items. For instance, answering "true" to the statement "People talk about me" might indicate a touch of paranoia. However, it could also indicate a source of pride. That is, it could be interpreted as proof that you are important enough that people are interested in discussing you. Similarly, believing that you are an agent of God *could* be an indication of some kind of distortion in your thought processes. On the other hand, it could simply be a statement of faith that all people are, in some way, agents of a higher spiritual power.

Still another problem is that the test score itself gives no clue about how well the person is handling life. Saying "I certainly feel useless" appears on the surface to express a personal problem. However, it tells us nothing about whether the person sees that as a serious difficulty with no solution in sight. He or she may feel that it is just an occasional fact of life to be endured until it passes and is of no particular significance. Even if it is seen as a problem, the person may also have a plan for resolving it.

Personality inventories are useful for general screening in order to locate those who might need help. Caution is always called for, though. A score that indicates the existence of a problem must always be followed up by a face-to-face discussion with a counselor or psychologist to avoid serious error (Anastasi, 1988).

▲ *Psychological tests are sometimes used by school counselors.*

California Psychological Inventory (CPI) personality inventory most often used in schools

Pause for Thought

1. Why is it necessary to standardize procedures for administering personality tests?
2. How do you achieve validity and reliability in personality tests?
3. What is a personality inventory, and what are some examples of personality inventories?

Critical Thinking
....

4. You apply for a job that requires you to complete a personality inventory. Explain to a friend your reactions to this requirement. Be sure to include some of the material from the critical thinking feature.

Thinking Critically about Psychology

Personality Inventories

Businesses have used objective personality tests in selecting employees and predicting job performance. Most psychologists question whether the tests should be used in these ways, but others believe they can be helpful (Hogan, Hogan, & Roberts, 1996). Specifically, it has been claimed that personality inventories can predict success in particular occupations. We want to examine the validity of these claims.

What specifically is being claimed or stated? Personality inventories are reasonably good predictors of occupational success or job performance and are appropriate to use for this purpose.

What is the objective evidence for and against this claim? Most studies in this area have been done with the MMPI, although a few have used the CPI. Generally, investigators single out certain scales of these tests for predictive purposes rather than using the entire test. Among the jobs that have been investigated are such diverse activities as police work, management, student teaching, dentistry, and truck driving. Overall, comparisons of test scores and later performance on the job have shown the tests to be successful to a "moderate" extent (Groth-Marnat, 1990). In general, they predict job performance about as well as IQ tests do (Hogan, Hogan, & Roberts, 1996; Vane & Motta, 1990). (See Chapter 9 for a discussion of IQ tests.)

Because these inventories measure personality, they include questions that many people find both irrelevant for hiring purposes and personally sensitive as well. For instance, they may include items referring to a person's sexual history, religious beliefs, or personal hygiene. What business does an employer have knowing this information? One pattern on the MMPI supposedly measures how likely a person is to become an addict (Keller, Butcher, & Slutske, 1990). If you are not a substance abuser and never

▲ *Applying for a job may mean answering a lot of questions.*

have been, should a prospective employer nevertheless be able to refuse you a position because of a suspicious test score? Needless to say, there are additional issues to be considered.

What other interpretations might be made instead? The research findings indicate that personality tests are only moderately useful. Are other tests or approaches more useful? Well, interviews are not any better. And on occasion, personality tests outperform tests specifically constructed for a particular job (Groth-Marnat, 1990). It would appear, then, that we don't have many ways to predict job performance that hold up well. The best approach, perhaps, is to use several different measures (Cronbach, 1990). However, that still leaves a serious question unanswered: Are these tests sufficiently useful to overcome their inherent problems? In other words, how do you balance the job applicant's right to privacy against the employer's right to hire the best person for the job?

What are the most logical conclusions to draw? In light of the potential for misuse of information obtained from a personality inventory, plus the possibly offensive nature of some of the questions, plus the fact that these tests are only moderately good at predicting job performance, it is doubtful that they are the best choice for this use. To us, the downside clearly outweighs the possible upside. However, if you are asked to complete such a test as part of a job application, you will have to determine for yourself whether the consequences of refusing to do so are worth it.

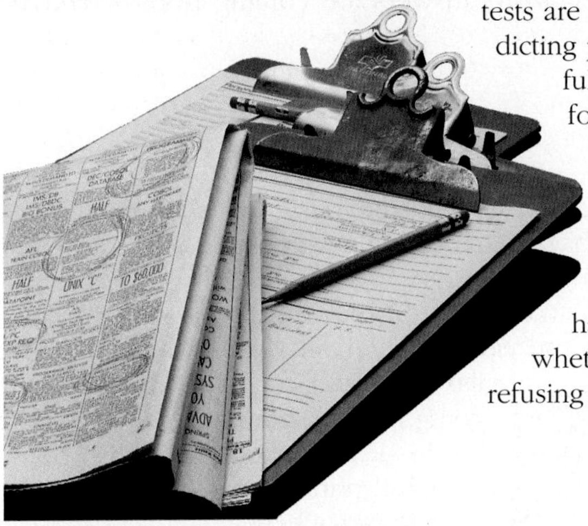

▲ *Should personality tests be part of the hiring process?*

See if **COOL** works for you....

Claim?

Objective evidence for and against claim?

Other interpretations?

Logical conclusions?

Applying Critical Thinking Skills

If after completing a job application you were asked to either complete a personality inventory or agree to be interviewed, which would you choose, and why?

projective tests tests measuring inner feelings elicited by a vague stimulus, such as an ink blot or an unclear picture

▲ *Figure 15.1* *Example of a Projective Test*

Rorschach test an ink blot projective test developed by Hermann Rorschach

Projective Tests

It is not too hard to "fool" a personality inventory by merely checking items to reflect the way you *wish* to be or the way you see yourself (which might not be that accurate). The inventories do have built-in lie scales to catch those who are not telling the truth. For example, one of them has a question, "I read every editorial in the newspaper every day." Nobody does that, so the question may trip up some people who are faking. Also, personality inventories seem to deal pretty much with the surface, rather than getting down to the nitty-gritty of our deeper personalities.

To try to offset these problems, **projective tests** may be used. *Projection* here means the same thing it does for a singer. A singer must project (throw) the voice outward until it lands on the audience. The same is true of the projective test. The test taker projects his or her innermost self onto the stimulus provided.

For example, look at Figure 15.1. What is it? Some will say a cactus, some a fork, some a flower, and so forth. The answers vary, depending on the person's experiences in life. Such an example is simple, but it shows the principle of the projective test. If the stimulus is more complex and the test taker is told to list a number of things it looks like, psychologists assume that some of the answers are coming from deeper in the personality.

The Ink Blot Test

The most famous projective test is the "ink blot," called the **Rorschach** (ROAR-shock) **test** after the designer, a Swiss psychiatrist named Hermann Rorschach. (Incredible as it seems, his nickname in school, "Klex," means "ink blot.")

Rorschach spent a lot of time in his basement splashing ink onto the middle of pieces of paper and then folding them together to get designs similar to that shown in Figure 15.2. After going through hundreds, he finally settled on 10 of them, some in color, which he then had printed on cards.

Rorschach believed that those who look at a card and see something moving in the blot (projection) have a lot of emotion and a good fantasy life. Those seeing color are explosive people. Those seeing lots of white space are negative people. What Rorschach based his conclusions on has never been clear, and the validity of the Rorschach is terrible. So is its reliability.

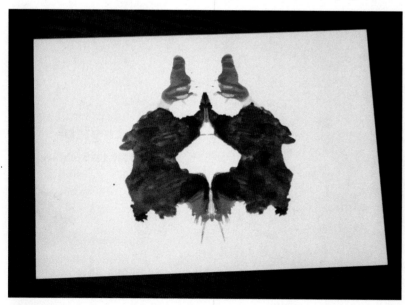

◀ *Figure 15.2* *Ink Blot from the Rorschach Test*

The TAT

The **Thematic Apperception Test,** or **TAT** for short, is another projective test. In the TAT, test takers are shown pictures that are vague and can be interpreted in many ways. They are asked to make up stories about what is happening in the pictures. The themes of their stories (hence the word *thematic* in the name of the test) are then interpreted by the psychologist.

If you look at Figure 15.3, you will see a picture of two women. One person might say that the woman in front is listening to the evil part of herself, telling her to do something. Such an answer might indicate a conflict in the test taker. Or it might just be a theme from a television show or novel. But if the test taker sees enough cards and tells enough similar stories about personal problems of the same type, the tester can get a rough idea of some of the core problems that might exist. Again, validity and reliability are low, but they are better with the TAT than with the Rorschach.

The Principle of Projection

According to the principle of projection, you see a vague stimulus, and you are asked to give responses. The more responses given, the more likely you are to dig into your deeper self. Even if this works, though, it is still hard to know what the responses given really mean.

In Their Own Words . . .

Swiss psychiatrist **Hermann Rorschach**'s *instructions illustrate what he felt was most significant about interpreting the ink blot test (1961/1921):*

> The subject is given one [card] after the other and asked, "What might this be?" He holds the [card] in his hand and may turn it about as much as he likes. (p. 921)

> In scoring the answers given by subject, the content is considered last. It is more important to study the function of perception. . . . The [testing result] depends primarily on the pattern.

> Protocols of the [responses to the blots] are examined according to the following scheme:

> **1.** How many responses are there? What is the reaction time? How frequently is refusal to answer encountered for the several [cards]?
> **2.** Is the answer determined only by the form of the blot, or is there also appreciation of movement or color?
> **3.** Is the figure conceived and interpreted as a whole or in parts? Which are the parts interpreted?
> **4.** What does the subject see?
> (p. 924)

Interpreting Primary Sources

What do you think Rorschach meant by the term *function of perception*? Why was he less interested in what the subject saw in the ink blot than in other factors?

Are projective tests of any use? Probably some, but not as much as you might think. They do offer the counselor or psychologist a chance to talk to the test taker, and they give some idea of how the test taker approaches problems. If the test taker is very disturbed, he or she might see bizarre, strange objects and events in the pictures (Anastasi, 1988). Some psychologists ignore the poor validity and claim the tests help them understand the person. While they are entitled to their views, in general, high validity is much preferred.

◀ *Figure 15.3* *This picture is like those used for the Thematic Apperception Test.*

Thematic Apperception Test (TAT) a projective test using unclear pictures about which people make up stories

443

Focus Question

- What do aptitude and achievement tests measure?

aptitude one's special skills

aptitude tests tests that measure one's special skills (in carpentry, medicine, and so forth)

▲ **Figure 15.4** *A Mechanical Aptitude Test Item. If the gear on the left turns in the direction of the arrow, what direction does the gear on the right turn?*

Aptitude and Achievement Tests

The major goal of any kind of testing is to sort out individual skills or characteristics when dealing with large numbers of people. An attempt is made not only to understand people but also to aim them in the right direction. For instance, a person whose eyes widen and who secretly begins to feel terrified and wants to scratch the floor on an airplane in an attempt to escape should avoid working toward being a flight attendant or pilot. People who love small detail and are precise should check out their skills in bookkeeping or accounting to see if these might be fields for them to pursue.

We will discuss some of the tests available in these areas, but first we have to sort out some confusing terminology. *Intelligence,* which was discussed at length in Chapter 9, is supposed to be a measure of our overall ability to handle general mental problems. The word *general* is used because intelligence is not thought to be specific. The two types of tests we will cover here *are* specific; they deal with specific, not general, abilities.

Aptitude Tests

The word **aptitude** is part of our everyday vocabulary. We say so-and-so has an aptitude for medicine, or for law, or carpentry, or engineering. We mean that this person seems to have special skills in that area.

Aptitudes are hard to measure with tests. But there are some **aptitude tests** available. These tests are usually grouped together, in the sense that the person takes all of them to see in which categories he or she scores highest. Here are some examples:

Mechanical Comprehension. This test attempts to predict success in fields involving repair of autos, refrigerators, air-conditioning equipment, and the like. A typical item is shown in Figure 15.4. If gear Y is moving in the direction of the arrow, will gear X move: (a) clockwise or (b) counterclockwise? This item and many *very* complex ones are used to measure a person's understanding of mechanical devices. The scores are compared with the scores of people who are already in these fields to see how well the test taker does. (Remember norm groups and validity?)

Verbal Skills. This test measures a person's interest in and knowledge about words. We assume that someone who scores poorly in this area will not do well in occupations requiring a great deal of reading or writing. An example of a simple test item in this area is: Which word is spelled incorrectly? (a) horse (b) house (c) humit (d) hanger.

Clerical Speed and Accuracy. Attempts to measure some of the skills necessary in clerical and office jobs fall into this category. This particular test is a timed speed test because even though you might be able to get the answers, if it takes you forever to do so, you won't be much use on the job. Here is a typical item: As quickly as you can, find the underlined test items and mark them on your answer sheet.

Test Item	Answer Sheet
MS MQ <u>MP</u> MF	A. MF MQ MP MX
A7 B2 AB <u>C3</u>	B. C3 B3 B2 A7

This sampling should give you an idea of the kinds of aptitude tests available. None is accurate enough to predict success in a field. But they can give clues to areas in which you might do well or that you should avoid. Their validities and reliabilities are good, but they measure only a small part of what would be involved in any given occupation (Cronbach, 1990).

Achievement Tests

Another kind of test is given in elementary school and high school to measure student progress. These tests are often used to determine how well a school system or class is doing, but they can also be useful in counseling an individual student. They resemble the exams given in history, English, or math courses, but they are usually normed for the whole country or for certain segments of it. Sometimes they are used to give advanced placement in a certain subject to a student.

Such tests are called **achievement tests** because they contain specific content that was (or should have been) learned in the classroom. Those who do best in class achieve the most in a certain area. The tests are not designed to predict future performance or skills, as is the case with an aptitude test—even though we assume that if you do well now in a particular area on the test, you will do so in the future.

achievement tests tests that measure the amount of specific material remembered from the classroom

Most students who plan to go to college will run head-on into one of life's more dreaded experiences: taking the **Scholastic Assessment Test, or SAT** for short. It used to be called the Scholastic *Aptitude* Test, which created a lot of controversy. The name change may help, but problems remain nonetheless. The issue is whether the SAT measures potential for learning, one's aptitude, or instead taps what one has already learned, one's achievement.

Scholastic Assessment Test (SAT) test designed to measure ability to do college work

The SAT is made up of advanced verbal and mathematical problems. You have to be able to define the meaning of words as they fit into certain sentences, solve word puzzles, and deal with fairly complex logic and mathematics problems.

But there are some difficulties. The SAT is supposed to be a *predictor* of college work, not an achievement test. Is that even possible? Doesn't the test require that you have learned specific math techniques in order to answer the questions? Or that you have had a course in social science in order to deal with verbal social science problems? That certainly seems to be the case. For example, let's take this:

Columbus discovered America in: (a) 1492 (b) 1700 (c) 1859 (d) 1950.

This item is a good *achievement* test item for a history test in fourth grade. We would expect this information to be part of a course in basic American history. It is assumed that by high school, everyone has already

▲ *It is not clear whether the SAT predicts future academic success or measures what students already know—probably a bit of both.*

445

learned the answer and remembers it. We certainly hope you do (it's not 1950). So this same item can become part of an *aptitude* test for high school students.

How is this possible? Aptitude tests use such items based on the assumption that as one goes through school life, those who absorb and retain the most material are also going to be the best in that area in the future because by then they will know even more.

You see how complicated this is? There seems to be no way to write an aptitude test item without getting involved in how well you've done in school and how much you remember from school. Thus, the SAT does measure achievement, in large part, especially the verbal section. The mathematics part relies more on reasoning than remembering formulas (Cronbach, 1990).

The biggest problem with the SAT is that environments differ so much from one person to another. We knew a psychologist who had never before been out of New York City and had never seen a live horse, cow, or pig. He was giving a talk to some grade-schoolers in a rural part of West Virginia. The children couldn't believe it when he asked them if any of them had the task of milking the cows that were in a pen next to the school. The problem was that the "cows" were pigs.

It is, then, impossible to measure aptitude without at the same time measuring achievement, which makes the SAT somewhat questionable. Since schools vary as much as does the overall environment, the test leans toward those from well-to-do schools. There are other problems: A low score can damage a person's self-esteem, and the test *can* err as much as 30 points in either direction just by chance. Expensive coaching for the test beforehand can help some students, again giving an advantage to those with money. But on the average, coaching doesn't help to an extent that matches the cost. Some people claim that the test is biased against minorities, and there is support for this (Morgan, 1984).

On the positive side, the test has good validity and reliability for enough students to make it worthwhile. And it does a much better job of predicting college success than an interview or letters of recommendation (Kaplan, 1982). While high school grade averages are better predictors of college success than the SAT, the test can add a little bit to predicting a person's chances for success (Weiss & Davidson, 1981). (Note, though, that college success is only about 50 percent predictable, no matter how many or what measures are used.)

Pause for Thought

1. How are projective tests different from personality inventories?
2. Describe two main types of projective tests.
3. What is the difference between an aptitude test and an achievement test? Describe examples of each.

Critical Thinking
....
4. Write a paragraph arguing for or against the use of SAT scores by college admission officers.

Vocational Interest Tests

Focus Question

- Can vocational interest tests really match aptitudes with jobs?

Probably one of the most important long-term goals any of us ever strives for is the one involving occupation. If things turn out well, most of us stay in the same general field throughout life, even though we may change where we work a number of times.

Areas of interest keep changing for most students until their junior or senior year in high school. Then they begin to become focused—at least in a general sort of way.

One of the most useful tests a student can take is the **vocational interest test.** Fortunately, the major tests in this area have some of the highest validities in psychological testing. Hence, their ability to predict is exceptional compared with the other tests we have discussed. Over 50 percent of people in some studies have been checked up on for more than 20 years after taking the test and are still reasonably happy in the selected occupation (Walsh & Betz, 1985).

vocational interest test a test that attempts to predict what occupational area an individual will like

The Strong-Campbell Interest Inventory

The interest test most often used is called the **Strong-Campbell Interest Inventory.** It is named after the two developers of the test. The test taker is provided with a test booklet answer sheet. The test contains hundreds of statements and choices to which the test taker responds with "like" or "dislike," "agree" or "disagree." Or the person is asked to choose among such things as being an actor, being an artist, or being a botanist.

This is simple enough, but the test is actually more clever than it may seem at first. Most people starting out, when faced with a choice of occupations, aren't sure at all what they want to be. Hence, it might do no good to ask these questions. If you already knew the answers, you wouldn't need the test.

So the test's authors took thousands of people reasonably successful in all kinds of occupations and gave these occupational questions to them. Also included in the test were all kinds of questions not related directly to occupation, such as "Would you rather drive along the side of a mountain, discuss the purpose of life, or go fishing?"

Strong-Campbell Interest Inventory the most widely used vocational interest test; based on answers of people successful in certain fields

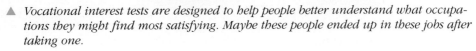

▲ *Vocational interest tests are designed to help people better understand what occupations they might find most satisfying. Maybe these people ended up in these jobs after taking one.*

▲ *Regardless of your occupational interests, you need the proper talents and abilities as well to succeed.*

Next, all the test answers (occupational and otherwise) for all these people were divided up according to what occupation they were in, *not* according to how they answered the questions. When new test takers answer questions, a computer compares their answers with those of the people in each of hundreds of occupations and points out the occupational groups with which the test taker has the most in common. The content of the item is *not* important, which might well be the key to the success of the test (Ackerman & Heggestad, 1997).

For example, if you agree that you would like to be an "auctioneer," this carries a *negative* weight for a score high on engineering, since real-life engineers don't want to be auctioneers. We don't know why—they just don't. It turns out that as a group, real-life lawyers might prefer to be skydivers—at least on paper—and so, if you check the same answer they do on that item, you are given a plus toward a career in law. Hence, the test is showing you how similar you are in hobbies, activities, interests, and the like to people already in various occupations. If you have that much in common with them, you will probably like that occupation (Cronbach, 1990).

The results from the test are reported on a computer printout showing many occupations that fall into such categories as working outdoors, working in science, engaging in artistic tasks, helping people directly, working in sales or politics, and doing business or clerical work. How high you score in these areas is shown as you are compared with others in the various fields.

One of the biggest problems faced in using these tests is a misunderstanding about how they work. Students might score high on an occupation like "funeral director" and come away from the test saying, "Oh, ick, I don't want to deal with dead bodies." But none of the occupations is to be taken at face value in that way. A funeral director is interested in running a small business, dealing with the public, helping people who are in need, and the like. If used in the right spirit, the test can be enormously helpful. Finally, the test is very good at helping you to eliminate certain occupations. If you score low in most occupations within a certain area, the chance that you will like any of those occupations is quite remote (Walsh & Betz, 1985).

Cautions about Interest Tests

It is critical to understand that the interest test does not show that you have the aptitude or ability for an occupation in which you score high. So try not to set your sights on jobs that, deep in your heart, you know you are not qualified for. But we all can adapt our goals within the fields we like. For example, in real life, the pilots think they are the most important part of an airline, the mechanics believe *they're* the most important, the flight attendants feel the airline would fail without their aid and public relations work, and the executives think they are really keeping it all together. The point is that a person with clear-cut aviation interests will probably fit into one (or more) of these subcategories better than the others. Whichever aviation job the person is best suited to, it is still a job in his or her desired field.

The Job Applicant

Case Study

In 1989, a 25-year-old man, Siri Soroka, applied for a position as a plainclothes security guard at a Target store in California. The interview went well, and he felt confident he would get the job. Before he could be hired, however, he had to complete a three-hour test that included hundreds of questions on a variety of topics.

The test booklet was a version of the MMPI and the California Psychological Inventory tests that psychologists use to assess personality. In the booklet were true/false items, yes/no questions, and numerous multiple choice sections. Soroka had to respond to questions such as these: "People talk about me . . . I have never lied . . . Sexual things make me uncomfortable . . . I have never had a problem with bowel movements." He also had to answer questions about religion, personal hygiene, and drug use.

Soroka was upset by the nature of the test: "I couldn't believe the questions that were in it. It made me physically sick" (Gavzer, 1990). Soroka got the job but was fired 10 days later. He then filed suit against the company that owned Target, claiming that the tests constituted an invasion of privacy.

Soroka's lawyers argued that employees should have to answer questions related only to job performance. A person's bathroom or bedroom behavior and his or her attitudes about sex and religion should not be subject to examination in the hiring process.

The store's lawyers countered that employee theft was a big problem, and the paper-and-pencil tests they used helped to reduce such crime by identifying dishonest people. Furthermore, federal law now restricted them from using lie-detector tests, so they had no other alternative. Whether these tests are accurate in identifying dishonesty is controversial. Some psychologists believe that the tests are valid and that employers should be able to use them. Others argue that the tests do not accurately predict if a person will be a risk on the job (Saxe, 1991). Furthermore, the results could be wrong, especially if they are administered by a business person who has little or no training in personality assessment. Regardless, if the company was only or mainly interested in theft, why did the test include so many other kinds of personal items?

The simplest answer has to do with cost. The tests were fairly inexpensive to buy—about $10 per test—and they were easy to administer. And until Soroka came along, no one had complained. To order new tests, or to have the publisher revise the tests, probably seemed costly and a waste of time.

A California court ultimately decided that the test was indeed a violation of Soroka's right to privacy. Thanks in part to Soroka, companies now have to tailor personality tests to job performance in order to ensure that a person's right to privacy is protected. (Note: Just before the court handed down its decision, the company settled the case with Soroka for a little over a million dollars.)

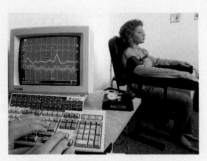

▲ *Federal law now prohibits the use of lie-detector tests by employers.*

Review the Case Study

Can you think of any situations in which violating a potential employee's right to privacy would be acceptable?

Second Look at Test Validity

Tests of all kinds have a way of seeming more powerful and accurate than they really are. This is a lot like the idea that if you read something in print, it *must* be true. Stop and think about any obnoxious or goofy people you know. Someday some of them will be writing things that find their way into print. Would you believe something you read if you knew they had written it? The same principle applies to tests.

This is a good place to look again and a little more closely at *validity*. We will use completely imaginary numbers just to help you grasp the point. Suppose you have a tub filled with 100 red marbles and 100 white marbles, mixed. We will blindfold you and have you pull out 100 marbles. White means no error; red, an error. We will call perfect validity 100 white marbles. You pull out 53 white and 47 red ones. That means you made an "error" 47 times.

Such is the case with validity—which is never perfect. In fact, in real life, tests that produce results like this would be considered to have good validity. Why? Because, as you'll see in the next section, many methods, such as inter-

In Focus

Tests and More Tests

	Personality Inventory	Aptitude Test	Achievement Test	Vocational Interest Test
General Purpose	Reveals beliefs, habits, hopes, needs, desires	Reveals or measures one's special skills	Measures amount of material remembered from classroom—*not* designed to predict future performance	Predicts suitable occupation Does *not* show aptitude for an occupation or ability
Positive Aspects	Locates those who might need help	Locates areas in which one might do well and areas one should avoid	Can be used to evaluate a school system or an individual—can help with advanced placement	Usually high validity—helps one eliminate certain occupations
Problems	Sometimes singles out those who don't really have problems	Not accurate enough to predict success in a field	Sometimes used as a predictor of future performance	Individuals may misinterpret their scores
Examples	California Psychological Inventory, MMPI	Mechanical comprehension Verbal skills	SAT	Strong-Campbell Interest Inventory

Imagine that you are an expert at interpreting test results. Subject A completes all of the above tests. Assuming you avoid the problems listed above, what information about A would the tests still not reveal?

viewing, will only produce perhaps 20 white marbles. Hence, tests work better than interviewing. In any case, always check with a counselor about any test results, and then, assuming you are being truly honest and reasonable with yourself, go with your instincts about whether the results are right or not.

Alternatives to Testing

Despite the problems we have mentioned, a test remains the most valid and reliable method for getting information. All of us like to think we are as objective as the tests if we are called on to be so, but that apparently isn't the case.

Interviews

Interviewing involves several problems. One of the worst is the **halo effect.** The halo effect applies when a person with one positive characteristic is assumed to have other positive traits as well. No one checks to see if this is actually the case; it is simply assumed to be so. We all know students who play up to the teacher so much that they seem to have a "halo" glowing above their heads. Often, these students get special treatment and recommendations when everyone in the class knows they are unpleasant and devious people. In almost any kind of interview, they will come off well, making the interviewer think they are bright, helpful, useful—all of which may be false.

There is also the **reverse halo,** where a negative characteristic leads to the assumption that the person has other negative aspects. The student who does dumb things, like throwing objects in class, may have great potential, but it is hidden by this behavior. So in this case, too, the teacher and the interviewer tend not to see the real person; they are taken in by the reverse halo.

Since the interview takes place in person, there is another pitfall, called **standoutishness.** In a job interview, for example, a male wearing a red-and-yellow-checked jacket and a tie that lights up or a female wearing four-inch-long birdcage earrings complete with miniature chirping birds will completely distract the interviewer, who will not notice whatever qualities the applicant possesses that are appropriate to the job. This description is deliberately exaggerated to get across a point. While such things shouldn't have any effect on how your intelligence or skills are viewed,

• Are interviews better than tests for assessing personality?

• What is the major drawback of situational assessment?

halo effect the situation in which a person who has one positive characteristic is assumed to have other positive traits

reverse halo the situation in which a person with one negative characteristic is assumed to have other negative traits

standoutishness doing or wearing something that is so startling it distracts observers from noticing one's real abilities

◀ *What do you think the halo situation is for each of these women? Which one really "stands out"?*

451

they clearly do, and there's no way to get around it. A test measures the relevant qualities better because it doesn't know what you look like or how you act.

Should the interview be skipped? No, it can add important information if well done, but it must always be viewed with caution.

Situational Assessments

Another alternative to testing is secret observation of people in action. Especially for research purposes, people are watched to see how they act when they think they are alone. For example, researchers wanted to understand what might lead people to help others in trouble. One study used stooges who faked a "flat tire" at the side of the road. Few people stopped to help. But then, the researchers set up another situation in which stooges were obviously helping someone who had a flat tire. When people saw this scene and *then* arrived on the scene of the second "flat tire," they tended to stop and help. Clearly, this results from a form of imitation, but it also shows that the specific situation alters behavior (Bryan & Test, 1969). The researchers in this study were engaging in what is called **situational assessment.**

The biggest difference between testing and the situational approach is that with the latter, the researcher is observing and can't interfere or ask questions. Hence, we can never know what is going on in the minds of those whose behavior is changing. The moment we start to ask questions, we are testing, not observing.

situational assessment the process of looking at how the circumstances surrounding an event influence people responding to that event

Focus Question

• What should you know about the ethics of taking or giving tests?

Ethics of Testing

When you take a test in math, history, English, psychology, or what have you, the worst outcome is that it will show that you haven't studied or that you have trouble with that subject. It is not a personal threat to you. Such is not the case with the personality tests we have been discussing. They almost always require answers to things that many of us prefer not to talk about. Hence, they can be extremely threatening. As a result, certain ethical standards exist to protect the test taker. Here are some of the core ones:

1. Depending on your age and state or federal law, someone—either you or your parent(s)—must give permission for you to take personality tests. And the reason for giving such a test should be spelled out.

2. Your privacy must be respected. Remember, however, that somehow law enforcement people can always find a way to see just about anything. So be careful when you take a personality test. You might be merely joking when you agree to answers that are strange, but they could become part of your permanent record. If you are truly deeply worried about personality problems, which can happen to almost anyone at some point, it is worth taking the test if you have a counselor in whom other students have faith. Often these counselors can help a great deal.

3. When personality tests are being given for research, you always have the right to refuse to take them. That's standard practice.

Here are some general tips on testing that might be of use:

1. Whether or not you have to take an intelligence test is controlled by many state and federal laws. Court battles are going on in this area all the time. Your counselor can inform you of your rights.

2. If you *do* take an intelligence test for some reason, a record will be made of the score. If you have any reason to doubt its accuracy, you should request a reexamination before you leave high school. This is important because these test scores can reflect measurement errors at times, and you might carry along on your permanent record a lifetime score that does not reflect your real ability.

3. It is to your benefit to take a vocational interest test. We know of none that is a disguised personality test. Taking the SAT or a similar test is also a good idea. Many colleges require one for admission. You can always take the test again or go to some school that doesn't require it if you don't like your scores. Most colleges *do* look at your high school records, so if the SAT scores are below average and your grades have been good, the grades tend to carry more weight with most admission committees. Remember that the SAT, at its best, *only* indicates school potential and has nothing to do with the possibility of great success in thousands of occupations.

4. As mentioned, anyone who takes a personality test may feel exposed and vulnerable. The worst part about this is that you might begin to feel that there *really* is something wrong with you just from the types of questions on the test. The chances are overwhelming that you are sane and about as normal or abnormal as most of the rest of us. The test has not made you the victim of some all-seeing, all-knowing psychologist. To illustrate this last point, we have developed the Learned Pig Personality Test. Maybe it will help you rest more easily.

 Pause for Thought

1. Are vocational interest tests usually valid? Describe one type of interest test.
2. Describe several problems that may arise in conducting interviews and situational assessments.

Critical Thinking

3. Create a simple chart that outlines the ethics of testing and general tips on taking tests. Use visuals and captions.

APPLYING
Psychology to Life

The Learned Pig Personality Test

Please identify each of the following eight statements as either true or false as it applies to you. At the end, we will tell you how to score your answers, and we will discuss the test.

1. I worry more often than I wish I did about the future. While sometimes the future seems reasonably clear, at other times it's too unknown.
   True   False

2. I have had a recent upsetting experience that is hard for me to forget. Sometimes it will pop into my mind at the strangest times.
   True   False

3. I worry about my body. It doesn't seem to be all that it should be, especially when I compare it with some other people's.
   True   False

4. I worry that I don't have enough really close friends. Many of my relationships seem too superficial.
   True   False

5. I'm not sure who I *really* am. Sometimes I feel like my personality is pretty good, but it doesn't feel right at other times.
   True   False

6. I'm uncomfortable about sexual matters. Lots of other people seem to know what's going on; but sometimes this subject makes me uncomfortable, and most of all it doesn't always make a lot of sense. Also, it seems to be out of proportion—but I'd never tell anyone that because they'd think there was something wrong with me.
   True   False

7. Being in love feels so good, and it's supposed to be a natural state. But I worry because sometimes things are so messed up about it that I wish it would go away.
   True   False

8. People always say that adolescence is the time when you don't really have any worries or burdens. There must be something wrong with me because that sure doesn't seem to be what my life is like.
   True   False

Scoring Key: Count the number of "true" responses you made. If you checked seven to eight "true," you are normal. If five or six, you're either awfully lucky or fooling yourself. If you checked four or fewer, you're either lying or not human.

There are several goals behind this little experiment. First, it should make you feel a little more at ease about your personality. We are all worried more often than we wish we were, and things don't always go smoothly no matter what area of life we're dealing with. Second, you can see that a test can be made up in such a way that persons can be made to *appear* abnormal when, in fact, they are not. And third, the test should show you that what may seem to be a deep, all-knowing question from a psychologist is often just a statement of the obvious made to look like there is special knowledge behind it.

Around the turn of the century, a famous circus called Barnum and Bailey's thrived. P. T. Barnum, one of the founders, said there was a "sucker born every minute." He was referring to the fact that you can fool people with great ease. Such foolery is still done today through palm reading and horoscopes, and the few remaining circuses usually have a "fortune-teller." All these people merely state the obvious or the common in such a way that it seems they know the deep, inner recesses of our minds. This is called the *Barnum effect,* and it is a serious problem because so many of the things these people say seem to be mysteriously probing us when they aren't.

We called our test the Learned Pig Test because for about 100 years, starting in the late 1700s, pigs became the "in" thing in touring acts and stage performances. The pigs were supposed to have incredible abilities: They supposedly could sing, dance, spell, tell time, tell your age, and speak in many languages. In those days, people sometimes believed that women were very frail and would "swoon" (fall into a faint) if they weren't dealt with very carefully. As a result, the promoters had to promise that ladies who attended the performance would not have their personalities revealed by the Learned Pig—thus, no one would know the ladies' secrets (Jay, 1987). The point is that the personality test we made up is similar to the one used by the pigs (on men only). The pigs would stick their snouts toward certain items on a big card that listed personality characteristics—in that way, they "revealed the truth."

▲ *Beware the learned pigs! They'll give away your deepest secrets!*

CHAPTER 15 REVIEW & APPLY

Summary

1. Tests must be standardized and norms must be established by use of different groups. Tests also must have good validity and reliability to work.

2. Personality tests are of two general types. The first is objective and uses factual questions to which the person responds. An attempt is made to build a picture of the person's personality using these statements.

3. Personality inventories don't seem to reach "deep" enough and are subject to problems like faking. Thus a second type of test—projective tests, like the ink blot—are sometimes used. These tests are designed to get material from the test taker that is hidden, since the stimulus he or she is responding to is so vague.

4. An achievement test is designed to measure what has already been learned. An aptitude test is intended to predict how well a person will do in the future, but these tests still have to use the person's current knowledge.

5. Vocational interest tests are used to predict a person's satisfaction in certain job areas. These tests measure interest only, not aptitude.

6. Interviews provide information, but it is usually less accurate and more subjective than test results.

7. Situational assessments are used primarily for research purposes. They involve observation of how people behave when they think they are alone. They do cast light on behavior, but they don't provide an opportunity to find out why the people are doing what they are doing.

Vocabulary

psychological test	projective tests	vocational interest test
standardization	Rorschach test	Strong-Campbell Interest
norms	Thematic Apperception	Inventory
validity	Test (TAT)	halo effect
reliability	aptitude	reverse halo
personality inventory	aptitude tests	standoutishness
MMPI-2	achievement tests	situational assessment
California Psychological	Scholastic Assessment	
Inventory (CPI)	Test (SAT)	

Review Questions

Matching

On a sheet of paper, match terms in the second list to descriptions in the first list. Answers may be used more than once.

1. Measures how much one has learned in the past
2. Helps one to eliminate certain career choices
3. Helpful in singling out people who need help
4. Designed to predict future performance, but sometimes not accurate enough
5. Reveals special abilities
6. Has a very high ability to predict

    a. aptitude test

    b. personality test or inventory

    c. achievement test

    d. vocational interest test

Fill in the blank

On a sheet of paper, write the word or words that best complete each statement.

7. If we take a test in April and score high and take the same test in May and score low, the test may not be highly ▓▓▓▓.
8. Teachers' pets may benefit from the ▓▓▓▓.
9. If 98 percent of the population answer a question in a similar way, they are establishing a pattern, or a ▓▓▓▓.
10. Test A is supposed to measure intelligence, and it *does!* The test therefore has a high degree of ▓▓▓▓.
11. Gathering information by observing people in different settings and situations is called ▓▓▓▓.

True/False

On a sheet of paper, answer each statement true or false. *If false, rewrite the statement to make it true.*

12. A personality test can usually be administered to someone without permission.
13. You need not take the results of a personality test too seriously, since the score will probably not be recorded on your permanent record.
14. You have the right to refuse to take a personality test used for research.
15. Certain laws exist that control whether you have to take an intelligence test.
16. Vocational interest tests are usually disguised personality tests.

Discussion Questions

1. Pretend you are writing a personality inventory and want to catch liars. Write three true-false questions that might serve to do this. Sample: "I always tell people what I think." Anyone who answers "true" is likely to be lying.

2. Personality inventories, sometimes used to predict job performance, may include personal questions about sexual history, religious beliefs, or hygiene. Can you think of any jobs where the employer should have a right to know this sort of personal information?

3. Just for fun, take another look at one of the projective test items in the chapter and describe what you would write down in response to the item. Then briefly explain whether you think your answer reveals much about your personality.

4. You've probably taken your share of achievement tests in school. Describe how you approach these tests. Do you prepare? Do the tests cause you great anxiety? Have the results from these tests accurately measured what you know?

5. Interest inventories help you rank your career interests. They usually take about 30 minutes or so to complete. You can probably make a fairly accurate prediction of the results in just a few minutes, however. Rank the following six items from greatest interest to least interest, then briefly explain your rankings: working outdoors, working in science, engaging in artistic tasks, helping people directly, working in sales or politics, doing business or clerical work.

Activities and Projects

1. Your school counselor probably has a great deal of knowledge about the purposes and uses of various aptitude, achievement, and vocational interest tests. Prepare a list of questions and interview your counselor. Include questions about: (a) the differences and similarities among the three types of tests; (b) the general strengths and weaknesses of each type of test; (c) the main kinds of tests your counselor uses and why—and whether these tests are valid and/or reliable; (d) students' rights in regard to testing—especially intelligence testing.

   Write a report of the interview and include your reactions.

2. Conduct an experiment to see if a halo effect or reverse halo effect can be created through brief positive and negative descriptions. Neatly print or type the following on an index card: "Denise Smith. 16 years old. GPA: 2.1. Job Objective: Computer programmer. Job Experience: Denise volunteers at a nursing home. She had a job as a waitress for a few months but quit because she didn't have enough time to study." Print the same information on a second index card, but replace the GPA score with "4.1."

   Take a third index card and write the following: "Based on the description of Denise, indicate how you would rate her (a) friendliness, (b) honesty, (c) generosity, (d) confidence level, (e) chances of succeeding as a computer programmer." Include a scale on the card: (1) poor, (2) below average, (3) average, (4) above average, (5) excellent.

   Present the first card to 15 subjects, and present the second card to 15 different subjects. Record their responses and analyze your results. Did Denise's GPA seem to create a halo effect? Which categories got the highest or lowest ratings? Why do you think you got the results you did? Do you think teachers are sometimes influenced by this halo effect?

3. Visit your school counselor to see if you can complete a vocational interest test. You'll need about 30 minutes to complete the test. Write a brief essay on what you learned in filling out the test. Look at the areas in which you scored highest and lowest. Any surprises? Do you think the test is highly valid, somewhat valid, or not valid at all?

4. As you may have gathered from reading the chapter, many of the personality and achievement tests commonly used often inspire controversy. Collect several articles that clarify and explain some of these controversies. Then design a detailed chart that presents the pros and cons of using these tests. Finally, in about a page, argue either for or against using the tests.

5. Imagine you are an advice columnist and you have just received this letter: "Dear_____, I'm a high school senior who suffers from test anxiety. I need to take the SAT next month and I'm afraid I'll flop. Can you help? Signed: Testaphobic." What advice would you give Testaphobic? Try to incorporate some of the material from the article and the chapter in your advice.

CHAPTER 16

Conflict, Stress, and Coping

Frustration, conflict, and stress are basic parts of life. They are most destructive when bottled up and turned into an inner anger or rage. Those who take change and problems in stride can often use the stress as motivation to achieve greater things. Those who cannot cope effectively may turn to alcohol or other drugs.

Frustration

If you plan on wearing something that matches your blue sweater, this item is bound to be either lost or all rolled up in a ball. If you are really in a hurry to get somewhere, the traffic will be unbelievable, and all the stoplights will turn red just as you reach them. If there is a sale and there is one CD you want badly, there are two possibilities: (1) you don't have enough money, or (2) you have the money and get the CD, but your player breaks down.

These are the frustrations of daily life, which do take their toll. While these problems may not be earthshaking in and of themselves, they gradually wear us down, since each of them causes us to tighten our muscles, clench our teeth, and want to run screaming down the street. Such frustrations can't be good for us—and they aren't.

Frustration occurs when we are blocked or hindered from reaching goals we are seeking. Most frustrations are relatively minor, if we can keep them in perspective. The problem is that since there are so many of them, we can get buried and lose that sense of perspective. Some minor frustrations are still hard to handle for almost anyone—try those irritating busy signals seven calls in a row. And frustrations can be serious, as when someone doesn't have the skills to play a particular sport or lacks some other talent in an activity that is special to him or her.

▲ *Endless frustration can make just about anyone break down and cry.*

Conflict

Conflicts are particularly difficult to deal with because they demand a decision. A **conflict,** then, is a situation in which we must decide between two or more alternatives (to do one thing or another, or to do or not to do something). Conflicts will not go away by themselves. There are four types of conflict.

Approach-Approach Conflict

The **approach-approach conflict** is not all that bad. It involves two attractive alternatives. We have to choose between two things we want to do (approach). There are two movies you want to see, for example, but you have money for only one. You have to choose.

Approach-Avoidance Conflict

The **approach-avoidance conflict** can be distressing. One part of the situation makes it attractive, but the other part makes you want to run away. You want to go out with someone, say, but are afraid you won't really be liked. The process of trying to decide what to do can leave you drained and feeling hopeless for the moment.

Focus Question

• What are four types of conflicts we commonly encounter?

frustration the process by which we are blocked or hindered from reaching goals

conflict a problem that demands a choice between alternatives

approach-approach conflict a conflict involving a choice between two attractive alternatives

approach-avoidance conflict a conflict involving a situation with both good and bad features

Avoidance-Avoidance Conflict

avoidance-avoidance conflict a conflict involving a choice between two unattractive alternatives

You can't win with the **avoidance-avoidance conflict,** the worst of the three because it involves two unattractive alternatives. If you don't go to the dentist, your teeth will rot (bad), but if you do go, he or she will bring out the whirling monster that sends bits of teeth and water flying all over the room while you squirm in agony (also bad).

Double Approach-Avoidance Conflict

double approach-avoidance conflict a conflict involving a choice between alternatives, both of which have good and bad parts

The **double approach-avoidance conflict** is the one we face most often. It is called "double" because there are both good and bad parts no matter which way we go. For example, suppose you have a vote on whether your family moves to another city. The school might be better there, but you aren't used to it. Special new friends could be there, but you have to leave behind those you already know and care about.

All of these types of conflict are normal. They can't be avoided. Still, a steady diet of painful conflicts, especially when one feels alone and not supported, can result in feelings of hopelessness. After a while, a person in this situation will begin to make incorrect decisions or will be unable to make any decision, and eventually he or she can develop psychological and physical symptoms from the steady drain on the body and psyche.

Anxiety

anxiety the feeling that something is wrong and disaster is imminent

Conflict and frustration lead to **anxiety,** a feeling of dread that something is seriously wrong and that disaster sits right around the corner. Anxiety results when we cannot resolve a conflict or when frustration builds too high. Any feeling of helplessness when we are trying to solve problems can lead to anxiety. This, in turn, can become a general feeling that we can't cope. If such anxiety goes on for a long time, it can eventually do a person in. Severe attacks of anxiety can cause a rapid heartbeat, fatigue, breathlessness, chest pains, dizziness, fainting, feelings of doom, and headaches.

▶ *Sometimes it all gets to be too much.*

Stress

Stress is defined as the *physical* pressure and strain that result from demands or changes in the environment (Mandler, 1984). Stress arises whenever we have to readjust. Conflict, frustration, and anxiety can all lead to stress. But *any* kind of change, even a positive one, causes stress, because we must adapt to a new environment. We'll talk more about this shortly.

Good Stress

Stress is not necessarily a bad thing in and of itself. Its impact is relative to the individual: What is terribly difficult for one person can make another person feel interested and alive. For example, meeting new people can be a very stressful situation. Most of us are uncomfortable if the person we are meeting is someone we want to like us or someone who might be important to us. But since never making any new friends or getting a job or leaving home is much worse than stress, we have to go ahead and do these things.

In fact, in these cases, stress turns out to be a good thing because it keeps the body going, and this, in turn, keeps us moving toward a new goal. Similarly, at least in theory, stress from doing homework is good in the long run because one learns. When stress is "good," leading to something desirable, it is called **eustress.**

Bad Stress

On the other side of the coin, the negative effects of stress are great. These include confusion, inability to make decisions, and avoidance of people, as well as, eventually, physical or psychological illness. When stress is "bad," or overwhelms our ability to cope, it is called **distress** (Cohen & Williamson, 1991).

How we view a particular problem has a lot to do with whether stress is bad or good. Moving to another city, for instance, can be seen as a chance to make a new and better life for ourselves, or it can be seen as a hassle and a loss. Making up your mind to make the best of a situation—even though this is often easier said than done—can work wonders in terms of how stress affects you.

Physical Changes with Stress

The effects of stress come from the physical responses that occur whenever we are facing change, conflict, or frustration. To understand this, we need to look for a moment at the animal world, where these effects are a little simpler to observe.

Focus Questions

• Can stress be positive?

• What physical changes occur during stress?

stress the physical strain that results from demands or changes in the environment

▲ *Stress is part of everyday life.*

eustress stress that motivates us to do something desirable

distress stress that is overwhelming or that causes problems

463

**Focus**

Conflicts

Approach-Approach

Two attractive alternatives, but you can only choose one:
"Should I eat a hamburger or pizza? I only have enough money for one."

Avoidance-Avoidance

Two unattractive alternatives; avoiding one brings you closer to the other.
"I hate broccoli, but if I don't finish it, Mom will never let me hear the end of it."

Approach-Avoidance

One goal or choice that is both attractive and unattractive; the person reaches for the positive feature of the goal, but the goal includes both positive and negative features:
"I want to have a candy bar, but I don't want to get another cavity."

Double Approach-Avoidance

Both alternatives include attractive and unattractive features:
"Should I eat broccoli, which is not very tasty but is nutritious, or should I have the dessert, which is rich in calories but makes my mouth water just thinking about it?"

Colleen has to decide which college to attend in the fall. How could each of these types of conflict be involved in her decision?

Fight or Flight.   In the wild, animals are designed to deal first of all with physical safety. The key to safety for them is an environment that remains the same. Any change in the environment, such as an unusual sound followed by some type of movement, immediately signals the possibility of danger. Some life-threatening event could be about to happen—a predator might be creeping up—and the sound and movement are warning signs. As a result, the vision and hearing systems of all animals (including humans) are physically designed to detect immediately *any* change in the surroundings. (How about when you are at home alone some night, especially after seeing a horror movie? You are sitting there and it is completely quiet, when all of a sudden you hear scratching and creaking sounds, and you see some kind of movement outside the window. Your body goes into full alert.) Thus, any kind of change triggers a physical alarm. That is nature's design.

Assume that the animal is correct about coming to alert status: There is a creature on its way to attack. The animal's body is fully mobilized to do one of two things—fight or flee. There is no third choice. Thus begins what is called the **fight or flight reaction.** In nature, the animal either wins, loses, or escapes. If the battle is won or the animal runs away, special chemicals are then sent through the body to cancel out the ones that were triggered in order to handle the emergency.

The Human Response. The major parts of the human that respond to emotional stress are the higher brain, the part we do our thinking with; the lower brain, the part that controls all the basic bodily functions; and the **adrenal** (ah-DREE-nal) **glands,** which sit above the kidneys and stir up the body's activity level. Here are three examples of the kinds of things that can trigger an emotional response: anticipating having an operation, going out on a first date with a new person, and having to accept the fact that a loved one has died. Notice that all three of these human problems involve a *psychological* change because they deal with *mental* issues. This does not reduce their potential for distressing us. Instead, it makes them harder to handle than real life-and-death physical struggles.

In each case, the higher brain assumes that threat and danger exist. It signals the lower brain about the emergency. The lower brain secretes a special chemical called the **stress hormone,** which signals the adrenal glands to send *adrenaline* (ah-DREN-ah-lin) to the body. This causes the muscles to tense, the heart to beat faster, and the liver to send out more sugar to be used by the muscles when we either fight or flee (Axelrod & Reisine, 1984). Thus, the body can't tell the difference between a physiological threat and a psychological threat and will respond in the same way to either kind of "danger."

If we were able to solve these problems immediately, the body would go back to normal quickly. But because our concerns are often more abstract than physical, it is tough to find an end to them. Hence, the stress lasts a long time. Eventually, it can cause physical problems because we are running (on the inside) at full alert too much of the time.

Examining Stress

Some stress results from change, whether the change is good or bad. In this regard, the listing in Figure 16.1 might be of some interest.

This listing is interesting because it suggests how upsetting certain events can be. For example, getting failing grades and gaining a new family member are not that far apart as stressors. But one would hope that acquiring a new sibling would quickly pass from a stressful event to developing a warm, happy relationship. Hence, one cannot add up these scores and predict how much damage will occur. Those who are subjected to major stressors, however—such as the death of a spouse, loss of a family member, or getting fired—are more likely to develop disease or sickness later on, especially if a couple of these stressors happen at about the same time (Krantz & Manuck, 1985).

fight or flight reaction the body's reaction to a crisis; the organism is mobilized to either fight or run away

adrenal glands glands that cause excitement in order to prepare the body for an emergency

stress hormone a special chemical that signals the adrenal glands to activate the body

▲ *The loss of a loved one is a major life stressor.*

Stress research also focuses on things that do not cause actual changes in one's life. For example, a continued beating from all of life's little annoyances, such as we discussed at the beginning of the chapter, if added to an environment of poverty, overcrowding, poor health, or the like, weakens a person's defenses to illness. In fact, some researchers feel that the accumulation of many moderately stressful problems might well be the real cause of early sickness or death.

Stress and Personality

The higher brain, as mentioned, makes our problems abstract. How many dogs or cats do you know who fret and worry about a history exam? Our concerns are certainly real enough, but we make life so complicated. People in groups—that is, societies—do the same thing. For instance, there are rules against punching a rude salesperson.

We couldn't survive as a group without such restrictions. But all these restraints *do* cost us something. The angrier we get without being able to do something about it, the more the walls of the stomach engorge (fill up) with blood, putting pressure on that organ; the more our muscles tighten up; the higher our blood pressure gets—until we make ourselves sick (Krantz & Manuck, 1985). In fact, physically healthy people who have strong hostile feelings much of the time have higher blood pressure than people who don't feel this way very often. They also describe their general everyday moods in more negative terms (Räikkönen, Matthews, Flory, & Owens, 1999).

Unrelieved Tension.   In one study, researchers deliberately frustrated the subjects. Then the researchers allowed half of the group a chance to get back at them verbally (no injuries allowed). The other half weren't allowed to do that. The blood pressure and heart rate of those who were able to pay the researchers back dropped noticeably, while those of the other subjects did not.

So, bottling up your feelings *too much* isn't good for you. There's a limit to this, however. No one wants to be around people who have no control over themselves. The point seems to be that a person needs to learn to pass off most things and to take a stand only on things that really matter. In actuality, there aren't that many things that matter deeply, if we are truthful.

The General Adaptation Syndrome.   Any creature put under major stress for long periods of time will eventually collapse. The events that occur under such stress have been outlined in what is called the **general adaptation syndrome.** Translated, this term refers to "the overall (general) process by which the creature adjusts (adapts) to various levels of stress." The word *syndrome* means a set of symptoms or signs.

The general adaptation syndrome assumes that the same pattern is followed each time stress is heavy. As with all things, we can't make a rule that fits every case, but the following three-part sequence of the general adaptation syndrome seems to occur frequently (Selye, 1956).

The first stage is called an **alarm reaction.** The body sends out emergency signals that stir it up in preparation for an attack—either psychological or physical.

Next, the **stage of resistance** occurs. This means that the organism tries to fight back against the attack. The organism wants to restore psychological and physical balance. If the threat is removed at this point, the body

Focus Question

• What are the three stages of stress response?

general adaptation syndrome sequence of behavior that occurs in reaction to prolonged stress. It is divided into stages: **alarm reaction,** preparation for an attack; **stage of resistance,** trying to restore balance; and **exhaustion,** giving up the battle.

and psyche begin to restore themselves to their normal chemical and emotional balance.

If the stress doesn't let up, continuous fighting becomes impossible. This third stage, **exhaustion,** means the battle is over, and we have lost—or at least, have quit.

The three-stage sequence is easiest to see in an accident. For example, suppose you break your leg. When the limb is broken, the first response is one of panic or alarm. Your body starts your heart beating rapidly, increases your breathing rate, and so forth. Next comes an attempt to see if the leg will move despite the pain, trying to offset it somehow, to make it all go away (resistance). Finally, when the pain is too much and the break is obvious, you give in and lie there helplessly.

Note that this is the case if the break happens around others. But if it occurs when you are alone, then the stage of resistance is seen very clearly because you struggle, fight, and drag yourself toward help before you collapse.

One thing might be bothering you: Stress, frustration, conflict, and anxiety have been defined. They are all slightly different, but they all interact. Stress can cause anxiety; anxiety can cause stress; conflict can cause frustration; frustration can cause stress. So just learn the differences among them in a formal sense, and don't be too concerned about the fact that they seem to get mixed together when we talk about them.

In Focus

The General Adaptation Syndrome

Alarm   **Resistance**   **Exhaustion**

Can you think of any other situations that you encounter at school that might produce this kind of reaction to stress?

 ## Pause for Thought

1. Briefly describe four kinds of conflicts that often cause frustration. What happens when we can't resolve conflict?
2. What is stress, and what is the difference between eustress and distress?
3. What are some basic physical changes that occur as a result of stress?

Critical Thinking

4. You find out that your grades will be lower than usual this semester. You agonize over how to tell your parents. According to the general adaptation syndrome, what kinds of changes will you go through?

Thinking Critically about Psychology

Personality Types

type A personality personality type associated with people who are always operating at full speed, are impatient, and are filled with distress

type B personality personality type associated with people who are open to change, are flexible, enjoy life, and have low levels of stress

A great deal of research has focused on the connection between developing stress-related illnesses and having what is called the **type A personality.** People with this personality type are always running full speed ahead. They are highly impatient and competitive people who frequently compare how they are doing with how others do. In conversation, they often seem to be distracted, thinking of other things (Yarnold & Grimm, 1982; Friedman & Rosenman, 1974). People with the **type B personality** are the opposite. They are open to change and are flexible. They enjoy life because they don't put competition first, and they like a variety of activities (Weinberger et al., 1979). Type B personalities are also said to be considered somewhat resistant to the ill effects of stress.

What specifically is being claimed or stated? There are really two parts to this claim. First, having the characteristics defined as a type A personality increases the risk of developing an illness associated with high levels of life stress, such as heart problems or chronic high blood pressure. Second, having the characteristics defined as a type B personality decreases this risk.

What is the objective evidence for and against this claim? A number of studies have found that people with a type A personality do indeed develop stress-related illnesses at a higher-than-average rate. However, not all studies have gotten these results, and not all type A people suffer major problems. In fact, some seem to be no more prone to these illnesses than the average person (Case, 1985). As for type B's, one study compared over 150 male executives from the same company. Roughly half the group had become physically ill following some stressful life events, and the other half had not. Both groups had experienced roughly the same amounts and kinds of stress, so they didn't differ in that respect. Analysis of the men showed that those who didn't get sick were type B's—those who were more open to change and who viewed problems more as a challenge than as a threat (Kobasa et al., 1981).

What other interpretations might be made instead? We might wonder if there is more than one kind of type A personality, since some don't seem that vulnerable to stress. Or we might ask if some people with type A personalities have other characteristics that influence these findings.

▲ *Type A's are always on the run.*

Another consideration might be whether the kind of job the type A person has makes a difference. To an extent, all these possibilities have some truth to them. For instance, lawyers expect stress and conflict to be a central part of the give-and-take of their profession and seem to thrive on them. Furthermore, the type A's

▲ *A high level of stress on the job is challenging to some, but exhausting to others.*

who appear to be at highest risk are not just competitive and impatient. They also distrust other people and are angry most of the time. The type A's who see others as a threat, who misinterpret events, and who refuse to accept the fact that they act the way they do are the ones most prone to physical disorders such as heart problems (Miller et al., 1991; Case, 1985; Friedman, 1984).

What are the most logical conclusions to draw? It does appear that the type B personality offers some protection against the negative effects of stress. As for having a type A personality and being at risk for stress-related illness, we need to alter our original claim. It seems that the elements of sus-piciousness, hostility or anger, and lack of self-awareness must be added into the mix before stress will take such a heavy toll.

Applying Critical Thinking Skills

Describe the type A and the type B personalities. In what ways do you fall into one or both of these categories? Provide examples.

See if **COOL** works for you....

Claim?

Objective evidence for and against claim?

Other interpretations?

Logical conclusions?

Case Study

Managing Everyday Stress

In his book entitled *Flow*, psychologist Mihaly Csikszentmihalyi (1990) describes several coping strategies people use to deal with stress. We may not have great control over the many stressors we encounter in life—the car breaks down, the job application is rejected, a friend moves away—but we have ultimate control over how we respond to the stress.

In general, we can respond to a stressful event in two ways—positively or negatively. Csikszentmihalyi calls the negative option *regressive coping.* We sleep too much, avoid or deny the problem, take out our anger on friends and family, and maybe even adopt destructive habits such as drinking. The more positive option is *transformational coping,* which means creating something good out of something bad. We admit our anger, address the problem more logically, adjust our priorities, and explore solutions.

Most of us, when faced with stress, rely on both strategies. We may withdraw from the problem for a while, try to tackle the problem directly, retreat, and then try out a number of solutions.

Read through the following case studies. For each one, think about how the characters might use both transformational coping and regressive coping to deal with their problems.

Case Study 1. Sixteen-year-old Roger lives in a single-parent home with his mother, who has recently lost her job. Roger has a 10-year-old brother who lives with them, and they've been fighting more than usual lately. Last week their gas and electricity were turned off for a while. Roger is struggling with his grades at school, and he feels he has no true friends.

Case Study 2. A freshman in college, Becky wants to become a doctor. She thinks she needs to earn straight A's to get into medical school. She also plays on the girls' basketball team because she received a partial athletic scholarship. Practices are long and interfere with her studying. Also, she wishes she had more time for a social life.

Csikszentmihalyi admits that psychologists don't know why some people rely more on one strategy over another, but maybe having a label for the two options will heighten self-awareness. Knowing you have a choice may encourage you to see the big picture when coping with stress.

▲ *A source of stress may be trying for balance between academic demands and athletic activities.*

Review the Case Study

Think about a recent stressful event in your own life. How did you use regressive coping or transformational coping to deal with the stress?

Psychological Stressors for High School Students

High school students ranked these events according to how stressful they perceived them to be. Note that some "happy" events are included here. Individual people may score these events higher or lower than they are scored here, and other individuals may be stressed by events not named here.

	Stress Points
• Death of parent	119
• Divorce of parents	98
• Death of a close family member (except parent)	92
• Breakup with boyfriend/girlfriend	79
• Expulsion from school	79
• Major personal injury or illness	77
• Death of a close friend	70
• Pregnancy	66
• Getting a job	62
• Money troubles	61
• Dating	57
• Gain of new family member	57
• Change of finances	56
• Major illness of family member or close friend	56
• Failing grades at school	54
• Change in number of arguments with peers	51
• Marriage	50
• Parent beginning or stopping work	46
• Peer difficulties	45
• Loss or death of loved pet	44
• Change in responsibilities at home or school	43
• Brother or sister leaving home	42
• Moving away	41
• School beginning or ending	38
• Trouble with parent	38
• Outstanding personal achievement	37
• Change in schools	35
• Christmas	30
• Change in recreation	29
• Trouble with teachers/principal	29
• Change in personal appearance	27
• Change in social activities (joining new group)	27
• Change in eating habits	27
• Change in sleeping habits	26
• Change in number of get-togethers	26
• Vacation	25
• Change in church activities	22
• Traffic tickets or other minor violations of the law	22

Check the list, and identify the events that have happened to you in the past year or that you expect within the next year. Use the number system to determine how many stress points you are experiencing in this period of your life. Then score yourself as follows:

Over 200: Urgent need of intelligent stress management.   100–149: Stressful life: Keep tabs on your mental health.
150–199: Careful stress management indicated.   Under 100: No present cause for concern about stress.

Your answers are personal and private. Share them with others only if you are comfortable doing so.

Source: Events and stress points adapted from the work of M. A. Miller and R. H. Rahe, "Life Changes Scaling for the 1990s," *Journal of Psychosomatic Research* 43 (1997): 279–292.

▲ *Figure 16.1*   *Psychological Stressors for High School Students*

Focus Question

• How is stress related to how much control we have over our lives?

Coping with Stress

Real problems in the real world have a definite impact on our well-being. However, a lot of the frustration and anxiety we feel has little to do with reality. To a large extent, the amount of stress we experience will depend on how much threat we perceive, how much we dwell on problems, and what we do about them.

Issue of Control

It is obvious that we can affect our health by the way we view life. Those who see themselves as worthless and who are anxious, depressed, angry, or hostile increase stress dramatically and set themselves up for problems.

One of the most important factors seems to be the degree to which we feel we have lost control of our lives. In one experiment using a pair of rats, researchers placed the rats in separate cages with wires attached to the rats' tails. Both were then subjected to a series of shocks.

One of the rats was an "executive." It was able to stop the shock by turning a wheel with its paws. This ended the shock for the other rat also—but the other rat had no control over what was happening. Hence, both rats got the same amount of shock, but only one of them was "in charge," so to speak,

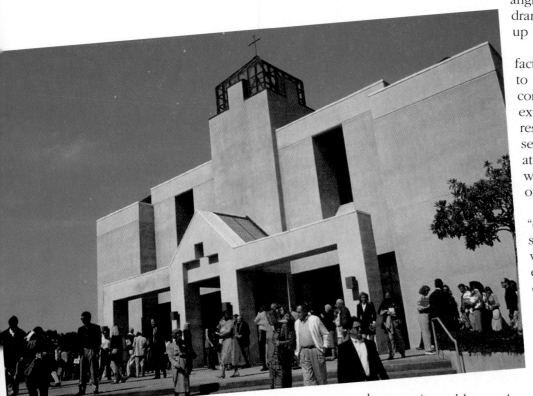

▲ *Religious beliefs that emphasize the power of forces outside the individual do not necessarily interfere with one's sense of control.*

because it could turn the wheel. The health of the rat controlling the wheel remained good, while the other one suffered ulcers and sickness—despite experiencing exactly the same level of shock (Weiss, 1972).

The key here seems to be the ability to *feel* in control of a stressful situation, even though the stress must still be faced. Also important, in cases where control isn't really possible, is whether there is a sense of *complete* helplessness. If an event can be predicted or at least partially controlled, the negative effects are reduced dramatically (Burger & Arkin, 1980). Many studies on many different types of creatures, including humans, support these claims.

It should be noted that some people and cultures find strength through strong spiritual or religious beliefs that do not emphasize the individual's power. In such cases, they believe that the control starts from outside them, but they still benefit because they believe (inside) that there *is* some control somewhere on their behalf over what is happening.

In Focus

Locus of Control Scale

Instructions

Answer the following questions the way you feel. (Do not write in your textbooks. Use a separate sheet of paper.) There are no right or wrong answers. Don't take too much time answering any one question, but do try to answer them all. One of your concerns during the test may be, "What should I do if I can answer both yes and no to a question?" It's not unusual for that to happen. If it does, think about whether your answer is just a little more one way than the other. For example, if you'd assign a weight of 51 percent to "yes" and 49 percent to "no," mark the answer "yes." Try to pick a response for all the questions.

The Scale

_____ 1. Do you believe that most problems will solve themselves if you just don't fool with them?

_____ 2. Do you believe that you can stop yourself from catching a cold?

_____ 3. Are some people just born lucky?

_____ 4. Most of the time do you feel that getting good grades means a great deal to you?

_____ 5. Are you often blamed for things that just aren't your fault?

_____ 6. Do you believe that if somebody studies hard enough he or she can pass any subject?

_____ 7. Do you feel that most of the time it doesn't pay to try hard because things never turn out right anyway?

_____ 8. Do you feel that if things start out well in the morning, it's going to be a good day no matter what you do?

_____ 9. Do you feel that most of the time parents listen to what their children have to say?

_____ 10. Do you believe that wishing can make good things happen?

_____ 11. When you get punished, does it usually seem it's for no good reason at all?

_____ 12. Most of the time, do you find it hard to change a friend's mind (opinion)?

_____ 13. Do you think that cheering more than luck helps a team to win?

_____ 14. Do you feel that it is nearly impossible to change your parent's mind about anything?

_____ 15. Do you believe that parents should allow children to make most of their own decisions?

_____ 16. Do you feel that when you do something wrong there's very little you can do to make it right?

_____ 17. Do you believe that most people are just born good at sports?

_____ 18. Are most of the other people your age stronger than you are?

_____ 19. Do you feel that one of the best ways to handle most problems is just not to think about them?

_____ 20. Do you feel that you have a lot of choice in deciding who your friends are?

_____ 21. If you find a four-leaf clover, do you believe that it might bring you good luck?

_____ 22. Do you often feel that whether or not you did your homework has much to do with what kind of grades you get?

_____ 23. Do you feel that when a person your age is angry at you, there's little you can do to stop him or her?

_____ 24. Have you ever had a good-luck charm?

_____ 25. Do you believe that whether or not people like you depends on how you act?

_____ 26. Do your parents usually help you if you ask them to?

(continued)

In Focus

Locus of Control Scale

(continued)

_____ 27. Have you felt that when people were angry with you, it was usually for no reason at all?

_____ 28. Most of the time, do you feel that you can change what might happen tomorrow by what you do today?

_____ 29. Do you believe that when bad things are going to happen, they just are going to happen no matter what you try to do to stop them?

_____ 30. Do you think that people can get their own way if they just keep trying?

_____ 31. Most of the time, do you find it useless to try to get your own way at home?

_____ 32. Do you feel that when good things happen, they happen because of hard work?

_____ 33. Do you feel that when somebody your age wants to be your enemy, there's little you can do to change matters?

_____ 34. Do you feel that it's easy to get friends to do what you want them to do?

_____ 35. Do you usually feel that you have little to say about what you get to eat at home?

_____ 36. Do you feel that when someone doesn't like you, there's little you can do about it?

_____ 37. Do you usually feel that it is almost useless to try in school because most other students are just plain smarter than you are?

_____ 38. Are you the kind of person who believes that planning ahead makes things turn out better?

_____ 39. Most of the time do you feel that you have little to say about what your family decides to do?

_____ 40. Do you think it's better to be smart than to be lucky?

Scoring the Scale

The scoring key is reproduced below. Circle your response on your answer sheet each time it corresponds to the keyed response below. Add up the number of responses you circle. This total is your score on the Locus of Control Scale. Record your score at the top of your answer sheet.

1. Yes	14. Yes	27. Yes
2. No	15. No	28. No
3. Yes	16. Yes	29. Yes
4. No	17. Yes	30. No
5. Yes	18. Yes	31. Yes
6. No	19. Yes	32. No
7. Yes	20. No	33. Yes
8. Yes	21. Yes	34. No
9. No	22. No	35. Yes
10. Yes	23. Yes	36. Yes
11. Yes	24. Yes	37. Yes
12. Yes	25. No	38. No
13. No	26. No	39. Yes
		40. No

What the Scale Measures

Locus of control is a personality dimension originally described by Julian Rotter (1966). According to Rotter, people vary in regard to how responsible they feel for their own fate. Individuals with an _internal_ locus of control tend to believe that we are responsible for our own successes and failures. Conversely, people with a relatively _external_ locus of control tend to attribute successes and failures to luck, chance, or fate.

The scale you just responded to was developed by Stephen Nowicki and Marshall Duke (1974) in order to remedy some technical prob-

Reprinted by permission of Stephen Nowicki. From the Instructor's Manual prepared by Wayne Weitan for _Psychology Applied to Modern Life,_ Second Edition, by Nowicki and Duke, published in 1986 by Brooks/Cole Publishing Company.

(continued)

Focus

Locus of Control Scale

(continued)
lems that were characteristic of the original Rotter (1966) scale. Like the original, it measures one's belief about whether events are controlled internally or externally.

Interpreting Your Score

Norms

External Score:	16–40
Intermediate Score:	7–15
Internal Score:	0–6

External Scorers: A score above 15 suggests that you have a fairly strong belief that events are beyond your control. In other words, you do not feel that there is much of a connection between your behavior and your outcomes. This means that you are less likely than others to take credit for your successes or to take the blame for your failures. Instead, you tend to believe that success and failure are primarily a matter of luck and chance.

Intermediate Scorers: A score in this range means that you have inconsistent views about the degree to which you control your own fate. You probably believe that you do control your own fate in some areas of your life but have little control in other areas.

Internal Scorers: A score below 7 indicates that you have a firm belief in your ability to influence your outcomes. Your score means that you generally do not attribute your successes and failures to good and bad luck or chance factors. Instead, you feel that you can influence the course of what happens to you. An internal locus of control is often associated with relatively high stress tolerance.

Self-Concept

What we define as troublesome and how we react to it are related to how we perceive ourselves. For example, if we feel confident in a social situation with new people, we won't see the situation as much of a problem, and we will probably enjoy ourselves. If we don't feel confident, we may well become anxious and withdraw instead of striking up a conversation.

These different views and reactions come from different **self-concepts.** A person's self-concept is the image that person has of herself or himself. Our self-concepts are mixtures of characteristics that we see as belonging to us, which make up who we believe we are. They may or may not be in line with the way others see us.

All of us can think of people whose self-concepts are not very accurate—a boring person who thinks she's hilariously funny, a drop-dead gorgeous guy who thinks he's ordinary looking. When a *large* gap exists between our self-images and others' images of us, we may be failing to see a problem that can get worse if we keep ignoring it. However, most of us see ourselves in a somewhat more positive light than is realistic. Is that a dangerous thing to do? Probably not, as long as it is within reason. In fact, it may help us maintain a sense of well-being. It is interesting to note that depressed people are usually both more negative and more accurate about their self-concepts than nondepressed people are (Haaga, Dyck, & Ernst, 1991).

There is another way in which a gap between our self-images and others' images of us can cause problems. Childhood versions of

self-concepts the images we have of ourselves

475

▲ *How we feel about ourselves should not be dependent upon other people's opinions.*

self-esteem the degree to which we think we are worthwhile

Focus Question

• What are some ways people "trick" themselves into feeling better?

defense mechanisms psychological distortions we use to remain psychologically stable, or in balance

repression the process of pushing a painful event or thought out of consciousness

self-concepts come from what other people tell us about ourselves. As we grow older, we add our own information and experience. But when important other people, such as our families, hold up an unrealistic idea of who we should be, we usually end up feeling inadequate. As a consequence, our **self-esteem** suffers.

Self-esteem refers to how worthwhile we think we are. Self-esteem is different from self-concept, but the two are related. For instance, a self-described nasty, ugly, mean, lazy slob can have high or low self-esteem, depending on the value those characteristics have for that individual. Similarly, people you think are kind, attractive, intelligent, athletic, and socially adept can still have low self-esteem. They may see themselves as not really having those characteristics or not having enough of them.

When we are expected to meet impossible standards, we often stop trying altogether and just give up (Heatherton & Baumeister, 1991). The key is to develop our own positive idea of who we are—one that is not so dependent on other people's opinions.

Psychological Defense Mechanisms

When threatened, we all do our best to keep some kind of balance. We protect our inner selves from too much attack by using **defense mechanisms**—psychological distortions, or "tricks," designed to keep us stable. If someone says you are a slimy, rotten worm of a person, for example, your defenses go into action instantly. You either think how terrible that person is or try to make yourself look better to offset the comment. Thus, we use defense mechanisms to reduce threats to ourselves and to feel better about ourselves. Defenses are normal, but they can be used too often. When that happens, we are refusing to face reality, and this is not adaptive.

In the next subsections, we cover several defense mechanisms. Usually, they are not fully conscious, because we use them to protect ourselves. If we fully admit that we are using a defense mechanism, it loses its effectiveness; we have to believe at least partially in what we are saying to and about ourselves while we are saying it. As you may have guessed by now, the idea of defense mechanisms comes from psychoanalytic, or Freudian, theory.

Repression. When we use **repression,** we do not allow ourselves to remain aware of painful material; we push it out of consciousness. Thus, if we hate someone and want to do him or her in, we force these feelings and impulses out of our awareness (repress them). Repression operates to some extent in all defense mechanisms. After all, if we are going to distort something, we cannot afford to remember it clearly.

Repression is usually unhealthy. For example, those who repress the feeling that someone important, like a parent, doesn't love them are asking for trouble. Pushing this feeling away can interfere with the ability to give and receive love. Better to find out where this belief comes from and resolve it.

◀ *Sticking your head in the sand is a gritty form of denial.*

Denial. When we engage in **denial,** we refuse to admit that anything bad has happened. In some ways, denial is similar to repression. With repression, though, we are at least partly aware of the problem, and then we push it out of consciousness. With denial, we don't let the problem into consciousness in the first place.

denial the process of refusing to admit that there is a problem

When given some terrible news, the first thing people usually say is something like, "Oh, no! That can't be true." Denial, then, is a common *first* response to tragedy. Most of us, however, go on to accept reality.

People who routinely deny having done or said things whenever they cause a problem are in for trouble. They may avoid facing the music for a short while, but eventually they lose out. Because they are less than truthful and do not take responsibility for their actions, others cannot trust them. Also, you simply cannot get anywhere in solving a problem if you cannot admit that one exists in the first place.

Displacement. Sometimes we have trouble directly expressing what we feel because of the threat (real or imagined) that something terrible will happen as a result. So we vent our feelings elsewhere or on someone else, engaging in **displacement.**

displacement the process of venting our feelings on something or someone other than the true or original target

This behavior is so commonplace that even animals do it. If a male bird is threatened by a more dominant male, he may, instead of responding directly, turn away and furiously peck at a leaf. In the human arena, if we dare not talk back to our boss, for instance, we might yell at a friend instead. Most of us have had this experience when we were in a bad mood because of something that happened earlier in the day.

Again, a little of this type of behavior is to be expected. However, too much displacement causes trouble because it allows us to avoid facing a problem that may only get worse rather than going away. Another problem is that when we displace anger onto innocent bystanders, we unnecessarily hurt people we care about.

Reaction Formation. In **reaction formation,** what we express is the opposite of what we really feel. Say that a man feels extremely hostile toward his mother and even thinks about physically harming her. This same man feels very guilty about his hostility because he believes that people should love their parents. He is horrified and terrified by his wish

reaction formation the process of expressing the opposite of what we feel

477

In Focus

Defense Mechanisms

Repression (to forget)

Rationalization (to make excuses)

Projection (to point finger)

Regression (to go backward)

Denial (to not admit)

PAINFUL THOUGHTS PUSHED INTO UNCONSCIOUS

I HATE MY AUNT!

WHAT WAS I THINKING ABOUT?

REAL REASON FOR BEING UPSET

CONVERTED TO REASON THAT SOUNDS GOOD

I DIDN'T GET A PROMOTION

WELL I DIDN'T WANT THE JOB ANYWAY.

PERSON'S REAL FEELINGS ARE THROWN AT ANOTHER PERSON

WHAT DO YOU MEAN, I'M UPSET; I'M NOT UPSET. YOU'RE UPSET!

FRUSTRATION EXPRESSED IN CHILDISH WAY

I SHOULD HAVE GOTTEN THE PROMOTION!

REAL PROBLEM BECOMES CANCELLED

I DON'T HAVE A BLACK EYE. I JUST HAVEN'T BEEN GETTING ANY SLEEP.

Reaction Formation (to stifle extreme hostility)

Displacement (to redirect anger)

Identification with Aggressor (to adopt another's characteristics)

(to stifle emotions)

Sublimation (to channel impulses)

FEELING ONE WAY EXPRESSED OPPOSITE WAY

HMM. THIS PROGRAM IS INTERESTING.

CENSOR THIS FILTH!

ANGER AT ONE SOURCE DIRECTED AT DIFFERENT SAFER SOURCE

YOU'RE FIRED!

WATCH WHERE YOU ARE GOING!

ANOTHER'S CHARACTERISTICS BECOME MY CHARACTERISTICS

I HATE HIM BUT SOMETIMES I WANT TO BE LIKE HIM...

HIGH EMOTIONS EXPRESSED OBJECTIVELY

YES, HE ENDED THE RELATIONSHIP. HE WAS READY TO MOVE ON. WE HAD TROUBLE COMMUNICATING

EXPRESSED IN ACCEPTABLE MANNER UNACCEPTABLE IMPULSES

BULLY NICK NEVER STOPPED FIGHTING WHEN HE GREW UP.

WORLD CHAMP

Should we try to avoid using defense mechanisms entirely?

to harm his mother. In order to keep these feelings both secret and under control, he displays a high degree of protectiveness and concern for her. He calls her often to ask about her health and well-being. He runs errands for her. He never misses a birthday or Mother's Day, and so on.

Reaction formation is sometimes a little hard to see in operation, since we can't read people's minds. Grade school, though, offers a perfect and harmless example. How does a little girl know that a little boy likes her? Because he studiously and deliberately ignores her in the hallway and makes faces at her on the playground.

Intellectualization.   When the emotions we feel are too overwhelming, we may try to eliminate them altogether. Talking coolly and "rationally" about a tragedy as if it were simply an event that we observed is called **intellectualization.** We have taken all the feelings out of our description.

Intellectualization can be somewhat healthy, at least for a short while. People who have been widowed or seriously assaulted, for instance, may appear very calm at first. They may concentrate on seemingly unimportant tasks and talk about what happened to them as if they were objective observers, uninvolved and untouched. It is only when this approach goes on too long that it becomes troublesome. The problem is that the emotions have not really disappeared. Refusing to express them, face them, and deal with them on an emotional level gives them more power, not less.

intellectualization the process of removing our feelings about an event and discussing it in a coolly rational and unemotional way

Identification with the Aggressor.   When we are mistreated for a long time by someone much more powerful than we are, we may take on some of that person's characteristics, or *identify* with him or her, to try to curry favor. By being like that person, perhaps we can avoid the abuse, perhaps that person will like us better, or perhaps we can also become powerful, at least in our own minds.

This defense mechanism—called **identification with the aggressor—** can help explain some puzzling events. For instance, some people who are held for long periods of time as prisoners of war become like their guards. Instead of treating the guards as the enemy, they treat them as friends— despite the fact that they have been beaten or tortured by these same people. When the war is over, the psychological conflicts begin. These former prisoners usually have great difficulty explaining their behavior to themselves and often come to feel like traitors. Although the behavior has stopped, the confusion and guilt they feel have not.

identification with the aggressor the process of taking on characteristics of someone who has mistreated us in order to psychologically avoid the abuse

Similarly, a child may take on the characteristics of an abusive parent. Thus, he or she may end up engaging in the very actions that were so hated and feared in childhood. Such people often find themselves doing things to their own children that they swore they would never do. As was true in our other example, guilt is often one result. However, in this case, the abusive behavior has no clear-cut built-in stopping point, so the cycle may continue to repeat itself.

▲ *Kidnapped heiress Patty Hearst came to identify with her kidnappers before she was taken into custody.*

regression the process of going backward in behavior and thought to a period when we were taken care of as a child; childish behavior

Regression. With **regression,** we defend ourselves by "moving backward" and behaving like children. This defense is a reaction to the extreme frustration of having to be an adult and take responsibility. We regress (move backward) to a time when we were helpless children and someone had to take care of us. What we want when we are on the firing line is to be home in bed with someone bringing us chicken noodle soup.

Regression is sometimes seen in sports events when the player lies down on the ground and has a temper tantrum, just as a child would. It is also seen in general behaviors such as pouting, sulking, and name-calling. If we can find someone willing on occasion to take care of us, regression might offer some comfort, but usually it tends to make others reject us, since anyone acting this way appears ridiculous.

rationalization the process of explaining away a problem so that we don't have to accept the blame

Rationalization. With **rationalization,** we explain what we do in such a way that we avoid any responsibility for a bad outcome. Say we take some money that we need for something important and spend it on something frivolous. We could rationalize this behavior by saying that we are all entitled to *some* enjoyment in life. However, we still need whatever it was, but now we don't have the money to pay for it.

On the other hand, rationalization can be used to our benefit to deal with something we can't do anything about anyway. If someone we have loved very much tells us to shove off, we could rationalize by thinking of some defect that he or she has (terrible breath? strange smile? who knows what?). So we are "tricking" ourselves into believing we didn't want the other person anyway.

▶ *Breaking up is hard to do. But then you can rationalize by saying that he really wasn't much to begin with, was he?*

projection the process of attributing our thoughts to someone else

Projection. **Projection** refers to the process of mentally giving to someone else our own thoughts or feelings. For example, if a person is fired from a job for genuinely poor performance, he or she might claim that it is the supervisor who is incompetent. In this way, the responsibility is shifted onto someone else. All of us, at times, have a few bad days in a row. We decide that those around us are acting strangely and making life difficult for us on purpose. A continued pattern of such behavior is self-destructive, since it doesn't help us face up to how *we* might be causing the problems.

sublimation the process of channeling emotional energy into constructive or creative activities

Sublimation. **Sublimation** occurs when we channel our emotional energy into a constructive or creative activity. It is the only defense mechanism that is truly healthy and adaptive. Instead of giving in to unacceptable aggressive impulses, we become gymnasts or play football. Sublimation allows us to express through painting or writing poetry the lingering sadness we feel over losing someone close to us. Similarly, rather than just getting angry about social injustice, we may become active in an organization designed to change an unfair law.

Healthy Characteristics

Focus Question

....

- What general characteristics do psychologically healthy people share?

Psychology often tends to emphasize what goes wrong rather than what goes right. We know much more about various mental disorders than we do about healthy behavior. However, certain personal characteristics are common to people who are resistant to stress and cope well with life's problems.

At the top of the list is accepting yourself, along with accepting and being interested in others. Being able to perceive reality fairly accurately is another important characteristic. This means not distorting things to suit your own purposes or denying that problems exist.

Psychologically healthy people feel basically in control of their lives, at least in Western cultures. They have a few close personal relationships and are able to make commitments. They are tolerant of and try to understand different points of view. They have a sense of purpose in their lives and are problem centered. People who are problem centered set specific goals and then go about reaching those goals. They do not just sit for hours stewing and worrying about things. They take steps to make constructive changes. In fact, they have developed the ability to accurately foresee problems and are able to take action before trouble strikes—or at least before it gets too bad (Aspinwall & Taylor, 1997).

Solving Problems

We have mentioned problem-solving skills at several points, so it seems like a good idea to provide some specific steps here. They are important both in dealing with everyday foul-ups and in maintaining a general sense of having some control over what happens to you.

1. The first step is to define the problem. Not only is this the first step but it is also the most important step. How you define a problem will determine the direction you take in trying to solve it. Your definition needs to be workable, objective, specific, and goal oriented. The statement, "I am not very happy," may be true, but it's not a good definition of the problem. Saying "I want to be happier" makes it more goal oriented, but it is still too vague to be of much use. So, pare it down further. What's the real issue? Is it money? Is it your social life? Is it making friends? Is it grades? The goal you choose needs to be as narrow as you can make it, at least for starters. Virtually all big problems can be broken down into smaller, more manageable ones. The more you do that, the less overwhelmed you will feel. Once you have selected the subject and defined the problem, *write it down*. We know this sounds trite, but it really does work.

2. Now that you have your problem defined, think about different ways it can be approached. Let's say you want to improve your grades. There are several ways to go about this. One is to spend more time studying. Another is to pay more attention in class. Another is to find better ways of learning. Still another is to get outside help. Think carefully about what you, as a unique individual, need. Write down all the approaches you have come up with. Again, be as specific as possible.

In Their Own Words . . .

*Social psychologist **David G. Myers** writes about what is the best predictor of whether a person will be happy:*

Let's pretend: I want you to guess whether a particular person I have in mind feels happy and views life with deep satisfaction. . . . I *won't* give you any important clues by telling you whether the person is male or female; age fifteen, fifty, or seventy-five; black or white; living in a city or rural area; high-school- or college-educated. Even more surprisingly, I also give you no vital clue by telling you whether my person was questioned thirty years ago or today, whether the person three years ago won a state lottery or was paralyzed in an accident, whether the person lives on an estate and drives a new Mercedes or in an apartment and drives a 1972 Volkswagen.

So, what would clue you? One clue comes from psychological research: The best predictor of behavior is past behavior in similar situations. The best predictor of grades is not aptitude scores, but past grades. The best predictor of job performance is not an interviewer's intuition, but past job performance. The best predictor of violent tendencies is not a prison psychologist's hunch, but past violence. Likewise, a good predictor of future well-being is past well-being. At the top of your wish list of clues should be knowing the person's happiness and life satisfaction at some earlier time. (*The Pursuit of Happiness*, New York: William Morrow & Co., 1992, pp. 105–106.)

Interpreting Primary Sources

Myers suggests that someone who was paralyzed in an accident can be just as happy as someone who won the lottery. How is this possible? Do you agree with Myers? Explain.

3. Now, assess or evaluate how workable you think each approach is. You can make up a scale from 1 to 5, for instance, and label each approach. Just be sure that the labeling is yours and yours alone. What sounds good to other people may not be right for you. You know what will work for you, so trust your own judgment.

4. From all the approaches you have evaluated, select the best one, and come up with as many specifics for implementing it as you can think of.

5. Put your implementations into action for a specific time period. This is probably the hardest part of problem solving. Making the changes a habit can help. For example, if you decided to study for an hour after supper, do it every evening, whether you have any assignments or not. Read ahead in one of your textbooks, or outline a chapter, or do extra-credit work; just *do something*.

You may have noticed that this step has a time limit to it. The goal is to give yourself enough time to succeed but not keep you stuck doing something that isn't going to work. For the time you have, though, don't waste your energy wondering if your choice is the right one. Put all your efforts toward making that choice work.

6. Once the time period is over, evaluate your success, being as honest with yourself as you possibly can be. For instance, did you really spend that time studying? Or did you spend it doodling in the margins and staring into space, daydreaming? Did you actually succeed quite well, but you are disappointed because in the back of your mind, you somehow imagined that you could go from all C's to all A's if you really applied yourself? Depending on the evaluation you make, you might want to continue with this plan, make a few changes, or try a different approach altogether.

Other Traits

Related to all these characteristics is a sense of responsibility. This means both taking credit for successes *and* taking the blame for failures. Some people do only one or the other, and leaving either one out is a bad idea. For example, some people take complete responsibility for nearly everything that goes wrong in their lives. This not only makes these people feel terrible most of the time but also allows other people to behave irresponsibly (Folkman & Lazarus, 1988).

◀ *Taking time to enjoy life is a basic part of psychological health.*

A certain amount of independence is also part of the recipe for psychological health. Healthy people have respect for social order, but they are not overly conforming. They also like their privacy and like to have some time alone. This means that they enjoy their own company and are not too dependent on other people. They are not rigidly locked into a specific philosophy or way of doing things but are open to new ideas, concepts, and activities.

"Take time to stop and smell the roses." Psychologically healthy people are experts here. They have a fresh appreciation of life, even things they have experienced many times before. They continue to marvel at a blossoming tree or the beauty of a snowfall or the changing shapes of the clouds or the miracle of being alive, regardless of how old they are.

Finally, healthy people do not take themselves too seriously. They are able to laugh at the absurdities of life. Having a sense of humor smoothes the roughest and most difficult of times. A good laugh not only releases tension but can help you see things in their proper perspective (Miller et al., 1991; Kobasa et al., 1979, 1980; Maslow, 1968).

 ## Pause for Thought

1. What is meant by the term *self-concept?*
2. How can self-esteem affect one's self-concept?
3. Describe several characteristics of people who exhibit healthy behaviors.

Critical Thinking
. . . .
4. Provide a brief, original example for each of the defense mechanisms listed in this section.

Focus Questions

- Which drugs do people commonly abuse?
- How do drugs affect the body?

substance abuse use of a drug to the extent that relationships or occupational demands suffer

substance dependence abuse of a drug; the abuser has physical symptoms when the drug is not used, uses more and more of the drug, and devotes large amounts of time to drug use

Substance Abuse

There are many ways of handling stress, conflict, and frustration—some reasonable, some disastrous. In this section, we cover one of the worst methods for handling problems: substance abuse.

Misuse of drugs is formally called either substance abuse or substance dependence. In **substance abuse,** the person's use of a drug has gotten bad enough to cause problems in his or her daily life—in relationships with other people, work on the job, or schoolwork. **Substance dependence** occurs when the person has physical symptoms when not using the drug, uses more and more of it, and spends large amounts of time involved in drug use. The two problems are closely related, and it is sometimes difficult to distinguish between them.

Using drugs to alter consciousness is not just a human activity. Reindeer, cattle, and rabbits eat intoxicating mushrooms; tobacco plants are preferred by baboons; elephants in the wild seek out fermented grain such as would be found in beer. There is some indication that stress is a factor in these behaviors, because when elephants are restricted in the amount of space they have, they dramatically increase their consumption of the grain (Siegel, 1983).

For humans, most scientists agree that stress, conflict, and frustration are major factors in drug use. The user is trying to alter the world enough to make it more tolerable. Also important is peer pressure: Some who get started on drugs do so because others are doing it and they don't want to feel left out of the group (Petraitis, Flay, & Miller, 1995).

One of the biggest problems we face in writing this section on drug abuse is that people have been lied to so often and in such exaggerated terms that it is hard to get anyone to listen to what the scientific findings are. For instance, a poster (Figure 16.2) put out by the government in the 1930s about marijuana warned that the drug caused murder, insanity, and death. It does none of these things.

▶ *Figure 16.2 1930s poster warns against using marijuana. (From* Marihuana Reconsidered *by Lester Grinspoon, Harvard University Press, 1971, p. 324.)*

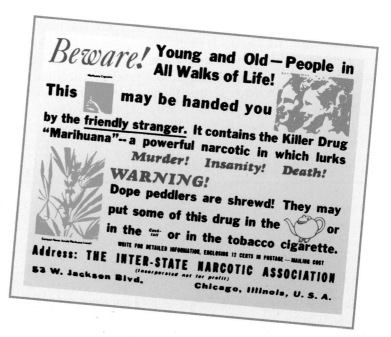

◀ *Peer pressure can help people avoid drug use.*

On the other hand, there *are* problems with telling the truth about drugs. Many people have the ability to read what they want into whatever is actually said. For example, bypassing the fact that some believe that drinking alcohol in any form or quantity is wrong, we can report that the scientific evidence does not support the claim that alcohol is dangerous in and of itself. It is illegal to drink alcohol unless you are 21 years of age or older, but for adults, a glass of wine with dinner can be enjoyable and even has some health benefits. The problem with saying this is that some will read it as meaning that if one glass of wine is safe every now and then, so are three or four—or more. That is not true. The chances of becoming an alcoholic increase as one increases the amount and frequency of drinking.

Another point is that over the years roughly half the population have used alcohol in one way or another on a fairly regular basis. To avoid the stigma attached to "drug" use, people often discuss alcohol as if it were not a drug. This is false. Alcohol works exactly the same way other drugs do, as we will describe in a moment. In fact, its general method of action is about the same as that of the popular tranquilizer Valium.

A final point should be made: Once a drug habit really gets started, it takes heroism to get rid of it. This does not mean that a person who has taken a drug a few times can never stop or is already damaged. But no matter what "they" say, everyone who has a steady intake of a drug eventually winds up in a very messy and painful situation. This is just common sense. The user becomes too attached to the sensations the drug produces to give it up. Such users keep saying, "I'll give it up tomorrow," but it doesn't work that way. If tomorrow ever *really* comes, a battle must take place before the person can win.

How Drugs Work

It is hard to grasp some of the issues surrounding drugs without at least a rough idea of how they work. So that's what we want to give you now.

Drugs all operate on the same general principle. If you look at Figure 16.3, you will see a nerve junction. The brain has billions of nerve cells, connected one to the other by these junctions. The spaces between the junctions help keep different thoughts and feelings separate from one another.

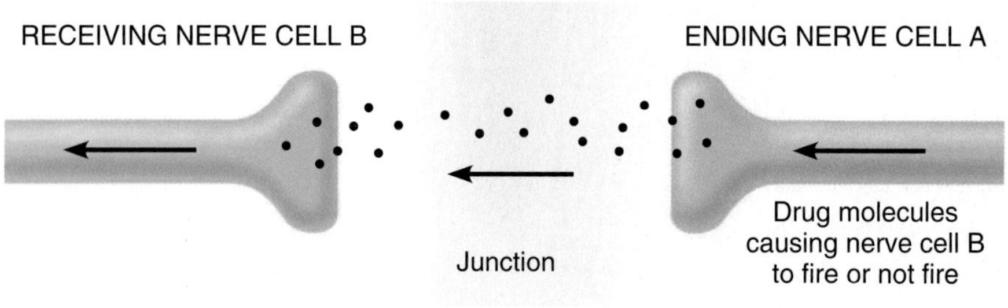

If certain nerve cells have to connect in order to complete a feeling or thought, chemical messages are sent across the junction to the next nerve and then, if needed, on to the next nerve and so forth, until the whole thought or feeling is complete. So at the end of each nerve cell, there are chemicals that send a message across the junction telling the next cell to either fire or not fire.

Drugs have molecular structures that physically resemble those of various chemicals already in the nerve cells. Hence, when we take in a drug, it lodges in the endings of specific nerve cells designed to receive certain types of chemical molecules. The body will do what these drug molecules say because it thinks they are coming from inside, not outside.

For instance, alcohol and tranquilizers have a structure similar to that of the chemicals that tell the nerve cells *not* to fire. When these drugs arrive in the brain, they hook onto certain nerve cell endings and give a message to stop firing. As more and more cells are stopped, the person becomes slower or "thicker" and more dazed and eventually can lose consciousness.

Drugs that speed up the body are molecularly similar to the nerve cell chemicals that make the cells fire. Hence, as a person takes in greater quantities of these drugs, more and more cells begin to fire, and the person becomes more and more agitated.

A third kind of drug causes its effect because normally the nerve cells keep different parts of the brain separate—hearing, seeing, smelling, and so on. Drugs like LSD lodge in different systems of the brain and cause the circuits in more than one of these areas to start firing together (Jacobs, 1987). As a result, people who take such drugs feel like they are "hearing colors" and "seeing sounds" and often wind up in a world so strange that it is terrifying.

RECEIVING NERVE CELL B

ENDING NERVE CELL A

Junction

Drug molecules causing nerve cell B to fire or not fire

▲ *Figure 16.3* *Nerve Junction*

486

Alcohol

Certain drugs tend to become fads for a while. For instance, in colonial America, alcoholism was twice as prevalent as it is today. Not unusual was the party given by the governor of New York for 120 guests: They consumed 120 bottles of Madeira, 36 bottles of port, 60 bottles of beer, and 30 bowls of rum punch (Rorabaugh, 1979).

Around 30 years ago, LSD was very popular. Its popularity then declined greatly until a few years ago, when it began to increase again. Marijuana was also very popular 25 or 30 years ago and then declined in popularity. In recent years, its use among teenagers has begun to increase again (Sarason & Sarason, 1996).

Through all the years and all the fads, alcohol has remained the most used drug. Roughly 70 percent of all teenagers have used alcohol—not all of them necessarily to excess. Obviously, not everyone who uses alcohol is an alcoholic, but there are more than 11 million known alcoholics across all age groups, and probably many more.

Chemical Effects. Because many people who seem halfway reasonable when sober do wild things when they drink too much, some believe that alcohol is a stimulant. What actually happens is that the first few drinks remove a person's inhibitions about making a fool of himself or herself. This creates an impression of freedom.

Alcohol is really a *depressant,* though, which is why country and western songs have so many drinkers crying in their beer. As the amount of alcohol in the body increases, more and more cells are shut off. Eventually, this leads to unconsciousness.

Alcohol is absorbed by the body in two to six hours, depending on how much is taken in, how much the person weighs, and, to a large extent, how much the person has eaten. Eating before or during drinking helps reduce the effects notably, if we're talking about a reasonable amount of alcohol.

Physical Effects. Repeated heavy drinking causes serious damage, but it takes a while to show up. About 10 percent of alcoholics develop permanent liver damage. Alcohol over time can directly destroy the liver.

About the same percentage of alcoholics—10 percent—develop irreversible brain damage. The situation here is less straightforward, however. You will hear that every time people take a drink, they destroy large numbers of brain cells. There is no real support for this claim (Blum, 1988). Hundreds of brain cells do die every day all by themselves. We have so many of them (100 billion) that most people can get to over 100 years of age and still function quite well.

The real trouble comes from the fact that alcohol is basically a food product: It fills you up and is high in calories but very low in nutrients. Hence, as people continue drinking over time, they gradually reduce their regular food intake, causing a vitamin loss. Another problem is that alcohol

Focus Questions

- How does the body react to the heavy intake of alcohol?
- What are the signs that a person may be an alcoholic?

▲ *Alcohol is a depressant.*

487

alcohol withdrawal delirium
mental confusion that occurs in
severe alcoholism in the absence
of alcohol

hallucinations seeing or hearing things that are not physically
present

synergistic effect effect in
which, when two drugs are taken
in combination, each is more
potent than it would be if it were
taken by itself

interferes with the absorption of some vitamins. Vitamin deficiency is one
of the few things that directly and permanently damage brain cells.

Severe cases of alcoholism can lead to nightmarish experiences.
When alcoholics can't get to a drink, they may experience the "horrors,"
or **alcohol withdrawal delirium.** The first symptoms are weakness, anxiety, and severe stomach cramps. These are followed by gross and terrifying **hallucinations**—that is, seeing or hearing things that are not really
there. Typically, the person is being attacked and eaten up by bugs,
snakes, and other crawling things. The delirium progresses from confusion
to disorientation, to stupor, and often to death. Ironically, one translation
of the word *alcohol* is "the water of life" (Blum, 1984).

The Synergistic Effect. The liver gets rid of foreign substances in the
body. But it cannot handle two chemicals of slightly different structure at
the same time. In fact, when two drugs are present in the liver, each of
them *increases* in its potency. This is called a **synergistic** (sin-er-JIS-tic)
effect. Hence, people run a notable risk when they take both barbiturates,
or tranquilizers, and alcohol in the same period of time, since the effect of
each will increase and the combined effects can be fatal.

Causes of Alcoholism. You will hear that body chemistry, allergies,
brain waves, and who knows what have been discovered as the cause of
alcoholism. We obviously assume that the alcoholic is or has been under
some kind of stress, but are there other factors that lead to alcoholism? We
don't know for certain. While many studies find some common problem
in one group of alcoholics, the problem doesn't show up in the next group
that is studied. Thus, there is no known "cause."

Heredity is sometimes cited as the origin. We don't know that, either.
We do know that if the parents are alcoholic, then the chances are higher
that the offspring will be also. But this finding does not separate out the
influence of environment. Someone living in an alcoholic family is clearly
exposed to an alcoholic environment.

To show you how difficult studies of heredity are—even with rats—
here is a typical finding: Some types of rats prefer alcohol as a drink while
other kinds of rats don't. This certainly would suggest that some rats have
an inherited desire or need for alcohol. But other studies show that some
groups of rats like to drink alcohol in one type of laboratory setting but
not in another. Hence, environmental factors could be at work as well.

Studies of humans show a possible link to genetic defects—that is,
certain abnormalities appear in alcoholic parents and in their offspring
who also become alcoholic—but again, this finding does not appear consistently. For the moment, we are stuck with the possibility of a genetic
(inherited) factor but not enough evidence to prove it.

An indication of the importance of social factors in drinking is the
consistent finding that among Orthodox Jewish people the rate of alcoholism is hardly more than zero. This is probably because alcohol is used
as a basic part of their religious tradition and is frequently part of family
celebrations at home during religious holidays. Excessive drinking is not
considered clever or funny, which is certainly at least one factor that influences many people to start drinking. From their early years, Jewish children drink small amounts of wine and other alcoholic beverages. As a
result, alcohol becomes just another "thing" in their environment, not
something to be sought after because it is forbidden—which is another
reason people start drinking (Blum, 1984).

Indicators of Alcoholism. A person clearly has a serious problem with alcohol if any of the following signs show up:

1. Frequent drinking sprees. "Frequent" is a little vague, but drunkenness once a week suggests real trouble.

2. A steady increase over time in the amount of alcohol drunk at one sitting.

3. Morning drinking. To almost everyone, alcohol in the morning is nauseating, so if the day starts off with a drink, then alcohol has become a crutch the person needs to get started.

4. Going to school or work drunk. This shows that the alcohol has taken over life to the point that *it* has become the major goal rather than anything else.

5. Blackouts. Rather than periods of unconsciousness, this term refers to loss of memory of events that occurred while the person was drinking.

6. Drinking whenever faced with a crisis. Most people drink on occasion to "relax," but when drinking goes along with facing most problems, it has become a serious problem itself.

Concerns about Alcoholism as a "Disease." Of late, many scientists have expressed concern about calling alcoholism a "disease." Over time, alcohol can certainly devastate the body, but that alone does not qualify it as a disease. Being beaten up repeatedly can have similar effects, but no one would put that in the same category as something like cancer. Excessive use of alcohol seems to be an individual behavior that people engage in for almost as many reasons as there are people who drink.

Normally, what we're saying here would seem to be little more than an argument about which words to use, but as you will see, the issue is far more important than that. In most cases, a disease is something that continues on its own course with very little chance for the victim to control it. If medicine can't help, people are at the mercy of the disease, and that can make them just give up trying to fight it.

◀ *These young people are learning early about the dangers of alcohol abuse.*

By assuming that alcoholism is this kind of disease, we become its victims, unable to do anything about it. The evidence to date, however, is pretty strong that anyone can stop the heavy use of alcohol. The keys to ending the problem are (1) really wanting to stop and (2) stabilizing one's psychological well-being enough to do so.

The major problem with calling alcoholism a disease, then, is that it tends to make the alcoholic feel hopeless. Another problem is that younger people overall feel quite good (at least compared with the rest of us), and the suggestion that they are suffering from a disease is usually seen as ridiculous, so it is ignored.

Since there is almost no evidence that alcoholism is indeed a disease in the formal sense, a leading researcher in the field of alcohol use and abuse has suggested calling the problem "heavy drinking" (Fingarette, 1988). At first, this seems to be a simpleminded distinction. But not so.

A heavy drinker is headed for trouble—physically, legally, financially, and what have you. Too many people who are heavy drinkers talk themselves into thinking that they are not alcoholics and thus do not have a problem. But if society sees heavy drinking itself as the problem, then these people will have to look at what they are doing.

For example, if certain people get drunk at most parties, it may mean any number of things, but most clearly it suggests that they are unable or unwilling to be themselves. They can't trust who they are when they're sober; they can't relate well to others unless they are in a fog. They are afraid. By avoiding the label *alcoholic,* they can also avoid the obvious fact that they need to stop depending on alcohol and gain the strength simply to be whoever they really are. Since there is no question that they are drinking to excess, it would be much harder for them to avoid the label *heavy drinker,* which would let them know they need to get help.

One final point should be mentioned. Alcoholics Anonymous has had considerable success with a number of heavy drinkers and considers alcoholism a disease. None of the current researchers desires to take anything away from this organization's fine work. But many researchers do feel that the term *heavy drinker* is more appropriate than *disease* for general use, experimentation, and understanding.

Marijuana

The use of marijuana today is much lower than it was in the 1960s and 1970s (Sarason & Sarason, 1996; *Statistical Abstracts . . . ,* 1986). Among those who use the drug on occasion, there are no obvious personality defects. But the heavier smokers—those who use the drug once or more a day—seem to have more than their share of personal problems. The effects of the drug are also influenced by social surroundings. Thus, those taking it alone tend to be quiet and subdued; those using it in groups are more talkative and outgoing.

Marijuana is a **psychedelic** (sigh-kuh-DEL-ik) **drug,** which means it distorts or confuses the user's perception of the world. Especially notable effects are that time seems to stretch out longer than usual and that the person becomes sleepy and has a floating feeling. While alcohol causes more problems with coordination and makes people more aggressive than marijuana, it still is not safe to perform any task involving coordination when taking this drug. When experienced pilots took marijuana and then were studied in flight simulators, the pilots made all kinds of serious errors (Blum, 1984; Zeichner & Pihl, 1979).

Focus Question

• What are the harmful effects of using marijuana, nicotine, and steroids?

psychedelic drug a drug that distorts or confuses the user's perception of the world

Many studies suggest that marijuana reduces the level of the male sex hormone in the user. The major concern here is the danger involved in a pregnant woman's use of marijuana. During the first four months of pregnancy, the male fetus's sex characteristics are developed by this hormone. Hence, if a pregnant woman uses marijuana, damage to the developing male fetus is possible.

The most serious clear-cut effect of marijuana involves the memory system. People have short- and long-term memories, as we discussed in Chapter 8. Everything we learn must first go into the short-term system and then be transferred to long-term, permanent storage. While the drug does not affect long-term memory, it does wipe out short-term storage for a few hours after being taken, so newly learned material is never transferred and hence not retained. The result is that frequent use of marijuana typically leads to very poor school achievement.

Nicotine

Nicotine, a stimulant, is the active ingredient in tobacco. It raises the user's heart rate and blood pressure and increases the brain's receptivity to certain neurotransmitters (Restak, 1994). The most common type of tobacco use is smoking, although tobacco can also be chewed or inhaled directly. Long-term smoking leads to higher risk of heart disease, lung disease, and various cancers. It negatively affects the user's breathing and physical endurance.

The harmful effects of tobacco are particularly devious because they don't cause terrible trouble right off the bat or prevent people from doing their work and living normal lives. In fact, the more serious effects often can't be seen until the person has used the substance for several years. This situation can make it difficult to convince young people that tobacco is as harmful as it really is. And most people who smoke started before the age of 20.

Smoking is a very difficult habit to break. Some say it is harder to stop smoking than to stop using various illegal drugs, such as cocaine (Petraitis, et al., 1995; Prochaska, DiClemente, & Norcross, 1992).

◄ *This billboard attempts to counter the appeal for young people of cartoon characters promoting smoking.*

Amphetamines

tolerance the body's adaptation to a drug, requiring larger and larger dosages to get the original effect

Stimulants called amphetamines are very dangerous. They do create a feeling of excitement, freedom, and energy, but they also create a heavy **tolerance** in the user. In other words, if at first the person takes, say, one tablet, then two tablets will soon be needed to produce the same effect, then three, and so on. Hence, tolerance means that the body adapts to each dosage. In a short time, the user is taking a dosage hundreds of times greater than the original one in order to get the same effect. Heavy dosages, in turn, result in bizarre mental images, trembling, convulsions, and notable **paranoia** (pair-uh-NOI-ya), the belief that others are out to get you.

paranoia the belief that others are out to get you

Amphetamines should never be used for weight loss. They do a poor job, and tolerance will build up quickly. Continued use to stay awake for studying will backfire, too, not only because of the buildup of tolerance but also because of the temporary memory loss that begins to occur.

Cocaine

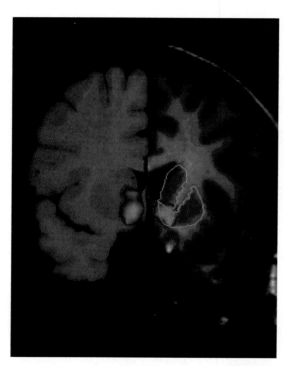

▲ *Heavy cocaine use over time can damage brain processes.*

Cocaine, which comes from coca leaves, is also a stimulant. It produces many of the same sensations as amphetamines. The first soda fountains in the 1800s in the United States served soda pop that contained cocaine. Among the brand names were Koca Nola, Nerve Ola, Wise Ola, and, believe it or not, Dope. The best known, of course, is Coca-Cola, which originally contained alcohol as well (Musto, 1989). These drinks were quite a success, as you might have guessed, until some of the dangers of cocaine were noted and the drug was made illegal. Today's Coca-Cola uses caffeine to provide stimulation (Blum, 1984).

Sniffing (snorting) is the most popular way to take cocaine. It creates a warm "rush," which radiates through the body for about 10 minutes. Cocaine in any form leads to severe hallucinations, mental confusion, and paranoia after a time (Siegel, 1985).

Crack is very dangerous because it is a highly purified form of cocaine with great potency. It is cocaine in paste form, normally smoked, which means that within a very brief time it is absorbed by the lungs and quickly enters the brain through the blood, causing an intense, although short-lived, "high."

psychological dependence a craving of the psyche for a drug

Cocaine produces a very strong **psychological dependence,** which means that although the body doesn't demand it, the user wants it so much that life becomes empty and intolerable without it. Most people who use cocaine do not die from it. Nonetheless, it can cause an instant heart attack and death in young and apparently healthy people who are using only an average dose. The exact cause of the heart spasms is not clear, and there is no way to know beforehand whom or when it will kill.

Opiates

opiates sedatives; drugs that reduce body functioning

Heroin, morphine, and opium are all **opiates**—that is, sedatives—that dramatically depress nerve operation in the brain. At first, they make the user feel very good and on top of the world, but suddenly the person comes crashing down into a deep depression.

492

Opiates produce psychological dependence and create a drug tolerance. Not only that, but they also cause **physical dependence,** which means that the body itself, not just the psyche, begins to crave the drug.

physical dependence a craving of the body for a drug

People can be killed by opiates from the additives put into them, from accidental overdoses, and from unsterile equipment (Ruttenber & Luke, 1984). These drugs can make those addicted to them so desperate that some have been known to cut open a vein in order to pour the drug in if they can't find a syringe (Stephens & Cottrell, 1972).

LSD

LSD is a very potent psychedelic drug called a **hallucinogen** (ha-LOOSE-en-uh-jen) because it produces major hallucinations. Doses as small as 1/250,000 of an ounce can cause marked changes in behavior. LSD makes the brain cells from different areas fire at random and mixes the senses, as we discussed earlier. Much of the danger from this drug arises when users who can't cope with the sensations become panicky, often running around or mutilating themselves.

hallucinogen a drug that produces major hallucinations

Steroids

Steroids are hormones that occur naturally in the body, some of which promote muscle growth. Steroids are also manufactured as drugs, and are used by many athletes, mostly males but also a few females hoping to increase their body size and strength.

steroids naturally occurring hormones some of which promote muscle growth

While steroids do help increase muscle mass, many users experience severe problems. They lose control of their emotions, often going way up and then way down. They begin to feel an unrealistic sense of power. For example, some have thought they could jump out of a window three or four stories high without hurting themselves (they couldn't). One deliberately drove a car into a tree at 40 miles an hour while his friend made a videotape of the scene. With short-term use, the symptoms usually end when intake of the drug is stopped. While on it, though, the individual is quite unpredictable (Pope & Katz, 1987). Continued use over a long period of time can cause a number of serious physical problems, including damage to body tissue, increased risk of heart trouble, and infertility.

 ## Pause for Thought

1. Briefly explain how drugs affect the nervous system.
2. What are some physical and chemical effects of using alcohol?
3. What are some possible causes and signs of alcoholism?
4. Describe some effects of using marijuana, nicotine, amphetamines, cocaine, opiates, LSD, and steroids.

Critical Thinking

5. Create your own In Focus feature to highlight some of the dangers of using the drugs mentioned in this section.

APPLYING Psychology to Life

Preventing and Overcoming Substance Abuse

Substance abuse is a serious problem in our society. Of all the categories of psychological problems, it affects the largest number of people (Neal & Turner, 1991). It is associated with unemployment, dropping out of school, violent crime, and child abuse and neglect. The financial cost to society is tremendous in terms of general health care, mental health care, incarceration, and drug and alcohol treatment programs. The emotional costs are staggering. Substance abuse destroys individuals and tears families apart. While adequate treatment

▲ *Help and support are a big part of preventing or overcoming substance abuse.*

is an important goal, prevention is a much better alternative. When you can avoid the problem beforehand, you are way ahead of the game.

High Risk Factors

Probably no one is completely immune to the temptations of chemical substances. However, some people are at higher risk than others. If prevention programs are to be effective, these risk factors must be identified. The adolescent years, for example, are a particularly vulnerable time.

We tend to assume that social class and drug use are automatically related, but that's not true. Only *extreme* poverty is a factor, and even its effects are limited. Children with behavior problems who also live in extreme poverty are at higher risk for substance abuse in adolescence or young adulthood. The risk

increases dramatically when the neighborhood in which they live is unstable. An unstable neighborhood is one where there are many vacant buildings, where the people do not identify much with their community and move frequently, and where there is general chaos and disorder. In areas where drugs are readily available, there is also a higher rate of drug use.

In addition to these societal or cultural factors, personal factors contribute to risk. Children with certain characteristics are more likely to become adolescent substance abusers. For instance, very impulsive children who are big risk takers or thrill seekers are more vulnerable than others. We used to think that coming from a broken home increased one's risk of substance abuse. Now, however, we know more about this issue. The problem is not divorce but the absence of any real bond between children and their parents, along with a great deal of family conflict.

Obviously, if adults in the family use drugs or have permissive attitudes about the children's use of drugs, the child is at risk. This finding holds regardless of ethnic or racial background. It is true for whites, Hispanics, African Americans, Native Americans, and Asian Americans. Other family factors include a lack of parental involvement in children's activities and a lack of firm, consistent, and humane discipline.

Associating with drug-using friends is an especially powerful factor for adolescents. Where substance abuse is involved, peers have a stronger influence than parents do. And again, this is true whether you are white, African American, Hispanic, Native American, or Asian American (Hawkins, Catalano, & Miller, 1992).

Simple Test for Substance Abuse

In this chapter, we listed several signs of alcoholism. There is, however, a simpler test for substance abuse, if people can be truly honest with themselves. Feeling a strong need for the substance or looking forward with real anticipation to its use indicates a problem, regardless of how often a person uses it. Also, if someone's life is being damaged by substance use, that person should take a very close look at his or her behavior. Finally, if a person's family and friends repeatedly say that person has a problem, it is most likely true.

Becoming Substance Free

Treatment programs are many and varied. We are not in any position to evaluate the ones in your area. However, the process one goes through in

▲ *Associating with people who do not use drugs can provide important emotional back-up.*

overcoming substance abuse seems to take the same general course. Stopping for a short while is not that difficult. Staying off the substance, though, is very difficult indeed. People often become discouraged and think it can't be done. However, relapsing and trying again are part and parcel of eventually winning out over an addiction.

There are several stages to becoming substance free. In the first stage, others see a problem, but the substance abusers do not. They may even quit using for a while because of the pressure from other people. However, they will quickly take it up again. Next comes the time when the person is aware that a problem exists but has no commitment to doing anything about it. Among smokers, this stage has been known to last for years. In the next phase, the person is preparing or intending to solve the problem or has done a little

something toward the goal of abstinence. For example, he or she may have cut down the number of cigarettes smoked or switched to a low-tar brand. This phase also can go on for quite a long time. The next-to-last step is changing behavior and actually abstaining from the substance. Why isn't this the last step? Because achieving abstinence is only part of the solution. Maintaining it is the real answer and the last step. Keep in mind that relapse is the rule, not the exception. Most people are embarrassed when a relapse happens, and they feel like failures. With each relapse, though, you gain a little bit over the last time and learn from your mistakes. The next time, you are more likely to succeed. The key is to keep at it and refuse to give up (Prochaska, DiClemente, & Norcross, 1992).

CHAPTER 16 REVIEW & APPLY

Summary

1. Frustration results from the blocking of goals. Conflict occurs when a choice must be made between alternatives. Stress and anxiety are brought about by frustration, conflict, and change.

2. With stress, the human body prepares for an emergency, just as the bodies of other animals do. But for humans, social restrictions make it more difficult to discharge the stress through either fighting or fleeing. Furthermore, our higher brains see abstract crises that are much harder to handle.

3. Any kind of change can trigger a stress response. Being under stress for too long can lead to physical problems, such as heart disease. Fighting off stress involves a three-part sequence called the general adaptation syndrome.

4. The key to handling many of life's problems seems to be either actual control of various situations or the belief that one is in control.

5. Self-concept is the image we have of ourselves. Self-esteem refers to how worthwhile we think we are. Either may agree or disagree with others' views of us.

6. Psychological defense mechanisms are used to keep the psyche in balance. By using them in moderation, we are able to protect our sense of well-being enough to recover from personality defects, mistakes, or problems. But using them often is not a healthy system for surviving.

7. Personal characteristics associated with a psychologically healthy personality include accepting yourself and others; being realistic, flexible, problem centered, and responsible; and having a good sense of humor.

8. Drugs affect the brain in a number of ways: blocking the firing of nerve cells, increasing their firing, or disturbing the normal ability to keep hearing, seeing, and smelling apart as different sensations. Drug tolerance, physical dependence, and/or psychological dependence can make it very hard to stop taking drugs.

Vocabulary

frustration	stage of resistance	projection
conflict	exhaustion	sublimation
approach-approach conflict	type A personality	substance abuse
approach-avoidance conflict	type B personality	substance dependence
avoidance-avoidance conflict	self-concepts	alcohol withdrawal delirium
double approach-avoidance conflict	self-esteem	hallucinations
anxiety	defense mechanisms	synergistic effect
stress	repression	psychedelic drug
eustress	denial	tolerance
distress	displacement	paranoia
fight or flight reaction	reaction formation	psychological dependence
adrenal glands	intellectualization	opiates
stress hormone	identification with the aggressor	physical dependence
general adaptation syndrome	regression	hallucinogen
alarm reaction	rationalization	steroids

Review Questions

Matching

On a sheet of paper, match terms in the second list to statements in the first list.

1. "Should I go to Europe or Florida for vacation?"
2. "Should I quit my job? If I do, I can spend time with my friends, but I won't have much money. If I don't quit, I can buy a new stereo, but I won't have much time to listen to it with my friends."
3. "I don't want to do my homework, but I don't want to fail."
4. "I want to stay home from school, but I know my dad will find out and punish me."

   a. avoidance-avoidance conflict
   b. double approach-avoidance conflict
   c. approach-approach conflict
   d. approach-avoidance conflict

Multiple Choice

On a sheet of paper, write the letter of the choice that best completes each statement.

5. Eustress is "good" because it
   a. helps us to live longer.
   b. helps push us toward new goals.
   c. blocks out "bad" stress.
   d. causes us less pain than "bad" stress.

6. Stress can be good or bad, depending primarily on
   a. the body's initial reaction to a problem.
   b. the number of problems a person encounters.
   c. the type of problem.
   d. how a person views a problem.

7. If an animal experiences a fight or flight reaction and then no longer needs to fight,
   a. chemicals will be released to balance or calm the body.
   b. chemicals will be released to further intensify the body's reaction.
   c. the animal will then run away.
   d. the animal will probably fight the next animal to come along.

8. According to the general adaptation syndrome, resistance occurs
   a. after alarm.
   b. before alarm.
   c. after exhaustion.

Matching

On a sheet of paper, match terms (a–h) in the second list to the situations described in the first list.

9. Will is unable to remember an accident he witnessed 24 hours ago because the accident was too traumatic.
10. Jill claims she flunked her math course because the teacher didn't like her.
11. Bill hates his teacher, but he won't admit it. Instead, he claims that the teacher hates him.
12. Phil runs to his dad for advice whenever problems become too intense.
13. Stan dislikes football but says he loves it.
14. Ann channels her anger by petitioning for social change.
15. Jan yells at her little brother when she's having a bad day.
16. Dan expresses his feelings unemotionally.

   a. rationalization   e. displacement
   b. regression   f. sublimation
   c. projection   g. reaction formation
   d. repression   h. intellectualization

497

Discussion Questions

1. Describe a recent conflict you've had, and then explain the conflict in terms of approach and/or avoidance.

2. Think of a situation that tends to create distress for many people but, for some reason, not for you. What advice can you offer these distressed people?

3. Suppose someone had followed you around with a video camera from the beginning of this school year to the present—and only filmed you at school. What conclusions would a person viewing the video draw about your personality? Would your behavior indicate a type A or a type B personality? Explain. What if you were filmed only at home?

Note: Conclusions should be based only on your behavior, not on your thoughts.

4. We all experience times when we feel that we have little control over circumstances. Do you tend to feel this way more often at school or at home? Explain.

5. It should be fairly obvious to you how advertisers glorify alcohol use. Some people claim that this type of glorification has little effect on non-drinkers—that it will not significantly alter drinking habits. Furthermore, the purpose of the ads is to promote or highlight a particular brand name, not drinking in general. Others argue that the constant barrage of alcohol ads certainly does affect drinking habits. The ads send the message that it is perfectly acceptable to drink. With which argument do you tend to agree, and why? Explain.

Activities and Projects

1. When we think of stress, we usually regard it as negative, as "distress." Conduct a simple experiment to see if a moderate amount of stress will actually improve performance.

   Procedure: Write out 10 multiplication problems, all involving three-digit numbers multiplied by two-digit numbers (336×75, for example). Find 20 subjects to solve the problems. Put 10 of the subjects under moderate stress and the remaining subjects under no stress. The stressed subjects should be told that they have only a minute to complete as many problems as they can as accurately as they can. The remaining subjects should simply be told to do their best—that it is just an assignment *you* need to complete. Don't tell them they are being timed. In other words, all 20 subjects will be allowed just one minute to solve the problems, but only half of them will know that they will be stopped at the end of a minute.

   Compare the results of your two groups. Which group solved more problems? Which group answered more problems correctly? Based on your results, would you say that moderate stress increases performance?

2. Pick any four of the defense mechanisms described in the chapter and find a song that seems to correspond well to each. For example, if a singer sings about not admitting his or her feelings for another, you might use this as an example of *denial*. Then write out the lyrics of each song and underline key words and phrases that reveal the defense mechanisms at work in the song. Finally, write about a paragraph on each song, explaining why the song appropriately illustrates the defense mechanism.

3. Take a look at the cartoons used in the In Focus feature on defense mechanisms. Pick any four of the defense mechanisms described and create your own visual for each. Feel free to deviate from the kinds of visuals used in the In Focus. Be creative. For example, instead of using a single cartoon, you might want to create a comic strip. Make the visuals large enough so that they can be displayed in class.

4. Write a three- to four-page paper describing the defense mechanisms that you typically use. How do others respond to your use of defense mechanisms? Do they use their own defenses? Include a paragraph or two assessing how the defense mechanisms you use are both beneficial and harmful.

5. There are numerous "self-help" books on the market today that are indeed helpful and very interesting. Books alone are obviously not going to make someone's personality healthy, but they often supply needed inspiration. Have your psychology teacher recommend several worthwhile self-help books, or simply go to a bookstore or library and choose your own (you will be surprised at the wide selection). Read any 20 pages out of one of them. Write a review of the pages and include the following information: (a) a summary of the pages, (b) your personal reactions to the pages, (c) whether the information seems practical and helpful, (d) whether you would recommend the book to a friend and why or why not.

6. Sift through several magazines, and cut out ads that clearly glorify alcohol or any other kind of drug use. Next, find several pictures that show some ugly realities of alcohol or other drug use. For example, you might use a picture of a vagrant sleeping on a bench with a pint of whiskey at his or her feet. Arrange both sets of pictures in a creative collage in which the message is clear that alcohol and drug use are often *not* glamorous activities. Your collage doesn't have to preach against anything; it should simply present two sides of an issue. It may be helpful to give a title to your collage or to include captions.

7. One of the most successful groups to deal with alcohol and drug abuse is Alcoholics Anonymous (AA). Contact an AA center in your area, and interview someone there. Possible questions:

What are some indicators that might reveal whether a person has an alcohol or drug problem?

How common is it for a person to deny these indicators, to deny that a problem exists?

In what ways does this denial often express itself?

What steps need to be taken in order for a person to recover?

Is there such a thing as a cure for alcoholism?

Write a report on your interview and include your reactions.

Unit 6

Psychological Disorders

501

Mental Disorders

Mental disorders in many cases involve an exaggeration of certain behavior patterns that are found in all of us. Most people with such disorders have been overwhelmed by the stress in their lives and can no longer cope. Another group of people, though, suffer from severe psychological disturbances induced primarily by chemical malfunctions.

The Nature of Mental Disorders

Focus Questions
....
- Are most emotionally disturbed people dangerous?
- What causes mental disorders?
- How do we know when someone needs help?

There are about 1.5 million people presently hospitalized in the United States for mental disturbances. An additional 4 to 5 million people annually seek psychological help of one sort or another. Despite these facts, it is surprising how incredibly difficult it is to define a mental disorder.

It is obvious that people who think they are someone famous like the president (but are not) or those who carry on loud conversations in public with themselves have something very amiss in their lives. But very few people with psychological problems are anything like that. Television depictions of those with severe problems are almost always inaccurate. The ax murderer who goes from house to house on Halloween chopping people up because of some early childhood experience shows little grasp of reality—on the part of the person who wrote the script.

While a handful of those with mental disorders are dangerous, the average mental patient is confused and withdrawn, bothering no one. Statistically, mental patients are less violent than those making up the "normal" general public.

If you pick an emotionally disturbed person at random, the odds are that he or she will not be that much different from you or your friends in most areas, except for an exaggeration of certain behaviors. In other words, the person distorts or exaggerates behaviors that are shared by all of us. It comes down to a matter of degree.

Causes of Mental Disorders

It may surprise you to learn that much of the time, the specific cause of a particular disorder cannot be determined. This is especially true when the problem is not extremely serious. Often the cause is a psychological one. For instance, a person may have learned not to trust people and so views the world as a fairly threatening place. As a result, this person may frequently feel anxious. Having a lot of stress in one's life can also cause problems. However, stress may produce general anxiety in one person, phobias in another, and depression in yet another, and no one knows why these differences emerge. Another factor that can play a part is the person's sociocultural background. A person may come from a culture in which expressing emotion or asking for help is seen as a weakness. Consequently, that person may become overwhelmed by some difficulty and feel unable to do anything about it. One possible result is that the problems get even worse and the person feels even more overwhelmed. Another example of cultural causes can be seen in current American society. Eating disorders, such as bulimia and anorexia, are rarely found outside the United States. It would seem, then, that something in our culture makes these problems more likely to occur. Another contributor can be one's biological nature. Some people seem to be physiologically prone to having attacks of extreme anxiety. Many cases of depression have biological as well as psychological causes. In many instances, then, the causes of the disorder may be psychological, biological, sociocultural, or some combination of these factors. For more severe disorders, the causes are frequently more clear-cut, and biological factors are usually at work. Most of the time, however, all these possible causes—biological, psychological, and sociocultural—must be taken into account.

▲ *Most of us have felt like this at one time or another.*

Definitions of Abnormal Behavior

It's important to note that there is something "abnormal" in all "normal" people. Have you ever done anything "strange" that you don't want others to know about? We have. By itself, this is not significant. One very workable definition of those who *do* need help has three parts to it:

1. The person may suffer from *discomfort* more or less continuously. The discomfort shows up as extreme anxiety, endless worry, or long periods of depression. In addition, the person feels that something is wrong with his or her life far more than the average person does.

2. The person may behave in a *bizarre* fashion. He or she constantly misinterprets what is going on and what others are doing or saying. For instance, this person could be afraid to go to work or school. He or she frequently comes completely apart over minor things or sinks into a depression about them.

3. Finally, people who need help may be very *inefficient*. This means that they are unable to perform their life roles properly. Examples include an alcoholic who refuses to accept that there is a problem; a person who does nothing while his or her family life is falling apart; a parent at home with the children who cannot even cope with the dirty dishes; and a student who reads no assignments, doesn't attend class, and has nothing but trouble with most of the teachers.

Any one of these symptoms or a combination can indicate trouble. In addition, just as the degree of disturbance varies, so does the number of symptoms. For example, the student just mentioned is in far worse shape if we add that he or she has no friends, locks himself or herself in a room most nights, and doesn't talk to family members (Buss, 1966).

Many people in need of help have trouble getting along with others and are typically *inflexible*. This means they can't go with the flow of life but instead plow ahead with a fixed set of responses to almost everything. Thus, a shy, withdrawn male goes to a party, and a few people are nice to him. This should help his self-image, but instead he misinterprets, just as he always does, and thinks they are only "feeling sorry" for him. Or a person who cannot tolerate elevators never accepts the fact that they are reasonably safe, even after hundreds of forced trips. So feelings, thoughts, and actions don't vary much. These people establish self-defeating boundaries around themselves that won't budge.

Another characteristic is that these people constantly see a *threatening environment*. A number of studies suggest that their world is colored a gloomy gray because the worst is always expected or seen. Their thoughts and feelings are hardly ever warm and outgoing but instead are tinged with fear. They see danger, rejection, and failure around every corner.

▼ *Is this normal or abnormal? It probably depends on whom you ask.*

InFocus

Mental Health—It's All a Matter of Degree

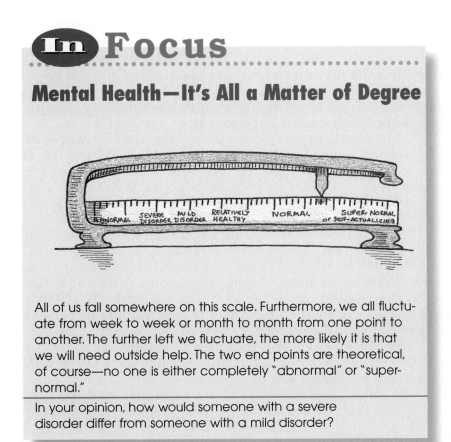

All of us fall somewhere on this scale. Furthermore, we all fluctuate from week to week or month to month from one point to another. The further left we fluctuate, the more likely it is that we will need outside help. The two end points are theoretical, of course—no one is either completely "abnormal" or "super-normal."

In your opinion, how would someone with a severe disorder differ from someone with a mild disorder?

A woman we knew a number of years ago provides a good example of disordered behavior. She was a secretary whose job was typing letters for the manager. This was during the days before word processors. She was determined to be the best secretary ever hired and began to put more and more pressure on herself to succeed. She tried to turn out a *perfect* letter each time with no corrections. Not only was this impossible to do, but she spent so much time on every single letter that her boss became impatient with her. She, in turn, was upset that he didn't appreciate her work, became irritable with other people, and finally grew quite depressed.

Throughout the rest of this chapter, we will cover many classifications of mental disorders. Before doing that, though, we want to warn you about something. A stigma is often attached to people who have been diagnosed with a mental disorder. The stigma is not as bad as it used to be, but it has not disappeared entirely. A major reason for this is that people tend to fear what they do not understand. Consequently, people suffering from a mental disorder may be avoided or treated unfairly by others. This is especially sad because usually what is most helpful for them is having the emotional support of family and friends.

As a society, we have come a long way in understanding abnormal behavior, but we still have a long way to go. So please remember that most people with mental disorders are not that different from the rest of us. They need and deserve our support and understanding, not our ridicule or our fear.

Classifying Disorders—The DSM-IV

Diagnostic and Statistical Manual of Mental Disorders IV (DSM-IV) a book published by the American Psychiatric Association that classifies the symptoms of mental disorders into formal categories

In the next sections, we discuss several classifications of mental disorders. These are part of a system in the mental health field that categorizes people according to the types of symptoms they have. There are hundreds of different sets of symptoms, each of which fits into a certain classification. The symptoms and classifications are contained in a book published by the American Psychiatric Association called the *Diagnostic and Statistical Manual of Mental Disorders IV,* or *DSM-IV.* Mental health workers use this book to determine what classification a particular person belongs in. The first *DSM* was published in 1952. Over the years, it has been revised several times to incorporate new information. The *DSM-IV* was published in 1994.

The classifications we will use are accurate, but we have taken some liberties with them just for the sake of clarity, since you are being exposed to them for the first time. In any case, remember that even though these categories have names and symptoms, no person really fits into any one category perfectly, and symptoms overlap with one another. The *DSM* system is used only to provide some degree of order when trying to decide the kind of problem the patient has.

Please refer to the In Focus titled "Mental Disorders" on page 513 as the chapter progresses. It contains the basic information you will need and will keep you from losing your way in all the details.

Focus Question

....

- What are two main disorders of childhood?

Disorders of Childhood

In this section, we cover two major disorders that are usually first diagnosed in childhood. As we discuss these disorders, keep in mind that almost any child can seem to behave abnormally on occasion. Only when problems are fairly continuous or extensive should we be concerned. After all, there are good reasons why society has very different guidelines for adults' behavior and children's behavior. For example, if a young child has an imaginary playmate, no one thinks too much about it. But what would you think if an adult had such a friend?

Attention Deficit/Hyperactivity Disorder

attention deficit/hyperactivity disorder a childhood disorder characterized by inattention, distractibility, impulsiveness, and/or excessive activity, and restlessness

Children with **attention deficit/hyperactivity disorder,** or **ADHD** (sometimes simply referred to as ADD) may have a great deal of trouble focusing on the task at hand, may be easily distracted and frustrated, may be impulsive, and may be constantly moving and restless. In school, intead of listening and doing their assignments, they are often squirming, wiggling, poking other children, giggling, getting out of their seats, and so on. Usually trouble at school is the first reason that parents become concerned. For some such children, difficulty paying attention is the biggest problem. For others, hyperactivity is the major issue. For still others, inattention and hyperactivity are about equally troublesome.

ADHD affects approximately 3 to 5 percent of the population of children. Far more boys than girls suffer from this disorder; about 80 percent of the children diagnosed with ADHD are males. ADHD is the single most common reason for children to be referred to a mental health professional.

The average age of the child when he or she is referred is between 8 and 10 years old. Some researchers worry that this problem may be over-diagnosed, especially by teachers. One study, for instance, found that grade school teachers believed nearly half the boys in their classrooms met the guidelines for ADHD (Wheeler & Carlson, 1994).

At present, we do not know what causes ADHD. A number of factors have been suggested, but no single one has held up over time. Some evidence indicates that there may be a malfunction in the prefrontal part of the brain, but what might cause that malfunction has not been determined (Barkley, 1997). You may have heard that hyperactivity is caused by eating too much sugar. This is simply not true. You may also have heard that it is often caused by allergies or reactions to food additives or dyes. While occasionally such a case arises, this is also generally not true. No laboratory tests can detect ADHD, and there are no physical features clearly associated with the disorder.

▲ *It's very hard for a hyperactive child to sit still for a long period of time.*

Even though we do not know what causes this problem, there are ways to help children deal with its symptoms. The most common treatment is a prescription drug called Ritalin. Ritalin is a stimulant, surprising as that may seem. Why in the world would you give a distracted, hyperactive child a stimulant? Because a child with ADHD usually doesn't react the same way another child or an adult might (Lubow & Gewirtz, 1995). Many children with ADHD become calmer and better able to focus when on Ritalin. It is not a miracle cure, though. For a number of patients, it doesn't work. For some others, side effects are a problem.

Another approach to treatment relies on structuring the child's world to a high degree. For instance, instead of asking the child to sit and pay attention for one long stretch, that time period is cut down into several shorter segments, with breaks in between. Distractions are reduced to a minimum—things such as background noises and other children moving around nearby.

The success of any treatment program is hard to predict. For children who respond well to the drug, Ritalin seems to be highly effective in reducing the symptoms associated with ADHD. For children who cannot take Ritalin and who are in other programs, the results are mixed.

For a long time, we believed that ADHD was a disorder that children eventually outgrew. Now we know that it can continue into adolescence and adulthood. Some researchers estimate that about half the cases diagnosed in childhood continue into adolescence. Of those cases, around one-third persist into adulthood.

Whether the problem is outgrown or not, it still should be dealt with. Otherwise, these children often don't do well in school, learn to hate it, and begin to see themselves as "bad kids" or "dumb kids."

Among the other difficulties associated with ADHD are poor relationships with both family and peers, delinquent behavior, substance abuse, and, later on, problems in one's marriage and occupation (Barkley, 1997; Wheeler & Carlson, 1994). The effects of this disorder on a child's self-esteem clearly can linger well into adult life.

Autistic Disorder

autistic disorder a childhood disorder characterized by a failure to develop normal patterns of communication, social interactions, and emotional responses

The symptoms of **autistic disorder,** or autism, center on a failure to develop normal communication patterns, social interactions, and emotional responses. The problems are usually quite severe, are present from birth, and appear very early in life (Kanner, 1943). Autistic disorder can be diagnosed before the age of three, and often its symptoms can be seen in infancy. It is a fairly rare disorder, affecting from 2 to 5 of every 10,000 children. Approximately three times as many males as females suffer from autism.

Autistic infants are difficult to feed, exhibit no social smiling, and do not respond well to being held or cuddled. As children, they frequently have tantrums. They may spin or rock themselves or stare off into space for long periods of time. They seem to have very little sensitivity to pain, and they may seriously injure themselves by repeatedly banging their heads or biting their own flesh. They rarely maintain eye contact with others.

Autistic children have a great deal of trouble forming attachments to people. They do become quite attached to objects, however, and have a powerful need to maintain "sameness" in their environment. In other words, they have an unusually strong and negative reaction to change.

echolalia an autistic symptom in which the person "echoes," or repeats, what has just been said

Few autistic children ever become capable of normal speech. Many of them remain mute, and some engage in what is called **echolalia,** simply repeating what has just been said. "Do you want to go to the store

▶ *The character played by Dustin Hoffman in the movie* Rain Man *was a fairly high-functioning autistic man.*

with me?" the mother asks, smiling. "Go to the store with me?" the child replies with no smile, no recognition, no visible response.

At present, we do not know what causes autistic disorder. Several structures in the middle and lower parts of the brain may malfunction, but what causes these malfunctions remains to be determined. The genetics of the disorder are also unclear. There are suggestions that heredity may play a part, but we cannot reach any absolute conclusions as yet (Piven et al., 1990). For a long time, one theory claimed that autism was caused by cold, indifferent parents. However, there is no evidence whatsoever to support this theory. Autism is the result of physiological or neurological problems, not bad parenting.

There is no cure for this disorder, no specific drug, and treatments vary widely in their success rates. Part of the inability to get good and consistent results comes from the fact that there are degrees of autism. Those who function at a high level profit the most from treatment. However, for most children with autistic disorder, progress is limited to helping them learn to care for themselves and control their aggressive behaviors.

For decades, psychologists have wondered about the inner life of those with autism, but because communicating with them was so difficult, answers were hard to come by. More recently, however, a few very high-functioning autistic adults have written books about their lives. One person in particular, a woman named Temple Grandin, has given us some extremely important insights (see In Their Own Words on this page).

In Their Own Words . . .

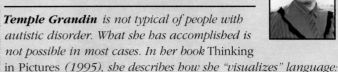

Temple Grandin *is not typical of people with autistic disorder. What she has accomplished is not possible in most cases. In her book* Thinking in Pictures *(1995), she describes how she "visualizes" language:*

I think in pictures. Words are like a second language to me. I translate both spoken and written words into full-color movies, complete with sound, which run like a VCR tape in my head. (p. 19)

Growing up, I learned to convert abstract ideas into pictures as a way to understand them. I visualized concepts such as peace or honesty with symbolic images. I thought of peace as a dove, an Indian peace pipe, or TV or newsreel footage of the signing of a peace agreement. Honesty was represented by an image of placing one's hand on the Bible in court. A news report describing a person returning a wallet with all the money in it provided a picture of honest behavior. (p. 33)

Elsewhere, Grandin discusses the difficulty she has had in understanding the subtle clues people give and respond to in social interactions.

Although business relationships can easily be learned by rote, dating is difficult. The social skills one needs to rent an apartment and keep a job were easier for me to learn than the social skills for dating, because I have very few emotional cues to guide me during complex social interactions. . . . When I have to deal with family relationships, when people are responding to each other with emotion rather than intellect, I need to have long discussions with friends who can serve as translators. I need help in understanding social behavior that is driven by complex feelings rather than logic. (p. 134)

Interpreting Primary Sources

What conclusions can you draw from these excerpts about how Grandin views and how she relates to the "outside" world?

Temple Grandin showed all the usual symptoms of autism from birth. She had terrible tantrums, rocked and spun herself for hours at a time, and showed no interest in other people. At the age of three, she was still unable to speak. Eventually, however, she overcame many of these problems in a big way. She earned a Ph.D. in animal science and became a well-known designer of livestock handling facilities. In addition, she has authored several books (Grandin, 1995).

Thinking Critically about Psychology

Communicating with Autistic Children

A few years ago, a new method for communicating with mute autistic children appeared on the scene. The method is called *facilitated communication*. To use this technique, a teacher or facilitator holds the autistic child's wrist over a keyboard. The child then types out words using one finger. Soon after this approach was introduced, autistic children who had never spoken before were reported to be typing out lengthy, emotional messages to their parents, some even writing poetry.

What specifically is being claimed or stated? The claim is that—although these autistic children could not speak or write—they could communicate if they were helped by having their hands supported over the keyboard.

What is the objective evidence for and against this claim? The evidence supporting the claim is largely anecdotal. That is, the evidence comes from stories of individual cases of breakthroughs. Many such stories were reported, and parents were truly convinced that their children were "talking" to them. But anecdotal evidence is not accepted as scientific proof, because it is not subject to any controls.

When controlled studies of the method were conducted at several institutions, researchers generally failed to achieve the same results (Rimland & Green, 1993). Why did these studies fail to support the original claims? One possibility is that the facilitators—not

▲ *Some very high-functioning autistic people do benefit from treatment and learn to communicate effectively. A few have written books about their lives.*

the children—were actually typing the messages. And indeed, when the facilitator does not know what the question is, the child usually cannot answer it.

In addition to the anecdotal nature of the evidence, there are some other problems with the claims. One is that the child is not usually looking at the keyboard while typing on it with one finger. Can anyone do this successfully? Try it. Take a computer keyboard, close your eyes, and try to type something with one finger. The odds are that what you type will be nonsense. Even expert touch typists cannot perform this task.

Another problem is that these children could not read. If they couldn't read, how could they spell out words? The suggestion was that they had somehow picked up this skill without anyone knowing about it. Does this seem likely to you? It doesn't to us, because it takes an enormous amount of time and patience to teach even high-functioning autistic children to read.

What other interpretations might be made instead? As mentioned, it may be that the facilitators, not the children, were actually typing the messages. But why would this have happened? Well, one might think that the people who proposed the method were deliberately trying to fool people so their program would appear to be very successful. That seems unlikely as well as unfair. Another interpretation is that the people involved wanted so badly to get through to these children that they ended up fooling themselves. Still another possibility is that the method may actually work for some children, those who can read and use words to some extent, but that the success rate was greatly exaggerated.

What are the most logical conclusions to draw? In light of all the evidence, it seems to us that the original claim must be rejected. To support the claim, carefully controlled observations would have to be made to ensure that the children could read and that the children, not the facilitators, were actually doing the communicating.

See if *COOL* works for you....

Claim?

Objective evidence for and against claim?

Other interpretations?

Logical conclusions?

Applying Critical Thinking Skills

This issue should remind us of the importance of controlled studies. What did researchers do in this case to make sure their study was controlled?

anxiety disorders disorders whose major symptom is anxiety

anxiety a generalized feeling of apprehension and pending disaster

panic disorder a type of anxiety disorder characterized by frequent and overwhelming attacks of anxiety that are not associated with specific objects or events

phobic disorder a type of anxiety disorder in which a person becomes disabled and overwhelmed by fear in the presence of certain objects or events. Examples include specific phobia and agoraphobia.

specific phobia a phobic disorder associated with a specific object or situation, such as snakes, dogs, elevators, and heights

Anxiety Disorders

The three categories of problems we are about to cover—panic disorder, phobic disorders, and obsessive-compulsive disorder—have in common one thing: The person suffering from them also suffers from severe anxiety. Hence, they are called **anxiety disorders.** Except for substance abuse, anxiety disorders are the most common type of mental disorder (Neal & Turner, 1991).

Anxiety is a generalized feeling of apprehension and dread that includes many bodily upsets. The palms sweat, the throat closes up, breathing is erratic, the heart pounds, hands tremble, and the armpits become a perspiration disaster. The feeling is a great deal like the one you get in a public speaking course when your turn comes to talk.

All of us experience anxiety, but people with anxiety disorders may have anxiety attacks a few times a day. In between, they are restless, sleep poorly, don't eat well, and are not capable of calming down.

Panic Disorder

The person with a **panic disorder** is afflicted by frequent and overwhelming attacks of anxiety. Sometimes a panic disorder originates in the person's psyche, probably developing from years of feeling insecure and helpless. But often such a disorder starts because something is physically or chemically wrong with the person. Once a panic attack has occurred, attacks tend to repeat themselves whenever the person is under stress.

In other words, the anxiety at first is not really connected to anything specific; it is a physical occurrence. Soon, however, the panic begins to spread, as the fear of dying or making a fool of oneself is associated with more and more objects, events, or people. Eventually, the person may reach a point where activities are severely limited because of these fears. When that happens, the problem is no longer simply physical but is psychological as well.

Many people who suffer from panic disorder can be treated with drugs that reduce the symptoms. Psychotherapy is also very effective and is discussed in the next chapter.

Phobic Disorders

In a **phobic disorder,** the person becomes disabled and overwhelmed by fear in the presence of certain objects or events. Anxiety is extraordinarily high but usually only in the presence of the problem. The word *phobia* means "fear of," and there are two basic types of phobic disorders.

A **specific phobia** centers on particular objects or situations: dogs, enclosed spaces, snakes, heights, elevators, water, even knives. Faced with the object of fear, the person becomes extremely anxious. (Note the difference here: A panic attack is not attached to something *specific,* as a phobia is.)

The most common explanation for phobias today is that they result from association or learning. Suppose that when a little boy cuts himself the parent begins screaming, crying, and running around shouting, "You're bleeding! You're bleeding!" The child, with repeated experiences of this kind, might develop hematophobia, a fear of blood *(hema).*

All of us have mild phobias. Many people fear that they will jump off high buildings. Others are hesitant to use public rest rooms for fear of getting germs. But for true phobics, the danger is so real that they live in mortal fear of being anywhere near the object.

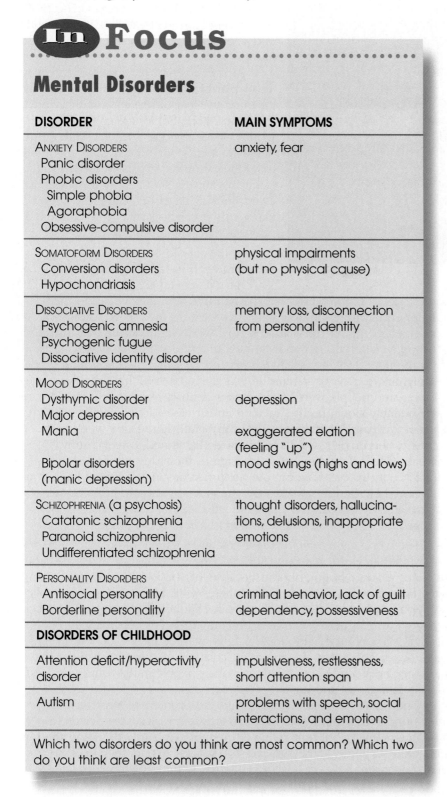

In Focus

Mental Disorders

DISORDER	MAIN SYMPTOMS

ANXIETY DISORDERS
 Panic disorder
 Phobic disorders
  Simple phobia
  Agoraphobia
 Obsessive-compulsive disorder
	anxiety, fear

SOMATOFORM DISORDERS Conversion disorders Hypochondriasis	physical impairments (but no physical cause)
DISSOCIATIVE DISORDERS Psychogenic amnesia Psychogenic fugue Dissociative identity disorder	memory loss, disconnection from personal identity
MOOD DISORDERS Dysthymic disorder Major depression Mania Bipolar disorders (manic depression)	 depression exaggerated elation (feeling "up") mood swings (highs and lows)
SCHIZOPHRENIA (a psychosis) Catatonic schizophrenia Paranoid schizophrenia Undifferentiated schizophrenia	thought disorders, hallucina- tions, delusions, inappropriate emotions
PERSONALITY DISORDERS Antisocial personality Borderline personality	 criminal behavior, lack of guilt dependency, possessiveness
DISORDERS OF CHILDHOOD	
Attention deficit/hyperactivity disorder	impulsiveness, restlessness, short attention span
Autism	problems with speech, social interactions, and emotions

Which two disorders do you think are most common? Which two do you think are least common?

▲ *These people obviously do not suffer from agoraphobia—or acrophobia either!*

agoraphobia the fear of leaving a familiar environment, especially home

Caution: Trying to get real phobics to overcome their fears by deliberately forcing them into the feared situation can be very dangerous. Phobics have been known to die from an overload on the system. The problem usually can be treated both efficiently and safely by a professional in a matter of a month or so.

A second type of phobia is called **agoraphobia** (ah-GORE-uh-pho-bee-a), meaning the fear of leaving a familiar environment. Agoraphobics are so fearful of the world outside that they become virtual prisoners in their own homes. The following case (McMahon & McMahon, 1983) is interesting because it shows how an accidental event, such as an ear infection, can trigger a mammoth psychological event—the agoraphobia—that will go on and on.

A 42-year-old married salesman had been in traveling sales work for ten years. One night when on the road at a motel, he developed an infection that spread to the inner ear, making him feel very dizzy. He decided to go to the bar and get a drink to "pick himself up." While sitting at the bar, things began to whirl around and the next thing he knew, he was lying on the floor, looking up at strangers all peering down at him as in a nightmare. He was certain he was dying because his heart was racing and people were saying things about a heart attack. He felt desperately alone, frightened, and embarrassed. The infection cleared up and everything seemed to be all right. But a week or so later, when driving down the highway, he started to feel "funny," weak, dizzy. He pulled off to the side of the road and waited the attack out. Instead of going on, he turned around and went back home where he felt safe. Within a matter of a month, he began to have anxiety attacks every time he left the house, and called in sick more and more often so he wouldn't have to leave home.

The word *agoraphobia* literally means a fear of open places. *Agora* is from the Greek for "marketplace" (an ancient shopping mall). We label the salesperson as agoraphobic because his basic fear is one of being away from the closed, secure atmosphere of his home and out in public.

Some believe such trouble starts in childhood when a child is accidentally lost in a place such as a department store. But many agoraphobics are women, especially homemakers without an outside job. In these cases, we suspect that the frequent isolation of this occupation makes them feel threatened about relating to other people in the "outside" world, and the fear grows and grows over time.

One oddity of agoraphobics might be of interest. Most have a specific boundary beyond which they cannot go. It varies from person to person. Thus, some people can go up to three blocks, some six, some another number, from home. If they go even a few feet beyond, they become anxious and fearful, but if they stay within the boundary, they feel safe.

Obsessive-Compulsive Disorder

An **obsession** refers to an endless preoccupation with some type of urge or thought. All of us experience this to a limited degree when we can't get a popular tune out of our minds. Eventually the tune disappears, but magnify such an occurrence many hundredfold and you have the

obsession a symptom characterized by an endless preoccupation with a certain urge or thought

Phobias

Achlophobia: Fear of crowds
Acrophobia: Fear of heights
Aerophobia: Fear of high objects
Agoraphobia: Fear of open spaces
Ailurophobia: Fear of cats
Algophobia: Fear of pain
Androphobia: Fear of men
Ankhophobia: Fear of flowers
Anthrophobia: Fear of people
Apiphobia: Fear of bees
Aquaphobia: Fear of water
Arachnephobia: Fear of spiders
Astraphobia: Fear of storms
Aviophobia: Fear of flying
Baccilophobia: Fear of microbes
Bacteriophobia: Fear of germs
Ballistophobia: Fear of bullets
Bathophobia: Fear of depth
Belonephobia: Fear of pins and needles
Botanophobia: Fear of plants
Brontophobia: Fear of thunder
Chromophobia: Fear of certain colors
Claustrophobia: Fear of enclosed places
Clinophobia: Fear of beds
Cynophobia: Fear of dogs
Decidophobia: Fear of making decisions
Demonophobia: Fear of demons
Domatophobia: Fear of being confined in a house
Entomophobia: Fear of insects
Equinophobia: Fear of horses
Ergophobia: Fear of work
Gephydrophobia: Fear of crossing bridges
Gynephobia: Fear of women

Hematophobia: Fear of blood
Herpetophobia: Fear of reptiles
Hydrophobia: Fear of water
Iatrophobia: Fear of doctors
Monophobia: Fear of being alone
Mysophobia: Fear of dirt
Necrophobia: Fear of dead bodies
Nucleomitiphobia: Fear of nuclear bombs
Numerophobia: Fear of numbers
Nyctophobia: Fear of night
Ombrophobia: Fear of rain
Ophidiophobia: Fear of snakes
Optophobia: Fear of opening your eyes
Pathophobia: Fear of disease
Peccatophobia: Fear of sinning
Pediphobia: Fear of children or dolls
Phobophobia: Fear of your own fears
Psychrophobia: Fear of cold
Pyrophobia: Fear of fire
Sitophobia: Fear of food
Sophophobia: Fear of learning
Syphilophobia: Fear of syphilis
Taphephobia: Fear of being buried alive
Technophobia: Fear of technology
Thalassophobia: Fear of the ocean
Thanatophobia: Fear of death
Topophobia: Fear of performing on stage
Trichophobia: Fear of hair
Triskaidekaphobia: Fear of the number 13
Tropophobia: Fear of moving
Verbophobia: Fear of words
Vestiophobia: Fear of clothing
Xenophobia: Fear of strangers
Zoophobia: Fear of animals

As you can see, people can develop phobias for just about anything. What are some phobias that might be added to the list because of technology? For example, videophobia could be the fear of programming a VCR!

compulsion a symptom involving repeated symbolic, ritualized behavior

obsessive-compulsive disorder an anxiety disorder characterized by both repetitive thoughts (obsession) and ritualized, repetitive behavior (compulsion)

concerns of the person suffering from an obsession. The person simply cannot control or get rid of the obsessive thoughts.

A **compulsion** is a symbolic, ritualized behavior that a person must repeatedly act out. Each time the person acts out the behavior, whatever anxiety he or she feels is decreased, so the behavior becomes self-rewarding and is repeated.

Most people have minor compulsions, such as a desire to step on a crack in the sidewalk. Genuine compulsions are different because the people *must* carry out the act or they get more and more anxious. Some, for instance, check dozens of times to be certain the front door is locked before going to bed each night. That's not normal.

The two words **obsessive-compulsive** are generally used together. Most compulsive people are obsessed with their compulsion. For instance, the compulsive hand washer is obsessed with the thought that he or she is "dirty." And being obsessed with cleanliness leads to compulsive washing.

The stranglehold that this disorder can exert is remarkable. Compulsive gamblers are examples. (These people are actually covered in the DSM slightly differently, but they serve our purposes well here.) They are constantly obsessed with the desire to keep on gambling no matter what. Every year, thousands of compulsive gamblers wipe out all the family finances, certain that the next hand of cards will change their luck.

The strength of the problem is illustrated by a man who entered a program in which he wanted to learn *not* to play a slot machine by having the act associated with something unpleasant, a shock. A slot machine was put in his hospital room, and he was wired up to receive a 70-volt shock to the forearm each time he pulled the lever. Over a period of time, he received 672 shocks. Only then did he decide to stop gambling. But his "cure" lasted only 18 months. At that point, he started again and had to go back to the hospital for a series of "booster shocks" (Barker & Miller, 1969).

Obsessive-compulsive behavior has been thought to result from faulty attempts to resolve guilt, anxiety, or insecurity. For instance, insecurity and anxiety can result in someone's *having to* get up and check the front door dozens of times before finally going to sleep.

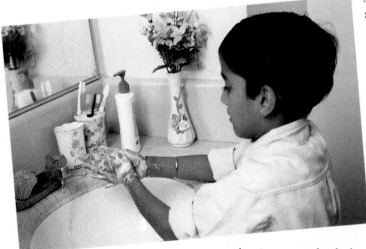

▼ *Repeated handwashing is a fairly common compulsion.*

Some behavior in this classification is quite symbolic. For example, many children are told that something they did was "dirty." This makes them associate cleanliness with goodness. Over time, whenever they feel "dirty" (guilty), they will wash their hands—up to hundreds of times a day. Just the act of doing *something* (even though it doesn't work) reduces their anxiety and guilt. Hence, they come to repeat it, rather than seeking a more sensible solution.

But obsessive-compulsive disorder has physical aspects as well. Recent research has found a defect in the amount of some brain chemicals in many people with this problem. The result is that circuits in the brain are triggered over and over to repeat endlessly actions that are reasonably normal for most of us. Certain drugs can help people begin to get the behaviors under control, at which point most can handle the problem effectively (Rapoport, 1989).

Somatoform Disorders

In **somatoform** (so-MAT-ah-form) **disorders,** psychological issues are expressed in bodily symptoms, but there is no actual physical problem. Most of us feel worse physically when life is not going well. Somatoform disorders, though, present a far more dramatic picture.

Conversion Disorder

You may have heard of "hysterical blindness" or "hysterical paralysis." The technical term for both of these conditions is **conversion disorder.**

In a conversion disorder, a serious psychological trauma is unconsciously changed (converted) into a symbolic physical dysfunction. For example, a person who has witnessed terrible human torture and slaughter may be overwhelmed by the horror, so the mind shuts the visual system down. The person can no longer see. Or perhaps someone was in a serious automobile accident and managed to get free of the car. He or she could hear other people screaming but, frozen by fear, was unable to move, to go get help. That person might develop some type of paralysis in response.

These people are not faking. Say that someone has, psychologically, lost feeling in the right leg. If you sneak up behind the person and stick a pin in that leg, he or she will not feel it. The dysfunction is real. There simply is no physical basis for it. Interestingly, however, such people show very little concern about their physical condition. As you might imagine, conversion disorders are quite rare.

Hypochondriasis

A less unusual somatoform disorder is **hypochondriasis** (high-po-con-DRY-ah-sis). Hypochondriacs are overly concerned about their health. They see disastrous illness in a minor physical complaint. Thus, a slight headache is interpreted as a symptom of brain cancer; a case of the sniffles is really pneumonia; and so on.

Often, such people, as children, were given affection or support from other people only when they were sick. They never learned better ways of getting attention. Now that they have spent years focusing on their health, they have trouble breaking the cycle. Needless to say, these people spend a great deal of time in doctors' offices.

somatoform disorder a condition in which psychological issues are expressed in bodily symptoms in the absence of any real physical problem

conversion disorder a somatoform disorder in which a serious psychological trauma is changed into a symbolic physical dysfunction

hypochondriasis a somatoform disorder characterized by feeling excessive concern about one's health and exaggerating the seriousness of minor physical complaints

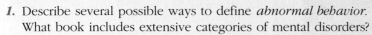 Pause for Thought

1. Describe several possible ways to define *abnormal behavior.* What book includes extensive categories of mental disorders?
2. Describe three types of anxiety disorders.
3. What is a somatoform disorder? Name two types.

Critical Thinking

4. Describe a typical anxious day for someone suffering from agoraphobia or some other specific phobia.
5. Write two brief journal entries, one from the point of view of an ADHD child, another from the point of view of an autistic child.

- How can someone forget who he or she is?

dissociative disorders disorders in which memory of a part of one's life becomes disconnected from other parts; amnesia, fugue, and dissociative identity disorder are examples

amnesia a dissociative disorder in which traumatic events seem to disappear from memory

selective forgetting forgetting only things that are very traumatic

Dissociative Disorders

Dissociative (dis-SO-see-ah-tiv) **disorders** are best known from soap operas on television. The major character develops amnesia and forgets she is married to a prominent attorney. She falls in love with a wealthy physician at the local hospital where she is treated for the flu. The physician is married to the head nurse, who has dissociative identity disorder and who got the woman-of-the-year award but steals drugs, which she sells on the street. Meanwhile . . . .

A person who took such television shows seriously might think that this sort of thing goes on all the time. Actually, dissociative disorders— amnesia, fugue, and dissociative identity disorder—are extremely rare.

The word *dissociative* refers to the fact that people with these disorders can disconnect, or "disassociate," certain events or behaviors from one another. There is a bit of this ability in all of us. We all have things we want to forget, and we can do a good job of getting rid of them. It is a rare individual who hasn't "absentmindedly" missed a doctor's appointment, for example. We have a bit of dissociative identity disorder also, which we carry out all the time—without getting confused as to which part we are playing. For instance, no one uses the same language or discusses the same thoughts at a family dinner as he or she does when alone with close friends. So, dissociative disorders are very elaborate behaviors that have seeds in our everyday activities. Most of us can change our behavior in different circumstances and rebound to whatever our "core" personality might be. People with dissociative identity disorder, however, are different because they have an aspect of themselves that causes such guilt (for example, a repeated tendency to violate the law) that they cannot face this aspect and thus block it off. Since this part won't disappear, for these people it grows and grows until eventually they form a separate personality that can do these acts and not be responsible and guilty for them when they return to their "good" personality.

Amnesia

In psychogenic **amnesia,** a dissociative disorder, memories related to a terrible trauma "disappear." They are still "in" the person, but they are cut off from consciousness. Some amnesias can be caused by a high fever or a blow to the head. In contrast, the term *psychogenic* refers to amnesia that is psychologically *(psycho)* caused *(genic)*. In fact, people with this problem often show little concern that parts of their past seem to be gone. Hence, there must be a psychological benefit involved, or they would indeed be alarmed at losing some of their memories.

A common and easily understood type of psychogenic amnesia is a soldier's loss of memory of nightmarish events that happened in battle. In such cases, **selective forgetting** is involved. This means that only the traumatic portions of the memories disappear. For example, a soldier may completely blot out the part of his identity connected with his fighting battalion and everything in

▲ *This character in the soap opera* General Hospital *suffers from (what else?) amnesia.*

the more recent past leading back to a horrible war experience. The terror and guilt these memories produce therefore disappear, occasionally reappearing in nightmares (Neal & Turner, 1991; Hartmann, 1984). But only certain events are gone: The soldier doesn't forget childhood friends, old memories, how to tie a shoe, and so forth. In fact, amnesia in all these cases is selective.

Fugue

The **fugue** (FYOOG) state is an extensive, complicated type of amnesia. The person disconnects all of his or her current life from awareness, moves somewhere else, and starts all over. More men than women exhibit this problem. It seems to be caused by serious and unresolved conflicts, often with a spouse. Fortunately, this condition usually does not last very long. When the person "comes out of it," he or she cannot remember what happened during the fugue state.

fugue a dissociative disorder in which a person forgets his or her current life and starts a new one somewhere else

Dissociative Identity Disorder

In its basic form, **dissociative identity disorder,** formerly called multiple personality disorder, is also similar to amnesia. Instead of forgetting specific events, though, such individuals "forget" a portion of themselves, and that portion begins to live a life of its own.

Multiple personalities are all over television and are usually called schizophrenics, which they AREN'T. In real life, though, they are actually extremely rare (Kluft, 1991).

Again, all of us have secret fantasy lives that we don't want others to know about. In a fashion similar to the true dissociative identity disorder, we make a division that is usually based on a "good" person and a "bad" person. But for the true dissociative identity disorder, the dissociative behaviors are exaggerated to the point of becoming at least partly independent of each other.

Dissociative identity disorder is probably so rare because a number of conditions must align themselves in just the right way to produce it. Such conditions typically include a haunted, confused personality, a history of very upsetting traumatic experiences or childhood abuse, and a long-term habit of escaping from almost every problem.

Usually, people with this disorder have very strong, conflicting desires and needs in their lifestyles. For example, a withdrawn and righteous man (call him A)

dissociative identity disorder a dissociative disorder in which a person divides himself or herself into separate personalities that can act independently

▼ *In the case of* Sybil *(portrayed here by Sally Field), a young woman supposedly had many, many different personalities. Today, experts seriously question the authenticity of Sybil's case.*

who desperately wants to give vent to animal impulses develops mammoth guilt over these desires. He needs to distance himself from this pain. Another personality gradually creeps into the picture containing these unacceptable desires. This is evil personality B. The man can then go about doing whatever he wants as long as he is B. When A returns, he becomes very self-righteous, even prim, and obnoxiously good. Complete amnesia can be involved, with A not knowing about B, and vice versa. Sometimes, however, the dominant or stronger personality knows about the weaker; the weaker rarely knows about the stronger one.

As noted, the dissociative identity disorder is not schizophrenia. In dissociative identity disorder, one person has two or more sides that tend to live independently. But the basic core personality is the same, and this core is well aware of general reality as we know it, does not have trouble thinking or communicating, and does not believe things that don't exist. The opposite is true in schizophrenia, discussed in detail later.

Focus Questions

- What are the different types of mood disorders?
- How is mania different from manic depression?

mood disorders disorders characterized by emotional states; include depression and mania

dysthymic disorder a mood disorder involving moderate depression

Mood Disorders

The *mood* of an individual is his or her emotional state—elated, depressed, angry, neutral, and so forth. Thus, mental disturbances characterized by a depressed mood, an exaggerated "up" mood, or an alternation between up and down are called **mood disorders.**

In the sections coming up, we discuss moderate and severe depression, mania, and bipolar disorders. Since the causes are similar in all these mood disorders, our discussion of the causes follows those sections. After that, we discuss suicide, which is most often associated with depression.

Dysthymic Disorder

The term **dysthymic** (dis-THIGH-mik) **disorder** comes from the Greek for "low spirits." Hence, it is a moderate depression. In any given year, between 4 and 12 percent of the population are affected by it. Thus, it is a fairly common problem. Of all the mental disorders in this chapter, dysthymic disorder is the most likely to clear up eventually without treatment. For both of these reasons, it is referred to as the common cold of mental health (Weissman, 1985).

Typical symptoms of dysthymic disorder are lack of energy, unhappiness, loss of interest in activities and people, loss of sense of humor, sadness, and rock-bottom feelings of self-worth (Beck, 1967). All of these feelings can occur in the normal person who, for instance, loses a loved one.

The best way to know whether depression of this sort is normal is to see if it has served its "function" or instead remains and lingers on. For instance, as mentioned, loss of a friend can trigger these problems in any normal person. But if the problems go on and on with the same degree of severity, something else is probably wrong. Or if the depression appears "out of nowhere" or arises following an insignificant event, again one's emotional makeup may include a tendency to become depressed.

Major Depression

Typical symptoms of severe depression, or **major depression,** are very slow speech, deep ongoing depression, disturbances in appetite and sleep patterns, lack of energy, a sense of hopelessness, extreme feelings of worthlessness, and frequent thoughts of death or suicide. Most people with major depression have trouble carrying out simple daily tasks. Some may even lie motionless in a rolled-up fetal position for hours at a time. It is as if all the joy has gone out of their lives. Underneath it all, though, there is frequently a great deal of anger, sometimes directed at the self, sometimes broad and unfocused. The depression may last from a couple of weeks to a matter of months.

major depression severe depression; involves loss of appetite, lack of energy, hopelessness, and suicidal thoughts

Mania

The word *mood* refers to any kind of emotion. Some people go in the opposite direction from depression and have extreme *up* moods. This might sound at first like something that wouldn't be bad, but unfortunately that is not the case.

This behavior, called **mania** (MAIN-ee-ah) from the Greek for "mad excitement," involves agitation, restlessness, inability to concentrate, and extremely rapid speech. The speech problem is the most notable part of the behavior. Thoughts are moving so quickly through the person's mind that they literally collide with one another into a mass of confused speech, making comprehension almost impossible. This problem is called a **flight of ideas,** meaning that thoughts are flying in all directions. Here is a brief example: "I went to the store where I kept the containers of milk which all babies should have in order to survive which not everybody can do because of the threat of nuclear war between countries which are divisions of various parts of the land which is filled normally with rock and dirt."

People with mania often get so excited that they begin to have delusions that they have special powers or great influence. They may make plans for controlling the world or some such project (Depue et al., 1981).

mania a mood disorder involving extreme agitation, restlessness, rapid speech, and trouble concentrating

flight of ideas a confused state in which thoughts and speech go in all directions with no unifying concept

◀ *Manic people often believe they are someone very special or powerful. Here, French Emperor Napoleon Bonaparte and British Prime Minister William Pitt are portrayed carving up the world to suit themselves.*

Bipolar Disorders

On occasion, people experience swings between the ups of mania and the downs of a major depression. The official term for this problem—which you may have heard of as "manic depression"—might confuse you at first, but it is logical.

First, remember that the word *bi* means "two." Next, recall that the earth has two poles, north and south. The word *pole,* in this sense, means "one of the two most extreme possibilities." One pole is at the top, the other at the bottom—they couldn't get farther from one another. So people who have these wild swings from up to down and back are categorized as having a **bipolar disorder.**

bipolar disorder a mood disorder involving high and low moods

Here is a case history of such a disorder (McMahon & McMahon, 1983):

> The patient, a 25-year-old woman, was admitted to the hospital for observation after the fire department was called by a neighbor who saw smoke. The patient was dressed in a grass skirt she had purchased in Hawaii during her honeymoon. She had built a "bonfire" in the middle of the living room floor and was dancing around the fire, leaping, jumping, and singing what seemed to be college football cheers.
>
> At the hospital she was not only dancing, but trying to throw touchdown passes at the same time, mixing obscenities and quarterback play calls in a continuous outpouring. She seemed only partially aware of her surroundings.
>
> The same patient was readmitted to the hospital 17 years later at the age of 42 with a diagnosis of bipolar disorder. Her husband brought her to the hospital because she had refused to eat for three days, slept only two or three hours a night, and spent long hours staring off into space. She would speak to others, but only after more or less continuous coaxing. In very slow, monotonous speech, she commented that she was talking to her dead sister who was wearing a white gown, but her face was eaten up by worms and part of her eye socket was missing. This hallucination was intermixed with a conversation with God, a combination of pleading with Him to do something about her sister and blaming Him for her hospitalization.
>
> In the years between her first hospitalization and her present admission, she had been treated on several occasions in the outpatient clinic for depressive episodes, but there had been one additional manic episode.

Note that in this case, the person suffered from hallucinations. Whenever hallucinations are present, the patient is considered to be *psychotic,* a term that is explained shortly. While most people with major depression are not psychotic, such elements are sometimes present. A similar situation exists with bipolar disorders, but psychotic elements are more frequent here. In fact, one type of bipolar disorder used to be classified as manic-depressive psychosis.

Causes of Mood Disorders

Mood disorders present a special problem when it comes to figuring out the causes. The problem is that most cases disappear all by themselves, without any treatment, within a few months. They often recur, however, so depression shouldn't be ignored.

Suffering a significant loss or extreme stress may trigger a bout of depression, particularly moderate depression. Major depression, especially when it occurs in repeated episodes, may come from a lifetime of many separations, losses, and serious setbacks. However, these two forms of depression are not two different disorders. Most research indicates that depression lies on a continuum from mild to severe and that moderate depression may, in fact, turn into major depression in some people (Flett, Vredenburg, & Kramer, 1997).

Starting in adolescence, clear gender differences in depression emerge (Wichstrom, 1999). Females are twice as likely to be moderately depressed—to suffer from dysthymic disorder—as males, and females are four times as likely as males to suffer from major depression. In bipolar disorder, however, the rates are the same for both genders. These ratios continue throughout the life span and hold true across many Western cultures. Furthermore, married women in the United States are more often depressed than single women, and the more children a woman has, the more likely she is to be depressed (Culbertson, 1997).

What might account for these findings? The issue is a fairly complex one. Differences and changes in the levels of sex hormones have been suggested. In the case of extreme changes, such as those that occur with pregnancy and childbirth, sex hormones are probably a major contributor. But hormones are not the only factor and may not even be the most important one.

A characteristic called **learned helplessness** is frequently associated with becoming depressed. People with this characteristic have accepted the generalized idea that there is nothing they can do about their situation. Even many nondepressed people lose their motivation, do poorly, and show some minor symptoms of depression when they are put into unpleasant situations where they are expected to perform a task but have no control (Seligman, 1978). Adolescent girls are more likely to feel this kind of helplessness than are adolescent boys. Not only that, they are also more likely to be pessimistic and say self-defeating things about various situations in their lives. Girls are under greater pressure to conceal their intelligence in order to be accepted, and they are also under more pressure to be physically attractive. Study after study shows that the typical adolescent girl's dissatisfaction with her body and general appearance is much greater than the typical adolescent boy's. These factors weigh more heavily on some females than on others, and males are not exempt from them. However, they are all related to females' being at higher risk for depression (Nolen-Hoeksema & Girgus, 1994).

Self-image is a related issue. People who are prone to depression usually have very poor self-images. They see themselves as responsible for everything bad in their lives and don't seem to struggle to put up a defense against this unrealistic burden.

Denying who you really are in order to have other people like you will eventually take its toll. While doing this is a particular problem in adolescence, it does not seem to go away in adulthood. And whether engaged

▲ *Adolescent females are at higher risk for depression than males are.*

learned helplessness a condition in which a person has accepted the generalized idea that he or she can do nothing to help himself or herself

in by men or by women, it is one more ingredient in the depression recipe (Gratch et al., 1995).

Chemistry also plays a part, and not only where sex hormones are concerned. A deficiency in the hormone thyroxin, produced by the thyroid gland, can cause depression in some people. Another culprit is the brain chemical, or neurotransmitter, called **serotonin** (ser-uh-TONE-in). Serotonin is associated with general brain activity and with feeling pleasure and being happy. Studies of mood disorders show a pretty clear relationship in the brain between serotonin level and mood. The level of serotonin is very high—much higher than normal—in many manics; the level is very low in depressives (Snyder, 1984).

What about the role of genetics? Could a chemical defect be inherited? There often is a family history of mood disorders, especially bipolar disorder. In the case of manic depression, then, genes may well play a part. However, the issue is still under study where depression is involved. Here's the problem: Even with a family history of depression, we can't be sure of the source of the disorder. We know that depression is psychologically "contagious," so it may be that being around depressed family members is as much a cause as having a genetic predisposition (Kidd, 1985). We'll have to wait for the results of further research for a final answer. For the moment, a combination of psychological factors and physical or chemical defects seems a good bet as the source of mood disorders.

Several approaches can be taken to treat depression. Various drugs are effective, particularly those that increase the amount of available serotonin. Psychotherapy can be highly effective. There are drugs to treat mania, as well, such as lithium, and they are usually quite successful.

Suicide

Suicidal thoughts and behaviors occur with a much higher than average frequency among people with mental disorders. The type of mental disorder most often associated with suicide is depression. This is true not only for adults but for adolescents as well (Wagner, 1997). Compared with the general population, almost three times as many people with mental disorders commit suicide.

Approximately twice as many people try to commit suicide as succeed at it. More males than females actually kill themselves, while females attempt it more often. For adolescent girls, the ratio of attempts to completions is four to one (Bettridge & Favreau, 1995). The major reason for these gender differences appears to be the method chosen. Males most often use a gun; females most often take a drug overdose. Hence, males have less of a chance of being rescued before it's too late.

Incidence of Suicide. For the population as a whole, about 12 people per 100,000 kill themselves every year. Among people aged 25 to 64 years, the rate is about 15 per 100,000; and for ages 65 to 74, about 18 per 100,000. For those 75 to 84, the figure jumps to 22 per 100,000 (Center for Disease Control, 1996).

The suicide rate for teenagers between 15 and 19 years of age is about 10 per 100,000, slightly below the overall national average. Although this rate is higher than it was decades ago, now it stays roughly the same year after year. It is not the teenager but the elderly man who is at highest risk of killing himself. The media's claim that adolescent suicide is taking over like the plague is clearly false. The press distorts the facts by

serotonin a brain chemical. Levels that are too high lead to mania; levels that are too low lead to depression.

Focus Question

• What are some risk factors for suicide?

using percentages. A small group of communities will have perhaps one adolescent suicide during a year. If, for whatever reason, two teens happen to commit suicide the following year, what we read is that suicide among teenagers has increased by 100 percent! However, when people so young choose to take their own lives, the tragedy is magnified, and the effects on those left behind are devastating.

Risk Factors. As mentioned earlier, depression is a serious factor in suicide and suicide attempts. Attention should always be paid when a depressed person talks about ending it all or makes repeated references to death and dying. But not all depressed people attempt suicide, and other factors seem to be involved.

Some of the most common stressors leading up to suicide are the loss of important people, substance abuse, serious conflicts within the family, and severe trouble at school or work. For adolescents, especially adolescent girls, attempting suicide can be associated with having few intimate relationships, little satisfaction with those relationships, and not much social support. Rejection by one's parents and a negative, unpleasant family life are other risk factors for adolescents, as is a history of physical or sexual abuse.

▲ *Suicide hot lines can literally save lives.*

Usually added to these specific problems is the feeling that everything is meaningless and hopeless and that there is no point in trying to make things better. Sometimes you will hear that the death of a parent in one's childhood puts that child at higher risk for committing suicide later on. However, this does not appear to be true (Wagner, 1997; Bettridge & Favreau, 1995).

Pause for Thought

1. What is meant by *dissociative disorder?* Name three types.
2. Describe the symptoms of dysthymic disorder, major depression, mania, and bipolar disorder.

Critical Thinking

3. You are a psychologist who wants to research the causes of depression, but you have only enough money to study one possible cause. Which cause would you focus on? Mention the many possible causes of depression and why you would focus on one over another.
4. You are asked to speak to an audience of high school freshmen on suicide. What might you include in your speech?

525

Focus Questions

• What are the common symptoms of psychotic disorders?
• What are the common symptoms of schizophrenia in particular?

psychosis (psychotic disorder) a severe mental disorder that may involve disorganized thought processes, hallucinations, delusions, and major problems with emotional responses

thought disorder a serious distortion in the ability to think or speak in a lucid and coherent way

hallucinating the act of seeing or hearing something that is not present

delusion a belief in something that is clearly not true

schizophrenia a psychosis involving disorganized thoughts and garbled speech as well as hallucinations and delusions; the most serious mental disorder

word salad speech in which words are mixed incoherently

clang associations rhythmic patterns associated with psychotic speech

Characteristics of Psychotic Disorders

A **psychosis** or **psychotic disorder,** involves a major disorganization of thought processes, confused and extreme emotional responses, and distorted perceptions of the world. There is a loss of contact with and difficulty in recognizing reality. Thus, a psychosis is a very serious mental disturbance. Most researchers do not think that it is an extension or outgrowth of less severe disorders but believe that it is a separate problem that arises all by itself.

Four major symptoms can appear in psychosis. All four may not be present in one individual, but typically at least two are.

1. The first symptom is a serious distortion of mental processes. Often it is hard to understand exactly what psychotic people are trying to say or to grasp what they are thinking. This behavior comes and goes so that they are lucid for a while, then very confused. This symptom is called **thought disorder.**

2. The second symptom involves seeing or hearing things that are not there. Again, this comes and goes. It is not unusual for psychotics to hear voices or see objects that are not present. This behavior is called **hallucinating.**

3. Next, many psychotics hold grossly inaccurate beliefs, such as thinking of themselves as avenging angels or as victims of persecution by some secret organization. Such a belief is called a **delusion.**

4. Finally, psychotics have a great deal of trouble with emotional responses. The emotions shown are quite inappropriate. They might show no response at all when something interesting happens, for example, or they might laugh at a tragic event. We seriously doubt that they really think it is funny. Instead, we think that they are quite confused and dominated by a malfunctioning brain.

Schizophrenic Disorders

Schizophrenia (skitz-oh-FREN-ee-ah), a psychosis, is the most serious of all mental disturbances. It affects about 1 percent of the population. Obvious symptoms of this problem are disorganized thoughts and garbled speech, as well as hallucinations and delusions.

In some cases, schizophrenics speak what is called **word salad.** Like the ingredients of a tossed salad, the words are all mixed together: "The house burnt the cow horrendously always." Or the speech has what we call **clang associations,** which means the speech has a rhythm like a bell: "You wear clothes and how much does this watch cost? Have you a sister? I have three and they are all fine girls, curls, furls, isn't that funny?" The clang comes with "girls, curls, furls."

Researchers doubt that schizophrenia is a single disorder but instead think that there are different causes and degrees of severity. For example, about a third of people with schizophrenia have one episode and get better, never to have it happen again. A third have very severe symptoms and do not respond to treatment very much at all. The final third are in and out of institutions most of their lives (Restak, 1984).

We suspect that schizophrenia results mostly from some physical or chemical problem because it appears in late adolescence or early adulthood, almost never earlier. This fact would tend to rule out the suggestion that the causes are mostly psychological. Psychological causes should result in a problem that could appear at almost any age.

Types of Schizophrenia

All schizophrenia has certain symptoms in common, especially thought disorders. However, there are several subtypes, three of which are described here.

Catatonic. The hallmark of **catatonic schizophrenia** is a disturbance of movement. Catatonics usually do not speak, or they say very little. They appear to be in a stupor much of the time. They may rigidly hold a peculiar posture or simply stand or sit, unmoving, for hours.

Paranoid. Paranoid schizophrenia is marked by strong feelings of persecution and suspiciousness. It often includes grandiose beliefs as well. For instance, a paranoid schizophrenic might believe that he or she has some kind of special or superhuman power.

Undifferentiated. Undifferentiated schizophrenia is just what the term implies. That is, there is nothing special to differentiate or distinguish it. Many professionals consider this a catchall category. In other words, this category is used when a schizophrenic does not fit into any other subtype.

Psychotic Episodes

Schizophrenics are not necessarily out of touch with reality all the time. Their unusual behavior (called **psychotic episodes)** often comes in cycles, and in between they are reasonably lucid. Even those who seem unaware of their surroundings may not be as completely lost as they may appear.

One story about this involves a loud and obnoxious student nurse who frequently made unflattering remarks about the patients. One day she leaned over to make a bed next to the one on which a catatonic schizophrenic patient had been sitting immobile for many hours. She commented on how stupid she thought his behavior was and suddenly received a good solid kick in the rear. By the time she had whirled around, the patient had "resumed his 'poker face' expression and former posture" (O'Kelly & Muckler, 1955).

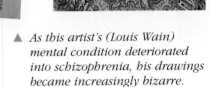

▲ *As this artist's (Louis Wain) mental condition deteriorated into schizophrenia, his drawings became increasingly bizarre.*

catatonic schizophrenia type of schizophrenia characterized by disturbances of movement

paranoid schizophrenia type of schizophrenia marked by strong feelings of suspiciousness and persecution

undifferentiated schizophrenia schizophrenia that lacks distinguishing symptoms

psychotic episodes periods of psychotic behavior; they can alternate with periods of relative coherence and calm

527

Case Study

Schizophrenia and Environment

Michael W., a 29-year-old married male, was brought to the hospital emergency room after refusing to eat or speak and staring out the window for four days. An interview with family members revealed that Mr. W. had had such episodes before, but they had never lasted this long. In addition, he had periods in which he was suspicious of everyone in his family and claimed they were trying to poison him. During these periods, he accused his wife of infidelity and became extremely agitated and hostile toward her. He had never been physically abusive, but his behavior was so irrational and out of control that she was quite fearful of him at those times.

Following high school graduation and vocational training, Mr. W. had been regularly employed in television repair until two years ago when economic conditions forced his employer to lay him off. Since that time, he worked occasionally at different jobs, the last one delivering for a local pizza parlor. He was fired from that job six months ago. Apparently, he would leave the parlor to make his deliveries, but would then become confused, park his truck, and sit for hours before returning with no deliveries made. Lately he had stopped seeking employment.

According to the older brother, he and Mr. W. had been reared by an unmarried aunt who was in her fifties when they came to live with her as small children. Their mother was killed in an automobile accident shortly after Mr. W.'s birth, and their father afterwards developed a drinking problem, eventually becoming totally unable to care for them. The brother described

▲ *People diagnosed with schizophrenia may also have other illnesses.*

his aunt as an emotionally cold woman who resented caring for her nephews, but he stated that they were well fed and clothed and their physical needs generally were attended to. Visits from their father were rare, and usually resulted in bitter arguments with their aunt, after which the boys were denied supper and confined to their room for the remainder of the day. Neither had seen nor heard from their father for over 10 years, and the aunt died six years ago.

During the interview, Mr. W. answered no questions, but merely stared at the opposite wall. Every now and then he would jerk his head sideways and inhale sharply. He sat in a very peculiar posture, his right hand and arm held rigidly at a 45° angle, the left stiffly at his side. When he walked, his knees bent only slightly with each step, giving him a robotlike appearance. He was admitted to the hospital and given antipsychotic drugs.

After several days of observation and drug treatment, Mr. W. began to respond to direct questions, but did so in a monotone. He revealed that he believed himself to be controlled by magnetic fields beamed at him by the Communists, and that he thought his wife and brother were working with them. Because of his severe motor problems, the diagnosis given was schizophrenia, catatonic type, with paranoid elements (McMahon & McMahon, 1983).

Review the Case Study

1. What "paranoid elements" did Michael W. exhibit?
2. Does this label seem accurate?

Hereditary and Environmental Factors in Schizophrenia

We know that heredity plays some role in schizophrenia. The odds of a person's becoming schizophrenic are moderately high if close family members have this problem. The studies of direct inheritance, though, are confusing. When we look at identical twins, we see that if one has the disorder, the odds are fairly good that the other will, too. For the population as a whole, however, the suggestion is strong that heredity is not the key factor.

• What are possible causes of schizophrenia?

For 90 percent of schizophrenics, there are no other schizophrenics in the immediate family. In addition, when children from schizophrenic families are adopted at a young age into other families, the children's risk of becoming schizophrenic is lowered somewhat. It is still fairly high but not as high as it would be if they had remained with their original families.

Environment, then, may play a small part in this disorder. As you can see from the case study of Michael W. (see page 528) the home life of the schizophrenic can be very disturbed. We suspect that a bizarre family may be enough to tip the balance for people who are already potentially schizophrenic. But in far more cases, the family is quite normal, things are very pleasant, and other children seem to be fine.

From the available evidence, then, it seems clear that environmental factors are not a major cause of this disorder. They may contribute to its development, but only if a predisposition already exists.

Chemical Factors in Schizophrenia

Think back to the last time you were at a party with some good friends and everyone was sitting in a circle. When the discussion really got going, people were talking rapidly and were agitated; thoughts were moving *very fast*. When that was happening, the level of one of the chemicals that fires nerve cells in the brain was quite high, causing a speed of speech and thought that eventually would exhaust most people. This chemical is called **dopamine** (DOUGH-pa-mean).

A major discovery about many schizophrenics is that they have abnormally high levels of dopamine in the brain. This certainly can explain many of their thought problems. If thoughts were running through their heads at maximum speed hour after hour, day after day, the end result would be confusion and eventually stupor from fatigue—which is just the way many schizophrenics act.

dopamine a brain chemical. It is present in excess in schizophrenics, which causes nerve cells to fire too rapidly and leads to confusion in thought and speech.

Studies with animals show that drugs that increase the levels of dopamine far beyond normal produce bizarre behavior in the form of strange posturing and robotlike movements—symptoms often seen with schizophrenics (Kokkinidis & Anisman, 1980). Finally, some schizophrenics get much better when they are given drugs that reduce dopamine levels.

The problem with drugs originally used to reduce dopamine levels was that they sometimes caused side effects, including uncontrollable tremors (Breggin, 1983). A newer class of drugs causes fewer side effects, but side effects have not been eliminated entirely. Of importance here is that scientists are on the right track. But they still need to refine the medication enough that it works safely for more people.

We should add that some researchers feel that psychological problems can cause the body to manufacture too much dopamine. That means schizophrenia may not simply be a physical problem that can be cured by chemical means alone. Still, we are on our way toward solving one of life's most destructive mental disorders.

Two additional points: (1) The rapidity of thought in the schizophrenic does not resemble that in the manic, discussed earlier. Schizophrenics speak and act as if they are exhausted from too much thought. (2) The chemical defect in mood disorders does not involve dopamine. That chemical, as mentioned, is serotonin. There is some very subtle difference in these chemicals that we don't completely understand yet.

Focus Question

- How do personality disorders differ from most other disorders?

personality disorder a disorder in which a person has formed a peculiar or unpleasant personality

antisocial personality disorder a personality disorder in which the person seems to have no conscience and is in constant conflict with the law

sociopath a person with antisocial personality disorder

▼ *In the movie,* Silence of the Lambs, *Anthony Hopkins played the ultimate sociopath, Hannibal "The Cannibal" Lector.*

Personality Disorders

The disorders we discuss next have nothing in common with the others discussed so far. Individuals with these disorders do not fit into the categories we have mentioned. They are not out of touch with reality, so they are not psychotic, and they do not show the guilt or anxiety so common in other disorders.

Instead, they seem to have formed peculiar and unpleasant personality patterns. For example, some are very secretive, some very self-centered and selfish, some suspicious all the time. We use the term **personality disorder** to indicate that their personalities are "off center."

Antisocial Personality Disorder

There are many personality disorders, but one in particular causes serious problems for society: the **antisocial personality disorder.** Originally, people with an antisocial personality were called *psychopaths,* a term you still sometimes hear. The label was given to those who committed crimes ranging from beating up little old ladies to committing ax murders.

A lack of conscience is central to this disorder. It is for this reason that the term **sociopath** is sometimes used, meaning that the behavior of these people toward society is clearly abnormal (*path* from "pathology," abnormal). Sociopaths don't even abide by the rules usually followed by criminals. Most criminals have at least some standards.

People with antisocial personality disorder repeatedly come into conflict with the law and show little or no concern, guilt, or anxiety. Nothing in the way of drug or psychological treatment works to help them. They are very smooth and agreeable on the outside and will go along with almost any treatment that is suggested. They will cooperate, tell you they are getting better, thank you, and seem to be well. But as soon as they are released, they go right back to whatever their favorite crime happens to be.

In truth, we don't understand how these people got the way they are or what to do with them. For many, there is a family history of neglect and rough treatment. The parents are often alcoholic and abusive, but millions of people over the years have had such a background and haven't acted this way. Measures of body chemistry and studies of genetic patterns have yielded nothing of any real significance regarding the origin of the sociopath's behavior.

Borderline Personality Disorder

The diagnosis of **borderline personality disorder** has only been around since 1980. Intense and unstable relationships with other people are a major characteristic. Borderline personalities are very dependent people, but they cannot admit this to themselves. So they constantly test other people's concern and often sabotage their own relationships.

People with this disorder appear to be "clingy" and emotionally needy. However, as soon as the slightest thing fails to go their way, they become extremely angry with the other person, often insulting and belittling him or her. In addition, they frequently use self-destructive behavior to manipulate others. Thus, they may make suicide threats and attempts, or deliberately cut themselves, or purposely have accidents.

It is as if they are so afraid of being abandoned that they are almost daring other people to do just that. Their emotions are also unstable, and they have trouble controlling their impulses. In some cases, their perceptions and thoughts are quite distorted (Millon, 1981).

The causes of borderline personality disorder are not yet clear. It does tend to run in families. However, because of the nature of this problem, it is hard to tell whether biology or learning is more involved. For instance, children who grow up with a borderline-personality parent will learn very little about how to develop and maintain healthy relationships. As adults, they may resort to angry outbursts or threats of suicide when things don't go their way. But this behavior could come from imitating the parent. In other words, their early home life is so chaotic and emotionally charged that it is almost impossible to separate hereditary and environmental factors.

People with borderline personalities are difficult to deal with in psychotherapy. Because they are so suspicious and manipulative, they have trouble developing a positive working relationship with a therapist. Consequently, they tend to switch from one therapist to another over and over again, rarely sticking with it long enough to be successful.

borderline personality disorder
a personality disorder marked by unstable emotions and relationships, dependency, and manipulative, self-destructive behavior

 ## Pause for Thought

1. What are four characteristics of psychotic disorders?
2. Some schizophrenics have peculiar speech patterns at times. Describe those speech patterns.
3. Describe several environmental and chemical factors in schizophrenia.
4. How are personality disorders different from the other disorders discussed in this chapter? Describe two types of personality disorders.

Critical Thinking
....

5. In one study, a psychologist faked some symptoms of psychosis and was admitted to a mental hospital (Rosenhan, 1973). After being admitted, he acted completely normal. Even so, he was never recognized by hospital staff as a phony patient. Can you explain why?

APPLYING
Psychology to Life

Not Guilty by Reason of Insanity

Some topics are almost guaranteed to provoke a heated argument. One such topic is use of the insanity defense in criminal trials. People have the idea that all across the country, every day, thousands of dangerous criminals are getting off scot-free after committing terrible and violent crimes by claiming they were or are insane. Actually, though, this claim is very rarely made. When it is made, the jury seldom accepts it as a defense. According to some estimates, it is used in fewer than one in every hundred cases; and in those cases, it succeeds only 10 percent of the time. When the crime involved is murder, the insanity defense is even less successful (Schmitt, 1997; Stone, 1982).

The first successful use of the insanity defense occurred in 1843 in England, when a man named M'Naghten killed the prime minister's private secretary. At his trial, he claimed that he suffered from "morbid delusions." He believed that the government was trying to do him in. The justices ruled that an act committed by a person operating under a delusion should be judged as if the delusion were fact. This "M'Naghten rule" formed the basis of the insanity plea.

Many decades later, the rationale for the plea was expanded. The Durham rule, established in 1954, came about when a man named Durham was tried for housebreaking and claimed he was not of sound mind. This decision opened the door for expert testimony in these cases and broadened the general scope of the plea.

Today, what exactly do we mean by the term *insanity?* Well, it doesn't necessarily have any-thing to do with the diagnostic categories we have discussed in this chapter. Psychotic disorders are the most common exception, because with these disorders, delusions and hallucinations are likely to affect the person's ability to function. However, most of the disorders we covered do not have much, if anything, to do with a person's overall capacity to make judgments about potential criminal acts. Indeed, it is often said that insanity is a legal term, not a psychological term.

▲ *Psychiatrist Phillip Resnick explains to the jury what schizophrenia is all about.*

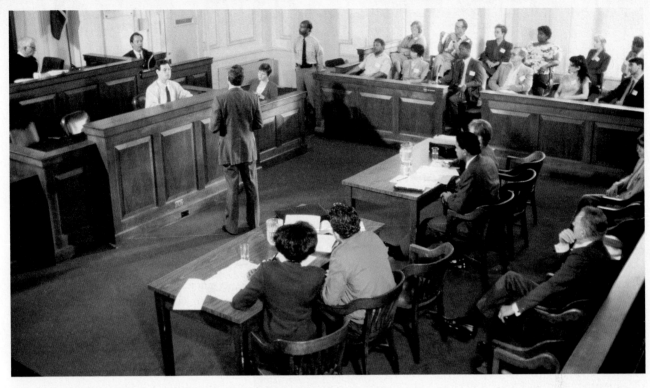

▲ *The insanity defense is rarely used and even more rarely used successfully.*

That is correct, but it doesn't clarify things all that much.

In determining the legal meaning of insanity, the Brawner rule is the one most often applied today. Under this rule, a person may be judged insane if, because of some mental problem, he or she was unable at the time the crime was committed (1) to know the difference between right and wrong or (2) to conform his or her behavior to the requirements of the law. For example, a man may be so utterly confused psychologically that he actually can no longer determine if a particular action is right or wrong. Or a woman may know that killing her terminally ill husband is wrong, but his pain may be so great and his pleas so heart-rending that she feels powerless to do otherwise. The overall concept is termed *diminished capacity* (to keep from doing something). In both of these examples, the person need not be diagnosed with a mental disorder to fit the criteria. But in both examples, a critical problem is how we can determine what someone else's state of mind was at some point in the past. We still have not addressed this problem satisfactorily.

Recently, several states have tightened their guidelines for the insanity defense. They have done so partly because the whole issue of diminished capacity is so vague that almost anything can be used as a defense for criminal behavior. One man claimed that he had eaten too much junk food and was suffering from sugar overload when he shot and killed a city official. This became known as the "Twinkie defense." More often, a history of child abuse or domestic violence is cited. Some states now allow a verdict of "guilty, but mentally ill." In most such cases, the person must undergo psychological treatment confined in a hospital. In some cases, he or she must then serve out a prison sentence as well.

CHAPTER 17 REVIEW & APPLY

Summary

1. Most people with mental disorders exhibit an exaggerated version of characteristics we all have. Symptoms include discomfort, bizarre behavior, and inefficiency. Such people often are inflexible and tend to find the environment threatening.

2. Childhood disorders include attention deficit/hyperactivity disorder (ADHD) and autistic disorder. Children with ADHD have trouble focusing on the task at hand and are restless, easily frustrated, and impulsive. Certain drugs are often useful in treating this disorder. In autistic disorder, the child does not develop normal patterns of communication, social interaction, and emotional response.

3. Anxiety disorders are characterized by apprehension and fear. A person with panic disorder has severe anxiety attacks unconnected to any particular thing. In specific phobias, the fear is attached to a certain object or situation. With agoraphobia, fear is triggered by anything outside one's familiar home environment. An obsession involves a preoccupation with a certain urge or thought. A compulsion involves repeated ritualized behavior usually related to an obsession.

4. Somatoform disorders are characterized by bodily symptoms without actual physical causes. Types include conversion disorder, in which the symptom symbolizes a psychological issue, and hypochondriasis, or exaggerated concern with one's health.

5. In dissociative disorders, part of the person's memory system is separated from the remainder. In amnesia, the person forgets certain upsetting things. In fugue, the person forgets his or her current life and starts over elsewhere. In dissociative identity disorder, instead of forgetting specific events, the person "forgets" a part of himself or herself, and that part begins to live a life of its own.

6. Mood disorders involve disturbances in people's emotional states. Dysthymia is a moderate depression. Major depression is a severe, disabling depression. In mania, the person's mood is extremely elevated. Bipolar disorders involve both mania and depression. We suspect that both physical and psychological problems exist in mood disorders.

7. Suicide and suicide attempts are often associated with depression. Those at highest risk are those who have experienced a serious loss, extreme stress, or family or job problems; have little social support; and feel hopeless about their situation.

8. Psychotic disorders involve major disorganization of thought processes, hallucinations (hearing or seeing things that are not there), delusions (false beliefs), and/or great difficulty with emotional responses.

9. Schizophrenia is an extremely serious psychotic disorder. Types include catatonic, paranoid, and undifferentiated schizophrenia. Severely disabled thought processes and bizarre speech patterns are notable symptoms. Schizophrenia usually appears in late adolescence or early adulthood. We suspect that it has a chemical or physical basis rather than psychological causes.

10. People with personality disorders have formed peculiar and unpleasant personality patterns. People with antisocial personalities have no conscience. People with borderline personalities are dependent, unstable, and emotionally intense. They are demanding, suspicious, and manipulative in their relationships with others.

Vocabulary

Review Questions

Matching

On a sheet of paper, match the terms (a–e) in the second list to definitions in the first list.

1. Associated with generalized anxiety attacks
2. Extreme anxiety at the sight of a dog
3. Thoughts that won't go away
4. Inability to leave a familiar environment
5. Repeated actions

   a. obsession
   b. agoraphobia
   c. compulsion
   d. specific phobia
   e. panic disorder

Fill in the Blank

On a sheet of paper, write the word or words that best complete each statement.

6. Someone who thinks he is Napoleon is having ▨▨▨▨.
7. Schizophrenics often mix words together in what is called ▨▨▨▨.
8. Schizophrenics also may use rhythmic patterns called ▨▨▨▨ in their speech.
9. The "up" part of an extreme mood swing is called ▨▨▨▨.
10. A person suffering from major up-and-down mood swings is suffering from a ▨▨▨▨ disorder.

(Review Questions continued on page 536)

535

Multiple Choice

On a sheet of paper, write the letter of the answer that best completes each statement.

11. A high level of serotonin might cause a person to become

    a. manic.   **c.** withdrawn.

    b. depressive.   **d.** dissociative.

12. The fact that the onset of schizophrenia usually occurs during late adolescence or early adulthood suggests that the cause of schizophrenia may be

    a. psychological.   **c.** learned.

    b. biological.   **d.** easily prevented.

13. A sociopath would most likely have

    a. a high level of serotonin.

    b. a high level of dopamine.

    c. abusive parents.

    d. all of the above.

14. Someone with a personality disorder would probably exhibit high levels of

    a. depression.   **c.** anxiety.

    b. guilt.   **d.** none of the above.

15. People who become blind because of a conversion disorder

    a. can suddenly see again when taught to relax.

    b. are usually faking their impairment.

    c. actually cannot see.

    d. have retinal damage.

16. Borderline personalities

    a. are easily angered.

    b. tend to be too dependent.

    c. are often self-destructive.

    d. are all of the above.

Discussion Questions

1. Other than violent behaviors, list five behaviors that our society considers abnormal. Then, for each of the five behaviors, describe a situation in which the abnormal behavior *might* be considered normal. For example, eating another human is certainly regarded as abnormal. But suppose a plane crashes and some people are killed. The survivors, after being stranded for three weeks, are forced to eat the remains to survive. In this case, the behavior *could* be construed by many as normal.

2. Your new job requires you to travel but you have a fear of flying. What do you do? Do you enlist in a program that teaches you how to reduce your fear? Do you take medication to relieve your anxiety? Do you drive instead? Explain.

3. Most people have at least one irrational fear. Describe a specific phobia you have. Offer a few guesses as to how you may have developed this phobia.

4. Roger complains constantly about aches and pains and a variety of other medical symptoms. His doctor knows he's a hypochondriac but never says anything. Instead, the doctor gives Roger placebos. If you were a member of Roger's family, would you confront him about his mental disorder or let him continue to take the placebos that seem to provide him with short-term relief?

5. Some researchers maintain that dissociative identity disorder is nothing more than a cultural creation fostered mainly by therapists who use hypnosis to encourage multiple personalities to emerge. What kind of evidence would you like to see to help you determine whether this disorder actually exists? For example, you might want to view a videotape of the sessions between the therapist and the patient.

Activities and Projects

1. A stigma is a mark of disgrace or discredit that sticks with a person for a long time. Acquiring a stigma is especially harmful when it involves a mental illness. Conduct an experiment to see how true this is. Type "Politics" at the top of a sheet of paper, and then add the following: "Rate this person's chances of being elected president of the United States. George Johnson. Age 54. Offices held: governor, 12 years; congressman, 10 years; lieutenant governor, 4 years. Background: Yale Law School, top 10% of class; married at age 25; treated for depression at age 43 with electroshock therapy but completely cured; practiced corporate law for 4 years." You can add other credentials if you'd like. Include a rating scale somewhere on the sheet: 1 = dismal; 2 = very poor; 3 = poor; 4 = average; 5 = high; 6 = very high; 7 = excellent.

    Now type the same information and rating scale on another sheet of paper, but replace the entire reference to depression with this: "divorced at age 43; remarried 3 years later." Show the first sheet to 20 people, and show the second sheet to 20 different subjects. Record subjects' ratings and any comments they may make, then compare your results. Explain why you think you got the results you did. Regardless of your results, discuss whether you think people in our society are stigmatized by the label of mental illness. What effect could a stigma have on the person who is labeled?

2. You'll need to find a partner from your psychology class to complete this project. Pick a controversial issue from this chapter and present a brief debate for the rest of the class. You might want to ask a debate teacher to help you with a format. Or you can try this: Round 1—state your position (2 minutes each). Round 2—rebuttal (1 minute each). Round 3—questions for opponent (1 minute). Afterward, the class can join in for an informal discussion. Possible issues:

    Should the insanity plea be allowed or revised?

    Is dissociative identity disorder a real disorder or simply a by-product of bad therapy?

    Does facilitated communication really help autistic children communicate?

    What can we do to eliminate the stigma of mental illness? (No one would argue *for* the stigma, but maybe you can debate how to go about eliminating it.)

3. Ask three of your teachers if you can use five minutes of class time to survey the classes about phobias. Copy the following onto a sheet of paper, and make enough photocopies for the three classes:

Phobias Survey

Use the scale below to rate how anxious you usually become around the following items.

Not anxious	Not very anxious	Somewhat anxious	Very anxious	Extremely anxious
1	2	3	4	5

Place a number from the scale next to each item below.

___ 1. Spiders   ___ 6. Snakes   ___ 11. Giving speeches

___ 2. Heights   ___ 7. Dogs   ___ 12. Open spaces

___ 3. Elevators   ___ 8. Tall buildings   ___ 13. Tests

___ 4. Water   ___ 9. Closed spaces   ___ 14. Cats

___ 5. Knives   ___ 10. Needles   ___ 15. Crossing bridges

    (Notice that we didn't list just 13 items—fuel for another phobia.) Tally your results and create a table.

    Place the phobia that received the highest average rating at the top, and work your way down to the phobia that received the lowest average rating. Transfer your table onto a poster and include appropriate captions—then put the poster up in class.

    In addition, you may want to create another chart that shows the differences between males' and females' phobias. In this case, ask each person to mark "male" or "female" at the top of his or her rating sheet.

CHAPTER 18

Treatment and Therapy

Therapy often helps people with emotional problems. In therapy, a professional is actively involved in working on the problems of another to try to help bring stability to the individual's life. This chapter discusses various methods by which help is provided.

Attitudes Toward Mental Illness

Focus Question

....

• How did one man change people's attitudes toward mental illness?

People typically are afraid of anything odd or unknown. Historically, reactions have been most violent to those with emotional disturbances, because the origin of the problem is often unclear. Before the 1700s in Europe, for example, mental problems were thought to be the result of influence by the devil or demons. Behavior such as hearing voices or speaking strangely usually led to torture and hanging. In some communities, such people were boiled alive, and their parts were hung on posts in the public square (Deutsch, 1946). When there were outbreaks of disease, such as the Black Death plague in the 1300s, people with mental disorders were blamed and "extremities were jerked from the . . . sockets, feet were torn from limbs, thumbs were squashed, and skin was torn with red-hot pincers" (Anderson, 1970).

With the arrival of the age of science, a search began for some method of treating those with serious mental problems. This new atmosphere was triggered by the work of a French physician, **Philippe Pinel** (Phil-LEAP Pea-NELL), who was put in charge of a hospital for the insane during the early 1700s. With great fanfare, he entered the hospital, which was really a dungeon, and freed the "patients," who were chained to the wall. Given their freedom, they did not go on a rampage and pillage the town but showed signs of improvement. This was the beginning of humane treatment.

People in the town were very suspicious of Pinel. When a cholera epidemic broke out later, they blamed him for poisoning the water supply, and an angry mob tried to kill him. The story has a romantic, but true, ending. Pinel was rescued from the mob by some of those he had freed (Reisman, 1966).

Even today, mental problems are one of the most feared maladies for people to be around, but attitudes have changed a fair amount regarding therapy or treatment. Therapy for those with such problems as phobias, moderate depression, and the like is so common that a person having treatment is no longer considered all that unusual.

◀ *This painting shows Philippe Pinel unchaining the inmates of his asylum.*

- What are the main tasks of various mental health workers?

counseling psychologists psychologists who deal mostly with problems not fitting into the formal classifications of mental disturbance

clinical psychologists psychologists who deal with emotional problems of any kind, including those fitting into the formal classifications of mental disturbance

psychiatrists medical doctors with special training in mental disorders

psychiatric social workers mental health workers with a degree in social work; help patients and families deal with problems

psychiatric nurses registered nurses with special education in psychiatric medicine

540

Types of Mental Health Workers

Many people use the terms *psychologist* and *psychiatrist* without being aware that these are different occupations. Before discussing therapies, we should make the differences clear.

Psychologists

Psychologists who work directly with people, seeking to assist them with their problems, are called either *counseling psychologists* or *clinical psychologists.* **Counseling psychologists** deal mostly with people who do not have formal classifications of mental disturbance. Typically, they work with people who have marital or family problems or general problems with living. **Clinical psychologists** perform all the tasks of the counseling psychologists, but some of them also work in mental hospitals and clinics with "classified" patients.

Many counseling psychologists have a doctor of education (Ed.D.) degree, while the typical clinical psychologist has a doctor of philosophy (Ph.D.) degree. After graduating from college, members of both groups continue in graduate school for an additional four to five years, studying psychology. Clinical psychologists must also have a year's internship in a mental health facility. Most states require an additional one to three years of supervised training.

Psychiatrists

Psychiatrists are medical doctors who spend four years as graduate students learning about physical medical problems rather than mental ones. After this general medical training, they can specialize in the mental health field. Training in their specialization can include one to three years of hospital residency, which resembles an apprenticeship.

The most striking difference between psychiatrists and psychologists is that the former can prescribe medicine. However, there is currently a strong movement among clinical psychologists to change this (DeLeon, Sammons, & Sexton, 1995). If the movement is successful, properly trained licensed psychologists would be legally able to prescribe drugs for psychological conditions such as anxiety and depression.

In any case, most psychologists downplay the role of medicine for the average person in treatment, and most psychiatrists do just the opposite. There probably is something to say for both sides. Your authors are psychologists, so, if you pick up any bias in how we cover the material, it is not intended—but we are probably right!

Other Mental Health Personnel

Other mental health personnel include psychiatric social workers and psychiatric nurses. **Psychiatric social workers** usually hold advanced degrees in social work. They help patients find jobs or housing and assist families, among others, in dealing with problems. **Psychiatric nurses** are registered nurses with special education in psychiatric medicine.

In the early years, mental health workers were mostly physicians (medical doctors) or ministers. Ministers today are still active in the field, but we can't specify their education or training because it varies so much from one individual to another.

Psychotherapists—The Blanket Term

In the next sections, we discuss the major methods used to try to help people with their problems. All these techniques are called **psychotherapies,** a term meaning that they involve an attempt to relieve *(therapy)* problems of the mind *(psyche)*. *Psychotherapist* is thus a broad term for any professional who tries to help others psychologically. A psychotherapist can be a psychologist, a psychiatrist, a social worker, a minister, or a psychiatric nurse.

As you will see, therapists use a number of different psychotherapies. But whatever the method used, the goal is for the therapist to help the person change views that are causing problems, to help reduce tension, to remove troublesome behavior patterns or habits, or to provide a source of support in a time of distress.

▲ *Talking it out is a major part of most forms of psychotherapy.*

Psychoanalytic Treatment

Psychoanalysis (analysis of the psyche, or mind) is a very symbolic and complicated treatment. It usually involves from three to five hours of treatment per week over a period of years. Its methods are based on the theory of the psychiatrist Sigmund Freud.

The Freudian system focuses on *anxiety* as the main problem people face. According to this theory, as you may remember from Chapter 14, anxiety arises from deep-seated animal impulses. We all have strong sexual and aggressive impulses that we want to act out. But since such expression is taboo, we live in constant anxiety that our impulses will break loose. And we suffer guilt whenever we partially act out the desires. This guilt in turn produces more anxiety.

These desires operate at the unconscious level, causing endless battles within the self. The self is caught between the animal desires, which go all the way back to childhood, and the conscience, which has, over the years, developed to try to prevent these behaviors.

The animal desires are viewed as a physical force within the person. This physical force is trying to be heard, and its voice can get louder and more demanding as it seeks expression. But since it is operating at the unconscious level, we are not aware of it. Psychoanalytic theory claims that some of the unconscious energy is released and can appear as symbolic dreams. On occasion, it is freed enough actually to express itself in the acts we perform. But most of the time it stays bottled up, building greater force, which increases anxiety. It is the task of the psychoanalyst to help the patient free some of this energy in a safe form.

The techniques we are going to discuss in the following sections are still in use. However, many Freudian therapists today use other techniques

Focus Questions
....
• What is the goal of psychoanalysis?

• How does it work?

psychotherapies broad term for any method used to try to help people with emotional and psychological problems

psychoanalysis therapy practiced by followers of Freud, who analyze the psyche via the unconscious

541

In Their Own Words...

Sigmund Freud summed up the task of the psychoanalyst this way:

The work of analysis which is necessary for the thorough explanation and complete cure of a case of sickness does not stop in any case with the experience of the time of onset of the disease, but in every case it goes back to the adolescence and the early childhood of the patient. Here only do we hit upon the impressions and circumstances which determine the later sickness. Only the childhood experiences can give the explanation for the sensitivity to later trauma(s) and only when these memory traces, which almost always are forgotten, are discovered and made conscious, is the power developed to banish the symptoms. We arrive here at the same conclusion as in the investigation of dreams—that it is the incompatible, repressed wishes of childhood which lend their power to the creation of symptoms. (1910/1957, pp. 23–24)

Interpreting Primary Sources

According to Freud, why does recalling childhood events help cure a patient of symptoms?

free association the process of saying whatever comes to mind; thought to uncover the unconscious in psychoanalysis

transference the process in which a person transfers emotional conflicts of earlier years onto the therapist

as well. They are more likely to have their patients sit in an armchair than lie on a couch. Modern psychotherapists who abide by Freudian concepts in general and tend to look beneath the surface for the root of problems may be called *psychodynamic* psychotherapists rather than psychoanalysts. Another term for this approach today is "insight" therapy.

Free Association

Free association is a major technique of psychoanalysis. People engaging in free association say *whatever* comes to mind, no matter how disconnected or unimportant the material might seem. The theory behind this is that since desires in the unconscious are seeking escape, they will often hook themselves onto what at first might seem innocent sentences. For instance, a person might claim that he wants to *tell* his parent something. Instead, he says, "I want to *kill* my parent." This "slip of the tongue" is the unconscious impulse escaping.

Freudians believe that the longer a person in psychoanalysis talks, the greater will be the amount of information coming from the unconscious. The therapist then points out to the person the kinds of things that are being said, asks what they might mean, and offers interpretations. In this way, the therapist puts the person more in control of those impulses. In other words, psychoanalysts believe they are allowing inner conflicts to come out, be explored in safety, and be resolved.

Transference

Another important aspect of psychoanalytic treatment is called **transference.** Here, a person transfers emotional conflicts of earlier years onto the therapist. Since the therapist is not personally part of any of these conflicts, he or she is emotionally objective. So here lies the crux of the treatment: Because the therapist is neutral, whatever the person claims about the therapist is made up by the person's unconscious trying to find expression.

Now, a person who can recognize this behavior for what it is will see that the therapist is being blamed for something he or she had no part in. As a result, the person's inner conflicts become visible. Once they are visible, they can be dealt with "out in the open," so to speak, rather than hidden where they can cause us grief without our understanding the source.

See the Case Study on page 543 for an illustration of the basic principle of transference.

A Case of Transference

Case Study

As you read through the following exchange between analyst and patient, pay close attention to the methods used by the analyst and how those methods evoke transference. The analyst first mirrors the patient, turns silent, acknowledges the patient's anger, then directly encourages transference.

Patient: I don't feel well today. I had a headache and I was going to stay in bed.

Analyst: You really didn't want to come in.

Patient: Yes, you might say that. I had a bad night, and I dreamed that I was falling and falling—off a building, you know—and I couldn't find anything to grab hold of.

Analyst: You feel like you might be losing control of the situation?

Patient: Well, of course. That's true. But I don't need a dream to tell me that. So I had a dream, so what?

Analyst: [silence].

Patient: No comment about that? You should say something, you know. [silence]. Well, why shouldn't you say something? You know I come

here endlessly—for what? I feel anxious right now and you say nothing. I feel like I'm losing control, just like in the dream, and when I come in here it just gets worse. So, why should I come? You don't know what it's like.

Analyst: You seem rather angry with me.

Patient: [silence]. Well, shouldn't I be? Angry, I mean? I keep trying to get myself straightened out and you just sit there—like a lump. So know-it-all and pompous.

Analyst: Do your feelings seem familiar? Do I remind you of someone?

Patient: Now let's not start that crap.

Analyst: [silence].

Patient: Well, OK. Sure. Who cares? Yes—yes, you remind me of my father. Isn't that beautiful? But you really have a lot in common. Every time I started to do something, there he was, like some kind of god, ready to jump all over me.

▲ *Therapists must be especially sensitive to what* isn't *being said as well as what* is.

Review the Case Study

Here, the person being analyzed transfers anger to the therapist. How does the analyst respond to the anger, and what will probably happen to the anger as a result?

Focus Questions

• • • • • • • • • • • • • • • • • • • •

- How do humanistic therapists view themselves?
- How do they view the people they help?

humanistic therapies therapies that emphasize the individual's ability to heal himself or herself with some assistance

person-centered therapy Carl Rogers's humanistic approach; reflects the belief that the person and his or her therapist are partners in therapy

nondirective therapy person-centered therapy

Humanistic Therapy

You may have felt when you read the previous section that the psychoanalyst lives in a pretty gloomy world regarding the human condition. We can't say that this view of the human is incorrect. Still, there are theories that take a different approach.

These therapies are based on the principle that people have within themselves the potential to know where they are heading. Eventually, they will be able to reach this potential and blossom like a flower. Thus, there is no unconscious filled with baser desires. It is the therapist's function to bring out the best in people, a "best" that is already in us from the beginning but that needs to be freed. These therapies are called **humanistic** because they emphasize the power within the individual human to control his or her own fate and movement toward fulfillment. In the sections that follow, we cover the major therapeutic methods in this area.

Person-Centered Therapy

Person-centered therapy was originally called *client-centered therapy,* and that term gives a clue to the orientation of the approach. At the time, it was common for therapists to refer to people in therapy as patients. But to humanists, *patient* had a one-above, one-below feeling to it. In contrast, *client* suggested a relationship in which the two (therapist and client) were partners working toward a common goal. Eventually, the word *client* was discarded as well and replaced with the term *person,* which is meant to imply completely equal status for both parties.

The person-centered approach, which is most closely associated with psychologist Carl Rogers, has also been called Rogerian therapy, or **nondirective therapy.** The word *nondirective* is designed to convey the idea that these therapists do not prod or push (direct) people but instead let them decide for themselves what is important to talk about and in which direction the therapy should be going.

The technique of person-centered therapy rests on the assumption that each of us aims toward living a meaningful life. To reach that state, we must accept ourselves for what we are, not for what others may think we should be. Since we are basically good, the humanists feel this is safe to do. Disturbed behavior, then, arises from worrying too much about the mismatch between what our inner selves are telling us and what others claim things should be like. Therefore, the therapist helps people to clarify and accept inner forces and directions.

What if the direction one is going in is wrong? This supposedly happens when a distorted environment blocks the inner forces for good. According to the humanistic theory, distressed people will be able, over time in therapy, to see for themselves that they are on the wrong track.

In the actual therapy, the therapist acts as a mirror that is held up to the person—a mirror that tries to reflect what the person is saying, *not* trying to put interpretations on the statements. Atmosphere is crucial: The therapist must provide a safe, nonjudgmental environment so the person can freely explore problems. To do so, the therapist reflects on and rephrases the person's own feelings and thoughts. You can see this in the small excerpt of dialogue that follows:

Person: I don't feel well today. I had a headache and I was going to stay in bed.

Therapist: You just didn't feel like coming today?

Person: Yes, you might say that. I had a bad night and I dreamed that I was falling and falling—off a building, you know—and I couldn't find anything to grab hold of.

Therapist: It sounds like that dream really bothered you and you feel insecure or afraid.

Person-Centered Therapy

The therapist's primary role in person-centered therapy, according to Carl Rogers, is to listen actively to the person in a non-judgmental way and to provide unconditional positive regard. Together, these factors provide a safe environment for the person, and in time, the person will shed the layers of defenses that he or she has created.

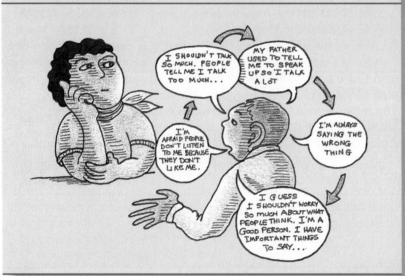

What are some ways in which a therapist can show that he or she is listening actively?

Unconditional Positive Regard

One final point about this treatment method: The critical thing that the therapist is to provide is called **unconditional positive regard.** This term means that the person's thoughts, feelings, hopes, and desires are to be accepted for what they are—a part of the growing individual. The people themselves are not to be judged. Obviously, a person who wants to

unconditional positive regard a principle of humanistic therapy in which the person's feelings and thoughts are accepted for whatever they are; Carl Rogers's term

kill someone is not holding an acceptable goal, but the Rogerians maintain that the *feeling* can be accepted as part of the person, even though the idea itself must be rejected. So there are no conditions on acceptance, and people are free to talk, to listen to themselves, and to grow.

This method of treatment may still seem a little vague to you. Basically, the therapist sits and listens, then rewords and reflects what the person is saying. The person "hears" himself or herself through the therapist's words. Over time, then, the person is talking to his or her inner self through the therapist. And since the person is basically good, eventually the right road will be discovered.

Focus Question

• What are some methods that behavioral therapists use to help people?

behavioral therapy therapy that uses principles of learning to alter the person's actions or behavior

Behavioral Therapy

Behavioral therapy involves techniques designed to bring about changes in people's behavior by using principles of learning. While the goals of behavioral therapy are the same as those of other therapies, its philosophy is different.

Behavioral therapists believe that most mental disorders are not complex problems but instead are the result of unacceptable behaviors learned over a period of years. Both "normality" and "abnormality" are learned. Thus, whatever symptom the person has comes not from some deep-seated problem but simply from having learned poor habits or responses to difficult situations.

Behavioral therapists say, basically, that if someone is afraid of elevators, it doesn't make any difference where the problem came from. Let's just get rid of the fear and ignore its origin, whatever that might be. We will bring about a relearning to reduce the fear.

This type of treatment is rapid (usually taking only a few months) and effective for dealing with problems that center on some kind of specific fear or bad habit. It is not as useful with issues that are complex, such as friction between members of a family. In such a case, the behaviors involved include so many factors that it is hard to focus on exactly what behavior one is trying to remove by using learning principles. As a result, behavioral therapists generally do not deal with this kind of case.

 Pause for Thought

1. How did Philippe Pinel change attitudes about mental illness?
2. Are psychologists and psychiatrists both psychotherapists? Explain.
3. Explain why humanistic therapists sometimes use the term *person-centered therapy*. According to humanists, what characteristics should therapists have?

Critical Thinking

4. You are a therapist who uses psychoanalysis, and you have a patient who fears his boss. How would you treat this patient? What would it mean in this case for transference to occur?

Systematic Desensitization

The goal of behaviorists is to weaken a habit that the person has and replace it with something that is newly learned. The most elaborate method in this area is called **systematic desensitization.** The term refers to a process in which the therapist step by step (systematically) increases the anxiety the patient feels. Each time it is increased, that level of anxiety is replaced by relaxation. In this way, the person becomes much less sensitive (desensitized) to the problem.

Here is a real case: A college student had a phobia (unreasonable fear) about dissection. She could not even enter a room where it took place. This meant that she was going to fail biology. First, the student was taught how to relax. The therapist then made up a list of items in order of increasing anxiety. The first item was presented to the student. Perhaps it was something like being on campus near the biology building. She was told to relax while thinking of this item. The next step was thinking about approaching the biology building. As anxiety built up at this thought, she was to relax once again. Then thoughts about the odors and atmosphere of the biology lab were introduced, creating greater anxiety. She again relaxed. Over time, she began to relax at the thought of cutting up a frog and hence was able actually to participate in such an activity. (McGlynn & O'Brien, 1972).

This procedure sounds almost simple-minded. But it works quite well with thousands of people every year.

▲ *Doesn't systematic desensitization look like fun?*

systematic desensitization a behavioral technique in which the therapist increases the patient's anxiety and counters it with relaxation in a graduated sequence

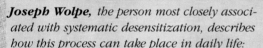

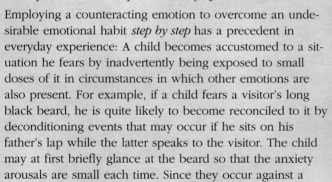

Joseph Wolpe, the person most closely associated with systematic desensitization, describes how this process can take place in daily life:

Employing a counteracting emotion to overcome an undesirable emotional habit *step by step* has a precedent in everyday experience: A child becomes accustomed to a situation he fears by inadvertently being exposed to small doses of it in circumstances in which other emotions are also present. For example, if a child fears a visitor's long black beard, he is quite likely to become reconciled to it by deconditioning events that may occur if he sits on his father's lap while the latter speaks to the visitor. The child may at first briefly glance at the beard so that the anxiety arousals are small each time. Since they occur against a background of warm and pleasant responses to the father, these small fear arousals are presumably inhibited, and gradually, as the fear subsides, the child tolerates lengthening inspections of the beard. (1982, p. 133)

Interpreting Primary Sources

Write a scenario that uses systematic desensitization to overcome a specific fear.

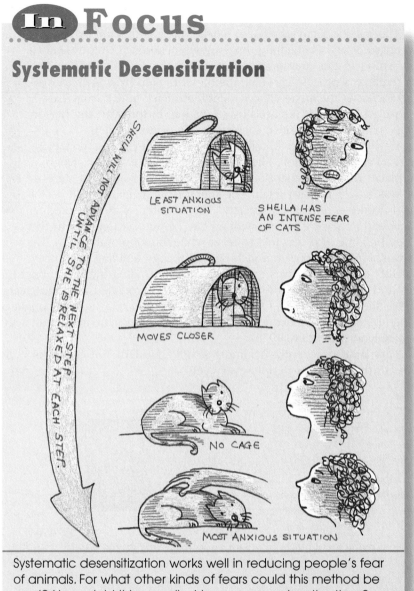

In Focus

Systematic Desensitization

SHEILA WILL NOT ADVANCE TO THE NEXT STEP UNTIL SHE IS RELAXED AT EACH STEP.

LEAST ANXIOUS SITUATION

SHEILA HAS AN INTENSE FEAR OF CATS

MOVES CLOSER

NO CAGE

MOST ANXIOUS SITUATION

Systematic desensitization works well in reducing people's fear of animals. For what other kinds of fears could this method be used? How might it be applied to more complex situations?

Aversive Conditioning

aversive conditioning a behavioral technique in which unpleasantness is associated with acts that are to be avoided

In **aversive conditioning,** the goal is to make certain acts unpleasant so that they will be avoided. For example, alcoholics can be given a medication that will make them nauseated when they take alcohol. Here, the goal of the relearning process is to associate the aversive (negative) feeling with taking the alcohol and hence reduce its use. The rate of improvement for this method is about 50 percent, with the "cure" lasting about six months. Thus, it is not a solution as much as a good beginning for a number of alcoholics.

The Token Economy

The **token economy** is a buying system (an economy) in which people use tokens to purchase things. This system may seem again like something a little too simple, but it works quite well with certain types of patients. The tokens—paper slips, poker chips, or the like—are given for good behavior, such as making the bed, brushing one's teeth, or taking a shower. In day-to-day living in close quarters, doing these things vastly improves the comfort of the living conditions and reduces episodes of frustration and increased abnormality. The tokens give the patients something to do along with a tangible reward.

Major changes take place using this method. Patients work for tokens with which they can buy extra walks on the grounds, more television time, candy, and the like. As a result, they become less withdrawn, have fewer confused thoughts, and improve their social relationships.

token economy a behavioral technique in which rewards for desired acts are accumulated through tokens, which represent a form of money

A Note about Behavioral Therapy

We need to add a word here about the term *behavioral.* Therapy can involve three processes: cognitive (mental processes), verbal (talking), and behavioral (performing actions). In the techniques just discussed, taking action (behavioral) is the most important aspect—going into the biology lab, not taking a drink, making a bed. The therapies do not involve the verbal (talking) aspects that the Rogerians and Freudians use. The therapies also downplay the mental (cognitive). You'll need to keep these distinctions in mind as you read the next section.

Cognitive Behavioral Therapy

We mentioned the limitations of straight behavioral therapy in terms of its inability to handle complex problems arising from mental, symbolic issues. Because of this failing, it wasn't long before some psychologists came up with the idea of uniting behaviors with cognitions (thoughts) as a method for helping people. Therapy of this kind involves actively working on the client's thought processes (cognitions) and having him or her change actions and emotional responses (behaviors) to be more appropriate. Thus, it is called **cognitive behavioral therapy.**

A leader in this area is **Albert Ellis** (b. 1913). Ellis's approach to problems is based on a belief that we humans are made up of two components: the rational (mental) and the emotional (emotive). Treatment focuses on getting emotions under control by using reason. Thus, the technique is called **rational-emotive therapy,** or **RET** (Ellis, 1980).

According to Ellis's view, most emotional upsets occur because we hold **irrational ideas,** ideas that don't hold up when challenged by careful logic. Put another way, we are disturbed "not by things but by the view we take of them."

External events can't do us in half as fast as how we think about them. Here's an example: (1) A woman loses a job. She becomes depressed. (2) A woman loses a job and looks forward to greater opportunities at a *new* job. These women have entirely different responses to the same set of circumstances. This scenario holds the key to Ellis's system.

Focus Question

....

• What techniques do cognitive therapists use?

cognitive behavioral therapy therapy in which thoughts are used to control emotions and behaviors

rational-emotive therapy (RET) Albert Ellis's form of cognitive behavioral therapy; aimed at getting emotions under control by using reason

irrational ideas ideas that do not hold up when challenged by careful logic

▲ *How you resolve the problem of losing your job depends on how you talk to yourself about your situation.*

internalized sentences what we say to ourselves in our own inner voices; Ellis's term

awfulize to see things in the worst possible light; Ellis's term

▲ *Psychologist Albert Ellis*

Each woman's beliefs are based on what Ellis called **internalized sentences.** To understand what he means, stop and listen to yourself for a few minutes. Notice how you talk "inside" all day every day. How well you do in life depends on what kinds of sentences you are giving yourself. If they are "I'm doomed," "I'm hopeless," or the like, you've got trouble.

Suppose someone who is important to us rejects us. We can **awfulize** (Ellis's term) the whole thing and say to ourselves, "This is just terrible. I'm no good, no good at all, and no one will ever like me again. I'm not worth anything. Doom. Doom." But we can change (behavioral) such internal sentences (cognitions) to read: "That's upsetting and disappointing. Maybe I'll have better luck next time." Sometimes this is very hard to do, but Ellis's ideas are well worth considering and trying to put into action for better mental health.

In therapy, Ellis and his followers assume people are straight thinkers and can be reached by reason to redo their internal sentences. Sometimes the therapy can get pretty rough, as the excerpt that follows shows, but the person knows the therapist cares, which offsets the roughness.

Client: I don't feel well today. I had a headache and was going to stay in bed.

Therapist: Well, why didn't you?

Client: Well, I . . . uh . . . well, I thought maybe I should come in because I was supposed to.

Therapist: That's not much of a motivation. Why are you coming here at all? Out of some obligation to me?

Client: No . . . I'm coming . . . well, you know, because . . .

Therapist: You tell me.

Client: Because . . . well, because I need some support. I need someone to talk to. I have some friends, but my parents . . . especially my father, don't *really* care about me. You know.

Therapist: So your father doesn't really care about you? So what? If you think that's the end of the world, then that's just stupid. Do you really believe that all fathers care about their children? I mean, just because it's written someplace that you should love your child doesn't mean everyone does. Don't you have friends? Didn't you just say that?

Client: Yes, but . . .

Therapist: No buts. If you've got friends, you should stop saying to yourself, "I'm not cared for, I'm not loved." That's just not true, is it? No! It's not true. If your father doesn't like you, he doesn't like you.

Albert Ellis explains:

Rational-emotive therapists do not believe a warm relationship between counselee and counselor is a necessary or a sufficient condition for effective personality change. They believe it is desirable for therapists to accept clients but criticize and point out the deficiencies of their *behavior.* RET therapists accept clients as fallible

In Focus

Major Psychological Approaches to Therapy

	Main Goal	How Goal Is Achieved	Main Technique(s)	Characteristic(s) of Therapist
Psychoanalysis	To reduce anxiety and guilt over unconscious impulses	Verbal processes	Free association Transference	Emotionally neutral
Humanistic Therapy	To help one see and fulfill one's potential	Verbal processes	Nondirective therapy	Nonjudgmental mirror—but demonstrates unconditional positive regard
Behavioral Therapy	To change one's unwanted or "abnormal" behaviors	Behavioral training	Systematic desensitization Aversive conditioning Token economy	Probably objective
Cognitive Behavioral Therapy	To unite behaviors and thoughts	Cognitive training	Rational-emotive therapy Analysis of internalized sentences	Analytical—perhaps rough, but caring

Which method would probably be most effective in treating depression? In eliminating phobias?

humans without necessarily giving *personal* warmth. . . . To keep clients from becoming and remaining unduly dependent, RET therapists often deliberately use hardheaded methods of convincing clients that they had . . . better resort to more self-discipline. (1984, p. 197)

Group Therapy

Group therapy has two purposes: (1) It is an attempt to treat more than one person at a time. This makes it cheaper for the person receiving treatment and more efficient for both that person and the therapist. (2) People can share their feelings and problems with one another and learn that they are not alone in their difficulties, a very important aspect of this method. Its usefulness is most noticeable in dealing with people suffering from grief or an addiction, not only because it offers companionship but also because if one or two can overcome the problem, the rest may be encouraged to follow suit.

Focus Question

• What are the purposes of group therapy?

group therapy therapy in which more than one person at a time is treated

551

The Group Method

In group therapy, people sit in a circle and talk to one another about problems under the guidance of a mental health worker. This type of therapy provides a more realistic world than individual therapy, in which there are only two people and very little of the give-and-take of interaction found outside the therapy. The group can provide support, go deeply into certain problems, or deal with social skills. As long as the therapist is skilled and knows how to handle the group, there is little danger to the group members. The odds that group members will be understanding and sympathetic with each other are very high.

Group therapists don't really follow a particular system, such as Freudian, behavioral, or cognitive. The therapy usually involves a mixture of a little bit of all of them. On occasion, a given therapist sometimes prefers one approach to another.

Encounter Therapy

You may have heard about **encounter groups.** In such a group, "normal" people are brought together to share their sensitivities and problems. The label *encounter* is used because people are forced to reveal inner conflicts and to share secret emotions and feelings. The purpose behind this is supposedly to expose people's psyches in order to make them more aware and stronger.

Give this therapy a wide berth. In regular group therapy with a professional, there are either implied or stated rules that prevent anyone from taking more psychological abuse than he or she can handle. In encounter groups, the goal is to expose oneself in order to get in touch with the "inner self." While some people survive and possibly even become better for the experience, the process is too dangerous for most to handle. Many wind up revealing inner feelings to others that they come to regret later. They feel exposed, betrayed, helpless, and too open to the world after it is all over and everyone has gone home.

▲ *Group hugs can be therapeutic.*

encounter groups therapy groups in which people are forced to share their inner conflicts and emotions

 Pause for Thought

1. How does behavioral therapy differ from other therapies?
2. What are the goals and techniques of the following: systematic desensitization, aversive conditioning, token economy?
3. What are some advantages of group therapy compared with other kinds of therapy? What is one problem with encounter therapy?

Critical Thinking

4. Describe a recent conflict or disappointment you've had, and explain how a cognitive behavioral therapist might view your situation. What might the therapist recommend?

Commonalities and Effectiveness of Therapy

Focus Questions
....
• What do the different therapies have in common?

• In what ways do people benefit from these therapies?

All the therapies we have discussed so far have certain factors in common that are important to note:

1. They are all designed to help the person resolve conflicts and problems, especially "Who am I, what do I want in life, and how do I get it?"

2. There is some direct relationship with a therapist for the purpose of trying to answer these questions.

3. There is the anticipation of some kind of positive change.

People benefit from these therapies in a number of ways, usually the following:

1. They start some kind of program to find better methods for handling problems.

2. They learn new rules for understanding and correcting their behavior.

3. They feel better for having developed a relationship with someone who wants to help.

4. They overcome present problems and are therefore better equipped to handle new ones that will arise later on.

You will sometimes hear that people with problems often get better all by themselves. While that is possible, it is unlikely. Certain factors work behind the scenes to help those who don't enter formal therapy. For example, those with a higher education tend to do better in the long run because this usually reduces financial and environmental stresses. Those who are married tend to get better because they have a spouse who can care for and support them emotionally. And those who have a job get better more quickly because they have something that provides income and meaning to life. It doesn't seem to be the passage of time itself that cures people but rather this "informal therapy."

We will discuss the effectiveness of psychotherapy shortly. Before doing that, though, we want to talk about the different types of research done in this area. Throughout this chapter and the preceding one as well, case studies frequently have been presented. Case studies are used a lot in the study of abnormal psychology because they provide detailed examples of various mental disorders and psychotherapies. Thus they can be very helpful in illustrating a problem or process. They are not helpful, though, in coming to any kind of general conclusion. Because they deal with only one instance of something, what is found in any one particular case study may or may not apply to other cases.

▼ *Having a job can be part of an "informal therapy" process.*

553

Thinking Critically about Psychology

Which Therapy is Best?—or, the "Dodo Bird Effect"

In the 1950s, a psychologist investigated the usefulness of psychotherapy and concluded that it was no more effective than having your name placed on a waiting list to see a therapist at some future date (Eysenck, 1952). His results jolted the psychological community and stimulated a tremendous amount of additional research. Since that time, numerous studies of psychotherapy have been done, and we are happy to report that these conclusions no longer hold true. Study after study has found that psychotherapy does indeed work, and the vast majority of clients are helped with their problems to a significant degree (Wampold, et al., 1997; Jacobson & Christensen, 1996; Barlow, 1996; VandenBos, 1996; Seligman, 1995). The question we want to examine more closely is whether a particular kind of problem should be dealt with by a particular kind of psychotherapy. For instance, is behavioral therapy more effective for anxiety-related problems than person-centered therapy is?

What specifically is being claimed or stated? Specific therapeutic approaches are particularly effective with specific types of problems.

What is the objective evidence for and against this claim? Some studies have found that behavioral therapy works better with phobias, smoking, and overeating and that cognitive therapy works best for depression (Matarazzo, 1985; Simons, 1984). Other research suggests that person-centered therapy and behavioral approaches are most helpful with anxiety (Phillips & Bierman, 1981). Finally, there is the suggestion that psychoanalytic or psychodynamic therapies in general are not terribly useful—that they have a below-average success rate (Garfield, 1981; Kernberg et al., 1972). But not all research on psychoanalysis has agreed with this finding (Brody, 1962).

The most recent and most complete analyses of studies done on various kinds of psychotherapy have found, over and over again, that the specific approach taken is not generally relevant to how successful the therapy is. In other words, there are no real differences in success rates among the different kinds of psychotherapy. With the possible exception of psychotic disorders, this holds true for all types of problems (Wampold et al., 1997; Barlow, 1996; Jacobson & Christensen, 1996; Seligman, 1996, 1995). We even have a term to describe this finding—the *Dodo bird effect*. Yes, it is a strange term. It comes from a story in *Alice in Wonderland,* where a silly race was run that had no starting point and no end point. The Dodo bird was the judge,

▲ *This Dodo bird is a pigment of the artist's imagination.*

and he concluded that everybody in the race had won and should have a prize. Thus, the conclusion is that in regard to psychotherapy, every approach is successful.

Where medications are involved, the picture is a little fuzzier. Certain drugs can be beneficial for certain problems. For instance, antidepressants are quite useful in cases of depression. However, it has been noted that psychotherapy provides longer-lasting improvement and is better at preventing a recurrence of the problem. Even with serious problems like bipolar disorders and schizophrenia, adding family therapy to drug treatment increases the level of improvement and helps prevent relapses (Barlow, 1996; Hollon, 1996).

A related issue is whether all professions that treat psychological disorders are equally effective. It has been found that psychologists, psychiatrists, and social workers have the same overall success rates. Marriage counselors, however, have a lower rate. Also, family doctors and ministers are not very effective in dealing with psychological problems (Barlow, 1996; Jacobson & Christensen, 1996; Seligman, 1996, 1995).

What other interpretations might be made instead? If the type of therapy doesn't, in general, determine the likelihood of success, then what does make a difference? Feeling comfortable with and trusting the therapist carry a lot of weight in determining how effective the therapy is. Psychotherapists today have broad training and often employ a variety of techniques. And as we have already noted, all psychological therapies have certain factors in common. Occasionally, studies do find that one approach is somewhat better than others in dealing with certain problems, but overall these differences tend to wash out. Finding a therapist one can relate to and work with is more important than trying to find a particular approach designed to treat a particular type of problem.

What are the most logical conclusions to draw? Generally speaking, the original claim does not hold up. The only partial exception to this conclusion involves disorders where medication is also helpful, such as depression, bipolar disorder, and schizophrenia.

See if **COOL** works for you....

Claim?

Objective evidence for and against claim?

Other interpretations?

Logical conclusions?

Applying Critical Thinking Skills

While specific therapies may not be particularly effective for specific types of problems, people who seek therapy may have preferences. If you were depressed and decided to seek therapy, which method of therapy would you prefer?

To obtain information from many people, instead of just one, surveys are often taken. For example, in trying to determine whether psychotherapy is effective, we might conduct a survey of people who have been in therapy and have agreed to answer our questions. This approach would give us information from many sources, but it also has its problems. The major one, as far as this subject matter goes, is that it relies completely on what the clients think about their therapy.

In other words, the question that has not yet been answered is whether real change has occurred or the client simply thinks that change has occurred. To answer that question, we need some outside measure of change. One possibility would be to ask friends and family members if things are actually different. Another might be to see if job performance or grades have improved. Whatever measures of therapeutic change we use, we need something to compare them with. Why? Perhaps time alone is responsible for any change we have found. In other words, maybe just by waiting it out positive things happen all by themselves. So, we need to measure change in another group of people—people who have not been in therapy at all. To keep things equal between the groups, it would be even better if this group of people had similar problems as well. One way to do this is to compare people who are on a waiting list for therapy with people who have already been accepted. If those who had therapy experience greater change than those who did not, then we can conclude that the therapy was in fact responsible.

All of these approaches have been used in researching the effectiveness of psychotherapy—each has provided essentially the same results.

Biomedical Therapies

So far we have discussed several psychological approaches to helping people with their problems. Another major category of treatment relies not on talking to someone or attempting to change one's behavior patterns but on actual physical intervention in the brain itself. This is the biomedical approach, and it is handled only by psychiatrists. There are three basic types of biomedical therapy: drug therapy, electroconvulsive therapy, and psychosurgery.

Focus Questions

• Are drug therapies effective?

• Why would someone choose to receive electroconvulsive therapy?

Drug Therapy

Drug therapy involves the use of drugs to relieve psychological symptoms. The main ones used are antianxiety drugs, antidepressants, and antipsychotics. The drugs alter the firing of nerve cells in the brain or the amounts of certain neurotransmitter substances available (Hollon, 1996; Tosteson, 1981). Thus, a psychiatrist dealing with a depressed person would choose a drug that increases the level of brain firing or the neurotransmitters responsible for a feeling of well-being. With someone very nervous and anxious whose nerve cells are already firing too rapidly, an antianxiety drug or tranquilizer would be appropriate. A different type of drug is used to calm people suffering from the manic episodes found in bipolar disorder.

Given in moderation and with careful supervision, these drugs can be quite useful in lessening anxiety or depression and reducing psychotic symptoms. Many patients are able to function in life after taking the drugs when that was not the case before. Thus, there is no question about their usefulness. However, today there is considerable concern about relying too heavily on drugs and not heavily enough on psychotherapy.

Part of the problem is that because drugs offer fairly rapid relief of symptoms and don't require much time from a professional, health care providers find them much less costly than psychotherapy. Another part of the problem is that our society as a whole seems to prefer a "quick fix" to the prospect of having to work hard at making changes. However, psychotherapy works better over a longer time with many problems and prevents relapses better, especially for things like anxiety and depression (Barlow, 1996; Newman & Tejeda, 1996).

An additional problem is that these drugs don't work for everyone. And although the majority of drugs currently used do reduce a person's symptoms, there is no drug that makes the person "well." Furthermore, none of the drugs is without its side effects, sometimes serious ones.

Yet another problem is that, in too many cases of schizophrenia, the patients are helped enough to be able to leave the hospital but not enough that they are able to function on their own. Once outside, they often stop taking their medication, and their symptoms come back. Consequently, the streets of every major city are populated by homeless and lost schizophrenics who don't know what to do, where to go, or how to get the help they need.

Finally, the dosage given is often too high. Some workers in the field are concerned that at times hospitalized patients are being "helped" only by being made semiconscious. In some hospitals, for instance, the daily dosage of a tranquilizer for psychotics is the same one used by veterinarians to subdue a 400-pound lion. It is no wonder that these patients complain of "empty feelings" in their lives (Breggin, 1983).

▼ *This patient is being prepared for electroconvulsive therapy (ECT).*

Electroconvulsive Therapy

In **electroconvulsive therapy (ECT),** a shock is deliberately sent through the patient's brain to produce convulsions. The procedure is not painful, but it certainly is quite terrifying to many patients. The treatment is very controversial. A major objection to it is that no one knows what it does, why it works when it does, and whether the risks involved are worth it (Weiner, 1984; Scovern & Kilmann, 1980).

The actual physical changes that occur after ECT are best summed up as confusion and loss of memory, which disappear after a few hours. With continued shock treatments,

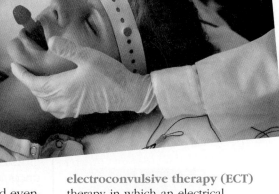

electroconvulsive therapy (ECT) therapy in which an electrical shock is sent through the brain to try to reduce symptoms of mental disturbance

however, the memory loss persists for longer and longer periods, and eventually ECT can result in brain damage (Freeman, 1985; Squire, 1985; Breggin, 1984).

What also makes the treatment worrisome is the fact that it is so primitive. It resembles a treatment used in the very early days of mental hospitals around Pinel's era, called the "snake pit." Patients who were depressed or behaving strangely were thrown in a pit that contained dozens of nonpoisonous snakes. Patients were left there until they "quit acting strangely." But from the previous chapter, you may remember that all psychotic patients have periods when the symptoms disappear. The hospital personnel were convinced that these patients were getting better as a result of the "treatment."

There are two final things to say about ECT that are important. First of all, it will lift some people out of a deep, suicidal depression, so there is some justification for using it in such cases. Second, it doesn't work with any category of mental disturbance other than depression and should not be administered to people who fall into those other categories. For example, it makes schizophrenics worse, probably convincing some of them that their false beliefs about someone trying to hurt them are true.

In a way, it may seem that we are being too harsh on this treatment. But it's difficult to overlook the negative factors involved. There is a real stigma attached to any person getting electroshock treatment. People think something really horrible is wrong with them. And most patients fear it. Since it *is* useful with some cases of *severe* depression, one could hardly fault its use in many of those cases. Nonetheless, the evidence is pretty clear that it does little good and sometimes harm with cases other than severe depression.

Psychosurgery

Any technique that involves entering the brain to alter the person's psychological state is called **psychosurgery.** The most common operation involves destruction of part of the front portion of the patient's brain, just behind the forehead. This part, the *prefrontal area,* contains nerve connections that control what we call "personality," especially our complex emotional responses. Usually a laser or probe is aimed at this portion, and enough tissue is damaged to try to slow the patient down.

Unfortunately, brain tissue never restores itself, so the effects are permanent. Another problem: If the wrong area is hit, the patient can get much *more* violent and unmanageable. This is a treatment that is very hard to justify. Fortunately, it is almost never done today. When it is, the grounds are that the patient is uncontrollable otherwise. This justification is hard to believe, given our arsenal of tranquilizing drugs.

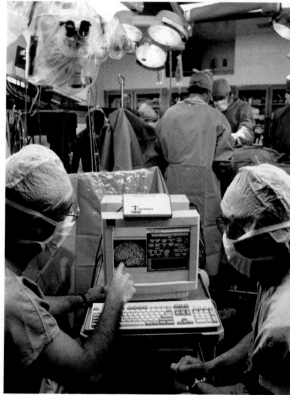

▶ *Psychosurgery is a drastic and nonreversible procedure.*

psychosurgery surgery that destroys part of the brain to make the patient calmer, freer of symptoms

Controversy: Mental Illness

As discussed in the previous chapter, the evidence mounts that psychotics have a physical or chemical problem. They probably could, in the broad sense, be said to have an "illness," a term that implies a physical defect. But psychotics are a minority among those with mental problems.

For the rest of the people who have serious problems, the issue is whether they should be listed as having a mental *illness*. Once people have an illness, they are supposed to be either "cured" or removed from society—a distressing idea. It has recently been suggested that even the term *mental disorder* should be applied with care (Wakefield, 1992).

In any case, if you say someone has a "disease," you are labeling him or her forever. Is that justified? What about the Uncle Harrys and Aunt Marthas who spend a lot of their time in the attic chatting with imaginary friends? Are they really hurting anyone? Should they be removed from society just because they are a little quirky?

One psychiatrist has suggested that rather than "disease" or "illness," we should say a person has "problems in living" (Szasz, 1961). Look what a difference just a change in wording would make, and decide for yourself: A man you slightly know is behaving strangely and seems distracted, so you ask a mutual friend what's wrong with him. Answer: "He has some problems at work. His marriage is in trouble. It's all getting to him." Now, here's the second scenario: "Charlie has a mental illness and had to be hospitalized."

Both describe the same person. Is there any difference in how you would respond to Charlie the next time you saw him, depending on which version you got?

 ## Pause for Thought

1. Describe several common elements of therapy.
2. Explain whether specific types of therapies are particularly effective in treating specific kinds of disorders.
3. What are some uses and some possible dangers of biomedical therapies?

Critical Thinking
....

4. Assume you have a relative who suffers from major depression and who is considering ECT. What would you advise? Why?

APPLYING
Psychology to Life

Seeking Professional Help

Reading about emotional problems in this chapter and the preceding one, you may have decided you have a serious problem. You could be right. But chances are excellent that you do *not* have a serious mental disturbance or illness. There is an enormous difference! A serious mental disturbance involves seeing things that are not there, believing things that never have happened, and having extremely confused thought processes. If these applied to you, chances are close to zero that you would even be reading this.

Everyone Has Problems

As mentioned several times, everybody has problems. Quite a number of people cross the line from having day-to-day problems to being involved with one that is so disruptive that it makes it hard to function. If this is true of you, it still does not mean that you have a serious mental disturbance. It means that someone will have to help you get back on track. The odds of your doing it on your own are remote because the problem gets distorted when it fills up so much of your time and thinking. You need someone objective.

Only a handful of counselors or psychologists today are very interested in trying to uncover deep dark secrets. Most of them are interested in rapid, clear results. They want to work with you to get to the heart of the problem and get you over it, not delve into every nook and cranny of your personal life. Most therapies today are measured in months, not years, to completion.

Finding a Therapist

One of the most important ingredients in getting yourself repaired, so to speak, is some degree of confidence in the therapist. In finding a therapist, you might start with a school counselor.

School counselors are like people in every other profession. There are good ones and bad ones. You can get a feel for what one is like by discussing other areas, such as occupational choice, with him or her to see if you think he or she might be the kind of person who can help you deal with more personal issues. Go to your school counselor if you feel good about doing so. And don't base your decision on

▲ *It's important to find the right therapist for you—one you can easily work with.*

bizarre rumors that crop up among students. Sort out what seems to be real from fiction.

From the outset, you can count on the fact that for a counselor or a psychologist, the problem you have is not something new and startling. Lots of other people have had it—whatever it is. If you decide to go to the counselor, be certain to ask him or her what the rules are about confidentiality. Counselors will be happy to tell you. The rules vary, and you don't want to get yourself into a position in which your problems become part of a school record.

If you decide to go to an outside psychologist, you will need your parents' cooperation and help in most states—but not always. It is likely that your parents will be somewhat upset if you approach them about it. But that is not because you are so weird. It's because they endlessly worry that somehow they haven't done right by you. It's almost inevitable that they have done the best they can and that they have little to do with what is bothering you. When you talk to them about the problem, be direct, but don't exhaust them with details so they think you are worse off than you are.

With or without parents, one of the best sources for finding help is a hot line, such as a suicide prevention hot line or runaway hot line. You don't have to have that particular problem to

call. All these organizations have endless sources of help available in almost any problem area. Another place to look is your local mental health association.

Rights and Protections

You should be aware that psychotherapy clients are protected by the law in several

▲ *If you think you need help, don't hesitate to get it.*

ways. For example, professional psychotherapists are bound by their code of ethics to provide competent treatment to their clients. If you believe you are not receiving proper care, you may contact the therapist's professional organization or licensing body and make a complaint.

Professional psychotherapists are also obligated to keep what is discussed in therapy confidential. They cannot discuss a case with the client's parents, for instance, unless the client gives permission. As was true for school counselors, however, it is also true here that confidentiality is not absolute. In other words, there are limits to confidentiality.

For instance, if a therapist has good reason to believe that a client is about to commit a serious violent crime or already has done so, that therapist must inform the authorities. And in some cases, the courts may order a therapist to turn over therapy notes. If you are concerned about this, ask the therapist for specific limitations on confidentiality. One last thing: Just as you have the right to competent treatment, you also have the right to refuse treatment. That is, if your therapist wants you to have ECT, for example, you have the right to say no.

Two things to trust us about: (1) You will find that therapy, when conducted properly, is very close to just sitting down and talking with a friend. Nothing strange or really different goes on. (2) *Don't* stick with a therapist you are not comfortable with. If you do, you will wind up fighting two battles—first, your problem, and second, your negative feelings about the therapist. Change therapists. But be aware that if you keep wanting to change, your expectations are probably too high.

Summary

1. A psychologist has an advanced degree in psychological principles and methods. A psychiatrist is a medical doctor who also has training in mental disorders. *Psychotherapist* is a broad term applied to almost any professional working with psychological problems.

2. Psychoanalysis is based on a theory that assumes unconscious animal impulses are seeking expression. Treatment focuses on free association and transference to reveal the inner forces and to reduce their strength and the anxiety they cause.

3. Humanistic therapy centers on the belief that the person is basically good. The therapist mirrors the thoughts of the person to bring out the potential that lies inside.

4. Behavioral therapy tries to change people's behavior or actions. Three methods used are systematic desensitization, aversive conditioning, and the token economy.

5. Rational-emotive therapy, a type of cognitive behavioral therapy, tries to reorient internal sentences so the individual has better control over his or her emotions.

6. Group therapy benefits the people receiving treatment because it is closer to real-life relationships than one-on-one therapy. This treatment is also cheaper because more than one person is handled at a time.

7. No single therapy seems to be the "best." People benefit most from working with a therapist they can trust. Therapy in general is effective.

8. Drugs in reasonable doses seem beneficial to many, but there are dangers. Electroconvulsive therapy is controversial but seems to help some people who are severely depressed. Psychosurgery is a highly questionable method involving brain destruction in an attempt to make the patient more manageable.

Vocabulary

counseling psychologists
clinical psychologists
psychiatrists
psychiatric social workers
psychiatric nurses
psychotherapies
psychoanalysis
free association
transference

humanistic therapies
person-centered therapy
nondirective therapy
unconditional positive regard
behavioral therapy
systematic desensitization
aversive conditioning
token economy
cognitive behavioral therapy

rational-emotive therapy (RET)
irrational ideas
internalized sentences
awfulize
group therapy
encounter groups
electroconvulsive therapy
  (ECT)
psychosurgery

Review Questions

Matching

On a sheet of paper, match the terms in the second list with the statements in the first list.

1. Client's thought processes are analyzed.
2. The therapist reflects what the client is saying.
3. Patient transfers emotional conflicts onto therapist.
4. Disorders are the result of learned responses.

   a. behavioral therapy
   b. humanistic therapy
   c. psychoanalysis
   d. cognitive behavioral therapy

True/False

On a sheet of paper, answer each statement true or false. If false, rewrite to make true.

5. Psychoanalysis tends to become a very expensive method of treatment.
6. In group therapy, "normal" people get together to share feelings without the guidance of a mental health worker.
7. The goal of most encounter groups is to train group members to become therapists themselves.
8. Psychologists often use drug therapy to treat disorders.
9. One or two treatments of electroconvulsive therapy will tend to cause long-lasting memory loss.
10. One reason why electroconvulsive therapy is still used today is that it seems to work well on deeply depressed individuals.
11. Psychosurgery is sometimes used on patients who are difficult to control.

Discussion Questions

1. If you decided to see a therapist, what qualities would you want the therapist to have? Think about your answer in terms of the types of therapists described in this chapter. Which kind of therapist best matches your requirements?

2. Therapy often involves a lot of hard work on the part of the person receiving it. If you had to decide between this hard work and medication, with its potential side effects, which would you probably choose, and why?

3. Describe a person, in your past or present, who consistently has demonstrated unconditional positive regard toward you. What effect, if any, did (or does) this have on you? Explain.

4. Suppose your principal wants to incorporate a token economy system at your school. Describe several ways to do this. Be specific. Do you think adopting your suggestions would realistically have any effect on students' behaviors? Explain.

5. The chapter describes how aversive conditioning can be used to curb alcoholism. Can you think of any other uses for aversive conditioning?

6. Imagine that someone in your family has been severely depressed for several months, that he or she has been completely listless and uncommunicative. All kinds of treatments have been ineffective. The last resort seems to be ECT; however, the hospital needs your approval to administer it. Do you give your approval? Why or why not? Explain.

Activities and Projects

1. On a sheet of paper, write down the first 10 things that come to mind when you think of a mental hospital. Your list should be somewhat detailed—not just single words and phrases. Then contact a mental health hospital and interview someone there, focusing on the accuracy or inaccuracy of the items on your list. Ask other questions about the hospital as well. (Prepare a list of questions beforehand.) Write a report on the interview.

2. Contact someone who conducts therapy on a more or less daily basis and interview this person. Possible questions:

   What are the most common kinds of problems that you treat? Would your answer to the preceding question have been the same five or ten years ago? What are the typical kinds of treatments and therapies that you use? What is the average length of treatment time for your clients? What are your feelings about drug therapy? Do you ever get tired of listening to other people's problems?

   Write a report on your interview, and include your specific reactions.

3. You will need to do this next project with a classmate. Choose a hypothetical problem on which you want to focus: depression over the breakup of a relationship, anxiety over a weight problem, frustration with parents, or the like. Second, select three of the four main types of therapists presented in the chapter and brainstorm how each would deal with the problem. You might refer back to Chapter 14 on personality theories for more insight. Next, write a dialogue between a person receiving therapy and one type of therapist. Then write dialogues for the other two types of therapists. Try to make each dialogue about two or three minutes long. Finally, rehearse your dialogues. One of you will be the therapist, the other will be the client. Arrange with your teacher a time when you can present the dialogues in class. *Note:* Your dialogues do not have to be entirely serious—have some fun with them—but they should be informative and accurate. Also, as we mentioned, be sure the problem you choose is *hypothetical*. A classroom is not the ideal setting in which to discuss personal problems.

4. You are probably familiar with therapists who conduct therapy on television or on the radio. As with anything, some of these therapists seem qualified and helpful while others should seek therapy themselves. Regardless of the therapists' qualifications, this kind of "fast-food" therapy is a natural target for parody. We want you and a classmate to prepare a five- to six-minute skit in which one of you will be a new TV or radio therapist and the other a person seeking the therapist's advice. Again, arrange a time when you can present the skit in class. Definitely have fun with this one!

5. In the next couple of days, pay special attention to the problems of two of your close friends. *Friend* can be broadly defined: family member, boyfriend or girlfriend, and so on. What you will be looking for is a time when your friends seem to feel a need to talk about a problem. The problems can range from frustration over studying for a test to irritation over serious family problems. If in the next couple of days your friends don't seem to have any problems in mind, perhaps you can prompt them with a simple question about a past problem. If, on the other hand, you encounter five or six friends with problems, pick the two with the most serious ones.

As your friends (one at a time) begin to discuss their problems, we want you to try to act as a mirror and simply rephrase your friends' own feelings and thoughts. In other words, you will be using Rogers's nondirective technique. Reread the sample dialogue from the chapter to get an idea of how to do this. Some pointers to keep in mind: (1) Don't give *any* advice. (2) Simply put their words into your words. (3) Be completely nonjudgmental—show unconditional positive regard. This entire experience may seem like a game at first, like you are simply repeating or mimicking what your friends say. But if you are sincerely concerned with your friends' problems, you will probably find that the experience is worthwhile.

Once you've tried this on two friends, write a report describing your reactions. Include how you felt at the time, whether you thought the experience was worthwhile and effective, whether you would use the technique again—for real, not just for an assignment. Be specific about your reactions, but do NOT disclose the content of your conversations—which should remain confidential.

6. We want you to practice identifying negative internalized sentences and supplying more rational responses. You can work with the two following situations:

Situation A: You have to give a speech tomorrow in front of your entire psychology class.

Situation B: You decide you are going to ask someone out for a date.

First, write down these situations on two separate sheets of paper. For each one, write down 10 possible negative internalized sentences, leaving plenty of room after each sentence. For example: "No one will like my speech; everyone will think I'm stupid." Next, after each sentence, write down a more rational response. For example, after the sentence above, you might write: "Even if the speech as a whole is not that good, there will be parts of it that will be OK—and there will be *some* people who will recognize this. People in class know how difficult it is to give a speech." Notice that the rational response is not just a single sentence: You will need to explain yourself. So you will be writing a total of 20 sentences with rational responses after each. This is typical of the approach cognitive behavior therapists might use.

As mentioned, this whole exercise is just practice. If you'd rather use two real situations from your own life, go ahead. It will probably make the activity much more meaningful. Your answers will not be read aloud in class.

Once you complete your two lists and the rational responses, write down your reactions to the exercise. How did you feel as you wrote the sentences and responses? Was it difficult? If you were to choose real situations, and if you had more practice, do you think this kind of exercise would be helpful? Why or why not? Explain.

Unit 7

Sociocultural
Influences
and Self

CHAPTER 19

This chapter focuses
on the social and
cultural factors that
guide our feelings and
actions toward one another.
We look at the external
influences that interact with
an individual's personality to
create beliefs about and
actions toward other people.

Sociocultural Influences and Relationships

Hidden Influences in Behavior

Focus Question

....

- How do we form our opinions of other people?

We all do things that at times surprise even us. The surprise is not necessarily pleasant, especially when we discover things about ourselves that we don't like. For example, say that you are walking down the sidewalk on a busy street. A person falls down in front of you moaning, rolling up into a ball. Would you stop and help? You claim you would. But is that true?

Since we don't know you personally, we can't say you won't, but statistically, in real life, the odds are staggering that you will walk on by. Later we will discuss why this happens so often. But first let's look at some of the details about how people think in their relationships with others and how they view the actions of others.

Attribution Theory

Much social interaction is colored by our own psychological makeup. A major factor in how we interpret the behavior of others is covered by **attribution** (at-trih-BYOO-shun) **theory,** which concerns the process by which we form opinions about another. Attribution theory can be divided into three parts, each of which interacts with the others. The first consists of **antecedents,** a word that means "things that come before"—that is, we rely on information, beliefs, and motivations we already have in forming our opinions. The next part is the actual **attribution,** which refers to the causes that we come up with to explain why people do what they do. In other words, we *attribute* (give) reasons to them for their actions. The final part involves **consequences,** such as our behavior (what we do about the situation), our emotional responses, and our expectations (what we think will happen in the future).

Here is an example of what we are talking about: You have an acquaintance named Maria, a classmate you know casually. The two of you speak when you meet at school. You are going home at 4:00 on a Tuesday afternoon, and you see Maria coming down the sidewalk. As usual, you say, "Hi." *Not* as usual, however, she replies, "Go away!" and stalks off.

Maria is usually a friendly, pleasant person and has always seemed to like you. You, in turn, value knowing her. Those beliefs are part of the *antecedents* (what existed before you were rejected). You had already formed a concept of what Maria was like, and now you must try to explain her behavior within this framework.

There are two possibilities. Either something about the situation caused her to act this way, or something personal is involved. Perhaps something happens on Tuesday afternoons that

attribution theory theory that describes how people explain the causes of behavior. The process includes antecedents, attribution, and consequences.

antecedents in attribution theory, information and beliefs a person already has about another

attribution in attribution theory, the act of making judgments about the causes for another's behavior

consequences in attribution theory, the emotional responses, behavior, and expectations that result from the attribution

◀ *When things don't go as expected, we can blame either the person or the situation.*

In Focus

Attribution Theory

Situation: Ann sees her boyfriend talking with her best friend.

Assume that you know Ann is a jealous person. With this antecedent in mind, what is *your* attribution for her thoughts above?

causes Maria to behave that way. Because you want to find out what is going on, you keep trying. So the following day you say "Hi" to her again, and this time she says "Hi" back. The same thing happens the next day, and the next, and so on. The following Tuesday, however, at 4:00, when you say "Hi," she says "Go away!" and stalks off.

Now you have additional information, characteristics that can be noted and that are consistent. Only on Tuesday does she act this way. On further investigation, you find that Maria has a standing appointment with the dentist at 4:30 on that day, is having painful procedures done, and hates going. Now you can make an *attribution*. That is, you can make up a cause for her weird behavior. You perceive it as being rooted in the fact that she has to go to the dentist.

Once an attribution is made, it leads to *consequences*. You can now explain Maria's behavior and not take it personally. If the antecedents had been different—if you had viewed her as an unpredictable, explosive person, for instance—you might have attributed her actions to instability, not bothered to investigate, and avoided her in the future.

Understanding the causes of events, particularly social events, helps to provide us with our sense of reality. It plays a crucial part in making our day-to-day world predictable and understandable (Weary, 1997). This is especially true when a social event has some personal impact, as in the case of Maria's behavior (Schlenker et al., 1994).

Thus, we are always seeking an explanation for why something happens, even if we unknowingly come to a false conclusion. Using such a system can lead us to accept or reject others. For instance, if a Republican publicly praises another Republican, most people pay no attention to what is said, since both politicians belong to the same political party and since politicians are not very high on people's lists of most trusted people. But if we hear a Democrat praising a Republican, we are much more likely to attribute honesty to that person and to tend to believe in him or her, even though that might not be sensible.

Now that you grasp attribution, note that its principles are used all the time. We use it to explain the behavior of our friends, our families, and people we work with. For groups we don't like, we attribute all kinds of strange things to group members—they don't bathe, they perform strange rituals—and then look for clues that might support our beliefs. With groups we like, such as the ones we belong to, we see the members as having all kinds of positive characteristics, some of which don't really exist.

Attributions can be quite distorted. When it was discovered that the earth was round, many famous people of the time believed that there was a whole race of creatures who lived "upside down" on the opposite side of the earth. They were called *Antipodes*. *Anti* means "opposite," and *podes* is another word for "feet." These Antipode people had feet growing in the opposite direction, or upside down. They lived at the bottom of the earth where trees grew upside down and rain fell upward. They were not creatures at all like the rest of us.

Some people did object to this strange idea, but they tried to fight it by claiming that the earth was a *cube* (Boorstin, 1983). That wasn't much of a solution, because using the logic of the day, you would then have some people who grew sideways as well as some who grew upside down!

Attributions are a subtle part of any relationship. In the very early stages, however, the critical factor in how people get together is how they view one another emotionally. Hence, in the next section, we review the factors involved in what seems to attract one person to another.

 ## Pause for Thought

1. Describe the process we go through when we form opinions about others, according to attribution theory.
2. What kinds of factors influence liking and loving?

Critical Thinking

3. Describe a situation in which a person's attributions would affect interpersonal attraction.

Focus Question
....
• What attracts one person to another?

Interpersonal Attraction

One of the more difficult subjects to handle scientifically is "love." Equally hard is trying to tell the exact differences between "like" and "love." We know what we feel, but we cannot define it very well. So we report here the valiant attempts of scientists to understand these feelings.

We can start with that overwhelming feeling we all have had at one time or another, "falling madly in love." There is no feeling quite like it. It can consume us one minute, make us feel wonderful the next, and leave us miserable and lost the minute after that. The most obvious characteristics of this state are the physical responses: rapid heartbeat, stomach contractions, and general body chaos.

Ironically, these "symptoms" are identical to those of fear and anxiety. The major difference is that the behaviors have become associated with someone we find physically attractive. When this association occurs, we know it isn't "fear" but "love." So we start off with a physical base, add emotional responses, and then top it all off by getting involved psychologically with the person.

Importance of Associations

We know that there is a considerable amount of high-level emotional association going on in this state, which is what makes it so special. For example, most people in love have a special song that "belongs" to them. They heard the song during a special moment together. Now it is associated with them and the emotions they felt the first time they heard it. Thus, each time they hear the song again, the emotions recur.

Often, people in love also have special places they have gone. Like the song, these places and the things connected with them are associated with this high level of emotional arousal. As a result, more and more associations are connected to the core response the couple had at the beginning. The more connections, the more associations and the stronger the feeling. What starts off as a physical feeling takes on broad emotional and mental associations.

Ingredients in Liking and Loving

Creatures don't fall in love with just anyone. Something special occurs. Many species of birds pick a specific mate for life. The wolf is quite selective in choosing a mate, and the couple tends to stay together as a unit with the "family." A male peacock spreads out its beautiful plumage to attract a female. Some females like what a particular male shows; others don't and prefer a different male. Finally, as is also true for humans, the female peacock is far more selective than the male.

Among people, how do these relationships begin? Often, the beginning involves flirting—something social psychologists refer to as "courtship signaling." We tend to think of males as the ones who usually start a conversation; and on the surface, this appears to be the case. However, when a male approaches a female, he generally does so *after* she has given him some kind of signal. In fact, some research indicates that men are more likely to approach a woman who has flirted with them than a more attractive woman who has not (Moore, 1995; Moore & Butler, 1989).

Much of what we consider to be flirting is nonverbal—actions such as glancing at the person, smiling, and nodding, for instance. A woman also gives less direct or obvious signals, such as tossing her head, flipping or smoothing her hair, primping, and playing with objects, such as keys or rings. Compared with adult women, adolescent girls tend to give somewhat exaggerated signals and often imitate the actions of the dominant girl in their group. In addition, adolescents engage in more playful flirting—things like pinching, tickling, and sticking out their tongues at someone (Moore, 1995).

Physical attractiveness is a large factor in interpersonal attraction when people first meet and get to know one another. At that point, there is little else on which to judge someone. The pitfall here is that we tend to see more attractive people in a generally more positive light—to see them as competent, confident, and so forth. In fact, just from appearance, we attribute all kinds of good things to those who are more in line with society's expectations of attractiveness. In this regard, females are far more discriminating than males; that is, they are more likely to view the whole person rather than just the body or hairstyle.

▲ *Physical attraction may get a relationship started, but other factors keep it going.*

People who are less attractive by society's standards are at a disadvantage—but only in the beginning. There is a saying that "beauty is in the eye of the beholder." Scientifically, this saying seems to be true. Studies show that in general people tend to match up with others who are similar to them in attractiveness (Cash & Janda, 1984). In any case, over time, personalities become more important to others than looks. While physical looks can often get a person a first date, whether or not there will be a second one usually relies heavily on personality. So there is at least some hope for most of us.

Both liking and loving are based on *familiarity*. In other words, the more we see specific people, the more we like them (if there is something to them), since we tend to find the familiar less threatening. This principle holds true as long as the interactions are spaced over time. There is a lesson here: In beginning relationships as well as in long-standing ones, we can exhaust the other person no matter how wonderful we are. Too much closeness too fast often reduces attractiveness. It is better to maintain *some* distance at first so that there is still psychological territory for the other person to explore and be fascinated by.

Revealing oneself to the other person has its place, time, and limits. While love seems to grow with mutual understanding and sharing of intimate feelings, endless exposure of the self turns the other person off, especially if it comes early in the relationship and involves ongoing baring of the soul. Believe it or not, our problems, shared in excess, are rather boring to others. Limited sharing, though, can deepen a relationship. At the very least, the partner needs a chance to talk about *some* of his or her problems.

Love can be a fragile mixture of ingredients.

Focus Questions

• How does the brain influence aggressive behavior?

• How do the culture and society influence aggressive behavior?

You will hear that those with opposite interests are best suited for a long-lasting relationship, but there is no evidence to support this claim. Hundreds of studies have explored this area, and most conclude that those who stay together the longest are more alike than they are different. Variation is interesting, but major differences are threatening.

While it is probably not applicable to your life at present, this is a good place to mention a few tips from seasoned marriage counselors. These ideas are too important to ignore:

1. Marrying someone with the intention of helping him or her get over a drug or alcohol problem almost never works. Things inevitably get worse.

2. A little jealousy goes a long way. Most experts agree that someone who is very, very jealous will make daily life miserable, and the odds against getting rid of this problem are staggeringly high.

3. Any kind of violence in a relationship is there to stay. The odds that the victim will be able to avoid it are so low that the time to end the relationship seems to be immediately, before it gets a foothold.

4. Love in the best of circumstances is a *very* fragile mixture of self-esteem and self-importance, of both giving and taking, and of trying to keep a decent balance between the two (Davis, 1985).

Aggression and Violence

War and violence are as old as human records. Fossil remains from the Neanderthals (100,000 years ago) show wooden weapons and spear tips embedded in human bone. As a result of such findings, many people claim that aggression appears naturally among humans, just as it does among animals of other kinds. However, virtually all animal species can and do control their aggressive impulses. Such control is absolutely necessary for survival.

At the human level, there are societies in which daily activities center on chances to cheat and be as cutthroat as possible toward one another. Other societies exist in which violence is absent or very rare, and people live in basic harmony.

Most of the evidence suggests that humans began as hunter-gatherers. When hunter-gatherers wandered in the forests, where food was usually available, violence would be at a minimum. Similar groups still exist in remote forest lands and show little aggression. This finding leads some to think that aggression may have arisen from some natural disaster that stripped the forest bare and left people fighting for food.

Whether we are supposed to be carnivores (meat eaters) or not is still argued. The evidence is ambiguous. Our intestinal systems are long, winding mazes, the kind that are normally found in creatures that require a lengthy digestion process for vegetation, as opposed to the relatively short and direct intestine of a meat eater such as a dog.

Be all that as it may, though, violence does indeed erupt all around us. Since most of us have more than enough to eat, we have to assume that at least part of such behavior is the result of imitation or social learning.

One last comment: The recent upsurge of violence in schools has created a sense of urgency about dealing more effectively with this issue. The truth, however, is that at present we simply do not have enough reliable information to come up with any clear solutions. So we will cover what we do know about aggression in general terms. Perhaps in the future better explanations will be available.

Influence of the Brain

With our elaborate brains, we produce all kinds of variations on situations. We can be either peaceful or violent, depending on how we *interpret* situations. For instance, in one study, people leaving a movie that had aggressive content who were "accidentally" pushed (by experimenters) were more likely to get aggressive than those who had just seen a peaceful movie. The people were stirred up, but they didn't know that it was from the movie. Hence, they attributed their arousal (remember attribution?) to the person who had jostled them (Rule & Nesdale, 1976). In fact, just having been exposed to the word *hostile* makes people more likely to interpret someone else's behavior as hostile when the behavior is ambiguous, or could be something else (Basic Behavioral Task Force, 1996b).

Thus, the current hypothesis for aggression focuses on mental activity rather than on the fulfillment of basic needs (such as getting food). At least once a week, we read about someone stabbing or shooting a family member to death because they lost the *TV Guide* or some equally absurd reason. A moment's reflection suggests that this aggression is the end product of some kind of symbolic issue, rather than of deprivation, starvation, or a specific basic need that has not been met.

▲ *Violence on school compuses has caused some schools to install metal detectors.*

Culture and Aggression

Human aggression also develops from environment and culture. The United States has always been a very violent country, and despite recent declines in the crime rate, it still is. You are between seven and ten times more likely to be murdered in America than in most European countries. In fact, homicide is the second highest cause of death among our youth, killing more people between the ages of 15 and 24 than anything else except accidents (Lore & Schultz, 1993). Japan, in contrast, is relatively free of violence despite notable overcrowding. Although violence is on the rise in Great Britain, the rule is still that police officers do not carry firearms, even when they are capturing thieves, burglars, or petty criminals.

▲ *For most ordinary citizens, the Old West was not such a violent place.*

Many experts believe that the high value Americans place on individual rights and freedoms plus our emphasis on competition have contributed to this problem. In other words, when the individual is overemphasized, getting along with others becomes less important. When one person is strongly encouraged to win over another, hostility and aggression are likely to result. Some other cultures place greater value on the welfare of the group, which in turn encourages people to cooperate and find ways to get along with other people. One study of over 20 peaceful societies found that the vast majority of them virtually prohibit competition among individuals. These societies clearly believe that competition leads to aggression and that aggression, in turn, leads to violence (Bonta, 1997).

To get another perspective on how humans vary in their aggressive behavior, we might consider the frontier West, which is often thought to have had very high crime rates. This was not the case. Murder was very rare among ordinary citizens. In Bodie, California, from 1878 to 1882, bodies did pile up at a rate three times that in today's most murderous urban areas. But these were the bodies of young men who wanted to go around "shooting it out," not of everyday citizens. During this four-year period, only one woman was robbed, and there were no reported rapes. Juvenile crimes were nonexistent (McGrath, 1985). In fact, even among the worst of criminals, it was taboo to bother a respectable woman. That was the code of the West.

Humans also seem to set up special places for aggression, such as football games, boxing matches, and bars. One psychological study focused on all the bars in one city—185 of them. Only a few accounted for the majority of the aggression that took place in bars. The psychologists found that people who entered these few bars *expected* either to attack or to be attacked before the evening was over. Such bars had certain characteristics in common: unclean and cheap surroundings, ill-kempt patrons, patrons drinking rapidly, people talking loudly to themselves, unfriendly bartenders, downtown location, and poor ventilation (Graham et al., 1980).

 ## Pause for Thought

1. Name several potential cultural influences on aggression.
2. Describe several social and biological factors in aggression.

Critical Thinking
....

3. Write a journal entry from the point of view of a parent who is deciding if she should allow her two children to watch a horror movie with some violent scenes. Assume the parent has just read the critical thinking discussion in this section.

Social Factors in Aggression

There is much more violence among men than women. One can make a case for hormones as the cause of this. However, social learning—that is, childhood training—seems equally, if not more, important. Males and females often receive training that is very different in this regard.

More often than not, aggressive behavior starts early in life and continues through adolescence. Most of it seems to result from family upbringing focusing on "masculine" activities that are typically aggressive—such as fighting back and standing up to someone "like a man." This kind of training has to be tempered very early, many feel, or it is too late to do anything about it. Aggressive patterns apparently are somewhat set by middle childhood.

In addition to family influence, psychologists point to the anonymous nature of groups as a cause of aggressive behavior. People in groups may engage in antisocial behaviors that they would not perform if they were by themselves. The term used for this phenomenon is **deindividuation** (DE-in-di-vi-ju-AYE-shun), meaning a loss of one's sense of individuality. A study performed on Halloween supports this hypothesis.

When children were given an opportunity to steal change from a money bowl about two feet from the candy bowl, they stole about 8 percent of the time if they were alone and if the person answering the door knew who they were. But they stole about 20 percent of the time under the same conditions if they were *with a group*—probably the result of group "bravado."

The figure jumped to 57 percent when the group was *not* known to the person answering the door. In one case, an experimenter answering the door told the children that she was going to leave the room, pointed to the smallest child, and said if she found any money missing when she came back, she was going to hold that child responsible. The stealing soared to 80 percent, since the group then had someone to blame (Diener et al., 1976).

As you can see, individuals lose some sense of their own responsibility when they are with other people. In other words, in a group, each person apparently feels less responsible for what happens. Also, the individual feels more powerful and less vulnerable when with other people. This situation has been called the **risky shift phenomenon,** meaning that in a group, the risk or danger for each individual is shifted (divided up) among all the group members. Hence, group behavior fosters risk taking. The risky shift phenomenon may help explain horrible events like mob lynchings, gang beatings, and mass riots.

Biological Factors in Aggression

There is evidence that some aggressive behavior can have physical causes. We discussed in Chapter 3 the fact that in the inner core of the brain, roughly midway between the nose and the back of the head sits a unit called the *hypothalamus,* which controls rage, anger, pleasure, and other behaviors. We believe that the rage portion of the hypothalamus might well be responsible for uncontrolled outbursts of violence.

Here are a few examples: Allergies to certain substances can cause dramatic changes in a person's behavior. There was a case of a child who was perfectly normal until he ate bananas. After doing so, he would try to

deindividuation a process in which a person loses his or her sense of individuality and responsibility as the result of being in a group

risky shift phenomenon a situation in which the risk associated with an act is split among the members of a group; hence, the risk is smaller for each person

▲ *Allergies to certain ingredients in foods can cause some people to act aggressively, while others are not affected at all.*

tear up the room and destroy his toys. This only occurred after eating that fruit. Another child would bang his head against the wall whenever he ate wheat.

We personally knew about a very sweet, normally calm mother who every now and then at breakfast would throw dishes against the wall and stomp on the silverware. This behavior was restricted to breakfast time and lasted only about 20 minutes. Of course, very few people can witness small children in action at breakfast without feeling a little crazy, but this was truly out of the ordinary.

After careful exploration, it was discovered that just before these episodes, she would sample pancakes she was cooking. She normally didn't eat them. It turned out that she was allergic to the yellow dye some manufacturers use to make the pancakes look more "eggy."

Normally, when people are allergic, they break out in hives, but in these cases, they were "breaking out" inside their heads, causing the brain tissue to swell and put pressure on the rage center in the hypothalamus (Moyer, 1975). Thus the woman's uncontrollable morning episodes erupted as a result of her allergy.

Amphetamines ("speed"), used over time, can cause brain cells to start firing at random and can make the world so confusing that the person feels threatened and begins striking out at others to protect himself or herself from being harmed—even though no one is really even paying attention to that person. Alcohol, too, can change the psychology of the person who uses it. Alcohol reduces inhibitions and leads to violence in people who are insecure or aggressive to begin with and who, when they drink, can no longer hold these traits in check.

Focus Question

• Does watching violent movies and TV shows make people more aggressive?

Effects of Mass Media

Recent attention has focused on other factors as contributors to aggression, especially in television and movies. We take a look at that here.

It may seem hard to believe, but for 50 years in colonial America, newspapers and books were considered a danger to the general public. Printing presses were carefully controlled, and what few things were published had to have government approval. The fear was that freedom of publication might damage the morals of the general public. In the 1600s, a highly spiritual book (today considered a Christian classic), the *Imitation of Christ,* was banned because it might lead to differing views about religion.

Much later, in Nathaniel Hawthorne's classic novel *The Scarlet Letter,* a woman had to wear a large red letter "A" (for adulteress) on her clothing because she had a child as the result of an adulterous affair. The book was banned in the 1850s. Later, in 1925, censors would not allow the movie based on the book to be shown unless the main characters were married to each other—which destroyed the whole point of the story (Tebbel, 1974).

Today, movies and television programs are at the center of attention in the same general way, with much concern expressed about violence and sex in their content. While important issues may well be involved here, we have to move cautiously to keep from winding up with the same restrictions and censorship that existed in earlier centuries. A few studies have addressed the issue of sex in movies and television, but many more have investigated violence, so we will focus on the latter to try to get some perspective.

Basic Film Studies. An early classic study on the influence of film violence involved showing part of a movie called *The Champion,* starring actor Kirk Douglas. In the part shown to subjects, Mr. Douglas received a grotesque beating.

After seeing the movie, subjects were told to judge the merit of a drawing made by a young man whose outline could be seen behind a screen. If they didn't like his work, they were to administer shocks to him. The shocks were not real, but the subjects thought they were, because after administering one, they could hear the person groan.

In one variation of the experiment, the "artist" was introduced as "Kirk" to some subjects and by another name to other subjects. The intensity of shock administered to "Kirk" was much greater than that administered to the person with another name (even though the same drawings were shown to the two different groups of subjects). These findings suggest that we can identify with violent behavior and carry the activity seen on the screen into real life (Berkowitz & Geen, 1967).

In a second version that used the same arrangement, some subjects were told before viewing the scene from the movie that a bad guy was receiving the beating. Another group was told that a good guy was getting the blows. In other words, for the first subjects, the beating was justified. For the second, it was unjustified. This study showed that *justified violence* bred greater violence (shocks) against the stooges than unjustified violence.

Some principles emerged from these studies. First, violence can breed violence. Second, justified violence is likely to breed greater violence than unjustified violence does. Thus, violence in the name of right, honor, and good in movies and television actually leads to more violence, at least in laboratory settings (Diener & Woody, 1981). In a way, society has condoned violence if it is "right." This is important because few of us ever feel that we are *not* justified in "paying someone back."

Children and Television Viewing. These studies are based on the principle that people imitate all kinds of behavior, including violence. What, then, are the effects of television viewing on children? First of all, in the laboratory, if children see a movie with violence, they tend to become violent themselves through a process called **imitation learning.** Logic, then, suggests that TV can contribute to imitation and aggression.

But the evidence is not all one sided. "Good" (nonviolent) television leads to imitation for a short while, but children seem to lose interest in it. Instead, they actively seek out the novelty in strange and wild programs such as the *Three Stooges* series. Some suspect the key to appropriate TV programming, for children at least, is plenty of nonviolent novelty.

Catharsis. Before ending the discussion, we should make one more comment. You will hear that seeing violence might help us get rid of our aggressive impulses—that is, that it can "discharge" the energy connected with those impulses. The psychological term for this is **catharsis** (ca-THAR-sis), which comes from the Greek meaning "to cleanse or purify."

▲ *The movie, "The Champion," was used in an experiment to see if people identify with violent behavior.*

imitation learning the process of learning behaviors by viewing and imitating others

catharsis a supposed process in which a person gets rid of aggressive energy by viewing others acting aggressively

Thinking Critically about Psychology

Violence in Television and Film

The studies discussed in the text strongly suggest that viewing violent or aggressive behavior on television or in films increases violence or aggression in the viewer. This issue has clearly been settled once and for all, hasn't it? That's the question we want to pursue.

What specifically is being claimed or stated? Viewing violent movies or television programs increases subsequent aggressive or violent behavior in the viewer.

What is the objective evidence for and against this claim? It is hard to get an issue in perspective once it "goes public" and becomes controversial. This is especially true where television is concerned, since the average child watches for 28 hours a week (Cheny, 1994).

One psychologist brought together all the research on TV and aggression and concluded that there was no clear-cut and strong relationship (Freedman, 1984). More recently, though, other psychologists looked at nearly 30 studies done in this area and reached very different conclusions. According to these researchers, media violence is directly linked to aggressive behavior, not only in children but among people of all ages (Wood, Wong, & Chachere, 1991).

▲ *Aggressive children often become more aggressive after viewing violent television programs.*

Here are some basic findings: Government reports and newspaper accounts say that there are 2,500 or more studies on TV and aggression. This number is misleading. The same studies are being reported over and over, but each time a little information is added to one of them. Actually, there are about 100 studies directly relating to the subject, most of them from the laboratory. Most such studies show a relationship between TV and aggression. But the fact that filmed or videotaped aggression leads to aggressive behavior in a laboratory may or may not reflect what happens in real life, so let's turn our focus to the nonlaboratory studies.

In *field studies,* behavior is directly observed in a natural, nonlaboratory setting. In this case, subjects are watched after they view violent and nonviolent TV programs. Taken as a whole, these studies give only weak support to the belief that TV aggression causes real-life aggression. In fact, some aggressive people are *less* aggressive after seeing violence, and some nonaggressive people are *more* aggressive. Why this happens is not clear. In any case, there is insufficient evidence in field studies to conclude that TV viewing leads to aggression. Some unclear but important difference exists between laboratory studies and the behavior of people outside the laboratory.

Examination of the overall behavior of children (not just their television viewing) does show something important. Children who are already aggressive and view a lot of TV get progressively worse. In addition, already aggressive children actively seek out aggressive television.

One clear finding is that the short-term effect of violent TV programs and movies is a very high level of *physical* arousal, which could lead to aggression if the person is then provoked in some way. The arousal lasts only about 20 minutes (Doob & Climie, 1972). No one disputes this short-term effect. It is the long-term effect that remains in question.

Some people seem to have a predisposition to view the world in a certain way—to see people as generally dishonest, for example. This predisposition also applies to hostility and aggression. When people tend to see other people's behavior as insulting or potentially harmful to them, they are more likely to respond aggressively. Additionally, when children experience a lot of violence and aggression in their homes, they are likely to carry that legacy out into the larger community (Basic Behavioral Task Force, 1996b).

What other interpretations might be made instead? Violence increases when a society accepts violent behavior. It may not be television or movies themselves that contribute to violence as much as our general attitude toward it. In other words, movies and television shows are just part of our generally tolerant view of violent behavior. Other cultures allow a great deal of violence in movies, for instance, but severely punish it when it occurs in real life. In these cultures, violent crime rates are much, much lower than they are in the United States. We have already touched on our society's emphasis on the importance of the individual and aggressive competition. This emphasis may well contribute to the problem. And we have seen that certain people are more likely to be negatively affected by viewing violence. Perhaps their numbers grow when the culture does little to curb this tendency.

What are the most logical conclusions to draw? The research leans toward supporting the original claim. But studies show mixed results concerning the relation between TV viewing and later violence *in the average person* in the real world. Aggressive people seek out aggressive programs and then become even more aggressive (Basic Behavioral Task Force, 1996b; Eron & Huesman, 1985).

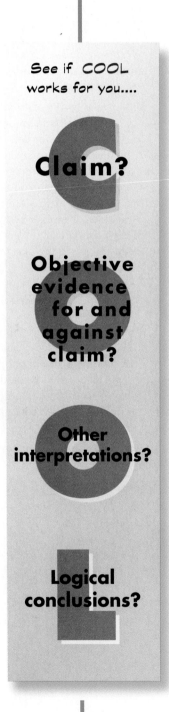

See if COOL works for you....

Claim?

Objective evidence for and against claim?

Other interpretations?

Logical conclusions?

Applying Critical Thinking Skills

Imagine you are a parent of an eight-year-old. Using the information provided in this section, decide whether you will allow your child to watch a TV program that includes violence. Explain your decision.

*Most studies of violence in our society focus on crimes of individual citizens against one another. Another aspect of violence—violence by the government—has been studied by the social scientists **Dane Archer** and **Rosemary Gartner** (1984). They made the following observations:*

> Violence by the State is strangely absent from most discussions of the problem of violence. Books about aggression, for example, often treat topics ranging from hormones to homicidal criminals without mentioning capital punishment, the shooting of looters, the beating of protesters, or even that most impressive form of "official" violence: war. . . .
>
> Why, then is official violence nearly invisible in discussions of murder and aggression? The most obvious explanation is that wars and other forms of official violence are unique in that they wear the mantle of government legitimacy. (p. 215)

The invisibility of official violence in scientific discussions of aggressions . . . is . . . disturbing. . . . Perhaps we are all, scientists included, socialized to accept the State's monopoly on legitimate violence—and perhaps this socialization influences our curiously selective use of the label *violence*. (pp. 216–217)

Interpreting Primary Sources

Why is violence by the government considered "legitimate"? Is it morally different in any way from acts of violence by individuals? Explain your answer.

The idea is that by fantasy, we can purify ourselves of this need in real life. As much as one might like this theory to be true, the evidence over a number of years shows that it doesn't work. Instead, people may merely get more agitated (Wood, Wong, & Chacheren, 1991).

Witnessing Real-Life Violence

We have discussed the effects of viewing filmed violence. However, we have not talked about the effects of witnessing real violence. And today, more and more people are exposed to violent crime than ever before. Homicide has become the second leading cause of death among young people in our society, and our homicide rate has doubled since 1950 (Osofsky, 1995; Stokols, 1995).

Among the problems associated with exposure to real-life violence are an almost constant state of anxiety, sleep problems, nightmares, and withdrawal from interaction with others. Many people living in communities where there is chronic violence resemble soldiers suffering from the effects of traumatic stress (Osofsky, 1995).

This finding leads into yet another area: violence by the government. See the In Their Own Words feature on this page for a discussion of this topic.

Violence in whatever form obviously leads to victims who need help. As a result, social psychologists also study the other side: Under what circumstances will people come to the aid of someone in an emergency? The answer is surprising.

Helping Behavior

Two experimenters wanted to learn why people will not help others who are in obvious distress (Latané & Darley, 1970). They set up situations in which people were sitting in a room when one of the following events occurred: Smoke began to creep through one of the air vents, a man had an epileptic seizure (fake), or a woman fell down in an adjacent room and was apparently seriously injured, indicated by all kinds of noise, moans, and groans. Each of these events was staged in such a way that the behavior of those who were "bystanders" to the event could be observed.

1. In the smoke experiment, different arrangements were tried: A student was alone in a room taking a test when it happened, then two students were in the room, three students, and so forth, all observed through a two-way mirror.

2. In the epileptic experiment, subjects were isolated from one another but "found out" that one of the subjects was epileptic. The subjects were to carry on a discussion with one another via earphones and microphones, so they could hear but not see one another. They were told that this was to allow them more freedom of speech. When the "seizure" came, they could hear it going on and could get help if they wanted it just by getting up and looking for the laboratory assistant.

3. The "injured" woman experiment used the same basic setup as the smoke experiment, but the door to the testing room was left open so that whoever was in the room could hear the woman.

The findings from these experiments are quite consistent and strong. First of all, though, we should note that no particular personality type responded to the need for help more than others. Furthermore, all the subjects were quite concerned about the plight of the person in need, so there was no lack of feeling. But although some subjects came to the rescue, large numbers did not.

What was the difference? The answer is so simple that it is startling and at first unbelievable. This type of study has been done so often over the years, though, that there is no question about it.

The factor that controlled whether or not someone helped others was how many people were present at the time the emergency arose. That makes sense, doesn't it? But there's a twist to it. The *more* people present at the emergency, the *less* likely any one person was to give aid to the victim, and this held true for all the experiments. The results, part of which are shown in Figure 19.1 on page 585, are striking.

How do the experimenters explain why this happens? Here are some of the conclusions that have been clearly demonstrated over time:

1. When others are present, we are inhibited from acting for fear we will make fools of ourselves in public.

2. If others are also observing the emergency, we use them as a guide for how to act—just as, when we go to a party with people we don't know, we use others at the party as a guide for how to behave. If the others don't help, we don't; if they do, we do.

3. People who think or know that others are present at an emergency are less likely to take personal responsibility because they feel that it is someone else's job. This is called **diffusion of responsibility,** meaning that the more people there are, the less responsibility each of us has to take (because responsibility is diffused, or spread out, among the members of the group).

In Their Own Words . . .

In the late 1960s, **J. M. Darley** (pictured) and **Bibb Latané** investigated why people do not help in a crisis and came to the following conclusion:

Once an event is noticed, an onlooker must decide if it is truly an emergency. Emergencies are not always clearly labeled as such; "smoke" pouring into a waiting room may be caused by a fire, or it may merely indicate a leak in a steam pipe. Screams in the street may signal an assault or a family quarrel. A man lying in a doorway may be having a coronary—or he may simply be sleeping off a drunk.

A person trying to interpret a situation often looks at those around him to see how he should react. If everyone else is calm and indifferent, he will tend to remain so; if everyone else is reacting strongly, he is likely to become aroused. This tendency is not merely slavish conformity; ordinarily we derive much valuable information about new situations from how others around us behave. It's a rare traveler who, in picking a roadside restaurant, chooses to stop at one where no other cars appear in the parking lot.
(1968, p. 120)

Interpreting Primary Sources

Why do you think a person facing a new situation feels a need to observe other people's reactions before reacting too?

diffusion of responsibility a process in which responsibility for helping others is spread out among group members; thus, each member's responsibility is less than it would be if the person were alone

Case Study

No One Called the Police

Just before 3:00 A.M. on a cold March night in 1964, Kitty Genovese finished her shift as a manager at a bar near her apartment. She lived in a middle-class neighborhood of New York City in the borough of Queens. After she parked her car and began walking toward her apartment, she was attacked on the street by a man bent on killing her.

The man slashed her with a knife several times but fled when a neighbor called out to leave her alone. Several apartment lights went on, but no one came out to help the wounded Genovese who lay helpless in the street. After a few minutes, the neighborhood quieted down again, and the attacker returned. Once again he was scared away by lights going on in some apartments and by a neighbor's call to leave her alone. He waited again, and when he returned a third time, he killed Genovese.

It took the man over half an hour to murder the young woman. During that time, according to police estimates, 38 of her neighbors had seen all or part of the attack. Some stood at their windows and watched. One of the neighbors was seen opening his door, going to the top of the stairwell, watching the attack going on in the street, and then returning to his apartment. Fifteen minutes later that man was the first person to call the police—from a neighbor's apartment so he wouldn't be identified (Seedman & Hallman, 1974).

▲ Some psychologists study why people watch crimes happening without taking any action to stop it.

Years later, after the case had gained national attention, several of the neighbors tried to present a different picture. They said that the neighborhood was loud, that it was difficult to hear Genovese's screams. They maintained that they did call or that they did try to assess the seriousness of the situation (Sexton, 1995). This much is true: no one called the police *during* the attack. The police arrived about two minutes after they were called. And Kitty Genovese was already dead when they arrived.

For years Genovese's murder baffled psychologists. Why didn't a single neighbor come to Genovese's aid? Why would so many people hesitate to simply pick up a phone and call the police? What factors could have increased helping and might possibly have saved Genovese's life? In an attempt to answer these questions, psychologists have since conducted literally hundreds of studies on helping behavior. Believe it or not, most bystanders in these types of situations do feel anguish and they do care. But a variety of other factors often keep them from lending a hand. You can read about many of these factors in the rest of the chapter.

Review the Case Study

In this particular case, what factors probably kept Kitty Genovese's neighbors from offering more help than they did?

In Focus

Helping Others

Diffusion of Responsibility

SOMEONE ELSE MUST HAVE CALLED THE POLICE. NO QUESTIONS ABOUT IT... BESIDES, SOMEONE HERE WILL BREAK IT UP SOON.

No Opportunity for Diffusion of Responsibility

I BETTER CALL THE POLICE. IF I DON'T DO IT, NO ONE WILL...

How could evaluation apprehension play a role in the situation on the left?

Speed of Response

Group Size	Percent Who Respond by End of Seizure	Percent Who Ever Respond
2 (subject and victim)	85	100
3 (subject, victim and one other)	62	85
6 (subject, victim, and 4 others)	31	62

▲ *Figure 19.1* *Effects of Group Size on Likelihood and Speed of Response to Epileptic Emergency*

The subject is the person being observed to see if he or she will respond to the cry of the epileptic. The victim is the epileptic. "Others" are just added people put into the situation by the experimenter. (Latané & Darley, 1970)

4. But why don't people at least phone for help? Calling the police, in and of itself, admits that there is an emergency. If we admit that, then we get ourselves into a bind. If there is indeed an emergency, we should do more about the problem than just hang up the phone and wait for help to arrive!

5. We won't help in a strange environment where we don't know the rules. Here is a study that shows that: A well-dressed man on crutches fell down. (He was a stooge for an experimenter and was not really injured.) Would someone help? The first series of

▲ We are more likely to help some-one when we are alone, rather than in a group.

evaluation apprehension con-cern about how others will judge us

experiments was done in a subway, and 83 percent of passersby came to his aid. In a second series of experiments, he fell down at an airport. Only 41 percent tried to help. Do these results reflect some kind of social class difference? No. The people were interviewed, and here is the finding: Those familiar with the airport were more likely to respond to the need for help; those familiar with the subway were likewise more likely to help. The difference comes from the fact that an airport is familiar to far fewer people; this was the deciding factor in whether or not help was forthcoming (Pearce, 1980).

The issue of familiarity is critical to behavior. We are always concerned about proper behavior and what others will think about us. This feeling is called **evaluation apprehension.** Without our even knowing it, we are apprehen-sive, or concerned, about how others will judge our performance. If we see someone helping someone, we tend to join in because that is expected; if no one is helping, we tend to stand back.

Finally, you may think that these studies might somehow have seemed "fake" to the subjects, but that was not the case. To prove the point, experimenters used experienced stuntmen to enact an apparently genuine violent situation, with people fighting in public, beating each other up over an allegedly stolen item. The results were identical to those in the previous studies. We are without doubt influenced by those around us—especially by the number of them. But none of the subjects later inter-viewed ever was aware of this influence (Shotland, 1985).

Focus Question

....

• How can the physical envi-ronment affect one's behavior?

territoriality an attachment to a fixed area designated as ours alone and the tendency to defend it against intruders

personal space an "invisible bubble," or portable area, around each person; each of us tries to keep this space from being invaded

Environmental Influences on Behavior

How we feel and how we interact with others can be strongly influ-enced by the physical environment. For example, a noisy environment can be distracting and nerve-racking. Students from schools with a great deal of noise are edgy and uncomfortable and tend to have higher blood pres-sure than students from other schools.

All animals have a sense of **territoriality,** an attachment to a fixed area set aside for their use, and they will attack anything that comes within this space. While humans may not immediately attack any and all intruders, we are also territorial. We acknowledge this when we knock on someone's door instead of simply entering unannounced. The invasion of our territory is highly likely to be seen as a direct threat. In fact, this connection is so strong that the law usually allows us to defend our homes aggressively.

Human territoriality can also be "carried around." Think for a moment about how uncomfortable you feel when someone moves too close to you. The "invisible bubble" we carry around with us is our **personal space.**

An invasion of personal space does not cause quite the same kind of reaction as an invasion of territory, but it is usually seen as threatening.

On the average, with strangers, our personal space is roughly two feet. If a stranger comes any nearer, we feel uncomfortable. Your psychological closeness to another person determines the exact distance you place yourself from him or her. With someone you truly love, personal space can approach zero most of the time.

Males generally have a larger personal space than females. And cultures differ in this regard as well. In many Middle Eastern countries, for example, people stand very close together in conversation. An American caught in this situation will probably start backing away and be seen as very rude in the process.

Overcrowding is a related problem. When animals are in crowded conditions, their behavior patterns become abnormal. Some of them kill one another, they fail to breed, they develop brain defects, and many die from the stress of the situation.

Human reactions to such situations are highly psychological. Thus, 10 people living in a 500-square-foot room for a couple of days may be overwhelmed by the feeling of closeness. The same number of people sharing about the same amount of space on a train for a day or so can feel lonely.

Psychologists therefore make a distinction between **density** and **crowding.** Density is the actual number of people per square foot, while crowding is the *feeling* of being too close. At a rock concert, density can be high but crowding low. Sitting at a restaurant counter with someone on your right and someone on your left can feel very crowded, although density is low compared with density at the rock concert.

Much work has been done with prison density, since high density can create such serious problems as riots. One very workable system that is far cheaper than dealing with trouble in a prison is to give each prisoner an individual cell. Interestingly, it makes no difference how small the cell is (as long as the person can move!) or how cheap it looks (Cox et al., 1984).

▲ *Feeling crowded depends more on psychological factors than on the actual number of people around us.*

density the number of people per square foot in a given space

crowding a psychological feeling of having too little space

Pause for Thought

1. List several conclusions about helping behavior.
2. How can the environment influence behavior? Discuss territoriality, personal space, and crowding.

Critical Thinking
....
3. Describe a time when you helped or failed to help a stranger. What factors may have contributed to your response?

APPLYING
Psychology to Life

Abusive Relationships

When personal attraction and violence come together, a physically abusive relationship exists. However, it is extremely important to keep in mind that abuse can occur without any actual physical violence. This is what is referred to as emotional or psychological abuse.

In an abusive relationship, one person dominates the other through physical harm or threats or by belittling, degrading, and demeaning the other person. Such a relationship lacks any sense of equality. One person has far more power and freedom than the other. Mutual respect and love, in the real sense of these words, simply cannot exist in this type of situation. In the overwhelming majority of cases, the male is the abuser.

How Does Abuse Begin?

Abusive men as a rule do not start off being violent or abusive. In the beginning, they are often quite charming. Abusive behavior is a problem that usually starts small and then escalates, following a fairly predictable pattern. In addition, when people fall in love, they tend to overlook or explain away things that would otherwise make them wary. In our society, women are expected to give and forgive more in a relationship than men and usually make more compromises.

The pattern of abuse is cyclical. First, there is a buildup of tension, with increasingly frequent arguing. Then comes the violent outburst. It may or may not include physically hurting the other person. Next come profuse apologies, pledges of love, and promises that it will never happen again. These are followed by a "honeymoon" period, when everything seems to be better than ever. Eventually, however, the cycle repeats itself. Each time it does, the interval between cycles is shorter, the violence increases, and the "honeymoon" period is shorter and less intense.

Warning Signs

Recently, there has been an alarming increase in domestic violence among married couples. However, there are also signs of an increase in abusive dating relationships, and that is what we want to focus on. In the fol-lowing paragraphs, we discuss several warning signs—behaviors that are associated with actual or potential abuse. Most of them involve a desire for control and/or a failure to take responsibility for one's actions, blaming the other person instead. It is not necessary for all of these behaviors to be present. Even two or three should be enough to send up a large red flag. Although occasionally females are the abusers, it is extremely rare. We want to simplify this section and not have to use "he or she" and "his or her" repeatedly because it's awkward. So we are assuming the abuser is male, for purposes of this discussion.

1. Does the man try to control the woman by telling her what she can and cannot do, where she can and cannot go, whom she can and cannot see? This is sometimes interpreted as having an interest in her welfare, but it also shows a lack of respect for her decisions, interests, and needs. When there are *major* and *frequent* disagreements in this area, the man is probably more concerned about himself than about her.

2. Is he extremely jealous? A certain amount of jealousy in a close relationship is probably to be expected, and most people find it flattering. However, too much jealousy can quickly become a serious problem. This is especially true if he blames her for encouraging the attention of other men.

3. Does he try to isolate her from her friends and family? By cutting off or damaging her relationships with other people, he increases his own control. If she has no one to turn to, to discuss her problems with, to seek help from, she is more likely to stay with him.

4. Does he frequently belittle or insult her? Is he quick to point out her flaws or faults? Love should make us feel better about ourselves, not worse. Humiliation is just another weapon for gaining control.

5. Do they as a couple always do what he wants to do and rarely or never what she wants to do? Again, this shows a lack of respect for her and increases his control in the relationship.

6. Does he blame her for his own mistakes, problems, or shortcomings? When he mistreats her, does he use his love for her to excuse his behavior? This is simply another indication of his failure to accept responsibility for his own actions. Also, she is more likely to forgive his abuse if he can make her believe that either she or his love for her is somehow responsible. Neither is true, period. No one can *make* someone else do something.

7. Does he have a short fuse? Someone who is very quick to anger is likely to act without thinking first. This behavior by itself does not necessarily mean the person is abusive, but in combination with one or more other warning signals, it usually means trouble.

8. Does he become angry and difficult when he drinks? Does he use being drunk as an excuse? The problem here is that it is his choice to drink in the first place. And once he knows how he acts when he is drunk, his behavior is solely his responsibility. Alcohol is frequently involved in cases of domestic violence.

9. Do her friends repeatedly ask her why she puts up with him and with the way he treats her? When those who know us really well become this concerned, it is usually a sign that we should take a very close look at what is going on. People outside of an emotional situation sometimes have a more objective and clearer perspective.

10. Has he ever forced her to do something sexually that she truly did not want to do? If so, his behavior is not only abusive, but he has broken the law. This is true even if an actual rape was not committed. The goal of both sexual assault and rape is to demean and dominate the victim. These behaviors simply have no place in an intimate relationship.

Finally, just about the only way an aggressive or violent person learns to control that aggression is when the negative consequences of the behavior are swift and sure (Lore & Schultz, 1993). It is usually best to leave the relationship after the very first instance of physical abuse. You should never give anyone more than one second chance. Failing that, it is never too late to get out. Having invested a lot of time and energy in a relationship is not a good reason to stay when it has gone this bad. No relationship is worth being abused. No one deserves to live that way—no one.

▲ We all have the power to control our aggressive impulses.

Summary

1. According to attribution theory, we rely on what we already know, try to interpret and explain the present event, and then guide our beliefs and behavior by combining the two.

2. Feelings of love and like seem to start from a physical base. This base is typically related to how attractive the person seems to us. After that, closeness develops by a process of association. Many events and actions become associated with the other person, and the person is viewed in more ways than just the physical.

3. Aggression and violence may be natural to humans in some situations. But evidence suggests that in most cases, human violence has psychological and sociocultural causes. Some instances of violence have physical causes, such as allergies.

4. Research on the connection between viewing violence in movies or television programs and behaving aggressively provides mixed results. Most laboratory studies show a connection, but field studies are less conclusive. Those who are already aggressive seem to be negatively influenced by the aggression they see on television or in movies.

5. Whether or not we help other people in an emergency seems primarily related to the size of the group we are part of when the emergency arises. The more people present, the less likely any one person is to help.

6. Humans have a sense of territoriality. We also have personal space, the distance we wish to maintain between us and the people interacting with us. Crowding represents how "closed in" we feel, whereas density is a measure of how many people occupy a given physical space.

Vocabulary

attribution theory	risky shift phenomenon	territoriality
antecedents	imitation learning	personal space
attribution	catharsis	density
consequences	diffusion of responsibility	crowding
deindividuation	evaluation apprehension	

Review Questions

Multiple Choice

On a sheet of paper, write the letter of the answer that best completes each statement.

1. According to attribution theory, our opinions about others are influenced by
   a. our own motivations.
   b. our emotional responses.
   c. our beliefs.
   d. all of the above.

2. An antecedent refers to the information we
   a. have before an event.
   b. receive during an event.
   c. conclude after an event.

3. Studies show that couples who stay together a long time are
   a. more different than alike.
   b. more alike than different.
   c. exactly the same.

4. The risky shift phenomenon suggests
   a. that we take fewer risks when in a group.
   b. that we take more risks when in a group.
   c. that risk in a group is shifted to other group members.
   d. both b and c.

True/False

On a sheet of paper, answer each statement true or false. If false, rewrite to make it true.

5. Studies show that we tend to form relationships with others who are about as attractive as we are.

6. Revealing personal information about ourselves is best done in small doses, especially at the beginning of a relationship.

7. Men tend to be more violent than women.

8. Deindividuation leads to a stronger sense of personal identity.

9. People are more likely to be violent when they think that their violence is justified, or right.

10. Most people agree that exposure to violence on TV has long-term effects on children.

11. Field studies clearly show that violence on TV causes real-life violence.

Fill in the Blank

On a sheet of paper, write the word or words that best complete each statement.

12. The feeling of being closed in is called ▓▓▓▓.

13. If there are three fans at a football game, we can assume that the ▓▓▓▓ is low.

14. Worrying about what others expect during an emergency is called ▓▓▓▓.

15. If we stand so close to someone that we can count his or her cavities, we are probably violating that person's ▓▓▓▓.

16. Animals who have a strong sense of ▓▓▓▓ will attack others who attempt to invade their "space."

17. Spreading our responsibility for our actions to others is called ▓▓▓▓.

18. ▓▓▓▓ is the process of getting rid of aggression by watching aggression.

19. Losing your sense of individuality is called ▓▓▓▓.

20. ▓▓▓▓ usually comes before attributions.

Discussion Questions

1. A nonhuman but intelligent being captures you and explains that it will set you free only if you adequately define the concept of *love*. Define it.

2. Researchers have found that females are more likely to initiate flirting, both verbal and nonverbal. Do these findings match what you've seen? Explain. Also, describe the ways in which men flirt and the ways in which women flirt. How do they differ?

3. Try to assess your own immediate reaction to violence on TV or in the movies. First, do you seek out or avoid such movies? Do you root for violence while viewing? Afterward, do you find yourself pushing your friends around or driving faster or acting aggressive in any other way, or does the violence seem to have no effect?

4. Imagine a high school where there is a real possibility for violence on a daily basis. You can probably assume that a certain amount of deindividuation exists at the school. Give several possible reasons for this deindividuation. For example, you might say, "The school is probably very large." Then describe several ways in which you might decrease this deindividuation.

5. The chapter explains that evaluation apprehension decreases the likelihood that a person will help in an emergency. In what ways could evaluation apprehension help to *create* emergencies? Offer several real-life examples of emergencies that might have been caused by evaluation apprehension. For example, one could argue that those who saw problems with the *Challenger* space shuttle before it exploded did not voice their opinions loudly enough because of evaluation apprehension.

6. Describe a personal experience where density was low but crowding was high and an experience where density was high but crowding low. Be specific.

Activities and Projects

1. Conduct an experiment to determine the role of antecedents in people's judgments. What you will do is supply the antecedents and then measure attributions and consequences. Write all of the following on an index card:

   Read the description below and answer the two questions beneath it.

   Melissa Weeber is 28 years old. She has been a high school counselor for six years. She enjoys the job but feels that her role has been reduced simply to scheduling students for classes. She now wants to become a marriage counselor. When asked to describe her, students commonly use the following adjectives: caring, dependable, and hardworking.

   Use the scale below to rate your answers to all the following questions.

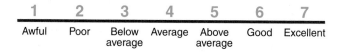

1	2	3	4	5	6	7
Awful	Poor	Below average	Average	Above average	Good	Excellent

   How would you rate this person's chances of becoming an effective marriage counselor?

   If you were responsible for hiring this person as a marriage counselor, what would be the likelihood that you would hire her?

   Write down the same information on another index card, but this time replace the adjective *caring* with *efficient*. Show the first card to 20 people, and show the second card to 20 other people. Record their ratings.

   Analyze your results. The first question measures attribution; the second measures consequences.

Were the subjects' answers to the first question similar to their answers to the second question? What were the average ratings for both questions on the first card? On the second card? Discuss why you think you got the results that you did.

2. As mentioned in the chapter, attractive people are initially perceived as more competent than others. Conduct a simple experiment to test this assertion.

First, find a paragraph or poem that you had to write for one of your classes, or use a poem or paragraph from a book. Neatly copy the material onto an index card.

Next, sift through some magazines and photocopy four pictures: an "attractive" male, an "attractive" female, an "unattractive" male, and an "unattractive" female. Your choice of photos will be subjective, so maybe a few classmates can help you with your final decision.

Now, write the following information on another index card:

How would you rate this person's writing skills?

Show the paragraph (or poem), *one* of the pictures, and the rating scale to 20 males and 20 females. Five males and five females will see the attractive male; five males and five females will see the unattractive male; five males and five females will see the attractive female; and and five males and five females will see the unattractive female.

Record your subjects' ratings on a separate data sheet and analyze your results. Were the attractive pictures rated higher? Were female subjects less influenced by attractiveness, as suggested in the chapter? Half the time, subjects saw pictures of the opposite sex. Were these ratings higher than the same-sex ratings? Discuss why you think you got the results that you did. Also, make a chart summarizing all your results.

3. Conduct an experiment on helping behavior. The procedure will be simple: Fall down, and stay on the ground for about 15 seconds, holding your ankle the whole time. Do this in exactly the same way 20 times.

This time *you* will supply the hypothesis. For example, your hypothesis might be that people are more likely to help when they are in a familiar environment. To test this hypothesis, you can fall in an environment familiar to your subjects 10 times and in an unfamiliar environment 10 times. Look back through the chapter for other ideas, or think of an original hypothesis. Be sure to have your teacher approve your hypothesis.

Get a friend to help record responses. A few remarks about responses: Devise a data sheet that will outline the degree of help that your subjects offer. The following is one example:

Level 1 = completely ignored
Level 2 = stopped, but did not help
Level 3 = offered help
Level 4 = helped immediately

In addition to recording these levels, write down as much information as possible about each subject. This information will give you something on which to base your conclusions.

As always, analyze your results in detail, and draw conclusions. You might consider videotaping this experiment and showing it to the class—perhaps your teacher will give you extra credit for this.

One final option: If you do not think you are bold enough to fall in front of strangers, consider testing helping behavior in another way—maybe by dropping money or a wallet—and see who helps. Be creative.

4. Stand close to someone you do not know in the hallway and gradually move closer. Do this to about 10 different people, and record their reactions.

(a) Did they ignore you completely?

(b) Did they look at you, then look away?

(c) Did they move slightly or turn away?

(d) Did they get up?

(e) Did they swear at you?

Notice that these questions are measuring the degree of your influence. Your data sheet should reflect these degrees. Write a report analyzing your results and describing your reactions in detail.

CHAPTER 20

Sociocultural Influences: Attitudes and Beliefs

Although it may seem that we arrive at attitudes and beliefs on our own, closer examination shows that many of them are based on the behavior and actions of others. This chapter looks at the cultural and group origins of many of the thoughts and feelings that people have.

Cultural Diversity

The United States is often called a "melting pot" that combines a wide variety of cultures, races, and ethnic groups. These terms are similar but not identical. A **culture** consists of a set of beliefs, attitudes, and values that are held in common by a fairly large number of people and passed down from one generation to the next. **Race** refers to a set of hereditary physical characteristics that distinguish one major group of people from another. An **ethnic group** is made up of people who share important cultural and racial features, often including national origin.

Historically, the United States is largely a country of immigrants, and religious freedom is one of our basic constitutional rights. Primarily for these reasons, we enjoy a great deal of cultural and religious diversity. You should be aware that other countries operate very differently. China, for instance, just recently opened its borders to foreigners. Only a decade or two ago, it was extremely difficult even to visit there.

Much has been said about racial problems and disharmony in the United States. These are serious issues, and much of this chapter is aimed at addressing them. To get some perspective, though, we should note that these concerns are as old as the human race itself. Furthermore, almost no other country has our level of cultural diversity *and* the expectation that we will all learn to live together in peace.

One of the few countries that included many races, cultures, and ethnic groups was the Soviet Union. The Communist government of the Soviet Union collapsed in the early 1990s. Without the control of a strong central government, it quickly broke up into warring factions. These factions were often based on ethnic and cultural differences. In contrast, when almost the entire population shares the same culture, race, religion, and history, as is true in many places, the risk of intergroup conflict is much lower.

Our point is *not* that multicultural harmony is impossible. Our point is to acknowledge that it is difficult. Because of that difficulty, we must never become complacent or let up in our efforts to achieve a tolerant and peaceable society. After all, war is also as old as the human race, but peace is still a better alternative.

Focus Question

- What do people mean when they call the United States a "melting pot"?

culture a set of beliefs, attitudes, and values held in common by a large number of people and passed down from one generation to the next

race a set of hereditary physical characteristics that distinguishes a major group of people

ethnic group a group of people who share important cultural and racial features, often including national origin

◄ *Many schools and campuses enjoy a great deal of cultural diversity.*

Multicultural America

The multicultural composition of the United States is changing. Since the early days of U.S. history, whites have made up the majority of the citizenry. Today, non-Hispanic white people account for about 72 percent of the population. This margin is smaller than ever before, and it continues to shrink. Within that majority are numerous groups with origins in many different countries, each with its own customs and values.

African Americans are the next largest group, comprising roughly 12 percent of the total. It is the only major group whose members did not choose to come to this country. Because their ancestors were sold into slavery, they were forced to leave much of their cultural heritage behind. That heritage originated in a variety of places on the African continent. Most African countries are, in turn, made up of various tribes. Each tribe has its own culture and often its own language as well.

Approximately 11 percent of our population is Hispanic, a growing minority. The number of Hispanic people in the United States increased by nearly one-third in the 1980s, and they are still the fastest-growing minority in the country. Within this group are many subgroups that differ from one another. Puerto Rican Americans are not exactly the same as Mexican Americans, who are also different from Spanish Americans or Argentinean Americans, and so on.

About 4 percent of the total population in the United States is Asian American (U.S. Bureau of the Census, 1998). This group is also diverse. Korean or Vietnamese Americans may have little in common with Japanese Americans or Chinese Americans, for example. Their countries of origin don't even share the same language.

Native Americans make up the smallest major group. There has been no notable increase here, and they comprise less than 1 percent of the total population. We tend to think of this group as a single entity, but that is far from the truth. In fact, there are hundreds of separate tribes, each with its own beliefs and traditions (Coughlin, 1993; Yetman, 1991).

To further complicate the picture, we cannot make many assumptions about any individual member of any particular ethnic group. For instance, it has been shown that African Americans, Hispanics, Asian Americans, and American Indians all emphasize interdependence within the family and family obligations more than whites do. However, it has also been shown that there are greater differences among individuals within a given ethnic group than between such groups. One major reason for this is that some people identify more strongly with their ethnic background than other people do (Phinney, 1996).

In the face of this head-spinning diversity, we may sometimes feel overwhelmed. Actually, though, we in this country are very fortunate. Most people have to travel far and wide to experience different cultures. All we have to do is look around us.

Multicultural Psychology

All of us are shaped by the culture in which we live. It influences how we dress and speak, our daily activities, our goals and dreams, and how and what we think. It even has an impact on simple physical reactions. Take, for instance, an impending sneeze. Does the person try to hold it back or loudly let it go? Do others look away or say something?

What do they say? The correct answers will depend on the culture (Segall, Dasen, Berry, & Poortinga, 1990). What does this have to do with psychology? These things are behaviors and as such are part of the field.

Psychology has primarily been studied in the United States, Europe, and Canada. Consequently, it has a North American and European bias (Mays, Rubinn, Sabouria, & Walker, 1996). The truth is that we do not know whether much of our information can be generalized to other places. Within the United States, our focus and research subjects are most often white and middle class (Graham, 1992). American psychology has not ignored minority groups. But it has failed to give them enough attention.

When psychology does study minorities, too often it simply makes a direct comparison with the dominant white culture. The frequent implication is that one culture is better or worse than the other. Sometimes, though, different is just that: different. Such comparisons are not necessarily called for. In addition, too often we simply assume that what is true for whites is true for other groups as well. Such an assumption is not necessarily accurate. We know, for instance, that psychological tests designed by and for white middle-class people may not be appropriate for other groups. We also know that family roles and the relative influence of peers and family are determined partly by one's ethnic group. Consequently, at least some of the information we have gathered from white subjects is probably not applicable to subjects with other backgrounds.

Regrettably, psychology does not have a very enviable record in its dealings with diversity. Throughout the 1800s, for instance, racial inferiority of some groups was accepted as fact. As late as 1920, the notion of mental or intellectual differences based on racial group was also accepted as fact. Only around 1940 did psychology begin in earnest to study prejudice as an unjustified or irrational attitude (Duckitt, 1992).

America casts its own cultural influence on a variety of racial and ethnic groups.

We have made substantial progress since then, but we still have a long, long way to go. With the current heightened interest in multicultural issues, our perspective should broaden. In the meantime, we must be alert to our biases and proceed with caution.

Group Influences

The groups people belong to clearly influence how they think, feel, and behave. For example, normally the school principal is set apart from other teachers, the teachers form their own group, and the students are a third group. The principal and possibly a vice-principal are often symbolically alone, and they behave and dress as they believe all principals do. Teachers normally do not dress as formally as the principal. Students follow their own dress code, which is designed to resemble that of the other two groups as little as possible.

Our dress, eating habits, patterns of speech, hobbies, entertainment—all these depend partly on the group we belong to. The more

Focus Question
....
• How do groups influence individuals?

internalize to take the attitudes or beliefs of others as our own

important a particular group is to us and the longer we have associated with it, the stronger its hold on us will be. In other words, the more we identify with a group, the more we **internalize** (take as part of ourselves) the attitudes, beliefs, and uniform of that group.

Group Effects

We have noted that members of a group tend to have similar attitudes and hold similar beliefs. When group members discuss these ideas with one another, the ideas become more firmly established and sometimes more extreme. For instance, a conservative (or liberal) who talks politics with other like-minded people will eventually become even more conservative (or liberal). Through this kind of discussion the group's existing characteristics are enhanced.

When everyone in a group thinks alike, both good and bad things can happen. Such single-minded focus gives encouragement and strength to the actions of every member. This can lead to very positive results, as can be seen in the civil rights movement of the 1960s, but can also have very harmful effects, as in the mass suicides associated with certain cults.

One result of everyone thinking alike is clearly negative. Group members tend to dismiss or ignore negative or critical information in order to stick to their original ideas. Most social scientists believe that that tendency was directly involved in the explosion of the space shuttle *Challenger* in the 1980s. Because of a long string of successes, the group in control thought that nothing could go wrong. When the engineers warned of danger, their warning was ignored and their information was not forwarded to people who should have had it. Consequently, the decision to go ahead and launch was made, with tragic results.

▲ *Members of a group tend to share similar goals and attitudes.*

Reference Groups

reference group a group with which one identifies and that provides standards of behavior

A **reference group** is a group with which a person identifies and that provides standards of behavior. A person can have more than one reference group—for example, family, church, workplace, and school groups. Reference groups often provide us with a particular way of seeing things in the world. In fact, they can sometimes actually control *what* we see.

Here is an example of this effect involving cultural reference groups. An experimenter used what is called a *stereoscope,* which can show two separate pictures to a subject, a different one to each eye. Quickly flashed to one eye was a picture of a baseball player. Flashed to the other, at the same time, was a picture of a bullfighter. Mexican subjects almost always saw only the bullfighter, while U.S. subjects saw only the baseball player, if the viewing time was kept short (Bagby, 1968). In another study without the stereoscope, experimenters showed subjects obviously satirical cartoons making fun of prejudice. Prejudiced subjects saw the cartoons as *supporting* their distorted and biased ideas (Cooper & Tahoda, 1964).

Fitting Attitudes to the Group

As we've said, people with whom we associate help form our attitudes. The term *attitude* needs some further discussion here because it has a special meaning in social psychology (Cacioppo & Bernston, 1994). An **attitude** is a general, enduring evaluation of something that includes emotional responses and tendencies to act in certain ways toward it. Attitudes, then, are fairly broad and long-lasting ways of categorizing things in our world that also bring about feelings in us and predispose us to behave in particular ways. Attitudes have a cognitive component (our opinions or evaluations), an emotional component (our feelings), and a behavioral component (our tendencies to act in certain ways).

Many of our attitudes begin very early, in the family, and tend to remain firmly implanted. But when new reference groups come along, they can bring about changes in these attitudes. A study of college students demonstrated this power. A group of conservative students entered a liberal college, where they formed new reference groups. By the time the students graduated, they were quite liberal in their outlook, except for the ones who did not form strong ties to a new group but stayed close to their families. Twenty-five years later, these two groups (both those who had changed and those who hadn't) had held onto their college attitudes, showing the staying power of group influences (Newcomb, 1963).

The case study feature on page 600 describes a famous experiment that was controversial both in what the researchers discovered as well as the methodology of the experiment itself. Twenty-five years later, these researchers note certain changes in our society, changes that make this study and others like it especially relevant and distressing. Our society imprisons more people for more types of crime every year. In fact, we imprison more people than just about any other industrialized society. At the same time, punishment, rather than rehabilitation, seems to have become the goal. Our society seems fairly unconcerned about the kind of environment prisoners must endure. Given what happened to these college students in a matter of days in a mock prison, the likely effects on real prisoners are frightening to imagine. From the researchers' view, we need to think carefully about what our prison system is doing to people. After all, most prisoners will eventually be released. We should consider the consequences that will have for society in the long run (Haney & Zimbardo, 1998).

attitude general, long-lasting evaluation that includes emotions and behavioral tendencies

 ## Pause for Thought

1. Explain how the terms *culture, race,* and *ethnic group* differ.
2. What is an attitude, and what does it mean to internalize an attitude or belief?
3. How do reference groups affect our attitudes? How did reference groups play a role in the prisoner-guard experiment?

Critical Thinking
....

4. Think of three or four stereotypes you have. Which of these stereotypes probably are fairly accurate, and which probably are not? Provide evidence. Based on your answers, what conclusions would you draw about stereotypes?

The Prisoner-Guard Experiment

Case Study

One of the most dramatic examples of reference-group influence occurred in an experiment that took place in the basement of a building at Stanford University in 1971. Psychologist Philip Zimbardo (1972) set up a mock prison there, complete with cells, security doors, and drab surroundings. He hired 20 male student volunteers for a "live-in" experiment. He interviewed the students and gave them personality tests to make sure they were emotionally stable and generally law abiding. Half of the students were randomly assigned the role of guards, and the other half were assigned to be prisoners.

The prisoners were picked up by actual police officers, handcuffed, brought to a police station, then transported to the mock prison. Meanwhile, the guards were told they could create their own rules to control the prisoners. They decided that the prisoners should not be allowed to talk during meals, during rest times, nor after the lights were turned off for the night. They decided that prisoners could eat only during meals. Finally, they wanted prisoners to address the guards as "Mr. Correctional Officer." When prisoners addressed each other, they could use only their ID numbers.

Each group was then given the proper attire—guard uniforms or prison garb. In addition, the guards were given billy clubs, whistles, and the keys to the cells. These symbols helped increase the students' expectations within their new reference groups. The prisoners were placed in their cells, and then the two groups were left on their own. An experimenter acted as "warden" but did not intervene in any situations that arose. The result was a nightmare no one expected.

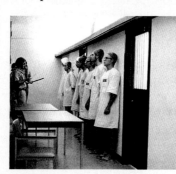

▲ *Participants in the mock prison experiment.*

The guards began viewing the prisoners as troublemakers, while the prisoners saw the guards as bullies. On the second day of the experiment, the prisoners organized a rebellion. They ripped off their ID numbers and pushed their beds against their cell doors. The guards used fire extinguishers to push the beds back and stormed the cells to regain order. During the next few days, the guards devised new rules to show their domination. They forced prisoners to complete meaningless tasks, while the prisoners thought of new ways to rebel. By the end of six days, the guards had become genuinely brutal and vicious toward the prisoners, who in turn had become docile and bitter. The experiment had to be stopped because it was literally getting out of control. The prisoners, as you would expect, were relieved and happy to end the ordeal. Disturbingly, though, some of the guards were actually disappointed.

Afterward, most of the men were embarrassed or shocked by their behavior. A number of them experienced emotional disturbances that had not been evident prior to the experiment—which explains why such an experiment would never be permitted again. During an investigation, two consultants—a 16-year inmate of a real prison and a prison chaplain—commented on how closely the behavior of the students had come to resemble that of real prisoners and guards (Zimbardo, 1972).

Review the Case Study

What kinds of rules could the guards have written that might have prevented the problems that arose during this experiment?

How We View Others

We assume we judge others objectively, relying on their individual characteristics. But that generally is not the case. All of us use stereotypes, and any of us may sometimes be guilty of prejudice and discrimination.

Stereotypes

Stereotypes originally were printing plates used to reproduce printed material. When the word **stereotype** is used in the realm of human relations, it refers to one group's ability to turn out *identical* information about every member of another group. For instance, a group may believe that all members of group A are good at math or that all people in group B have a bad character trait such as laziness.

Stereotypes can become so broad and familiar that dozens of meanings are summarized by just one name. When someone uses this name, all within hearing range are supposed to know the characteristics of the group being stereotyped.

The origin of stereotypes can be seen in studies in which subjects were given descriptions of a certain group of foreigners whom they never actually met. Most of the subjects preferred those people who were said to have characteristics similar to their own.

Prejudice and Discrimination

As we have seen, stereotypes are not, in and of themselves, bad. If we think of a member of a specific group, for instance, even though every single person looks different, we "take an average" and come up with a stereotype of what "those people" look like. We have an idea regarding what a teacher will look like, a mechanic, or a nurse. The nurse will likely be female and will wear white, even though many hospitals allow different-colored uniforms today, and many nurses are male.

We need a basis, then, for understanding and simplifying our environment, and the stereotype helps us do this. The problem arises when stereotypes cause **prejudice,** a biased judgment of other people based on the group they belong to rather than on their own individual characteristics. Given human nature and the world we live in, most of us find it very difficult to erase all of our prejudices completely. However, we can become aware of them. And we can refuse to participate in **discrimination,** mistreating or denying certain rights to people because they are members of a particular group.

Focus Question
• How can stereotypes affect how we view others?

stereotype a fixed set of beliefs about a group that is generalized to all or most group members. Stereotypes may or may not be accurate.

Focus Questions
• How do people learn prejudice?
• How can prejudice be overcome?

prejudice a biased judgment of people based on the group they belong to rather than their individual characteristics

discrimination mistreatment or denial of rights based on group membership

◀ *Do you think these groups have stereotypes of each other?*

Thinking Critically about Psychology

What Is a Stereotype?

The term *stereotype* has negative connotations attached to it. We tend to think of a stereotype as always being both inaccurate and uncomplimentary. In fact, some psychologists have defined it in those very terms. We want to look at this issue more closely.

What specifically is being claimed or stated? Stereotypes are negative, inaccurate generalizations.

What is the objective evidence for and against this claim? To begin with, most evidence suggests that stereotypes cannot be avoided. It is impossible for us to evaluate everything we see and hear on a case-by-case basis, and stereotypes help us to categorize and analyze our environment. In fact, stereotyping may have its basis in aiding the group's survival. If we have to compete with another group for food, then we must be able to identify its members in order to protect our supply. If a particular area holds certain dangers for us, then we want to avoid all such areas.

One purpose that stereotypes serve is to solidify the "in-group," thereby increasing the group's self-esteem by making the stereotyped group seem inferior or strange. Stereotypes also tend to ward off the possibility that different cultural ways will "take over." In other words, the in-group wants things to stay the way they are. Ridiculing the other group reduces that group's importance and influence. Clearly, then, stereotypes *can be* negative and inaccurate, but that does not mean they always are.

Some stereotypes are positive. For example, "Doctor" and "Reverend" generate stereotypes associated with those titles. Society reserves such titles for properly trained individuals to ensure the well-being of its members and to reassure them that they are in good hands.

▲ *Wording can determine whether a stereotype is positive or negative. Is this guy a computer whiz or a techno-geek?*

Furthermore, whether generalizations are negative depends in part on the wording. For instance, we can say that this group of people is thrifty or we can say that they are cheap. We can say that those people are lazy or that they have a more flexible view of time than we do (Jussim, McCauley, & Lee, 1995). (This principle can apply to environments as well. Is a city noisy and crowded and dangerous, or is it lively and interesting and challenging?)

Interestingly, some research has shown that people usually tend to *underestimate* the degree to which various characteristics apply to members of other groups. For instance, the idea that business majors in college wear "preppie" clothes and vote for Republicans is a stereotype, as is the idea that men drink beer and watch sports. One study investigated these stereotypes and found that in both cases, outside groups—that is, non–business majors and women—underestimated the extent to which these descriptions were valid (McCauley, 1995). Another study looked at whether teachers' actions differed on the basis of students' social class, gender, and ethnicity. Were they prejudiced against students because of these aspects? The answer was clearly "no." Regardless of what the stereotype would lead one to expect in terms of academic performance, the teachers did not rate the students or assign grades with a negative bias in mind (Jussim & Eccles, 1995).

This whole issue has taken on increased importance as our society has become more global in nature. When dealing with people from other countries, we have to draw a careful line between understanding the general ways in which their culture differs from ours and applying a rigid stereotype to individuals. Trouble can result when we fail to do either one accurately. Thus, an American employee in a Japanese company created problems in the working relationship by failing to grasp the deference to authority that is expected and required. Similarly, Americans working with a Mexican company caused unnecessary conflict when they did not take into account the fact that their hosts' idea of time was different from their own. Because neither group understood the other, the Americans viewed the Mexicans as lazy, and the Mexicans viewed the Americans as robots (Lee & Duenas, 1995).

What other interpretations might be made instead? While stereotypes do involve generalizations, they are not absolute, and people are quite capable of seeing exceptions to the rule. In addition, stereotypes do not just materialize out of thin air. They may come from a misunderstanding of behavior or from an overgeneralization where none is warranted, but there is usually some basis for them. Even so, we have to be careful in dealing with stereotypes. One important concern is that stereotypes lead people to exaggerate the characteristics of groups and then react to individual members of a group on that basis. In this regard, groups that have little power or status are likely to suffer the most (Stangor, 1995).

What are the most logical conclusions to draw? There is evidence that stereotypes are not always negative. There is also evidence that they are not always inaccurate. However, we must be careful not to overgeneralize, especially when dealing with individual members of a group.

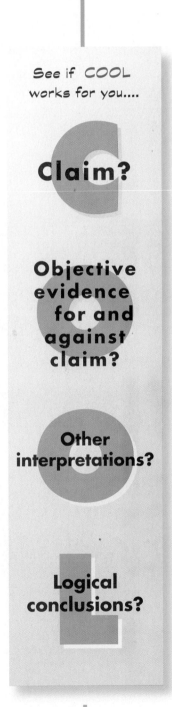

See if COOL works for you....

Claim?

Objective evidence for and against claim?

Other interpretations?

Logical conclusions?

Applying Critical Thinking Skills

Explain the purpose of stereotypes and explain why they cannot be avoided.

illusory correlations seeing relationships between things that match already held beliefs and ignoring what does not match these beliefs

Illusory Correlations. A stereotype will fight off incoming information that contradicts it. This is because we tend to form **illusory** (il-LOOSE-uh-ree) **correlations.** That is, we see relationships that match our previously set beliefs, and we ignore others. Because these relationships match (correlate), we think we have seen the two together far more often than is really the case (illusion), thus making the stereotype even stronger.

A simple experiment illustrates the principle. Subjects are shown several pairs of words an equal number of times. One of the pairs of words is *bacon-eggs,* a connection we already have. Even though *bacon-eggs* appears the same number of times as other pairs, subjects think it has appeared far more frequently.

In the same way, if we have a stereotype that the fictitious "Slobian" race is lazy, all we have to do to start the "bacon-egg" process is to see a couple of "Slobians" on different occasions lying down under a tree instead of working. We will then be convinced they "all" act that way.

Here is another example. Most males of a certain generation are convinced that females are bad drivers—at least compared with males! What happens to feed this illusory correlation is that the males store in their memories every incident in which they see a female doing something stupid in a car, while ignoring males who do the same thing or females who drive very well. If these males do store positive events that involve female drivers, they put them into the "chance happening" category (Basic Behavioral Science Task Force, 1996b).

Perception is clearly changed by such correlations. For instance, if you flash on a screen a picture of a well-dressed man holding a spoon while he stands on a subway train, adult viewers are puzzled by the spoon. But if you show them a teenage male holding a spoon in the same situation, they more often than not see the spoon as a knife.

Overcoming Prejudice. On the positive side, when students from a mixed-race class rate one another *individually* on personal characteristics, stereotypes do not show up—not even across social class or race (Sagar & Schofield, 1980). This suggests that even though stereotypes may exist for a group, an individual member may be viewed differently. Again on the positive side, the longer one lives around a different culture, the more the original negative beliefs toward that culture begin to fade.

In the same vein, the odds that someone will help another across races are affected by whether the helping behavior is face to face or "remote." In face-to-face studies, experimenters set up a situation in which a black or a white man dropped a grocery bag at a market. There was no difference in helping regardless of the race of the helper or the individual helped. The result was the same if a black or a white man with a cane fell down in a subway car.

But a difference does show up in the "remote" setup because no "real person" is present—just a stereotype. In one study, different college applications *with pictures* were left in a phone booth at an airport, with a stamped, addressed envelope and a note to "Dad" to please mail (hence, "Dad" must have dropped it on the way to his plane). In this situation, people did not respond as they did in the face-to-face arrangement. Those applications with an opposite-race picture were mailed less often (Lerner & Frank, 1974). So there is no question that prejudice is still around—that we do not deal even-handedly with all people, regardless of race or ethnic background. However, generally prejudice is not expressed as openly, face-to-face, as it used to be (Ransford & Palisi, 1992).

Perhaps you have heard of the "blue eyes–brown eyes" experiment. It was designed to increase students' awareness of the negative effects of prejudice and discrimination. In this study, a teacher divided her class according to eye color. She then announced that people with brown eyes are smarter, better students, and generally superior to those with blue eyes. For the next two days, the "brown eyes" got special privileges and extra praise. The "blue eyes" were treated like second-class citizens.

Then the teacher made a second announcement: It is not people with brown eyes who are superior, after all, but those with blue eyes. The students' roles were reversed. For the next two days, the "blue eyes" were treated specially and the "brown eyes" viewed as inferior. As you undoubtedly know, eye color actually has no bearing on intelligence or other abilities.

When the study was over, both groups had learned a great deal. They were all much more sensitive to the issue of prejudice (Peters, 1971). In daily life, it might be a good idea for us to stop now and then and try to put ourselves in someone else's situation.

Prejudice can be reduced. For example, groups "at war" with one another, as in a sports competition, feel strongly toward their own group and "hate" the other group. In one experiment, when a truck taking two opposing teams back to town from a game broke down (courtesy of the experimenter), the two groups had to cooperate and thus became one group working toward a common goal. The rivalry disappeared (Sherif, 1982). If students in racially tense classes are given projects requiring every group member's help to complete them, racial barriers also go down.

On a personal level, we can speak up to help reduce prejudice. When someone makes a racial or ethnic slur, we can let that person know how we feel. Often, even when we are uncomfortable hearing such a remark, we don't say anything, just to avoid creating a touchy situation. The trouble is that our silence may be interpreted as agreement or approval.

605

Scapegoats

If things go wrong at school or at home, most of us tend to blame someone else. Even if we are fairly open-minded, we are likely to say, "Yes, it was partly my fault, but *he* (or *she*) was mostly responsible—at least, *he* (or *she*) started it," or some variation on this theme. Psychologically, we retain balance—keep ourselves safe—by not taking the full blame.

The same mechanism works with groups; others are blamed for whatever goes wrong. Prejudice is built on this process, called **scapegoating,** in which group A blames group B for its ills. The word *scapegoat* comes from the biblical reference to a sacrificial goat. Sins were symbolically laid on the goat before it was killed as an offering.

A blatant example of scapegoating was the Nazi movement of the 1930s, which managed to incite people to the point of mass murder. Germany had been plunged into despair after its defeat in World War I. In 1933, millions of Germans were unemployed. Adolf Hitler, a scrawny man who had been rejected by the army, came up with just the right formula: "We are the result of the stress *for which others [the Jews] are responsible,*" he shouted (Bullock, 1953).

Things got so far out of control that eventually a group of 80,000 "technicians" (experts at efficient murder) exterminated approximately 6 million Jews. Assembly lines were set up in the camps, and each worker was assigned a gruesome specific task. One removed the clothing; another formed victims into lines; some took out gold fillings to get money for the Nazi cause; others worked on methods of increasing the heat to burn the bodies that were piling up. All of this resulted from Germany's identifying a scapegoat to blame for its ills.

▲ *A chilling example of scapegoating.*

scapegoating blaming someone else for what goes wrong

Removing Those Who Deviate

In less dramatic but still serious cases, group members try to "drive out the demons" by ejecting those whom they feel threaten the group's integrity. In other words, they try to remove anyone who might make the group look different from the desired image.

A group may also be threatened by the prospect of including people who compromise its goals or ideals. In group workshops, for example, where people explore ways to improve their lives, their business conditions, and so forth, the group will on occasion turn against "masculine" women who express anger or against "feminine" men who express supposedly nonmasculine emotions (Kahn, 1980).

Group behavior of this kind can become quite cruel. At school or in the workplace, for example, someone may be "boycotted" or kept out of a group because of certain characteristics that the group doesn't like, such as manner of speech, body size, appearance, or a physical defect.

Changing Attitudes

Focus Question
• How do attitudes change?

We join groups that believe the same things we do, and thus we strengthen our ideas by associating with those who agree with us. The more frequent the contact with the group, the greater the emotional investment, and the harder it is to alter one's opinion.

How, then, do attitudes change? We have already seen the influence of new reference groups. The subjects in the prison experiment discussed earlier had no idea that they would adopt the attitudes they eventually did. So playing a role, such as that of guard, can be a powerful agent in attitude change. There is more than a grain of truth in the old saying that you will understand people better after you have walked a mile in their shoes. None of us can be sure how we will respond to certain circumstances until they occur.

Cognitive Dissonance

If we find that our beliefs (cognitions) are contradictory (dissonant), it makes us uncomfortable and puts us in a state called **cognitive dissonance** (DIS-o-nance). Suppose you fall madly in love with someone who later tells you that you are stupid and a bore. Since you can't reconcile the love with the insults, you are in a state of cognitive dissonance. (Cognitive dissonance, then, creates an imbalance of beliefs.)

cognitive dissonance a contradiction between actions or events and beliefs, which causes discomfort and so must be reconciled or justified

You must do something to relieve the discomfort this causes. You must find some way to justify what happened, since it is not in harmony with what you feel about yourself or about the other person. Since you cannot change what happened, you change your beliefs, thus providing a justification and saving face. After the initial hurt, you will probably decide that your "loved one" wasn't that great a bargain after all.

Let's apply this to a topic we discussed earlier, prejudice. Traditionally, psychology has generally agreed that prejudice arises from hostility toward a group and incorrect generalizations made about that group. The basic idea is that we do this to clearly define the "other"—those outsiders who could be a threat to our own group's safety or welfare. Because we fear and are hostile toward these people, we either avoid them or treat them badly. Since we have attributed all kinds of negative characteristics to them, we see our behavior as reasonable—thus, no cognitive dissonance.

▲ *Mistreating others can lead us to believe that they deserve it in some way.*

However, a different view has recently been proposed. This view states that prejudice arises from the mistreatment of another group of people. In other words, the actions come first, and then these actions are justified by the prejudicial beliefs or attitudes (Gaines & Reed, 1995). Individual behavior can serve as an example. For instance, a girl who continually mistreats and insults her little brother can come to dislike him and believe he possesses all kinds of awful traits (Basic Behavioral Science Task Force, 1996b).

Avoiding cognitive dissonance is a very strong motivator. We like to believe that our behavior is justified—that what we think and do makes sense. Further, we will distort reality to reach that goal, if that is what it takes.

Many experiments demonstrate cognitive dissonance in operation. For instance, psychologists have measured people's attitudes on a particular topic and then had them take the *opposite* position by giving speeches and writing essays to get others to believe that point of view. Just completing the exercise had some effect. But if the subjects were then led to believe that their arguments had been successful and had changed other people's minds on the subject, the subjects became very uncomfortable indeed, especially if they knew the people they had affected. As a result, their own attitudes shifted in the direction of what they had been preaching (Cialdini et al., 1981).

Yielding to Others

Group pressure toward conformity can be very hard to fight. In a classic experiment, subjects were asked to judge the length of different lines drawn on a piece of cardboard. Specifically, the subjects had to choose which of three lines matched another line.

Subjects were formed into groups, but only one member of each group was not "in" on the experiment. All the other members worked for the experimenter. These people had the task of giving an answer that was wrong. They chose a line that was clearly too short. The goal was to put pressure on the subject to see whether or not he or she would yield and go along with the others, even though they were obviously wrong.

So the study was aimed at finding out how much people will conform to pressure from those around them. Roughly 25 percent of the subjects consistently buckled under and agreed with the rest of the group. About the same portion held on to their beliefs and gave the right answer, despite pressure from the others to agree. The remaining subjects went back and forth in their judgments. This study showed just how strong is the need of most people to "go along with the crowd."

Using basically the same experimental setup, researchers had just one of the stooges go over to the subject's side. With this small change, what had been unanimous group pressure disappeared, and the subject's agreement with the group declined dramatically (Asch, 1952).

 Pause for Thought

1. What is prejudice? What is discrimination?
2. How might illusory correlations help to strengthen stereotypes?
3. This section describes four studies on prejudice. What were the conclusions of these studies? How does scapegoating fuel prejudice?

Critical Thinking
....
4. Describe a situation you've recently experienced in which cognitive dissonance played a part. How did you overcome this dissonance?

InFocus

Conformity to Group Pressure

Which of the three lines on the right is most like the one on the left?

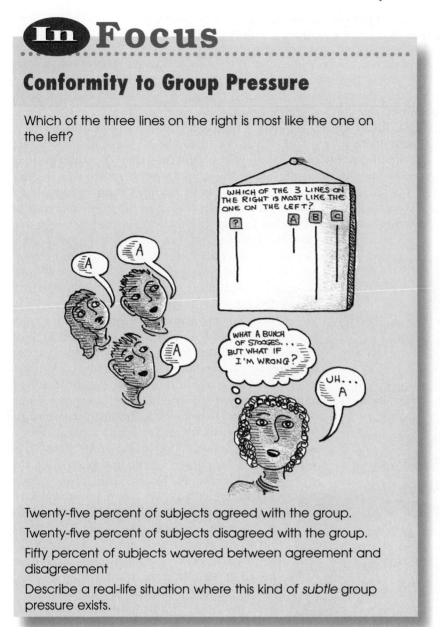

Twenty-five percent of subjects agreed with the group.

Twenty-five percent of subjects disagreed with the group.

Fifty percent of subjects wavered between agreement and disagreement

Describe a real-life situation where this kind of *subtle* group pressure exists.

Compliance with Authority

Unquestioning obedience can be very dangerous. In a now-famous laboratory experiment, the subjects, young adults, were told that they were to be a part of a "learning experiment." The task was simple.

On the other side of a screen from the subject sat a person who was a "learner." This person was a confederate of the experimenter, but the subject didn't know that. Each time the learner made an error, the subject was to send a shock to the learner by turning a dial marked off in voltages. With every error, the subject was to send a stronger shock. The dial was labeled from "mild shock" through "danger," all the way to a setting of 450 volts. The final point was marked in red, suggesting that it might trigger a fatal charge of electricity.

Focus Question

• Why do people obey authority?

At a certain point, the stooges began to cry out "in pain" (they were not really receiving shocks). Even then, many subjects obediently continued to give the erring "trainees" seemingly agonizing shocks.

In fact, a full 65 percent of the subjects obeyed instructions to give severe shocks as a penalty for failure to answer questions properly. Interviews after the experiment indicated that the subjects had been genuinely concerned that they might be injuring the people (Milgram, 1974a). Incidentally, there was no difference between male and female behavior in this experiment.

Sometimes people are skeptical, thinking that the subjects had somehow caught on to the experiment and would not do this in "real life." But in an identical experiment, with puppies right in view, subjects were willing to shock them at the command of the researcher as a "training" device. The shocks did cause the puppies to yelp and squirm uncomfortably, but the shocks were not great (again unknown to the subjects). As in the other experiment, the subjects had a dial in front of them that indicated increasing voltages (Sheridan & King, 1972).

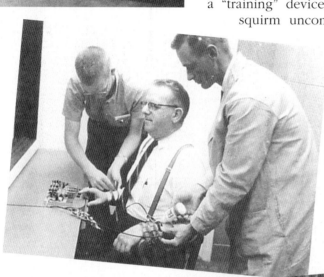

Psychologist **Stanley Milgram,** who pioneered these studies, was very distressed at how things turned out. He decided to try the experiment using physical contact with the victim, figuring *that* would make a difference. And it did. Few subjects were willing to administer shock to someone sitting right there next to them. However, some subjects ordered to force the victim's hand onto a shock plate supposedly containing 150 volts were willing to grab the person's hand and place it on the plate (Milgram, 1977).

Another study was set up at a real hospital. Twenty-two nurses were *telephoned* by a "physician" unknown to them. They were told to administer a drug to a patient while the physician was en route to the hospital, so the drug would have started taking effect by the time he got there. The experimenters used the name of a fictitious drug. They had already placed the bottle, clearly labeled with a maximum dosage, in the nursing station drug locker. On the phone, the "physician" prescribed an amount *double* the safe dosage. Twenty-one of the 22 nurses had to be stopped as they left the nurses' station, medicine in hand, to give it to the patient as ordered (Hofling et al., 1966).

▲ *Scenes from the Milgram experiments.*

Is there any saving grace in this mess? A little, at least in terms of learning a lesson. As two social psychologists have noted, the key to a lot of this destructive obedience may lie in the fact that people are often not given full responsibility for their own actions. When subjects are told that they are in charge and must account for what happens, obedience to these outlandish commands drops dramatically (Worchel & Cooper, 1983).

Verbal Persuasion

Verbal persuasion is all around us. It runs the gamut from a radio commercial to a defense attorney's plea to a jury. Persuasion by itself is neither good nor bad; each of us tries to convince others of our point of view. None of us is totally immune to the effects of persuasion. How resistant we are to an appeal depends on a number of factors.

Defenses Against Persuasion

Psychologists have studied various techniques for fighting off persuasion, called **immunization.** Can a subject be immunized against propaganda as if it were the measles? Results are inconsistent, but a few points do stand out.

For one thing, a two-sided argument in which opposing viewpoints are stated and compared seems to be a more effective immunizer than a one-sided lecture. This technique helps prepare the listener before he or she hears the propaganda from the actual "persuader," so the propaganda loses some of its punch.

In the same way, lawyers gain an advantage by presenting some of the opponent's views in watered-down form or in a way that makes those views seem insignificant. Doing this may impress judges and juries, since the lawyer seems more "open" about the issues, less biased. As a result, when the opposing attorney gets up, everyone has "already heard that argument"—but heard it from the first attorney, who probably slipped in his or her own slant (Cialdini et al., 1981).

A second point is that passively reading arguments is not as effective as having to work out one's own case for or against something. Suppose we are asked to present an argument supporting a point of view that is opposite the one we actually hold—our point of view on the death penalty, for example. Actively working on this argument results in our becoming more certain of the side we are taking, and we begin to think that this was our view all along. Of some interest, if we hear a counterargument before this new argument is settled in our brains, we tend to return to our original beliefs (Rogers & Thistlethwaite, 1969). People *gradually* change beliefs so that their beliefs match what they are saying, but it requires work on their part.

In Their Own Words . . .

Stanley Milgram *was worried that ordinary citizens in our society would behave so brutally. He stated his concerns shortly after his original experiments:*

Obedience, as a determinant of behavior, is of particular relevance to our time. It has been reliably established that from 1933–1945 millions of innocent persons were systematically slaughtered on command. Gas chambers were built, death camps were guarded, daily quotas of corpses were produced with the same efficiency as the manufacture of appliances. These inhumane policies may have originated in the mind of a single person, but they could only be carried out on a massive scale if a very large number of persons obeyed orders. (1963/1984, p. 23)

The problem of obedience is not wholly psychological. The form and shape of society and the way it is developing have much to do with it. There was a time, perhaps, when people were able to give a fully human response to any situation because they were fully absorbed in it as human beings. But as soon as there was a division of labor things changed. Beyond a certain point, the breaking up of society into people carrying out narrow and very special jobs takes away from the human quality of work and life. A person does not get to see the whole situation but only a small part of it, and is thus unable to act without some kind of overall direction. He yields to authority but in doing so is alienated from his own actions. . . . Thus there is a fragmentation of the total human act; no one is confronted with the consequences of his decision to carry out the evil act. The person who assumes responsibility has evaporated. Perhaps this is the most common characteristic of socially organized evil in modern society. (*Perils of Obedience,* 1974b)

Interpreting Primary Sources

Can you think of two or three reasons why soldiers during World War II obeyed orders to slaughter innocent people?

immunization a process in which a person is trained in how to resist persuasion or propaganda

One more human characteristic needs mentioning here. We prefer not to believe that we are influenced by others even when our actions tell a different story. For instance, although we "know" we are buying a product because of the advertising, we discount its effects. The strange part is that even when we are aware we are being persuaded by others and want to correct for it, we still usually go in the direction we have been influenced to take (Wilson & Brekke, 1996).

So defenses against persuasion work to some extent. Complete resistance to new points of view is impossible and a fiction. Long-standing beliefs can be very resistant to change.

The Sources of Information

As a rule, we are more likely to listen to a genuine expert on a subject (or one who seems to be!) than to an appealing but relatively unknowledgeable person. Advertisers should pay more attention to this fact, given their tendency to use movie or television personalities in ad campaigns. Having a tennis star advertise sports equipment works reasonably well, but having the same person push a laundry detergent is a different matter, since the viewer knows full well that stars rarely do their own laundry.

In many cases, *what* a person is saying in a commercial or a persuasive argument doesn't make as much difference as *how* it is said. If you make up lots of "impressive" statistics and claims, the true facts of the situation may be hidden and may not play a role in the opinion the listener forms.

Consciously or unconsciously, realistically or not, we are always evaluating the source of information before we act on it. If we feel it is reliable, we tend to agree; if not, we don't. Consider the following experiment: Trying to determine the influence of source credibility on saving energy, experimenters sent out two batches of identical "consumer energy-saving tips." One was sent from the electric company and the other from a "public service group." Those who received the utility's letter did not cut their energy use, while those who thought the letter was from the service group reduced their use by 7 percent (Stern, 1984).

▲ *Michael Jordan is likely to be seen as credible when advertising sports equipment, but not as much so for other products.*

Social Persuasion: Brainwashing

Focus Question

• How can friendliness and rewards be used to brainwash someone?

In war and in terrorist actions, it is not unusual for a captive to "confess" to something that is untrue or even to defect to the enemy. This results from what is commonly called brainwashing. Why this happens is very complex, but we do have clues that might help explain it.

Friendliness

Having a common enemy usually unites a group of prisoners around the prisoners' own ideals and goals. In World War II, torture was common in prison camps, thus bringing the prisoners closer together. In such situations, they did a good job of resisting pressure to expose secrets or confess.

But in the Korean and Vietnam wars, prisoners dealt with a new situation—captors who at times were unusually friendly. This approach was unexpected and, as a result, caused the prisoners confusion about resisting the enemy (Lifton, 1961). It was a calculated technique that weakened the prisoners' resolve to resist.

Sensory Deprivation

Other prisoner-of-war incidents have called attention to a severe type of punishment called **sensory deprivation.** This punishment involves no physical torture, as such, but deprives the person of the use of his or her senses. Sensory deprivation is accomplished by placing gloves, earmuffs, and a blindfold on the person and, in some cases, suspending the person in water set at body temperature. Because our bodies require stimulation, this treatment becomes intolerable very quickly.

Many a cocky college student has been taken down a peg or two by this procedure. In one study, students were asked to volunteer for a sensory deprivation experiment in which they had to do absolutely nothing but wear some of the equipment mentioned above. They were paid the equivalent of about $100 a day. Despite this, only the stoutest students could last a full three days.

Deprivation induces a fear rather like that of being lost in a vast wasteland without a sight or sound around. Because there is no stimulation, the brain begins to call on its own inner resources to make things up. For instance, visual hallucinations—seeing things that are not there—are common (Heinemann, 1970). Confusion, worry, disorientation, regret, and panic are also common symptoms (Zubek et al., 1971).

One has to assume that the students' symptoms were moderate, since they knew they could quit at any time. Prisoners are left in a state of deprivation until they agree to whatever the captors want. As far as we know, everyone eventually gives in to this psychological pressure.

You will hear about a "therapy" using isolation chambers. People lie in an enclosed tank of water and meditate. This has helped some people get more in touch with themselves, but it is completely voluntary, relatively brief, and not externally controlled. Hence, there is no comparison with psychological torture.

sensory deprivation technique used in brainwashing in which all external sensations and stimulation are removed

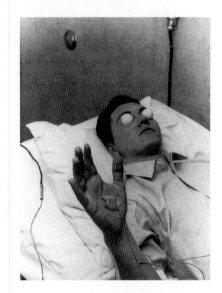

▲ *Participant in a sensory deprivation experiment.*

In Focus

How to Persuade

Present *both* sides. You'll seem more open-minded.

Actively involve your audience.

Have experts sell your message.

How you say something is often more important than *what* you say.

Suppose you wanted to convince your audience not to abuse alcohol and other drugs. How could you use each of these suggestions?

Reward System

Difficult to fight is a reward system in which prisoners are given, say, extra food for providing basically useless information about others. This technique is clever because once the captors have convinced the prisoner to give in a little, each similar behavior is a bit easier to obtain. Along the same line, minor (but useful) confessions may be elicited for a reward. Larger confessions soon follow.

Probably the most destructive aspect of this method is that it undermines the prisoners' group structure. Every person walking around with extra food is immediately suspected by the other prisoners, and they don't know exactly who is giving significant information to the enemy and to what extent.

The same basic approach is often used by police officers, and it rarely fails. They bring in two suspects who were working on a "job" together. They question each one separately. Neither knows what the other said, but the police officers make one of them think that the game is up by being very friendly, suggesting that a confession has already been obtained from the other suspect.

Brainwashing and the Consumer

Brainwashing and other forms of control are often based on the principle of compliance with a small request, followed by a reward, followed by a larger request. This same system is used by advertisers who invite you to enter a contest by simply writing down the name of their product or sending in a box top. The advertisers assume that if you perform this one small act, you will probably engage in the larger behavior of buying their product.

Studies have been fairly consistent in showing that making small requests is a good method for getting people to comply with larger ones. In one study of such techniques, women were called on the phone and asked a few questions about some household product, such as soap. A few days later, the same women were called and asked if the experimenter could bring *five men* and take a two-hour inventory of the products in the home. Having given in to the small request, 52 percent of the women agreed to the larger request.

To see if the first request had made a difference, the experimenters contacted another group and made only the larger request. Only 22 percent of the women in this group agreed to allow the inventory (Freedman & Fraser, 1966). To be sure, giving in on an issue involving soap is different from giving in on a major issue; but the principle is fairly sound.

Finally, despite the commotion we hear on occasion about thought control and such, rarely does a person change deep-seated opinions. We may be willing to "change" our beliefs for a short while. When the pressure is over, though, lifelong philosophies reappear.

▲ *Food can be a powerful incentive for a prisoner to inform on others.*

 ## Pause for Thought

1. Briefly describe the procedures used in the Milgram and Asch obedience studies discussed in the section on compliance with authority. List several conclusions of these studies.
2. Describe several methods of immunization against persuasion. What effect does an expert have on the persuasiveness of a message?

Critical Thinking
. . . .
3. Bill has a friend who seems to be interested in joining what Bill perceives to be a cult. What advice can Bill offer his friend about brainwashing?

APPLYING Psychology to Life

Resisting Peer Pressure

Throughout this chapter, we have discussed ways in which we are influenced by others. Armed with this knowledge, we can choose whether or not to let these social pressures sway us.

Peer Pressure and Risky Behavior

A problem that many teenagers face is the pressure they encounter from peers to do things they would not otherwise do. Peer pressure often emerges when some kind of risky behavior is involved—behavior the individual really does not want to engage in.

Tips on Resisting Pressure

Most teenagers have trouble resisting peer pressure, but we can give you some tips from the material covered in this chapter. While you are reading these tips, imagine how you might use them to resist pressure to do something you really do not want to do.

• First of all, realize that you are being manipulated—

that others are deliberately trying to get you to change your mind. Just knowing that can make resisting a bit easier.

• In the Asch experiments on the length of lines (p. 608), most individuals gave in and agreed with the group, even though they knew the group's answer was wrong. But subjects with only one ally tended to stick to their correct response. If you are the only holdout, you are more likely to give in. Try to get just one other person on your side, and you will feel much stronger about your position.

• People want their behavior and attitudes to be in harmony. Consequently, even if they know of some negative effects of what they are doing, they probably won't own up to them, because to do so would cause cognitive dissonance. Thus, you should be aware that you are probably not getting the whole story from the group.

• For all age groups, peers are more persuasive than other people are. The more

prestige particular peers have, the greater their influence. But peer pressure is especially important in adolescence. Consequently, what teachers, parents, or other adults say may have less impact right now. However, that does not mean that peers are more accurate. In other words, know that you are not being objective in listening more closely to them. Another way to use this tendency to your advantage is to find peers who have had a bad experience with whatever you are being urged to do and listen to what they have to say.

• Minority opinions can have an effect on the majority. One way to increase this effect is to give consistent and repeated statements of your position. Often, this technique has a private impact on the others—one that is not publicly expressed (Wood et al., 1994). So don't give up.

• If all the members of a group are on one side, doesn't that mean they are more likely to be right than a single, lone individual? Actually, a group's decision making is usually not as accurate as an individual's, particularly if the individual is well informed and highly rational (Gigone & Hastie, 1997).

• When attempting to persuade someone, group members often try to make that person feel embarrassed for not going along. Embarrassing people is an age-old tool for making them conform (Keltner & Buswell, 1997). If you know that ahead of time, perhaps it will have less impact on you.

• One of the best ways to resist conformity is to be exposed to all the arguments in favor of some risky behavior and then learn how to refute these arguments, one by one. Practicing the arguments in a role-playing situation is particularly helpful (Basic Behavioral Science Task Force, 1996b). You can do this with some friends, and you will then be in an excellent position to stand successfully on your own.

• Remember that we don't want to think we are being influenced, so we tend to discount the effects of influence. But be honest with yourself. When you realize that the only reason you are even considering doing something is because other people want you to, the odds are strongly in favor of your resisting their social pressure.

▲ *With a little preparation, it's possible to resist peer pressure.*

Summary

1. The United States is made up of many different cultures, races, and ethnic groups. Whites make up the majority. African Americans are the largest minority group, followed by Hispanics, Asian Americans, and Native Americans.

2. The field of psychology has a North American and European bias. Some of our research information may not apply to minority groups.

3. We identify with reference groups that help form and continue to support a set of beliefs that we internalize.

4. We form stereotypes because they bring organization to our world. They are not bad in and of themselves but can lead to prejudice and discrimination. Once prejudice starts, it is kept going by illusory correlations. Scapegoats are people whom we blame for our problems, even though they are not responsible.

5. We sometimes change our attitudes because of cognitive dissonance. In this situation, contradictions in our beliefs cause us to feel uncomfortable, so we realign our beliefs. We also often yield to pressure from others without even knowing it. Obedience studies show that any of us might yield too much to the pressure of authority.

6. Brainwashing is not a technique that normally has lasting effects. Methods used in brainwashing include friendliness, sensory deprivation, and rewards.

▲ *People wander among teepees during the One Mind, One Heart, One Voice, One Prayer Vigil for peace and the environment. Representatives of the Native nations of North and South America gathered on the Mall near the Washington Monument for the event.*

Vocabulary

Review Questions

Fill in the Blanks

On a sheet of paper, write the word or words that best complete each statement.

1. The statement "All Slobians are lazy," is an example of a ▐▐▐▐▐▐▐.

2. Treating all members of an ethnic group the same way is a sign of ▐▐▐▐▐▐▐.

3. When we ▐▐▐▐▐▐▐ a group's beliefs, we adopt them as our own.

4. We often perceive the world differently because of the various ▐▐▐▐▐▐▐ with which we identify.

5. If we blame tall people for indirectly raising clothing prices, tall people then are ▐▐▐▐▐▐▐.

6. When we use ▐▐▐▐▐▐▐, we see in others only what we want to see and ignore other information.

7. Two-sided arguments often lead to ▐▐▐▐▐▐▐.

8. Contradictory beliefs lead to ▐▐▐▐▐▐▐.

True/False

On a sheet of paper, answer each statement true *or* false. *If false, rewrite to make it true.*

9. Stereotypes often lead to prejudice.

10. Illusory correlations tend to weaken stereotypes.

11. Recent studies indicate that face-to-face prejudice seems to be decreasing.

12. When faced with cognitive dissonance, most people will change their beliefs.

13. Milgram's subjects delivered high voltages of shock because they suspected that no one was actually getting hurt.

14. Someone who will be held responsible for his or her actions is less likely to obey an authority.

15. Without external stimulation, the brain creates its own stimulation.

16. Sensory deprivation can cause hallucinations.

17. Immunization helps us resist persuasion.

18. Most of Zimbardo's subjects quit the experiment.

19. Friendliness is one technique used to brainwash prisoners of war.

20. Reference groups provide standards of behavior.

Discussion Questions

1. Describe two of your most important reference groups. Discuss several similarities and differences between these two groups. Overall, are there more similarities or differences? Explain.

2. List several stereotypes of teachers and discuss (without using names) whether your teachers this year fit these stereotypes.

3. If you were dating someone for several months and then found out that this person was extremely prejudiced against a certain ethnic group, do you think you might eventually stop dating the person for this reason? Explain.

4. Compare some of the attitudes you have today with those you had when you were in junior high school. Have they remained basically the same? If yes, do you *express* them differently? Explain. If your attitudes have changed, in what ways? Explain.

5. While Milgram's obedience studies are fascinating, they also put the subjects involved under a great deal of stress at times. Experimenters always need to strike a balance between *how* they get their results and *what* they find out. Some might argue that Milgram's studies do not achieve this balance—that it is not ethical to put subjects under so much stress, regardless of what is learned. Do you agree? Why or why not? Explain.

6. How do advertisers establish credibility for their products? Describe several real advertising examples to support your answer.

7. As noted in the chapter, sensory deprivation may cause hallucinations. What kinds of occupations would be most affected by this problem? Explain. Keep in mind that not all the senses need to be deprived at one time to cause problems.

8. Most of us admit that peer pressure is out there, but we'd like to believe that this pressure doesn't affect us. Describe several of your behaviors that might be affected by subtle peer pressure.

Activities and Projects

1. Write a "letter to the editor" to your school newspaper on the issue of multicultural harmony. If your school has achieved what you perceive to be true harmony, the letter could be written in a congratulatory tone and might include reasons why people are getting along. Or you can discuss how other schools can adopt your school's policies and attitudes. If your school needs improvement in multicultural harmony, state the problems, and then offer numerous concrete, practical solutions to the problems. Ask your teacher about the length of the letter and about the possibility of actually submitting the letter to the newspaper.

2. Pick two people who have helped to shape your attitudes and beliefs, and write a letter of appreciation to each of them. Be specific as to the kinds of things that the person did or said and what effect these things have had on your past and present values and beliefs.

Something unexpected usually happens after you've written these kinds of letters: You not only feel better about the people to whom you wrote but you also tend to feel better about yourself! No one will force you to do this, but once you receive credit for the letters from your teacher, why don't you mail them and spread some of the positive feelings you experience to others?

3. Conduct the illusory correlation (or "bacon-eggs") experiment described in the chapter. Think of five familiar word pairs: bacon-eggs, lion-roar, and so on. Think of five unfamiliar word pairs: night-fork, gamble-bed, and so on. Write *each* word pair, both familiar and unfamiliar, on five separate index cards. In other words, five cards will say "bacon-eggs," five will say "lion-roar," and so on. You will have a total of 50 index cards.

    Procedure: Mix up the cards and hand them to your first subject. (*Note:* Do *not* mix them blindly as you would with playing cards. Make sure the same word pair does not appear two times in a row.) The subject will look at the first card for three seconds (yes, time it), and then you will announce, "next." The subject will then put the card face down onto the table or desk and look at the next card. After the subject has gone through all the cards, give him or her a separate sheet of paper with all the word pairs listed. Ask the subject to indicate how many times each word pair appeared on the cards. This list should mix the familiar and unfamiliar word pairs evenly: Word pair number 1 would be familiar, number 2 would be unfamiliar, and so on. Record the subject's answers. Repeat this entire procedure on 20 subjects. Analyze your results in detail.

4. Conduct research on an extreme kind of reference group: cults. Find out: (a) the broad definition of a cult; (b) *how* new cult members internalize the beliefs and attitudes of the cult; (c) what the established members of the cult do to promote this internalization process; (d) why people join cults; (e) how and why people leave cults. Organize this information into a report and include your reactions.

    You will probably acquire your information from books or magazines, but at least consider another source: a police station. Often, someone there has, through necessity, become a sort of expert on the topic.

5.   This chapter mentions that advertisers often use celebrities to promote products about which they probably know little. These ads do not seem highly credible. Flip through several magazines and find a bunch of ads that *do* strike you as credible for one reason or another. Also find ads that do *not* strike you as credible. Organize these ads into a creative collage. Be sure that the collage somehow presents the message about credibility versus incredibility. Perhaps you can do this by including appropriate captions—for example, "Would this man do his own laundry?" Once the collage is completed, display it in class.

Statistical Measures: Reporting Experimental Findings

Statistics are nothing more than a kind of shorthand, a way to collapse large groups of numbers into one or two, so comparisons can be made easily. **Statistics,** then, include any numerical process used to group, assemble, organize, or analyze information.

Graphical Analysis

In some studies, the experimenter varies the instructions on a particular task in order to vary the amount of pressure put on the individual who has been asked to solve a problem. As pressure to solve the problem increases, anxiety increases. With high anxiety, efficiency decreases drastically.

One study shows the effect of anxiety on test performance. Discussing the results will show how graphs work and how they help to clarify the findings of a psychological study.

The experimenter administered a questionnaire to a large group of students (Sarason et al., 1952). From the information he obtained about their feelings and responses to test situations, he was able to pick out two groups. One group was what might be called "high-anxious"—or, in everyday terminology, high-strung, prone to nervousness, or quite jumpy in a tight situation. The other group was low on the anxiety rating, meaning these people were calm, not nervous or jumpy under pressure.

The two groups were given a test. Each subject worked individually on the task of matching various symbols with numbers using a key (see Figure A.1). The test was too long to be completed in the time allotted, yet the subjects were told that they were "expected to finish."

The subjects were given five chances to succeed at the task. In other words, they took the test five times in succession. In psychological terminology, these five chances are called five **trials.**

Here is a report of the results: The scores varied from 27 through 43 on the five trials for the two groups. The low-anxious group scored consistently higher (better) for each of the five trials. In every case, they did better on the task than the high-anxious group. Even on the fifth trial, the low-anxious group continued to score better than the high-anxious group.

Although this verbal report is accurate, it does not help us to visualize the results of the experiment. Such results are difficult to visualize from verbal accounts, no matter how well organized or written. This problem comes up frequently in the reporting of psychological experiments. **Graphs** are used to clarify and organize facts visually. A graph of this experiment is shown in Figure A.2.

The horizontal line, or axis, at the base of Figure A.2 is marked off to indicate the number of trials (1, 2, 3, 4, 5). The vertical line, or axis, at the left indicates the scores obtained by the subjects. A legend, similar to one found on a road map, shows the reader which line represents which group in the study. The lines themselves connect a series of dots. Each dot represents a point on the horizontal axis (trial line) and a point on the vertical axis (score line).

The two arrows you see in Figure A.2 do not normally appear in graphs. They have been added here to explain how the position of the dots is determined. Assume that the experimental results show that, on trial 2, the average score of all the subjects in the high-anxious group was 35. An arrow moves from 35 on the score axis (vertical) over to the right

Key

1	2	3	4	5
v	X	T	<	Z

2	5	1	4	2	3
X	Z				

5	4	1	3	2	3

Test taker writes in symbols using key above.

▲ *Figure A.1* *Digit-Symbol Task*

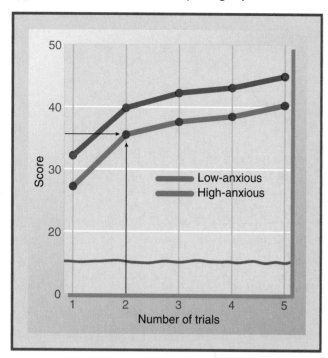

Score

Number of trials

Low-anxious
High-anxious

▲ *Figure A.2* *Performance of High- and Low-Anxious Subjects on Digit-Symbol Task*

until it meets an arrow coming up from trial 2 on the trial axis (horizontal). The point at which they meet is the point at which the dot is placed. Put another way, the dot represents trial 2, for which the average score of high-anxious subjects equaled 35.

With that out of the way, notice how easy it is to see the results of the experiment just by looking at the graph. The dotted line (high-anxious) is consistently below the straight line (low-anxious). High anxiety, then, appears to keep the level of performance low through all five trials. If this explanation is not completely clear, go back to the paragraph in which the results of the experiment were described, and compare the verbal description with the graph in Figure A.2.

You will see hundreds of graphs in scientific reports. They all follow the same principle as the one we've just shown you.

Correlation

Almost all psychological studies involve comparisons. The intelligence of a student is compared with school grades; problems in the home are compared with delinquency rates; amount of narcotics taken is compared with amount of disorganized behavior; and so on. One statistical tool used to make these comparisons is **correlation.**

Correlation is simply a measure of how things are related to one another, or co-related. For example, look at Figure A.3, which lists the heights of parents and their grown children. Nothing could be more obvious than the fact that the heights of children are correlated with the heights of their parents. Parents who are tall have children who are taller than the children of parents who are short. For example, the offspring in family C (69.5 inches) are taller than the offspring in family E (68.2 inches). And the parents in family E are shorter than those in family C. Therefore, a relationship must exist between height of parents and height of children.

How do we go about putting this relationship into numbers? Mathematicians have figured out a way. Look at Figure A.4. In this figure, each point represents the height of a set of parents (vertical axis) and the height of their children (horizontal axis). A diagonal line extends from the lower left to the upper right. This line must come as close as possible to all the points while remaining a straight line. The amount of distance *between the dots and the line* indicates how close a relationship there is between the two characteristics (height of parents and height of offspring). In other words, it shows the correlation.

Graphs like this can show different strengths in relationships. For example, Figure A.5 (hypothetical) shows a perfect relationship; there is no difference between the points and the straight line. Figure A.6 (hypothetical) shows a weak relationship; there is a great difference between the points and the line.

It is possible, with highly accurate graph paper, actually to measure the distances between the points and the diagonal line and to place them in a formula to determine the degree of relationship. Rather than do all

Family	Parents	Offspring
A	72.5	72.2
B	71.5	69.9
C	70.5	69.5
D	69.5	68.9
E	68.5	68.2
F	67.5	67.6
G	66.5	67.2
H	65.5	66.7
I	64.5	65.8

▲ *Figure A.3* *Average of Heights of Parents and Offspring (in Inches)*

624

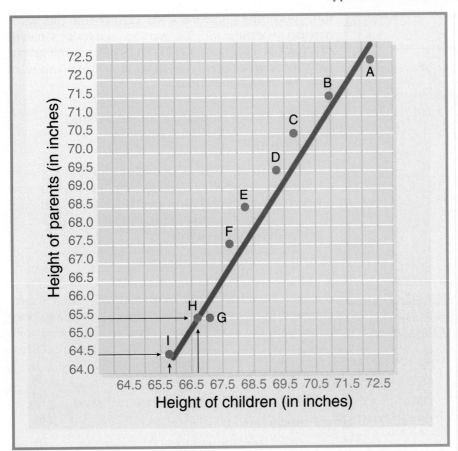

◀ **Figure A.4** *Correlation of Average Heights of Parents and Children*

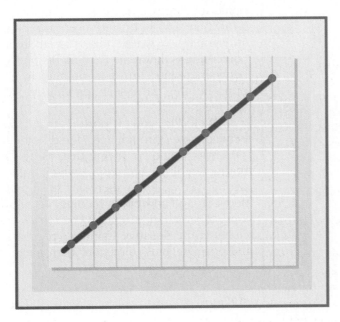

▲ **Figure A.5** *Perfect Correlation*

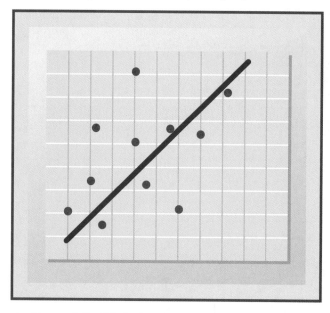

▲ **Figure A.6** *Weak Correlation*

this measuring, however, we can obtain the same results by dealing with the numbers *directly* by means of a mathematical formula. The reason for using graphs here for correlations is to provide a visual image of what we are talking about.

Reading, Interpreting, and Reporting Correlations

Correlation, then, is a measure of the apparent relationship between two things. The numbers for correlation, called **correlation coefficients,** vary from 0 to 1. Zero means no relationship exists, while 1 means a perfect relationship exists.

Words of caution: It is a rare student who does not confuse correlation with percentages at the beginning. A correlation is not in any sense the same as a percentage. Correlation numbers *look like* percentages. They are *not*. Nonetheless, at least one similarity does exist—the higher the number, the more the two items seem to be related.

So the size of the correlation indicates the strength of the relationship; the higher the number, the stronger the relationship:

Typical correlations:

| .00 | .15 | .38 | .59 | .70 | .89 | .90 | 1.00 |

Relationship getting stronger →   →   →

Here, the number .00 means no correlation exists; 1.00 means perfect correlation exists. A correlation coefficient can be *any* number between 0 and 1.

Now, suppose we examine the relationship between bottle feeding and age. As age increases, bottle feeding will decrease. At age five, there are a few hangers-on; by age seven, maybe one. Look at Figure A.7, where this correlation is plotted. Something is different. The line fits pretty squarely between points, but it is running in a direction opposite the ones seen previously. What does this mean?

Well, if you reported that "correlation between age (through age 7) and bottle feeding is .90," you would be saying that, as age *increases,* bottle feeding *increases,* which obviously is wrong. Yet we know there is a strong relationship between age and bottle feeding. To allow for this kind of situation, scientists use correlation coefficients in the negative (minus) direction as well as the positive (plus) direction. Both mean the *same*

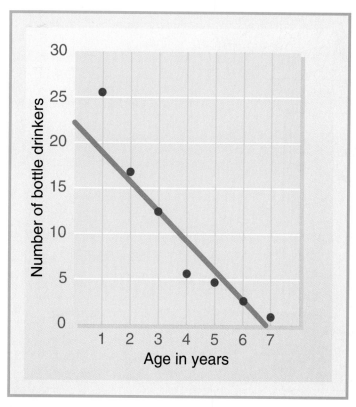

◀ **Figure A.7** *Correlation of Bottle Feeding with Age*

thing in terms of *degree* of relationship. A negative .90 correlation (−.90) is just as strong as a positive .90 correlation (.90).

The negative correlation means that, as one variable (age) goes one way (increases), the other variable (bottle feeding) goes the other way (decreases). The positive correlation means that, as one variable goes one way, the other variable goes the same way (as height of parents goes up, that of the children goes up).

The following *rough* guides can be used to interpret correlation coefficients:

- From .00 to +.20 or −.20 means an indifferent or negligible relationship exists.
- From +.20 or −.20 to +.40 or −.40 means a low correlation exists. A relationship is present, but it is slight.
- From +.40 or −.40 to +.70 or −.70 means a substantial or marked correlation exists.
- From +.70 or −.70 to +1.00 or −1.00 means a strong to perfect relationship exists.

A Word of Caution

Correlation coefficients show the degree to which two things are related to each other. They do *not* necessarily show a cause-and-effect relationship. For instance, suppose we find that students with good grades in school tend to do well on achievement tests. Given these two numbers, grade point average and achievement-test performance, can we say that grades cause the test scores or vice versa? No. Instead, it is far more likely that both are caused by other things, like basic intellectual ability, study habits, quality of education, home atmosphere, motivation, and so on. Similarly, the length of one's arms and the length of one's legs are correlated with one another, but it is not very likely that one causes the other. Instead, both are probably caused by a "program" in the genes that directs the body's overall development, with nutrition and general health playing a role.

The Normal Curve: Fitting People into Groups

All sciences must bring order to a large number of facts. This holds true for psychology as well. Somehow people and their characteristics have to be brought together in an orderly fashion. Otherwise, people can't be studied in a way that permits comparison.

The scientist putting things and people into categories often uses diagrams to represent these categories. Take the case of investigators who, using numbers, must show the difference in wealth among various groups in a country called Moolahland. The citizens are extremely normal, and the national currency is the bucko **(B)**. The investigators want to show how many families in Moolahland make 10,000 buckos a year, how many make 50,000 buckos, and how many make 90,000 buckos. They have found that approximately 3 million families fall into the first category, 15 million into the second, and 3 million into the third.

Suppose that you draw a line to equal, in length, the number of families in each category:

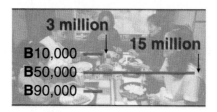

You have created a visual representation of income and families divided by categories. If you wanted to include more data (assuming you had such data), you could draw a line for each of a large number of income categories. You might obtain something approximating this diagram:

(The larger the number of families, the longer the line.)

Now you can turn the diagram on its side, connect the highest points, and remove the lines, as shown in Figure A.8. The curve that results is called a bell-shaped or **normal curve.** This same curve represents (in a rough fashion) the distribution of a large number of things in the world. Psychologists use it frequently to illustrate characteristics of people as a whole or to categorize people along a certain dimension. It is used to represent visually how large numbers of people are distributed.

You can see how the normal curve works by examining the hypothetical curve of cleanliness in Figure A.9. Most people (the norm, or normal—that is, what is to be expected) are going to be in the middle in the more-or-less clean group (see the rectangle in Figure A.9). Some people are

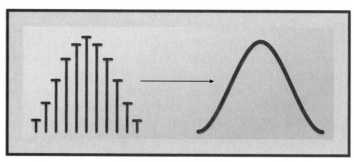

▲ *Figure A.8* *A Bell-Shaped Curve*

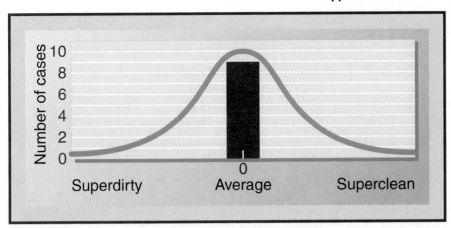

going to deviate from this norm. At the far right of the curve in Figure A.9 might be the superclean, the bathtub dwellers. As we move along the curve toward the superclean, the number of individuals becomes smaller and smaller. Sliding to the left, we move away from the norm toward the superdirty, represented at the far left (and fortunately also in the minority).

The technical name for Figure A.9 is a *normal frequency distribution*. This means that, after having counted (determined frequency), we have a distribution (arrangement) that fits the normal (quite frequently found) arrangement of things: few superdirty, few superclean, most in the middle. Figure A.10 describes this arrangement in more detail.

Height of individuals is a characteristic that fits the normal frequency distribution curve. Another is intelligence-test results, which would include the very bright at one end of the curve, the very dull at the other, and the average in the middle.

Figure A.11 shows the percentage of subjects (persons, things, events, and so on) that would fall within a certain area of the curve if the curve were perfect. (It is never perfect, but sometimes it comes close.) The largest group of subjects fall into the middle (68 percent); 95 percent of the subjects are included within the second set of lines; and at 99 percent,

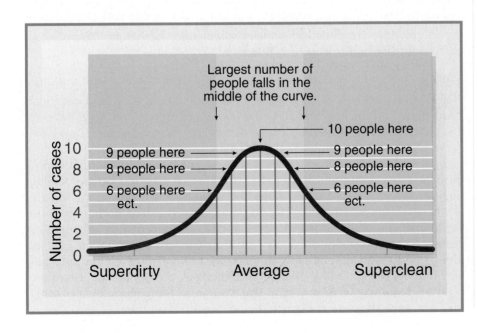

◀ *Figure A.10* *Normal Frequency Distribution*

▶ **Figure A.11** *Breakdown of Normal Curve*

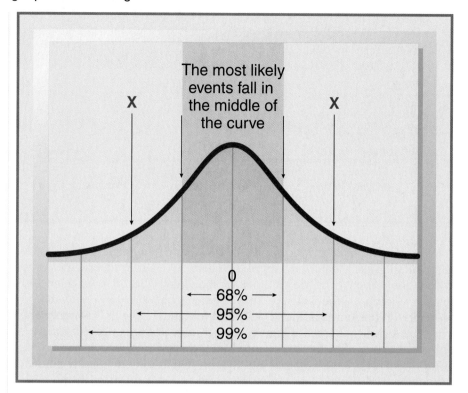

the third set of lines, nearly all subjects are accounted for. For example, 68 percent of the people in a typical group are average in cleanliness. (In other words, if we studied and categorized 100 individuals, 68 of them would fall between the two lines indicated.) All people vary somewhat, but they can be classified according to these individual differences. Some are cleaner than others, some brighter than others.

The purpose of this discussion has been to acquaint you in a general way with a distribution curve. The normal curve is a representation of the way in which people are distributed through a given population according to certain characteristics, such as intelligence or height. The normal curve does not fit all situations, however.

The normal curve is an idealized one, so of course, the psychologist will run into other curves, some of them very oddly shaped. For example, if fifth-grade children were given a third-grade test, they would get most items right, and the curve would look something like Figure A.12. Reverse the procedure and give the fifth-grade test to the third-graders, and the curve will look something like Figure A.13.

Since Figures A.12 and A.13 deviate so much from the normal curve, they serve the useful function of showing immediately that we are dealing with an unusually distributed behavior or occurrence. These curves are not normal curves, and the percentages discussed earlier do not apply to them. The curves do, however, give a visual representation of numbers pertaining to grouped individuals, and they can quickly supply a general idea of performance, removing the need for tedious research into the specific numbers obtained for each subject. Since all these kinds of curves are used so frequently, it is important that you grasp the general idea of what they are, how they are constructed, and how to read them.

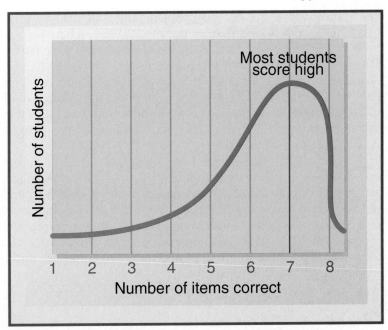

Mean, Median, and Mode: Representative Numbers

Three other mathematical measures are used in psychology to condense information into accessible form. Suppose, for example, we have five scores: 25, 26, 24, 24, and 21. If we add them together and divide by 5 (the number of scores), the result is 24—very close to representing all these scores. This number is called the arithmetic **mean.** In everyday language, it is called the average.

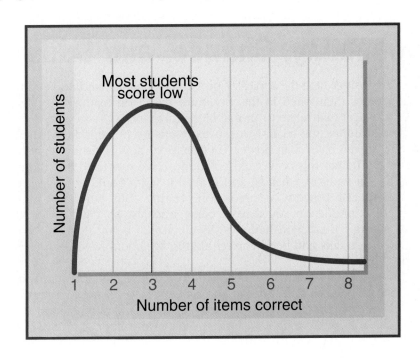

The scores above present no problem. But suppose we took the scores 3, 5, 6, 7, and 30 and figured the mean. We'd obtain 10.2, which would not be very representative of the many small scores we have (four out of five are below 10). The major problem with the mean, therefore, is that it can be inflated or deflated by a few extremely high or low numbers. (We should note, though, that this problem is sometimes an advantage, since the mean is sensitive to extreme scores and includes them in its calculation. As you will see, neither the median nor the mode takes extreme numbers into consideration.)

In the case of the numbers just listed (3, 5, 6, 7, and 30), we can get the best possible representative number by using what is called the **median,** or halfway mark—the midpoint of a list of ordered numbers. Since we have an odd number of digits in our list, the midpoint or median will be the middle number, 6. This number is much more representative of the scores than 10.2. To find the median in a list with an even number of entries, we merely take the middle two numbers in the list, add them together, and divide by 2. For example:

Scores: 3, 5, 5, 6, 7, 30

5 + 6 = 11

11 ÷ 2 = 5.5

Median: 5.5

The third representative numerical measure is the **mode.** It is simply the most frequently appearing number. The mode is adequate if you have a set of scores such as 3, 7, 9, 9, 12, and 14, because here the mode (9) occurs close to the middle of the series. But the most frequent number might appear at a strange place. For instance, consider 3, 3, 3, 9, 9, 12, 14, and 17. Here, the mode is 3 and certainly does not represent the group of numbers.

Of the three kinds of representative numbers we have discussed, the mean is the most frequently used. It is typically used with other statistics, but it can be used by itself.

Probability, Chance, and Odds

We consider next the topics of probability, chance, and odds. Almost all the studies mentioned in this book are based on mathematical measures (statistics) that relate to probability and chance.

For example, the basic issue in extrasensory perception is whether individuals even have such power. Let's consider how statistics might help determine whether this power exists. Suppose we predicted that the next flip of a coin would be heads, and indeed it was. Would you agree that we had special powers of prediction? Hardly. But why not? Simply because our prediction could have come true just by chance. In other words, a single prediction had a 50-50 chance of being right. We could have predicted tails and been correct; that is, we could have been correct just by chance.

No one knows what chance is. We do, however, assume that certain fixed laws operate in the universe and influence, for example, the roll of dice. In addition to these laws, there is chance: the unknown factors influencing the roll, which might include the tilt of the floor, the particles in the air, the angle of the hand, and so on. Even though the universal laws operate, unknown or chance factors constantly enter into any occurrence. So at any given time, almost anything could occur just by chance once, or maybe twice, or maybe even a few more times.

Now suppose we could correctly predict the roll of dice 99 percent of the time for 1,000 throws. We assume you would then give us the credit we deserve for our special abilities. Why? Because something other than chance must be operating.

The same considerations apply to studying extrasensory perception or even the finding that a person is a delinquent and comes from a broken home. We might be able to guess what card someone is holding by chance alone. Or a delinquent could come from a broken home by chance; there might be no relationship between the home and the child's later behavior.

We need a statistic that will determine just how far-fetched it is to assume that chance is operating. If, for example, we were to apply a statistic to our 99-percent-correct predictions of dice rolls, we would find that the likelihood that chance alone is working *this often* is quite remote. In fact, we can be almost certain that something other than chance is operating, even if it is nothing more than our having loaded the dice.

Statistics on how far the results of a given study are removed from the effects of chance are reported in the same fashion as other statistics are. We will get to this in a moment. First, it might be worthwhile to start the discussion all over again with another example to clarify these concepts.

One universal fact about human beings is that not everyone behaves in the same way. How, then, is it possible to make *any* statements about human behavior? We have already discussed correlation, but other statistical methods also give information about experimental findings.

Suppose, for example, that we take a group of men we find loitering on the corner somewhere and discover their weights to be 150, 165, 140, 160, and 325 pounds. Immediately, we are struck by the highly deviant weight of 325, something expected very rarely. Also, we begin to speculate on how this man became so heavy. Maybe a glandular problem, maybe overeating. No one, however, tries to speculate on how a man comes to weigh 140 or 160 pounds. There's nothing unusual about it.

Reverse the situation. Experimenters think they have found a drug that induces weight increase. They administer it to a group of four males and then examine them 10 years later, finding that their weights are 140, 150, 180, and 175 pounds. Assuming that their physiques correspond roughly to these weights, we can conclude that this is a very ineffective drug for increasing weight.

Using another drug, the experimenters find 10 years later that the subjects weigh 325, 298, 310, and 170 pounds. The heavier weights are rare. Because of this rarity, the researchers can entertain the hypothesis that the drug induces weight gain. Chance might have given them one unusual weight, but it is highly unlikely that they would have obtained three out of four strikingly deviant weights just by chance. In other words, the likelihood that this event occurred just by chance is remote. The scientist is always trying to demonstrate that the results obtained would have been highly improbable if chance had been the only factor operating.

Notice that in this latter study, the results were not totally consistent. Three of the weights were unusually high, but the fourth, 170, was not. Similarly, psychological experiments, including ESP experiments, intelligence testing, predictions of group behavior, and so on, never produce results that

633

are 100 percent rare. The psychologist is looking for results that *approach* statistical rarity. The best way to understand this is to return to coin tossing.

In coin tossing, using a fairly new and untampered-with coin, the **probability,** or odds, that you will get either heads or tails is, in lay terminology, 50-50 (in statistical language, $p = .50$, where p stands for probability). In other words, *in theory*, every 100 tosses of a coin should yield 50 heads and 50 tails.

In actuality, for any given set of 100 coin tosses, you might get 40 heads and 60 tails, 55 heads and 45 tails, and so on. Chance (unknown or accidental) factors are operating to give slight variations in the numbers of heads and tails. The nature of these chance factors is unspecified, but they are assumed *not* to operate in a consistent fashion. In other words, sometimes, owing to chance, heads will appear a few more times; sometimes, tails will appear a few more times. Eventually, these variations will cancel one another out to result in overall figures close to 50-50.

If you have any money riding on the flips and they come up 20 tails and 80 heads, you should investigate the coin immediately on the grounds that something other than chance is operating—for example, a weighted coin. The discrepancy is too far removed from what normally occurs by chance alone.

This is exactly what experimenters do: They look for results that are very remote from chance, just as it is very remote that 20 tails and 80 heads would occur merely by chance. Note that it *is* physically possible for this to happen, but it is so rare as to be considered improbable. It is more logical to search for a reason—a loaded coin—than to assume chance is the cause.

It is interesting to see what happens if you toss 10 different coins at the same time 1,024 times. First of all, even with so many coins, the law of probability will still work. We could expect 5 heads and 5 tails from the 10 coins more often than any other combination. Next most probable would be 4 heads and 6 tails or 6 heads and 4 tails. Something to be expected *very* rarely would be 10 tails or 10 heads.

Figure A.14 shows a curve that closely represents the results obtained from throwing a group of 10 coins 1,024 times. Note that a toss of 10 heads or 10 tails comes up only once in 1,024 tosses. The odds are 1,024 to 1 of getting either 10 heads or 10 tails.

Figure A.14 is the normal curve again. In Figure A.15, we mark off the percentage of occurrences of various combinations on the curve. Take the combination of 10 heads. It falls at a point (indicated by the arrow that points off the page) beyond the 99 percent level of the curve—actually, a little beyond the 99.9 percent level—meaning that over 99.9 percent of all other combinations fall below this point on the curve. Looked at another way, 10 heads leaves only .1 percent ($\frac{1}{10}$ of 1 percent) of the curve.

The whole curve, 100 percent, is going to equal 1.00 when the percentage is changed to a decimal (1.00). To find out how much of the curve representing 10 heads is left, we change 99.9 percent to .999 and subtract it from 1.00; .001 is the remainder. This figure as a fraction is $\frac{1}{1,000}$ and means that one time in 1,000 (actually, in our case, $\frac{1}{1,024}$) could this occur by chance alone. Thus, it is *extremely* rare.

In the sciences, even though we know that an event *could* conceivably occur with a p (probability) of .001 and still result from chance, such an event is so rare that scientists assume that it is more likely caused by the variable studied than by chance. Thus, if scientists find that statistics demonstrate that what they found in a study could occur only once in

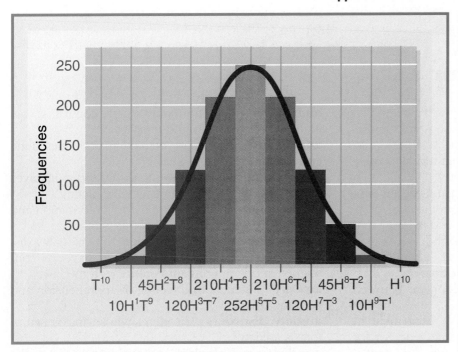

◀ *Figure A.14* *Normal Frequency Distribution in Coin Tossing*

1,000 times by chance alone, they assume that chance is not the important factor. Another way of saying this is that the results reached the .001 level of **significance,** meaning that only 1 out of 1,000 times would such a finding occur by chance.

The .001, .01, and .05 levels are typically agreed on by scientists as indicating significant (important) findings. These levels are reported in scientific studies as $p = .001$, $p = .01$; $p = .05$, respectively. The experimenter decides before the experiment what level of significance will be acceptable. For most studies, a level of .05 is considered good enough. If the results turn out to be even more significant—say, .01 or .001—so much the better.

◀ *Figure A.15* *Breakdown of Normal Curve*

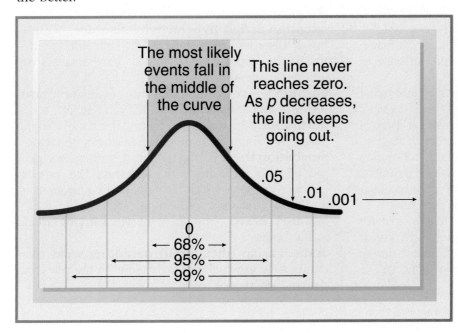

GLOSSARY

A

absolute threshold the level of sensory stimulation necessary for sensation to occur

acetylcholine neurotransmitter that regulates basic bodily processes such as movement

achievement tests tests that measure the amount of specific material remembered from the classroom

acoustic memory a very brief sound memory that can be sent to the short-term memory

adaptation the gradual loss of attention to unneeded or unwanted sensory information

adolescence the period of development between childhood and adulthood

adrenal glands glands that cause excitement in order to prepare the body for an emergency or for some important activity; also involved in sexual maturation

adrenaline chemical that prepares the body for emergency activity by increasing blood pressure, breathing rate, and energy level

afterimage image that remains after stimulation of the retina has ended. Cones not used fire to bring the visual system back in balance.

age regression process of reliving one's very early childhood under hypnosis

agoraphobia the fear of leaving a familiar environment, especially home

alarm reaction first stage of the general adaptation syndrome—preparation for an attack

alcohol withdrawal delirium mental confusion that occurs in severe alcoholism in the absence of alcohol

alpha waves fairly relaxed brain waves that occur in stage 1, just before we go to sleep

Alzheimer's disease a disease involving loss of chemical nerve cell transmitters and other damage to nerve transmission that result in mental deterioration

amnesia a dissociative disorder in which traumatic events seem to disappear from memory; the blocking of older memories and/or the loss of new ones

amygdala limbic system structure responsible for emotional responses, particularly aggression and fear

anal stage Freudian stage of development during which toilet training is the child's major concern

androgen the male sex hormone

androgens male hormones; they control sexual interest in both males and females

androgyny the quality of having both masculine and feminine characteristics

anorexia nervosa an eating disorder that involves severe loss of weight from excessive dieting

antecedents in atttribution theory, information and beliefs a person already has about another

antisocial personality disorder a personality disorder in which the person seems to have no conscience and is in constant conflict with the law.

anxiety a generalized feeling of apprehension and pending disaster

anxiety disorders disorders whose major symptom is anxiety

applied psychologists psychologists who make direct use of the findings of research psychologists; they deal directly with clients

approach-approach conflict a conflict involving a choice between two attractive alternatives

approach-avoidance conflict a conflict involving a situation with both good and bad features

aptitude one's special skills

aptitude tests tests that measure one's special skills (in carpentry, medicine, and so forth)

archetypes Jung's term for inherited universal human concepts

attention alert focusing on material

attention deficit/hyperactivity disorder a childhood disorder characterized by inattention, distractibility, impulsiveness, and/or excessive activity and restlessness

attitude general, long-lasting evaluation that includes emotions and behavioral tendencies

attribution in attribution theory, the act of making judgments about the causes for another's behavior

attribution theory theory that describes how people explain the causes of behavior. The process includes antecedents, attribution, and consequences.

audition the sense of hearing

auditory nerve bundle of nerves carrying sound to the brain

authoritarian (dictatorial) parenting style parenting style in which parents rigidly set the rules and demand obedience

authoritative parenting style parenting style in which parents seek input from children; parents are consistent but flexible in enforcing rules

autistic disorder a childhood disorder characterized by a failure to develop normal patterns of communication, social interactions, and emotional responses

autonomic nervous system the automatic control system of the body; regulates breathing, heart rate, digestion, and so on

aversive conditioning a behavioral technique in which unpleasantness is associated with acts that are to be avoided

avoidance-avoidance conflict a conflict involving a choice between two unattractive alternatives

awfulize to see things in the worst possible light; Ellis's term

axon part of the neuron that carries messages away from the cell to the dendrites on another neuron

B

behavioral approach an approach that views behavior as the product of learning and associations

behavioral therapy therapy that uses principles of learning to alter the person's actions or behavior

behaviorism a personality theory that focuses on overt acts or behaviors

belongingness needs needs at the third level of Maslow's hierarchy: friendship, closeness with another

beta waves rapid brain waves; appear when a person is awake

biological clocks internal chemical units that control regular cycles in parts of the body

biopsychological approach an approach that views behavior as strongly influenced by physiological functions

bipolar disorder a mood disorder involving high and low moods

blind spot the portion of the retina through which the optic nerve exits and where there are no receptors for light waves

blood-sugar level the amount of sugar contained in the blood, which indicates the level of hunger

borderline personality disorder a personality disorder marked by unstable emotions and relationships, dependency, and manipulative, self-destructive behavior

break set come up with unusual, unexpected ideas; use something in a way different from the way in which it is normally used

brightness constancy the ability to keep an object's brightness constant as the object is moved to various environments

bulimia nervosa an eating disorder that involves binging on food and purging by vomiting or using laxatives

C

California Psychological Inventory (CPI) personality inventory most often used in schools

Cannon-Bard theory theory of emotion proposing that the bodily reaction and the emotional response to an event occur at the same time

cardinal traits Allport's term for very strong personality characteristics that affect most of what a person does

case study method research that collects lengthy, detailed information about a person's background, usually for psychological treatment

catatonic schizophrenia type of schizophrenia characterized by disturbances of movement

catharsis a supposed process in which a person gets rid of aggressive energy by viewing others acting aggressively

central nervous system the brain and spinal cord

central traits Allport's term for personality traits that are highly characteristic of a person

cerebellum part of the lower brain that coordinates and organizes bodily movements for balance and accuracy

cerebral arteriosclerosis blockage of blood vessels to the brain; it can result in loss of mental faculties

cerebral cortex the outermost layer of the brain; controls high-level mental processes such as thought

chaining reinforcing the connection between the parts of a sequence

chromosomes structures containing genes; all human cells contain 46 chromosomes, except reproductive cells, which contain 23

chunking putting items into clusters or "chunks" so that the items are learned in groups rather than separately

cilia hairlike extensions on cells

circadian rhythm sequences of behavioral changes that occur every 24 hours

clang associations rhythmic patterns associated with psychotic speech

classical conditioning Ivan Pavlov's method of conditioning, in which associations are made between a natural stimulus and a learned, neutral stimulus

clinical psychologists psychologists who deal with emotional problems of any kind, including those fitting into the formal classifications of mental disturbance

clique a very tightly knit group with limited membership and strict rules of behavior; normally tied to school activities

closure the process of filling in the missing details of what is viewed

cochlea a snail-shaped part of the ear, filled with fluid and small hairs that vibrate to incoming sound

cognition higher-order thought processes, such as reasoning and problem solving

cognitive approach an approach that emphasizes how humans use mental processes to handle problems or develop certain personality characteristics

cognitive approach (in learning) an approach to the study of learning that emphasizes abstract mental processes and previous knowledge

cognitive behavioral therapy therapy in which thoughts are used to control emotions and behaviors

cognitive development the ways in which thinking and reasoning grow and change

cognitive dissonance a contradiction between actions or events and beliefs, which causes discomfort and so must be reconciled or justified

cognitive map a mental image of where one is located in space

cognitive theory theory of emotion proposed by Stanley Schachter; it holds that people label a bodily response by giving it the name of the emotion they think they are feeling

collective unconscious Jung's term for the portion of a person that contains ideas or archetypes (such as hero, mother, and so on) shared by the whole human race

color blindness inability to perceive certain colors, such as red and green

color constancy the ability to perceive an object as the same color regardless of the environment

compulsion a symptom characterized by a symbolic, ritualized behavior that a person must keep acting out in order to avoid anxiety

concrete operations stage Piaget's third stage of child development, from about 7 to 11 years of age, in which the child understands that there is a real world with real objects, which exist apart from the child and which can be manipulated

conditioned response a response to a stimulus that is brought about by learning—for example, salivating at the word *pickle*

conditioned stimulus a previously neutral stimulus that has been associated with a natural (or unconditioned) stimulus

cone a visual receptor that responds during daylight; "sees" color

conflict a problem that demands a choice between alternatives

consciousness the organism's awareness of, or possibility of knowing, what is happening inside or outside itself

consequences in attribution theory, the emotional responses, behavior, and expectations that result from the attribution

conservation Piaget's term for the idea that some of an object's characteristics can be changed while others remain the same; for example, changing shape does not change volume

consolidation process by which a memory solidifies over time, eventually becoming permanent

construct a concept requiring a belief in something that cannot be seen or touched but that seems to exist

contact comfort the satisfaction obtained from pleasant, soft physical stimulation

continuous reinforcement reinforcement given each time a behavior occurs

control group the group that does not participate in the critical part of the experiment

conventional level Kohlberg's middle stage of moral development, in which moral reasoning is based on the expectations of others regarding what is right or wrong

conversion disorder a somatoform disorder in which a serious psychological trauma is changed into a symbolic physical dysfunction

cornea the clear outer covering of the eye, behind which is a fluid

corpus callosum a large bundle of nerve fibers that transfer information from one half of the cerebral cortex to the other

counseling psychologists psychologists who deal mostly with problems not fitting into the formal classifications of mental disturbance

creativity the mental processes that result in original, workable ideas

critical period a specific period of development that is the only time when a particular skill can begin to develop or a particular association can occur

cross-sectional method a method of research that looks at different age groups at the same time in order to understand changes that occur during the life span

crowding A psychological feeling of having too little space

crowds large groups with loose rules and changeable memberships

culture a set of beliefs, attitudes, and values held in common by a large number of people and passed down from one generation to the next

curiosity motive a drive that moves a person to seek new and different things

cutaneous receptors nerve receptors in the skin that respond to pressure, temperature, or pain

D

decibels a measure of how loud a sound is (its intensity)

defense mechanisms psychological distortions we use to remain psychologically stable, or in balance

deindividuation a process in which a person loses his or her sense of individuality and responsibility as the result of being in a group

delta waves slow, lazy, deep-sleep brain waves

delusion a belief in something that is clearly not true

dendrites parts of neurons that receive information from the axons of other neurons

denial the process of refusing to admit that there is a problem

density the number of people per square foot in a given space

dependent variable the factor in a study that changes or varies as a result of changes in the independent variable

depth perception the ability to see the relation of objects in space

Diagnostic and Statistical Manual of Mental Disorders IV (DSM-IV) a book published by the American Psychiatric Association that classifies the symptoms of mental disorders into formal categories

dictatorial parenting style (see **authoritarian parenting style**)

diffusion Marcia's term for the state in which the adolescent has no clear idea of his or her identity and is not attempting to find that identity

diffusion of responsibility a process in which responsibility for helping others is spread out among group members; thus, each member's responsibility is less than it would be if the person were alone

discrimination learning learning to tell the difference between one event or object and another; the reverse of generalization

discrimination mistreatment or denial of rights based on group membership

displacement the process of venting our feelings on something or someone other than the true or original target

dissociative disorders disorders in which memory of a part of one's life becomes disconnected from other parts; amnesia, fugue, and dissociative identity disorder are examples

dissociative identity disorder a dissociative disorder in which a person divides himself or herself into separate personalities that can act independently

distress stress that is overwhelming or that causes problems

dizygotic twins twins who develop from different eggs fertilized by different sperm; they are not identical in their genetic makeup

dominance control; either the right or left hemisphere of the cerebral cortex is dominant in each individual; hence, one of them is preferred and controls the majority of actions performed

dopamine neurotransmitter involved in the control of bodily movements; present in excess in schizophrenics, causing nerve cells to fire too rapidly and leading to confusion in thought and speech

double approach-avoidance conflict a conflict involving a choice between alternatives, both of which have good and bad parts

double-blind study a study during which neither participants nor researchers know to which group any subject belongs

drives forces that push an organism into action to reach a goal

dysthymic disorder a mood disorder involving moderate depression

E

eardrum a piece of skin stretched over the entrance to the ear; vibrates to sound

early maturer someone whose physical development is one and one-half years or more ahead of average development

eating disorders conditions in which a person cannot read the body's nutritional needs and eats or refuses to eat for the wrong reasons

echolalia an autistic symptom in which the person "echoes," or repeats, what has just been said

eclecticism the process of making your own system by borrowing from two or more other systems

ego Freudian psychological unit that is based in reality; the "self" that allows controlled id expression within the boundaries set by the superego

eidetic imagery an iconic memory lasting a minute or so that keeps images "in front of" the viewer so objects can be counted or analyzed; also called *photographic memory*

elaboration the process of attaching a maximum number of associations to an item to be learned so that it can be retrieved more easily

electroconvulsive therapy (ECT) therapy in which an electrical shock is sent through the brain to try to reduce symptoms of mental disturbance

emotion a state of the body causing feelings, such as of hope, fear, or love

emotional intelligence the ability to properly feel, deal with, and recognize emotions

emotional stability Eysenck's term for the personality dimension that concerns how much a person is affected by feelings

empty-nest period the time of life when one's children have grown and moved away from home; for some people, this event leads to feelings of uselessness and depression

encounter groups therapy groups in which people are forced to share their inner conflicts and emotions

endocrine system system that includes all the glands and their chemical messages taken together

endorphins neurotransmitters that relieve pain and increase our sense of well-being

entrainment the process of altering the free-running cycle to fit a different rhythm

environment a person's surroundings, which influence the person's characteristics and development

estrogen the female sex hormone; controls the female reproductive cycle

ethnic group a group of people who share important cultural and racial features, often including national origin

eustress stress that motivates us to do something desirable

evaluation apprehension concern about how others will judge us

exhaustion third stage of the general adaptation syndrome—giving up the battle

expectancies beliefs about our ability to perform an action and to get the desired reward

experimental group the group on which the critical part of the experiment is performed

extended family nuclear family plus other relatives

extinction the gradual loss of an association over time

extraversion Eysenck's term for the personality dimension of being outgoing and sociable

extrinsic motivation motivation that comes from outside the individual

F

feral children children supposedly reared by animals

fidelity Erikson's term for faithfulness to one's ideals and values; loyalty

field study research that takes place outside the laboratory

fight or flight reaction the body's reaction to a crisis; the organism is mobilized to either fight or run away

fissure a depression marking off an area of the cerebral cortex

fixed interval schedule schedule in which reinforcement occurs after a desired act is performed following a fixed amount of time

flight of ideas a confused state in which thoughts and speech go in all directions with no unifying concept

foreclosure Marcia's term for the state in which the adolescent accepts the identity and values he or she was given in childhood

forgetting an increase in errors in bringing material back from memory

forgetting curve graphic representation of the rate and amount of forgetting that occurs

formal operations Piaget's term for the ability to reason in abstract ways and use complex thought processes

formal operations stage Piaget's fourth stage of child development, beginning at about 11 years of age, in which the ability to deal with the highly symbolic and abstract thoughts found in logic, math, philosophy, and ethics begins to appear

free association the process of saying whatever comes to mind; thought to uncover the unconscious in psychoanalysis

free-running cycles cycles set up by biological clocks that are under their own control, ignoring the environment

frontal association area part of the frontal lobe that engages in elaborate associations or mental connections; it plays an important part in integrating personality and in forming complex thoughts

frontal lobe division of the cerebral cortex that contains the motor strip, prefrontal area, and frontal association area

frustration the process by which we are blocked or hindered from reaching goals

fugue a dissociative disorder in which a person forgets his or her current life and starts a new one somewhere else

fully functioning individual Rogers's term for someone who has become what he or she should be

G

gang a rebellious, antisocial group with strict rules; not connected with accepted school or social organizations

gender role behavior acts that reflect society's view of what is appropriate for males and what is appropriate for females

gender the sex of an individual, male or female

general adaptation syndrome sequence of behavior that occurs in reaction to prolonged stress. It is divided into stages: alarm reaction, preparation for an attack; stage of resistance, trying to restore balance; and exhaustion, giving up the battle

generalization a behavior that spreads from one situation to a similar one

genital stage Freudian stage of development during which the individual seeks an appropriate marital partner and earlier conflicts reappear

gerontology the branch of psychology that studies the aging process and the problems of older people

gestalt organized whole, shape, or form

glands units of the body that contain the hormones

glucose another name for sugar in the blood

goal the target of a set of behaviors

gonads the sex glands; they make sperm or eggs for reproduction

group identity versus alienation Erikson's idea that early adolescents either belong to a group or feel lost (alienated)

group intelligence tests IQ tests administered to many people at one time; tests are highly verbal and use paper and pencil

group therapy therapy in which more than one person at a time is treated

growth cycles orderly patterns of development

growth hormone the hormone that regulates the growth process; it is controlled by the pituitary gland

growth spurt a rapid increase in growth during puberty

H

hair cells receptor cells for hearing found in the cochlea

hallucinating seeing or hearing something that is not present

hallucinations images or sounds that are not physically present

hallucinogen a drug that produces major hallucinations

halo effect the situation in which a person who has one positive characteristic is assumed to have other positive traits

hemisphere one half of the cerebral cortex; each half controls the opposite side of the body

heredity characteristics obtained directly from the genes

hierarchy of needs a system that ranks human needs one above the other, with the most basic needs for physical survival at the bottom of the pyramid; proposed by the psychologist Abraham Maslow

hippocampus limbic system structure involved in forming memories

homeostasis bodily process of maintaining a balanced internal state

hormones chemical regulators that control bodily processes such as emotional responses, growth, and sexuality

hospice care care for terminally ill people that emphasizes pain management, comfort, and quality of life

humanism a personality theory that emphasizes the positive potential of the person

humanistic approach an approach that views people as basically good and capable of helping themselves

humanistic therapies therapies that emphasize the individual's ability to heal himself or herself with some assistance

hypnosis a state of relaxation in which attention is focused on certain objects, acts, or feelings

hypochondriasis a somatoform disorder characterized by feeling excessive concern about one's health and exaggerating the seriousness of minor physical complaints

hypothalamus part of the lower brain that regulates basic needs (hunger, thirst) and emotions such as pleasure, fear, rage, and sexuality

hypothesis a statement of the results that the experimenter expects

I

iconic memory a very brief visual memory that can be sent to the short-term memory

id Freudian psychological unit containing basic needs and drives

ideal self   Rogers's term for the goal of each person's development; the self each person would like to be

identification   the process of modeling behavior patterns after (usually) a member of the same sex

identification with the aggressor   the process of taking on characteristics of someone who has mistreated us in order to psychologically avoid the abuse

identity   a sense of oneself as a unique person

identity achievement   Marcia's term for the state in which the adolescent has developed well-defined personal values and self-concepts

identity confusion   Erikson's term for uncertainty about who one is and where one is going

illusions   inaccurate perceptions

illusory correlations   seeing relationships between things that match already held beliefs and ignoring what does not match these beliefs

imitation learning   the process of learning behaviors by viewing and imitating others

immunization   a process in which a person is trained in how to resist persuasion or propaganda

imprinting   a biological process in which the young of certain species follow and become attached to their mothers

inclusion   the practice of keeping children with disabilities in regular academic classrooms

independent variable   the factor that the experimenter manipulates or changes in a study

individual intelligence tests   IQ tests administered on a one-to-one basis—one examiner to one test taker

information processing   the methods by which we take in, analyze, store, and retrieve material

insomnia   the inability to get enough sleep

intellectualization   the process of removing our feelings about an event and discussing it in a coolly rational and unemotional way

intelligence quotient (IQ)   a measure of intelligence originally obtained by comparing mental age, as determined by testing, with chronological age

intelligence   the ability to understand and adapt to the environment by using a combination of inherited abilities and learning experiences

intensity   how loud a sound is

interference theory   the idea that we forget because new and old material conflict (interfere) with one another

internalize   to take the attitudes or beliefs of others as our own

internalized sentences   what we say to ourselves in our own inner voices; Ellis's term

interview   a research method that involves studying people face to face and asking questions

intrinsic motivation   motivation that comes from within the individual

introspection   the process of looking into yourself and describing what is there

iris   a colored circular muscle that opens and closes, forming larger and smaller circles to control the amount of light getting into the eye

irrational ideas   ideas that do not hold up when challenged by careful logic

J

James-Lange theory   theory of emotion proposing that first the body responds and *then* one feels the emotion

juvenile delinquency   repeated violations of the law by those aged 17 and younger

L

late adolescence   the period from 16 to 19 years of age

late maturer   someone whose physical development is one and one-half years or more behind average development

latency stage   Freudian stage of development during which the child's earlier conflicts are hidden or go below the surface

latent learning   learning that is not obvious but goes on under the surface

learned helplessness   a condition in which a person has accepted the generalized idea that he or she can do nothing to help himself or herself

learning curve   a gradual upward slope representing increased retention of material as the result of learning

lens   the part of the eye that focuses an image on the retina

libido   Freudian term for internal energy forces that continuously seek discharge

limbic system   lower brain area whose structures are involved in basic emotions and memory

lobes   major divisions of the cerebral cortex

long-term memory   memory system that retains information for hours, days, weeks, months, or decades

longitudinal method   a method of research that studies the same group of people over an extended period of time

lower brain   part of the brain common to animals and humans that regulates basic functions such as breathing

M

major depression severe depression; involves loss of appetite, lack of energy, hopelessness, and suicidal thoughts

mania a mood disorder involving extreme agitation, restlessness, rapid speech, and trouble concentrating

manipulation motive a drive that moves a person to handle and use objects in the environment

maturation the automatic, orderly, sequential process of physical and mental development

meditation a form of self-control in which the outside world is cut off from consciousness

menopause the "change of life" period for women, when menstruation and ovulation stop; some women experience major physical symptoms, such as dizziness and "hot flashes"

menstrual cycles monthly cycles that revolve around the elimination of the lining of the uterus when the egg has not been fertilized

mental age the level of intellectual functioning in years, which is compared with chronological age to derive IQ

mental retardation below-average intellectual functioning that prevents a person from being able to perform at the level appropriate for his or her age

metabolism the speed at which the body operates or the speed at which it uses up energy

middle adolescence the period from 14 to 16 years of age

MMPI-2 latest version of the Minnesota Multiphasic Personality Inventory, the most widely used personality inventory

mnemonic devices unusual associations made to aid memory

modeling Bandura's term for learning by imitating others

monozygotic twins twins who develop from one fertilized egg; they are identical in their genetic makeup

mood disorders disorders characterized by emotional states; include depression and mania

moratorium a term used by both Erikson and Marcia to describe the adolescent's delay in making the commitments normally expected of adults

motivation the drive to seek a goal, such as food, water, or friends

motor strip band running down the side of the frontal lobe that controls all bodily movements (called motor functions)

Müller-Lyer illusion illusion in which one line in a picture with two equal-length lines seems longer

N

narcolepsy disorder in which a person falls instantly into sleep no matter what is going on in the environment

naturalistic observation a research method that involves studying subjects without their being aware that they're being watched

nature/nurture controversy contrasting views of how we gain certain characteristics: *nature* refers to heredity, *nurture* to environment

need for achievement psychological need for personal accomplishment

need for affiliation psychological need to belong to and identify with groups

need for approval psychological need to have other people think highly of oneself

negative identity Marcia's term for an identity that results from defining oneself as bad or as a troublemaker

negative reinforcement reinforcement that involves strengthening a response by following it with the removal of something unpleasant

negative transfer interference with learning that results from differences between two otherwise similar tasks

neo-Freudians those psychoanalysts who broke away from Freud to emphasize social forces in the unconscious

neuron a nerve cell; neurons transmit electrical and chemical information (via neurotransmitters) throughout the body

neurotransmitters chemicals in the endings of neurons that send information across synapses

night terror a horrible dream occurring during NREM, when the body is not prepared for it; also called an *incubus attack*

nightmare frightening dream that occurs during rem

nondirective therapy person-centered therapy

norms patterns of test answers from different types of people

NREM sleep non–rapid eye movement sleep; sleep involving partial thoughts, images, or stories that are poorly organized

nuclear family parents and their children

O

object permanence Piaget's term for the awareness that specific objects are real and exist all by themselves

observational learning a form of social learning in which the organism observes and imitates the behavior of others

obsession a symptom characterized by an endless preoccupation with a certain urge or thought

obsessive-compulsive disorder an anxiety disorder characterized by both repetitive thoughts (obsession) and ritualized, repetitive behavior (compulsion)

occipital lobe division of the cerebral cortex that interprets visual information

olfaction the sense of smell

olfactory bulbs units that receive odor molecules and communicate their nature to the brain

operant conditioning conditioning that results from the individual's actions and the consequences they cause

opiates sedatives; drugs that reduce body functioning

opponent-process theory theory that the presence of one emotion triggers its opposite, which then emerges somewhat later

oral stage Freudian stage of development during which feeding and weaning are the child's main issues

ovaries the female sex glands; they make eggs

overlearning learning something beyond one perfect recitation so that the forgetting curve will have no effect; the development of perfect retention

P

panic disorder a type of anxiety disorder characterized by frequent and overwhelming attacks of anxiety that are not associated with specific objects or events

paranoia the belief that others are out to get you

paranoid schizophrenia type of schizophrenia marked by strong feelings of suspiciousness and persecution

parasympathetic nervous system a division of the autonomic nervous system that conserves bodily activity; works in opposition to the sympathetic system to calm us down

parietal lobe division of the cerebral cortex that contains the sensory strip

partial reinforcement schedule reinforcement not given each time an act is performed

perception the process of assembling and organizing sensory information to make it meaningful

performance scale IQ test items that try to bypass verbal material and focus on problem solving without words

peripheral nervous system all the nerves outside the brain and spinal cord

permissive parenting style parenting style in which parents let children do as they wish; few rules are made or enforced

person-centered therapy Carl Rogers's humanistic approach; reflects the belief that the person and his or her therapist are partners in therapy

persona Jung's term for a "mask" people wear to hide what they really are or feel

personal space an "invisible bubble," or portable area, around each person; each of us tries to keep this space from being invaded

personality a person's broad, long-lasting patterns of behavior

personality disorder a disorder in which a person has formed a peculiar or unpleasant personality

personality inventory a list of items about a person's beliefs, habits, hopes, needs, and desires

personality traits more or less permanent personality characteristics

phallic stage Freudian stage of development during which the child experiences romantic interest in the opposite-sex parent and hostility toward the same-sex parent

pheromones odor chemicals that communicate a message

phobic disorder a type of anxiety disorder in which a person becomes disabled and overwhelmed by fear in the presence of certain objects or events. Examples include specific phobia and agoraphobia.

physical dependence a craving of the body for a drug

physiological needs needs at the bottom of Maslow's hierarchy: hunger and thirst

pitch how high or low a sound is

pituitary gland the master gland that controls other glands and hormones, as well as producing its own hormone that regulates growth

placebo a "medicine" that has no active ingredients and works by the power of suggestion

positive reinforcement reinforcement that involves strengthening the tendency to repeat a response by following it with the addition of something pleasant

positive transfer transfer of learning that results from similarities between two tasks

postconventional level Kohlberg's last stage of moral development, in which personal ethics and human rights come into play

preconventional level Kohlberg's early stage of moral development, in which morality is determined by the sheer power of outside authority

prefrontal area part of the frontal lobe that enables us to re-experience personal past events

prejudice a biased judgment of people based on the group they belong to rather than their individual characteristics

premenstrual syndrome (PMS) anxiety, irritability, and mental confusion resulting from monthly female hormonal changes

preoperational stage Piaget's second stage of child development, from about two to seven years of age, in which children acquire language and the ability to use symbols but are still not capable of logical thought

primary reinforcement something necessary for psychological or physical survival that is used as a reward

principle learning a method of learning in which an overall view (principle) of the material to be learned is developed so that the material is better organized

projection the process of attributing our thoughts to someone else

projective tests tests measuring inner feelings elicited by a vague stimulus, such as an ink blot or an unclear picture

proximity a perceptual cue that involves grouping together things that are near one another

psychedelic drug a drug that distorts or confuses the user's perception of the world

psychiatric nurses registered nurses with special education in psychiatric medicine

psychiatric social workers mental health workers with a degree in social work; help patients and families deal with problems

psychiatrists medical doctors with special training in mental disorders

psychoanalysis therapy practiced by followers of Freud, who analyze the psyche via the unconscious

psychoanalytic theory a theory that personality is based on impulses and needs in the unconscious

psychological dependence a craving of the psyche for a drug

psychological test systematic measure of what people know; how they act, think, and feel; or what their goals are

psychological tests objective methods for observation and measurement of subjects in various areas, such as intelligence

psychology the scientific study of mental processes and behavior

psychosis (psychotic disorder) a severe mental disorder that may involve disorganized thought processes, hallucinations, delusions, and major problems with emotional responses

psychosurgery surgery that destroys part of the brain to make the patient calmer, freer of symptoms

psychotherapies broad term for any method used to try to help people with emotional and psychological problems

psychotic episodes periods of psychotic behavior; they can alternate with periods of relative coherence and calm

puberty the time of sexual maturation

punishment the process of weakening a response by following it with unpleasant consequences

pupil the opening in the eye

R

race a set of hereditary physical characteristics that distinguishes a major group of people

rational-emotive therapy (RET) Albert Ellis's form of cognitive behavioral therapy; aimed at getting emotions under control by using reason

rationalization the process of explaining away a problem so that we don't have to accept the blame

reaction formation the process of expressing the opposite of what we feel

recall the ability to bring back and integrate many specific learned details

recognition the ability to pick the correct object or event from a list of choices

reference group a group with which one identifies and that provides standards of behavior

reflex an automatic behavior of the body involving movement that is activated through the spinal cord without use of the higher brain

regression the process of going backward in behavior and thought to a period when we were taken care of as a child; childish behavior

reinforcement something that follows a response and strengthens the tendency to repeat that response

reinforcement value the preference for certain types of reinforcement over other types

reliability measure of a test's consistency

REM sleep rapid eye movement sleep; dreams occur during REM sleep

REM rebound increase in the number of dreams after being deprived of REM sleep

representative sample a group that truly reflects a selected characteristic of a larger population

repression the process of pushing a painful event or thought out of consciousness; the process of pushing the needs and desires that cause guilt into the unconscious

research psychologists psychologists who study the origin, cause, or results of certain behaviors

response a reaction to a stimulus

reticular activating system (RAS) the alertness control center of the brain that regulates the activity level of the body; also called the reticular formation

reticular formation unit in the brain that registers and controls activity level, increases excitement, and helps generate sleep

retina the back of the eye, which contains millions of receptors for light

retinal disparity the difference between the images provided by the two retinas. When the images are brought together in the brain, they provide a sense of depth.

reverse halo the situation in which a person with one negative characteristic is assumed to have other negative traits

reversibility Piaget's term for the idea that a relationship that goes in one direction can go in the other direction also

reversible figure illusion in which the same object is seen as two alternating figures—first one, then the other

risky shift phenomenon a situation in which the risk associated with an act is split among the members of a group; hence, the risk is smaller for each person

rite of passage a socially recognized and ritualized change in status, such as the passage to adulthood

rod a visual receptor most sensitive to the violet-purple wavelengths; very sensitive for night vision; "sees" only black and white

Rorschach test an ink blot projective test developed by Hermann Rorschach

S

safety needs needs at the second level of Maslow's hierarchy: shelter, nest egg of money

sample a group that represents a larger group

savant syndrome condition in which a person with below-normal mental capacity possesses a special talent or mental ability to an extremely high degree

scapegoating blaming someone else for what goes wrong

schedules of reinforcement different methods of reinforcing

schema an organized and systematic approach to answering questions or solving problems

schizophrenia a psychosis involving disorganized thoughts and garbled speech as well as hallucinations and delusions; the most serious mental disorder

Scholastic Assessment Test (SAT) test designed to measure ability to do college work

secondary reinforcement anything that comes to represent a primary reinforcer, such as money

secondary traits Allport's term for weak personality traits that appear only on occasion

selective forgetting forgetting only things that are very traumatic

self-actualization needs needs at the top of Maslow's hierarchy: establishing meaningful goals and a purpose in life

self-actualized Maslow's term for the state of having brought to life the full potential of our skills

self-concepts the images we have of ourselves

self-esteem the degree to which we think we are worthwhile

self-esteem needs needs at the fourth level of Maslow's hierarchy: liking and respecting yourself, feeling important and useful

senile dementia loss of mental faculties in old age

sensation the process of receiving information from the environment

sensorimotor stage Piaget's first stage of child development, from birth to about two years of age, in which knowledge is tied to movements and objects in the environment

sensory deprivation technique used in brainwashing in which all external sensations and stimulation are removed

sensory memory system system that includes direct receivers of information from the environment—for example, iconic, acoustic

sensory strip band running down the side of the parietal lobe that registers and provides all sensation

separation anxiety the baby's fear of being away from the parent; the desire to avoid strangers

serotonin a brain chemical. Levels that are too high lead to mania; levels that are too low lead to depression.

set a tendency to solve problems in the same way over and over

set point the body-regulating mechanism that determines a person's typical weight

shape constancy the ability to perceive an object as having the same shape regardless of the angle at which it is seen

shaping the process of gradually refining a response by successively reinforcing closer approximations of it

short-term memory memory system that retains information for a few seconds to a few minutes

similarity a perceptual cue that involves grouping like things together

situational assessment the process of looking at how the circumstances surrounding an event influence people responding to that event

size constancy the ability to retain the size of an object regardless of where it is located

sleep apnea condition in which a person's breathing often stops while the person is asleep

social contracts Kohlberg's term for agreements based on what's "best for everyone"

social learning all learning that occurs in a social situation

sociocultural approach an approach that views behavior as strongly influenced by the rules and expectations of specific social groups or cultures

sociopath a person with antisocial personality disorder

somatic nervous system a division of the peripheral nervous system containing sensory and motor nerves

somatoform disorder a condition in which psychological issues are expressed in bodily symptoms in the absence of any real physical problem

source traits Cattell's term for personality traits that underlie surface behavior

space constancy the ability to keep objects in the environment steady by perceiving *either* ourselves *or* outside objects as moving

spatial skills skills involving the ability to imagine how an object would look if it was moved about in space

specific phobia a phobic disorder associated with a specific object or situation, such as snakes, dogs, elevators, and heights

spinal cord part of the body that functions as an automatic "brain" in its own right and as a relay station for impulses to and from the higher brain

spontaneous recovery the sudden reappearance of an extinguished response

stage of resistance second stage of general adaptation syndrome—trying to restore balance

standardization the process of developing clear directions for taking, scoring, and interpreting a test

standoutishness doing or wearing something that is so startling it distracts observers from noticing one's real abilities

Stanford-Binet Intelligence Scale intelligence test developed by Alfred Binet and later refined at Stanford University

state-dependent learning learning that occurs in one chemical state and is best reproduced when the same state occurs again

stereotype a fixed set of beliefs about a group that is generalized to all or most group members; stereotypes may or may not be accurate

steroids naturally occurring hormones, some of which promote muscle growth

stimulus anything that elicits a response

stimulus generalization process in which a response spreads from one specific stimulus to other stimuli that resemble the original

strategies methods for solving problems

stress hormone a special chemical that signals the adrenal glands to activate the body

stress the physical strain that results from demands or changes in the environment

Strong-Campbell Interest Inventory the most widely used vocational interest test; based on answers of people successful in certain fields

subconscious consciousness just below our present awareness

subjects people or animals on whom a study is conducted

sublimation the process of channeling emotional energy into constructive or creative activities

subliminal perception stimulation presented below the level of consciousness

substance abuse use of a drug to the extent that relationships or occupational demands suffer

substance dependence abuse of a drug; the abuser has physical symptoms when the drug is not used, uses more and more of the drug, and devotes large amounts of time to drug use

superego Freudian psychological unit roughly synonymous with the conscience

surface traits Cattell's term for characteristics that can be easily observed by others

survey a method of research that involves asking subjects questions about their feelings, opinions, or behavior patterns

sympathetic nervous system a division of the autonomic nervous system that energizes and prepares for emergencies

synapse the junction point of two or more neurons; a connection is made by neurotransmitters

synergistic effect effect in which, when two drugs are taken in combination, each is more potent than it would be if it were taken by itself

systematic desensitization a behavioral technique in which the therapist increases the patient's anxiety and counters it with relaxation in a graduated sequence

T

taste receptors chemical receptors on the tongue that decode molecules of food or drink to identify them

temporal lobe division of the cerebral cortex responsible for hearing and some speech functions

territoriality an attachment to a fixed area designated as ours alone and the tendency to defend it against intruders

testes the male sex glands; they make sperm

texture gradient how rough or smooth objects appear; used in depth perception

thalamus part of the lower brain that functions primarily as a central relay station for incoming and outgoing messages from the body to the brain and the brain to the body

thanatology the study of death and of methods for coping with it

Thematic Apperception Test (TAT) a projective test using unclear pictures about which people make up stories

theory a general framework for scientific study; smaller aspects can be tested

theory of multiple intelligences Howard Gardner's theory that intelligence is made up of seven abilities—language, logical/mathematical, visual/spatial, musical, bodily movement, intrapersonal, and interpersonal

thought disorder a serious distortion in the ability to think or speak in a lucid and coherent way

thyroid gland the gland that controls and regulates the speed of bodily processes, called metabolism

timbre the complexity of a sound

token economy a behavioral technique in which rewards for desired acts are accumulated through tokens, which represent a form of money

tolerance in relation to drug use, the body's adaptation to increasing dosages. Larger and larger dosages are needed to get the effect produced by the original dosage.

trance another word for the state of deep relaxation that can occur during hypnosis

transfer of training learning process in which learning is carried over from one task to another based on similarities between the tasks

transference the process in which a person transfers emotional conflicts of earlier years onto the therapist

twilight state relaxed state just before we fall asleep

type A personality personality type associated with people who are always operating at full speed, are impatient, and are filled with distress

type B personality personality type associated with people who are open to change, are flexible, enjoy life, and have low levels of stress

U

unconditional positive regard a principle of humanistic therapy in which the person's feelings and thoughts are accepted for whatever they are; Carl Rogers's term

unconditioned response an automatic response to a particular natural stimulus, such as salivation to meat

unconditioned stimulus a stimulus that automatically elicits a response, as meat causes salivation

unconscious according to psychoanalytic belief, the part of the mind that is beyond consciousness. Although we are unaware of its contents, they strongly affect our behavior; thoughts or desires about which we have no direct knowledge

undifferentiated schizophrenia schizophrenia that lacks distinguishing symptoms

universal ethical principles Kohlberg's term for concepts such as justice and honor

V

validity the extent to which a test measures what it is supposed to measure

variable interval schedule schedule in which reinforcement occurs after a desired act is performed following a variable amount of time

variable ratio schedule schedule in which reinforcement occurs after a desired act is performed a particular but variable number of times

variables factors that change in an experiment

verbal scale IQ test items that rely heavily on word comprehension and usage

vesicles bubblelike containers of neurotransmitters, located at the ends of axons

visual cliff an apparatus used to demonstrate depth perception

vocational interest test a test that attempts to predict what occupational area an individual will like

W

Wechsler Adult Intelligence Scale (WAIS) an intelligence test for adults that provides three IQs: verbal, performance, and full-scale (total)

Wechsler Intelligence Scale for Children (WISC) an intelligence test for children aged 6 to 16 that provides three IQs: verbal, performance, and full-scale

white light light as it originates from the sun or a bulb before it is broken into different frequencies

word salad speech in which words are mixed incoherently

Z

zygote fertilized egg

GLOSARIO

A

absolute threshold (umbral absoluto) nivel de estimulación sensoria necesaria para que ocurra una sensación

acetylcholine (acetilcolina) neurotransmisor que regula los procesos básicos del cuerpo, tales como el movimiento

achievement tests (pruebas de evaluación) pruebas que miden la cantidad de material específico que se recuerda después de una clase

acoustic memory (memoria acústica) memoria de un sonido muy breve que puede ser enviada a la memoria reciente

adaptation (adaptación) pérdida gradual de atención de la información sensoria innecesaria o no deseada

adolescence (adolescencia) período de desarrollo entre la infancia y el ser adulto

adrenal glands (glándulas suprarrenales) glándulas que provocan exitación, con el objeto de preparar al cuerpo en caso de emergencia o para cierta actividad importante; participan también en la maduración sexual.

adrenaline (adrenalina) producto químico que prepara al cuerpo para una emergencia, aumentando la presión sanguínea, el ritmo de la respiración y el nivel de energía

afterimage (sobreimagen) imágen que permanece impresa aún después de haber terminado la estimulación de la retina. Podemos experimentar sobreimágenes luego de haber observado detenidamente algo durante cierto lapso; los conos no utilizados se estimulan con el fin de equilibrar el sistema visual

age regression (regresión) proceso de revivir bajo hipnosis, los primeros a–os de la infancia

agoraphobia (agorafobia) temor a abandonar el círculo familiar, en especial, el hogar

alcohol withdrawal delirium (crisis por abstinencia acohólica) delirio acarreado por un alcoholismo agudo; incluye debilidad, ansiedad, calambres y alucinaciones

alpha waves (ondas alfa) ondas cerebrales muy relajadas que aparecen en la fase 1, justo antes de dormirse

Alzheimer's disease (enfermedad de Alzheimer) enfermedad que comprende pérdida de los transmisores químicos de las células nerviosas y otros da–os en la transmisión nerviosa, lo que produce un deterioro mental

amnesia (amnesia) desorden disociativo por el cual parecen desaparecer de la memoria, ciertos eventos traumáticos. Bloqueo de la memoria anterógrada y/o pérdida de la memoria reciente

amygdala (amígdala, almendra) estructura cerebral que produce respuestas emocionales frente a la agresión y el miedo. Estructura del sistema límbico relacionada con las emociones, en especial, la agresión

anal stage (fase anal, control de esfínteres) estado de desarrollo freudiano en el cual aprender a controlar los esfínteres, es la mayor preocupación del niño

androgens (andrógenos) hormonas masculinas; controlan el deseo sexual tanto en hombres como mujeres

androgyny (androginia) característica de tener ambos sexos: masculino y femenino; hermafrodita

anorexia nervosa (anorexia nerviosa) desorden del comer que produce una severa pérdida de peso, debido a una dieta excesiva

antecedents (antecedentes) en la teoría de la atribución, informes y creencias que una persona ya tiene de otra

antisocial personality disorder (personalidad antisocial) desorden de la personalidad en el que el individuo está en conflicto constante con la ley y parece no tener conciencia

anxiety (ansiedad) sensación generalizada de aprehensión y zozobra. Sentimiento de que algo anda mal y de peligro inminente

anxiety disorders (desórdenes por ansiedad) desórdenes cuyo síntoma principal es la ansiedad

applied psychologists (psicólogos especializados) psicólogos que hacen uso directo de los descubrimientos de psicólogos investigadores; tratan directamente con los pacientes

approach-approach conflict (conflicto entre dos propuestas) conflicto de elección entre dos alternativas igualmente atrayentes

approach-avoidance conflict (conflicto con propuesta dispar) conflicto sobre una situación con características buenas y malas

aptitude (aptitud) capacidad de una persona

aptitude tests (pruebas de aptitud) pruebas que miden la capacidad de alguien (como ser: carpintería, medicina)

archetypes (arquetipos) término de Jung para los conceptos humanos universales heredados

attention (atención) enfoque alerta sobre cierto material

attention deficit/hyperactivity disorder (déficit de atención/ hiperactividad) desorden de la niñez caracterizado por falta de atención, distracción, irreflexión, y/o actividad excesiva y desasosiego

attitude (actitud) evaluación general y prolongada que incluye las emociones y tendencias de la conducta

attibution (atribución) en la teoría de atribución, acto de juzgar las causas del comportamiento de otro

attribution theory (teoría de atribución) teoría que describe cómo la gente explica las causas del comportamiento. El proceso incluye antecedentes, atribución y consecuencias

audition (audición) sentido del oído

auditory nerve (nervio auditivo) haz de nervios que llevan el sonido al cerebro

authoritarian (dictatorial) parenting style (paternidad autoritaria; dictatorial) estilo de educación en el que los padres aplican duras reglas y demandan obediencia

authoritative parenting style (paternidad autorizante) estilo de educación al que contribuyen tanto padres como hijos; los padres son consistentes pero también flexibles al imponer reglas

autistic disorder (autismo) desorden de la infancia caracterizado por la falta de desarrollo normal de los patrones de comunicación, interacción social y respuestas emocionales

autonimic nervous system (sistema nervioso autónomo) sistema automático de control del cuerpo; regula la respiración, el ritmo cardíaco, la digestión, etc.

aversive conditioning (condicionamiento por aversión) técnica de la conducta por la que se asocia cierto disgusto por las acciones que se deben evitar

avoidance-avoidance-conflict (conflicto para evitar) conflicto que involucra una elección entre dos alternativas no atractivas

awfulize (abrumar) ver algo del peor modo posible; término de Ellis

axon (axón) parte de la neurona que lleva mensajes desde la célula hacia las dendritas de otra neurona

B

behavioral approach (propuesta de conducta) alternativa que toma a la conducta como un producto del aprendizaje y de las asociaciones

behavioral therapy (terapia conductista) terapia que emplea los principios del aprendizaje para alterar las acciones o comportamiento de una persona

behaviorism (conductismo) teoría de la personalidad dedicada a acciones o comportamientos hostiles

belongingness needs (necesidad de pertenecer) necesidad del tercer nivel de la tabla de Maslow: amistad, cercanía con el prójimo

beta waves (ondas beta) veloces ondas cerebrales; aparecen cuando la persona está despierta

biological clocks (relojes biológicos) unidades químicas internas que controlan los ciclos regulares, en varias partes del cuerpo

biopsychological approach (propuesta biopsicológica) alternativa que considera que la conducta está fuertemente influenciada por las funciones fisiológicas

bipolar disorder (desorden bipolar) desorden del temperamento que varía entre altos y bajos

blind spot (punto ciego) porción de la retina por la que pasa el nervio óptico, pero donde no hay receptores de ondas luminosas

blood-sugar level (nivel de azúcar en la sangre) cantidad de azúcar en la sangre, que indica el nivel de hambre

borderline personality disorder (desorden de personalidad al límite) desorden de la personalidad caracterizado por emociones y relaciones inestables, dependencia y conducta manipulativa y autodestructiva

break set (desprenderse) traer ideas inusuales o inesperadas; utilizar algo de un modo totalmente diferente al usual

brightness constancy (constancia luminosa) capacidad que tiene un objeto de mantener constante su luminosidad, a pesar de ser transportado a varios entornos

bulimia nervosa (bulimia nerviosa) desorden de la alimentación por el que uno come en exceso para luego purgarse por vómitos o el uso de laxantes

C

California Psychological Inventory (CPI) (Inventario Psicológico de California) inventario de la personalidad usado más comúnmente en las escuelas

651

Cannon-Bard theory (teoría de Cannon-Bard) teoría de la emoción que propone que la reacción física y la respuesta emocional ante un hecho, ocurren al mismo tiempo

cardinal traits (rasgos cardinales) término de Allport para indicar características muy definidas de la personalidad, que afectan casi todo lo que hace una persona

case study method (estudio del caso) método de investigación que genera mucha información detallada sobre los antecedentes de una persona, en general para tratamiento psicológico

catatonic schizophrenia (esquizofrenia catatónica) tipo de esquizofrenia que afecta el movimiento

catharsis (catarsis) supuesto proceso por el cual una persona elimina su agresión, al observar el comportamiento de otros individuos agresivos

central nervous system (sistema nervioso central) el cerebro y la médula espinal

central traits (rasgos centrales) término de Allport para los rasgos de personalidad profundamente característicos de un individuo

cerebellum (cerebelo) parte del cerebro inferior que coordina y organiza los movimientos físicos de equilibrio y precisión

cerebral arteriosclerosis (arteriosclerosis cerebral) bloqueo de los vasos sanguíneos del cerebro; puede producir pérdida de las facultades mentales

cerebral cortex (corteza cerebral) membrana más externa del cerebro; controla los procesos mentales de alto nivel, como el pensamiento

chaining (encadenado) refuerzo de la conexión entre las partes de una secuencia

chromosomes (cromosomas) estructuras que contienen genes; todas las células humanas contienen 46 cromosomas, excepto las células reproductoras, que tienen 23

chunking (trozado) agrupar las unidades en ramos o "trozos" para aprenderlas en grupo, y no separadamente

cilia (cilios) extensiones filamentosas de las células.

circadian rhythm (ritmo circadiano) secuencias de cambios de conducta que ocurren cada 24 horas

clang associations (asociación por ritmo, por tañído) patrones rítmicos asociados con el habla psicótica

classical conditioning (condicionamiento clásico) método de condicionamiento de Ivan Pavlov, en el que se asocia un estímulo natural con un estímulo neutral aprendido

clinical psychologists (psicólogos clínicos) psicólogos que tratan problemas emocionales de cualquier clase, incluyendo aquellos que se encuadran dentro de las clasificaciones formales de perturbación mental

clique (camarilla) grupo firmemente unido de limitados miembros y estrictas reglas de conducta, asociado por lo general, con actividades escolares

closure (conclusión, clausura) proceso por el que se completan los últimos detalles de lo visto

cochlea (caracol del oído) parte del oído con forma de caracol, llena de fluído y pequeños pelos, que vibra al entrar el sonido

cognition (cognición, conocimiento) procesos de alto nivel del pensamiento, como ser: el razonamiento y la resolución de problemas

cognitive approach (método cognoscitivo) método que explica el modo en que los humanos emplean los procesos mentales para enfrentar problemas o desarrollar ciertas características de la personalidad. Propuesta sobre el estudio del aprendizaje, basado en los procesos mentales abstractos y el conocimiento previo

cognitive behavioral therapy (terapia de conducta cognoscitiva) terapia en la que se usa el pensamiento para controlar las emociones y la conducta

cognitive development (desarrollo cognoscitivo) modos en que crecen y cambian, el pensamiento y el razonamiento

cognitive dissonance (disonancia cognoscitiva) contradicción entre acciones o hechos y las creencias, lo que provoca molestias que deben ser subsanadas o justificadas

cognitive map (mapa cognoscitivo) imagen mental de donde se halla uno ubicado en el espacio

cognitive theory (teoría cognoscitiva) teoría de la emoción propuesta por Stanley Schachter; sostiene que la gente designa una respuesta física, con el nombre de la emoción, que dice sentir

collective unconscious (subconsciente colectivo) término de Jung para la porción de una persona que contiene ideas o arquetipos (tales como héroe, madre, etc.) compartidos por toda la raza humana

color blindness (daltonismo) incapacidad para distinguir ciertos colores, tales como rojo y verde

color constancy (constancia cromática) capacidad para distinguir un objeto con el mismo color, sin tener en cuenta el entorno

compulsion (compulsión) desorden de la ansiedad que se caracteriza por una conducta simbólica, ritual, que la persona debe representar para evitar la ansiedad

concrete operations stage (fase de operación concreta) etapa tercera del desarrollo del niño, de Piaget, entre los 7 y 11 años de edad, en que el niño entiende que existe un mundo real con objetos reales que son ajenos al niño y que pueden ser manejados

conditioned response (respuesta condicionada) respuesta a un estímulo que ocurre a partir del aprendizaje—por ejemplo, aumento de la saliva ante la palabra pan

conditioned stimulus (estímulo condicionado) estímulo previamente neutral que ha sido asociado con un estímulo natural (o incondicionado)

cone (cono) receptor visual que responde ante la luz; percibe los colores

conflict (conflicto) problema que demanda la elección entre dos alternativas

consciousness (estado consciente) conocimiento del organismo, o posibilidad de saber lo que sucede dentro y fuera de si mismo

conservation (conservación) término de Piaget sobre la idea de que algunas características del objeto se pueden cambiar, mientras que otras permanecen iguales; por ejemplo, el cambio de la forma no cambia el volumen

consolidation (consolidación) proceso por el cual la memoria se solidifica durante el tiempo, llegando eventualmente a ser permanente

construct (elaborar) concepto que requiere creer en algo que no se puede ver ni tocar, pero parece existir

contract comfort (placer del contacto) satisfacción que se obtiene a partir de una placentera, suave, estimulación física

continuous reinforcement (reafirmación contínua) reafirmación dada cada vez que ocurre un comportamiento

control group (grupo de control) grupo que no participa de la parte crítica del experimento

conventional level (nivel convencional) etapa media del desarrollo moral de Kohlberg, en la que el razonamiento moral está basado en las expectativas de los otros con respecto a lo que está bien, o está mal

conversion disorder (desorden de conversión) desorden somatoforme en el que se cambia un serio trauma psicológico por una anormalidad física simbólica

cornea (córnea) cubierta clara exterior del ojo, detrás de la cual hay un fluído

corpus callosum (cuerpo calloso) haz grande de fibras nerviosas que transmiten información desde una mitad de la corteza cerebral hacia la otra

counseling psychologists (psicólogos consultores) psicólogos que tratan mayormente los problemas ajenos a la clasificación formal de anormalidad mental

creativity (creatividad) procesos mentales que producen ideas originales, adaptables

critical period (período crítico) período específico del desarrollo: es el único momento en que comienza a desarrollarse cierta capacidad, o sucede una asociación en particular

cross-sectional method (método cruzado) método de investigación que estudia simultáneamente a grupos de distintas edades, con el objeto de comprender los cambios que se dan durante toda la vida

crowding (amontonamiento) sentimiento psicológico de tener poco espacio

crowds (muchedumbre) grandes grupos con ligeras reglas y miembros intercambiables

culture (cultura) conjunto de creencias, actitudes y valores que mantienen en común, un gran número de personas y que se pasan de generación en generación

curiosity motive (curiosidad) impulso que mueve a una persona hacia cosas nuevas y diferentes

cutaneous receptors (receptores cutáneos) receptores nerviosos de la piel que responden a presión, temperatura o dolor

D

decibels (decibeles) medida de volumen de un sonido (su intensidad)

defense mechanisms (mecanismos de defensa) distorsiones psicológicas que usamos para permanecer psicológicamente estables y en equilibrio

deindividuation (des-individualización) proceso por el cual una persona pierde su sentido de la individualidad y responsabilidad, como resultado de estar en un grupo

delta waves (ondas delta) ondas del cerebro: lentas, perezosas, de sueño profundo

delusion (ilusión, divague) creencia en algo que no es claramente verdadero

dendrites (dendritas) partes de las neuronas que reciben información desde los axones de otras neuronas

653

denial (negación) proceso en que se resiste a admitir que existe un problema

density (densidad) en un lugar dado, cantidad de gente por pie cuadrado

dependent variable (variable dependiente) en un estudio, el factor que cambia o varía como resultado de los cambios de la variable independiente

depth perception (percepción en produndidad) capacidad para ver la relación de los objetos en el espacio

Diagnostic and Statistical Manual of Mental Disorders IV (DSM-IV) (Manual de Estadística y Diagnóstico de Desórdenes Mentales-IV (DSM-IV) libro publicado por la Asociación Americana de Psiquiatría, que clasifica dentro de categorías formales, los síntomas de los desórdenes mentales

dictatorial parenting style (paternidad dictatorial) (ver authoritarian parenting style-paternidad autoritaria)

diffusion (difusión) término de Marcia para el estado en que el adolescente no tiene idea clara sobre su identidad y no está tratando de hallar tal identidad

diffusion of responsibility (difusión de responsabilidad) proceso en el cual la responsabilidad de ayudar a los demás se distribuye entre miembros de un grupo, de modo que la responsabilidad de cada uno, es menor que si estuviera solo

discrimination learning (aprendizaje por discriminación) aprender a diferenciar entre un evento u objeto, y otro; opuesto a generalización

discrimination (discriminación) maltrato o negación de los derechos por ser un grupo

displacement (desplazamiento) proceso de concentrar nuestro sentir en algo o alguien que no es exactamente el foco real o verdadero

dissociative disorders (desórdenes disociativos) desórdenes en los que la memoria de una parte de nuestra vida, se desconecta de las otras partes: la amnesia o la fuga, son ejemplos de desorden disociativo de la identidad

dissociative identity disorder (desórden disociativo de la identidad) desorden disociativo en que una persona se divide en personalidades separadas, que pueden actuar independientemente

distress (zozobra, angustia) estado de estrés que no es productivo y provoca problemas físicos

dizygotic twins (mellizos no-cigóticos) mellizos que se desarrollan en óvulos distintos a partir de distintos espermatozoides; no son idénticos en su constitución genética

dominance control (control dominante) en la corteza cerebral de cada individuo, puede ser dominante el hemisferio derecho o el izquierdo, por lo tanto, uno de ellos, es el preferido y controla la mayoría de las acciones

dopamine (dopamina) producto químico del cerebro. Se presenta en exceso en los esquizofrénicos, lo que provoca un encendido muy rápido de las células nerviosas, trayendo confusión de pensamiento y palabra. Neurotransmisor dedicado al control de los movimientos físicos

double approach-avoidance conflict (conflicto con doble propuesta dispar) conflicto que requiere decisión entre dos alternativas, ambas con partes buenas y malas

double-blind study (estudio a ciegas por partida doble) estudio durante el cual, ni los participantes ni los investigadores conocen a qué grupo pertenece el objeto

drives (impulsos) fuerzas que ponen un organismo en acción, para lograr un objetivo

dysthymic disorder (desorden distímico) desorden del ánimo que provoca una moderada depresión

E

eardrum (tambor del oído) trozo de piel extendido sobre la entrada del oído; vibra con el sonido

early maturer (madurez precoz) alguien cuyo desarrollo físico está un año, o año y medio, o más, más avanzado que el desarrollo promedio

eating disorders (desórdenes del comer) condiciones en las que una persona no entiende las necesidades nutricionales de su cuerpo, y come, o se resiste a comer, por razones equivocadas

echolalia (ecolalia) síntoma autístico en el que una persona hace "eco" o repite lo que recién se ha dicho

eclecticism (eclecticismo) proceso de elaborar su propio sistema, a partir de otros dos o más sistemas

ego (ego) unidad psicológica freudiana basada en la realidad; el "yo" que permite controlar las expresiones de uno, dentro de los límites establecidos por el superego

eidetic imagery (imágen eidética) memoria icónica que dura alrededor de un minuto, y que mantiene imágenes "frente" al espectador, para poder contar o analizar los objetos; llamada también *memoria fotográfica*

elaboration (elaboración) proceso de acoplar a una unidad de aprendizaje, el mayor número de asociaciones, con el objeto de retenerla más fácilmente

electroconvulsive therapy (ECT) (terapia electroconvulsiva) terapia por la que se aplica a través del cerebro, un shock eléctrico, para tratar de reducir los síntomas de perturbación mental

emotion (emoción) estado del cuerpo que produce sensaciones tales como: esperanza, miedo o amor

emotional intelligence (inteligencia emocional) capacidad de sentir, tratar y reconocer correctamente las emociones

emotional stability (estabilidad emocional) término de Eysenck que designa la dimensión de la personalidad en lo que se refiere al efecto de los sentimientos

empty-nest period (período del "nido vacío") etapa de la vida en que los hijos han crecido y volado fuera del hogar; para algunos, este evento provoca sentimientos de depresión e inutilidad

encounter groups (grupos de encuentro) grupos de terapia en los que la gente se ve forzada a compartir emociones y conflictos internos

endocrine system (sistema endocrino) sistema que incluye todo el conjunto de glándulas y sus mensajes químicos

endorphins (endorfinas) neurotransmisores que alivian el dolor y aumentan nuestro sentido de bienestar

entrainment (encadenado) proceso por el que se altera el ciclo normal, por un ritmo diferente

environment (entorno) lo que rodea a una persona e influye en sus características y desarrollo

estrogen (estrógeno) hormona sexual femenina. Hormona que controla el sistema reproductivo de la mujer

ethnic group (grupo étnico) grupo de gente que comparte características culturales y raciales, a menudo, de la misma nacionalidad

eustress (eustrés, estrés positivo) estrés que nos motiva a hacer algo útil

evaluation apprehension (aprehensión al "qué dirán") miedo a ser juzgados

expectancies (expectativas) concepto sobre nuestra capacidad para realizar un acto y obtener la deseada recompensa

experimental group (grupo experimental) grupo con el cual se realiza la parte crítica del experimento

extended family (familia extendida) núcleo familiar más los demás parientes

extinction (extinción) pérdida gradual de una asociación, a lo largo del tiempo

extraversion (extraversión) término de Eysenck que define una personalidad sociable y amistosa

extrinsic motivation (motivación extrínseca) motivación que viene de afuera del individuo

F

feral childen (niños ferales, salvajes) niños supuestamente criados por animales

fidelity (fidelidad) término de Erikson que designa la honradez hacia nuestros ideales y valores; lealtad

field study (estudio de campo) investigación que se realiza fuera del laboratorio

fight or flight reaction (reacción de pelear o huir) reacción del cuerpo ante una crisis; el organismo se moviliza ya sea para pelear o huir

fissure (fisura) depresión que marca un área de la corteza cerebral

fixed interval schedule (plan a intervalos fijos) esquema en que ocurre una reafirmación después de haber realizado una acción durante un tiempo determinado

flight of ideas (desparramo de ideas) estado de confusión en que los pensamientos y el habla van en todas direcciones, sin concepto que los unifica

foreclosure (rendición, cierre) término de Marcia que designa el estado en que los adolescentes aceptan la identidad y valores, que les fueron dados en su infancia

forgetting (olvido) aumento de errores al traer material desde la memoria

forgetting curve (curva de amnesia) representación gráfica de la proporción y cantidad de olvidos

formal operations (operación formal) término de Piaget que designa la capacidad de razonar en forma abstracta y de usar procesos complejos de pensamiento

formal operations stage (fase de operación formal) cuarta fase de Piaget del desarrollo del niño, a partir de los 11 años aproximadamente, en la que aparece la capacidad de concebir ideas altamente simbólicas y abstractas, halladas en la lógica, matemáticas, filosofía y ética

free association (asociación libre) proceso freudiano en el que una persona dice todo lo que aparece en su mente, aunque las ideas o imágenes parezcan desconectadas. Proceso de decir cualquier cosa que viene a la mente; pensamiento de descubrir el subconsciente, en el psicoanálisis

free-running cycles (ciclos de libre acción) ciclos establecidos por los relojes biológicos, que están bajo su propio control, ajenos al entorno

frontal association area (área frontal de asociación) parte del lóbulo frontal que elabora asociaciones o conecciones mentales; tiene papel importante en integrar la personalidad y formar pensamientos complejos

frontal lobe (lóbulo frontal) división de la corteza cerebral que contiene la banda motriz, la zona prefrontal y el área frontal de asociación

frustration (frustación) proceso por el cual estamos bloqueados o imposibilitados de lograr nuestros objetivos

fugue (fuga) desorden disociativo en el que la persona se olvida de su vida actual y comienza una nueva en otro lado

fully functioning individual (individuo en total funcionamiento) término de Roger que designa a alguien que se ha transformado en quien debe ser

G

gang (pandilla) grupo rebelde y antisocial con estrictas reglas; no se vincula con organizaciones escolares o sociales aceptables

gender role behavior (conducta del género) actos que reflejan el punto de vista de la sociedad sobre lo que es apropiado para hombres y para mujeres

gender (género) sexo de un individuo, masculino o femenino

general adaptation syndrome (síndrome de adaptación general) secuencia de conducta que ocurre en reacción a un estrés prolongado; está dividida en etapas: alarma, preparación para el ataque, fase de resistencia, intento de restablecer el equilibrio, agotamiento, entrega

generalization (generalización) conducta que se extiende desde una situación, a otra similar

genital stage (fase genital) fase freudiana de desarrollo, en la que el individuo busca un socio matrimonial adecuado y reaparecen los conflictos anteriores

gerontology (gerontología) rama de la psicología que estudia el proceso del envejecimiento y los problemas de la gente mayor

gestalt (unidad de Gestalt) un todo organizado, figura o forma

glands (glándulas) unidades del cuerpo que contienen las hormonas

glucose (glucosa) otro nombre para el azúcar en la sangre

goal (objetivo) dirección hacia donde apuntan una serie de conductas

gonads (gonadas) glándulas sexuales; fabrican óvulos o esperma para la reproducción

group identity versus alienation (identidad de grupo versus enajenación) idea de Erikson de que los adolescentes o pertenecen a un grupo o se sienten perdidos (alienados)

group intelligence tests (pruebas de inteligencia en grupo) pruebas de cociente intelectual suministradas a muchas personas simultáneamente; estas pruebas pueden ser orales o escritas

group therapy (terapia de grupo) terapia en la que se trata a más de una persona por vez

growth cycles (ciclos de crecimiento) patrones metódicos del desarrollo

growth hormone (hormona de crecimiento) hormona que regula el proceso de crecimiento; está controlada por la glándula pituitaria

growth spurt (crecimiento espontáneo) aumento rápido del crecimiento durante la pubertad

H

hair cells (células capilares) células receptoras del sonido, halladas en el caracol del oído

hallucinations (alucinaciones) cosas que se ven u oyen, y que no están físicamente presentes

hallucinogen (alucinógeno) droga que produce severas alucinaciones

halo effect (efecto de halo) situación en la que una persona tiene una característica positiva, por lo que se asume que tiene más rasgos positivos

hemisphere (hemisferio) mitad de la corteza cerebral; cada mitad controla el lado opuesto del cuerpo

heredity (hereditarias) características obtenidas directamente de los genes

hierarchy of needs (tabla de necesidades) sistema que selecciona las necesidades humanas, siendo las inferiores de la pirámide aquellas necesidades físicas básicas de supervivencia; propuesto por el psicólogo Abraham Maslow

hippocampus (hipocampo) estructura del sistema límbico, dedicada a la formación de memorias

homeostasis (homeostasis) proceso físico que mantiene un estado de equilibrio interno

hormones (hormonas) reguladores químicos que controlan los procesos físicos tales como las respuesas emocionales, el crecimiento y la sexualidad

hospice care (internación en hospicio) cuidados dados a enfermos incurables que se especializan en control del dolor, confort y calidad de vida

humanism (humanismo) teoría de la personalidad que enfatiza el potencial positivo de una persona

humanistic approach (encuadre humanístico) propuesta que considera a la gente como básicamente buena y capaz de ayudarse entre sí

humanistic therapies (terapias humanísicas) terapias que enfatizan la capacidad del individuo en curarse a si mismo, con un poco de ayuda

hypnosis (hipnosis) estado de relajación en el cual la atención está enfocada en ciertos objetos, acciones o sentimientos

hypochondriasis (hipocondriasis) desorden somatoforme caracterizado por sentir demasiada preocupación por la salud personal y por una exagerada seriedad de las menores complicaciones físicas

hipothalamus (hipotálamo) parte del cerebro inferior que controla las necesidades básicas de hambre y sed, y emociones tales como placer, miedo, rabia y sexualidad

hypothesis (hipótesis) enunciación de los resultados a los que se piensa llegar

I

iconic memory (memoria icónica) memoria breve, visual, que puede ser enviada por la memoria reciente

id ("id") unidad psicológica Freud, que contiene necesidades e impulsos básicos

ideal self (yo ideal) término de Roger que define el objetivo del desarrollo de cada persona; el yo que cada persona desearía ser

identification (identificación) proceso de modelar los patrones de conducta (por lo general) ante un miembro del mismo sexo

identification with the aggressor (identificación con el agresor) proceso de tomar las características de alguien que nos ha maltratado, con el objeto de evitar psicológicamente, el abuso

identity (identidad) sentido de uno mismo como ser único

identity achievement (logro de la identidad) término de Marcia que designa el estado en que el adolescente ha desarrollado valores y autoestima personales bien definidos

identity confusion (confusión de identidad) término de Erikson que define la incertidumbre de quién es uno y hacia dónde va

illusions (ilusiones) percepciones inexactas

illusory correlations (correlaciones ilusorias) concebir relaciones entre cosas que corresponden con creencias ya existentes, e ignorar lo que no corresponde con tales creencias

imitation learning (aprendizaje por imitación) proceso de aprender una conducta, viendo e imitando a otros

immunization (inmunización) proceso en el que una persona está entrenada para rechazar la persuasión y la propaganda

imprinting (impresión, apego) proceso biológico en el cual los pequeños de cualquier especie, siguen y se apegan a sus madres

inclusion (inclusión) costumbre de ubicar a niños incapacitados, en escuelas comunes

independent variable (variable independiente) factor que se manipula o cambia, en un estudio

individual intelligence tests (pruebas individuales de inteligencia) exámenes de cociente intelectual IQ, aplicados en forma individual (uno a uno)—un examinador por un examinado

information processing (procesado de información) métodos por los cuales tomamos, analizamos, almacenamos y extraemos material

insomnia (insomnio) incapacidad de poder dormir

intellectualization (intelectualización) proceso de extraer nuestros sentimientos sobre un hecho y discutirlos en forma fríamente racional y no emotiva

intelligence quotient (IQ) (cociente intelectual) medida de inteligencia obtenida originariamente al comparar la edad mental que se obtiene mediante pruebas, con la edad cronológica

intelligence (inteligencia) habilidad para entender y adaptarse al entorno, usando una combinación de capacidades hereditarias y experiencias aprendidas

intensity (intensidad) cuán fuerte es un sonido

interference theory (teoría de la interferencia) idea que olvidamos porque entran en conflicto el material antiguo con el nuevo; (se interfieren)

internalize (internalizar) tomar como nuestras, las actitudes o creencias de los otros

internalized sentences (parecer interno) opinión de nosotros mismos, que nos formamos prestando atención a nuestro interior; término de Ellis

interview (entrevista) método de investigación que se dedica a estudiar a las personas cara a cara, mediante preguntas

intrinsic motivation (motivación intrínseca) motivación que nace dentro del individuo

introspection (introspección) proceso de buscar dentro de sí y describir lo que se halla

iris (iris) músculo coloreado circular que se abre y cierra, formando círculos mayores y menores para controlar la cantidad de luz que llega al ojo

irrational ideas (ideas irracionales) ideas que no se sostienen al ser desafiadas por la lógica

657

J

James-Lange theory (teoría de James-Lange) teoría de la emoción que propone que primero el cuerpo responde y que después se siente la emoción

juvenile delinquency (delincuencia juvenil) violaciones repetidas de la ley, por parte de jóvenes menores de 17 años

L

late maturer (maduración tardía) alguien cuyo desarrollo físico está un año, o año y medio, o más, por debajo del desarrollo promedio

latency stage (fase latente) fase freudiana del desarrollo, en la cual los conflictos previos del niño están escondidos y corren bajo la superficie

latent learning (aprendizaje latente) aprendizaje que no es óbvio pero que se da bajo la superficie

learned helplessness (impotencia aprendida) condición en la que la persona ha aceptado la idea generalizada de que no puede hacer nada para ayudarse

leaning curve (curva de aprendizaje) pendiente gradual ascendente que representa el incremento retentivo del conocimiento, como resultado del aprendizaje

lens (lente) parte del ojo que enfoca una imagen en la retina

libido (libido) término freudiano que define las energías internas que buscan descargarse contínuamente

limbic system (sistema límbico) zona del cerebro inferior cuya estructura controla las emociones básicas y la memoria

lobes (lóbulos) divisiones principales de la corteza cerebral

long-term memory (memoria prolongada) sistema de memoria que retiene información durante horas, días, semanas, meses o décadas

longitudinal method (método longitudinal) método de investigación que estudia al mismo grupo de gente durante un extenso período de tiempo

lower brain (cerebro inferior) parte del cerebro común, de animales y humanos, que regula funciones básicas tales como la respiración

M

major depression (depresión aguda) depresión grave; comprende pérdida del apetito, falta de energía, desasosiego y estado suicida

mania (manía) desorden del ánimo que comprende agitación extrema, inquietud, habla acelerada y falta de concentración

manipulation motive (manipulación obsesiva) impulso que mueve a alguien a toquetear y usar objetos de su entorno

maturation (maduración) proceso automático, ordenado y secuencial, del desarrollo físico y mental

meditation (meditación) forma de auto-control en la que el mundo exterior se desasocia del subconsciente

menopause (menopausia) el período del "cambio de vida" para las mujeres, en que ya no hay menstruación ni ovulación; algunas mujeres experimentan graves síntomas físicos, como mareos y calores

menstrual cycles (ciclos menstruales) ciclos mensuales en que se elimina la membrana del útero, cuando el óvulo no ha sido fertilizado

mental age (edad mental) nivel de funcionamiento intelectual a lo largo de los años, comparado con la edad cronológica, para llegar al cociente intelectual (IQ)

mental retardation (retraso mental) rendimiento intelectual inferior al promedio, lo que evita que una persona pueda rendir al nivel apropiado para su edad

metabolism (metabolismo) velocidad en que el cuerpo funciona, o la velocidad en que gasta energía

MMPI-2 última versión del Inventario Multifasético de la Personalidad, de Minnesota, el inventario de personalidades de mayor uso

mnemonic devices (reglas nemotécnicas) asociaciones inusuales para facilitar la memoria

modeling (modelar) término de Bandura para el aprendizaje imitando a otros

monozygotic twins (gemelos monocigóticos) gemelos que se desarrollan a partir de un óvulo fertilizado; son idénticos en su configuración

mood disorders (desórdenes del ánimo) desórdenes que comprenden los estados emocionales de las personas; incluyen la depresión y las manías

moratorium (moratorio) término usado tanto por Erikson como por Marcia, para describir los retrasos del adolescente en emprender los cometidos que normalmente se espera de los adultos

motivation (motivación) impulso para lograr los objetivos, como ser alimentos, agua o amigos

motor strip (banda motriz) banda que corre a lo largo del lóbulo frontal y que controla todos los movimientos del cuerpo (llamados funciones motrices)

Müller-Lyer illusion (ilusión de Müller-Lyer) ilusión por la que una línea de un dibujo de dos líneas iguales, parece ser más larga

N

narcolepsy (narcolepsia) desorden por el cual una persona se duerme instantáneamente, sin tener en cuenta lo que sucede a su alrededor

naturalistic observation (observación naturalista) método de investigación que comprende el estudio de sujetos, sin que ellos perciban que está siendo observados

nature/nurture controversy (controversia entre natural y adquirido) puntos de vista contrastantes sobre cómo obtenemos ciertas características: la naturaleza se refiere a la herencia, lo adquirido al ambiente

need for achievement (necesidad de triunfos) necesidad psicológica en obtener logros personales

need for affiliation (necesidad de afiliación) necesidad psicológica de pertenecer o identificarse con grupos

need for approval (necesidad de aprobación) necesidad psicológica de que los demás piensen bien de uno

negative identity (identidad negativa) término de Marcia aplicado a la identidad que resulta cuando uno se define a si mismo como malo o perturbador

negative reinforcement (reafirmación negativa) reafirmación que consiste en reforzar una respuesta, mediante la eliminación, a continuación, de algo desagradable

negative tansfer (transferencia negativa) interferencia con el aprendizaje, porque hay diferencias entre tareas que de otro modo, hubieran sido similares

neo-Freudians (neo-freudianos) psicoanalistas que se separaron de Freud para enfatizar fuerzas sociales en el subconsciente

neuron (neurona) célula nerviosa; las neuronas transmiten información eléctrica y química a través del cuerpo, via neurotransmisores

neurotransmitters (neurotransmisores) productos químicos en los extremos de las neuronas, que envían información a través de sinapsis

night terror ("noche de terror") sueño terrible que ocurre durante el MONR (NREM) cuando el cuerpo no está preparado para ello; se llama también "ataque del incubo(demonio)"

nightmare (pesadilla) sueño espantoso que ocurre durante el MOR (movimiento ocular rápido)

nondirective therapy (terapia no-dirigida) terapia personal

norms (normas) modelos de respuestas a tests tomados por distintas personas

NREM sleep (fase MONR del sueño) sueño de movimiento ocular no-rápido; sueño que comprende pensamientos, imágenes o historias parciales, poco organizados

nuclear family (núcleo familiar) padres e hijos

O

object permanence (permanencia del objeto) término de Piaget para determinar objetos específicos que son reales y existen por sí mismos

observational learning (aprendizaje por observación) forma de aprendizaje social en el cual el organismo observa e imita el comportamiento de otros

obsession (obsesión) desorden de la ansiedad caracterizado por una preocupación interminable, con cierto apremio e insistencia

obsessive-compulsive disorder (desorden de obsesión compulsiva) desorden de la ansiedad, caracterizado por pensamientos repetitivos (obsesión) y rituales, y por una conducta repetitiva también (compulsión)

occipital lobe (lóbulo occipital) división de la corteza cerebral que interpreta la información visual

olfaction (olfato) sentido del olor

olfactory bulbs (bulbos olfatorios) unidades que reciben las moléculas del olor y comunican su naturaleza al cerebro

operant conditioning (operación condicionada) condición que resulta de las acciones del individuo y de las consecuencias que producen

opiates (opiatos, narcóticos) soporíficos; drogas que reducen el funcionamiento del cuerpo

opponent-process theory (teoría de proceso opuesto) teoría que indica que la presencia de una emoción provoca, una opuesta, la cual aparece con posterioridad

oral stage (fase oral) fase freudiana del desarrollo, durante la cual el llanto y el comer, son los actos principales del niño

ovaries (ovarios) glándulas sexuales femeninas; producen óvulos

overlearning (sobreaprender) aprender algo por sobre la perfección, de modo que la curva de memoria no tiene efecto; desarrollo de una retentiva perfecta

P

panic disorder (pánico) tipo de desorden por ansiedad, caracterizado por ataques de ansiedad frecuentes y agobiantes, que no están asociados con objetos o hechos específicos

paranoia (paranoia) creencia de que alguien le está persiguiendo

paranoid schizophrenia (esquizofrenia paranoica) tipo de esquizofrenia marcada por profundos sentimientos de sospecha y desconfianza

parasympathetic nervous system (sistema nervioso del parasimpático) división del sistema nervioso autónomo que mantiene la actividad del físico; trabaja en oposición al sistema simpático que nos calma

parietal lobe (lóbulo parietal) división de la corteza cerebral que contiene la banda sensorial

partial reinforcement schedule (plan parcial de reafirmación) reafirmación que no sucede todas las veces, que se ejecuta una acción

perception (percepción) proceso de armado y organización de la información sensoria, para darle significado

performance scale (escala de rendimiento) unidades de las pruebas de cociente intelectual IQ, que tratan de saltear el material oral, y fijarse en la solución de problemas, sin hablar

peripheral nervous system (sistema nervioso periférico) todos los nervios ajenos al cerebro y la médula espinal

permissive parenting style (paternidad permisiva) educación paterna en la que los padres permiten que los niños hagan lo que quieran; existen y se ejecutan pocas reglas

person-centered therapy (terapia personal) propuesta del humanista Carl Rogers; refleja la convicción de que la persona y su terapista, están asociados en su terapia

persona (la persona) término de Jung para designar la "máscara" que usan algunos para esconder lo que realmente son o sienten

personal space (espacio individual) "burbuja invisible" o área alrededor de cada persona; cada uno de nosotros trata de evitar que este espacio sea invadido

personality (personalidad) patrones de conducta de un individuo: amplios y duraderos

personality disorder (desorden de la personalidad) desorden en el que la persona ha formado una personalidad peculiar, o desagradable

personality inventory (inventario de la personalidad) lista de datos sobre una persona: sus creencias, costumbres, necesidades y anhelos

personality traits (rasgos de la personalidad) características de la personalidad más o menos permanentes

phallic stage (fase fálica) etapa del desarrollo, de Freud, durante la cual el niño experimenta interés romántico por el padre del sexo opuesto y hostilidad hacia el del mismo sexo

pheromones (feromonas) productos químicos con olor, que comunican un mensaje

phobic disorder (fobia) tipo de desorden por ansiedad en el que la persona queda incapacitada y abrumada por el terror, en presencia de ciertos objetos o eventos. Ejemplo:agorafobia

physical dependence (dependencia física) deseo desesperado del cuerpo, por una droga

physiological needs (necesidades fisiológicas) necesidades al pie de la tabla de Maslow: hambre y sed

pitch (amplitud) cuán alto o bajo es un sonido

pituitary gland (glándula pituitaria) glándula principal del cuerpo; controla y activa a otras glándulas y hormonas; produce su propia hormona, que regula el crecimiento

placebo (placebo) "medicina" que no tiene ingrediente activo y actúa bajo el poder de la sugestión

positive reinforcement (reafirmación positiva) reafirmación que refuerza la tendencia de repetir una respuesta, cuando a continuación se le agrega algo placentero

positive transfer (transferencia positiva) transferencia de aprendizaje que surge por similitud, entre dos tareas

postconventional level (nivel pos-convencional) fase última del desarrollo moral, de Kohlberg, en la cual vienen a participar la ética personal y los derechos humanos

preconventional level (nivel pre-convencional) primera fase del desarrollo moral, deKohlberg, en la cual se determina la moralidad, mediante el poder cabal de una autoridad externa

prefrontal area (zona prefrontal) parte del lóbulo frontal que nos permite experimentar nuevamente, eventos personales pasados

prejudice (prejuicio) juicio parcial de la gente, en base al grupo al que pertenecen, en lugar de considerar sus carcterísticas individuales

premenstrual syndrome (PMS) (síndrome premenstrual) ansiedad, irritabilidad y confusión mental, como resultado de los cambios hormonales mensuales femeninos

preoperational stage (fase pre-operativa) segunda fase del desarrollo infantil, de Piaget, entre los dos y siete años de edad, en que los niños adquieren el lenguaje y la capacidad para usar símbolos, pero todavía no emplean la lógica del pensamiento

primary reinforcement (reafirmación primaria) algo necesario para sobrevivir física o psicológicamente, y que es usado como premio

principle learning (aprendizaje fundamental) método de aprendizaje por el cual se desarrolla un panorama completo (fundamental) del material a aprender, para poder organizar mejor, dicho material

projection (proyección) proceso de atribuir nuestros pensamientos a algún otro

projective tests (pruebas de proyección) pruebas que miden sentimientos internos extraídos de un estímulo vago, tal como un manchón de tinta o un dibujo(o foto) poco claros

proximity (proximidad) clave perceptiva que comprende la agrupación de cosas que están muy juntas unas de otras

psychedelic drug (droga psicodélica) droga que deforma o confunde la percepción del mundo

psychiatric nurses (enfermeras psiquiátricas) enfermeras certificadas, con especialidad en medicina psiquiátrica

psychiatric social workers (trabajadores sociales psiquiátricos) trabajadores de salud mental con título de trabajador social; ayudan a pacientes y familiares, a sobrellevar problemas

psychiatrists (psiquiatras) doctores en medicina, con especialidad en desórdenes mentales

psychoanalysis (psicoanálisis) terapia practicada por los seguidores de Freud, que analizan la psiquis vía el subconsciente

psychoanalytic theory (teoría del psicoanálisis) teoría de que la personalidad está basada en impulsos y necesidades del subconsciente

psychological dependence (dependencia psicológica) deseo extremo de la psiquis por una droga

psychological test (prueba psicológica) medida sistemática del conocimiento de la gente; de como actúan, piensan o sienten; y cuales son sus objetivos. Métodos objetivos de observación y evaluación del sujeto, en varias áreas, tales como la inteligencia

psychology (psicología) estudio científico de los procesos mentales y de la conducta

psychosis (psychotic disorder) (psicosis) desorden mental agudo que puede comprender procesos desorganizados del pensamiento, alucinaciones, divagaciones o graves problemas con respuestas emotivas

psychosurgery (psicocirugía) cirugía que destruye parte del cerebro para calmar al paciente y aliviarle los síntomas

psychotherapies (psicoterapia) término general para cualquier método usado para tratar a la gente con problemas emocionales o psicológicos

psychotic episodes (episodios psicóticos) períodos de conducta psicótica; pueden alternar con períodos de relativa coherencia y calma

puberty (pubertad) tiempo de maduración sexual

punishment (castigo) proceso por el que se debilita una respuesta, cuando se prosigue con consecuencias desagradables

pupil (pupila) abertura del ojo

R

race (raza) conjunto de características físicas hereditarias que distingue a un grupo considerable de gente

rational-emotive therapy (RET) (terapia racional-emotiva) forma de terapia de la conducta cognoscitiva de Albert Ellis, destinada a controlar las emociones, mediante el uso de la razón

rationalization (racionalización) proceso de justificar un problema, con el objeto de no tener que aceptar la culpa

reaction formation (elaborar la reacción) proceso de expresar lo opuesto a lo que sentimos

recall (recordar) capacidad de traer e integrar muchos detalles específicos aprendidos

recognition (reconocer) capacidad de elegir el objeto o evento específico, dentro de una lista de posibilidades

reference group (grupo de referencia) grupo con el que uno se identifica y que provee bases de conducta

reflex (reflejo) conducta automática del cuerpo mediante el movimiento, activada a través de la médula espinal, sin utilizar las partes altas del cerebro

regression (regresión) proceso de retroceso en conducta y pensamiento, hasta un período en que nos cuidaban como niños; comportamiento infantil

reinforcement (reafirmación) algo que viene después de una respuesta y que refuerza la tendencia a repetir dicha respuesta

reinforcement value (valor de la reafirmación) preferencia por ciertos tipos de reafirmación, en lugar de otros

reliability (precisión) consistencia de una prueba

REM sleep (sueño de MOR) sueño de movimiento ocular rápido; los sueños ocurren durante esta fase MOR

REM rebound (recaída en mor) aumento de la cantidad de sueños, luego de haber sido desprovisto de la fase MOR

661

representative sample (muestra representativa) grupo que refleja con veracidad, las características específicas de una población mayor

repression (represión) proceso de eliminar de la conciencia, un evento o pensamiento doloroso. Proceso de transladar al subconsciente, las necesidades y deseos que acarrean culpas

research psychologists (psicólogos investigadores) psicólogos que estudian el origen, las causas o los resultados de ciertos comportamientos

response (respuesta) reacción ante un estímulo

reticular activating system (RAS) (sistema de activación reticular—SAR) centro del control alerta del cerebro, que regula el nivel de actividad del cuerpo; llamado también formación reticular

reticular formation (formación reticular) centro del cerebro que registra y controla el nivel de actividad, aumenta la excitación y ayuda a generar el sueño

retina (retina) parte posterior del ojo que contiene millones de receptores de la luz

retinal disparity (disparidad retinal) diferencia entre las imágenes provistas por ambas retinas. Cuando las imágenes se encuentran en el cerebro, producen un sentido de profundidad

reverse halo (halo contrario) situación en la que se considera que una persona con una característica negativa, puede tener más rasgos negativos

reversibility (reversibilidad) término de Piaget sobre la idea de que una relación que va hacia una dirección dada, también puede ir en otra dirección

reversible figure (figura reversible) ilusión en la que el mismo objeto es visto como dos figuras alternadas: primero una, luego la otra

risky shift phenomenon (fenómeno de compartir el riesgo) situación en la cual el riesgo asociado a una acción, es dividido entre los miembros de un grupo; por lo tanto, el riesgo es menor para cada persona

rite of passage (crisis evolutiva normal) cambio de estado socialmente reconocido y ritualizado, tal como el paso a ser adulto

rod (bastón) receptor visual más sensible a la longitud de onda violeta-púrpura; muy sensible a la visión nocturna; "ve" sólo en negro y blanco

Rorschach test (prueba de Rorschach) test de proyección del manchón de tinta, desarrollado por Hermann Rorschach

S

safety needs (necesidades de seguridad) necesidades del segundo nivel de la tabla de Maslow; un techo, y dinero a resguardo

sample (muestra) grupo que representa a un grupo mayor

savant syndrome (síndrome del sabio) condición en la que una persona con capacidad mental bajo lo normal, posee un talento especial, o habilidad mental, de grado extremadamente alto

scapegoating (chivo expiatorio) acusar a otro, por lo que sale mal

schedules of reinforcement (planes de reafirmación) diferentes métodos de reafirmación

schema (diagrama) método organizado y sistemático para contestar preguntas o resolver problemas

schizophrenia (esquizofrenia) psicosis que comprende pensamientos desordenados y habla cortada, al igual que alucinaciones y divagues; es el desorden mental más serio

Scholastic Assessment Test (SAT) (Prueba de Evaluación Escolástica-SAT) exámen destinado a medir la capacidad para ingresar a la universidad

secondary reinforcement (reafirmación secundaria) cualquier cosa que puede representar un reafirmador principal, por ejemplo: el dinero

secondary traits (rasgos secundarios) término de Allport para los rasgos débiles de la personalidad, que aparecen sólo en raras ocasiones

selective forgetting (olvido selectivo) olvido solamente de lo que es muy traumático

self-actualization needs (necesidad de auto-realización) necesidades al tope de la tabla de Maslow, que establecen objetivos muy significativos y un propósito en la vida

self-actualized (auto-realizado) término de Maslow para el estado de haber alcanzado en la vida, el mayor potencial de nuestra capacidad

self-concepts (concepto propio) imágenes que tenemos de nosotros

self-esteem needs (necesidades de auto-estima) necesidades del cuarto nivel de la tabla de Maslow: amarse y respetarse a uno mismo, sentirse importante y útil

senile dementia (demencia senil) pérdida de las facultades mentales, con la vejez

sensation (sensación) proceso de recibir información del entorno

sensorimotor stage (fase sensomotriz) primera fase del desarrollo del niño, de Piaget, entre el nacimiento y los dos años de edad, en que el conocimiento está ligado al movimiento y los objetos del entorno

sensory deprivation (privación sensoria) técnica usada en el lavado del cerebro, en la que se eliminan todas las sensaciones y estímulos externos

sensory memory system (sistema de memoria sensoria) sistema que contiene receptores directos de información externa; por ejemplo: acústica, icónica

sensory strip (banda sensoria) banda que corre a lo largo del lóbulo parietal, y que registra y provee todas las sensaciones

separation anxiety (ansiedad por separación) temor del bebé de estar lejos de sus padres; deseo de evitar extraños

serotonin (serotina) producto químico del cerebro. En niveles muy altos, produce manías; en niveles bajos, crea depresión

set (direccional) tendencia a resolver los problemas siempre del mismo modo

set point (punto determinado) mecanismo regulador del cuerpo que determina el peso típico de una persona

shape constancy (forma constante) capacidad de percibir un objeto siempre con la misma forma, sin tener el cuenta el ángulo desde el que se mira

shaping (pulir) proceso de afinar una respuesta, dirigiéndola, mediante sucesivas aproximaciones

short-term memory (memoria reciente) sistema de memoria que retiene información durante algunos segundos, hasta algunos minutos

similarity (semejanza) clave perceptiva por la que se agrupan en conjuntos, elementos similares

situational assessment (evaluación de la situación) proceso de observar cómo las circunstancias que envuelven un evento, influyen en la respuesta de la gente a tal evento

size constancy (constancia por volumen) capacidad de recordar el tamaño de un objeto, sin considerar donde está ubicado

sleep apnea (apnea del sueño) condición en la que se detiene la respiración de una persona, mientras está durmiendo

social contracts (contratos sociales) término de Kohlberg para los acuerdos basados en lo que está "bien para todos"

social learning (aprendizaje social) todo aprendizaje que ocurre en situación social

sociocultural approach (propuesta sociocultural) propuesta que considera que las reglas y expectativas de grupos o culturas sociales específicos, influyen profundamente en la conducta

sociopath (sociópata) persona con un desorden de personalidad antisocial

somatic nervous system (sistema nervioso somático) división del sistema nervioso periférico que contiene los nervios sensoriales y motores

somatoform disorder (desorden psicosomático) condición en la cual los hechos psicológicos son expresados en síntomas físicos, aunque no haya un problema físico real

source traits (rasgos fundamentales) término de Cattell para los rasgos de la personalidad que son la base de la conducta superficial

space constancy (constancia espacial) capacidad de sentir fijos a los objetos del entorno, al sentir nosotros o los otros objetos, como en movimiento

spatial skills (habilidad espacial) habilidad de concebir un objeto, como si se moviera en el espacio

specific phobia (fobia específica) fobia asociada con un objeto o situación específicos, tales como víboras, perros, elevadores y alturas

spintal cord (médula espinal) parte del cuerpo que funciona como un "cerebro" automático por sí misma y como una estación reguladora de los impulsos, de ida y vuelta, al cerebro superior

spontaneous recovery (recuperación espontánea) reaparición súbita de una respuesta extinta

standardization (generalización) proceso de desarrollo de instrucciones claras, para tomar, calificar e interpretar, una prueba

standoutishness (sobresalir) hacer o lucir algo tan destacado, que impide que los observadores noten las reales habilidades de uno

Stanford-Binet Intelligence Test (Prueba de Inteligencia de Stanford-Binet) test de inteligencia desarrollado por Alfred Binet y pulido luego por la Universidad de Stanford

state-dependent learning (aprendizaje dependiente) aprendizaje que sucede bajo un cierto estado químico y se reproduce mejor, cuando dicho estado se repite

stereotype (estereotipo) conjunto fijo de conceptos sobre un grupo, que es generalizado hacia todos o la mayoría de sus miembros; los estereotipos pueden ser correctos, o no

steroids (esteroides) componentes naturales hormonas. Producidas artificialmente, ciertas hormonas sexuales masculinas, mejoran el crecimiento muscular y a veces, son utilizadas por los atletas

stimulus (estímulo) algo que provoca una respuesta

stimulus generalization (estímulo generalizado) proceso por el cual una respuesta se distribuye desde un estímulo específico, a otros estímulos que se parecen al original

strategies (estrategias) métodos para resolver problemas

stress hormone (hormona del estrés) producto químico especial que ordena a las glándulas suprarrenales, para que activen el cuerpo

stress (estrés) esfuerzo físico como resultado de exigencias o cambios en el entorno

Strong-Campbell Interest Inventory (Inventario de Orientación Vocacional de Strong-Campbell) prueba de orientación vocacional de más amplio renombre; basado en respuestas de gente que ha prosperado en ciertos campos

subconscious (subconsciente) conciencia justo por debajo de nuestro conocimiento consciente

subjects (sujetos) gente o animales con los cuales se conduce un estudio

sublimation (sublimación) proceso de canalización de la energía emotiva, en actividades constructivas o creativas

subliminal perception (percepción subconsciente) estimulación presentada bajo el nivel consciente

substance abuse (abuso narcótico) uso de drogas hasta el punto en que se perjudican el trabajo y las relaciones

substance dependence (dependencia narcótica) abuso de una droga; el usuario presenta síntomas físicos cuando no consume la droga, entones consume más y más, y dedica mucho tiempo al consumo

superego (superego) unidad psicológica freudiana, en general, sinónimo de conciencia

surface traits (rasgos superficiales) término de Cattell que designa las características que pueden ser fácilmente observadas por otros

survey (reconocimiento) método de investigación por el que se pregunta a los sujetos sobre sus sentimientos, opiniones o patrones de conducta

sympathetic nervous system (sistema nervioso del gran simpático) división del sistema nervioso autónomo que se energiza y prepara para emergencias

synapse (sinapsis) punto en que se juntan dos o más neuronas; la conección es realizada mediante neurotransmisores

synergistic effect (efecto sinérgico) efecto por el cual, cuando se toman dos drogas en combinación, cada una es más potente que si se la tomara individualmente

systematic desensitization (desensibilización sistemática) técnica de la conducta, por la cual el psicólogo aumenta la ansiedad del paciente y la contrarresta con relajación, en una secuencia gradual

T

taste receptors (receptores gustativos) receptores químicos de la lengua, que decodifican las moléculas de la comida y bebida, para identificarlas

temporal lobe (lóbulo temporal) división de la corteza cerebral relacionada con el oído y algunas funciones del habla

territoriality (territorialidad) apego a un área fija que consideramos únicamente nuestra y la tendencia a defenderla contra intrusos

testes (testículos) glándulas sexuales masculinas; producen espermatozoides

texture gradient (textura) percepción de la estructura de los objetos: rugosos o suaves; usada para apreciar la profundidad

thalamus (tálamo) parte del cerebro inferior que funciona principalmente como estación central reguladora de entrada y salida de mensajes, desde el cuerpo hacia el cerebro y vice versa

thanatology (tanatología) estudio de la muerte y de los métodos para sobrellevarla

Thematic Apperception Test (TAT (Prueba de Apercepción Temática-TAT) prueba de representaciones proyectadas que utiliza figuras no muy definidas, sobre las cuales las personas inventan historias

theory (teoría) sistema general para un estudio científico; los aspectos menores pueden ser examinados

theory of multiple intelligences (teoría de inteligencias múltiples) teoría de Howard Gardner sobre la composición de la inteligencia en siete capacidades: lenguaje, lógica/matemática, visual/espacial, musical, movimiento físico, intrapersonal e interpersonal

thought disorder (desorden del pensamiento) deformación aguda de la capacidad de pensar o hablar, de modo lúcido o coherente

thyroid gland (glándula tiroides) glándula que controla y regula la velocidad de los procesos del cuerpo, llamados metabolismo

token economy (economía de premios) técnica de la conducta por la que se da premios por actos logrados, los cuales representan cierto tipo de dinero

tolerance (tolerancia) con respecto al uso de drogas, adaptación del cuerpo a dosis en aumento. Se necesitan, cada vez dosis mayores de drogas, para obtener el efecto producido por la dosis original

trance (trance) otra denominación para el estado de relajamiento profundo que ocurre durante hipnosis

transfer of training (transferencia de entrenamiento) proceso de enseñanza en el que el aprendizaje se transporta de una tarea a otra, basado en la similitud entre ambas tareas

transference (transferencia) proceso en el cual una persona transfiere al terapista, sus conflictos emocionales de años anteriores

twilight state (narcosis, estado crepuscular) estado relajado justo antes de dormirnos

type A personality (personalidad grupo A) personalidad asociada con las personas que están siempre a toda velocidad, impacientes, llenos de ansiedad

type B personality (personalidad grupo B) personalidad asociada con la gente que está dispuesta al cambio, es flexible, disfruta de la vida y tiene bajo índice de estrés

U

unconditional positive regard (consideración positiva incondicional) principio de la terapia humanística por el que los sentimientos y pensamientos de una persona, son aceptados por lo que son en realidad; término de Carl Rogers

unconditioned response (respuesta incondicional) respuesta automática a un estímulo natural en particular, como ser la salivación ante la comida

unconditioned stimulus (estímulo incondicional) estímulo que automáticamente despierta una respuesta, como la comida produce salivación

unconscious (subconsciente) de acuerdo con la creencia psicoanalítica, parte de la mente más allá de lo consciente. A pesar de que no sabemos su contenido, afecta profundamente nuestro comportamiento. Pensamientos o deseos sobre los que no tenemos conocimiento directo

undifferentiated schizophrenia (esquizofrenia indescifrable) esquizofrenia que carece de síntomas que la distinguen

universal ethical principles (principios éticos universales) término de Kohlberg que define conceptos tales como la justicia y el honor

V

validity (validez) límite hasta donde una prueba mide lo que se supone que tiene que medir

variable interval schedule (plan de intervalos variables) plan en que ocurre una reafirmación por haberse cumplido la acción deseada, en cierto período variable

variable ratio schedule (plan de proporción variable) plan en que ocurre una reafirmación por haberse cumplido la deseada acción, una variable cantidad de veces

variables (variables) factores que cambian en un experimento

verbal scale (escala verbal) unidades en una prueba de cociente intelectual (IQ), que dependen profundamente de la comprensión y uso de vocabulario

vesicles (vesículas) ampolletas que contienen a los neurotransmisores, ubicadas a los extremos de los axones

visual cliff (abismo visual) aparato usado para demostrar la percepción en profundidad

vocational interest test (prueba de orientación vocacional) prueba que intenta predecir la ocupación que le gustaría a un individuo

W

Wechsler Adult Intelligence Scale (WAIS) (Escala de Wechsler de Inteligencia en Adultos-WAIS) prueba de inteligencia para adultos, que suministra tres IQ, cocientes intelectuales: verbal, rendimiento y combinado (total)

Wechsler Intelligence Scale for Children (WISC) (Escala de Wechsler de Inteligencia en Niños-WISC) prueba de inteligencia en niños de 6 a 16 años, que suministra tres IQ (cocientes intelectuales): verbal, rendimiento y combinado

white light (luz blanca) luz tal cual es originada por el sol o una lámpara, antes de ser descompuesta en diferentes frecuencias

word salad (ensalada de palabras) discurso en el cual las palabras son mezcladas sin coherencia

Z

zygote (cigoto) óvulo fertilizado

REFERENCES

A

Ackerman, P. L., and Heggestad, E. D. (1997). Intelligence, personality, and interests: Evidence for overlapping traits. *Psychological Bulletin, 121,* 219–245.

Adams, A. B. (1969). *Eternal quest: The story of the great naturalists.* New York: Putnam's.

Adams, G. A., & Jex, S.M. (1999). Relationships between time management, control, work-family conflict, and strain. *Journal of Occupational Health Psychology,* 4, 72–77.

Adler, A. (1969). *The science of living.* Garden City, NY: Doubleday and Company. (Originally published in 1929).

Alcock, J. E. (1990). *Science and supernature: A critical appraisal of parapsychology.* Buffalo, NY: Prometheus.

American Psychiatric Association. (1994). *Diagnostic and statistical manual of mental disorders, 4th ed.* Washington, D.C.: Author.

American Psychological Association. (1992). *Ethical standards of psychologists and code of conduct.* Washington, D.C.: Author.

Anastasi, A. (1988). *Psychological testing* (6th ed.). New York: Macmillan.

Anderson, J. R. (1983). *The architecture of cognition.* Cambridge, MA: Harvard University Press.

Anderson, R. D. (1970). The history of witchcraft: A review with some psychiatric comments. *Amer. J. Psychiat., 126,* 1727–1735.

Archer, D. and Gartner, R. (1984). Peacetime casualties: The effects of war on the violent behavior of noncombatants. In E. Aronson (Eds.) *Readings about the social animal,* 4th ed. New York: W. H. Freeman and Co. (Original work published in 1978). *Readings About The Social Animal* by Aronson © 1973, 1977, 1981, 1984, 1988, 1992, 1995, 1998 by W. H.Freeman and Company. Used with permission.

Archer, J. (1996). Sex differences in social behavior, *American Psychologist, 51,* 909–917.

Arkes, H. R., & Garske, J. P. (1982). *Psychological theory of motivation* (2d ed.). Monterey, CA: Brooks/Cole.

Asch, S. E. (1952). *Social psychology.* Englewood Cliffs, NJ: Prentice-Hall.

Aspinwall, L. G., and Taylor, S. E. (1997). A stitch in time: Self-regulation and proactive coping. *Psychological Bulletin, 121,* 417–436.

Axelrod, J., & Reisine, T. D. (1984). Stress hormones: Their interaction and regulation. *Science, 224,* 452–459.

B

Bagby, J. W. (1968). Quoted in J. D. Frank, The face of the enemy. *Psychol. Today, 2,* 24–29.

Bahrick, H. P., Bahrick, P. O., & Wittlinger, R. P. (1974). Long-term memory: Those unforgettable high school days. *Psychol. Today, 8*(7).

Baltes, P. B., & Kliegl, R. (1992). Further testing of limits of cognitive plasticity: Negative age differences in a mnemonic skill are robust. *Develop. Psychol., 28,* 121–125.

Bandura, A. (1991). Social cognitive theory of moral thought and action. In W. M. Kurtines & J. L. Gewirtz (Eds.) *Handbook of moral behavior and development: Theory, research and applications* (Vol. 1, pp. 71–129). Hillsdale, NJ: Erlbaum.

Bandura, A., & Walters, R. (1963). *Social learning and personality development.* New York: Holt, Rinehart and Winston.

Bandura, A., Barbaranelli, C., Caprara, G., and Pastorelli, C. (1996). Mechanisms of moral disengagement in the exercise of moral agency. *Journal of Personality and Social Psychology.* 71, 364–374.

Barber, B., & Eccles, J. (1992). Long-term influence of divorce and single parenting on adolescent family- and work-related values, behaviors, and aspirations. *Psychol. Bull., 111,* 108–126.

Barker, J. C., & Miller, M. B. (1969). Quoted in T. Wolpe, *The Practice of Behavior Theory.* New York: Pergamon Press.

Barkley, R. A. (1997). Behavioral inhibition, sustained attention, and executive functions: Constructing a unifying theory of ADHD. *Psychological Bulletin, 121,* 65–94.

Barlow, D. H. (1996). Healthcare policy, psychotherapy research and the future of psychotherapy. *American Psychologist, 51,* 1050–1058.

Barron, F., & Harrington, D. M. (1981). Creativity, intelligence, and personality. *Ann. Rev. Psychol., 32,* 439–476.

Basic Behavioral Science Research for Mental Health. (1995). A report of the national advisory mental health council. Washington, D.C.: NIH, No. 96–3682.

Basic Behavioral Science Task Force of the National Advisory Mental Health Council, (1995). Basic behavioral science research for mental health: A national investment: Emotion and motivation. *American Psychologist, 50,* 838–845.

Basic Behavioral Science Task Force of the National Advisory Mental Health Council, (1996b). Basic behavioral science research for mental health: Social influence and social cognition. *American Psychologist, 51,* 478–484.

Basic Behavioral Science Task Force of the National Advisory Mental Health Council. (1996a). Basic behavioral science research for mental health: Family processes and social networks. *American Psychologist, 51,* 622–630.

Baumeister, R. F., and Sommer, K. L. (1997). What do men want? Gender differences of belongingness: Comment on Cross and Madson (1997). *Psychological Bulletin, 122,* 38–44.

Beck, A. T. (1967). *Depression.* New York: Harper & Row.

Beckwith, J., & Woodruff, M. (1984). Achievement in mathematics. *Science, 223,* 1247.

Beilin, H. (1992). Piaget's enduring contribution to developmental psychology. *Developmental Psychology, 28,* 191–204.

Belmont, L. and Marolla, F. A. (1973, December 14). Birth order, family size, and intelligence. *Science, 182,* 1096–1101.

Belsky, J. (1990). Parental and nonparental child care and children's socioemotional development: A decade in review. *J. Marr. and Fam., 52,* 885–903.

_____. (1992). The research findings on gender issues in aging men and women. In B. R. Wainrib (Ed.) *Gender issues across the life cycle.* New York: Springer Publishing Co.

Bem, S. L. (1975). Sex role adaptability: One consequence of psychological androgyny. *J. Pers. Soc. Psychol., 31,* 634–643.

Benbow, C. P., & Stanley, J. C. (1983). Sex differences in mathematical reasoning ability: More facts. *Science, 222,* 1029–1031.

Benjamin, Jr., L. T., Durkin, M., Link, M., Vestal, M., & Acord, J. (1992). Wundt's American doctoral students. *American Psychologist, 47,* 123–131.

Benjamin, L. T., and Dixon, D. N. (1996). Dream analysis by mail: An American woman seeks Freud's advice. *American Psychologist, 51,* 461–468. © 1996 A. W. Freud *et al,* by arrangement with Mark Paterson & Associates.

Benner, S. A. (1980). Quoted in: Biological information storage: How to fold proteins. *Science News, 125,* 231.

Bergland, R. (1985). *The fabric of mind.* New York: Viking Press.

Berkowitz, L., & Green, R. G. (1967). Stimulus qualities of the target of aggression: A further study. *J. Personal. Soc. Psychol., 5,* 364–368.

Bettridge, B. J., and Favreau, O. E. (1995). The dependency needs and perceived availability and adequacy of relationships in female adolescent suicide attempters. *Psychology of Woman Quarterly, 19,* 517–531.

Bickerton, D. (1984). The language bioprogram hypotheses. *Brain Beh. Sci., 7,* 173–221.

Bjorklund, D. F. (1997). The role of immaturity in human development. *Psychological Bulletin, 122,* 153–169.

Blackman, S., & Catalina, D. (1973). The moon and the emergency room. *Percept. Mot. Skills, 37,* 624–626.

Block, J. (1979), *Socialization influence of personality development in males and females.* American Psychological Association Master Lecture, Convention of the American Psychological Association, New York City, Sept. 1979.

References

Blum, K. (1984). *Handbook of abusable drugs*. New York: Gardner Press.

Blum, K. (1988). Personal communication.

Blume, E. S. (1990). *Secret survivors: Uncovering incest and its aftereffects in women*. New York: Ballantine.

Bonta, B. D. (1997). Cooperation and competition in peaceful societies. *Psychological Bulletin, 121,* 299–320.

Boorstin, D. J. (1983). *The discoverers*. New York: Random House.

Bouchard, T. J., Jr. (1983). Twins. *Yrbk. Sci. and the Future. Encyclopedia Britannica.*

Bouchard, T. J., Jr. (1997) "Twins—nature's twice told tale," *Yearbook of Science and the Future*. Chicago: Encyclopedia Britannica.

Bouchard, T. J., Lykken, D. T., McGue, M., Segal, N. L., and Tellegen, A. (1990). Sources of human psychological differences: The Minnesota study of twins reared apart. *Science, 250,* 223–228.

Bradshaw, J. (1992, August). Incest: When you wonder if it happened to you. *Lear's, 5,* 43–44.

Brasch, R. (1967). *How did it begin?* New York: McKay.

Braudel, F. (1981). *The structures of everyday life* (Vol. 1). (S. Reynolds, Trans.). New York: Harper & Row.

Breggin, P. R. (1983) *Psychiatric drugs: Hazards to the brain*. New York: Springer.

_____. (1984). Electroshock therapy and brain damage: The acute organic brain syndrome as treatment. *Brain Beh. Sci., 7,* 24–25.

Bringmann, W. G., & Tweney, R. D. (Eds.). (1980). *Wundt studies: A centennial collection*. Toronto, Canada: Hogrefe.

Brislin, R. W. (1983). Cross-cultural research is psychology. *Ann. Rev. Psychol., 34,* 363–400.

Brody, N. (1997). Intelligence, schooling, and society. *American Psychologist, 52,* 1046–1050.

Brome, V. (1967). *Freud and his early circle*. New York: William Morrow.

Bronfenbrenner, U., and Ceci, S. J. (1994). Nature-nurture reconceptualized in developmental perspective: A bioecological model. *Psychological Review, 101,* 568–586.

Brown, K. D., and Rodin, J. (1994). The dieting maelstrom: It is possible and advisable to lose weight? *American Psychologist, 49,* 781–791.

Bruner, J. S. (1968). Foreword. In A. R. Luria, *The mind of a mnemonist*. New York: Basic Books.

Bryan, J. H., & Test, M. A. (1969). Models and helping: Naturalistic studies in aiding behavior. Quoted in P. H. Mussen and M. R. Rosensweig (Eds.), *Annual review of psychology*. Palo Alto, CA: Annual Review.

Buchanan, C., Eccles, J., & Becker, J. (1992). Are adolescents the victims of raging hormones: Evidence for activational effects of hormones on moods and behavior at adolescence. *Psychol. Bull., 111,* 62–107.

Buckhout, R. Figueroa, D., & Hoff, E. (1972, November). *Psychology and eyewitness identification: A preliminary report*. Ctr. Responsive Psychol. Rep. (CR–1).

Bullock, A. (1953) *Hitler: A study in tyranny*. New York: Harper &Row.

Burger, J. M., & Arkin, R. M. (1980). Prediction, control, and learned helplessness. *J. Pers. Soc. Psychol., 38,* 483–491.

Burros, M. (1988, February 23). Women: Out of the house but not out of the kitchen. *New York Times,*1, 18.

Buss, A. H. (1966). *Psychopathology*. New York: Wiley.

Buss, D. M. (1994). Mate preferences in 37 cultures. In W. J. Lonner & R. Malpass (Eds.). *Psychology and culture*. Boston: Allyn and Bacon.

Butler, R., and M. Nisan. (1986). Effects of no feedback, task-related comments, and grades on intrinsic motivation and performance. *Journal of Educational Psychology, 78* (3, June): 210-216. EJ 336 917.

C

Cacioppo, J. T., and Berntson, G. G. (1994). Relationship between attitudes and evaluative space: A critical review, with emphasis on the separability of positive and negative substrates. *Psychological Bulletin, 115,* 401–423.

Campbell, D. E., & Beets, J. L. (1980). Lunacy and the moon. *Psychol. Bull., 85,* 1123–1129.

Cannon, W. B. (1939). *The wisdom of the body*. New York: Norton.

_____. (1942). Voodoo death. *Amer. Anthropol, 44,* 169.

Caplan, P. J. (1984). The myth of women's masochism. *Amer. Psychol., 40,* 786–799.

Carr, J. G., Gilroy, F. D., and Sherman, M.F. (1996). Silencing the self and depression among women. *Psychology of Women Quarterly, 20,* 375–392.

Carstensen, L., Isaacowitz, D., & Charles, S. (1999). Taking time seriously: a theory of socioemotional selectivity. *American Psychologist,* 54, 165–181.

Carter, Jimmy (1998). *The virtues of aging*. New York: Ballantine Publishing.

Case, R. B. (1985). Quoted in "Type A's maybe now you can relax." *Science 85, 6*(5).

Cash, T. F., & Janda, L. H. (1984). The eye of the beholder. *Psychology Today, 18*(12).

Ceci, S. J., and Williams, W. M. (1997). Schooling, intelligence, and income. *American Psychologist, 52,* 1051–1058.

Chomsky, N. (1980). Rules and representations. *Beh. Brain Sci., 3,* 1–15.

Cialdini, R. B., Petty, R. E., & Cacioppo, J. T. (1981). Attitude and attitude change. *Ann. Rev. Psychol., 32,* 357–404.

Clark, R. W. (1980). *Freud: The man and the cause*. New York: Random House.

Cleland, C. C., Case, J., & Manaster, G. J. (1980). IQs and etiologies: The two-group approach to mental retardation. *Bull. Psychon. Soc., 15,* 413–415.

Cohen, D. (1979). *J.B. Watson*. Boston: Routledge & Kegan Paul.

Cohen, S., & Williamson, G. (1991). Stress and infectious disease in humans. *Psychol. Bull., 109,* 5–24.

Cohn, L. (1991). Sex differences in the course of personality development: A meta-analysis. *Psychol. Bull., 109,* 252–266.

Coile, D. C., & Miller, N. E. (1984). How radical animal activists try to mislead humane people. *Amer. Psychol., 39,* 700–701.

Coleman, R. M. (1986). *Wide awake at 3:00 A.M.,* New York: W. H. Freeman.

Colombo, J. (1982). The critical period concept: Research, methodology, and theoretical issues. *Psychol. Bull., 91,* 260–275.

Conger, J. J., & Peterson, A. C. (1984). *Adolescents and youth*. New York: Harper & Row.

Consumer Union. (1993, June). Rating the diets. *Consumer Reports, 353*–357.

Coon, Dennis (1998) *Introduction to psychology,* West Publishing/ International Thomson Publishing, p. 112–113.

Cooper, E., & Tahoda, M. (1964). Quoted in W. W. Lambert and W. E. Lambert, *Social psychology*. Englewood Cliffs, NJ: Prentice-Hall.

Corballis, M. C., & Morgan, M. J. (1978). On the biological basis of human laterality: Evidence for a maturational left-right gradient. *Behav. Brain Sci., 1,* 261–269.

Coren, S. (1996). *Sleep thieves*. New York: The Free Press.

Costa, P. T., Jr., & McCrae, R. R. (1986). Cross-sectional studies of personality in a national sample: 1. Development and validation of survey measures. *Psychol. Aging, 1,* 140–143.

Costa, P. T., Jr., Zonderman, A. B., McCrae, R. R., Cornoni-Huntley, Locke, B. Z., & Barbano, H. E. (1987). Longitudinal analysis of psychological well-being in a national sample: Stability of mean levels. *J. Gerontol., 42,* 50–55.

Coughlin, E. (1993, March 24). Conflicts over census categories mirror struggles in society at large. *The Chronicle of Higher Education,* p. A8.

Cowart, B. J. (1981). Development of taste perception in humans: Sensitivity and preference throughout the life span. *Psychol. Bull., 90,* 43–73.

Cox, V. C., Paulus, P. B., & McCain, G. (1984). Prison crowding research: The relevance for prison housing standards and a general approach regarding crowding phenomena. *Amer. Psychol., 30,* 1148–1160.

Cronback, L. (1990) *Essentials of psychological testing*. Reading, PA: Addison Wesley.

Cross, S. E., and Madson, L. (1997). Models of the Self: Self-construals and gender. *Psychological Bulletin, 122,* 5–37.

Csikszentmihalyi, M. (1990). *Flow*. New York: Harper & Row.

References

Culbertson, F. M. (1997). Depression and gender. *American Psychologist, 52,* 25–31.

Curtiss, S. (1977). *Genie: A psycholinguistic study of a modern-day "wild child."* New York: Academic Press.

D

Dadds, M. R., Bovbjerg, D. H., Redd, W. H., and Cutmore, T.R.H. (1997). Imagery in human classical conditioning. *Psychological Bulletin, 122,* 89–103.

Daniel, J. (1996). Learning to love (gasp!) growing old. In K. L. Freiberg (Ed.). *Annual editions in human development.* Guilford, CT: Dushkin Publishing Group. (Original work published in 1994).

Daniel, M. H. (1997). Intelligence testing: Status and trends. *American Psychologist, 52,* 1038–1045.

Darley, J. M., and Latané, Bibb (1968). Why people do not help in a crisis. Psychology Today, 120+.

Davies, P. T., and Cummings, E. M. (1994). Marital conflict and child adjustment: An emotional security hypothesis. *Psychological Bulletin, 116,* 387–411.

Davis, K. E. (1985). Near and dear: Friendship and love compared. *Psychology Today, 19*(2).

Deary, I. J., and Stough, C. (1996). Intelligence and inspection time: Achievements, prospects,and problems. *American Psychologist, 51,* 599–608.

DeCasper, A., & Fifer, W. (1980). Of human bonding: Newborns perfer their mothers' voices. *Science,* June 6.

Degler, C. N. (1980). *At Odds.* New York: Oxford University Press.

DeLeon, P. J., Sammons, M. T., and Sexton, J. L. (1995). Focusing on society's real needs: Responsibility and prescription privileges? *American Psychologist, 50,* 1022–1032.

Delgado, J. M. R. (1969). *Physical control of the mind.* New York: Harper & Row.

Denmark, F. (1992). The thirty-something woman: To career or not to career. In B. R. Wainrib (Ed.), *Gender issues across the life cycle.* New York: Springer Publishing Co.

Denton, D. (1983). *The hunger for salt.* New York: Springer-Verlag.

Depue, R. A., Slater, J. F., Wolfstetter-Kausch, H., Klein, D., Goplerud, E., & Farr, D. (1981). A behav-ioral paradigm for identifying persons at risk for bipolar depressive disorder: A conceptual framework and five validation studies. *J. Abn. Psychol. Monog., 90,* 381–437.

Detterman, D. K., and Thompson, L. A. (1997). What is so special about special education? *American Psychologist, 52,* 1082–1090.

Deutsch, A. (1946). *The mentally ill in America* (2d ed.). New York: Columbia University Press.

Diagnostic and Statistical Manual of Mental Disorders (4th ed.). (1994). Washington, DC: American Psychiatric Association.

Diener, E. (1976). Effects of prior destructive behavior, anonymity, and group presence on deindividuation and aggression. *J. Pers. Soc. Psychol., 33,* 497–507.

Diener, E., & Woody, L. W. (1981). Television violence, conflict, realism, and action. *Comm. Res., 8,* 281–306.

Dindia, K., & Allen, M. (1992). Sex differences in self-disclosure: A meta-analysis. *Psychol. Bull., 112,* 106–124.

Doob, A. N., & Climie, J. R. (1972). Delay of measurement and the effects of film violence. *J. Exp. Soc. Psychol., 8,* 136–142.

Duckitt, J. (1992). Psychology and prejudice. *Amer. Psychol., 47,* 1182–1193.

Dunn-Rankin, E. D. (1978). The visual characteristics of words. *Sci. Amer.,* 238(1).

Dweck, C. S., Goets, T. E., & Strauss, N. L. (1980). Sex differences in learned helplessness: 4. An experimental and naturalistic study of failure generalization and its mediators. *J. Pers. Soc. Psychol., 38,* 441–452.

E

Eagley, A. H., Karau, S. J., and Makhijani, M. G. (1995). Gender and the effectiveness of leaders: A meta-analysis. *Psychological Bulletin, 117,* 125–145.

Egeland, B. & Sroufe, L. A. (1981). Attachment and early maltreatment. *Child Development, 52,* 44–52.

Eisenberg, N. (1989). The development of prosocial values. In N. Eisenberg, J. Reykowski, & E. Staub (Eds.), *Social and moral values: Individual and social perspectives.* Hillsdale, NJ: Erlbaum.

Eisenberger, R., and Cameron, J. (1996). Detrimental effects of reward: Reality or myth? *American Psychologist, 51,* 1153–1166.

Ekman, P. (1994). Strong evidence for universals in facial expressions: A reply to Russell's mistaken critique. *Psychological Bulletin, 115,* 268–287.

Ellenberger, H. F. (1970). *The discovery of the unconscious.* New York: Basic Books.

Ellis, A. (1980). Rational-emotive theory and cognitive behavior therapy: Similarities and differences. *Cog. Ther. Res., 4,* 325–340.

_____. (1984). Rational-emotive therapy. In R. Corsini (Eds.) *Current Psychotherapies (3d ed.),* Itasca, IL: F. E. Peacock Publishers, Inc.

Engen, T. (1987). Remembering odors and their names. *Amer. Sci., 75*(5).

Epstein, S. (1994). Integration of the cognitive and the psychodynamic unconscious. *American Psychologist, 49,* 709–724.

Ericsson, K. A., and Charness, N. (1994). Expert performance: Its structure and acquisition. *American Psychologist, 49,* 725–747.

Erikson, E. H. (1968). *Identity: Youth and crisis.* New York: Norton.

Erikson, E. H., Erikson, J. M., & Kivnick, H. Q. (1986). *Vital involvement in old age.* New York: W. W. Norton.

Eron, L. D., & Huesman, L. R. (1985). Quoted in "Once a bully, always. . . ." *Psychology Today, 19*(7).

Evans, C., & Evans, P. (Eds.), *Landscapes of the night.* New York: Viking Press.

Evans, G. W. (1980). Environmental cognition. *Psychol. Bull., 88,* 259–287.

Evans, R. I. (1964). *Conversations with Carl Jung.* New York: D. Van Nostrand Co.

Eysenck, H. J. (1952). The effects of psychotherapy: An evaluation. *Journal of Consulting Psychology, 16,* 319–324.

F

Falbo, T., & Polit, D. F. (1986). Quantitative review of the only child literature: Research evidence and theory development. *Psychological Bulletin, 100,* 176–189.

Fancher, R. E. (1979). *Pioneers of psychology.* New York: Norton.

Feingold, A. (1988). Cognitive gender differences are disappearing. *Amer. Psychol., 43,* 95–103.

_____. (1994). Gender differences in personality: A meta-analysis. *Psychological Bulletin, 116,* 429–456.

_____. (1992). Gender differences in mate selection preferences: A test of the parental investment model. *Psychol. Bull., 112,* 125–139.

Fingarett, H. (1988). *Heavy drinking.* Berkeley: University of California Press.

Flett, G. L., Vredenburg, K., and Kramer, L. (1997). The continuity of depression in clinical and nonclinical samples. *Psychological Bulletin, 121,* 395–416.

Flexner, J. T. (1974). *Washington: The indispensable man.* New York: New American Library.

Folkman, S., & Lazarus, R. (1988). Coping as a mediator of emotion. *J. Pers. Soc. Psychol., 54,* 466–475.

_____. (1980a, July 27). Animal bulletin. In "Animal doctor." *St. Louis Post Dispatch.*

_____. (1980b). *The soul of the wolf.* Boston: Little, Brown.

_____. (1983). Humane ethics and animal rights. *Int. J. Stud. Anim. Prob., 4,* 286–289.

Frank, J. D. (1974). *Persuasion and healing: A comparative study of psychotherapy.* Baltimore, MD: Johns Hopkins University Press.

Forgas, J. P. (1995). Mood and judgment: The affect infusion model (AIM). *Psychological Bulletin, 117,* 39–66.

Fredrickson, R. (1992). *Repressed memories: A journey to recovery from sexual abuse.* New York: Simon & Shuster.

Freedman, J. L. (1984). Effect of television violence on aggressiveness. *Psychol. Bull., 96,* 227–246.

Freedman, J. L., & Fraser, S. C. (1966). Compliance without pressure. *J. Pers. Soc. Psychol., 4,* 196–202.

Freeman, C. (1985). Quoted in "The patients' perspective on ECT." *Sci. News, 127,* 74.

Freud, S. (1895). *Freud-Fleiss.* In Gay, P. (1988). *Freud: A life for our time.* New York: W. W. Norton.

_____. (1953). Fragment of an analysis of a case of hysteria. In J. Strachey (Ed. and Trans.), *Standard* edition of the complete psychological works of *Sigmund Freud* (Vol. 7). London: Hogarth Press. (First German edition, 1905). A. W. Freud *et al.*, by arranagement with Mark Paterson & Associates.

_____.. (1957). The origin and development of psychoanalysis. In J. Richman, (Ed.). *A general selection from the works of Sigmund Freud*. Garden City, NY: Doubleday & Company, Inc. (Original work published in 1910).

_____. (1938). The history of the psychoanalytic movement. In A. A. Brill (Ed.), *The basic writings of Sigmund Freud*. New York: Random House.

Friedman, H. S. Tucker, J. S. Schwartz, J. E., Tomlinson-Keasey, C., Martin, L. R., Wingard, D. L., and Criqui, M. H. (1995). Psychosocial and behavioral predictors of longevity: The aging and death of the "Termites." *American Psychologist, 50,* 69–78.

Friedman, M. (1984). Quoted in "Type A: A change of heart and mind." *Sci. News, 126,* 109.

Friedman, M. A., and Brownell, K. D. (1995). Psychological correlates of obesity: Moving to the next research generation. *Psychological Bulletin, 117,* 3–20.

Friedman, M., & Rosenman, R. (1974). *Type A behavior and your heart.* New York: Knopf.

G

Gagnon, D. (1986). *Videogames and special skills.* Mimeograph from author.

Gaines, S. O., Jr., and Reed, E. S. (1995). Prejudice: From Allport to Dubois. *American Psychologist, 50,* 96–103.

Gardiner, H. W., Mutter, J. D., and Kosmitzki, C. (1998). *Lives across cultures: Cross-cultural human development.* Boston, MA: Allyn and Bacon.

Gardner, H. (1993). *Multiple intelligences.* New York: Basic Books.

Gardner, Howard (1994) *Creating minds,* New York: Basic Books.

Gardner, J. (1997). *Extraordinary minds.* New York: Basic Books.

Garfield, S. L. (1981). Psychotherapy: A 40-year appraisal. *Amer. Psychol., 36,* 174–183.

Gavzer, B. (1990). Should you tell all? *Parade,* May 27, 4–7.

Gay, P. (1988). *Freud: a life for our time.* New York: W.W. Norton & Company.

Gazzaniga, M. S. (1970). *The bisected brain.* Englewood Cliffs, NJ: Prentice-Hall.

Geller, J., and Harris, M. (1994). *Women of the asylum.* New York: Doubleday.

Geschwind, N. (1983). Quoted in Kolata, G. Math genius may have hormonal basis. *Science, 222,* 1312.

Getzels, J. W., & Jackson, P. W. (1962). *Creativity and intelligence.* New York: Wiley.

Gibson, E. J. and Walk, R. D. (1997). In T. F. Pettijohn (Ed.). *Sources.* Guilford, CT: Dushkin Publishing Group/Brown & Benchmark Publishers. (Original work published 1960).

_____. (1960). "The Behavior of the Children . . . they may discriminate depth," from *The Visual Cliff. Scientific American,* April, Vol. 202, p. 64.

Gigone, D., and Hastie, R. (1997). Proper analysis of the accuracy of group judgments. *Psychological Bulletin, 121,* 149–167.

Gilbert, S. (1985). Noise pollution. *Sci. Dig., 93*(3).

Gill, R., & Keats, D. (1980). Elements of intellectual competence. Judgments by Australian and Malay university students. *J. Cross-Cult. Psychol., 11,* 233–243.

Gilligan, C. (1982). *In a different voice: Women's conception of self and morality.* Cambridge, MA: Harvard University Press.

Gise, L. H. (1991). Premenstrual syndrome: which treatment helps? *Medical Aspects of Human Sexuality, 25,* 62–68.

Goleman, D. (1980, February). 1,528 little geniuses and how they grew. *Psychology Today,* 28–53.

_____. *Emotional intelligence.* New York: Bantam Books. Copyright © 1995 by Daniel Goleman. Used by permission of Bantam Books, a division of Random House, Inc.

Goodall, J. (1971). *In the shadow of man.* Boston, MA: Houghton Mifflin.

_____. (1986). *The chimpanzees of Gombe: Patterns of behavior.* Cambridge, MA: Harvard University Press.

Goodman, S., Barfoot, B., Frye, A., Belli, A. (1999). Dimensions of marital conflict and children's social problem-solving skills. *Journal of Family Psychology,* 13, 33–45.

Gough, H. G. (1960). *Manual for the California Psychological Inventory* (rev. ed.). Palo Alto, CA: Consulting Psychologists Press.

Gould, J. (1985). Quoted in "To honeybees, a picture is worth a thousand line angles." *Sci. News, 127,* 196.

Gould, J. L. (1984). Quoted in "Mind maps." *Sci. News, 125,* 62–63.

Graber, E. (1988). Personal communication.

Graesser, A. C., Singer, M., and Trabasso, T. (1994). Constructing inferences during narrative text comprehension. *Psychological Review, 101,* 371–395.

Graf, P., Squire, L. R., & Mandler, G. (1984). The information that amnesiac patients do not forget. *J. Exp. Psychol.: Lrn. Mem. Cog., 10,* 164–178.

Graham, K., LaRocque, L., Yetman, R., Ross, J. G., & Guistra, E. (1980). Aggression and barroom environments. *J. Stud. Alcoh., 41,* 277–292.

Graham, S., (1992). "Most of the subjects were white and middle class." *Amer. Psychol., 47,* 629–639.

Grandin, T. (1995). *Thinking in pictures.* New York: Doubleday.

Gratch, L. V., Bassett, M. E., and Attra, S. L. (1995). The relationship of gender and ethnicity to self-silencing and depression among college students. *Psychology of Women Quarterly, 19,* 509–515.

Greeno, C. G. & Wing, R. R. (1994) "Stress-induced eating," *Psychological Bulletin,* 115.

Greenough, W. (1985). Quoted in "The brain branches out." *Science 85,* 6(5).

Greenwald, A. G. (1992). New Look 3: Unconscious cognition reclaimed. *American Psychologist, 47,* 766–779.

Gresham, W. L. (1959). *Houdini: The man who walked through walls.* New York: Holt, Rinehart & Winston.

Grolnick, W. S., and R. M. Ryan. (1987). Autonomy in children's learning: an experimental and individual investigation. *Journal of Personality and Social Psychology,* 52: 890-898.

Groth-Marnat, G. (1990). *Handbook of psychological assessment.* New York: John Wiley & Sons.

Gutmann, D. (1997). *The human elder in nature, culture, and society.* Boulder, CO: Westview Press.

_____. (1987). *Reclaimed power: Towards a psychology of later life.* New York: Basic Books.

H

Haaga, D., Dyck, M., & Ernst, D. (1991). Empirical status of cognitive theory of depression. *Psychol. Bull., 110,* 215–236.

Hall, C. S., Lindzey, G., Loehlin, J. C., & Manosevitz, M. (1985). *Introduction to theories of personality.* New York: Wiley.

Hamilton, E. (1942). *The Greek way.* New York: Norton.

Haney, C. and Zimbardo, P. (1998). The past and future of U.S. prison policy: Twenty-five years after the Stanford prison experiment. *American Psychologist, 53,* 709–727.

Harlow, H. F. (1959). Love in infant monkeys. *Sci. Amer., 22*(6).

Harlow, H. F., Blazek, N., & McClearn, G. (1956). Manipulatory motivation in the infant rhesus monkey. *J. Comp. Physiol. Psychol., 49,* 444–448.

Harmon, L. D. (1973). The recognition of faces. *Sci. Amer., 229*(5).

Hartmann, E. (1984). *The nightmare.* New York: Basic Books.

Hartrup, W. W. and Stevens, N. (1997). Friendships and adaptation in the life course. *Psychological Bulletin, 121,* 355–370.

Harvey, E. (1999). Short-term and long-term effects of early parental employment on children of the National Longitudinal Survey of Youth. Developmental Psychology, 35, 445–459.

Haugeland, J. (1978). The nature and plausibility of cognitivism. *Behav. Brain Sci., 1,* 215–225.

Hawgood, J. A. (1967). *America's western frontiers.* New York: Knopf.

Hawkins, J. D., Catalano, R., & Miller, J. (1992). Risk and protective factors for alcohol and other drug problems in adolescence and early adulthood: Implications for substance abuse prevention. *Psychol. Bull., 112,* 64–105.

References

Hayflick, L. (1979). The cell biology of human aging. *Sci. Amer., 242*(1), 58–65.

_____. (1994) *How and why we age.* New York: Ballantine.

Heatherton, T., & Baumeister, R. (1991). Binge eating as escape from self-awareness. *Psychol. Bull., 110,* 86–108.

Heilman, M. E. (1984). Information as a deterrent against sex discrimination: The effects of applicant sex and information type on preliminary employment decisions. *Organizational Behavior and Human Performance, 33,* 174–186.

Heinemann, L. G. (1970). Visual phenomena in a long sensory deprivation. *Percept. Mot. Skills, 30,* 563–570.

Hellige, J. B. (1990). Hemispheric asymmetry. *Ann. Rev. Psychol., 41,* 55–60.

Helms, J. (1992). Why is there no study of cultural equivalence in standardized cognitive ability testing? *Amer. Psychol., 47,* 1083–1101.

Helwig, C. C. (1997). Making moral cognition respectable (again): A retrospective review of Lawrence Kohlberg. *Contemporary Psychology, 42,* 191–195.

Hilgard, E. R. (1980). Consciousness in contemporary psychology. *Ann. Rev. Psychol., 31,* 1–26.

Hinshaw, S. P. (1992). Externalizing behavior problems and academic underachievement in childhood and adolescence: Causal relationships and underlying mechanisms. *Psychological Bulletin, 111,* 127–155.

Hofling, C. K., Brotzman, E., Dalrymple, S., Graves, N., & Pierce, C. M. (1966). An experimental study in nurse-physician relationships. *J. Nerv. Ment. Dis., 143,* 171–180.

Hogan, R., Hogan, J., and Roberts, B. W. (1996). Personality measurement and employment decisions: Questions and answers. *American Psychologist, 51,* 469–477.

Holden, C. (1980). Twins reunited. *Science 80,* 55–59.

Holden, C. (1993). Wake-up call for sleep research. *Science, 25,* 748.

Hollis, K. L. (1997). Contemporary research on Pavlovian conditioning. *American Psychologist, 52,* 956–965.

Hollon, S. D. (1996). The efficacy and effectiveness of psychotherapy relative to medications. *American Psychologist, 51,* 1025–1030.

Hopkins, J. R. (1995). Erik Homburger Erikson (1902–1994). *American Psychologist, 50,* 796–797.

Hoptman, M. J. & Davidson, R. J. (1994). How and why do the two cerebral hemispheres interact? *Psychological Bulletin, 116,* 195–219.

Horm, J., and Anderson, K. (1993). Who in America is trying to lose weight? *Annals of Internal Medicine, 119,* 672–676.

Horney, K. (1945). *Our inner conflicts.* New York: Norton.

_____. (1950). *Neurosis and human growth.* New York: Norton.

Hulicka, I. M. (1978). Cognitive functioning of older adults. *Master lectures on the psychology of aging.* Tape 14/15. Washington, DC: American Psychological Association.

Hurd, T. L., and Brabeck, M. (1997). Presentation of women and Gilligan's ethic of care in college textbooks, 1970–1990: An examination of bias. *Teaching of Psychology, 24,* 159–167.

Hyde, J. S. & Linn, M. C. (1988) "Gender differences in verbal ability: a meta analysis." *Psychological Bulletin,* 104.

Hyde, J. S. (1990). *Understanding human sexuality.* New York: McGraw-Hill.

_____. (1994). *Understanding human sexuality (5th ed).* New York: McGraw-Hill Publishing Co.

I

Itard, J. M. G. (1932). *The wild boy of Aveyron.* New York: Appleton-Century-Crofts.

Izard, C. (1994). Innate and universal facial expressions: Evidence from developmental and cross-cultural research. *Psychological Bulletin, 115,* 288–299.

J

Jack, D. C. (1991). *Silencing the self: Women and depression.* Cambridge, MA: Harvard University Press.

Jackson, D. D. (1984). If women needed a quick pick-me-up, Lydia provided one. *Smithsonian, 15*(4).

Jacobs, B. L. (1987). How hallucinogenic drugs work. *Amer. Sci., 75,* 386–392.

Jacobson, J. W., Mulick, J. A., and Schwartz, A. A. (1995). A history of facilitated communication. *American Psychologist, 50,* 750–765.

Jacobson, N. S., and Christensen, A. (1996). Studying the effectiveness of psychotherapy: How well can clinical trials do the job? *American Psychologist, 51,* 1031–1039.

James, W. (1890). *Principles of psychology.* 2 vols. NY:Holt.

Jay, R. (1987). *Learned pigs & fireproof women.* New York: Villard Books.

Johnson, H. M. (1994). Process of successful intentional forgetting. *Psychological Bulletin, 116,* 274–292.

Joiner, G. W., and Kashubeck, S. (1996). Acculturation, body image, self-esteem, and eating disorder symptomatology in adolescent Mexican American women. *Psychology of Women Quarterly, 20,* 419–435.

Jones, M. C. (1924). A laboratory study of fear: The case of Peter. *Pedagog. Semin., 31,* 308–315.

———. (1974). Albert, Peter, and John B. Watson. *Amer. Psychol., 29,* 581–583.

Jouandet, M., & Gazzaniga, M. S. (1979). The frontal lobes. In M. S. Gazzaniga (Ed.), *Handbook of behavioral neurobiology.* New York: Plenum.

Jung, C. G. (1933). *Modern man in search of a soul.* New York: Harcourt Brace Jovanovich.

———. (1958). Transformation symbolism in the mass. In V. S. deLaszio (Ed.), *Psyche and symbol: A selection of writings of C. G. Jung.* New York: Doubleday.

Jussim, L. J., and Eccles, J. (1995). Are teacher expectations biased by students' gender, social class, or ethnicity? In Y. Lee, L. J. Jussim, and C. R. McCauley (Eds.). *Stereotype accuracy.* Washington, D.C.: American Psychological Association.

Jussim, L. J., McCauley, C. R., and Lee, Y. (1995). Why study stereotype accuracy and inaccuracy? In Y. Lee, L. J. Jussim, and C. R. McCauley (Eds.). *Stereotype accuracy.* Washington, D.C.: American Psychological Association.

K

Kagan, J. (1984). *The nature of the child.* New York: Basic Books.

———. (1996). Three pleasing ideas. *American Psychologist, 51,* 901–908.

Kahn, L. S. (1980). The dynamics of scapegoating: The expulsion of evil. *Psychother. Theory Res. Pract., 17,* 79–84.

Kamil, A. C., & Roitblat, H. L. (1985). The ecology of foraging behavior: Implications for animal learning and memory. *Ann. Rev. Psychol., 36,* 141–169.

Kamin, L. J. (1978). Comment on Munsinger's review of adoption studies. *Psychol. Bull., 85,* 194–201.

Kanner, L. (1943). Autistic disturbances of affective contact. *Nervous Child, 2,* 217–250.

Kapatos, G., & Gold, R. M. (1972). Tongue cooling during drinking: A regulator of water intake in rats. *Science, 176,* 685–686.

Kaplan, R. M. (1982). Nader's raid on the testing industry. *Amer. Psychol., 37,* 15–23.

Kary, S. (1984). Personal communication. (My thanks to Dr. Kary for his suggestion.)

Kaslow, F. (1992). Thirty-plus and not married. In B. R. Wainrib (Ed.), *Gender issues across the life cycle.* New York: Springer Publishing Co.

Kassin, S. M., Ellsworth, P. C., & Smith, V. L. (1989). The "general acceptance" of psychological research on eyewitness testimony. *Amer. Psychol., 44,* 1089–1098.

Kavanaugh, R. E. (1974). *Facing death.* Baltimore: Penguin Books.

Keller, L. S., Butcher, J. N., and Slutske, W. S. (1990). Objective personality assessment. In G. Goldstein & M. Hersen (Eds.). *Handbook of psychological assessment.* New York: Pergamon Press.

Kellman, P.J. (1997). From chaos to coherence. *Psychological Science Agenda, 10 (4),* 8–9.

Kellogg, W. N., & Kellogg, L. A. (1933). *The ape and the child.* New York: McGraw-Hill.

Keltner, D., and Buswell, B. N. (1997). Embarrassment: Its distinct form and appeasement functions. *Psychological Bulletin, 122,* 250–270.

References

Kelton, E. (1993). Visions of a lost world. *American History Illustrated,* January-February, 50–59.

Kernberg, O. F., Bernstein, C. S., Coyne, R., Applebaum, D. A., Horwitz, H., & Voth, T. J. (1972). Psychotherapy and psychoanalysis: Final report of the Menninger Foundation's psychotherapy research project. *Bull. Menninger Clin., 36,* 1–276.

Kessler, D. (1991). Birth order, family size, and achievement: Family structure and wage determination. *Journal of Labor Economics, 9,* 413–426.

Kidd, K. K. (1985). Quoted in "Depression and the family." *Sci. News, 127,* 360.

Kihlstrom, J. F., Barnhardt, T. M., & Tataryn, D. J. (1992). The psychological unconscious: Found, lost, and regained. *Amer. Psychol., 47,* 788–791.

Kimble, D. P. (1990). Functional effects of neural grafting in the mammalian central nervous system. *Psychol. Bull., 108,* 462–479.

Kimble, G. A. (1994). A new formula for behaviorism. *Psychological Review, 101,* 254–258.

Kirsch, I., and Lynn, S. J. (1995). The altered state of hypnosis: Changes in the theoretical landscape. *American Psychologist, 50,* 846–858.

Kitayama, S., & Markus, H. (Eds.). (1994). *Emotion and culture.* Washington, D.C.: American Psychological Association.

Kluft, R. (1991). Multiple personality disorder. In A. Tasnan, & S. Goldfinger, Eds. *Review of psychiatry, vol. 10.* Washington, DC: American Psychiatric Press.

Kobasa, S. C., Hilker, R. R., & Maddi, S. R. (1979). Who stays healthy under stress? *J. Occ. Med., 21,* 595–598.

Kobasa, S. C., Maddi, S. R., & Kahn, S. (1981) *Hardiness and health: A prospective study.* Mimeograph received from authors.

Kohlberg, L. (1963). Moral development and identification. In H. W. Stevenson (Ed.), *Yearbook of the national society for the study of education: 1. Child psychology.* Chicago: University of Chicago Press.

———. (1969). "The cognitive-developmental approach to socialization." In A. Goslin (Ed.), *Handbook of Socialization Theory and Research.* Chicago: Rand McNally.

———. (1981). Excerpt, as submitted, from *Essays on Moral Development: The Philosophy of Moral Development* (Volume 1) by Lawrence Kohlberg. Copyright © 1981 by Lawrence Kohlberg. Reprinted by permission of HarperCollins Publishers, Inc.

Kohn, A. (1993*). Punished by rewards: the trouble with gold stars and incentive plans, A's, praise, and other bribes.* Boston: Houghton Mifflin.

Kokkinidis, L. K., & Anisman, H. (1980). Amphetamine models of paranoid schizophrenia: An overview and elaboration of animal experimentation. *Psychol. Bull., 88,* 551–579.

Krantz, D. S., & Manuck, S. B. (1985). Acute psychophysiologic reactivity and risk of cardiovascular disease: A review and methodologic critique. *Psychol. Bull., 96,* 435–464.

Krech, D. (1962). Cortical localization of function. In W. Postman (Ed.), *Psychology in the making.* New York: Alfred A. Knopf.

Kübler-Ross, E. (1969). *On death and dying.* New York: Macmillan.

L

Lang, P. J., & Melamed, B. G. (1969). Case report: Avoidance conditioning therapy of an infant with chronic rumative vomiting. *J. Abnorm. Psychol., 74,* 1–8.

Latané, B., & Darley, J. M. (1970). *The unresponsive bystander: Why doesn't he help?* Englewood Cliffs, NJ: Prentice-Hall.

Laursen, B., and Collins, W. A. (1994). Interpersonal conflict during adolescence. *Psychological Bulletin, 115,* 197–209.

Leary, D. E. (1992). William James and the art of human understanding. *Amer. Psychol., 47,* 152–160.

Lee, Y., and Duenas, G. (1995). Stereotype accuracy in multicultural business. In Y. Lee, L. J. Jussim, and C. R. McCauley (Eds.). *Stereotype accuracy.* Washington, D.C.: American Psychological Association.

Lemley, B. (1986). I'n not a nerd. *Parade,* June 22, 8–9.

Lerner, R. M., & Frank, P. (1974). Relations of race and sex to supermarket helping behavior. *J. Soc. Psychol., 94,* 201–203.

Levant, R. (1992). The new father roles. In B. R. Wainrib (Ed.), *Gender issues across the life cycle.* New York: Springer Publishing Co.

Levanthal-Belfer, L., Cowan, P., & Cowan, C. (1992). Satisfaction with child care arrangements: Effects on adaptation to parenthood. *American Journal of Orthopsychiatry, 62*, 165–177.

Levine, R. V., West, L. J., & Reiss, H. T. (1980). Perceptions of time and punctuality in the United States and Brazil. *J. Pers. Soc. Psychol., 38*, 541–550.

Levinson, D. J. (1978). *The seasons of a man's life.* Copyright © 1978 by Daniel J. Levinson. Excerpt reprinted by permission of Alfred A. Knopf, Inc.

Lifton, R. (1961). *Thought reform and the psychology of totalism.* New York: Norton.

Linville, P. W., & Jones, E. E. (1980). Polarized appraisals of out-group members. *J. Pers. Soc. Psychol., 38*, 689–703.

Loewenstein, G. (1994). The psychology of curiosity: A review and reinterpretation. *Psychological Bulletin, 116*, 75–98.

Loftus, E. F. (1984). Eyewitnesses; Essential but unreliable. *Psychology Today, 181*(2).

_____. (1997, September). Creating false memories. *Scientific American*, 70–75.

Loftus, E. F., & Klinger, M. R. (1992). Is the unconscious smart or dumb? *American Psychologist, 47*, 761–765.

Loftus, E. F., and Ketcham, K. (1994). *The myth of repressed memories: False memories and allegations of sexual abuse.* New York: St. Martin's Press. Copyright © 1994 by Elizabeth Loftus and Katherine Ketcham. Extract reprinted by permission of St. Martin's Press, Incorporated.

Loftus, E. F., Polonsky, S., and Fullilove, M. T. (1994). Memories of childhood sexual abuse: Remembering and repressing. *Psychology of Women Quarterly, 18*, 67–84.

Lombroso-Ferrero, G. (1911). *Criminal man.* New York: Putnam's.

Lopez, B. H. (1978). *Of wolves and men.* New York: Scribner's.

Lore, R., & Schultz, L. (1993). Control of human aggression. *Amer. Psychol., 48*, 16–25

Lorenz, K. (1952). *King Solomon's ring.* New York: Crowell (Division of HarperCollins) Excerpt reprinted by permission of HarperCollins Publishers, Inc. For additional rights, please contact Routledge, 11 New Fetter Lane, London ECAP4EE, England.

Lubow, R. E. and Gewirtz, J. C. (1995). Latent inhibition in humans: Data, theory, and implications for schizophrenia. *Psychological Bulletin, 117*, 87–103.

Luce, G. G. (1971). *Body time.* New York: Random House.

Luria, A. R. (1968). *The mind of a mnemonist.* New York: Basic Books.

Lytton, H., & Romney, D. (1991). Parents' differential socialization of boys and girls: A meta-analysis. *Psychol. Bull., 109*, 267–296.

M

Maccoby, E. E. (1990). Gender and relationships: A developmental account. *American Psychologist, 45*, 513–520.

Maccoby, E. E., & Jacklin, C. N. (1974). *The psychology of sex differences.* Stanford, CA: Stanford University Press.

Maddison, S., Wood, R. J., Rolls, E. T., Rolls, B. J., & Gibbs, J. (1980). Drinking in the rhesus monkey: Peripheral factors. *J. Comp. Physiol. Psychol., 94*, 365–374.

Mandler, G. (1984). *Mind and body: Psychology of emotion and stress.* New York: Norton.

Mandler, J. M., & Ritchey, G. H. (1977). Long-term memory for pictures. *J. Exp. Psychol.: Hum. Lrn. Mem., 3*, 386–396.

Marcia, J. E. (1980). Identity in adolescence. In J. Adelson (Ed.), *Handbook of adolescent psychology.* New York: Wiley.

Margules, D. L., & Olds, J. (1962). Identical "feeding" and "rewarding" systems in the lateral hypothalamus of rats. *Science, 135*, 374–375.

Marks, I. (1979). Conditioning models for clinical syndromes are out of date. *Beh. Brain Sci., 2*, 175–176.

Martin, C. L., and Ruble, D.N. (1997). A developmental perspective on self-construals and sex differences: Comment on Cross and Madson (1997). *Psychological Bulletin, 122*, 45–50.

References

Martinko, M. J., & Gardner, W. L. (1983). A methodological review of sex-related access discrimination problems. *Sex Roles, 9,* 825–839.

Martz, D. M., Handley, K. B., and Eisler, R. M. (1995). The relationship between feminine gender role stress, body image, and eating disorders. *Psychology of Women Quarterly, 19,* 493–508.

Maslow, A. (1997). A theory of human motivation. In T. F. Pettijohn (Ed.) *Sources.* Guilford, CT: Dushkin Publishing Group/Brown & Benchmark Publishers. (Original work published 1943).

Maslow, A. H. (1954). *Motivation and personality.* New York: Harper.

_____. (1970) *Motivation and personality.* New York: Harper & Row.

_____. (1968). *Toward a psychology of being* (2d ed.). New York: D. Van Nostrand.

Matarazzo, J. D. (1985). Psychotherapy. In G. A. Kimble and K. Schlesinger (Eds.), *Topics in the history of psychology.* Hillsdale, NJ:Erlbaum.

_____. (1990). Psychological assessment versus psychological testing: Validation from Binet to the school, clinic, and courtroom. *Amer. Psychol., 45,* 999–1017.

Mays, V. M. Rubin, J., Sabouria, M., and Walker, L. (1996). Moving toward a global psychology: Changing theories and practice to meet the needs of a changing world. *American Psychologist, 51,* 485–487.

McCauley, C. R. (1995). Are stereotypes exaggerated? A sampling of racial, gender, academic, occupational, and political stereotypes. In Y. Lee, L. J. Jussim, and C. R. McCauley (Eds.). *Stereotype accuracy.* Washington, D.C.: American Psychological Association.

McCloskey, M., & Zaragonza, M. (1985). Quoted in "How malleable are eyewitness memories?" *Sci. News, 127,* 164.

McConkey, K. M. (1992). The effects of hypnotic procedures on remembering: The experimental findings and their implications for forensic hypnosis. In E. Fromm and M. R. Nash (Eds.). *Contemporary hypnosis research.* New York: Guilford Press.

McConnell, J. V. (1989). Reinvention of subliminal perception. *The Skeptical Inquirer, 13,* 427–428.

McConnell, J. V., Cutler, R. L., & McNeil, E. B. (1958). Subliminal stimulation: An overview. *Amer. Psychol., 13,* 229–242.

McCrae, R. R. and Costa, P. T. (1997). Personality trait structures as a human universal. *American Psychologist, 52,* 509–516.

McDonald, D. G. (1997). Psychology's surge in undergraduate majors. *Teaching of psychology, 24* (1), 22–26.

McGee, M. (1980). Faith, fantasy, and flowers: A content analysis of the American sympathy card. *Omega, 11,* 25–35.

McGlynn, F. D., & O'Brien, L. (1972). The semiautomated treatment of a phobia: A case study. *J. Clin. Psychol., 28,* 228–230.

McGrath, E. (1992). New treatment strategies for women in the middle. In B. R., Wainrib (Ed.), *Gender issues across the life cycle.* New York: Springer Publishing Co.

McGrath, R. D. (1985, February 26–28). The myth of frontier violence. *Harpers.*

McMahon, F. B., & McMahon, J. W. (1983). *Abnormal behavior: Psychology's view.* Homewood, IL: Dorsey Press.

McMahon, J. (1987). [Untitled John Wesley Hardin poem.]

McWilliams, N. (1992). The worst of both worlds: Dilemmas of contemporary young women. In B. R. Wainrib (Ed.), *Gender issues across the life cycle.* New York: Springer Publishing Co.

Meece, J. L., Parsons, J. E., Kaczala, C. M., Goff, S. B., & Futterman, R. (1982). Sex differences in math achievement: Toward a model of academic choice. *Psychol. Bull., 91,* 324–348.

Mesquita, B., & Frijda, N. H. (1992). Cultural variations in emotions: A review. *Psychol. Bull., 112,* 179–204.

Messick, S. (1995). Validity of psychological assessment: Validation of inferences from persons' responses and performances as scientific inquiry into score meaning. *American Psychologist, 50,* 741–749.

Milgram, S. (1974a) *Obedience to authority.* New York: Harper & Row.

_____. S. (1974b) "The perils of obedience" as it appeared in *Harper's Magazine*. Abridged and adapted from Obedience to Authority.

_____. (1977). *The individual in a social world*. Reading, MA: Addison-Wesley.

_____. (1984). Behavioral study of obedience. In E. Aronson (Ed.). *Readings about the social animal*. New York: W. H. Freeman. (Original work published 1963).

Miller, G. A. (1962). *Psychology: The science of mental life*. New York: Harper & Row.

Miller, J. A. (1983). Lessons from the lab. *Sci. News, 124,* 394–396.

Miller, M. A., and Rahe, R. H. (1997). Events and stress points adapted from the Life changes scaling for the 1990s, *Journal of Psychosomatic Research, 43*: 279–292.

Miller, T., Turner, C., Tindale, R. S., Posavac, E., & Dugoni, B. (1991). Reasons for the trend toward null findings in research on Type A behavior. *Psychol. Bull., 110,* 409–485.

Millodot, M. (1982). Accommodation and refraction of the eye. In H. B. Barlow and J. D. Mollon (Eds.), *The senses*. New York: Cambridge University Press.

Millon, T. (1981). *Disorders of personality*. New York: John Wiley & Sons.

Mills, J. A. (1997). An unquiet grave. *Contemporary Psychology, 42,* 785–786.

Mollon, J. D. (1982). Colour vision and colour blindness. In H. B. Barlow and J. D. Mollon (Eds.), *The senses*. New York: Cambridge University Press.

Money, J. (1974). Differentiation of gender identity. *Master lectures on physiological psychology*. Tape. Washington, DC: American Psychological Association.

_____. (1980). *Love and love sickness*. Baltimore: Johns Hopkins University Press.

Moore, M. M. (1995). Courtship signaling and adolescents: "Girls just wanna have fun"? *Journal of Sex Research, 32,* 319–328.

Moore, M. M. and Butler, D. L. (1989). Predictive aspects of nonverbal courtship behavior in women. *Semiotica, 3*(4), 205–215.

Moore, T. E. (1984). Subliminal delusion. *Psychology Today, 19*(7).

Moore-Ede, M. C. (1986, December 26). [Interview.] *New York Times*.

Moore-Ede, M. C., Sulzman, F. M., & Fuller, C. A. (1982). *The clocks that time us*. Cambridge, MA: Harvard University Press.

Morgan, D. (1984, February 20). If you want good schools, stop doting on a test like the SAT. *Washington Post Nat. Week. Edition*.

Moyer, K. E. (1975). *The psychobiology of aggression*. New York: Harper & Row.

Mueller, C. G. (1979). Some origins of psychology as science. *Ann. Rev. Psychol., 30,* 9–29.

Mueller, C., and C. Dweck. (1998). Praise for intelligence can undermine children's motivation and performance. *Journal of Personality and Social Psychology*, 75 (1, July): 33-52

Munsinger, H. (1975). The adopted child's IQ: A critical review. *Psychol. Bull., 82,* 623–659.

Murchison, C. (Ed.) (1927). *Psychologies of 1925*. Worcester, Mass.: Brandeis University.

Musto, D. (1989). America's first cocaine epidemic. *The Wilson Quarterly, Summer,* 59–64.

Muuss, R. E. (1975). *Theories of adolescence* (3d ed.). New York: Random House.

Myers, David G. (1992). *The pursuit of happiness*. New York: William Morrow & Co. Copyright © 1992 by David G. Myers. Excerpt reprinted by permission of William Morrow and Company, Inc.

Myers, J. J. (1984). Right hemisphere language: Science or fiction? *Amer. Psychol., 39,* 315–319.

N

Neal, A., & Turner, S. (1991). Anxiety disorders research with African Americans: Current status. *Psychol. Bull., 109,* 400–410.

Neisser, U. (1997). Never a dull moment. *American Psychologist, 52,* 79–81.

Neisser, U., Boodoo, G., Bouchard, T. J., Jr., Boykin, A. W., Bordy, N., Ceci, S. J., Halpern, D. F., Loehlin, J. C., Perloff, R., Sternberg, R. J., and Urbina, S. (1996). Intelligence: Knowns and unkowns. *American Psychologist, 51,* 77–101.

References

Newcomb, T. (1963). Persistence and repression of changed attitudes: Long-range studies. *J. Soc. Issues, 19,* 3–14.

Newman, B. M., & Newman, P. R. (1984). *Development through life: A psychosocial approach.* Homewood, IL: Dorsey Press.

Newman, F. L. & Tejeda, M. J. (1996). The need for research that is designed to support decisions in the delivery of mental health services. *American Psychologist, 51,* 1040–1049.

Nicholson, J. (1984). *Men and women: How different are they?* New York: Oxford University Press.

Nielsen, A. C. (1985, February 18). Survey quoted in *U.S. News & World Report.*

Nigg, J. T., and Goldsmith, H. H. (1994). Genetics of personality disorders: Perspectives from personality and psychopathology research. *Psychological Bulletin, 115,* 346–380.

Nolen-Hoeksema, S., & Girgus, J. S. (1994). The emergence of gender differences in depression during adolescence. *Psychological Bulletin, 115,* 424–443.

Nowicki, Stephen, Jr., (1986). Reprinted by permission of Stephen Nowicki, Jr. From the Instructor's Manual prepared by Wayne Welton for *Psychology Applied to Modern Life,* Second Edition, by Nowicki and Duke, published in 1986 by Brooks/Cole Publishing Company.

O

O'Kelly, L. I., & Muckler, F. A. (1955). *Introduction to psychopathology.* Englewood Cliffs, NJ: Prentice-Hall.

Olds, J. (1956). Pleasure centers in the brain. *Sci. Amer., 195*(4).

Oltmanns, T. F., Neale, J. M., and Davison, G. C. (1995). *Case studies in abnormal psychology.* New York: John Wiley & Sons. Reprinted by permission of John Wiley & Sons, Inc.

Olton, D. S. (1978). Characteristics of spatial memory. In S. H. Hulse, H. F. Fowler, and W. K. Honig (Eds.), *Cognitive aspects of animal behavior.* Hillsdale, NJ: Erlbaum.

_____. (1979). Mazes, maps and memory. *Amer. Psychol., 34,* 583–596.

Orenstein, P. (1994). *School Girls.* New York: Doubleday.

Osofsky, J. D. (1995). The effects of exposure to violence on young children. *American Psychologist, 50,* 782–788.

Oster, G. (1970). Phosphenes. *Sci. Amer., 222*(2).

Owens, J., Bower, G. H., & Black, J. B. (1979). The "soap opera" effect in story recall. *Mem. Cogn., 7,* 185–191.

Ozer, E. M. (1995). The impact of childcare responsibility and self-efficacy on the psychological health of professional working mothers. *Psychology of Women Quarterly, 19,* 315–335.

P

Paikoff, R. L., & Brooks-Gunn, J. (1991). Do parent-child relationships change during puberty? *Psychol. Bull., 110,* 47–66.

Papalia, D. E., & Olds, S. W. (1995). *Human development.* New York: McGraw-Hill.

Papalia, D. E., Camp, C. J., and Feldman, R. D. (1996). *Adult development and aging.* New York: McGraw-Hill.

Patterson, K. E., & Baddeley, A. D. (1977). When face recognition fails. *J. Exper. Psychol.: Hum. Lrn. Mem., 3,* 406–417.

Pazy, A. (1992). Sex-linked bias in promotion decisions: The role of candidate's career relevance and respondent's prior experience. *Psychology of Women Quarterly, 16,* 209–228.

Pearce, P. L. (1980). Strangers, travelers, and Greyhound terminals: A study of small-scale helping behaviors. *J. Pers. Soc. Psychol., 38,* 935–940.

Pederson, P. B. (1991). Multiculturism as a generic approach to counseling. *J. Couns. Devel., 70,* 6–12.

Pendergrast, M. (1997). Memo to Pope: Ask the real questions, please. *American Psychologist, 52,* 989.

Penfield, W. (1959). The interpretive cortex. *Science, 129*(6).

Penn, D. L., Corrigan, P. W., Bentall, R. P., Racenstein, J. M., and Newman, L. (1997). Social cognition in schizophrenia. *Psychological Bulletin, 121,* 114–132.

Peters, J. (1971). *A class divided.* Garden City, NY: Doubleday.

Petersen, A. (1987). Those gangly years. *Psychology Today, 21*(9), 28–34.

Peterson, L., & Brown, D. (1994). Integrating child injury and abuse-neglect research: Common histories, etiologies, and solutions. *Psychological Bulletin, 116,* 293–315.

Petraitis, J., Flay, B. R. and Miller, T. Q. (1995). Reviewing theories of adolescent substance use: Organizing pieces in the puzzle. *Psychological Bulletin, 117,* 67–86.

Pettijohn, T. F., (Ed.). A theory of human motivation. *Sources.* Guilford, Ct: Dushkin Publishing Group/Brown & Benchmark Publishers. (Original work published 1943).

Phares, V. (1992). Where's Poppa? The relative lack of attention to the role of fathers in child and adolescent psychopathology. *Amer. Psychol., 47,* 656–664.

Phares, V., & Compas, B. (1992). The role of fathers in child and adolescent psychopathology: Make room for Daddy. *Psychol. Bull., 111,* 387–412.

Phillips, J. S., & Bierman, K. L. (1981). Clinical psychology: Individual methods. *Ann. Rev. Psychol., 32,* 405–438.

Phinney, J. S. (1996). When we talk about American ethnic groups, what do we mean? *American Psychologist, 51,* 918–927.

Piaget, J. (1929). *The child's conception of the world.* New York: Harcourt, Brace Jovanovich.

Pike, K. M. (1995). Bulimic symptomatology in high school girls. *Psychology of Women Quarterly, 19,* 373–396.

Pion, G. M., Mednick, M. T., Astin, H. S., Hall, C. C. I., Kenkel, M. B., Keita, G. P., Kohout, J. L., and Kelleher, J. C. (1996). The shifting gender composition of psychology: Trends and implications for the discipline. *American Psychologist, 51,* 509–527.

Piven, J., Berthier, M. L., Starkstein, S. E., Nehme, E., Pearlson, G., and Folstein, S. (1990). Magnetic resonance imaging evidence for a defect of cerebral cortical development in autism. *American Journal of Psychiatry, 147,* 734–739.

Plomin, R., and DeFries, J. C. (1998, May). The genetics of cognitive abilities and disabilities. *Scientific American,* May, 62–69.

Plous, S. (1996). Attitudes toward the use of animals in psychological research and education. *American Psychologist, 51,* 1167–1180.

Poole, D. A., & White, L. T. (1991). Effects of question repetition on the eyewitness testimony of children and adults. *Developmental Psychology, 27,* 975–986.

Poole, D. A., Lindsay, D. S., Memon, A., and Bull, R. (1995). Psychotherapy and the recovery of memories of childhood sexual abuse: A national survey of psychologists' clinical practices, beliefs, and personal experiences. *Journal of Consulting and Clinical Psychology, 63,* 426–437.

Poole, D. A., Lindsay, D. S., Memon, A., and Bull, R. (1997). Did Pope (1996) read a different Poole, Linsay, Memon, and Bull (1995)? *American Psychologist, 52,* 990–993.

Pope, H. G., Jr., & Katz, D. L. (1987). Of muscles and mania. *Psychology Today, 21*(9).

Pope, K. S. (1996). Memory, abuse, and science: Questioning claims about the False Memory Syndrome epidemic. *American Psychologist, 51,* 957–974.

Posner, M. I., & Raichle, M. E. (1994). *Images of mind.* New York: Scientific American.

Pratkanis, A. R., & Greenwold, A. G. (1988). Recent perspectives on unconscious processing: Still no marketing applications. *Psychology and Marketing, 5,* 337–353.

Pribram, K. H. (1971). *Languages of the brain: Experimental paradoxes and principles in neuropsychology.* Englewood Cliffs, NJ: Prentice-Hall.

Probst, T., Krafczyk, S., & Brandt, T. (1984). Interaction between perceived self-motion and object motion impairs vehicle guidance. *Science, 225,* 536–538.

Prochaska, J., DiClemente, C., & Norcross, J. (1992). In search of how people change: Applications to addictive behaviors. *Amer. Psychol., 47,* 1102–1114.

R

Ramachandran, V. S. (1998). *Phantoms in the brain.* New York: William Morrow & Co.

References

Ransford, H. E., & Palisi, B. (1992). Has there been a resurgence of racist attitudes in the general population? *Sociological Spectrum, 12,* 231–255.

Rapoport, J. L. (1989). *The boy who couldn't stop washing: The experience and treatment of obsessive-compulsive disorders.* New York: Dutton.

Reeves, L. M., and Weisberg, R. W. (1994). The role of content and abstract information in analogical transfer. *Psychological Bulletin, 115,* 381–400.

Reisman, J. M. (1966). *The development of clinical psychology.* Englewood Cliffs, NJ: Prentice-Hall.

Restak, R. (1994). *Receptors.* New York, Bantam Books.

Restak, R. (1995). *Brainscapes: An Introduction to What Neuroscience Has Learned About the Structure, Function and Abilities of the Brain.* New York: Hyperion. Copyright © 1995 by Richard Restak, M.D. Published by Hyperion. Excerpt reprinted by permission.

Retherford, R. D. and Sewell, W. H. (1991). Birth order and intelligence: Further tests of the confluence model. *American Sociological Review, 56,* 141–158.

Rhodes, N., & Wood, W. (1992). Self-esteem and intelligence affect influenceability: The mediating role of message reception. *Psychol. Bull., 111,* 156–171.

Rimland, B., and Green, G. (1993). Controlled evaluations of facilitated communication. *Autism Research Review, 7, 7.*

Rivlin, R., & Gravelle, K. (1984). *Deciphering the senses.* New York: Simon & Schuster.

Robinson, H., & Robinson, N. (1970). Mental retardation. In P. H. Mussen (Ed.), *Carmichael's manual of child psychology* (3d ed.). New York: Wiley.

Rochen, A., Ligiero, D., Hill, C., & Heaton, K. (1999). Effects of training in dream recall and dream interpretation skills on dream recall, attitudes, and dream interpretation outcome. *Journal of Counseling Psychology, 46,* 27–34.

Rodin, J. (1984). A sense of control. *Psychology Today, 18*(12).

Rogers, C. R. (1951). *Client-centered therapy: Its current practice, implications and theory.* Boston: Houghton Mifflin.

_____. (1961). *On becoming a person—A therapist's view of psychotherapy.* Boston: Houghton Mifflin.

_____. (1986). Client-centered therapy. In I. L. Kutash and A. Wolf (Eds.), *Psychotherapist's casebook: Therapy and technique in practice.* San Francisco: Jossey-Bass.

_____. (1980). *A way of being.* Boston: Houghton Mifflin Co. Excerpt reprinted by permission of Houghton Mifflin Company. All rights reserved.

Rogoff, B. (1990). *Apprenticeship in thinking: Cognitive development in social context.* New York: Oxford University Press.

Rogoff, B. and Chavajay, P. (1995). What's become of research on the cultural basis of cognitive development? *American Psychologist, 50,* 859–877.

Romain, D. (1997). *Thinking things through.* Mountain View, CA: Mayfield Publishing Co.

Rorabaugh, W. J. (1979). *The alcoholic republic.* New York: Oxford University Press.

Rorschach, R. (1921, reprinted 1942 and 1961) *Psychodiagnostics.* Bern: Hans Huber.

Rosenthal R. (1965) *Clever Hans: a Case study of scientific method.* Opfungst: New York: Holt, Rinehart & Winston.

Rosenzweig, M. (1962). The mechanisms of hunger and thirst. In L. Postman (Ed.), *Psychology in the making.* New York: Knopf.

Rosenzweig, M. R. (1984). Experience, memory, and the brain. *Amer. Psychol., 39,* 365–376.

Ross, A. O., & Pelham, W. E. (1981). Child psychopathology. *Annual Review of Psychology, 32,* 243–278.

Rotter, J. B. (1982). Social learning theory. In N. T. Feather (Ed.). *Expectations and actions: Expectancy-value models in psychology* (pp. 241–260). Hillsdale, NJ: Erlbaum.

Rotton, J., & Kelly, I. W. (1985). Much ado about the full moon: A meta-analysis of lunar-lunacy research. *Psychol. Bull., 97,* 286–306.

Rowe, D. C. Vazsonyi, A. T., and Flannery, D. J. (1994). No more than skin deep: Ethnic and racial similarity in developmental process. *Psychological Review, 101,* 396–413.

Rubenstein, A. (1992). Clinical issues in the treatment of adolescent girls. In B. R. Wainrib (Ed.), *Gender issues across the life cycle.* New York: Springer Publishing Co.

Rule, B. G., & Nesdale, A. R. (1976). Emotional arousal and aggressive behavior. *Psychol. Bull., 83,* 851–863.

Ruttenber, A. J., & Luke, J. L. (1984). Heroin-related deaths: New epidemiologic insights. *Science, 226,* 14–20.

Ryckman, R. M. (1997). *Theories of personality.* New York: Brooks/Cole Publishing Company.

Rymer, R. (1993) Genie: a scientific tragedy. New York: Harper Perennial.

S

Sacks, Oliver (1995) *An anthropologist on Mars.* New York: Alfred A. Knopf. Copyright © 1995 by Oliver Sacks. Excerpt reprinted by permission.

Sadker, M., & Sadker, D. (1994). *Failing at fairness.* New York: Charles Scribner's Sons.

Sagar, H. A., & Schofield, J. W. (1980). Racial and behavioral cues in black and white children's perceptions of ambiguously aggressive acts. *J. Pers. Soc. Psychol., 39,* 590–598.

Samuelson, F. (1980). J. B. Watson's Little Albert, Cyril Burt's twins, and the need for a critical science. *Amer. Psychol., 35,* 619–625.

Sarason, I., & Sarason, B. (1993). *Abnormal psychology.* Englewood Cliffs, NJ: Prentice-Hall, Inc.

_____. (1996). *Abnormal psychology.* Upper Saddle River, NJ: Prentice-Hall.

Saxe, L. (1991). Lying. *American Psychologist, 46* (4), 409–415.

Schachter, S., & Singer, J. (1962). Cognitive, social, and psychological determinants of emotional state. *Psychol. Rev., 29,* 379–399.

Schlenker, B. R., Britt, T. W., Pennington, J., Murphy, R., and Doherty, K. (1994). The triangle model of responsibility. *Psychological Review, 101,* 632–652.

Schmitt, R. B. (1996/1997). Insanity pleas fail a lot of defendants as fear of crime rises. In J. J. Palladino (Ed.). *Annual Editions in Abnormal Psychology 97/98.* Guilford, CT: Dushkin/McGraw-Hill.

Schultz, D. P. (1969). *A history of modern psychology.* New York: Academic Press.

Schwartz, G. E. (1979). The brain as a health care system. In G. Stone, N. Adler, and F. Cohen (Eds.), *Health psychology.* San Francisco: Jossey-Bass.

Schwartz, W. J. (1984). Quoted in "Fetuses watch the clock." *Sci. News, 126,* 266.

Scovern, A. W., & Kilmann, P. R. (1980). Status of electroconvulsive therapy: Review of the outcome literature. *Psychol. Bull., 87,* 260–303.

Scruggs, T., & Mastropieri, A. (1992). Classroom applications of mnemonic instruction: Acquisition, maintenance, and generalization. *Exceptional Children, 58,* 219–229.

Seedman, A., & Hellman, P., (1974). *Chief!* New York: Arthur Fields Books.

Seger, C. A. (1994). Implicit learning. *Psychological Bulletin, 115,* 163–196.

Seligman, M. E. P. (1995). *The Optimistic Child.* Boston: Houghton Mifflin. Copyright © 1995 by Martin P. Seligman, Ph.D., Karen Reivich, M.A., Lisa Jaycox, Ph.D., and Jane Gillham, Ph.D. Reprinted by permission of Houghton Mifflin Company. All rights reserved.

_____. (1978) Comment and integration. *Journal of Abnormal Psychology, 87,* 165–179.

_____. (1995). The effectiveness of psychotherapy: The *Consumer Reports* study. *American Psychologist, 50,* 965–974.

_____. (1996). Science as an ally of practice. *American Psychologist, 51,* 1072–1079.

Selye, J. (1956). *The stress of life.* New York: McGraw-Hill.

Senk, S., & Usiskin, Z. (1984). Quoted in "Inventing gender differences." *Science 85, 6*(5).

Serdula, M. K., Collins, M. E., Williamson, D. F., Anda, R. F., Pamuk, E. R., and Byers, T. E. (1993). Weight control practices of U.S. adolescents and adults. *Annals of Internal Medicine, 119,* 667–671.

Sexton, J. (1995). Reviving the Kitty Genovese case, and its passions. *New York Times,* July 25, B-1–B-4.

Sheldon, W. H. (1936). *The varieties of temperament: A psychology of constitutional differences.* New York: Harper & Row.

References

Sheridan, C. L., & King, R. G., Jr. (1972). Obedience to authority with an authentic victim. *Proceed. 80th Ann. Conv. Amer. Psychol. Assn.*

Sherif, C. W. (1982). Social and psychological bases of social psychology. In A. G. Kraut (Ed.), *The G. Stanley Hall lecture series* (Vol. 2). Washington, DC: American Psychological Association.

Shotland, R. L. (1985). When bystanders just stand by. *Psychology Today, 19*(6).

Sidorowicz, L. S., & Lunney, G. S. (1980). Baby X revisited. *Sex Roles, 6,* 67–73.

Siegel, R. K. (1983). Quoted in "Natural highs in natural habitats." *Sci. News, 124,* 300–301.

_____. (1985). Quoted in "Cocaine use: Disturbing signs." *Sci. News, 128*(14).

Silverstein, L. (1991). Transforming the debate about child care and maternal employment. *Amer. Psychol., 46,* 1025–1032.

Silverstein, L. B. (1996). Fathering is a feminist issue. *Psychology of Women Quarterly, 20,* 3–37.

Simons, A. D. (1984). Quoted in "Changing ideas in depression." *Sci. News, 125,* 58.

Simons, M. (1987, February 13). Brazil's health crisis: The plague is just one part. *New York Times.*

Skinner, B. F. (1953). *Science and human behavior.* New York: Macmillan. Excerpt reprinted by permission of Prentice-Hall, Inc., Upper Saddle River, NJ.

_____. (1957). *Verbal behavior.* Englewood Cliffs, NJ: Prentice-Hall.

_____. (1967). Autobiography. In E. G. Boring and Lindzey (Eds.), *A history of psychology in autobiography.* Englewood Cliffs, NJ: Prentice-Hall.

_____. (1990). Can psychology be a science of the mind? *Amer. Psychol., 45,* 1206–1210.

Small, B. & Baeckman, L. (1997). Cognitive correlates of mortality: evidence from a population-based sample of very old adults. *Psychology & Aging, 12,* 309–313.

Snarey, J. R. (1985). Cross-cultural universality of social-moral development: A critical review of Kohlbergian research. *Psychol. Bull., 97,* 202–232.

Snyder, S. H. (1984). Drug and neurotransmitter receptors in the brain. *Science, 224,* 22–31.

_____. (1986). *Drugs and the brain.* New York: W. H. Freeman.

Solomon, R. L. (1980). The opponent-process theory of acquired motivation. *American Psychologist, 35,* 691–712.

Spanos, N. P. (1994). Multiple identify enactments and multiple personality disorder: A sociocognitive perspective. *Psychological Bulletin, 116,* 143–165.

Spence, J. T., and Hahn, E. D. (1997). The attitudes toward women scale and attitude change in college students. *Psychology of Women Quarterly, 21,* 17–34.

Spitz, R. A. (1946). Hospitalism: A follow-up report. *Psychoanal. Study Child, 2,* 113–117.

Springer, S. P., & Deutsch, G. (1985). *Left brain, right brain.* New York: W. H. Freeman.

Squire, L. (1985). Quoted in "ECT: New studies on how, why, who." *APA Monitor, 16*(3).

Squire, L. R. (1987) *Memory and brain.* New York: Oxford University Press.

Stangor, C. (1995). Content and application inaccuracy in social stereotyping. In Y. Lee, L. J. Jussim, and C. R. McCauley (Eds.). *Stereotype accuracy.* Washington, D.C.: American Psychological Association.

Starr, R. H. (1979). Child abuse. *Amer. Psychol., 34,* 872–878.

Statistical Abstracts of the United States. (1986). Washington, DC: U.S. Government Printing Office.

Steinberg, L. (1987). Bound to bicker. *Psychol. Today, 21*(9).

Stephens, R., & Cottrell, E. (1972). A follow-up study of 200 narcotic addicts committed for treatment under the Narcotic Addict Rehabilitation act (NARA). *Brit. J. Addict., 67,* 45–53.

Stern, P. C. (1984, January). Saving energy: The human dimension. *Technology Rev.* (Mass. Inst. Technology).

Sternberg, R. J. (1997). The concept of intelligence and its role in lifelong learning and success. *American Psychologist, 52,* 1030–1037.

Sternberg, R. J., Wagner, R. K. Williams, W. M., and Horvath, J. A. (1995). Testing common sense. *American Psychologist, 50,* 912–927.

Stewart, A. J., & Winter, D. G. (1974). Self-definition and social definition in women. *J. Pers., 42,* 238–259.

Stillings, N. A., Feinstein, M. H., Garfield, J. L., Rissland, E. L., Rosenbaum, D. A., Weisler, S. E., & Baker-Ward, L. (1987). *Cognitive science: An introduction.* Cambridge, MA: MIT Press.

Stokols, D. (1995). The paradox of environmental psychology. *American Psychologist, 50,* 821–837.

Stone, A. A. (1982). The insanity defense on trial. *Hospital and Community Psychiatry, 33,* 636–640.

Stone, I. (1980). *The origin.* Franklin Center, PA: Franklin Library.

Suomi, S. J. (1983). Social development in rhesus monkeys: Consideration of individual differences. In A. Oliverio and M. Zappella (Eds.), *The behavior of human infants.* New York: Plenum Press.

Swartz, K. B., & Rosenblum, L. A. (1980). Operant responding by bonnet macaques for color videotape recordings of a social stimuli. *Anim. Learn. Behav., 8,* 322–331.

Szasz, T. S. (1961). *The myth of mental illness: Foundations of a theory of personal conduct.* New York: Harper & Row.

T

Tannen, D. (1990). *You just don't understand.* New York: Ballantine Books. Copyright © 1990 by Deborah Tannen. Excerpt reprinted by permission of William Morrow and Company, Inc.

Tavris, C. (1992). *The mismeasure of women.* New York: Simon & Schuster.

Tebbel, J. (1974). *The media in America.* New York: Crowell.

Thinus-Blanc, C., and Gaunet, F. (1997). Representation of space in blind persons: Vision as a spatial sense? *Psychological Bulletin, 121,* 20–42.

Thomas, K. (1983). *Man and the natural world.* New York: Pantheon Books.

Thompson, R. A., and Wilcox, B. L. (1995). Child maltreatment research: Federal support and policy issues. *American Psychologist, 50,* 789–793.

Thompson, R. F. (1994). Behaviorism and neuroscience. *Psychological Review, 101,* 259–265.

Todes, D. P. (1997). From the machine to the ghost within: Pavlov's transition from digestive physiology to conditioned reflexes. *American Psychologist, 52,* 947–955.

Tolman, E. C., Ritchie, B. F., & Kalish, D. (1946). Studies in spatial learning. *J. Exp. Psychol., 36,* 221–229.

Torrance, E. P. (1980). Creativity and futurism in education: Retooling. *Education, 100,* 298–311.

Tosteson, D. C. (1981). Lithium and mania. *Sci. Amer., 244*(4).

Treffert, D. A. (1989). *Extraordinary people.* New York: Harper & Row. Copyright 1989 by Darold. A. Treffert, M.D., reprinted with permission.

Trickett, P. K. & Susman, E. J. (1988). *Parents perceptions of child-rearing practices in physically abusive and non-abusive families. Developmental Psychology, 24* (2), 270–276 .

Tulving, E., & Partay, J. E. (1962). Concurrent effects of contextual constraint and word frequency on immediate recall and learning of verbal material. *Canad. J. Psychol., 16,* 83–95.

Turkheimer, E. (1991). Individual and group differences in adoption studies of IQ. *Psychol. Bull., 110,* 392–405.

Twenge, J. M. (1997). Attitudes toward women, 1970–1995. *Psychology of Women Quarterly, 21,* 35–51.

U

U.S. Bureau of the Census. (1998). *United States population estimates by age, sex, race, and Hispanic origin, 1990 to 1997.* Washington, D.C.: Author.

V

Valenstein, E. S. (1973). *Brain control: A critical examination of brain stimulation and psychosurgery.* New York: Wiley.

van der Gaag, N. (1996). Ageing with attitude. In K. L. Freiberg (Ed.). *Annual editions in human development.* Guilford, CT: Dushkin Publishing Group. (Original work published in 1995.)

VandenBos, G. R. (1996). Outcome assessment (of psychotherapy). *American Psychologist, 51,* 1005–1006.

Vane, J. R., and Motta, R. W. (1990). Group intelligence tests. In G. Goldstein & M. Hersen (Eds.). *Handbook of psychological assessment.* New York: Pergamon Press.

References

Vasta, R., Knott, J. A., and Gaze, C. E. (1996). Can spatial training erase the gender differences on the water-level task? *Psychology of Women Quarterly, 20,* 549–567.

Vaughter, R. M., Sadh, D., and Vozzola, E. (1994). Sex similarities and differences in types of play in games and sports. *Psychology of Women Quarterly, 18,* 85–104.

Verhaeghen, P., and Salthouse, T. A. (1997). Meta-analyses of age-cognition relations in adulthood: Estimates of linear and nonlinear age effects and structural models. *Psychological Bulletin, 122,* 231–249.

Von Frisch, K. (1963). *Man and the living world.* New York: Harcourt Brace Jovanovich.

W

Wadden, T. A., & Anderson, C. H. (1982). The clinical use of hypnosis. *Psychol. Bull., 91,* 215–243.

Wade, C. & Tavris, C. (1994). The longest war: Gender and culture. In W. J. Lonner & R. Malpass (Eds.). *Psychology and culture.* Boston: Allyn and Bacon.

Wade, C., & Tavris, C. (1993). *Critical and creative thinking.* New York: HarperCollins College Publishers.

Wagner, B. M. (1997). Family risk factors for child and adolescent suicidal behavior. *Psychological Bulletin, 121,* 246–298.

Wagner, R. K. (1997). Intelligence, training, and employment. *American Psychologist, 52,* 1059–1060.

Wainrib, B. (1992a). The aging female client: Developmental or disorder issues. In B. R. Wainrib (Ed.), *Gender issues across the life cycle.* New York: Springer Publishing Co.

_____. (1992b). Introduction: Gender issues in the aging population. In B. R. Wainrib (Ed.), *Gender issues across the life cycle.* New York: Springer Publishing Co.

Wakefield, J. (1992). The concept of mental disorder: On the boundary between biological facts and social values. *Amer. Psychol., 47,* 373–388.

Walsh, W. B., & Betz, N. E. (1985). *Tests and assessment.* Englewood Cliffs, NJ: Prentice-Hall.

Wampold, B. E., Mondin, G. W., Moody, M., Stich, F., Benson, K., and Ahn, H. (1997). A meta-analysis of outcome studies comparing bona fide psychotherapies: Empirically, "all must have prizes." *Psychological Bulletin, 122,* 203–215.

Watson, J. B. (1928). *Psychological care of infant and child.* NY: W. W. Norton.

Weary, G. (1997). Why ask why? The motive to reduce causal uncertainty. *Psychological Science Agenda, 10*(6), 8–9.

Wechsler, D. (1975). Intelligence defined and undefined: A relativistic appraisal. *Amer. Psychol., 30,* 135–139.

_____. (1981). *WAIS-R manual.* New York: Psychological Corporation and Harcourt Brace Jovanovich. Simulated items similar to those in the Wechsler Intelligence Scales for Adults and Children. Copyright 1949, 1955, 1974, 1981, 1997 by The Psychological Corporation. Reproduced by permission. All rights reserved.

Weinberger, D. A., Schwartz, G. E., & Davidson, R. J. (1979). Low-anxious, high-anxious, and repressive coping styles: Psychometric patterns and behavioral and physiological responses to stress. *J. Abn. Psychol., 88,* 369–380.

Weiner, R. D. (1984). Does electroconvulsive therapy cause brain damage? *Brain Beh. Sci., 7,* 1–47.

Weiss, D. J., & Davidson, M. L. (1981). Test theory and methods. *Ann. Rev. Psychol., 32,* 629–658.

Weiss, J. M. (1972). Psychological factors in stress and disease. *Sci. Amer., 226*(6).

Weissman, M. M. (1985). Quoted in "Growing up with depression." *Sci. News, 127,* 344.

Whalen, R. E., & Simon, N. G. (1984). Biological motivation. *Ann. Rev. Psychol., 35,* 257–276.

Wheeler, J., & Carlson, C. L. (1994). The social functioning of children with ADD with hyperactivity and ADD without hyperactivity: A comparison of their peer relations and social deficits. *Journal of Emotional and Behavioral Disorders, 2,* 2–12.

Wheeler, M. A., Stuss, D. T. & Tulving, E. (1997). Toward a theory of episodic memory: The frontal lobes and autonoetic consciousness. *Psychological Bulletin, 121,* 331–354.

Wichstrom, L. (1999). "The emergence of gender difference in depressed mood during adolescence: The role of intensified gender socialization. *Developmental Psychology, 35,* 232–245.

Williams, J. E., and Best, D. L. (1994). Cross-cultural views of women and men. In W. J. Lonner & R. Malpass (Eds.). *Psychology and culture.* Boston: Allyn and Bacon.

Wilson, T. D., and Brekke, N. (1994). Mental contamination and mental correction: Unwanted influences on judgments and evaluations. *Psychological Bulletin, 116,* 117–142.

Windholz, G. (1987). Pavlov as a psychologist. *Biol. Sci., 22*(3).

_____. (1997). Ivan P. Pavlov: An overview of his life and psychological work. *American Psychologist, 52,* 941–946.

Winfree, A. T. (1987). *The timing of biological clocks.* New York: W. H. Freeman.

Winner, E. (1997). Exceptionally high intelligence and schooling. *American Psychologist, 52,* 1070–1081.

Wolf, S., & Wolff, H. G. (1947). *Human gastric function.* London: Oxford University Press.

Wolpe, J. (1982). *The practice of behavior therapy.* New York: Pergamon Press.

Wolpe, J., and Plaud, J. J. (1997). Pavlov's contributions to behavior therapy. *American Psychologist, 52,* 966–972.

Wood, W., Lundgren, S., Ouellette, J. A., Busceme, S., and Blackstone, T. (1994). Minority influence: A meta-analytic review of social influence processes. *Psychological Bulletin, 115,* 323–345.

Wood, W., Wong, F., & Chachere, J. (1991). Effects of media violence on viewers' aggression in unconstrained social interaction. *Psychol. Bull., 109,* 371–383.

Worchel, S., & Cooper, J. (1983). *Understanding social psychology.* Homewood, IL: Dorsey Press.

Wright, B. J., & Isenstein, V. R. (1975). *Psychological tests and minorities.* Rockville, MD: Nat. Inst. Ment. Health.

Wundt, W. (1873). *Principles of physiological psychology.* (Vol. 1, translated by E. B. Titchener, 1904; author's preface to first edition). New York: Macmillan.

Y

Yarnold, P. R., & Grimm, L. G. (1982). Time urgency among coronary-prone individuals. *J. Abnorm. Psychol., 91,* 175–177.

Yates, A. (1989). Current perspectives on the eating disorders: I. History, psychological and biological aspects. *J. Amer. Acad. Child Adoles. Psychiat., 28,* 813–828.

Yetman, N. (Ed.). (1991). *Majority and minority: The dynamics of race and ethnicity in American life.* Boston: Allyn & Bacon.

Yoshikawa, H. (1994). Prevention as cumulative protection: Effects of early family support and education on chronic delinquency and its risks. *Psychological Bulletin, 115,* 28–54.

Z

Zajonc, R. B., and Bargh, J. (1980). The confluence model: Parameter estimation in six divergent data sets on family factors and intelligence. *Intelligence, 4,* 349–361.

Zajonc, R. B., and Mullaly, P. R. (1997). Birth order. *American Psychologist, 52,* 685–699 .

Zeichner, A., & Pihl, R. O. (1979). Effects of alcohol and behavior contingencies on human aggression. *J. Abn. Psychol., 88,* 153–160.

Zelinski, E., Crimmins, E., Reynolds, S., & Seeman, T. (1998). Do medical conditions affect cognition in older adults? *Health Psychology,* 17, 504–512.

Zigler, E., Taussig, C., & Black, K. (1992). Early childhood intervention: A promising preventative for juvenile delinquency. *Amer. Psychol., 47,* 997–1006.

Zimbardo, P. G. (1972, April). Pathology of imprisonment. *Society,* 3–8.

Zimbardo, Philip. From the *Instructor's Resource Book* to accompany *Psychology and Life,* tenth Edition. Copyright © 1979, 1977, 1975, 1971 Scott, Foresman and Company. Reprinted with permission of Addison-Wesley Educational Publishers Inc.

Zubek, J. P., Hughes, G. R., & Shepard, J. M. (1971). A comparison of the effects of prolonged sensory deprivation and perceptual deprivation. *Can. J. Behav. Sci. Rev. Can. Sci. Comp., 3,* 282–290.

Zuckerman, M., & Wheeler, L. (1975). To dispel fantasies about the fantasy-based measure of fear of success. *Psychol. Bull., 82,* 932–946.

INDEX

Index

Credits

Index